The Treasury and British Public Policy,
1906–1959

The Treasury and British Public Policy, 1906–1959

G. C. PEDEN

OXFORD

UNIVERSITY PRESS

OXFORD
UNIVERSITY PRESS

Great Clarendon Street, Oxford OX2 6DP

Oxford University Press is a department of the University of Oxford.
It furthers the University's objective of excellence in research, scholarship,
and education by publishing worldwide in

Oxford New York

Athens Auckland Bangkok Bogotá Buenos Aires Calcutta
Cape Town Chennai Dar es Salaam Delhi Florence Hong Kong Istanbul
Karachi Kuala Lumpur Madrid Melbourne Mexico City Mumbai
Nairobi Paris São Paulo Singapore Taipei Tokyo Toronto Warsaw

and associated companies in Berlin Ibadan

Oxford is a registered trade mark of Oxford University Press
in the UK and certain other countries

Published in the United States
by Oxford University Press Inc., New York

British Library Cataloguing in Publication Data
Data available

Library of Congress Cataloging in Publication Data
Peden, G. C.
The Treasury and British public policy, 1906–1959 / G. C. Peden.
Includes bibliographical references and index.
1. Great Britian.   Treasury—History.   2. Great Britain—Economic
policy—History.   I. Title.
HJ1030.P414   2000   338.941—dc21   99–38006

ISBN 0–19–820707–7

1 3 5 7 9 10 8 6 4 2

Typeset by
Jayvee, Trivandrum, India
Printed in Great Britain
on acid-free paper by
T. J. International Ltd.,
Padstow, Cornwall

For ALISON

Acknowledgements

Work on this book began in 1987, when I was awarded a British Academy Research Readership, but I have drawn upon research which began in the 1970s. Over the years I have accumulated many debts. Sir Alec Cairncross and Barry Supple supported the project from the outset. Gill Bennett, Kathleen Burk, Sir Alec Cairncross, Peter Clarke, Martin Daunton, José Harris, Roger Middleton, Alison Peden, Neil Rollings, Pat Thane, and Tom Wilson read and commented on parts or all of the draft text. Responsibility for remaining errors and omissions rests solely on the author. The late Lord Jay, Henry Jenkyns, Sir Thomas and Lady Rosalind Padmore, Sir Edward Playfair, Sir Leo Pliatzky, Enoch Powell, Sir Denis Rickett, the late Lord Sherfield, the late Lord Thorneycroft, the late Lord Trend, and Sir John Winnifrith were kind enough to allow me to interview them.

I have to thank the Bank of England; Birmingham University Library; the Bodleian Library; the British Library; the British Library of Political and Economic Science; Professor Christopher Clay; Cambridge University Library; Churchill College, Cambridge; the Franklin D. Roosevelt Library; Glasgow University Archives; the House of Lords Record Office; Lord Kennet; King's College, Cambridge; the National Archives of Scotland; the National Archives, Washington, DC; the Warden and Fellows of Nuffield College, Oxford; the Public Record Office, London; the Master and Fellows of Trinity College, Cambridge; and the Master and Fellows of University College, Oxford, for access to documents and other material; Jane Bonham-Carter; the Hon. Mrs L. Fleming; Sir Edward Ford; Sir Nicholas Henderson; Lord Lothian; the Trustees of Harold Macmillan's papers; Christie, Viscountess Simon; the Keeper of the Public Record Office, London; and the Clerk of the Records, House of Lords Record Office, with the agreement of the Beaverbrook Foundation, for permission to reproduce, or publish passages based on, copyright material; and to the following publishers for permission to include copyright material: Blackwell Publishers, Oxford (Figure 6.2 and Tables 3.4 and 7.2); Edward Elgar, Cheltenham (Figure 1.1); and the Macmillan Press Ltd. (Tables 3.1 and 3.2).

I also gratefully acknowledge the financial assistance of the British Academy, the Carnegie Trust for the Universities of Scotland, the Economic and Social Research Council, the Leverhulme Trust, and the Wolfson Foundation, and the generous hospitality of the Warden and Fellows of All Souls College, Oxford, where I spent a productive year as a visiting fellow.

Rosemary Berry and Margaret Hendry typed some early draft chapters before I learned to use a computer. Finally, more than conventional thanks are due to my family, who have provided just the right amounts of support and distraction.

G.C.P.
University of Stirling
1999

Contents

List of Figures

List of Tables

List of Abbreviations

FCO	Foreign and Commonwealth Office
FO	Foreign Office papers
HC Deb.	House of Commons Debates
HL Deb.	House of Lords Debates
HTRY	Hawtrey papers (Churchill College, Cambridge)
JMK	*Collected Writings of John Maynard Keynes*
NDE	National Debt Enquiry
n.d.	no date
NS	new series
PP	Parliamentary papers
PR	Policy Review paper
RG	Record Group
ser.	series
T	Treasury papers

CHAPTER ONE

The Treasury and its Roles,
1906–1959

INTRODUCTION

The Treasury has been described as 'the most political of departments'.[1]
Treasury control of public expenditure involves participation in decisions as to
which policies should be funded, and the Chancellor of the Exchequer has to
decide how to raise taxes or loans to pay for them. In conjunction with the Bank
of England, the Treasury is responsible for the soundness of the country's financial system. During the period covered by this book, the Treasury moved from
being a department of finance to being an economic ministry, with responsibility for managing the national economy. Finally, in addition to all these direct
influences on policy, the Treasury was responsible for the size and efficiency of
the Civil Service. The Treasury thus combined a range of functions that in other
countries would have been divided between different departments. For
example, in the United States there evolved, in addition to the US Treasury, the
Bureau of the Budget (for control of expenditure); the Federal Reserve Board
(for monetary policy); the Council of Economic Advisers (for co-ordinating
economic policy); and the Civil Service Commission.

Historians and political scientists have long been aware of the influence of
senior civil servants on policy.[2] However, it has not been easy to put that influence in its institutional context. The last comprehensive history of the Treasury,
by Henry Roseveare in 1969,[3] covered some nine centuries, and devoted just
over seventy pages to the period covered by this book. Moreover, Roseveare
completed his manuscript too early to be able to make use of the files that
became available under the 1967 Public Records Act, which reduced the period
for which material from government archives was withheld from the public
from fifty years to thirty years. His problem was compounded by the fact that
most Treasury files for the pre-1919 period are fragmentary and, until recently,

[1] Lord Welby, Permanent Secretary of the Treasury, 1885–94, cited by Lord Bridges, Permanent
Secretary, 1945–56, in id., *The Treasury* (1966), 41.
[2] See Max Beloff, 'The Whitehall Factor: The Role of the Higher Civil Service', in Gillian Peele and
Chris Cook (eds.), *The Politics of Reappraisal, 1918–1939* (1975), 209–31; D. C. Watt, *Personalities and Policies:
Studies in the Formulation of British Foreign Policy in the 20th Century* (1965).
[3] Henry Roseveare, *The Treasury: The Evolution of a British Institution* (1969).

were badly catalogued. Thus, down to the late 1960s, there was little material on how the Treasury had influenced policy, apart from official views in Parliamentary Papers, or stray glimpses offered by the writers of memoirs. Contemporary studies could also make use of interviews with members of the Treasury, and it was largely on the basis of such interviews that Professor Samuel Beer, of the Government Department at Harvard University, published in 1956 an account of how the Treasury co-ordinated economic and financial policy. However, Beer's account had been bowdlerized at the behest of senior officials, whose instinct was to 'keep something of a veil over our internal processes', and who believed that the opinions of officials should not be quoted in public.[4] Subsequent books based on interviews with Treasury personnel were less inhibited but still preserved the anonymity of officials.[5]

Although there are detailed accounts of the evolution of the Treasury's role in Whitehall, particularly in relation to its influence on the Civil Service,[6] the sheer volume of Treasury files that became available under the thirty-year rule has made it difficult for researchers to study the work of the department as a whole. There has been a tendency for economists and economic historians to focus on financial and economic policy, and in particular on the extent to which the Treasury had listened to Keynes's advice.[7] Economists have a professional interest in studying the impact of economic theory on policy, and have written memoirs or monographs, and edited diaries, all of which cast light on the Treasury's response to economists' advice regarding economic policy, albeit to the exclusion of many other aspects of the department's work.[8] The emphasis on

---

[4] Samuel H. Beer, *Treasury Control* (Oxford, 1956); James E. Cronin, 'Power, Secrecy, and the British Constitution: Vetting Samuel Beer's *Treasury Control*', *20th Cent. Brit. Hist.*, 3 (1992), 59–75.

[5] See Samuel Brittan, *The Treasury under the Tories, 1951–1964* (1964); Hugh Heclo and Aaron Wildavsky, *The Private Government of Public Money: Community and Policy inside British Politics* (1974).

[6] See G. K. Fry, *Statesmen in Disguise* (1969); Richard A. Chapman and J. R. Greenaway, *The Dynamics of Administrative Reform* (1980); Peter Hennessy, *Whitehall* (1989).

[7] Major monographs include: Alan Booth, *British Economic Policy, 1931–1949: Was There a Keynesian Revolution?* (1989); Peter Clarke, *The Keynesian Revolution in the Making, 1924–1936* (Oxford, 1988); Ian Drummond, *The Floating Pound and the Sterling Area, 1931–1939* (Cambridge, 1981); Susan Howson, *Domestic Monetary Management in Britain, 1919–38* (Cambridge, 1975); id., *British Monetary Policy, 1945–51* (Oxford, 1993); Roger Middleton, *Towards the Managed Economy: Keynes, the Treasury and the Fiscal Policy Debate of the 1930s* (1985); D. E. Moggridge, *British Monetary Policy, 1924–1931: The Norman Conquest of $4.86* (Cambridge, 1972); L. S. Pressnell, *External Economic Policy since the War*, vol. i (1986); Jim Tomlinson, *Employment Policy: The Crucial Years, 1939–1955* (Oxford, 1987). For other literature see G. C. Peden, *Keynes, the Treasury and British Economic Policy* (1988).

[8] See Donald MacDougall, *Don and Mandarin: Memoirs of an Economist* (1987); Edwin Plowden, *An Industrialist in the Treasury: The Post-War Years* (1989); Alec Cairncross and Nita Watts, *The Economic Section, 1939–1961: A Study in Economic Advising* (1989); Susan Howson and Donald Winch, *The Economic Advisory Council, 1930–1939: A Study in Economic Advice during Depression and Recovery* (Cambridge, 1977); Alec Cairncross (ed.), *The Robert Hall Diaries, 1947–1953* (1989), and *1954–1961* (1991); Susan Howson and Donald Moggridge (eds.), *The Collected Papers of James Meade*, vol. iv, *The Cabinet Office Diary, 1944–46* (1990); eid. (eds.), *The Wartime Diaries of Lionel Robbins and James Meade, 1943–45* (1990). For international comparisons see Mary O. Furner and Barry Supple (eds.), *The State and Economic Knowledge: The American and British Experiences* (Cambridge, 1990); Joseph Pechman (ed.), *The Role of the Economist in Government: An International Perspective* (1989).

economics and policy has been in no way diminished by the appearance of major biographies of Keynes himself.[9]

There have been studies by historians of other aspects of the Treasury's work, but these have usually dealt with particular topics, such as the impact of the First World War on the department, or the influence of the Treasury on rearmament in the 1930s.[10] The Permanent Secretaries who were in charge of the Treasury from 1919 to 1939, and from 1945 to 1956, have been the subject of biographies, but these were written primarily from the point of view of how they conducted themselves as heads of the Civil Service.[11] There are no studies of the Treasury in relation to public policy comparable to those commissioned by the Bank of England.[12]

The absence of such studies has in no way deterred critics of the Treasury. James Cronin, for example, has identified the 'bureaucratic self-interest' of Treasury officials, as taxpayers themselves, in keeping tax rates low, and the position of the Treasury at the centre of 'bureaucratic power', as major barriers to collectivist action by the state.[13] John Macnicol has likewise seen bias in favour of the taxpayer in attempts by the Treasury between 1908 and 1946 to alter the funding of old-age pensions from a tax-funded basis, which redistributed income, to one in which there was increased reliance on flat-rate national insurance contributions, which did not, and has questioned the 'right of unelected Treasury officials to exercise control over the political wishes of democratically elected politicians'.[14] Certainly there is evidence that Treasury parsimony limited the development of policies to deal with poverty, from the Liberal reforms before 1914 to the Beveridge Report of 1942.[15] On the other hand, parsimony was not restricted to social reform. The Treasury has also been accused of failing to finance adequate preparation for either world war.[16] One has to ask whether the Treasury could be expected to be other than parsimonious, if the combined demands by the civil and defence departments exceeded the willingness of politicians to levy taxes.

[9] D. E. Moggridge, *Maynard Keynes: An Economist's Biography* (1992); Robert Skidelsky, *John Maynard Keynes: Hopes Betrayed, 1883–1920* (1983); id., *The Economist as Saviour, 1920–1937* (1992).

[10] See Kathleen Burk, 'The Treasury: From Impotence to Power', in id. (ed.), *War and the State: The Transformation of British Government, 1914–1919* (1982), 84–107; G. C. Peden, *British Rearmament and the Treasury, 1932–1939* (Edinburgh, 1979).

[11] Richard Chapman, *Ethics in the British Civil Service* (1988), which deals with Sir Edward Bridges, and Eunan O'Halpin, *Head of the Civil Service: A Study of Sir Warren Fisher* (1989).

[12] R. S. Sayers, *The Bank of England, 1891–1944*, 3 vols. (Cambridge, 1976); John Fforde, *The Bank of England and Public Policy, 1941–1958* (Cambridge, 1992).

[13] James E. Cronin, *The Politics of State Expansion: War, State and Society in Twentieth-Century Britain* (1991), 5, 8.

[14] John Macnicol, *The Politics of Retirement in Britain, 1878–1948* (Cambridge, 1998), 291.

[15] José Harris, *Unemployment and Politics: A Study in English Social Policy, 1886–1914* (Oxford, 1972), 328, 332, 352–3, 356; id., *William Beveridge: A Biography* (Oxford, 1977), 410–12, 422–3.

[16] David French, *British Economic and Strategic Planning, 1905–1915* (1982), 44–6, 68–70, 77, 134–5; Robert Shay, *British Rearmament in the Thirties: Politics and Profits* (Princeton, NJ, 1977), 282–9.

In the sphere of economic policy, the Treasury has been castigated by, among others, Sidney Pollard for pursuing policies which favoured the financial interests of the City of London over those of industry, and which exacerbated, where they did not cause, unemployment in the inter-war period, and which destabilized the economy and retarded economic growth even when there was full employment after 1945.[17] However, Pollard used the term 'Treasury' as a 'shorthand' to 'designate the whole decision-making complex',[18] thereby begging the question of whether policy accurately reflected Treasury advice.

Explanation of why the Treasury has acted as it has done depends upon an understanding of what the Treasury was trying to achieve. The Treasury was part of a system of public finance, which had been established in the nineteenth century by Sir Robert Peel and William Gladstone, whereby, at least in theory, the state was not to favour any particular economic interest. The system was intended to involve the minimum distortion of market forces. Its three key characteristics were: first, the balanced budget, which imposed on the Treasury the tasks of raising revenue to match central government expenditure, and holding down that expenditure to a level that taxpayers were willing to pay for; second, the gold standard, whereby sterling had a fixed value in terms both of gold and of all other currencies on the gold standard, thereby giving the Bank of England a target that was independent of political pressure in its management of the monetary system; and third, free trade, which ensured that no group of producers could bargain for political favours. Both the gold standard and free trade acted to maintain Britain as an open economy, and it was widely believed that, if British industry encountered competition in home as well as in international markets, it would retain the competitive edge that it had gained as the world's first industrial nation.

Most senior figures in the Treasury down to the 1950s had been brought up in this tradition of public finance. However, from 1914 there were major changes in the role of the state, as a result of two world wars, and an unprecedented international depression in the inter-war period. Even before 1914 central government was becoming increasingly responsible for a wide range of social services, and by mid-century the welfare state had evolved. The inflationary financing of the First World War undermined the gold standard's supposedly automatic mechanism for ensuring the soundness of the currency. The high levels of unemployment experienced between the wars created political pressure for an active employment policy, and from 1947, when Sir Stafford Cripps became Chancellor of the Exchequer as well as Minister for Economic Affairs, the Treasury was the department with overall responsibility for managing the national economy. The 1950s were in fact years of increasing prosperity, but

[17] Sidney Pollard (ed.), *The Gold Standard and Employment Policies between the Wars* (1970), 2–10, 23; id., *The Wasting of the British Economy: British Economic Policy 1945 to the Present* (1982), esp. 34–5, 47–50, 86–8.
[18] Pollard, *Wasting*, 67.

there was a growing awareness that the economy was overloaded and that Britain's position as a leading exporter of manufactures was under threat. Consequently the Treasury took a leading part in policy reviews within Whitehall on the country's future role in world affairs.

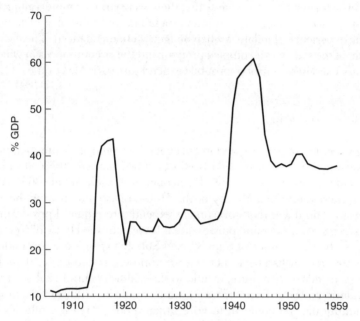

FIG. 1.1. *Total Public Expenditure in the UK as a Percentage of Gross Domestic Product, 1906–1959*

Source: Roger Middleton, *Government Versus the Market: The Growth of the Public Sector, Economic Management and British Economic Performance, c.1890–1979* (Cheltenham, 1996), 89.

Figure 1.1 shows how total public expenditure grew as a percentage of gross domestic product (GDP). In 1906/7 central government expenditure (excluding the cost of the National Debt) was about 5.3 per cent of GDP; by 1959/60 it was about 18.5 per cent, while the total of public expenditure which the Chancellor of the Exchequer might seek to influence, including current and capital expenditure by local government, and capital expenditure by nationalized industries, was about 37 per cent.[19] Public expenditure rose sharply in two world wars, and on neither occasion fell back to its pre-war level, leading the economists Alan Peacock and Jack Wiseman to put forward the thesis that war had a displacement effect on public expenditure, both by increasing the public's tolerance of

[19] The exact figures depend upon definitions of public expenditure and estimates of national income.

higher taxation, and by revealing social conditions that had adverse effects on the nation's health.[20] While war cannot be a complete explanation for changes in the level of state activity—if only because there was a tendency for the public sector to grow even in neutral states, such as Sweden and Switzerland—there is no reason to doubt that war was a shock to the British political system. However, a longer-term perspective suggests that there were strong countervailing forces against increasing public expenditure, including the resistance of taxpayers, and the experience of inflation when budgets were unbalanced. The growth in the role of the state was a complex process, and the circumstances in which the Treasury exercised control over public expenditure varied over time.

TREASURY CONTROL

Treasury control of central government expenditure and of the numbers of posts in government departments had been developed between the 1780s and the 1860s, culminating in Gladstone's Exchequer and Audit Act of 1866.[21] With a view to increasing the authority of the House of Commons over the executive, it was laid down that government expenditure required prior approval, both as regards amount and purpose, year by year, by the House of Commons, sitting as the 'Committee of Supply', and Supply expenditure was audited to ensure that money had been spent on the approved purposes. No department could incur new expenditure, or add to its establishment of civil servants, or their salaries, without Treasury assent, which would be withheld if the proposed expenditure did not conform to government policy. Treasury officials made detailed criticisms of proposals for new expenditure and no expenditure could be added to a department's Estimates during the financial year, unless a Supplementary Estimate were approved by the Treasury and submitted to Parliament, or unless overspending under one heading (known as a 'vote') in the Estimates could be matched by underspending in another, in which case the Treasury might grant the power of virement. Departments had to prepare annual accounts of expenditure, down to the last farthing (0.1p), and an independent official, the Comptroller and Auditor-General, could be asked by the Treasury to examine any expenditure that appeared to have been incurred without its authority, and to report any breach of the rules of public finance to the House of Commons's Committee of Public Accounts.

The Treasury was expected to ensure that the taxpayer's money was not unnecessarily or unwisely spent. In Gladstone's memorable words in 1877, 'the saving of candle-ends' was 'very much the measure of a good Secretary of the

---

[20] A. Peacock and J. Wiseman, *The Growth of Public Expenditure in the United Kingdom* (1961).

[21] What follows draws upon Bridges, *Treasury*, 23–45 and 51–3, and Sir Norman Chester, *The English Administrative System, 1780–1870* (Oxford, 1981), 169–220.

Treasury'.[22] The prevailing economic wisdom in the nineteenth century, based upon the writings of Adam Smith, David Ricardo, and John Stuart Mill, was that the things government spent money on did less to promote prosperity than the things private individuals spent money on. Given that the principal items of central government expenditure were defence and interest on the National Debt (itself largely representing the cost of past wars), there was something to be said for this view. Consequently, in another memorable dictum, Gladstone laid down that 'money should be left to fructify in the pocket of the taxpayer'.[23] The main aim of a Chancellor of the Exchequer, therefore, was to balance the expenditure and revenue of central government at as low a level as possible, using any surplus to reduce the National Debt. Contrary to a common misconception on the part of the Treasury's critics, the fact that budgets were presented to Parliament annually did not preclude a Chancellor from looking ahead more than one year at a time—Gladstone set out in his first budget in 1853 the steps by which he proposed to abolish income tax seven years hence[24]—but sound finance did preclude incurring a deficit in one year in anticipation of increased revenue in later years. The system of strict annual accounting was designed to prevent a government from committing its successors to expenditure or taxation in future years; however, from the time that central government took responsibility for old-age pensions (1908) and national insurance (1911), it was difficult to avoid moral, if not contractual, obligations in future years.

The convention of a balanced budget was the key to what might be called the fiscal constitution. Any increase in central government expenditure had to be matched by an increase in revenue from taxation, unless Parliament authorized borrowing for some specific purpose. Such borrowing was exceptional, being confined to expenditure which was necessary for national defence, usually in time of war, or which was 'capital' in nature, in the sense that it produced a tangible asset. Each loan for capital expenditure would have a separate sinking fund attached to pay off the loan over a fixed period of time. Consequently, the Treasury strongly preferred to confine borrowing to cases where there would be a money return capable of repaying the sum borrowed, plus interest, as, for example, was the case with investment in telephone systems by the Post Office. Generally speaking, the system of annual budgeting for expenditure and revenue ensured that any attempt by politicians to secure popularity through additional central government expenditure was likely to incur unpopularity with taxpayers. The balanced-budget convention meant that any attempt by one minister to increase the expenditure of his department was likely to reduce the funds available to other ministers. Consequently, although a minister who had been refused money by the Chancellor could appeal to the Cabinet, the

---

[22] Bridges, *Treasury Control*, 6.   [23] Ibid., 7.
[24] Sydney Buxton, *Mr Gladstone as Chancellor of the Exchequer* (1901), 9–17.

Chancellor was rarely without allies among other ministers, so long as expenditure could not be paid for by borrowing.

The Prime Minister in 1900, Lord Salisbury, remarked that 'by exercising the power of the purse it [the Treasury] claims a voice in all decisions of administrative authority and policy' and 'much delay and many doubtful resolutions have been the result'.[25] In fact it is by no means clear that the Treasury had as tight a grip over expenditure or the numbers of posts in other departments as Salisbury suggested.[26] Even in the nineteenth century it had to contend with the fact that there are always people who can think of new ways in which to spend public money. Moreover, whereas the Reform Act of 1832 had enfranchised the propertied classes, who tended to elect MPs committed to economical government, the Reform Acts of 1867 and 1884 extended the vote to a large part of the working classes, thereby creating the possibility of political pressure for more expenditure on social improvement. As it happened, until the Liberal governments of 1905–15, most new expenditure on social improvement (education being the largest item) fell upon the local ratepayer. The main expansion of central government expenditure in the quarter of a century from 1880 reflected the demands of the Admiralty and War Office. Technical change was making defence equipment more expensive, and more prone to obsolescence, in an age of mounting international political rivalries. As a result, 41 per cent of central government expenditure in 1905 went on defence, compared with 33 per cent in 1880.[27]

The technical and international pressures leading to higher defence expenditure continued after 1905, but domestic political pressures for central government to accept responsibility for improving social conditions increased markedly, partly because of the inadequacy of local authorities' revenues and partly because politicians believed that issues of social policy were electorally significant. Heavy sacrifices by the public in two world wars; a further widening of the franchise in 1918, including the extension of the vote to women; the experience of economic depression in the inter-war years; and growing political pressure to support the unemployed, the sick, and the elderly from central government funds, all tended to alter the political balance in favour of increased public expenditure. The Treasury's traditional role of guardian of the taxpayers' money was no longer sufficient, and instead its role became one of persuading spending departments and the Cabinet to establish priorities between competing claims on national resources. In 1919 the Permanent Secretary, Sir Warren Fisher, argued successfully that large sums of money could be saved only if the Chancellor, and by extension his official advisers, could question the

[25] Roseveare, *Treasury*, 183.
[26] See Maurice Wright, 'Treasury Control, 1854–1914', in Gillian Sutherland (ed.), *Studies in the Growth of Nineteenth-Century Government* (1972), 195–226.
[27] Ursula Hicks, *British Public Finances: Their Structure and Development, 1880–1952* (1958), 14.

policies of other departments. Fisher went on to try to make his department into a 'general staff' for Whitehall as a whole, with his officials exercising control of expenditure in the spirit of a 'candid friend', offering constructive criticism, rather than acting as the traditional 'abominable no-man'.[28] One of the purposes of this book is to show how successful, or otherwise, he was in achieving this aim.

FINANCE AND ECONOMIC POLICY

The original function of the Chancellor's budget was to give the House of Commons, sitting as the 'Committee of Ways and Means', an account of how central government expenditure and revenue had turned out in the previous financial year; to explain what changes could be expected in the coming financial year, in the light both of the annual Estimates for expenditure and of variations in revenue that could be foreseen on the basis of existing taxation; and finally to propose tax reductions or increases as required to balance the budget.[29] Even a balanced budget required a measure of borrowing, because the collection of revenue tended to be concentrated into the last quarter of the financial year, and therefore for the first nine months expenditure usually exceeded revenue. Under the Exchequer and Audit Departments Act of 1866, all revenue and other receipts were paid into the government's central cash account, the Consolidated Fund, also known as 'the Exchequer', from which all central government payments were made. During the period when expenditure exceeded revenue, demands on the Exchequer had to be paid for by borrowing, usually by selling short-term securities known as Treasury bills, which could be paid off when there was a surplus of revenue later in the year. In making choices on borrowing and repayment the Treasury worked closely with its banker, the Bank of England. Originally, questions of management of government debt were concerned almost entirely with deciding how much the Exchequer needed to borrow, taking account of the need to repay maturing debt, and the terms that would have to be offered to raise the money. However, the scale of government borrowing for the First World War was such that the terms offered clearly influenced the structure of interest rates in the economy as a whole, and it became necessary for the Treasury and the Bank to begin to think in terms of the economic effects of public finance.

Nevertheless, it was not until 1941 that the budget became an instrument of macroeconomic policy. John Maynard Keynes's *General Theory of Employment, Interest and Money* (1936) had little to say about budgetary policy, and his proposals

[28] Conversation with Sir John Winnifrith, 31 Jan. 1975. Winnifrith served in the Treasury from 1934 to 1959.
[29] For a full account see Sir Herbert Brittain, *The British Budgetary System* (1959).

for reducing unemployment had been largely concerned with raising the level of expenditure in the community, through increased investment by public authorities outside the budget. However, the concepts of his theory could also be applied to the problem of excess expenditure in the community. Under Keynes's direct influence, as an adviser to the Chancellor, the 1941 budget made use of an analysis of national income to estimate the level of taxation and savings which, in conjunction with controls over production and rationing of consumption, would be required to check inflation. Widespread acceptance by economists of Keynes's theory also helped to persuade the wartime coalition government that maintenance of high and stable employment was possible. The 1930s had also seen widespread advocacy of economic planning as an alternative to market forces and, although there was considerable disagreement across the political spectrum as to what form economic planning should take, Keynes's theory of aggregate demand could be applied to a mixed economy, incorporating both nationalized industries and private enterprise. Most members of the Labour party, however, had reservations about Keynesian macroeconomics and believed that government must also rely on physical planning of production, and post-war economic policy relied more upon direct controls than on financial instruments.[30] Treasury reactions to planning and controls therefore deserve attention, as well as its reactions to Keynes's ideas.

Even once the budget became an instrument of macroeconomic policy the question of how revenue was to be raised remained central to the Chancellor's budget. Over the period covered by this book taxation ceased to be simply a means of raising, as equitably as possible, the money required to meet government expenditure, and became both a means of redistributing income and an instrument of economic policy. The Chancellor traditionally enjoyed considerable independence in drawing up his budget. Any novel taxes would be discussed in Cabinet, but Lloyd George's 'People's Budget' in 1909 was quite exceptional in being the subject of no fewer than fourteen meetings. A Chancellor would normally reveal his detailed proposals orally to the Cabinet only a few days before he was due to present them to the House of Commons. In 1917 the Cabinet minutes recorded the budget discussion, but subsequently neither proposals nor discussions were recorded. In 1936 the Cabinet discussion took place twenty-one days in advance of the budget, owing to the Easter recess, but thereafter it took place on the day of the budget, or the day before, by which time it was too late to make substantial changes. The reason for this procedure was to minimize the risk of a leakage of information that might be used by speculators on the Stock Exchange—such as occurred in 1936. From 1950 onwards, in recognition of the budget's new importance as an instrument of economic policy, the drafting of the budget was preceded by a Cabinet discussion of the

[30] Elizabeth Durbin, *New Jerusalems: The Labour Party and the Economics of Democratic Socialism* (1985); Daniel Ritschel, *The Politics of Planning: The Debate on Economic Planning in Britain in the 1930s* (Oxford, 1997).

economic and financial situation, but the Chancellor continued to withhold his tax measures from his Cabinet colleagues until the last moment.[31]

Chancellors and their colleagues were, of course, concerned with the political impact of taxation, and proposals for raising revenue would not proceed without the Prime Minister's support.[32] However, Treasury officials had their own input into budget-making. Any proposals for changes would be examined by them from a number of points of view: what would be the effect on the overall balance of the budget? Would the proposals be accepted by taxpayers as fair, or would they meet with obstruction? In the case of indirect taxes, what would the effect be on demand for the goods or services in question, and was it desirable to curb demand, or to maximize revenue? In the case of direct taxes, what would be the effect on incentives to work, or in the case of businessmen, to take risks? Estimates of future revenue were prepared by the boards of Inland Revenue and Customs and Excise, and the opinion of the boards on whether proposals for taxation or tariffs were practical was usually decisive. Both the Board of Inland Revenue and the Board of Customs and Excise were independent of the departmental Treasury on matters relating to the collection of revenue, but were subject to the authority of the Chancellor, and were in practice subordinate to the Treasury on matters of policy.[33] Even so, relations between officials in the three financial departments were marked by mutual respect, which was strengthened by interchange of staff.[34]

Monetary policy involved the Treasury acting in partnership with the Bank of England to maintain the external stability of sterling; to control credit; and to manage the National Debt. On the other hand, it was not until December 1959 that the Bank was represented on the Treasury's Budget Committee. The partnership between what were known as the monetary authorities evolved over

[31] Sir Ivor Jennings, *Cabinet Government* (Cambridge, 1961), 237–9; 'Cabinet Business', 21 Apr. 1950, Treasury papers, series 273, file 322 (hereafter cited as T273/322), Public Record Office, London. The minister responsible for the 'leak' in 1936 was J. H. Thomas, the Colonial Secretary.

[32] There is a growing literature on the politics of taxation. Particularly useful works include: Bruce K. Murray, *The People's Budget, 1909/10: Lloyd George and Liberal Politics* (Oxford, 1980); Mary Short, 'The Politics of Personal Taxation: Budget-making in Britain, 1917–31', Ph.D. (Cambridge, 1985); M. J. Daunton, 'Payment and Participation: Welfare and State-Formulation in Britain, 1900–1951', *Past and Present*, 150 (1996), 169–216; id., 'How to Pay for the War: State, Society and Taxation in Britain, 1917–24', *Eng. Hist. Rev.*, 111 (1996), 882–919; R. C. Whiting, 'Taxation and the Working Class, 1915–24', *Hist. J.*, 33 (1990), 895–916; id., 'Taxation Policy', in H. Mercer, N. Rollings, and J. D. Tomlinson (eds.), *Labour Governments and Private Industry: The Experience of 1945–51* (Edinburgh, 1992), 117–34; id., 'The Boundaries of Taxation', in S. J. D. Green and R. C. Whiting (eds.), *The Boundaries of the State in Modern Britain* (Cambridge, 1996), 146–69; id., 'Income Tax, the Working Class, and Party Politics, 1948–52', *20th Cent. Brit. Hist.*, 8 (1997), 194–221.

[33] See Sir James Crombie, *Her Majesty's Customs and Excise* (1962); Sir Alexander Johnston, *The Inland Revenue* (1965).

[34] To take some notable examples: Sir Warren Fisher moved from the chairmanship of the Board of Inland Revenue to become Permanent Secretary of the Treasury in 1919, and his successor at the Inland Revenue, Sir Richard Hopkins, followed him to the Treasury in 1927, becoming Permanent Secretary in 1942. In 1930 P. J. Grigg moved from the Treasury to become Chairman of the Board of Customs and Excise and later Chairman of the Board of Inland Revenue.

time, and was not without tensions as the Treasury took on more responsibilities, and the Bank became more subject to political control.[35] Normally the principal instrument of monetary policy was Bank rate, technically the rate at which the Bank of England discounted bills of good security, and in practice the rate at which it would lend to other banks (thereby setting a floor to interest rates generally). Down to 1914 Bank rate, in the words of one Treasury official, was no more the Treasury's business than 'the colour which the Bank painted its front door'.[36] In that period the Governor of the Bank rarely had occasion to see the Chancellor—so much so that, when he did so during a financial crisis in 1914, his visit to the Treasury had to be concealed in case it caused further alarm.[37] The problems of financing the First World War brought the two institutions closer together, and the Governor became a frequent visitor. After the final suspension of the gold standard in 1931, no change in Bank rate was made without the prior approval of the Chancellor. Even so, notwithstanding nationalization of the Bank in 1946, it was not until 1959 that changes in Bank rate became formally decisions of the Chancellor. At all times, the Treasury relied heavily upon the advice of the Bank; indeed in 1958 a recently retired Permanent Secretary, Sir Edward Bridges, described Treasury officials as 'laymen' compared with the specialists at the Bank.[38]

The Bank also derived independent influence from its close relationship with financial markets and the banking system. References are sometimes made to the 'City–Bank–Treasury nexus'.[39] That there were bound to be connections between the three cannot be doubted, especially given the Bank's management of the state's debts by means of loans raised in the City. What is less certain is the degree and direction of influence. It is true that the need to maintain confidence in the direction of the financial system was such that hostile City opinion could block a politician's appointment as Chancellor.[40] On the other hand, the interests of the City, the Bank, and the Treasury were separate, although coincident, and the Treasury had its own reasons for pursuing policies of 'sound finance', even when these met with approval in the City.

[35] For a useful short account see David Kynaston, 'The Bank of England and the Government', in Richard Roberts and David Kynaston (eds.), *The Bank of England: Money, Power and Influence* (Oxford, 1995), 19–55.

[36] Sir Otto Niemeyer, cited in Moggridge, *British Monetary Policy*, 160.

[37] Sir Ralph Hawtrey, taped conversation with Sir Alec Cairncross, 1966, Hawtrey papers (hereafter HTRY) 13/5, Churchill College, Cambridge.

[38] (Radcliffe) *Committee on the Working of the Monetary System: Principal Memoranda of Evidence* (1960), iii. 47.

[39] Geoffrey Ingham, *Capitalism Divided? The City and Industry in British Social Development* (1984), 134; Scott Newton and Dilwyn Porter, *Modernization Frustrated: The Politics of Industrial Decline since 1900* (1988), p. xiii; P. J. Cain and A. G. Hopkins, *British Imperialism: Crisis and Deconstruction, 1914–1990* (1993), 283.

[40] For example, in 1923 Baldwin told Neville Chamberlain that Sir Laming Worthington-Evans would not be acceptable to the City—see David Dilks, *Neville Chamberlain*, vol. i, *1869–1929* (Cambridge, 1984), 335. Other examples, mentioned in this book, are Sir Robert Horne (1924) and Oliver Lyttleton (1951). For influence of City see E. H. H. Green, 'The Influence of the City over British Economic Policy, *c*.1880–1960', in Youssef Cassis (ed.), *Finance and Financiers in European History, 1880–1960* (Cambridge, 1992), 193–218.

One of these shared interests was the maintenance of the role of sterling as an international currency, both for trade and financial services, reflecting a belief that Britain would benefit from a continuation of the economic international-ism that had marked the nineteenth century. Prior to the First World War the Treasury had no division dealing with overseas finance, the maintenance of a fixed exchange rate under the gold standard being the responsibility of the Bank of England. The Treasury's limited role is indicated by the fact that it was left to the most junior official in the Treasury's Finance Division to record *once a week* the exchange rates on each of the leading money markets.[41] However, the dis-ruption brought about by both world wars, and the inter-war depression, led the Treasury to become involved in international talks relating first to the restor-ation of the gold standard in the 1920s and then to the designing of what came to be called the Bretton Woods system of stable exchange rates in the 1940s.

War and its aftermath also involved the Treasury in diplomacy concerning intergovernmental debts, including reparations. The Treasury's increasing par-ticipation in international relations inevitably led to some overlap between its work and that of the Foreign Office, and the history of the Treasury therefore casts some light on Britain's international relations. Within the Treasury over-seas finance work grew in importance, so that, whereas in the inter-war period there was one Overseas Finance Division, by the 1950s there were eight.

RELATIONS WITH PRIME MINISTER, CABINET, AND WHITEHALL

The Treasury was frequently described as the central department of govern-ment. Apart from the Prime Minister, the Chancellor of the Exchequer was the only Cabinet minister with responsibility for central government expenditure as a whole. Moreover, throughout the period covered by this book, the Prime Minister's private office was staffed by only three or four private secretaries, nor-mally (from 1929 exclusively) civil servants, of whom even the most senior would be of no more than middle ranking. Sometimes the Prime Minister would have additional support, as in the First World War, when Lloyd George had his 'Garden Suburb' of advisers drawn from academic life, business, or journalism, or in the Second World War, when Winston Churchill had his Statistical Section of economists, recruited mainly from universities, headed by a scientist, Profes-sor Frederick Lindemann (later Lord Cherwell).[42] However, the only perman-ent organization to rival the Treasury in its co-ordinating role was the Cabinet Office, and it was very small until the Second World War.

In 1919 the Permanent Secretary of the Treasury, Sir Warren Fisher, was rec-ognized as the Head of the Civil Service. As such, Fisher claimed that he was

[41] Sir Alec Cairncross, *The Wilson Years: A Treasury Diary, 1964–1969* (1997), 56.
[42] For these innovations see John Turner, *Lloyd George's Secretariat* (Cambridge, 1980); Thomas Wilson, *Churchill and the Prof.* (1995).

'the principal official adviser of the Prime Minister', to whom he had direct access. However, what this meant in practice depended on his personal relations with the incumbent of 10 Downing Street.[43] The Cabinet Secretary, whose post had been created in 1916, was in more continuous contact with the Prime Minister, by being present at meetings of the Cabinet and its principal subcommittees. The first Cabinet Secretary, Sir Maurice Hankey, became a confidential adviser to successive Prime Ministers, as did Edward Bridges (1938–46) and Norman Brook (1946–62). Even so, the post of Cabinet Secretary was still lower in rank than that of the Permanent Secretary of the Treasury when Bridges was appointed to the latter post in 1945. It was only when he retired in 1956, and his job was divided between Brook, who became Head of the Civil Service, while continuing to be Cabinet Secretary (with the title of Joint Permanent Secretary of the Treasury), and another Joint Permanent Secretary, Sir Roger Makins, who was responsible for the rest of the work of the department, that the Cabinet Secretary become equal in status to the permanent head of the Treasury.

As noted above, a minister whose department had been refused money or increased staff by the Treasury could appeal to the Cabinet. Treasury influence thus depended in part on the authority in Cabinet of the Chancellor, and on his ability to play the part of devil's advocate against new proposals. That ability in turn rested in part on the advice given to him by his officials in the divisions controlling public expenditure—hence Treasury insistence that sound government depended upon proposals for new expenditure being discussed with the Treasury in advance of being put to Cabinet. Treasury criticism would often be directed at the merits of the proposals, and whether they would establish undesirable precedents. Treasury control could make Cabinet government more effective by ensuring that ministers heard the arguments against, as well as for, new expenditure. However, the most promising line for the Treasury to pursue was to argue that the aggregate of expenditure would require increased taxation, thereby forcing ministers and departments to think in terms of priorities.

The Cabinet would swiftly have been overloaded with work if it had had to decide every question of policy or priority. Accordingly, the normal procedure was for spending departments to reach bilateral agreements with the Treasury, at the official level in the first instance, but with ministers being consulted on matters of policy. If no bilateral agreement could be reached, the matter would go to the Cabinet, whose decision was binding. However, normally the Cabinet was concerned only with matters of high policy, and details, including the speed with which policy was to be implemented, would remain subject to Treasury control. Consequently, there could remain ample room for dispute between the Treasury and a spending department even after the Cabinet had taken a decision. Moreover, it was not unknown for Cabinets to take contradictory decisions: for example, endorsing a general policy of economy, while also approving

[43] O'Halpin, *Head of the Civil Service*, 135.

particular proposals for expenditure which, in aggregate, conflicted with the policy of economy. Treasury control was necessary to ensure that departments were conforming to policy as laid down by the Cabinet. Even so, departments might still go their own way: for example, in the period of rearmament before the Second World War the Air Ministry, the Admiralty and the War Office all tended to go beyond what the Cabinet had authorized in carrying out their programmes.[44]

Inevitably the Treasury's role appeared to be negative to departments trying to get on with what they conceived to be their jobs, or to outsiders who believed that government should be more ambitious in its objectives. However, part of the Treasury's unpopularity arose from the tone which it adopted in its dealings with other departments. Sir Edward Hamilton, who was Joint Permanent Secretary from 1902 to 1907, thought that the Treasury would be more effective if its officials would avoid incivility, and thereby get other departments on to its side, instead of getting their backs up. Sir Warren Fisher felt the same. Yet as late as 1956 Sir Roger Makins, newly appointed as Joint Permanent Secretary, was struck by the rudeness of Treasury correspondence, and tried to persuade his officials to be more polite. On the other hand, at least one of these officials, Leo Pliatzky, took the view that, in relation to the control of public expenditure, Treasury correspondence was not rude enough.[45] Some allowance has to be made for Makins's diplomatic background—he had come from the Foreign Office—and there were occasions when Treasury officials were sorely provoked. For example, in 1953 the Secretary of State for War complained that detailed Treasury control of barrack-building was holding up measures necessary for boosting army morale. An internal Treasury paper noted that the War Office's plans were for buildings of higher standard than those of the other services or local authorities, and that, at a time when a five-bedroomed house in Belgravia could be bought for £5,000, the War Office wished to build officers' accommodation estimated to cost £2,500 a head—and 'that for young gentlemen of the Household Cavalry, whose morale boosting takes place mostly by night in the Piccadilly area'.[46]

More sinister than charges of incivility were claims that the Permanent Secretary's position as Head of the Civil Service gave him and his department too much influence. The Head of the Civil Service was responsible for advising the Prime Minister on senior appointments in all government departments, including, until the Second World War, the Foreign Office. Claims of excessive

---

[44] Peden, *British Rearmament*, esp. 157–66, 172.

[45] Hamilton to Asquith, 25 Sept. 1907, Asquith Papers, vol. 19, Bodleian Library, Oxford. Conversations with Lord Sherfield (formerly Sir Roger Makins) and Sir Leo Pliatzky, both 9 June 1988.

[46] G. P. Humphreys-Davies to I. P. Bancroft, 11 Dec. 1953, T225/350. Bridges noted that Humphreys-Davies's paper had been 'much praised' in the Treasury but made plain that something more restrained would be required for the Chancellor's reply.

influence were particularly strident with regard to Fisher. It was believed that civil servants might fear that their promotion prospects would suffer if they made too strong a fight with the Treasury for the policy of their departments.[47] Although it is hard to find any evidence to substantiate such a belief, it is always possible that some civil servants were influenced by rumour and played safe.

However, what seems more likely to have influenced attitudes towards the Treasury was the emphasis placed by Fisher and his successors on teamwork in the Civil Service, with much of the work of government being done through interdepartmental committees. Not every minister appreciated interdepartmental teamwork at the official level: Richard Crossman, when Minister for Housing and Local Government, complained in 1966 that 'all civil servants I worked with were imbued with a prior loyalty to the Treasury and felt it necessary to spy on me and report all my doings to the Treasury, whether I wanted then kept private or not'. It appears that Crossman's Permanent Secretary, Dame Evelyn Sharp, had told the Treasury that her minister was not telling the Chancellor the truth about the rate of housing approvals.[48] She was not the first official in a spending department to look to the Treasury for support against her own minister. For example, in 1936 a Treasury official noted that a decision regarding the building of a new barracks was 'the Secretary of State's, arrived at against the preponderance of opinion at the War Office' and that there was 'reason to believe that Treasury objection would be welcomed'.[49]

MINISTERS AND OFFICIALS

One of the enduring questions about Whitehall is who makes policy: ministers or civil servants?[50] The constitutional position is that the ministers are responsible for policy, and civil servants advise and warn. In practice the influence of civil servants over ministers varies according to policy issues and personalities, and therefore requires empirical research. Generally speaking, however, a minister could hardly hope to formulate a policy, or draw up a budget, without the help of civil servants. There is a story that Benjamin Disraeli, when he was invited by Lord Derby to join the latter's Cabinet as Chancellor of the Exchequer, pleaded ignorance of the duties he would have to perform. Derby replied that this was normal for a new Chancellor and that 'anyway, they [the Treasury officials] give you the figures'. That was in 1852, and in 1959 the then

---

[47] 125 HL Deb. 1942–3, col. 269. These charges have since been debated by historians: see O'Halpin, *Head of the Civil Service*, 75–8, 134–5.

[48] Richard Crossman, *The Diaries of a Cabinet Minister*, vol. i, *Minister of Housing, 1964–66* (1976), 615; Cairncross, *Wilson Years*, 84.   [49] Peden, *British Rearmament*, 169.

[50] For a useful debate on this question see *Public Admin.*, 43 (1965), 251–68, for contributions by Sir Edward Boyle, who was a junior minister in the Treasury in 1955–6 and again in 1959–62, and Sir Edward Playfair, who was a Treasury official in 1934–46 and 1947–56.

Chancellor, Derick Heathcoat Amory, recalling the story in a budget speech, remarked that 'fortunately that well-tried practice continues today'.[51]

The Chancellor of the Exchequer was not expected to be a financial expert, but he was expected to bring political judgement to bear on the figures that his officials gave him. In particular, he had to judge the likely reactions of his party and the electorate to different possible ways of raising revenue, and different possible ways of curbing government expenditure. To be successful, he also had to be a strong minister, and to enjoy the support of the Prime Minister, to win battles in Cabinet. Chancellors were usually substantial political figures in their own right, and in the period covered in this book the Treasury was more often a stepping stone to the premiership than was the equally prestigious Foreign Office.[52]

The Chancellor was, however, often a lonely figure. The post of Chief Secretary, the Treasury minister who now does much of the work relating to control of public expenditure, was not created until 1961. Until 1947 the Treasury had only one junior minister, the Financial Secretary, who acted as the Chancellor's lieutenant in Parliament and in matters relating to public expenditure, but who was normally excluded from the formulation of major policies. There were only two short periods, in 1915–16 and again in 1923, when the Financial Secretary was a member of the Cabinet. At the end of 1947, in recognition of the Treasury's wider economic responsibilities, a second junior ministerial post was created, that of Economic Secretary, but again its holder was not expected to exercise much influence on policy.

Normally the Chancellor looked to his senior officials for advice. It was the duty of civil servants both to ensure that a minister was aware of all the facts and arguments relating to a case on which he had to take a decision, and to advise which of the possible courses of action should be followed. Officials had to take the political complexion of the government of the day into account, but Bridges believed that a civil servant had a duty to draw upon 'the storehouse of departmental experience; and to let the waves of practical philosophy wash against the ideas put forward by his ministerial master'.[53] In practice, given the technical nature of many of the issues they had to deal with, most Chancellors tended to become the spokesmen of the departmental Treasury view much of the time. Lloyd George was described in the late 1920s as the only Chancellor who had made the Treasury do what it had not wanted to.[54] However, later examples can be found in this book of Chancellors who overrode officials' views.

[51]   603 HC Deb., 5s, 1958–9, col. 33.

[52]   Between 1906 and 1959 there were twenty Chancellors of the Exchequer, of whom seven later became Prime Minister (Asquith, Lloyd George, Bonar Law, Baldwin, Neville Chamberlain, Churchill, and Macmillan), compared with two out of fifteen Foreign Secretaries (Eden and Macmillan).

[53]   Sir Edward Bridges, *Portrait of a Profession: The Civil Service Tradition* (Cambridge, 1950), 19.

[54]   By P. J. Grigg, according to Robert Boothby, *Recollections of a Rebel* (1978), 46. Grigg joined the Treasury in 1913.

The Permanent Secretary of the Treasury outranked all other permanent heads of Whitehall departments. Between 1919 and 1932 there was a second tier of Treasury officials with the rank of 'Controller', each with the status equal to that of the permanent head of a first-class department in Whitehall. In 1932 the rank of Controller was abolished, being replaced by that of 'Second Secretary'. Controllers or Second Secretaries had the right to give advice directly to the Chancellor, as long as the Permanent Secretary knew what was going on. The detailed work of the department was carried out by more junior officials, organized into divisions, each of which had particular areas of responsibility. In 1906 there were twenty-seven officials in the 'upper establishment', only one more than when the Treasury had been reorganized in 1870, when Gladstone had been Prime Minister. It was this small group of officials, in what from 1921 was known as the 'administrative class', that dealt with all questions relating to finance, control of central government expenditure, Civil Service establishments and superannuation, and Civil List pensions. By 1948 there were 168 officials in the administrative class, a figure that fell after 1951 to 153 in 1958. However, given the increased range of the Treasury's responsibilities, a sixfold increase in personnel was by no means excessive, and it can be argued that increasing pressure of work meant that most Treasury officials had insufficient time to keep up with developments in economic theory or managerial practice.

The ethos of the pre-1914 Treasury was that of a cultured élite, its few new recruits frequently having come first in the Civil Service examinations.[55] Keynes, who came second in 1906, had to be content with the India Office. As an archetypal product of the period, one might take Sir David Waley, who joined the department in 1910, having studied classics at Oxford, and who could relax from negotiations over reparations after the Second World War by reading Ovid (in Latin) while several typists clattered away beside him.[56] Subsequent enlargement of the Treasury modified the department's ethos somewhat, but there continued to be recruits who were well up to pre-1914 standards. Sir Douglas Wass, who had studied mathematics at Cambridge, and had been employed on scientific research in the Admiralty before entering the Treasury in 1946, may be taken as an example. When he retired as Permanent Secretary

[55] The Treasury's upper establishment was also exclusively male until 1920, when Dame Maude Lawrence was appointed Director of Women's Establishments. It was not until 1925 that the Civil Service examination for the administrative class was opened to women, and down to the Second World War their careers normally ended with marriage, owing to a Treasury circular of August 1921 which laid down that all women civil servants should be unmarried or widows, unless an exception was granted in the interests of the service. Prejudice against women seems to have abated somewhat by the late 1930s, and by 1959 Mrs E. M. Abbott had reached the rank of Third Secretary, as Establishments Officer for the Treasury. For the entry of women into the administrative class see Meta Zimmeck, 'Strategies and Stratagems for the Employment of Women in the British Civil Service, 1919–1939', *Hist. J.*, 27 (1984), 901–24, and memoirs by senior women civil servants: Hilda Martindale, *From One Generation to Another, 1839–1944* (1944), 188–97, and Dame Alix Meynell, *Public Servant, Private Woman* (1988). The latter points out (p. 85) that in the inter-war period the state was a pioneer in recruiting women to positions of responsibility.   [56] MacDougall, *Don and Mandarin*, 51.

in 1983, he gave a series of Reith Lectures, the title of which was drawn from Milton's *Paradise Lost*; the first lecture began with a description of a fourteenth-century allegorical painting of good and bad government by Ambrogio Lorenzetti, followed by a discussion of the art of government with reference to Herodotus, John Locke, and Adam Smith.[57]

Keynes described the Treasury, in which he served as a temporary civil servant during the First World War, as 'very clever, very dry and in a certain sense very cynical; intellectually self-confident',[58] a description that would serve for the whole period. Treasury humour could certainly be very dry. A departmental favourite was a letter to the War Office written entirely in monosyllables. Drafted about 1890 by Lord Welby, the then Permanent Secretary, as a protest against the alleged thick-headedness of the War Office, the letter was still being circulated for the amusement of officials as late as 1956.[59]

Most Treasury officials had studied humanities at Oxford or Cambridge, or (less commonly) mathematics at Cambridge,[60] and as late as 1955 a Chancellor, R. A. Butler, could write comments in Latin on a memorandum relating to the budget.[61] Latin, Greek, and mathematics were originally given a greater weighting in the Higher Civil Service examinations compared with subjects like economics or modern languages, and in 1943 Professor Lionel Robbins, the Director of the Economic Section of the War Cabinet Offices, observed that it was difficult for a candidate with a training in economics or another social science to satisfy the requirements of the Civil Service examiners. He expected changes then being made to produce a 'larger recruitment of personnel with an expert training in economics and economic statistics',[62] but even in the 1950s

[57] The *Listener*, 24 Nov. 1983, 19.

[58] *Collected Writings of John Maynard Keynes* (hereafter *JMK*), vol. xvi. 299.

[59] Apparently the letter was never sent—Bridges to S. C. Leslie, 24 Oct. 1956, T199/362. Another copy of the letter is to be found in T172/1857, where a note to the Chancellor, 25 Nov. 1937, describes it as having 'long been a tradition in the Treasury'. The letter itself begins: 'Sir, The skilled men who are bound to see that in the case of war the State is safe at all points, wish that there should be a store of cash, or what would be as good as cash, kept at great Ports and Forts out of this realm, to meet the need which would rise if those Ports and Forts should be blocked by the foe, and for that end they ask that a store of notes of the Bank should be kept at the spots they name . . . . But . . . the notes you name can not be used in Law to pay debts out of this land, nor yet in this land but on this side of Tweed' (Bank of England notes were not then legal tender in Scotland) and ends: 'Tracts on wealth are used by School Boards. Some of these might be read with gain by those who have to plan schemes of the kind now in vogue. They might be bought out of Vote 8, if a small sum on the Vote could be saved for so good an end.'

[60] In 1906, of the twenty-five officials in the upper establishment (second class clerks and above), sixteen had gone to Oxford; seven to Cambridge; one to London and Berlin; and one had not been to university. In the period 1919–25, of the twenty-eight senior officials who served in the Treasury with the rank of principal clerk (subsequently assistant secretary) or above, eighteen had been to Oxford; four to Cambridge; one to Trinity College, Dublin; one to Manchester; and four had not been to university. Of the twenty-two whose university studies are known, sixteen had studied *literae humaniores* at Oxford or classics at Cambridge; three had studied mathematics or natural sciences; two had studied history; and one had studied law.

[61] The memorandum was by Sir Edward Bridges, 20 Jan. 1955, T171/450.

[62] 'Notes on the Role of the Economist in the Future Machinery of Government', 25 Jan. 1943, para. 27, Cabinet Office Papers, series 87, vol. 72 (hereafter CAB87/72), Public Record Office, London. For

most new entrants to the administrative class had studied one or more of the humanities. The traditional academic background of Treasury officials was not without its defenders. Oxford's degree in *literae humaniores*, combining as it did ancient history and philosophy, using Greek and Latin texts, with modern philosophy, including logic, was praised as an intellectual background by Treasury ministers in the 1950s; and Sir Leo Pliatzky, who reached the rank of Second Permanent Secretary in 1976, believed that *literae humaniores* provided an excellent training in the precise and accurate use of words.[63]

Until the opening of the Centre for Administrative Studies in 1963 officials received very little formal instruction; instead training was 'on the job'. New entrants learned their craft by drafting papers, including recommendations on policy issues. In theory, and originally in practice, experienced colleagues would discuss a new recruit's work with him, but by 1945 the pressure of business had become so great that it seems that they had little time to spare for this purpose, and the quality of training may have declined.[64] A Committee on the Training of Civil Servants, under the chairmanship of Ralph Assheton, the Financial Secretary, reported in 1944 in favour of formal post-entry training for civil servants,[65] and as a result a Training and Education Division was set up in the Treasury in 1945 to co-ordinate training in government departments and to run central courses. However, pleading a shortage of staff, the Treasury reduced the Assheton Committee's recommendation of a two- to three-month, part-time course for assistant principals (the grade of entry for the administrative class) to a two-week, full-time course on the machinery of government. In 1951 the Permanent Secretary, Bridges, in response to the Conservative government's demands for a reduction in the size of the Civil Service, told the Chancellor that the training of civil servants was one of the 'less essential' duties of the Treasury,[66] and the staff of the Training and Education Division was cut. Although the initial two-week course was supplemented by further opportunities for training, unfavourable comparisons were being drawn by the mid-1950s with the three-year course for the French administrative élite at the École National d'Administration.[67]

evolution of Civil Service recruitment over the period covered by this book see Richard A. Chapman, *Leadership in the British Civil Service* (1984).

[63] Arthur Salter, *Memoirs of a Public Servant* (1961), 31–2; Reginald Maudling, *Memoirs* (1978), 27–8; conversation with Sir Leo Pliatzky. Salter was Minister for Economic Affairs in 1951–2, and Maudling was Economic Secretary in 1952–5.

[64] Conversations with Mr Henry Jenkyns, 10 Oct. 1988, and Sir Leo Pliatzky. Jenkyns entered the Treasury in 1945 and Pliatzky in 1950. In contrast, P. J. Grigg and Frederick Leith Ross seem to have received very effective training from their divisional heads before the First World War—see P. J. Grigg, *Prejudice and Judgement* (1948), 35–6, and Sir Frederick Leith-Ross, *Money Talks* (1968), 22–3.

[65] *Report on the Training of Civil Servants* (Cmd. 6525), PP 1943–4, iii. 119.

[66] Bridges to Butler, 22 Nov. 1951, T273/323.

[67] For a defence of the British system see David Hubback, 'The Treasury's Role in Civil Service Training', *Public Admin.*, 35 (1957), 99–109.

As part of 'training on the job', officials would be moved from one division to another, often at intervals of only one to two years, with a view to broadening their experience of the work of the department, including finance, control of expenditure, and establishments work, with specialization deferred until they reached the rank of assistant secretary. In the inter-war period Fisher suspended direct recruitment into the Treasury and instead selected picked men from other departments, who would make the Treasury a 'corps d'élite'.[68] Direct recruitment to the Treasury resumed thereafter, but the tradition of the 'generalist' or 'all-rounder' continued with an increased number of transfers of officials between departments. In a famous essay entitled 'The Apotheosis of the Dilettante', first published in 1959, the Fabian economist Thomas Balogh condemned the lack of expert knowledge of Treasury officials,[69] and certainly it is not clear that on-the-job training alone was adequate for managing the economy.

On the other hand, lack of formal professional training was not a unique characteristic of the Civil Service; it was also then characteristic of business management, journalism, and, indeed, Balogh's own principal occupation, university teaching. Doubtless formal training is desirable in all occupations, but it would seem unwise of critics, who themselves have learned their trade on the job, to dismiss accumulated practical experience as 'amateurism', without at least allowing the possibility that exceptional intelligence may have allowed some civil servants to become competent administrators and advisers. Nor was the Treasury exceptional in not employing economists in the control of public expenditure: the same would have been true of the Bureau of the Budget doing the equivalent job in the United States. A Treasury official was supposed to be able to subject a proposal for expenditure to the same kind of cross-examination as a barrister applies to an expert witness, and to be able to advise the Chancellor when there was a dispute with the department making the proposal.[70] However, by the 1950s, much more was being demanded of 'intelligent laymen' in Whitehall than had been the case fifty years earlier, as the functions of government came increasingly to require managers rather than administrators, and it is not surprising that academic critics questioned whether the Treasury had responded adequately to this change.[71]

---

[68] See Fisher's evidence to Treasury Organisation Committee, 2 Nov. 1936, and the Committee's report, 10 Mar. 1938, T199/50c.

[69] Thomas Balogh, 'The Apotheosis of the Dilettante', in Hugh Thomas (ed.), *The Establishment* (1959), 83–126. Balogh's criticisms were subsequently repeated a decade later in the Fulton Report: *Report of the Committee on the Civil Service* (Cmnd. 3638), PP 1967–8, xviii. 129. The Fulton Committee's criticisms of the Civil Service received a mixed reception from informed opinion—see Geoffrey K. Fry, *Reforming the Civil Service: The Fulton Committee on the British Home Civil Service of 1966–1968* (Edinburgh, 1993), 241–59.

[70] T. H. Caulcott, 'The Control of Public Expenditure', *Public Admin.*, 40 (1962), 273; Sir John Woods, chairman of Treasury Organisation Committee, at first meeting of that committee, 2 Feb. 1950, T273/203.

[71] See, for example, Ely Devons, *Papers on Planning and Economic Development*, ed. Sir Alec Cairncross (Manchester, 1970), chs. 17 and 18.

Balogh also believed that the Civil Service was much too representative of the most privileged and conservative elements in British society. It is certainly true that most officials in the administrative class had been educated at independent schools and either Oxford or Cambridge University.[72] On the other hand, one should be cautious about assuming that social origins determine political opinions. Many socialists are living refutations of such a hypothesis. Nor were humble origins a bar to advancement. For example, P. J. Grigg, an influential private secretary to successive Chancellors in the 1920s, and later Permanent Under-Secretary of State at the War Office, was a carpenter's son; Sir Horace Wilson, who became Permanent Secretary of the Treasury in 1939, was the son of a furniture-maker and a boarding-house keeper. There can be no doubt, however, that the fact that the social background of many members of the Treasury's administrative class was similar to that of ministers made for easy and informal relations between them. For example, when Harold Macmillan became Chancellor in 1955, he noted that he had known the Permanent Secretary, Bridges, from schooldays at Eton more than forty years earlier.[73]

The most important influence on a Treasury official, however, was experience of work in the department itself. A new recruit could not fail to notice the department's austere, Gladstonian attitude towards expenditure of the taxpayer's money. The Treasury had also inherited Gladstone's belief that tariffs favoured particular economic interests, and as late as 1956, twenty-four years after the introduction of a general tariff, Bridges could remark that 'the general traditional slant of the Treasury is slightly "free trade".'[74] There were other relics of pre-1914 attitudes in the 1950s: Macmillan, as minister for housing, encountered anti-landlord attitudes among Treasury officials that he believed would not have been out of place among nineteenth-century radicals.[75] Even when the Treasury was concerned with macroeconomic management, officials continued to believe that all government expenditure tended to create vested interests, making it harder to reduce expenditure, and therefore taxation.[76]

ECONOMIC ADVICE

Given that Treasury officials were generalists, how did economics enter the policy-making process? Until 1919 the Treasury had nobody employed as an economist. One official, Henry Higgs, had been joint editor of the *Economic Journal* from 1892 to 1906, and had published books about the financial system. However, there is no evidence that Higgs was regarded in the Treasury as an

---

[72] For sociological survey see R. K. Kelsall, *Higher Civil Servants in Britain from 1870 to the Present* (1955).
[73] Harold Macmillan, *Riding the Storm, 1956–1959* (1971), 2.
[74] Bridges to Macmillan, 2 Feb. 1956, T273/339.
[75] Harold Macmillan, *Tides of Fortune, 1945–1955* (1969), 423.
[76] 'Notes for Cabinet', 20 Dec. 1951, T273/315.

economic expert during his years in the department (1907–21); latterly he was employed as Treasury Parliamentary Clerk, a post in which his training as a barrister would have been of more use than his interest in economics.[77] Economists had not yet achieved the professional status that they were to gain by mid-century, and when Lloyd George wanted economic advice when he was Chancellor before the First World War he turned to a financial journalist, George Paish, editor of the *Statist* (see Chapter 2). Down to the 1930s economics was something that officials who had studied philosophy or mathematics at Oxford or Cambridge were expected to be able to 'get up', if required, and many candidates for the Civil Service examination did so. Keynes himself studied mathematics at Cambridge, and his initial training in economics amounted to no more than directed reading over a summer vacation. Yet, in 1908, within three years of graduation, he was considered to be qualified not only as a lecturer in economics at Cambridge but also as joint editor of the *Economic Journal*. During the First World War he was recruited into the Treasury, where he became head of a new division dealing with overseas finance, but his duties differed only in subject matter from those of other officials.

In 1919 Ralph Hawtrey, who had been a Treasury official since 1904, was released from administrative duties to become Director of Financial Enquiries, and became the department's in-house economist for the rest of the inter-war period. Like Keynes, Hawtrey had studied mathematics at Cambridge, and had little formal training in economics. Indeed, he scored low marks in the political economy paper in the Civil Service examination, having crammed the subject by attending lectures by J. H. Clapham, the economic historian. Hawtrey later recalled that, on entering the Treasury in 1904, he found that officials were not generally interested in economics, which was not regarded as more important to their work than, say, a knowledge of local government. Nevertheless, he learned a lot from Sir John Bradbury, an official who enjoyed a reputation in the City as a financial expert and who, after his retirement, became President of the British Bankers' Association. Hawtrey made a study of the trade cycle, which was published as *Good and Bad Trade* in 1913. His second book, *Currency and Credit* (1919) was widely used by university students in the 1920s and 1930s, and in the academic year 1928/9 he went on leave to teach at Harvard. Keynes took Hawtrey seriously as an economist, corresponding extensively with him while working out the *General Theory*.[78] In 1936 Fisher told the Public Accounts Committee that the Director of Financial Enquiries concerned himself 'primarily

---

[77] I am grateful to Andrew McDonald for drawing my attention to Higgs's career. Higgs's publications included *The Financial System of the United Kingdom* (1914), *National Economy* (1917), and *A Primer of National Finance* (1919).

[78] For Hawtrey's contribution to economics see P. Deutscher, *R. G. Hawtrey and the Development of Macroeconomics* (1990), and more specifically on his contribution to Keynesian economics see Neville Cain, 'Hawtrey and the Multiplier Theory', *Australian Econ. Hist. Rev.*, 22 (1982), 68–78, and Robert W. Dimand, *The Origins of the Keynesian Revolution: The Development of Keynes's Theory of Employment and Output* (Aldershot, 1988), 107–11, 136–7.

with the theory of higher finance'; but that it was difficult to define his duties, which struck Fisher 'as a bit metaphysical'.[79] The following year, during an internal enquiry into the Treasury's organization, Sir Frederick Phillips, then one of the two most senior Treasury officials dealing with financial policy, said that he regarded the employment of an economist in the department as a necessity, and that when the time came for Hawtrey to retire he should be replaced by an economist from outside the Civil Service. Otherwise, Phillips noted, ministers 'would come to rely on unofficial advice from divers quarters'.[80]

The Treasury had good reason for not wishing ministers to rely on unofficial advice. Keynes, who had resigned from the Treasury in 1919 and returned to Cambridge, had subsequently established a reputation for proposing in the press unorthodox solutions to unemployment, to the point where Treasury officials carefully read what he had to say, in order to supply the Chancellor with counter-arguments. In 1930 Ramsay MacDonald, the Labour Prime Minister, established an Economic Advisory Council, with Keynes as one of its members, and one of the council's subcommittees, the Committee on Economic Information, provided economic advice through the Cabinet Office until the outbreak of the Second World War. It was the war itself, however, that gave economists a permanent position in Whitehall, with the creation in 1939 of a Central Economic Information Service, which later divided into the Central Statistical Office and the Economic Section, all located in the Offices of the War Cabinet. The war brought about a revolutionary improvement in the compilation and presentation of statistics which enabled the economists in the Economic Section, notably Lionel Robbins and James Meade, to apply macroeconomic concepts and to play a major role in introducing Keynesian ideas into official thinking, especially with regard to post-war employment policy.[81]

The Treasury recruited its own economic advisers during the war, including Keynes, who returned in 1940 as an (unpaid) adviser to the Chancellor, a position he retained until his death in 1946. Treasury officials, not being professional economists, looked to Keynes and then to successive Directors of the Economic Section, Meade (1946–7) and Robert Hall (1947–61), for a judgement of the macroeconomic variables, and the Economic Section was transferred from the Cabinet Office to the Treasury in 1953. It has been argued that, whereas the Treasury had generally excluded Keynes's ideas from policy-making in the inter-war period, the very authority of the department made it easier for Keynesian ideas to become established in Whitehall in the 1940s than was the case in the United States, where there was no comparable central department

---

[79] PP 1935–6, v. 439.

[80] Minutes of Treasury Organisation Committee, 9 Mar. 1937, T199/50c.

[81] Cairncross and Watts, *Economic Section*, chs. 2–7. There is a huge literature on how Keynes influenced economic thought and policy—see Mark Blaug, 'Second Thoughts on the Keynesian Revolution', *Hist. of Pol. Econ.*, 23 (1991), 171–92; Peter Clarke, 'Keynes in History', ibid., 26 (1994), 117–35, and sources cited therein.

in the administrative structure.[82] That may well be so, but it is also worth asking how Keynesian ideas were received in the Treasury, and how they were fitted into the traditional framework of public finance, as the way in which Keynesian ideas are applied depends very much upon historical circumstances.

At no time would Treasury officials have conceded that economists had a monopoly of economic knowledge. Most officials were employed on the control of expenditure or Civil Service establishments but some had spent many years working on financial questions and had their own experience to draw on. For example, Sir Richard Hopkins, who entered the Treasury in 1927 as Controller of the Finance and Supply Services departments and later became Permanent Secretary, had previously served for 25 years at the Board of Inland Revenue, and his experience of public finance, which he supplemented with private study of economics, won him admiration even from professional economists. Sir Roy Harrod, for example, compared him to 'an ancient sage . . . somehow wafted through the centuries to give wise counsel to a half-baked generation'.[83]

The Treasury also valued advice from people with practical experience of economic affairs. For example, Fisher, while Permanent Secretary between the wars, used his informal contacts with Reginald McKenna, a former Chancellor who had become Chairman of the Midland Bank, Sir William McLintock, the leading City accountant, and Lord Weir, the Glasgow industrialist.[84] Inevitably the Treasury's location in London, its responsibility for financial policy, and its links with the Bank of England, meant that informal contacts tended to be closer with finance than industry. The London bias of the Treasury's world view would also seem to have been reinforced by officials' choice of financial journalism which, to judge from cuttings in Treasury files, was dominated by the *Economist*, the *Financial Times*, the *Statist*, and *The Times*. It is doubtful whether advice from academic economists based in Cambridge or Oxford did much to broaden this world view.

PROBLEMS OF ASSESSING THE TREASURY'S PERFORMANCE

It is not easy to assess the Treasury's performance as a department, given the nature of the evidence. Winston Churchill, who was Chancellor from 1924 to 1929, subsequently referred to the often irresistible power of departmental advice 'based upon knowledge and on systematized and organized currents of opinion'.[85] However, ministers' diaries and other private papers contain

[82] Margaret Weir, 'Ideas and Politics: The Acceptance of Keynesianism in Britain and the United States', in Peter A. Hall (ed.), *The Political Power of Economic Ideas: Keynesianism Across Nations* (Princeton, NJ, 1989), 53–86.   [83] R. F. Harrod, *The Life of John Maynard Keynes* (1951), 529.
[84] O'Halpin, *Head of the Civil Service*, 139 n. 71. For a discussion of sources of economic advice see G. C. Peden, 'Economic Knowledge and the State in Modern Britain', in Green and Whiting, *The Boundaries of the State*, 170–87.   [85] 368 HC Deb., 5s, 1940–1, col. 258.

remarkably few references to officials or their advice, probably because that advice was so pervasive that ministers felt no need to mention it. On the other hand, official advice had to be tailored to the political preferences of the government of the day, and consequently Treasury documents, even those relating to advice offered by economists, have to be read in the context of Cabinet controversies, parliamentary debates, and elections.

There has been some debate among historians as to the value of Whitehall records, and certainly Treasury documents are no less problematic than other historical sources.[86] The manner in which officials would write varied markedly according to their purposes: an informal exchange of views between officials might reveal marked differences of opinion; minutes of meetings or reports for ministers, on the other hand, would normally only record conclusions. Whereas an academic would have set out the points at issue, the civil servant's instinct, when drafting a formal document, was to find a form of words with which everyone could agree, even if the document was internally inconsistent as a result. Even the authorship of Treasury papers may be in doubt. Most files begin with a paper (or 'minute') drafted by a junior official, acting on instructions from a senior colleague, and, depending upon the importance and complexity of the matter, there would be several subsequent drafts, incorporating the ideas of a number of senior officials, before the matter reached the Chancellor. Even a manuscript draft may have been partly dictated by someone other than the person who signed it. One official recalled an example when a very senior official, Sir Frederick Phillips, was writing furiously while a subordinate, Ernest Rowe-Dutton, who knew more about the matter in hand, told him what to write. Every now and then Phillips would look up and ask, 'Why?', when Rowe-Dutton made a point. At last Rowe-Dutton asked, 'Who is writing this minute—you or I?'. Phillips grunted, then wrote on in silence.[87] It is not easy, therefore, to identify either 'organized currents of opinion' in Whitehall, or the extent to which individuals helped to shape them. However, the effort is worthwhile, for some officials have had a great influence on policy over long periods.

Ideally, Treasury control of expenditure would be judged according to how resources were allocated or redistributed in the community as a whole. In practice such judgement is extremely difficult. Evidence would have to be sought in the files of departments other than the Treasury, to see how far these departments and the aspects of government for which they were responsible were affected by Treasury control—a massive task that cannot be carried out by one historian. A book based mainly on Treasury files and papers of Chancellors of the Exchequer can only trace the direction of Treasury influence, while bearing in mind that policy outcomes reflect the influences of other departments as well.

---

[86] See Rodney Lowe, 'Plumbing New Depths: Contemporary Historians and the Public Record Office', *20th Cent. Brit. Hist.*, 8 (1997), 239–65, and the articles cited therein.

[87] Conversation with Sir Edward Playfair, 21 Apr. 1975.

A quite different problem arises from the breakdown since the 1970s in the Keynesian consensus, which once provided an agreed basis on which to judge economic policy. Most accounts written from the 1950s to the 1970s assumed that the Treasury should have adopted Keynes's ideas more quickly or more wholeheartedly than it did. However, since the 1970s there has been a rival interpretation: public choice theory, which claims that, when the state provides more than minimal welfare services, collective choice always tends to produce suboptimal or even harmful outcomes. It is argued that whereas the individual making a private choice in a free market weighs costs against benefits, both governments and voters are able to avoid, or at least to postpone, the consequences of spending decisions. Voters are more aware of the benefits of particular policies to themselves than they are of the economic consequences of financing all the policies favoured by the electorate. Consequently, it is claimed, fear of being outbid by the opposition in making promises to spend money on vote-catching policies tends to discourage democratic governments from curbing public expenditure, especially when the burden of payment can be placed on future governments (and taxpayers) by increasing the public debt. It has also been claimed that the tendency to expand public services beyond what is either necessary or desirable is reinforced by the self-interest of bureaucrats in maximizing their own budgets and departments without due regard to the costs for the nation as a whole. While these claims were originally made with reference to American rather than British experience, public choice theory challenges earlier assumptions about the benevolence and competence of experts and planners.[88]

Peter Clarke has pointed out that the public choice model hardly applies to the Treasury itself, with its austere attitude to public expenditure and the size and pay of the Civil Service.[89] Indeed, Gladstonian rules of public finance, especially the balanced budget convention, may be said to have anticipated public choice theory, even before the electorate was extended beyond the property-owning classes by the Reform Acts of 1867, 1884, and 1918. The perspective of a Treasury official seeking to maintain control over public expenditure was very

[88] James M. Buchanan and Richard E. Wagner, *Democracy in Deficit: The Political Legacy of Lord Keynes* (New York, 1977); William A. Niskanen, *Bureaucracy and Representative Government* (New York, 1971). Public choice theory was applied to the British case in J. M. Buchanan, John Burton, and R. E. Wagner, *The Consequences of Mr Keynes* (1978); W. A. Niskanen, *Bureaucracy: Servant or Master?* (1973); and Gordon A. Tullock, *The Vote Motive: An Essay in the Economics of Politics* (1976). However, Peter Clarke, 'Keynes, Buchanan and the Balanced Budget Doctrine', in John Maloney (ed.), *Debt and Deficit: An Historical Perspective* (Cheltenham, 1997), 60–83, has shown that successive Chancellors had a surplus of current revenue over current expenditure from 1948 to 1972, which hardly suggests that Keynesian economics was incompatible with sound finance. For difficulties of applying the American model of bureaucracy to the British Civil Service see Alan Peacock, *The Economic Analysis of Government and Related Themes* (Oxford, 1979), ch. 17.
[89] Peter Clarke, 'The Twentieth-Century Revolution in Government: The Case of the British Treasury', in F. B. Smith (ed.), *Ireland, England and Australia: Essays in Honour of Oliver MacDonagh* (Canberra and Cork, 1990), 163.

different from that of an economist proposing to solve unemployment by borrowing for public expenditure. There is no a priori way of knowing which point of view was right: the historian must look at policies and their economic contexts case by case.

QUESTIONS RAISED IN THE BOOK

The period covered begins with the budget speech of 1906, when the Chancellor, H. H. Asquith, reasserted the financial orthodoxy that central government's current expenditure each year must be balanced by revenue raised in that year. It ends with the budget of 1959, when, for the first time, public expenditure was deliberately increased, and taxes cut, with a view to reducing unemployment according to Keynesian economic theory. How can one explain the evolution of the Treasury from the keeper of the central government's purse to the manager of the national economy, and to what extent were these roles reconciled? Was the Treasury able to offset the tendencies in democratic government identified by public choice theory? In other words, how successful were officials in formulating and maintaining rules of public finance that protected politicians from electoral pressures? The study of these rules is, or should be, integral to the study of how British government works. Indeed, the extent to which the Treasury succeeded, or failed, in influencing policy is itself a means of identifying the dominant political priorities of the period.

What was the relationship between civil servants and ministers, and to what extent did each set the agenda for the other, both in relation to public expenditure and taxation? How important were personalities in determining policies? To what extent did the Treasury as a department have aims that were independent of the political preferences of the government of the day? What was the nature of its relations with the Bank, the City, and industry? What was the influence of economists, and how were economic ideas incorporated into official thinking? How effective was the Treasury's control of expenditure and coordination of policy? If, to use a favourite Treasury metaphor, the proof of the pudding is in the eating, how successful was the Treasury, as measured by policy outcomes?

The book is organized into chapters which cover periods of five to eight years. Each chapter has an introduction outlining the main political or economic developments affecting the work of the Treasury, followed by sections on the department's leading personalities and how they interacted with each other, its sources of economic advice, its influence on public policies, and its relations with the rest of Whitehall. The main thesis is that the Treasury sought at all times to maintain rules that would ensure that the nation's financial system would remain sound, that government business was conducted in an orderly way, and that policy commitments did not outrun the prospective resources available. There is always a temptation for governments to try to do too much too quickly, in response to political pressures. The Treasury played a key role in enabling governments to establish priorities in relation to the economy, social services, defence, and international relations. The influence of the Treasury is open to criticism in respect of particular policies, but the issues were often more complex than critics have assumed. There has been a tendency for academics to specialize in one part of public policy only, and to assume that more resources could have been made available for the aspect of policy in which they are interested, without giving too much thought to what other purposes these resources might have been directed. This book may help to correct that tendency, since the Treasury was concerned with public policy as a whole.

CHAPTER TWO

Liberal Finance and Social Reform, 1906–1914

INTRODUCTION

Public finance occupied the centre of the Edwardian political stage, with the principal difference between the Conservative and Liberal parties in general elections being the question of how defence expenditure and social reform were to be paid for. From 1903 the orthodoxy of free trade was challenged by a tariff reform campaign, led initially by Joseph Chamberlain, who recommended that Britain should return to a policy of protection on three grounds: in order to weld the Empire into an imperial tariff union, to protect British industries and employment from foreign competition, and to broaden the sources of revenue with which to pay for social reforms such as old-age pensions. By December 1905 the Conservative Prime Minister, Arthur Balfour, could no longer keep his party united on the issue of free trade or protection. The Liberals, who were firmly wedded to their traditional policy of free trade, took office under Sir Henry Campbell-Bannerman and won the election that followed in 1906 by a landslide.[1] The Liberals aimed to avoid a need to raise revenue from tariffs, first by economies in defence expenditure, and then, when these proved to be insufficient or impracticable, by raising direct taxation on the more affluent members of society. The introduction of a tax on land values aroused such controversy in 1909 that the House of Lords rejected the budget, precipitating a constitutional crisis which was resolved only after two general elections in 1910, and by the passage of the Parliament Act of 1911, which eliminated the Lords' veto over money bills, and reduced the Lords' veto over other bills to a power to delay for two years.

On the expenditure side, the Liberals were confronted with an international arms race, punctuated by a series of crises that made war with Germany seem more than a possibility. At home policies to ameliorate poverty and unemployment were prompted not only by the ideology of what has been called the New Liberalism,[2] but also by electoral politics, for, after the 1906 election, the

---

[1] For a useful discussion of these issues see Peter J. Cain, 'Political Economy in Edwardian England: The Tariff Reform Controversy', in Alan O'Day (ed.), *The Edwardian Age: Conflict and Stability, 1900–1914* (1979), 35–59.
[2] See Michael Freeden, *The New Liberalism: An Ideology of Social Reform* (Oxford, 1978).

Liberals faced a new challenge in the form of the Labour party, which threat-ened to attract the Liberals' traditional working-class support. Social reform also had cross-party appeal as a contribution to Britain's ability to compete in the international environment, which was often represented as a Darwinian struggle in which only the fittest would survive: school meals, minimum wage legislation, and national insurance benefits, by preventing poor health or physique among the labour force or potential recruits, would promote what was called 'national efficiency'.[3]

Most nineteenth-century social services had been provided by local author-ities, including the Poor Law unions, but by the Edwardian period it was clear that in the poorer areas the limits of existing local taxation had been reached, so that a further expansion of social services would have to be paid for by central government. There were central government grants for various purposes, notably education, but Treasury officials, with a shrewd understanding of human nature, believed that local authorities would spend central government funds less carefully than their own ratepayers' money, so that grants were con-ditional on some proportion of expenditure being met out of rates. Short of major reconstruction of local government finance—something which was on the political agenda but which never happened in the Edwardian period—new expenditure on social welfare had to be taken on by central government. Whereas nearly all nineteenth-century social policy legislation was operated through local authorities, this was true of only three of the twelve major social policy enactments introduced under the Liberal governments of 1905–14.[4] Between the financial years 1907/8 and 1913/14 central government expend-iture on social services (education, old-age pensions, labour exchanges, and national insurance) increased from under £17 million to £38 million. The latter figure was still less than expenditure on the navy in 1913/14 but the 125.5 per cent increase in expenditure on social services since 1907/8 had been greater than the 49.1 per cent increase in naval expenditure (see Table 2.1).

Faced with what were then regarded as massive increases in expenditure, Treasury officials were determined to maintain the orthodox system of govern-ment finance. This task was made easier by the fact that the trade cycle moved from a recession in 1907–9 to a boom in 1912–14, and revenue was buoyant in consequence. To put the same point another way, public expenditure increased under the Liberals, but so did the wealth of the community which was being taxed, so that total central and local government expenditure, expressed as a percentage of gross domestic product (GDP) was almost exactly the same in

---

[3] See G. R. Searle, *The Quest for National Efficiency: A Study in British Politics and Political Thought, 1899–1914* (Oxford, 1971).

[4] José Harris, 'The Transition to High Politics in English Social Policy, 1880–1914', in Michael Bentley and John Stevenson (eds.), *High and Low Politics in Modern Britain* (Oxford, 1983), 60–1. The three were Acts relating to school meals (1906), school medical inspection (1907), and small holdings and allot-ments (1908).

TABLE 2.1. *Expenditure on Defence and Social Policy, 1905/6–1913/14 (£000)*

	Navy	Army	Total defence	Social policy[a]
1905/6	37,159	29,130	66,289	15,934
1906/7	34,600	28,366	62,966	16,477
1907/8	32,736	26,717	59,453	16,893
1908/9	33,512	26,338	59,850	18,925
1909/10	36,060	26,624	62,684	25,924
1910/11	41,119	26,923	68,042	28,032
1911/12	44,882	27,329	72,211	30,382
1912/13	45,617	27,633	73,250	35,582
1913/14	48,833	28,346	77,179	38,098

[a] Social policy comprised education, old-age pensions (from 1908), labour exchanges (from 1909), and national health and unemployment insurance (from 1911).

Source: Bernard Mallet, *British Budgets, 1887/88 to 1912/13* (1913), 503–4, 509; id. and C. O. George, *British Budgets, 1913/14 to 1920/21* (1929), 392; eid., *British Budgets, 1921/22 to 1932/33* (1933), 556.

1913 (11.9) as it had been in 1905 (11.8).[5] However, long-term commitments had been undertaken, especially with regard to unemployment insurance, which would be difficult to finance in future depressions (see Chapters 4 to 6).

In what follows, it will be shown how the Treasury adapted its Gladstonian traditions of public finance to the challenge of the New Liberalism. Under Asquith, who was Chancellor of the Exchequer from December 1905 to April 1908, the important 'Asquith doctrine' was laid down, establishing the principles by which central government borrowing for peacetime expenditure were to be guided until loans for defence were raised on the eve of the Second World War. Asquith also introduced the beginnings of graduation in income tax, and prepared the way for the introduction of the first big social reform to be financed directly from the Exchequer, old-age pensions. His successor, Lloyd George, was to push direct taxation close to what at the time was regarded as its political limit, while promoting social reform with such vigour that the Treasury at times acted like a spending department in initiating proposals for public expenditure.

International comparisons suggest that a British Chancellor of the Exchequer commanded a much more robust financial machine than that of other European states. In particular, the reforming budgets of 1907 and 1909 enabled the Chancellor to raise the money required for defence and social security through direct taxation. In contrast, it has been argued that the German Empire, relying, like other continental powers, on less elastic indirect taxes, found itself unable to finance armed forces in line with its manpower and industrial strength.[6] Income tax and supertax were powerful financial instruments

[5] Roger Middleton, *Government versus the Market: The Growth of the Public Sector, Economic Management and British Economic Performance, c.1890–1979* (Cheltenham, 1996), 648.
[6] See Niall Ferguson, 'Public Finance and National Security: The Domestic Origins of the First World War Revisited', *Past and Present*, 142 (1994), 141–68. For Britain's long-standing superiority in public finance see D. E. Schremmer, 'Taxation and Public Finance: Britain, France and Germany', in P. Mathias and S. Pollard (eds.), *The Cambridge Economic History of Europe*, vol. viii (Cambridge, 1989), 315–494.

that had to be balanced by effective Treasury control of expenditure, to check extravagance.

Several features of Treasury control of public expenditure are worth commenting on, as they show that what might seem to be novel features of the inter-war period, or later, were in fact firmly in place before 1914. One was the difficulty in controlling defence expenditure, with Treasury officials unable to match defence departments in technical arguments, and with financial arguments unable to prevail in Cabinet at times of international tension. A second feature was the need to go beyond the functions of a ministry of finance in respect of social reform, and therefore to have a less negative attitude than hitherto to proposals for public expenditure. On the other hand, when faced with proposals for the use of public expenditure to offset variations in the trade cycle and to stabilize aggregate demand for labour, the Treasury began to adopt counter-arguments which can be seen as the origins of the 'Treasury view' on public works as a cure for unemployment in the inter-war period. This negative Treasury view, together with the Asquith doctrine on borrowing by central government, was to form a powerful orthodoxy against which Keynes was to argue, largely in vain, in the 1920s and 1930s, and which provoked him to write his *General Theory of Employment, Interest and Money*. The Edwardian period thus forms essential background to the controversies involving the Treasury later in the century.

PERSONALITIES AND ORGANIZATION

The Treasury in 1906 had outwardly changed little since the early 1870s. The joint Permanent Secretaries, Sir Edward Hamilton and Sir George Murray, were decidedly Gladstonian in outlook, and indeed both had served Gladstone as private secretary during one or more of his premierships. Murray was proud of the fact that, below the rank of Permanent Secretary, the upper establishment of the Treasury was exactly the same, twenty-five, as when the department had been reorganized during Gladstone's first ministry, although the volume of work had increased by at least 50 per cent.[7] Exceptionally, there had been two Permanent Secretaries since 1902, instead of the usual one, with Hamilton handling the financial side of the Treasury's work and the other Permanent Secretary (Murray from 1903) handling the administrative side. However, on the eve of his retirement in October 1907, Hamilton advised Asquith that such an arrangement was only justified when the man designated to be Permanent Secretary was a 'financial man', like himself, and not a 'born administrator' like Murray. In future financial matters would be handled by a subordinate official,

[7] Murray to Asquith, 12 Oct. 1907, Asquith papers, vol. 19.

William Blain, who was given the rank of Assistant Secretary, with direct access to the Chancellor, when Hamilton retired.[8]

The Treasury's work was divided between five (from October 1908, six) divisions.[9] Of these, the First or Finance Division, comprising five officials, dealt with taxation, banking and currency, the National Debt and sinking funds for its reduction, loans for local authorities, and the Public Works Loan Board. Another division was concerned with the administration of superannuation and government gratuities to non-pensionable government employees, but its work was extended to include the Old Age Pension Act of 1908. The other divisions controlled the expenditure of central government departments and also the numbers and salaries or wages of their staffs. One of these divisions superintended regulations for the Civil Service as a whole, in consultation with the Civil Service Commission, but this was not regarded as enough work to occupy the division's three officials, who were therefore given some of the normal work of controlling expenditure and staffs of a range of Whitehall departments, including the boards of Trade, Agriculture and Fisheries, and Education, and also the Irish and Scottish departments. Another division, also of three officials, controlled the expenditure and civil staffs of the Admiralty and War Office—by far the biggest spenders in Whitehall—and also the India Office. Control of the expenditure and staffs of the Foreign Office, Home Office, Colonial Office, and law courts was allocated to another division, but the work was purely administrative, and the Treasury then claimed no more active role in foreign policy than it did in legal matters.[10]

In general, both in finance and administration, the Treasury's role was to enforce economy rather than to initiate policy. Over 90 per cent of Treasury business consisted of dealing with applications from other departments in connection with some form of expenditure (including additions to staff).[11] Nevertheless, both Liberal chancellors, Asquith and Lloyd George, were able to make their mark on policy. Asquith was deputy leader of the House of Commons and the heir apparent of a Prime Minister, Campbell-Bannerman, who was visibly failing before he was forced by ill health to retire in April 1908. Accordingly, Asquith felt free to concern himself with the whole field of government policy, including the introduction of state old-age pensions. His successor, Lloyd George, was even more inclined to initiate policy. He had long taken an interest

---

[8] Hamilton to Asquith, 25 Sept. 1907, Asquith papers, vol. 19. See also Hamilton to Asquith, 30 July 1907, Hamilton papers (Add. MS 48,614), British Library, London.

[9] What follows is based on 'Memorandum on the Duties of the Treasury and in Particular its Financial and Administrative Control', 30 Apr. 1913, T170/11, and Henry Roseveare, *The Treasury: The Evolution of a British Institution* (1969), 211, 203.

[10] It is noteworthy that the Treasury does not appear in the index of Keith M. Wilson, *The Policy of the Entente: Essays on the Determinants of British Foreign Policy, 1904–1914* (Cambridge, 1985). The Foreign Secretary, Sir Edward Grey, protested in 1908 about Lloyd George speaking publicly on international affairs (ibid., 32) but Lloyd George's views on international affairs owed nothing to Treasury briefs.

[11] Royal Commission on the Civil Service, *Minutes of Evidence* (Cd. 6210), PP 1912–13, xv. 113, q. 853.

in old-age pensions and he was one of the leading instigators of national insurance against interruption of earnings due to ill health or unemployment.

Not all Treasury officials could view with equanimity the Chancellor's determination to disburse money in the cause of social reform. In particular Murray never hid his dislike of Lloyd George's proposals or methods, and did not hesitate to gossip with leading Liberal politicians about his political master's alleged incompetence. Lloyd George disliked paperwork and often refused to read memoranda, insisting instead on being briefed orally. Murray refused to adapt to this method of business and Lloyd George soon learned to bypass his Permanent Secretary, by seeking advice from the Chairman of the Board of Inland Revenue, Sir Robert Chalmers, on more than revenue matters, or by dealing directly with more junior subordinates, notably John Bradbury, a principal clerk. When Murray retired in 1911 he was replaced by Chalmers, and when the latter fell out with Lloyd George and left two years later, Bradbury was promoted at the early age of 40 to be joint Permanent Secretary with Sir Thomas Heath, who was nine years his senior.[12]

Of successive junior ministers who filled the post of Financial Secretary in the Liberal governments, Lloyd George said 'they'd make good clerks or accountants'.[13] One exception was Charles Masterman (1912–14), an advocate of social reform whom Lloyd George asked to take on national insurance. Masterman was succeeded in February 1914 by Edwin Montagu, who was described by his private secretary as 'easily the most outstanding of my political chiefs', but also as a 'highly strung creature'.[14]

The Permanent Secretaries, Hamilton and Murray, were products of the system of patronage in a department which had come to pride itself as an intellectual élite. Whereas most of the younger officials in the Treasury's upper establishment had first-class degrees from Oxford or Cambridge, and all had entered the Civil Service under a system of competitive examination, both Hamilton and Murray had attained only third-class honours in *literae humaniores* at Oxford, and had entered the Civil Service under a system of limited competition after nomination by the minister in charge of the department into which they were first appointed. Hamilton's entry into the Treasury in 1870 was probably not unconnected to the fact that his father was one of Gladstone's best friends, although Gladstone was out of office at the time. Murray, as a relative of the Duke of Atholl, had influential social connections, and had originally entered the Civil Service via the Foreign Office in 1873, before transferring to the Treasury in 1880.

---

[12] For Lloyd George's relations with his officials see Edward David (ed.), *Inside Asquith's Cabinet: From the Diaries of Charles Hobhouse* (1977), 72–3, 76–7; John Grigg, *Lloyd George: The People's Champion, 1902–1911* (1978), 145–7; and Bruce K. Murray, *People's Budget, 1909/10* (Oxford, 1980), 76–81.

[13] Lucy Masterman, *C. F. G. Masterman: A Biography* (1939), 172.

[14] Sir Andrew McFadyean, *Recollected in Tranquillity* (1964), 52.

Hamilton had been Gladstone's private secretary from 1873 to 1874 and again from 1880 to 1885, but seems to have developed such expertise as he had in public finance only after joining the Finance Division in 1885. It is evidence of the mundane nature of public finance at the beginning of the twentieth century that Hamilton should have been the leading figure on the finance side of the Treasury. His reputation rested mainly on the conversion of the National Debt in 1888 from a 3 per cent to a 2¾ per cent basis, about which he had published a pedestrian, technical account, which (appropriately enough, as a son of a bishop) he had entitled *Conversion and Redemption*.[15] Most of the work on the budget in Hamilton's latter years was done by the principal clerk in charge of the Finance division, Blain. Blain also had a third-class honours degree, in classics, from Cambridge, but in his case his degree classification would seem to have been a result of the time he had devoted to the Cambridge Union, of which he had at one time been president. He had served for ten years in the Post Office before being transferred to the Treasury in 1894 and had risen rapidly to the rank of principal clerk in 1903.[16]

Chalmers, who had served in the Treasury for twenty-five years before becoming Chairman of the Board of Inland Revenue in 1907, was a more impressive Permanent Secretary than either Murray or Hamilton, both intellectually and otherwise. A man of wide interests, who had obtained first-class honours in classical moderations, and second-class honours in biology, at Oxford, Chalmers was the Treasury's first Permanent Secretary to have gained first place in the open competitive examination for the upper division of the Civil Service. Tough and efficient, he was notorious for his crushing remarks. There is a story that when Murray was appointed Permanent Secretary he said to Chalmers: 'Things have changed since you and I first joined the Treasury. Do you remember that in those days the Permanent Secretary was some old dodderer and we did most of the work without consulting him, so that he never knew much of what was happening in the office?' 'Humph', replied Chalmers. 'I fancy, George, that if you were to consult the juniors you might find that things haven't changed so much as you think.'[17]

Chalmers and Lloyd George got on well at first but Chalmers was no respecter of persons and, according to oral tradition in Whitehall, they fell out in 1913. Apparently, one day Chalmers, accompanied by his most senior subordinate, Heath, as a witness, went to the Chancellor's room, and told Lloyd George: 'What you said in the House of Commons yesterday was a lie, and when you said it you knew it was a lie.' Shortly afterwards, apparently at his own suggestion, Chalmers was appointed governor of Ceylon, where he could indulge his hobby of the study of Pali, the ancient language of that

---

[15] Unlike his colleagues, Hamilton was apparently not greatly amused to learn that this work was being sold alongside religious tracts (Roseveare, *Treasury*, 219).

[16] *The Times*, 29 Dec. 1908, 9e.   [17] Sir Frederick Leith-Ross, *Money Talks* (1968), 21.

country.[18] The story has the ring of truth. Certainly Chalmers was high minded. As a young man he had chosen to live in London's East End and do social work in addition to his duties at the Treasury. Chalmers also had a reputation as a vigilant watchdog over public expenditure, acquired when he was in charge of the Treasury's division dealing with the Admiralty and the War Office. He had also worked on the financial side of the Treasury and had written a *History of Currency in the British Colonies* (1893) which was the standard work on the subject.[19]

Chalmers' successors, the Joint Permanent Secretaries Bradbury and Heath, divided the work as Hamilton and Murray had done, with Bradbury handling finance and Heath the administrative side. The arrangement was not without its disadvantages: Bradbury later recalled that there was always a tendency for other departments to try to play off one Permanent Secretary against the other, and within the Treasury there was no single person responsible for arranging the work of the department.[20] Bradbury, who had a double first in *literae humaniores* and modern history from Oxford, was apparently prone to error in simple arithmetic, and his private secretary had to check his calculations.[21] Nevertheless, he showed a firm grasp of public finance when, as the principal clerk in charge of the Finance Division of the Treasury (from 1908) he was the main draughtsman of Lloyd George's budgets. Bradbury also took a leading part in the creation of the national health insurance scheme, serving for a time as an insurance commissioner in addition to his duties at the Treasury. He had a reputation for being argumentative; indeed one colleague, admittedly a hostile witness, claimed that anyone could get anything past Bradbury by proposing the opposite.[22]

Heath was no less difficult a character. Indeed, he was apparently regarded by other departments, in Asquith's words, 'as the special incarnation of all that is most angular and pedantic in Treasury traditions and practice'.[23] Of Heath's intellectual calibre there could be no doubt: he had passed with first-class honours both parts of the Cambridge tripos (classics and mathematics) and, like Chalmers, had passed first in the Civil Service examination. Also like Chalmers, Heath found time for intellectual interests outside public finance. He was an expert on Greek mathematics, and shortly after he left the Treasury he published a two-volume *History of Greek Mathematics*, which is still the standard work on the subject. However, like Murray, Heath was less happy giving oral

---

[18] Sir Denis Rickett, interviewed by author, 15 Feb. 1989. This story seems to have been transmitted by Hawtrey, as another version appears in the transcript of a taped conversation between him and Sir Alec Cairncross in 1966, HTRY 13/5.

[19] Sir Thomas Heath and P. E. Matheson, 'Lord Chalmers, 1858–1938', *Proc. Brit. Acad.*, 25 (1939), 321–32.

[20] Bradbury to Austen Chamberlain, 19 Aug. 1919, Austen Chamberlain papers, AC24/1/21, University of Birmingham Library.

[21] McFadyean, *Recollected in Tranquillity*, 45.

[22] William Braithwaite, *Lloyd George's Ambulance Wagon*, ed. Sir Henry Bunbury (1957), 68, 105.

[23] Asquith to Hamilton, 27 Sept. 1907, Hamilton papers.

advice than with paperwork, and consequently he exercised no perceptible influence on Lloyd George.[24]

The expansion of the Treasury's business under Lloyd George led to an increase in the department's staff, the higher establishment rising from twenty-six in 1908 to thirty-three by the outbreak of the First World War. The Edwardian Treasury attracted the pick of recruits to the Civil Service, and some were to play notable parts in the history of the department. These men (with dates of service in the department) included: Ralph Hawtrey (1903–47), who was to be the Treasury's in-house economist in the inter-war period; Basil Blackett (1904–22), who was appointed as the first Controller of the Finance Department in 1919; Otto Niemeyer (1906–27), Blackett's successor as Controller of the Finance Department; Frederick Phillips (1908–43), the most influential official on the finance side from 1932 until 1940, when he became Treasury representative in the United States; Frederick Leith-Ross (1909–32), who took part in international financial negotiations, both as Deputy Controller of the Finance Department from 1925 to 1932, and thereafter with the title of Chief Economic Adviser to the Government; Sigismund David Schloss (1910–47), who changed his name to Waley on the outbreak of war in 1914, and who became a leading official dealing with international financial questions in the 1930s and '40s; and Bernard Gilbert (1914–56), who, as the Permanent Secretary's deputy, was the senior official co-ordinating economic advice to the Chancellor in the mid-1950s. There was thus a remarkable continuity in personnel—and values and attitudes—between the Edwardian Treasury, with its attachment to Gladstonian principles of public finance, and the Treasury in the 'age of Keynes'.

LIBERAL FINANCE: BORROWING AND THE NATIONAL DEBT

The principles of public finance before 1914, and indeed until the Second World War, were simple. A Chancellor was judged by his ability not only to balance his budget but also to reduce the National Debt. The focus of the budget was on taxation and its incidence on different classes in the community.

The state could and did borrow for certain purposes, but few would have disagreed with the dictum in the leading study of public finance of the period that 'a nation cannot, any more than an individual, keep adding continuously to its liabilities without coming to the end of its resources'.[25] The nation's resources, in this context, meant its taxable capacity, for it was from tax receipts, less

[24] M. F. Headlam, 'Sir Thomas Little Heath', *Proc. Brit. Acad.*, 26 (1940), 429. Heath's *History of Greek Mathematics*, first published in 1921, was reprinted as recently as 1981.

[25] C. F. Bastable, *Public Finance* (1892), 581. This statement echoed the views of Adam Smith and David Hume over a century earlier. Treasury officials thought well enough of Bastable's work to include it in a reading list for the Russian ambassador in 1908 when he expressed a desire to study the British financial system (T1/1209/10859).

public expenditure, that interest upon the National Debt was paid and debt redeemed. Moreover, the soundness of a state's finances was held to be subject to the same test as those of an individual: at what rate of interest could the state borrow? Historically Britain had been able to raise loans on international money markets at lower rates of interest than had other countries, and this was believed to be a considerable advantage in time of war. When in his account of the conversion of the National Debt in 1888 Hamilton wrote of 'the credit of the British nation', he had in mind the state's credit rating in money markets, and it was for this reason that he wrote of the need for 'rigid observance of good faith towards the public creditor'.[26]

It was also believed that 'public borrowing is a demand for loanable capital which helps to raise its value, i.e. the rate of interest'.[27] Conversely, repayment of the National Debt was seen as releasing loanable funds, thereby tending to lower the rate of interest. For this reason a prudent Chancellor made provision every year in his budget not only for a sinking fund, but also for a small budget surplus, which would also be used to reduce the National Debt. New borrowing for the Boer War (1899–1902) had restored the National Debt to the size it had been in 1865 (£798 millions), and in Hamilton's view the British state's credit had been 'damaged . . . very materially' thereby.[28] The *Statist*, whose editor, George Paish, advised Lloyd George in economic matters from 1909, had no doubt that the National Debt, which 'was created almost entirely for war purposes, and is represented by few assets other than the wealth of individual [taxpayers]' ought to be redeemed as speedily as the revenue permitted.[29]

The Liberals themselves had criticized Conservative governments for borrowing for defence expenditure in peace, and Asquith took the opportunity to reinforce orthodoxy with regard to financing central government expenditure from loans. Under successive Naval and Military Works Acts his predecessors had raised loans for various 'permanent structures', such as dockyards and barracks, each loan having a sinking fund of its own. Asquith denounced this practice for encouraging 'crude, precipitate and wasteful' expenditure, and made it clear that henceforth the only tangible assets that would be financed by borrowing would be those which produced a money return, and did not rely on future taxation for the servicing and redemption of the debts incurred.[30] What he had in mind as examples of suitable assets to be financed by loans were Post Office telegraphs and telephones—forms of capital expenditure which amounted to about one million or £1.5 million annually, whereas the Conservatives

---

[26] E. Hamilton, *Conversion and Redemption* (1889), 5, 57.

[27] Bastable, *Public Finance*, 588.

[28] Hamilton to Asquith, 22 Oct. 1907, Asquith papers, vol. 19.

[29] *Statist*, 3 Feb. 1912, 237, filed in T171/35. For Paish's role as an economic adviser see Avner Offer, 'Empire and Social Reform: British Overseas Investment and Domestic Politics, 1908–1914', *Hist. J.*, 26 (1983), 125–7, 135–7. Paish was knighted in 1911.

[30] 156 HC Deb., 4s, 1906, col. 290. Orthodox political economy allowed that the purchase or creation of productive assets might fairly be financed by loans—see Bastable, *Public Finance*, 586–7.

had created a debt of some £51 million under the Naval and Military Works Acts between 1901 and 1905.[31] The Asquith doctrine of restricting loan finance in peace to objects that would produce an adequate money return to service and repay the debt incurred led the Treasury to insist that even the cost of building public offices should be met out of revenue. As Bradbury noted in 1911: 'whatever arguments there may be in favour of "spreading" capital expenditure generally, the question must be taken to have been argued out and settled in 1906.'[32] Consequently, central government expenditure was substantially limited to what taxpayers would bear in a given year.[33]

There were, however, exceptions to the rule of annual budgeting. Lloyd George's first budget, that of 1909, set up a Development Fund, to promote rural employment and fisheries, and a Road Fund, which made grants to local authorities for road works. The former fund was derived from general taxation, and the latter fund from new taxes on road users, and the accumulated funds were expended over a series of years. The amounts involved were not large, however, even at a time when total central government expenditure was in the range of £172 million (1910/11) to £208 million (1913/14). The total receipts and payments of the Development Fund over these four financial years were £2,900,000 and £540,000 respectively: the comparable figures for the Road Fund were £4,639,000 and £719,000 respectively.[34] Thus, in each case funds were being accumulated *in advance* of expenditure. A similar principle operated with the National Health Insurance and National Unemployment Insurance Funds, created by the National Insurance Act of 1911. The health insurance fund had receipts of £26,642,000 in its first 18 months from July 1912 but payments of only £14,341,597, while the unemployment insurance fund had receipts of £2,497,000 in the 12 months to July 1914 but payments of only £895,760 in the same period.[35]

Despite the novelty of these extra-budgetary funds, the Liberal government was more rigorously orthodox in relation to the National Debt than the Conservatives had been. In eight financial years between 1906/7 and 1913/14 Asquith and Lloyd George reduced the National Debt by a net annual average of £10,167,000—over three times the net annual average of £3,120,000

---

[31] *Statist*, 2 Feb. 1912, 237–8, filed in T171/35.

[32] Memorandum by Bradbury, 12 Oct. 1911, T1/11322/16991.

[33] Local authorities, on the other hand, were empowered by Parliament to borrow for a number of purposes, and had a range of activities that involved more capital expenditure—e.g. public utilities and transport systems—than central government. Thus, whereas the National Debt fell from £788,990,000 in 1906 to £762,464,000 in 1910, total local government indebtedness in the United Kingdom increased from £572,505,000 in 1906 to £629,635,000 in 1910 (B. Mallet, *British Budgets, 1887/88 to 1912/13* (1913), 495, 499).

[34] *Development Fund Accounts*, PP 1912–13, xlix. 206 and 210–11; PP 1914, l. 168–9, and PP 1914–16, xxxviii. 218–19; *Fourth Annual Report of the Road Board*, PP 1914, xlvii. 753–836, para. 4. Figures for receipts are net of profits and interest on investments and repayments of loans.

[35] *National Health Insurance Fund Accounts*, PP 1914–16, lvi. 2–3 and *Unemployment Fund Accounts*, ibid., 1254–5.

achieved by their immediate Conservative predecessors, C. T. Ritchie and Austen Chamberlain between 1903/4 and 1905/6, and more than any Victorian Chancellor. It is true that debt reduction proceeded more rapidly under Asquith than Lloyd George, but this was partly because of increased borrowing for Post Office investment in telephones after 1908. If this element is deducted, Lloyd George's rate of debt redemption was 97 per cent of that of Asquith's[36]— a remarkable figure in view of the fact that Asquith faced fewer problems than Lloyd George both on the expenditure and revenue sides of his budget. In his three budgets, those of 1906, 1907, and 1908 (the last of which he introduced shortly after he became Prime Minister), Asquith was able to keep expenditure practically level, whereas Lloyd George took over shortly before the Old Age Pensions Act was passed, and had to find funds for the first complete year of pensions in 1909/10, just as increased naval expenditure became necessary. These new demands on the Exchequer came at a time when the slump of 1908 and 1909 was beginning to have adverse effects on the revenue. There was consequently an estimated deficit of about £16 million for 1909/10 on the existing basis of taxation. This situation, together with the need to finance future social reforms, including labour exchanges and national health and unemployment insurance, led Lloyd George to seek new sources of revenue in his radical 'People's Budget' of 1909. Provision for debt redemption was reduced, but remained above the level which had been regarded as a maximum before the Boer War.[37]

Budget surpluses and debt redemption were not sufficient, however, to prevent a fall in the prices of gilt-edged stock. The securities most affected were Consols, which were undated, and which had originally paid interest of 3 per cent, but after the conversion operation of 1888 the interest had been reduced to $2\frac{3}{4}$ per cent immediately, with a further reduction to $2\frac{1}{2}$ per cent to be made in 15 years' time—1903. In 1896, during an international depression, when British funds were temporarily denied an outlet in overseas investment, Consols had stood at 114. By January 1906 they had already fallen to $89\frac{3}{8}$ and depreciation continued thereafter, so that by mid-1911 they were at $79\frac{1}{8}$ and by mid-1912 $76\frac{3}{8}$. Consols were an important element in the reserves of the banking system, and as Consols declined in value, banks had to write down their reserves.[38] City critics were not slow to blame the Liberals for reducing the credit-worthiness of the state, although by far the greater part of the decline in Consols had taken place under Conservative administrations. In particular, Lloyd George was attacked for his diversion in 1910/11 of half of his budget surplus from debt redemption so as to provide £1.5 million for the Development Fund, £1.5 million for hospitals, and £250,000 for railways and water works in East Africa. He was

[36] Calculated from statistics compiled by Basil Blackett in T171/56.
[37] 'Six Years of Liberal Finance', 30 June 1912, T171/2.
[38] See Offer, 'Empire and Social Reform', 131–2.

also accused of 'predatory' finance, notably his action in raising death duties, which, by taxing capital, was alleged to have contributed to the depreciation in gilt-edged securities.[39]

In contrast, Paish argued that the principal causes of the depreciation of Consols, as well as the greater part of their decline, antedated the Liberal governments. Prior to 1889 trustees had been very limited in the range of securities in which they could invest, and large amounts of trust money had been placed in Consols for want of alternatives. From 1889 the range of trustee securities was widened and from 1900 it included colonial government securities, with the result that the supply of trustee securities tended to exceed the supply of trust money, whereas before 1889 the reverse had been the case. As already noted, the Boer War saw an expansion of government borrowing, much of which had to be funded subsequently through the sale of gilt-edged securities, and then in 1903 the Conservative government adopted a plan for buying out Irish landlords, which involved the annual issue of large amounts of Irish Land Stock, absorbing funds that might otherwise have been invested in Consols. Finally, the revival of industrial dividends after the slump of 1908–9 tended to depress all fixed-interest securities, including those in the private sector and those of foreign governments.[40] To these factors might be added the fact that whereas prices had tended to fall between 1873 and 1896, they tended to rise thereafter; moreover, overseas investment was buoyant in the Edwardian period. There was, therefore, very little in the argument that Liberal financing of social reform was causing a decline in the state's credit, but clearly no risks could be taken with financial confidence.

Treasury officials had reasons other than the maintenance of confidence in government stock for wishing to preserve strict orthodoxy in budgets. When Lloyd George diverted £3,250,000 of his budget surplus in 1910/11 to the Development Fund, hospitals, and East Africa development, he was in breach of the convention, which had operated since 1829, that any surplus at the end of a year should be devoted to reducing the National Debt, for the money which he had diverted could not be spent until after the end of the financial year. Basil Blackett, then a second-class clerk in the Finance Division, pointed out that:

... there is much objection to using the chance surplus of one year for the ordinary expenditure of the next—such a system would lead to much political jobbery, as a strong government would build up a surplus in its early years and use it to remit taxation when its popularity was waning and leave its successors of the opposite party with an empty Exchequer.[41]

[39] 'Notes in Defence of Raids on Sinking Fund', by Blackett, 22 Nov. [1910], T171/9, and unsigned, undated notes, probably by Blackett, c. Dec. 1911, T171/14.
[40] Statist, 10 Feb. 1912, 295–7, and 20 July 1912, 107–8, filed in T171/35, and Paish to Lloyd George, 23 June 1914, T171/67. See also the Economist, 27 July 1912, also filed in T171/35.
[41] 'Finance Bill 1911', memorandum by Blackett, 22 Nov. [1910], T171/9.

Lloyd George's action was justifiable, Blackett thought, only because the budget for 1910/11 had included a substantial sum for debt redemption and because the funds being held over were to be used for capital rather than ordinary expenditure (although Blackett had doubts about the Development Fund, which he thought less justifiable on this basis than hospitals or East African railways). Blackett's comments go some way to explaining why the Treasury sought both to maintain public finance on an annual accounting basis and to exercise strict control over the Development and Road Funds (see below).

LIBERAL FINANCE: TAXATION

The main party conflicts over Liberal finance arose over the issue of taxation. Most Conservatives argued that social reform and naval expansion should be paid for by adopting tariffs. The Liberals, on the other hand, were determined to show that it was unnecessary to abandon free trade. It has been convincingly demonstrated that Lloyd George's budgets from 1909 to 1914 reflected a strategy of increasing expenditure in ways that would prevent a transfer of working-class support to the Labour party, while raising taxation in ways that would enable the Liberals to retain most of their middle-class support.[42] Accordingly, increased direct taxation did not fall on the main body of salary earners, who might have been attracted to tariff reform had it done so. Instead, new taxes or increased taxes on high incomes and property were introduced, in the belief that these would fall largely on people who would vote Conservative anyway, while major increases in licence duties would hit the drink trade, which funded the Conservatives.

Most Treasury officials were in favour of free trade. Chalmers, when an Assistant Secretary, had gone so far as to take an active part in 1902–3 in the defeat of Joseph Chamberlain's proposals for tariff reform, helping to brief the Prime Minister, Balfour, and other politicians as well as the Chancellor. On the other hand, some officials tended to waver, as Balfour did, on the issue, and Blackett, admittedly only a junior official, was a protectionist.[43]

Gladstonian views extended to the form of the income tax. When Asquith told Hamilton in 1906 that he proposed to introduce differentiation for the purposes of income tax between earned and unearned incomes, he was, as he recalled, 'at once met with the objection, which was considered fatal, that Gladstone had always declared that any such scheme was impracticable'.[44] The Board of Inland Revenue's experts were no more enthusiastic about the Chancellor's scheme, but Asquith was able to secure the support of an all-party Select

[42] Murray, *People's Budget*.
[43] Roseveare, *Treasury*, 222. Conversation between Hawtrey and Cairncross, HTRY 13/5.
[44] H. H. Asquith [Earl of Oxford and Asquith], *Memories and Reflections*, 2 vols. (1928), i. 253–4.

Committee, whose report not only recommended differentiation between earned and unearned income but also recommended graduation in income tax, through the imposition of a supertax on higher incomes. Asquith introduced differentiation in his budget in 1907 and Lloyd George introduced graduation in his budget of 1909, and it was from this time that the income tax began to acquire a generally progressive character. Asquith gave relief to income tax payers whose total income did not exceed £2,000 a year so that they paid only 9d. (3.75p) in the pound on earned income instead of the standard rate of 1s. (5p). In 1909 Lloyd George raised the standard rate of income tax to 1s. 2d. (5.8p) and imposed a supertax of 6d. (2½p) in the pound on incomes over £5,000 a year. Fewer than 1,200,000 people paid any income tax, and of these fewer than 11,500 had incomes over £5,000 in 1909/10. Lloyd George necessarily depended upon the technical expertise of his officials, but it was his idea to revive the allowance for children that Pitt's Income Tax Act of 1799 had given— indeed, Chalmers was opposed to this concession to 'brats'.[45]

Lloyd George later remarked that Chalmers was the only member of the Treasury staff to support the idea of supertax, and this has been repeated by one of Lloyd George's leading biographers.[46] In fact, Chalmers was not in the Treasury while the budget was being prepared, being chairman of the Board of Inland Revenue. As already noted, supertax was not a new idea in 1909, having been proposed by an all-party Select Committee two years earlier. When Chalmers and Bradbury, the principal clerk in charge of the Treasury's Finance Division, came to consider supertax for the 1909 budget, they were able to refer to what Bradbury called an 'excellent memorandum of 26 February 1907, to which it would be difficult to add anything'.[47] The author of the memorandum was William Blain, who had been head of the Treasury's Finance Division at the time. Both Blain and Bradbury, as well as Chalmers, had for some time been in favour of the supertax proposal, as against relying exclusively on increasing income tax, on the grounds that it would be easier to tax low incomes if the better off were paying at a higher rate.[48] Blain's career was cut short by his early death in December 1908, but his memorandum, and Bradbury's reaction to it, suggests that below the level of Hamilton and Murray the responsible officials fully grasped the need for supertax.

Blain argued that too much revenue was being raised from indirect taxation, which placed an unfair burden on the poorest classes, since people were taxed according to their consumption of certain commodities (chiefly tobacco and

---

[45] Murray, *People's Budget*, 165. For statistics see Mallet, *British Budgets, 1887–1913*, 484–6, and id. and C. O. George, *British Budgets, 1913/14 to 1920/21* (1929), 398.

[46] Bentley B. Gilbert, *David Lloyd George: A Political Life. The Architect of Change, 1863–1912* (1987), 369.

[47] 'Super Tax'—memoranda by Chalmers and Bradbury, circulated by the Treasury, 31 Mar. 1909, CAB37/99/57.

[48] Montagu to Asquith, 3 Mar. 1908, E. S. Montagu papers, box 3, AS/1/7/6, Trinity College, Cambridge.

alcohol) and not in proportion to their incomes. He pointed out that the Liberal government was committed to heavy additional expenditure on social reforms, and that no one now expected that reductions in existing expenditure would make it possible to do this without raising new revenue. Blain then argued that progressive, direct taxation was necessary for the preservation of free trade:

While the present position continues, it puts a powerful weapon in the hands of the advocates of Tariff Reform. They are able to point to the admitted desire of the Government to effect social changes, a desire which is thwarted by the want of elasticity in our present revenue. No better answer to the most specious argument on their side could be found than a fiscal change which would enable additional revenue to be raised at need without an increase—indeed, with a diminution—of the proportion of burden falling upon the most numerous classes.[49]

Blain favoured both an increase in death duties and the introduction of supertax. He admitted that the Board of Inland Revenue's experts had pronounced against supertax, on the grounds of administrative complexity, but argued that this objection was not insuperable. If the tax was introduced on a small and manageable scale, he suggested, valuable knowledge would be gained and it would be possible to establish the machinery for an extension of the tax when necessary. He added that it would be best to start with a moderate rate so as to make the risks of evasion not worthwhile.[50]

All of Blain's principles were followed by Bradbury, Chalmers, and Lloyd George in the 1909 and subsequent budgets. Supertax receipts even in 1913/14 were only £3,339,000, about 7 per cent of total receipts from income tax and supertax that year. Even so, increases in direct taxation, including death duties and land value duties, had raised the proportion of revenue which was raised from income or wealth to 57.4 per cent of total tax revenue by 1913/14, compared with 49.5 per cent in 1904/5.[51]

Increased rates of death duties in the 1909 budget provoked a major protest from the City. Thirty-six of its leading figures, headed by Lord Rothschild, wrote an open letter to the Prime Minister, in which they claimed that death duties were really paid out of capital, and that there was 'a danger of capital being reduced below the point necessary to the trade in which it is employed. We feel that the prosperity of all classes has been greatly due to the fact that this country has afforded indisputable safety for capital'.[52] On this occasion the Treasury was quite unmoved by City advice. By 1910/11 death duties raised £25,452,000, compared with £18,370,000 in 1908/9, and another revision in the duty included in the 1914 budget was calculated to produce a further £3 million in a full year. Josiah Stamp, then personal assistant to the Chief Inspector of

---

[49] 'Supertax', by Blain 26 Feb. 1907, T168/55.
[50] Ibid.
[51] Mallet and George, *British Budgets, 1921/22 to 1932/33* (1933), 554, 566, 576.
[52] *The Times*, 15 May 1909, cited in Offer, 'Empire and Social Reform', 123.

Taxes at Somerset House, was asked to produce a memorandum to meet the Opposition argument that death duties had an adverse effect on capital accumulation. Stamp responded with an argument which, having reviewed the opinions of such respected authorities as Gladstone, Mill, Bastable, and Professor   A. C. Pigou, concluded that there was no evidence that death duties reduced savings and capital any more than income tax did (indeed Pigou thought that duties postponed until after death had less effect than taxes from current income).[53]

What really aroused the fury of the Conservatives, and apprehension among a number of his Cabinet colleagues, was Lloyd George's proposal in his budget of 1909 for the valuation of land, with a view to taxation, including a tax on the capital value of 'undeveloped' land at an annual rate of $\frac{1}{2}d.$ (0.2p) in the pound and a 20 per cent duty on profits from unearned increments in land values, the latter tax being payable when land was sold or inherited.[54] Land taxation posed considerable problems for the Board of Inland Revenue, but Lloyd George did not consider these to be insuperable. Assessment involved a valuation of all land in the country, as at April 1909, and valuers had to differentiate between the gross value—that is the value of the property as it had been improved by building, etc.—and its site value—that is its value without these improvements— since the principal land taxes were to be charged with reference to its site value. The valuation was a task of considerable magnitude, requiring the recruitment and training of a staff of almost 5,000 by the Board of Inland Revenue, and was not expected to be completed until 1915. The technical problems were made no easier by the fact that professional surveyors and valuers were hostile to the land taxes. As one Inland Revenue official complained: 'surveyors are rather prone to consider themselves as representing a single class—the landowner.'[55] Lloyd George and the Cabinet decided to appease rural voters by exempting purely agricultural land from the increment duty, but the need to value such land remained because it might acquire value as a result of urban development.

All this trouble was to be undertaken for taxation which, on Lloyd George's own figures, would yield only £500,000 in 1909/10, and which was not expected to produce large yields for eight or ten years. The figure of £500,000 was little more than a token estimate to meet the constitutional requirement that, in order to be included in the budget, taxes had to yield revenue in the coming financial year. Indeed it was doubtful whether the tax could be made effective in 1909/10, which provided the Conservatives with grounds for claiming that the valuation should not be included in a finance bill, thereby, in their view,

---

[53] 'The Economic Effects of Estate Duty upon Capital', by J. Stamp, 20 June 1914, T171/85; A. C. Pigou, *Wealth and Welfare* (1912), 375–8.

[54] The complexities of land taxation can be followed in Avner Offer, *Property and Politics, 1870–1914: Landownership, Law, Ideology and Urban Development in England* (Cambridge, 1981), 363–9.

[55] 'Notes on Memorandum from Council of Surveyors' Institution', unsigned, n.d., for Finance Bill 1909, T171/8.

justifying the House of Lords in rejecting the budget. In fact, the estimate of £500,000 was not wide of the mark: in 1910/11, the first year in which land value duties were collected, the yield was £520,000. On the other hand, the maximum yield in any one year was £715,000, in 1913/14.[56] Sustained opposition by the landed interest, in the form of litigation over valuation and assessments, made the duties difficult to collect.

Even so, Lloyd George's fiscal radicalism was far from exhausted in 1914. For financing new grants to local authorities, and greatly increased naval estimates, in 1914/15, he relied in his budget proposals entirely on increases in income tax, supertax, and death duties, which, he proudly told the House of Commons, would raise the proportion of total revenue raised from direct taxation to over 60 per cent. In the event, the budget had to be amended at the second reading of the Finance Bill in June: instead of the original proposal to increase the standard rate of income tax from 1s. 2d. (5.8p) to 1s. 4d. (6.7p), the rate was altered to 1s. 3d. (6.25p). It has often been assumed that this change was forced on Lloyd George by opposition within the Liberal party, both from wealthy MPs and from traditional Gladstonians who were shocked by what they saw as his profligacy. However, recent research suggests that the problem was that he had failed to appreciate the complexity of his proposal to increase local authorities' revenue through the introduction of land value rating. Rates could not be levied on site values until 1916/17, after the valuation provided for in the 1909 budget had been completed. Lloyd George intended to provide local authorities with interim Exchequer grants totalling £2,550,000 for the last four months of 1914/15, and £11 million or £12 million in 1915/16, contrary to Bradbury's advice that it would be possible to reform the rating system without making large new Exchequer grants. In the event, the grants for 1914/15 had to be dropped, as they were linked to local government legislation that could not be put through Parliament in time for the 1914 budget; hence not all of the proposed increase in income tax was necessary.[57]

Total tax revenue increased from £125,550,000 in 1908/9 to £163,029,000 in 1913/14 (gross revenue, including items like income from Post Office Services, increased over the same period from £151,578,000 to £198,243,000).[58] The revenue benefited from buoyancy in existing taxes as the economy recovered from recession, and from 1910/11 revenue exceeded forecasts. Responsibility for forecasting revenue lay with the boards of Inland Revenue and Customs and Excise, both of which were inclined to be cautious. The task of the Board of Inland Revenue in predicting tax receipts was eased by the fact that income taxes were

[56] Mallet and George, *British Budgets, 1913–21*, 406.

[57] Ian Packer, 'The Liberal Cave and the 1914 Budget', *Eng. Hist. Rev.*, 111 (1996), 620–35. See also Bruce K. Murray, ' "Battered and Shattered": Lloyd George and the 1914 Budget Fiasco', *Albion*, 23 (1991), 483–507; Offer, *Property and Politics*, 392–9. Bradbury's memorandum on 'Reduction of Rates on Improvements', 21 Apr. 1914 is in T171/71.

[58] Mallet, *British Budgets, 1887–1913*, 474–5; Mallet and George, *British Budgets, 1921–1932*, 554.

collected yearly or half-yearly in arrears. (The modern pay-as-you-earn (PAYE) system dates from the Second World War.) It was also possible to vary revenue slightly by pressing taxpayers to pay income tax, supertax, or death duties before the end of the financial year, or by allowing payments to fall in the next financial year. Even so, the reliance of the boards of Inland Revenue and Customs and Excise on past trends meant that they tended to overestimate revenue in a recession and underestimate it when the economy was in the upward phase of the trade cycle.

For his budgets from 1910 onwards Lloyd George took advice on future economic trends from Paish, whose memoranda, with cuttings from the *Statist*, were supplemented by Treasury officials with cuttings from the *Economist* and memoranda from the Board of Trade. Paish believed that railway earnings were the most accurate indicator of the state of trade within Britain, while for foreign trade he looked at trends in overseas investments and gold production.[59] Paish's forecasts were more optimistic down to 1914 than those of the Chancellor's official advisers, and it seems probable that the forecasts made in budget speeches were higher than would otherwise have been the case. Even so, revenue was underestimated throughout the upswing in the economy (see Table 2.2).

TABLE 2.2. *Excess (+) or Shortfall (−) on Estimate of Total Revenue, 1906/7–1913/14*

	£000	Per cent
1906/7	+2,059	+1.4
1907/8	+3,703	+2.6
1908/9	−2,772	−1.8
1909/10	−30,893	−19.0
1910/11	+4,060	+2.0
1911/12	+3,469	+1.9
1912/13	+1,613	+0.9
1913/14	+3,418	+1.7

Source: Bernard Mallet, *British Budgets, 1887/88 to 1912/13* (1913), 390–405; 62 HC Deb., 1914, col. 57.

The margins of error, whether up or down on forecasts, were not insignificant, as major battles could occur between the Treasury and spending departments over sums which were much smaller than two or three million pounds. The large shortfall in 1909/10 was because of the refusal of the House of Lords to pass the budget of 1909, leading to delays in the collection of taxation. The experience of a shortfall in revenue in 1908/9, followed by the uncertainties of 1909/10, must have strengthened Treasury officials' determination to keep down the totals for expenditure. Moreover, there remained the problem of how

---

[59] See e.g. memoranda relating to the 1913 budget in T171/29 and T171/30.

the budget could be balanced once economic activity slackened, as Paish expected it would in 1915,[60] and revenue became less buoyant.

THE CONTROL OF EXPENDITURE: DEFENCE

The largest single item in the annual Estimates was the navy, the funds voted for it being greater than the combined votes for education, old-age pensions, labour exchanges, and national insurance (see Table 2.1). Asquith succeeded in having naval expenditure reduced from £33,300,000 in 1905/6 to £31,141,000 in 1907/8, years in which the First Sea Lord, Sir John Fisher, made a determined effort to scrap ships which were too old to fight and too slow to run away, as well as cutting down on extravagance in dockyards and stores.[61] Thereafter, however, the naval Estimates climbed steadily to over £46 million for 1913/14— twice what Germany was then estimated to be spending.[62] Asquith's decision to abandon the policy of financing permanent works, such as dockyards, by loans meant that the whole of the increase had to be met from current income, but the Accountant General of the Navy estimated that the difference this made to the naval Estimates in 1913/14 was only one million pounds. The comparable estimate by the War Office for the army was £500,000.[63]

Like other departments in Whitehall, the Admiralty and War Office were subject to detailed Treasury regulations. Thus, for example, in 1908 the Admiralty had to request Treasury sanction for a change in regulations relating to the supply of trusses to workers in naval dockyards, in order to be able to supply a replacement to a worker who had left the service. (On that occasion Hawtrey, who dealt with Admiralty correspondence, was prepared to argue that the proposal was wrong in principle, but the Permanent Secretary, Murray, minuted that it was hardly worth the Treasury's while to object.)[64] However, the cost of the armed services was largely beyond the Treasury's control. Whereas civil departments would consult with the Treasury about their Estimates for the coming year before the Estimates went to the Cabinet, the armed services' Estimates were regarded as highly confidential and not suitable for normal interdepartmental correspondence until after the First World War. Consequently, they were referred to the Cabinet in the first instance without previous consultation with Treasury officials, who were therefore not well placed to advise the Chancellor on any aspects apart from the financial ones.[65]

---

[60] Paish to Lloyd George, 23 June 1914, T171/67.

[61] Arthur J. Marder, *From Dreadnought to Scapa Flow: The Royal Navy in the Fisher Era, 1904–1919*, vol. i (1961), 23–5 and 38–40.

[62] 'Naval Expenditure of Great Britain, France and Germany in 1873 and 1913', forwarded by Chalmers to Lloyd George, 18 Apr. 1913, T171/31.

[63] 'Budget Statement 1913: Result of Abandonment of Loan Policy for Naval and Military Works', T171/31.   [64] T1/10962/31.

[65] 'Navy Estimates: Procedure for Settling the Total', by Hawtrey, n.d., but 1914, HTRY 1/9.

What the Treasury claimed to do was to make 'legitimate and necessary criticism' of details within the totals set by the Cabinet, and even then control of expenditure was less minute than in the cases of civil departments. Criticism was legitimate and necessary because the House of Commons was concerned that public money should not be spent wastefully, and no detail was too small for the Public Accounts Committee. For example, in 1912 the War Office was criticized for its contract procedure which allowed the Aldershot Command to pay higher prices for horses than other commands.[66]

This was not, however, the stuff of grand strategy. Treasury officials, as laymen, even if highly intelligent laymen, were always at a disadvantage in disputes with technical experts. The normal procedure, when Treasury officials came to look at the sketch Estimates in the autumn, was to take the Estimates for each department for the previous financial year as a base line and to raise questions about deviations from that line. The Treasury kept 'blue notes', setting out the history of each 'vote' (the Estimates being divided into different votes—for example, one for pay, one for stores, one for new construction, and so on in the case of the Admiralty), and this made it easier to identify the deviations from past practice, although not in great detail. Decisions about the size of the Estimates, however, were taken by ministers: the First Lord of the Admiralty and the Secretary of State for War would consult separately with the Chancellor as to the sum which the Chancellor was prepared to find in his budget. If the First Lord or Secretary of State for War would not agree to remain within the financial limits set by the Treasury, the matter would be thrashed out in Cabinet or a Cabinet committee.

In the Estimates for 1908/9 the Admiralty made a bid for what was then considered a substantial increase of £1.25 million, but Treasury officials advising the Chancellor saw no reason why the recent trend for reductions in the Admiralty budget should not be continued. The Permanent Secretary, Murray, focused on the Admiralty's proposals for new construction, and argued that not even a single new capital ship was justified. He assumed that the Royal Navy was at its authorized two-power standard, that is that it was equal to the combined strength of the next two largest navies, Germany and the United States, and that neither of these powers was likely to have a ship equal to *HMS Dreadnought*, the first of a new class of battleship, launched in 1906. Murray used the fact that *Dreadnought* had been completed in less than half the normal time for a capital ship to argue against laying down another in the immediate future:

If we can build a Dreadnought and commission her in 15 months, we ought to have little difficulty in overtaking the paper programmes of any other power which showed signs of accelerating its activities.[67]

[66] Public Accounts Committee, *Epitome of the Reports from the Committee of Public Accounts, 1857 to 1937 and of the Treasury Minutes Thereon* (1938), 543–5.

[67] 'Naval and Military Expenditure', 18 Nov. 1907, cited in P. P. O'Brien, 'The Cabinet, Admiralty

However, the Treasury's case was undermined by an amendment to the German Naval Law, accelerating the pace of new construction, and the Admiralty's request for new dreadnoughts was approved. On the other hand, minor reductions in the Estimates elsewhere held the overall increase to £900,000 instead of £1.25 million.

In December 1908 the First Lord of the Admiralty, Reginald McKenna, brought to the Cabinet a new shipbuilding programme of six dreadnoughts to be laid down in 1909/10—two of them in February 1910 near the end of the financial year. Lloyd George, aided by Winston Churchill, then President of the Board of Trade, vigorously attacked McKenna's proposals on the grounds that four new dreadnoughts would suffice to secure Britain's superiority at sea. Lloyd George was concerned about how he could finance both old-age pensions and increased naval expenditure, and he was aware that many Liberal supporters would oppose the latter.[68] He believed, on the one hand, that the Admiralty was panicking the Cabinet with false intelligence as to Germany's intentions, but, on the other, that if Admiralty forecasts as to German intentions were accurate, then McKenna's new construction programme would be inadequate. Accordingly, on 2 February 1909 Lloyd George suggested to Asquith that Parliament be asked to approve the building of a large fleet over a period of five to seven years, at a rate to be decided by the Cabinet in the light of evidence of German construction.[69]

The idea was that the Admiralty could then place orders for future years and arrangements for construction could proceed in advance of any payments by the Admiralty. Lloyd George consulted Murray, and, at a meeting of Asquith, McKenna, and Admirals Fisher and Jellicoe, claimed that the Permanent Secretary's advice was that, while the Admiralty could not pay contractors for work in future financial years, contracts could be drawn up in advance of the financial year in which work was to begin, provided that parliamentary authority was obtained. It was left to the First Commissioner of Works, Lewis Harcourt, who was a member of the Cabinet, to challenge this break in convention that government accounting was on an annual basis. Harcourt, the son of Sir William Harcourt, had been his father's private secretary when he had been Chancellor of the Exchequer in 1886 and 1892–5, and was more alert than most members of the Cabinet to the implications of Lloyd George's proposal. A precedent would be set, he pointed out, which would enable a Conservative government,

and Perceptions Governing the Formation of British Naval Policy, 1909, 1921–22, 1927–36', Ph.D. (Cambridge, 1992), 43.

[68] 'The Financial Situation—This Year and Next', by Lloyd George, printed for Cabinet, 19 May 1908, Lloyd George papers, series C, box 14, folder 1, document 2 (hereafter C/14/1/2), and Lloyd George to Asquith, 2 Feb. 1909, Lloyd George papers C/6/11/2, House of Lords Record Office, London.

[69] Randolph Churchill, *Winston S. Churchill*, vol. ii (1967), 516–17; Lloyd George papers C/6/11/2.

just before leaving office, to commit their successors to a large programme of naval construction, and leaving them the bill too.[70]

The suggestion that a five-year programme be authorized was dropped. Even so, the Cabinet agreed that four dreadnoughts would be laid down in 1909/10 and preparations would be put in hand so that, if necessary, the rapid construction of another four could begin on the first of April 1910 (that is only two months later than McKenna had originally proposed that the fifth and sixth dreadnoughts of its 1909/10 programme be begun). The First Sea Lord, Fisher, was not content with this compromise, and he covertly encouraged the Conservative opposition and press to campaign on the slogan: 'we want eight and we won't wait'. A reluctant Cabinet was forced to agree to include the additional four dreadnoughts in the 1909/10 programme. As Churchill wryly commented: 'the Admiralty had demanded six ships; the economists (Lloyd George and himself) offered four, and we finally compromised on eight.'[71] The Admiralty had won hands down, for eight dreadnoughts were as many as industry could supply with guns in one year. Indeed the Admiralty was unable to spend all the sums voted for new construction in subsequent years.

When Churchill took over from McKenna as First Lord in October 1911— the year of the Agadir crisis—he was quickly converted from being an advocate of economy to being a fervent advocate of naval expansion. Lloyd George himself had written to Churchill three months earlier that Foreign Office papers which he had been reading were 'full of menace' and that he was not at all satisfied that Britain was prepared for war.[72] In January 1912 Churchill provided Lloyd George with a five-year forecast of naval expenditure, which showed 1913/14 as a peak year at £44,192,000, with expenditure falling thereafter to just over £43 million. Six months later, experience of underspending and underestimating led Churchill to revise the forecast for 1913/14 to £46,164,000, on the assumption that contractors who had fallen behind schedule would catch up in that financial year.[73] However, by December 1913, following Supplementary Estimates, expenditure in 1913/14 was forecast to be £48,833,000.

In September 1913 Churchill had enquired of the Chancellor what was the maximum sum which could be afforded for the navy, if various financial measures were taken, and was told £50 million, if the sinking fund for redemption of the National Debt were reduced and if payments into the National Insurance Fund were rearranged, or £53 million if an additional penny in the pound were levied on unearned income and on incomes over £2,000 a year.[74] Lloyd George

[70] 'Navy Estimates': minutes of a conference, 23 Feb. 1909, Asquith papers, vol. 21; 'Navy Estimates 1909/10', by Harcourt, 24 Feb. 1909, CAB37/98/37.

[71] Winston S. Churchill, *The World Crisis, 1911–1914* (1923), vol. i. 37.

[72] Lloyd George to Churchill, 25 Aug. 1911, Lloyd George papers, C/3/15/6.

[73] Churchill to Lloyd George, 12 July 1912, Lloyd George papers C24/3/19.

[74] 'Note to Remind Chancellor of the Exchequer', 29 Sept. 1913 and unsigned copy of reply, Lloyd George papers C/24/3/20.

agreed to give Churchill more money for the navy if Churchill would support his land policy, and in November Churchill submitted a claim for £52,300,000. However, other ministers did not wish to see any increase in taxation, since 1914 was expected to be an election year, and Churchill was urged to knock at least £1.5 million off his Estimates by slowing down new construction. In December the Admiralty proposed £50,694,800 for 1914/15, but warned that a Supplementary Estimate of £2 million would be required if contractors kept up to time.[75]

These proposals provoked a counterblast from the Treasury in the form of a memorandum circulated to the Cabinet by Lloyd George, who professed to take the view that the programme of new construction put forward by the Admiralty was an unnecessary challenge to Germany.[76] Most unusually, the memorandum challenged the Admiralty's interpretation of the naval situation, using technical arguments. In his memoirs, Lloyd George remarked that the Treasury 'was not without information from expert naval sources', and Sir Ivor Jennings has suggested that these sources were opponents of Churchill's policy (and personality).[77] In fact, such evidence as can be gleaned from Lloyd George's papers and the relevant Treasury file does not support a conspiracy theory. Lloyd George's covering note to the Cabinet openly stated that the Treasury memorandum had been prepared on the basis of information supplied by the Admiralty, while the official chiefly responsible for drafting the memorandum, George Barstow, the principal clerk in charge of the Treasury's division dealing with Admiralty expenditure, seems to have applied an intelligent layman's mind to the information from the Admiralty plus published sources. Certainly he made no mention of private information from Admiralty experts, even in what was a confidential file, and the Admiralty did not find it difficult to challenge the Treasury memorandum on technical grounds.

The Treasury memorandum sought to support the suggestion by Herbert Samuel, the Postmaster-General and one of the members of the Cabinet in favour of economy in naval expenditure, that it would be sufficient to lay down two dreadnoughts in 1914/15 instead of the four planned by the Admiralty. The Treasury claimed that this would be enough to maintain a 60 per cent margin over Germany in this class of warship, and pointed to the Royal Navy's enormous superiority in most other classes except destroyers, comparisons being drawn in qualitative as well as quantitative terms. It was also argued that Britain had forced the pace in developing larger and faster dreadnoughts, with a consequent increase in costs, including fuel and crews. The Admiralty made a

[75] 'Points Discussed at Dinner at 11 Downing Street, November 12th', Lloyd George papers C/14/1/10; 'Navy Estimates, 1914/15', 5 Dec. 1913, Lloyd George papers C/24/3/21.

[76] 'Navy Estimates, 1914/15', Dec. 1913, with covering note by the Chancellor, T1/11598/25942 (also in Lloyd George papers at C/24/3/26).

[77] David Lloyd George, *War Memoirs*, vol. i (1933), 9; Sir Ivor Jennings, *Cabinet Government* (Cambridge, 1961), 161.

stinging reply, claiming that qualitative comparisons should be made only by the 'responsible technical experts'.[78] The Admiralty was able to demonstrate (all too accurately as the war was to prove) that the larger calibre of British guns did not confer so great an advantage in fire-power over the Germans as the Treasury supposed. The Admiralty also sifted out some of the ships from the calculation, either on qualitative grounds or because of political commitments made to Empire countries.

It proved to be impossible to defeat the Admiralty on its own ground, even when Churchill sometimes appeared to be in a minority of one in the Cabinet. Eventually, after discussions at no fewer than fourteen Cabinet meetings over five months, the Estimates for 1914/15 were fixed at £51,550,000, or only £750,000 less than the sum which Churchill had asked for in November 1913. Both Churchill and Lloyd George threatened to resign, and Asquith threatened to dissolve the government if either did so. Lloyd George was unwilling to sacrifice the prospect of implementing his land policy in the 1914 budget, and he had to be content with Churchill's promise that there would be a substantial reduction in the Estimates in 1915/16.[79]

The Treasury had grave doubts about whether a substantial reduction would be possible in 1915/16 or even later. As Hawtrey, Barstow's assistant, pointed out, the cost of maintaining the fleet—repairs, stores, and fuel—had increased considerably in recent years, so that the only possible way to reduce the Estimates would be to build fewer ships. However, the vote for new construction was quite uncertain: underspending in one year, owing to failure of contractors to keep up to time, led to an increase in expenditure the following year, and meanwhile the Admiralty would divert unspent funds to other purposes, sometimes without Treasury sanction, which was in any case very difficult to withhold. Such practices, which seem to have been revealed to Lloyd George by the Parliamentary and Financial Secretary to the Admiralty, T. J. Macnamara, a fellow radical, disorganized successive budgets and set an inflated standard for future Estimates.[80] Bradbury agreed, noting that by March 1915 there would be arrears in new construction totalling about £5 million, arrears which the Admiralty would be unable to make up within Churchill's proposed figure of £48,550,000 for 1915/16 unless there were improbable reductions in maintenance costs or in the number of new ships laid down.[81] The Treasury thus found itself in a situation by 1914/15 where the navy's Estimates had risen by about

[78] 'Enclosure III: Remarks on the Treasury paper "Navy Estimates", 1914/15', Jan. 1914, T1/11598/25942.
[79] For politics of this episode see B. B. Gilbert, *David Lloyd George: A Political Life. Organizer of Victory* (1992), 69–79.
[80] Memorandum by Hawtrey, 23 Jan. 1914, Lloyd George papers C/24/3/30; Gilbert, op. cit., 75–6.
[81] Memoranda by Bradbury, 24 Jan. and 26 Jan. [1914], Lloyd George papers, C/24/3/31 and C/24/3/32.

57 per cent compared with expenditure in 1907/8 and showed no prospect of declining. For its part, the Admiralty had benefited from the fiscal revolution represented by the People's Budget and was able to outbuild its German rival.[82]

By way of contrast, the army's Estimates for 1914/15, £28,845,000, had risen by only about 8 per cent compared with expenditure in 1907/8. The War Office's expenditure was reduced year by year from 1906/7 to 1909/10, and then rose slowly to a level that was still below that of 1905/6 (see Table 2.1). When Lord Haldane first took office as Secretary of State for War in 1905 he undertook to cut out waste and, out of the savings so achieved, to reorganize the army. By 1908/9 he had reduced the Estimates from £29,796,000 in 1906/7 to £27,459,000, but, as the Treasury pointed out, the reduced figure was still well above the level prevailing before the Boer War (£20,096,000) for almost exactly the same size of army. Haldane retorted that about a quarter of the increase was accounted for by pay alone, and, compared with 1898/9, there were more garrisons in the colonies, while ancillary services, notably the Medical Corps, had been expanded. He rejected any sudden reduction in the Estimates to assist Lloyd George with his 1909 budget, on the grounds that that would disrupt the reorganization of the army.[83]

As with the contemporary battle over naval expenditure in 1908/9, Lloyd George had a powerful ally in Churchill, then President of the Board of Trade. In a memorandum circulated to the Cabinet Committee on the Estimates, Churchill claimed that the planned expeditionary force of 166,000 men was 60,000 more than needed for plans for the immediate reinforcement of India, and that the expeditionary force could be cut to 100,000 men if the Cardwell system were abandoned. (Under that system a battalion was maintained at home for every battalion abroad, so that the size of the army was determined by the number of battalions abroad.) Churchill also challenged the need for additional transport for the army, unless it had definitely been decided to commit the expeditionary force to a European campaign.[84] Haldane dared not admit that the expeditionary force was designed to meet the requirements of a European war, for to do so would provoke the radicals in the Liberal party. As with the battle over the navy's Estimates in 1908/9, Treasury officials seem to have contributed nothing to the strategic debate. In the event, Haldane successfully resisted Lloyd George's pressure for substantial economies: the army Estimates for 1909/10, £27,435,000, were only £24,000 less than for 1908/9.[85]

The relative stability of army expenditure compared with the navy's could not be attributed wholly to budgetary constraints and the efficacy of Treasury

[82] Jon Tetsuro Sumida, *In Defence of Naval Supremacy: Finance, Technology and British Naval Policy, 1889–1914* (1989), 188–96.
[83] Documents circulated by Haldane to the Cabinet Committee on the Estimates, 25 May 1908, Lloyd George papers, C/18/3/1.
[84] Memorandum for Cabinet Committee on the Estimates, 14 June 1908, Lloyd George papers C/18/3/3.   [85] Edward Spiers, *Haldane: An Army Reformer* (Edinburgh, 1980), 64–73.

control, since Haldane himself tried, with some success, to enforce economy on the Army Council. The one aspect of military policy where the Treasury had a decisive influence was preparation for munitions production in war. In 1906/7 Murray, then Joint Permanent Secretary of the Treasury, chaired the Government Factories and Workshops Committee, which had been set up to enquire into 'the economy of production [of munitions] in time of peace and the power of expansion in time of war'. Unfortunately, Murray and his committee showed much more interest in economy than in the power of expansion, and their recommendations not only reduced the size of the Royal Ordnance factories, but also led to private manufacturers being kept short of orders so that the Royal Ordnance factories could be kept as fully employed as possible. As a result there was a serious shortage of industrial capacity for munitions when war broke out in 1914.[86]

THE CONTROL OF EXPENDITURE: SOCIAL REFORM

Whereas the Treasury sought only to restrain defence expenditure, Lloyd George took so active a part in framing new legislation in the field of social reform that the Treasury sometimes acted almost like a spending department. With the Chancellor determined to spend money on the relief of poverty, Treasury control became less concerned with the prevention or minimization of all new forms of public expenditure, and more concerned with the most prudent and economic spending of money on approved projects.

The first of the Liberal reforms to require large sums to be raised in taxation was the provision of state old-age pensions. Asquith had promised in 1906 to introduce old-age pensions on a non-contributory basis, and he claimed that his efforts to reduce the National Debt, and thereby the annual burden of interest on his budget, would make it possible to finance old-age pensions without additional taxation.[87] In this he was mistaken, since the cost of old-age pensions to the Exchequer had been greatly underestimated. Lloyd George's first major task as Chancellor was to pilot the Old Age Pensions Bill through the House of Commons, a task which he was very willing to undertake, since he had been associated with old-age pensions since 1899, when he had been a member of a Commons Select Committee which had recommended that the whole cost of pensions be paid for out of taxation. Asquith's private secretaries, Roderick Meiklejohn and Mark Sturgis, had already handled the preparatory work—which was an innovation in itself, since Treasury officials did not normally draw up plans for expenditure. However, one of the Treasury's divisions dealt with superannuation in the Civil Service and thus had the expertise necessary to

    [86] Clive Trebilcock, 'War and the Failure of Industrial Mobilisation', in J. M. Winter (ed.), *War and Economic Development: Essays in Memory of David Joslin* (Cambridge, 1975), 152–4.
    [87] Murray, *People's Budget*, 92.

devise a state pension scheme. Much of the work was to fall on the principal clerk in charge of this division, John Bradbury.

Following earlier schemes for old-age pensions, and in the light of evidence that increasing years beyond age 60 were a major cause of pauperism, Meiklejohn and Sturgis seem to have assumed that pensions would begin at age 65.[88] However, officials responsible for preparing the budget insisted on a limit of £7 million a year to be spent on pensions, and in consequence the pensionable age was raised from 65 years to 70 before the scheme was put before Parliament.[89] In the event old-age pensions cost the Exchequer £2,070,000 for the last quarter of 1908/9 (payments began on 1 January 1909) and £8,496,000 for 1909/10.

The increased cost was partly the result of concessions made by Lloyd George to parliamentary opinion. The original old-age pensions scheme, as announced by Asquith in his budget speech in May 1908, had provided 5s. (25p) a week for individuals over seventy with annual incomes of less than £26, and of 7s. 6d. (37½ p) a week for married couples with joint annual incomes of less than £39. In May Lloyd George told the Cabinet that the minimum cost of the scheme was £6 million and that concessions during the passage of the bill, together with possible errors in Treasury calculations, might raise the cost to nearer £7 million.[90] In the event he gave way to criticism of the fixed cut-off point at incomes of £26 a year, substituting a sliding scale, and likewise he removed the discrimination against married couples. These concessions were estimated to cost £100,000 and £334,000 respectively.[91] The main reason for underestimating the cost of pensions, however, was failure to calculate accurately the number of people who would be entitled to them. This was partly because it was impossible to calculate accurately the effects on the number of applicants of the sliding-scale income limit or of the provisions in the Bill excluding 'lunatics, paupers, criminals, loafers and wastrels'. A major problem, however, was lack of satisfactory statistics in Ireland, where in many districts there was no documentary proof of age and where the 1911 census was to show a remarkable 84 per cent increase over the 1901 figure for the population claiming to be aged between 70 and 80 years.[92] There were other imponderables: in March 1909, for example, Bradbury felt he could reduce the forecast for the cost of pension payments in the coming financial year, on the macabre grounds that 'the severe weather of the last ten days is certain to make the 1909 death rate higher than normal'.[93]

Another imponderable was what the take-up would be among those entitled to claim pensions. The fact that pensions were income related meant that they had to be means tested, and the most obvious people to do the means testing

[88] 'Old Age Pensions', by Meiklejohn and Sturgis, Dec. 1906, T168/55.
[89] Pat Thane, 'Non-contributory versus Insurance Pensions, 1878–1908', in id. (ed.), *The Origins of British Social Policy* (1978), 103.
[90] 'The Financial Situation—This Year and Next', 19 May 1908, Lloyd George papers, C/14/1/2.
[91] Murray, *People's Budget*, 85–6.   [92] Ibid., 126–7.
[93] 'Old Age Pensions: Estimate 1909/10', 6 Mar. 1909, T1/11134/23733.

were Poor Law officials, who were accustomed to such work. However, employment of Poor Law officials would involve the taint which came with recourse to
the Poor Law, and this was something Lloyd George was determined to avoid.
Instead, officials from the Customs and Excise were given the job of means testing—something which they continued to do until after the Second World
War—while pensions were paid through the Post Office, an expedient which
has endured to this day. The Edwardian Treasury deserves some credit for
bureaucratic innovation in the field of the relief of poverty.

The recession of 1907–9 induced the Liberal government to adopt a plan by
Winston Churchill, then President of the Board of Trade, for interdependent
schemes of labour exchanges and compulsory insurance against unemployment in certain trades. The organization of labour exchanges owed much to
William Beveridge, who was already, at the age of 29, recognized as a leading
figure in London social administration, and whom Churchill had been persuaded by Beatrice and Sidney Webb to recruit as a temporary civil servant in
1908. Beveridge hoped that the labour exchanges would reduce unemployment
by making labour markets more closely resemble economists' standard assumption of perfect information, but he also intended that the exchanges could be
used to test the willingness of workers to work.

The Treasury had its doubts about whether labour exchanges would be successful but focused its criticism on administrative costs. Beveridge originally estimated his scheme would cost £130,000 a year, a figure which the Treasury
queried, and before the Labour Exchanges Bill had been introduced the Board
of Trade had raised its estimate to £200,000 on the basis of 227 exchanges
throughout the country. Continued Treasury scepticism was justified, for by 1911
the Board wished to increase this number to 350, and by February 1914 there
were 423. The Board of Trade had wanted purpose-built exchanges, but the
Treasury, mindful no doubt that under the Asquith doctrine the cost of the
exchanges would have to be met out of current revenue, insisted that most
exchanges should be in hired or converted premises, until the scheme had proved
to be successful. The fact that such premises were often dismal and inconvenient
has been cited by José Harris as one reason why labour exchanges did not in fact
have a major impact on the labour market. Be that as it may, Treasury officials
accepted that labour exchanges were a matter of government policy, subject only
to small reductions on points of detail (apart from the question of premises). It
was doubtless provoking to Board of Trade officials when the Treasury sought to
save £1,600 a year by substituting boy clerks for adult statistical clerks, or £5,000
by cutting the 1911/12 estimate for the cleaning of exchanges, but Treasury
officials did not feel free to press their doubts about the effectiveness of labour
exchanges, at least until the exchanges had been given a longer trial run.[94]

---

[94] Harris, *Unemployment and Politics: A Study in English Social Policy, 1886–1914* (Oxford, 1972), 288–9,
295, 352–3; 'Labour Exchanges', memorandum by Barstow, 4 Feb., 1911, T1/11329/18383.

In fact, the introduction in 1912 of national insurance against unemployment for workers in certain trades such as building, engineering, and shipbuilding, which were particularly subject to fluctuations in the trade cycle, gave the exchanges an indispensable role in testing unemployment and paying benefits, as well as helping workers to find employment. The unemployment insurance scheme had been prepared by the Board of Trade in 1908, but Churchill agreed with Lloyd George to delay its introduction until the Treasury had prepared a scheme for national insurance against interruption of earnings on account of ill health, and unemployment and health insurance were included in a single National Insurance Bill introduced by Lloyd George in 1911. In the case of unemployment insurance each worker contributed $2^{1}/_{2}d.$ (1p) a week to a national fund; his employer made a matching contribution, and the state paid $1^{2}/_{3}d.$ (0.7p). Barstow wrote to Beveridge pointing out that the employer's contribution was bound to affect either his prices or his wages. If prices rose, demand would fall and unemployment would increase. If, as then seemed more likely, employers reduced wages, workers would really be paying twice for insurance, once directly and once indirectly. Barstow had to abandon this objection, however, once Lloyd George wished to introduce a similar health insurance scheme. In a curious reversal of roles, Beveridge then advised the Treasury that the cost of health insurance should be borne entirely by workers and the state, so as to reconcile employers to the burden of unemployment insurance—advice which the Treasury did not take.[95]

Lloyd George personally favoured national unemployment insurance— indeed, he regarded himself as the originator of the idea, although Churchill disputed his claim—but the Board of Trade had to fight hard to have its scheme adopted, and had to make concessions to the Treasury. It seems that Lloyd George's jealousy of the Board of Trade scheme and his desire to make unemployment insurance his own made him as eager as his officials to find fault in the Board's proposals. Early in 1911 he forced the Board of Trade to reduce the proposed contribution by the state to unemployment insurance from one-third to one-quarter, as in his health insurance scheme, and he complained about the political difficulty of including far fewer workers in the unemployment insurance scheme than in the health insurance scheme. On the latter point Sir Hubert Llewellyn Smith, the Permanent Secretary of the Board of Trade, stressed the administrative difficulty of including all trades at the outset.[96] Ironically, within three years it was the Board of Trade which was advocating, and the Treasury which was resisting, an extension of unemployment insurance to more workers. Originally about 2 million workers had been insured, and in November 1913 the Board of Trade proposed to include 850,000 more. Commenting on these proposals, Hawtrey noted that already the administration of

[95] Harris, *Unemployment and Politics*, 310–11, 322.   [96] Ibid., 322–4.

unemployment insurance had crowded out the job-finding aspect of the labour exchanges' work, with staff working overtime continually, and administrative costs were rising, although there had as yet been no experience of unfavourable trade conditions.[97] In the event, pressure from employers and trade unionists was such that some concession had to be made, and unemployment insurance was extended to a further 80, 000 workers in April 1914.

The story of Lloyd George's national health insurance scheme, and the part played by Treasury and Inland Revenue officials in drafting it, is well known. As the scheme emerged in the National Insurance Act of 1911, insured workers were entitled to receive 10s. (50p) a week and free medical treatment if they could not earn because they were sick, compared with 7s. (35p) a week, up to a maximum of fifteen weeks, if they were unemployed. There was also a maternity allowance of 30s. (£1.50). Employees covered by national health insurance were required to contribute 4d. (1.67) a week; their employers 3d. (1.25) a week, and the state would contribute 2d. (0.8p) a week—hence Lloyd George's claim that workers would get 9d. for 4d. Over 12 million workers were covered, including 75 per cent of the adult male population and 25 per cent of the adult female population, compared with only 2 million workers in the national unemployment insurance scheme. Whereas the Excise and the Post Office could handle old-age pensions, and the labour exchanges administer unemployment insurance, there was no government body which could take on the running of the vast health insurance scheme. Lloyd George had originally prepared to operate national health insurance through approved friendly societies, which would collect contributions and pay out benefits, but he was pressurized by commercial insurance companies into letting them share in the administration of the scheme.

Drafting this kind of legislation was an unfamiliar task for the Treasury. The senior official involved in 1909–11 was Bradbury, then a principal clerk, assisted from the end of 1910 by W. J. Braithwaite from the Inland Revenue. Hawtrey, as the Chancellor's private secretary, was also involved. Braithwaite was given the task of investigating the German scheme of sickness insurance, but he was not impressed by what he regarded as heavy-handed German administration, and used German experience largely for examples of what to avoid; in particular, he argued against detailed supervision of the friendly societies.[98] Braithwaite did not care for Bradbury, whom he described as 'all teeth, talk . . . spectacles and argument'. Even so, Braithwaite admitted that Bradbury's criticism, although sometimes captious and annoying, did result in considerable improvements in his drafts.[99] Perhaps the fairest comment is that of Sir Henry Bunbury, the

---

[97] 'Unemployment Insurance—Inclusion of Additional Trades', 17 Nov. 1913, T1/11659/16660.
[98] E. P. Hennock, *British Social Reform and German Precedents: The Case of Social Insurance, 1880–1914* (Oxford, 1987), 173–8.
[99] Braithwaite, *Lloyd George's Ambulance Wagon*, 68, 89, 105.

editor of Braithwaite's memoirs, to the effect that national health insurance legislation was the product of Bradbury's logic, Braithwaite's idealism, and Lloyd George's mastery of the political art of the possible.[100] Certainly, Bradbury's contribution, following upon his work on old-age pensions, seems to have enhanced the esteem in which Lloyd George held him, for it was within two years of the National Insurance Act that the Chancellor had him appointed Joint Permanent Secretary of the Treasury.

In addition to drafting legislation, the Treasury also took an active part in the early administration of national health insurance. It is true that Sir Robert Morant, Permanent Secretary of the Board of Education, was appointed chairman of the English National Health Insurance Commission, the largest of four commissions set up to administer the Act (the others being for Ireland, Scotland, and Wales). However, the Financial Secretary of the Treasury, Masterman, was the minister responsible for health insurance in Parliament, and Bradbury, as Treasury representative on the English Commission, exercised the power of the purse while commissioners debated how the many points of detail left undecided by the Act should be determined by administrative regulation. What Bradbury would pass the Treasury would sanction, a position which, in Braithwaite's opinion, made Bradbury, not Morant, the master of the commission.[101]

The administrative achievement of the commission was not Bradbury's alone, however; nor was he the only official whose work on health insurance impressed Lloyd George. By May 1912 it seemed doubtful if the national health insurance scheme would be ready to start on the date set by the Act, 1 April 1913, and a few promising young civil servants from various departments were sent to help the commission's staff. A number of men made their reputations as administrators thereby, including John Anderson, a future Chancellor of the Exchequer, and Arthur Salter, a future Treasury Minister of State for Economic Affairs. Foremost among this group, however, was Warren Fisher, who had already caught Lloyd George's eye with his work at the Inland Revenue; in 1919, with Lloyd George's support, Fisher was to become Permanent Secretary of the Treasury and head of the Civil Service. Masterman remarked: 'we never got going properly until Warren Fisher came in.'[102]

Accounts of the Liberal reforms frequently overlook the fact that not all possible social reforms were implemented. The most obvious omission was education. Educational reform was linked to the vexed question of local government finance. Since 1901 successive Chancellors of the Exchequer had promised to carry out a reform which would equalize financial burdens as between rich and poor areas. The provision of elementary education was the largest single item of local authority expenditure, but the education grant system was the outcome of

[100] Ibid., 113.   [101] Ibid., 284–5.
[102] Lucy Masterman, *Masterman*, 236.

thirty years of gradual accumulation, and was full of anomalies. Most grants for elementary education were paid at a fixed rate per child, without any differentiation between rich areas and poor ones. What the President of the Board of Education, Walter Runciman, called 'a dole' of £200,000 was provided annually by the Liberal government to 'necessitous areas' for the improvement of elementary education, but this subsidy benefited only forty out of the 328 authorities administering elementary education in England and Wales. Moreover, total Exchequer grants for elementary education actually fell by £210,000 between 1907/8 and 1909/10, and the proportion of the cost of such education borne on the rates rose from 46.4 per cent to about half. This led to what Runciman called a 'formidable deputation' from the local authorities in March 1909, and by November that year several local authorities were 'on the brink of revolt'. Runciman realized that a time when the government was locked in a struggle with the Lords over the People's Budget was not a propitious one for asking for more money, but he argued hard for another £1,000,000 to raise the Exchequer grant to a level which would allow redistribution without penalizing the better-off areas.[103]

The Treasury position had been that some increase in the Exchequer grants for education was inevitable but that the division of the burden between the taxpayer and ratepayer had reached ideal proportions at half-and-half. Murray believed that local education authorities were 'in many cases very extravagant', and quoted Board of Education figures showing that current expenditure (largely teachers' salaries) was over twice as high per child in the suburbs of London as in Falmouth. He argued that the cause of economy would not benefit from the ratepayer being able to place the burden of a locally administered service on somebody else. Any increase in the Exchequer grant should await legislation for more equitable redistribution, and there was always the hope that a drastic redistribution of grants would make an overall increase unnecessary.[104]

However, by 1914 Barstow could assume that, if there were to be an Education Bill in the coming parliamentary session, some attempt should be made to reform the existing system of grants, and that for political reasons the reform could only be carried out by increasing Exchequer grants. Treasury officials would have preferred not to undertake a revision of the education grant system in 1914/15 in advance of completion of land valuation for local authority rates, but accepted that educational reform could no longer wait upon the latter.[105] The 1914 Finance Bill provided £2,750,000 of new money for elementary education in England and Wales, as well as redistributing the grant in a way that

[103] Runciman to Lloyd George, 30 Nov. 1909, T172/27, and 'The Need for an Increase of Exchequer Grants in Aid of Elementary Education', Cabinet memorandum by Runciman, 12 Dec. 1909, Lloyd George papers C/18/5/1.
[104] 'Education Expenditure', by Murray, 16 Mar. 1909, and memorandum by Barstow, 27 Jan. 1909, T1/10973/2145.   [105] Barstow to Heath, 28 Jan. 1914, T1/11632/11015.

would be fairer than the old, as between rich and poor areas, with the intention that every authority would be able to spend £3 per child.[106]

The case of education reminds one how closely social reform and public finance were intertwined. This was even true of the 'fiscal question' of free trade or tariff reform. By 1914 the Treasury accepted that the direct bearing of technical education on the industrial welfare of the nation was self-evident, greater industrial efficiency being seen as 'the real alternative to Protection'.[107] Funds were therefore released for this purpose. Treasury parsimony was selective and could be overcome by arguments of economic utility as well as political necessity. In general, however, the Treasury believed in the efficacy of leaving social and economic questions to be resolved by market forces, with only highly selective public expenditure to alleviate destitution or raise national efficiency.

PUBLIC WORKS AND UNEMPLOYMENT

Just how many people were unemployed in the Edwardian period was a matter of obscurity, since the only available statistics were those collected by trade unions of unemployment among their members, and only a minority of the working population belonged to a trade union. Imperfect as the data were, however, it was clear that unemployment increased sharply between 1907 and 1908 (from 3.7 per cent to 7.8 per cent of the working population according to a later estimate).[108] As free traders, Treasury officials were concerned that distress arising from unemployment should not strengthen the case for tariff reform, but equally they were concerned that funds voted by Parliament should be properly administered with due concern for economy. The Poor Law offered relief to the destitute, but on terms which were designed to force the able-bodied into the labour market, and which involved social stigma. Since 1886 attempts had been made to provide work for the 'respectable' unemployed outside the Poor Law by encouraging local authorities to start public works, such as roads or sewage works, when unemployment was high, but the policy had been almost completely unsuccessful, partly because the Treasury had refused to sanction cheap loans to local authorities for such projects. A recession in 1903–5 led to the Unemployed Workmen Act of 1905, which was originally framed by Balfour's Conservative government as a temporary measure pending the report of a Royal Commission on the Poor Laws. The Act provided for the administration of relief schemes by local 'distress committees', the schemes being funded from charitable contributions and local rates. From 1906/7 the Liberal government

---

[106] 63 HC Deb., 5s, 1914, cols. 1784–5.
[107] Brief for Chancellor, 27 May 1914, T1/11632/11015.
[108] Charles H. Feinstein, *National Income, Expenditure and Output of the United Kingdom, 1855–1965,* (Cambridge, 1972), Table 57.

added an annual parliamentary grant, initially of £200,000 a year, to be allocated by the Treasury between the Local Government Boards of England and Wales, Scotland, and Ireland, with the details of expenditure being subject to Treasury approval.[109]

In the case of England and Wales, the Treasury had a powerful ally in the cause of economy in John Burns, the President of the Local Government Board from 1905 to 1914, who was hostile to schemes for 'artificial' employment, and handed back to the Treasury over half the English share of the grant for 1906/7. The Treasury was also satisfied that the Scottish Local Government Board administered its funds very economically. However, there was conflict with the Irish Local Government Board, arising out of differing interpretations of the function of distress committees. The Irish Local Government Board spent the bulk of its grant in 1906/7 in rural districts, but the Treasury, in the person of Sir George Murray, took the view that 'Connemara peasants' were 'not "workmen" and were not "unemployed" within the meaning of the Act'. Consequently, the grant available to Ireland was reduced and the Irish Local Government Board was told to apply it to urban districts only. Murray's justification for this action was that chronic distress should be relieved by the Poor Law, supplemented by a vote of Parliament when the Poor Law unions were too heavily burdened, whereas the Irish Local Government Board had allocated grants for relief works to which local rates had contributed nothing. As always, the Treasury was anxious to limit the demands on the taxpayer to bear the burdens of the ratepayer.[110]

The Treasury's own administration of the Act was extremely detailed—one can, for example, discover from Treasury records that in 1909 £110 was spent on the boundary wall of Bermondsey Church and £50 for improvement of land at Reading workhouse—revealing considerable concern that funds were disbursed according to the Treasury's interpretation of the Act. The Treasury's records also reveal a concern that grants for unemployment relief were leading men to relax their search for employment, thereby creating the unemployment which the Act was designed to relieve.[111] At the same time the Treasury was hardly alone in its scepticism about the efficacy of the Act: the Local Government Board agreed that 'relief works' had to be different from a local authority's normal programme of development (otherwise Exchequer funds would simply have been used for work which would otherwise have been paid for out of the rates), but this made it difficult to find suitable schemes, and experience showed that, after their maximum of sixteen weeks a year on relief works, men usually reverted to a life of casual labour and unemployment.[112]

[109] Harris, *Unemployment and Politics*, esp. 75–9, 98, 164–79.
[110] Murray to Asquith, 3 Dec. 1907, T1/10740A/22327.
[111] T1/11149/24652 *passim*.   [112] Harris, *Unemployment and Politics*, 180–4.

Such experience did not deter influential Fabians, Sidney and Beatrice Webb, from advocating programmes of public works worth £40 million in wages over ten years, with a view to countering variations in the trade cycle and regularizing the demand for labour.[113] The Liberal government itself was anxious in the recession of 1908–9 to do something for the unemployed, and the parliamentary grant to distress committees under the Unemployed Workmen Act was increased by 50 per cent to £300,000 in the financial year 1908/9. In the autumn of 1908 Lloyd George successfully urged the First Lord of the Admiralty, McKenna, to bring forward shipbuilding contracts that had been scheduled for the following year—a measure which would mean that an additional £200,000 would be spent on wages before 31 March 1909.[114]

Lloyd George's major policy measure for the provision of employment, however, was the Development and Road Improvement Funds Act of 1909. This established a Development Commission empowered to assist agricultural research, instruction and co-operation; forestry; land reclamation; rural industries; and fisheries, with grants or loans, or by improving rural transport and harbours. The Act also established a Road Board empowered to construct and maintain new roads and to give financial assistance to local highway authorities. Each grant or loan by the Development Commission or the Road Board was to be approved by the Treasury. The Act required the Development Commission and the Road Board to take account of 'the general state and prospects of employment' when considering applications for grants as loans, but Lloyd George himself told the House of Commons that it was not possible to eliminate fluctuations in the trade cycle and that it was 'no part of the function of Government to create work'. Instead, he stressed the advantages to the nation of profitable forestry, better roads, and healthy and useful employment, rather than the stabilization of aggregate demand for labour as advocated by the Webbs.[115] As already noted, the size of the funds was small, total receipts for both over the four financial years 1910/11–1913/14 being £7,539,000, of which only 30 per cent was disbursed, an average of £565,000 a year.

Treasury officials certainly did not see the Development and Road Improvement Funds Act as a carte blanche for work creation. As with the Unemployed Workmen Act, the Treasury seems to have been restrictive in its interpretation of what Parliament had intended. It was certainly not easy to administer the Development Act, since the drafting had been such that Bradbury commented that he had 'never fully grasped the principles on which the Act was framed', in terms of how the receipts of the Fund might be allocated between grants and loans. He was determined, however, to prevent the Development Commission from entering commitments to make recurrent annual grants on the assumption

---

[113] *Royal Commission on the Poor Laws, Minority Report* (Cd. 4499), PP 1909, xxxvii. 1195.
[114] Harris, *Unemployment and Politics*, 274–5.
[115] 4 HC Deb., 5s, 1909, cols. 488, 490–1, 495–7.

that additional parliamentary votes would be forthcoming.[116] The accumulation of money in the Road Fund seems similarly to have been motivated by a
concern to cover all future commitments, some of which were subject to long
delays as surveys were made and plans drawn up. Treasury officials resisted
demands from the Automobile Association that the Road Board should use its
borrowing powers: these, it was stated, should be held in reserve, to be used, 'if
at all, during periods of trade depression'.[117]

The lack of commitment implied in the phrase 'if at all' is not surprising.
Treasury officials seem to have had no faith whatsoever in the efficacy of
counter-cyclical public works. With regard to the ideas of the Webbs embodied
in the Minority Report of the Royal Commission on the Poor Laws, Hawtrey
wrote in his first book in 1913:

> The writers of the Minority Report appear to have overlooked the fact that the Gov-
> ernment by the very act of borrowing for this expenditure is withdrawing from the
> investment market saving which would otherwise be applied to the creation of capital.[118]

In common with classical economists such as Ricardo and Mill, he believed
that money which was saved would be spent 'sooner or later' on fixed capital or
invested abroad. Government expenditure would thus, in his view, merely
divert the demand for labour, either from industries which were concerned with
the construction of fixed capital or industries which relied on export markets.
(There was an unspoken assumption here that overseas investment stimulated
demand for British exports.) In both cases the industries which would suffer
would be those most affected by the trade depression. Hawtrey was a relatively
junior official at the time, but there is no reason to suppose that his more senior
colleagues would have disagreed with his belief that government expenditure
would 'crowd out' private investment.

It is true that Treasury officials were almost certainly aware of alternative
views. It is likely, for example, that some would have read Pigou's review of
Hawtrey's book, in which Pigou described Hawtrey's crowding out hypothesis
as 'a fallacy' that he believed he had dealt with in his own *Wealth and Welfare*
(1912), in which he had supported the counter-cyclical proposals of the Minority Report.[119] Moreover, in 1914 Stamp wrote that J. A. Hobson's undercon-
sumptionist theory of unemployment was 'well reasoned' and might have 'some
truth', even 'though not generally accepted as a full explanation'. Following
Hobson, Stamp noted that excessive accumulation of savings could lead to a dis-
proportionate amount of investment by industry in fixed capital, which would

---

[116] Memorandum by Bradbury, 26 Oct. 1911, and correspondence with Development Commission,
T1/11332/18893.

[117] 'Debate in the House of Commons, 25 July 1913. Points Likely to be Raised, and the Answers
Thereto', T171/44.

[118] R. G. Hawtrey, *Good and Bad Trade* (1913), 260–1.

[119] Pigou's review, *Econ. J.*, 23 (1913), 580–4.

then produce more consumer goods even although savings had diverted the community's income away from consumption. At such a time the community would benefit if the state taxed capital and spent it on current consumption, thereby steadying production.[120] However, Stamp was writing in connection with the economic effects of death duties, and there is no evidence of Treasury officials applying Hobson's theory to counter-cyclical investment.

The Treasury's sceptical attitude to an active employment policy was shown in 1913 when, under parliamentary pressure, the Prime Minister, Asquith, decided to set up an interdepartmental committee to consider what could be done, through the distribution of public contracts, to mitigate unemployment by regularizing the total demand for labour from year to year and in different seasons. The public contracts in question were to include those of local authorities as well as government departments. When the committee's terms of reference were being drawn up, Heath, by then Joint Permanent Secretary, endorsed the view of Barstow, Hawtrey's immediate superior, that:

Even if no practical result in the way of mitigating unemployment by this means followed the appointment of a committee, it would not necessarily follow that the committee would have been useless. At least it might have scotched a fallacy.[121]

Indeed, Masterman, the Financial Secretary, thought that 'from the Parliamentary point of view it was '*as* important to "kill a fallacy"'' as it was to find ways of rescheduling government contracts.[122]

The views of other departments suggested that there were practical problems in the way of counter-cyclical expenditure: some departments like the Post Office already did try to spread contracts appropriately; on the other hand, the biggest spenders, the Admiralty and the War Office, argued that their contracts were governed by the needs of national safety and could not wait for unemployment. The Irish Public Works Board pointed out that times of high unemployment were also times when revenue was difficult to obtain—leading Barstow to observe that the Road Improvement Fund and the Development Fund would be more easily able to increase expenditure in time of depression than would government departments financed out of annual budgets. The last observation, also endorsed by Heath, suggests that, despite fears of 'political jobbery' arising from a relaxation of annual budgeting, the Treasury was not totally opposed to some spreading of expenditure so long as the principle of the balanced budget could be observed. But both the Asquith doctrine that borrowing should only be for investments which would produce a money return that would redeem the debt, and the Treasury's administration of the Unemployed Workmen Act and the Development and Road Funds, suggest that the scale of work that could be

---

[120] 'The Economic Effects of Death Duties upon Capital', 20 June 1914, T171/85.
[121] Heath to Masterman, 4 Dec. 1913, and Barstow to Heath, 20 Aug. 1913, T1/11631/10551.
[122] Masterman to Heath, 6 Dec. 1913, ibid.

rescheduled would be far less than the annual average of £4 million in wages advocated by the Webbs and would be too small to have a significant counter-cyclical effect. In the event, the Committee to Consider the Distribution of Public Contracts never met; war intervened in August 1914, and the Treasury discouraged attempts by the committee's secretary to revive it during or after the war.[123] When the issue of unemployment resurfaced after the war the Treasury took a view on public works and unemployment that reflected Hawtrey's theory rather than Hobson's (see Chapters 4 and 5).

THE TREASURY AND WHITEHALL

The manner in which the Treasury controlled the Civil Service before 1914 followed from officials' belief in a restricted role for the state, and has therefore been criticized by people who have favoured a more managerial role. In particular, Roger Davidson has lamented the Treasury's opposition to the recruitment of statisticians by the Board of Trade's Labour Department, and the concomitant shortfall between the Labour Department's investigative aims and its achievements in compiling labour statistics. The Treasury's attitude to the utility of labour statistics was partly a product of scepticism, partly a concern with administrative costs, but also, Davidson believes, partly a fear that investigation of the incidence and causes of poverty would prove to be the thin end of the wedge of socialistic expenditure.[124]

Certainly, as regards scepticism, Barstow rejected the argument that the dissemination of more comprehensive labour and commercial statistics would produce an increasing volume of trade and should therefore be funded by the taxpayer,[125] and there is no doubt that concern with administrative costs was a normal feature of Treasury control. Alleged Treasury fears that social investigation would lead to socialistic expenditure are harder to document. Davidson cites a minute by Heath as evidence that 'Treasury officials were innately hostile to the work of the Labour Department . . . viewing it as a hotbed of social radicalism and a permanent conspiracy to extravagance'.[126] Heath's minute certainly shows a concern to check bureaucratic empire-building in connection with a proposed census of wages, but contains no reference to social radicalism, the minute being largely concerned with the technicalities of recruitment of temporary officials with a view to safeguarding their pension rights. Moreover, Heath's minute is followed in the relevant Treasury file by another minute, in

---

[123] T1/11631/10551 *passim*.

[124] Roger Davidson, *Whitehall and the Labour Problem in Late Victorian and Edwardian Britain* (1985), ch. 7.

[125] Memorandum by Barstow, 5 Nov. 1909, T1/11170/25785, cited ibid., 169–70.

[126] Minute by Heath, 9 Feb. 1905, T1/10241B/2068, cited in Roger Davidson, 'The Measurement of Urban Poverty: A Missing Dimension', *Econ. Hist. Rev.*, 2nd ser., 41 (1988), 299–300.

which Murray, the Permanent Secretary, expressed the opinion that: 'the wages census would be a very useful piece of work.'[127] These words hardly read like innate hostility towards the work of the Labour Department.

There is no reason to doubt that labour statistics would have been improved if the Treasury had been less restrictive in its control of recruitment of statisticians. Nevertheless, Davidson's own statistics provide evidence that, despite Treasury parsimony, the Board of Trade's Labour Department secured most of what it asked for when it had dynamic ministers, like Lloyd George (1905–8) and Churchill (1908–10), who carried weight in Cabinet. A comparison of the Board of Trade's sketch Estimates for statistical staff and investigations with financial appropriations agreed with the Treasury reveals that the proportion of the Board's requests that were accepted rose between 1906 and 1910 from 55 per cent to nearly 90 per cent.[128] Some people might regard dependence of bureaucracy on ministers to secure support in Cabinet for an increase in the number of bureaucrats as entirely proper.

A similar picture of Treasury resistance (but also of grudging concessions) to requests for increases in staff or pay has emerged from a study of the Local Government Board for a rather earlier period.[129] No doubt Treasury attempts to restrict bureaucratic growth generated a good deal of frustration in Whitehall, but one can be certain that, left to themselves, departments would have expanded staffs and increased pay to a degree unacceptable to Edwardian public opinion. The two main aims of Treasury control, both of departmental establishments and central government expenditure in general, were to ensure that departments did not go beyond the bounds set by parliamentary statute, and to restrict growth of expenditure to what could be accommodated within a balanced budget. The effectiveness and scope of Treasury control varied according to circumstances: it was difficult for the Treasury to resist demands from a department once a particular policy had been endorsed by the Cabinet, or when the support of the Cabinet could be anticipated. It was also difficult for laymen in the Treasury to counter arguments based on professional—for example, medical—opinion. It was also the case that some departments, notably the Foreign Office, had prestige and self-confidence that made them much harder to control than 'second-class' departments like the Board of Trade, the Local Government Board, or the Board of Education.

In the Victorian and Edwardian periods the Treasury's internal organization did not reflect a recognition that control of the Civil Service was a very different function from control of Supply expenditure. As already noted, one Treasury division dealt with superannuation questions, and another division

[127] Minute by Murray, 9 Feb. 1905, T1/10241B/2068.
[128] Davidson, *Whitehall and the Labour Problem*, 171.
[129] Roy M. MacLeod, *Treasury Control and Social Administration: A Study of Establishment Growth at the Local Government Board, 1871–1905* (1968).

superintended regulations for the Civil Service, but the latter division also took charge of both Supply Services and establishment questions for a group of government departments, as did three other Treasury divisions, each dealing with its own group of departments. This system reflected the relatively simple and decentralized machinery of government before 1914, compared with what was to develop after 1919. Civil servants were organizing themselves into associations before 1914, but their right to negotiate their conditions and terms of employment was only beginning to be recognized. Consequently, it mattered little if there were disparities in conditions or pay between departments.[130] Moreover, the Treasury took little interest in questions relating to what were later to be called 'organization and methods'. Indeed, the senior Treasury official in charge of establishment questions, Heath, had a record of being an extreme reactionary. He had, for example, opposed the introduction of telephones to the Treasury, on the grounds that they would impair the ability of officials to write concisely.[131]

The Treasury was also reluctant to impinge upon departmental autonomy in Whitehall. As Chalmers, when Permanent Secretary, explained to the Royal Commission on the Civil Service in 1912, both discipline and normal promotion to established posts were matters for the minister in charge of a department. Treasury approval was required where promotion bypassed regulations regarding public examinations: for example, where an official was promoted from a lower to a higher division of the Civil Service, but there had been only one case where approval of a proposed promotion had been refused since 1895, and Chalmers knew of no similar case before that. One consequence of departmental autonomy was that promotions between departments were very rare,[132] which must have militated against a sense of corporate identity in the Civil Service as a whole.

Chalmers took a restricted view of the Treasury's responsibilities in relation to the Civil Service. The co-ordination and control of pay scales he regarded as 'an essential function of the Treasury'. On the other hand, while the Treasury was empowered under an Order in Council of 1910 to require an inquiry to be made into the pay and numbers of officials employed in a department, at intervals of not less than five years, Chalmers said that he would use this power only 'in a very bad case'. He would prefer the initiative to come from the department itself, as tended to happen anyway when a department was making out a case for an increase in its establishment. He thought that the Treasury's powers were quite adequate, given the assumption that a measure of departmental autonomy was desirable—a judgement with which his predecessor, Murray, who also

---

[130] Treasury Organization Committee, Report, Feb. 1938, T273/201.

[131] E. O'Halpin, *Head of the Civil Service: A Study of Sir Warren Fisher* (1989), 30.

[132] Chalmers' evidence on these points is to be found in *Royal Commission on the Civil Service, Appendix to First Report: Minutes of Evidence* (Cd. 6210), PP 1912–13, xv. 149–74.

gave evidence, concurred. Chalmers summarized his position by saying that he was 'no centraliser'.[133]

In the light of Chalmers' and Murray's evidence it is not surprising to find that the Permanent Secretary of the Treasury did not occupy quite the same position in the Edwardian Civil Service as he was to occupy as head of the Civil Service after 1919. Warren Fisher was to claim that the Permanent Secretary of the Treasury had been official head of the Civil Service since 1867, but a memorandum submitted to the Royal Commission on the Civil Service in 1913 claimed no more than that the Permanent Secretary of the Treasury was 'ex officio the doyen of the permanent officials of the Civil Service'.[134]

The Royal Commission did not share the satisfaction expressed by Chalmers and Murray concerning the role of the Treasury. The Commission's *Fourth Report* in 1914 stated that the Treasury did not exercise sufficiently effective control over the organization of departments, except when questions of finance were involved—that is when a department wished to increase its establishment of officials—and recommended the creation within the Treasury of a special division devoted to the general supervision and control of the Civil Service, including methods of working.[135] Nothing was said about the position of the Permanent Secretary of the Treasury in relation to the Civil Service, but, in retrospect, the Commission's report can be seen as pointing towards the centralization of control that was to occur under Warren Fisher in the inter-war period. As it happened, the First World War delayed implementation of the report, and it was not until February 1919 that a new division was set up in the Treasury to specialize in Civil Service matters.

The pre-1919 system whereby the Treasury division controlling the expenditure of a department also dealt with staff questions relating to that department was not without its merits. As Keynes noted, in the light of his experience as a Treasury official during the First World War, officials who were familiar with the general work of a department were in a much better position to judge the reasonableness of additions to staff or alterations to salary than officials who dealt with 'a staff question *in vacuo*' would be.[136] Effective control of the Civil Service cannot be divorced from questions of finance or policy, and the academic study of public administration in Britain had not reached a point in 1914 (or, indeed, until much later) where theory could be applied to practice in Whitehall. The disadvantage of the pre-1919 system of Treasury control over establishments was that it was essentially negative, ensuring that such expansion of staffs as took place was necessary for the conduct of government policy and was not simply a result of bureaucratic empire-building. On the other hand, economies or greater efficiency that might have been achieved by better organization and methods were not actively pursued by the Treasury.

[133] Cd. 6210, qs. 856, 958–61, 990, 1903.
[134] 'Memorandum on the Duties of the Treasury', 30 Apr. 1913, T170/11.
[135] Cd. 7338, PP 1914, xvi. 1, paras. 96–101.   [136] *JMK*, xvi. 293–4.

SUMMARY

The Treasury was the department that, more than any other, was at the centre of Edwardian political controversy. Asquith's 1906 budget had restated Gladstonian financial orthodoxy. Maintenance of free trade required new forms of progressive taxation to meet the rising costs of the navy and social reform. Particularly under Lloyd George, the Treasury had to adapt itself to more active participation by central government in the relief of poverty and had to begin to act like a central department of government, seeking value for money, while at the same time holding firmly to the canons of public finance. Reviewing old-age pensions, national insurance, and the Development and Road Funds, one can see the Treasury combining administrative innovation with traditional parsimony. Both elements are probably necessary for good government, but some officials, notably Murray and Heath, were a good deal more at home with parsimony than with innovation. Others, notably Chalmers and Bradbury, could cope with the changes wrought by Lloyd George, and their careers benefited accordingly. However, the department was still too small to act effectively as a central department of government, and the independence of other departments was indicated by the lack of Treasury control over the Civil Service, other than over increases in establishments. Issues such as how to control defence expenditure, how to secure value for money across a wider range of government activities, and how to deal with unemployment, all of which were to bulk large in the inter-war period, had already surfaced before 1914, but the scale of these problems was to be transformed by the First World War.

CHAPTER THREE

The First World War,
1914–1919[1]

INTRODUCTION

The First World War had a threefold effect on the Treasury: the functions of the department were extended on the finance side, particularly with regard to a wholly new responsibility for external financial relations; Treasury control over expenditure and establishments was greatly weakened in all aspects of government related to the war; and, finally, in reaction to the consequences of the weakening of Treasury control during the war, there was strong political pressure after the war to make Treasury control over both expenditure and Civil Service establishments more effective in future. The focus of this chapter, however, is on the period from the outbreak of war in August 1914 to the conclusion of the peace treaties in the summer of 1919, leaving over to the next chapter the reorganization and strengthening of the Treasury in the autumn of the latter year.

The Treasury's role in 1914–19 has to be seen in the context of expectations and experience of the nature of the war itself.[2] Pre-war plans had been based on a strategy of naval blockade, with only the regular army of about 160,000 men being committed to war on the European continent. Lord Kitchener, who was appointed Secretary of State for War in August 1914, had a very different conception of warfare. By December 1914 he had raised an army of over one million volunteers, who had to be equipped. Even before Kitchener's mass

---

[1] The Treasury's records for the First World War are particularly fragmented. As Sir Otto Niemeyer noted on 22 Dec. 1924: 'much is not recorded anywhere where the future historian can find it and exists only in the memories of Bradbury, Blackett, Keynes and others.' However, although the possibility of publishing a Treasury war history had been mooted, Niemeyer (with the agreement of Bradbury and the Governor of the Bank of England) took the view that the Treasury had no 'stirring episodes' like the fighting services, and that much of what had happened could not be published yet. Instead, Niemeyer suggested that 'we shall get as much as can be rescued from Lethe' by asking Hawtrey to compile a study for the Treasury's private records (T176/14). However, although Hawtrey was later to produce an unpublished 'Financial History' which chronicled the Treasury's role in the Second World War (T208/204), there is nothing in the Treasury's records or library to suggest that he completed a corresponding work on the First World War (Miss Y. Woodbridge, Treasury, to author, 1 May 1990).

[2] The relationship between economics and strategy can be followed in David French's trilogy: *British Economic and Strategic Planning, 1905–1915* (1982); *British Strategy and War Aims, 1914–1916* (1986); and *The Strategy of the Lloyd George Coalition, 1916–1918* (Oxford, 1995).

army took the field, it was discovered that the scale of operations on the western front was greater than expected, and the supply of munitions became a first-class political issue. When a coalition government was formed with the Conservatives, in May 1915, with Asquith continuing as Prime Minister, Lloyd George left the Treasury to head a new Ministry of Munitions.

In previous European wars, since the beginning of the eighteenth century, Britain's strategy had been to limit her own military operations and to use her wealth to finance those of her allies. In the First World War she attempted to maintain both a mass army and to subsidize her allies, and found herself increasingly dependent upon imports of munitions from the United States, for which she could only pay by borrowing dollars. Loans were raised from the American public in 1914–17 on a scale which strained British credit. Indeed, Britain would have been unable to wage war on the scale that it did in 1917–18 had not the American government provided loans from April 1917, when the United States entered the war.[3] American intervention could not have been counted upon earlier, and there was therefore considerable point to Treasury warnings from 1915 that financial and economic stability had a part to play in victory as well as the supply of men and munitions.

Opposition to conscription was led by Reginald McKenna, Lloyd George's successor as Chancellor, and Walter Runciman, the President of the Board of Trade, on the grounds that further diversion of labour from industry would cripple exports, and thereby undermine Britain's ability to subsidize her allies and bankrupt her before the Germans were beaten. The conscriptionists in the Cabinet nevertheless carried the day in January 1916. McKenna considered resignation, but Asquith, who was inclined to share the Treasury view, was able to placate him. In May that year McKenna circulated a paper to the Cabinet, giving figures that showed that there was a danger that after September Britain would be unable to pay for orders placed in the United States. However, the Cabinet supported Lloyd George in rejecting McKenna's argument that greater control must be exercised over war expenditure. What little political restraint that remained on the scale of Britain's war effort was removed in December, when Lloyd George replaced Asquith as head of the coalition, with Asquith, McKenna, and Runciman all out of office.

From August 1914 war expenditure was financed out of votes of credit, the Treasury being empowered by Parliament to borrow as much as was required over and above tax receipts. Financial policy thus became the handmaiden of the war departments, whose activities determined the size of funds that had to be raised. The Treasury, however, had to try to raise funds in a manner which would minimize inflation, and the activities of 1D, the finance division, became very much more technical than before the war. Borrowing in America meant that, for the first time, the Treasury became involved in overseas finance,

[3] R. H. Brand, *War and National Finance* (1921), pp. viii–x, 284–7.

including management of the exchange rate, hitherto the exclusive province of the Bank of England, and the Treasury established its dominance over the Bank in 1917.

The Treasury exercised little control over war-related expenditure, but was able to retain control over normal expenditure. As Hawtrey wrote later, the problem was to adapt each civil department to the purposes of war and 'to cut down all its other activities to a bare minimum'.[4] The Treasury's hand was strengthened towards the end of the war by reports in 1917 and 1918 by the parliamentary Select Committee on National Expenditure, which showed that, in the absence of effective Treasury control, there had been much wasteful expenditure by the Ministry of Munitions and the War Office. On the other hand, political pressures in 1919 for social improvement, and fears about the political consequences of unemployment among ex-soldiers and munitions workers, were too great to allow the Treasury to reimpose financial orthodoxy immediately.

PERSONALITIES, ORGANIZATION, AND ECONOMIC ADVICE

As always, the Treasury depended for its effectiveness not only upon events but also upon the personalities and attitudes of ministers. Lloyd George continued to be a powerful member of Cabinet as Chancellor, but he was increasingly interested in expediting the supply of munitions rather than in exercising control over finance. In January 1915 he had a row with Bradbury, who, according to Lloyd George, was suffering from a swollen head on account of his rapid promotion to Joint Permanent Secretary, and therefore had to be reminded of the proper relations between minister and official. Asquith noted that Lloyd George's 'curious tactlessness' had provoked something like a mutiny in the Treasury.[5] Worse followed: on 20 May Asquith received a letter from Bradbury, asking to be transferred to another post, as he could no longer work with Lloyd George. Bradbury reported that he had seen the Chancellor only rarely in the last few months and that the post of Permanent Secretary had sunk to the level of a minor clerkship.[6]

As it happened, on that date Asquith was reconstructing his Cabinet, following a decision to enter a coalition with the Conservatives, and it has been suggested that the prospect of the Treasury losing Bradbury so soon after it had lost Chalmers may have encouraged the Prime Minister to move Lloyd George to the new Ministry of Munitions.[7] McKenna's appointment as Chancellor was

[4] R. G. Hawtrey, *The Exchequer and the Control of Expenditure* (Oxford, 1921), 64.
[5] Lloyd George to Montagu, 24 Jan. 1915, quoted in Peter Rowland, *Lloyd George* (1975), 296–7; *H. H. Asquith: Letters to Venetia Stanley*, ed. Michael Brock and Eleanor Brock (Oxford, 1982), 26 Jan. 1915.
[6] Bradbury to Asquith, 20 May 1915, Asquith papers, vol. 14.
[7] By B. B. Gilbert, *David Lloyd George: Organizer of Victory* (1992), 200–1.

originally understood to be provisional, in the expectation that Lloyd George would return to the Exchequer once he had dealt with the problem of munitions—an arrangement which, Lloyd George later admitted, was a mistake, since it made personal relations between the two ministers difficult. Lloyd George, who was himself cavalier in the use of figures, described McKenna as 'a competent arithmetician . . . a master of finance in blinkers'.[8] From the Treasury's point of view, McKenna's crucial weakness was that he did not have the weight in Cabinet to restrict expenditure, especially by the Ministry of Munitions.

From the time that Lloyd George became Prime Minister, December 1916, until January 1919, there was a War Cabinet of five to seven ministers, all bar one of whom had no departmental responsibilities. The exception was the Chancellor of the Exchequer, Bonar Law, who, however, was included because of his standing as leader of the Conservative party and leader of the House of Commons, rather than because of the importance of the Treasury. Although the ministers in charge of the Admiralty and the War Office were not members of the War Cabinet, they were commonly in attendance, and decisions were often taken without reference to finance. Indeed, throughout the war, proposals involving expenditure were constantly being presented to the Cabinet without Treasury officials having been given a chance to criticize them. Bonar Law was described on taking office at the end of 1916 as 'feeling . . . like a lost stranger among the wolves of a melancholy Treasury'.[9] His successor from January 1919, Austen Chamberlain, was both a senior Conservative politician and a former Chancellor. Chamberlain had to insist on Cabinet membership as a condition for accepting the appointment. He disliked the job, doubted whether Lloyd George would back him, and soon showed signs of stress that led his family to fear that he might suffer a breakdown.[10]

Owing to the novelty and complexity of the financial problems thrown up by the war, Lloyd George asked Lord Reading, the Lord Chief Justice, to assist him. Reading's practice at the Bar had included most of the important financial cases of the day, and he had shown great mastery of figures (never Lloyd George's strong point), while grasping the general principles of high finance, even though he had had time only for elementary study of the subject. Reading took a principal part in devising measures to deal with the financial crisis caused by the outbreak of the war, and he was given a room at the Treasury where he spent part of each day dealing with financial problems, while continuing with his judicial functions.[11]

    [8] David Lloyd George, *War Memoirs*, vol. ii (1933), 744.
    [9] By J. C. C. Davidson, Bonar Law papers, box 65, folder 3, document 1 (hereafter 65/2/51), House of Lords Record Office, London. Davidson was Law's private secretary.
    [10] Sir Austen Chamberlain, *Down the Years* (1935), 135–42; *The Austen Chamberlain Diary Letters*, ed. Robert C. Self, Camden 5th ser., vol. v (Cambridge, 1995), 104–8.
    [11] Marquess of Reading, *Rufus Isaacs, First Marquess of Reading, 1914–1935* (1945).

There seems to have been an effort to strengthen the Chancellor's position in Cabinet in January 1916 by making the Financial Secretary of the Treasury, Montagu, a member, with the title of Chancellor of the Duchy of Lancaster. The arrangement was continued when T. McKinnon Wood succeeded him in July, but lapsed when Asquith resigned as Prime Minister. Lloyd George appointed a City accountant, Sir Samuel Hardman Lever, as Financial Secretary in December 1916, but, as Lever had no seat in the House of Commons, and left early in 1917 to be Treasury representative in New York, the parliamentary aspects of the post were handled by Stanley Baldwin, who was named Joint Financial Secretary from June. Baldwin proved to be popular in the House, but Treasury officials found that he had difficulty in making up his mind for himself.[12]

The Treasury's official staff did not expand proportionately to its work. The number in the upper establishment (Permanent Secretaries down to second-class clerks), which had been 33 before the war, was raised to 37 in 1914, 38 in 1916, and 40 in 1918, a total which included David Waley, who had gone off to join the army, with whom he won the Military Cross. In addition, there were about a dozen additional temporary officials, serving mainly in the overseas finance division, by 1917. The Treasury's financial experts were astonishingly few in number. The most senior in 1914 was Bradbury. (Heath, the other Joint Permanent Secretary, was concerned with control of expenditure and Civil Service establishments.) In December 1915 Chalmers was asked to return from Ceylon and on 4 March 1916 he became a third Joint Permanent Secretary, handling financial questions in partnership with Bradbury. However, Chalmers was absent again from the Treasury from May to September 1916, when he acted temporarily as Under-Secretary for Ireland. He was due to retire in August 1918 but agreed to stay on, at Bonar Law's request,[13] and did not leave until March 1919. Next to Bradbury and Chalmers, the most senior official on the financial side was Malcolm Ramsay, the head of 1D, who was promoted Assistant Secretary in 1914. However, the Treasury's new responsibility for overseas finance gave relatively junior officials the opportunity to make their names. Lloyd George very much preferred to have Blackett, then a first-class clerk in 1D, rather than Ramsay, at his side in negotiations in Paris with the French and Russian finance ministers in 1915,[14] and Ramsay seems to have played no significant part in overseas financial policy, whereas Blackett played an important role in financial missions to the United States.

Among the temporary officials was a young Cambridge economist, J. M. Keynes, who had published a book on *Indian Currency and Finance* in 1913 and had served on a Royal Commission on that subject. In August 1914 Keynes was asked by Blackett, who had been secretary of the Royal Commission, to advise on how to deal with the financial crisis caused by the outbreak of war. Then in

[12]   A. McFadyean, *Recollected in Tranquillity* (1964), 63.
[13]   Chalmers to Chancellor, 10 June 1918, Bonar Law papers 65/2/51.
[14]   Peter Rowland, *Lloyd George*, 296–7.

January 1915 he was invited back to the Treasury as assistant to Sir George Paish, who, as editor of the *Statist*, had advised Lloyd George on his budgets since 1910, and who had been appointed special adviser to the Chancellor on the outbreak of war. According to Keynes, Lloyd George had soon got bored with Paish and had stopped reading his lengthy memoranda; indeed, before the end of 1914 Treasury officials had put Paish in a room at the Road Board building, a considerable distance from the Treasury.[15] However, Keynes was given a seat in Blackett's room and worked independently of Paish, who had a breakdown and retired a few months later.

Keynes soon picked up Treasury manners. While on a mission to France he listened to the Chancellor, Lloyd George, giving an exposition of the situation there. Asked to comment, Keynes replied: 'with the utmost respect, I must, if asked for my opinion, tell you that I regard your account as complete rubbish.'[16] In May 1915 Keynes joined the Finance Division (1D), where his duties differed little from that of other officials. When in January 1917 'A' Division was hived off from 1D to deal with overseas finance, Keynes was put in charge, as a Temporary Principal Clerk, reporting directly to Chalmers and the Chancellor. By the end of the war his staff numbered seventeen, including Dudley Ward, a fellow of St John's College, Cambridge, who was a former student of Keynes and a former Berlin correspondent of the *Economist*, and Oswald Falk, a stockbroker with an interest in statistics. Work in A Division provided intensive on-the-job training for a number of young established officials, including Andrew McFadyean and Ernest Rowe-Dutton, both of whom were to have opportunities after the war to apply what they had learned.

The increased scope of the Treasury's activities was also indicated by the appointment of a Director of Financial Enquiries in April 1915. Hitherto, Whitehall had had no organized arrangements for collecting information on international currency matters or movements of capital, and the new Director was to be responsible for this as well as for collating trade and finance statistics gathered by the Foreign Office, the Board of Trade, and the revenue departments.[17] The first Director of Financial Enquiries was Hartley Withers, a financial journalist and merchant banker, who was given Dudley Ward as his assistant. Withers does not seem to have found his Treasury appointment a very satisfactory one, for in 1916 he left to be editor of the *Economist*. He was an advocate of increased taxation,[18] but he seems to have had little influence on Chancellors, and the post of Director of Financial Enquiries was not filled again until after the war.

What the recruitment of men like Withers, Ward, and Falk indicates is an increasing interaction between the City and the Treasury. The Governor of the

[15]   D. E. Moggridge, *Maynard Keynes: An Economist's Biography* (1992), 243–4. One of Paish's memoranda, in connection with the budget of May 1915, runs to forty-three pages of typescript (T171/110).

[16]   R. F. Harrod, *The Life of John Maynard Keynes* (1951), 201.

[17]   Treasury minute dated 24 Mar. 1915, T1/11791/13516.

[18]   See Hartley Withers, *Our Money and the State* (1917).

Bank of England, Lord Cunliffe, now called to see the Chancellor and senior officials quite frequently. However, whereas Lloyd George had got on well with Cunliffe, relations between McKenna and the Governor were so bad that the Prime Minister, Asquith, twice had to intervene. On the first occasion, in July 1915, Cunliffe seems to have resented the interest that the Chancellor was taking in the financing of purchases of supplies in the United States, and threatened to resign. On the second occasion, in August 1916, Cunliffe's complaints led Asquith to draw the conclusion that there was an estrangement and lack of confidence between the Bank and the Treasury. On both occasions Asquith urged McKenna to make greater efforts to co-operate with Cunliffe, and on the latter occasion set up a secret committee of himself, McKenna, and one or two other ministers to confer with representatives of the Bank and the City.[19] Both McKenna and Cunliffe could be difficult characters, but the real problem was that Cunliffe resented any interference in what he considered to be the Bank's business.

A number of Treasury officials became increasingly familiar with financial questions and were prepared to use their own judgement. For example, at one committee dealing with silver currency, on which Cunliffe, Keynes, and officials from the Colonial and India Offices sat under Chalmers' chairmanship, Cunliffe produced some figures that were out of date. Keynes disputed the figures and appealed to the chair. Chalmers remarked gently but acidly, 'Mr Governor, I fear that you are obsolete.'[20] As will be described below, relations between Cunliffe on the one hand, and Keynes and Chalmers on the other, deteriorated to a point in 1917 where the Chancellor, Bonar Law, had to assert his authority over the Governor. The war also strengthened informal City–Treasury links. In 1917 the Tuesday Club was formed to bring together City men, financial journalists, academic economists, and civil servants, with Blackett and Keynes among the first members.

TABLE 3.1. *Adjusted Budget Balance for Financial Years 1913/14–1918/19 (£m.)*

	Adjusted revenue	Adjusted expenditure	Adjusted balance	Published balance
1913/14	196.6	189.9	+6.7	+0.7
1914/15	225.4	487.0	−261.6	−333.8
1915/16	333.9	1228.9	−895.0	−1222.4
1916/17	564.7	1638.5	−1073.8	−1624.7
1917/18	659.6	2189.4	−1529.8	−1989.0
1918/19	844.6	2368.1	−1523.5	−1690.3

Source: E. V. Morgan, *Studies in British Financial Policy, 1914–1925* (1952), 98, 104. The principal adjustment made by Morgan to the published figures was to omit loans to the dominions and allies from the expenditure column, on the grounds that these transactions, together with interest payments abroad, had their impact on the foreign balance rather than on the level of demand in the domestic economy.

[19] Asquith to McKenna, 25 and 26 July 1915, and 15 Aug. 1916, Reginald McKenna papers 5/8, Churchill College, Cambridge.
[20] J. C. C. Davidson, *Memoirs of a Conservative: J. C. C. Davidson's Memoirs and Papers, 1910–37*, ed. Robert Rhodes James (1969), 61.

TABLE 3.2. *National Debt Outstanding at End of Financial Years 1913/14–1918/19*

	Domestic debt (£m.)	Percentage of domestic debt floating[a]	Foreign debt (£m.)	Total debt (£m.)
1913/14	649.8	2.0	nil	649.8
1914/15	1105.1	7.0	nil	1105.1
1915/16	2072.7	28.3	70.9	2143.6
1916/17	3643.8	18.7	473.3	4117.1
1917/18	4876.6	23.9	1048.7	5925.3
1918/19	6142.1	23.0	1364.8	7506.9

[a] The floating debt comprised Treasury bills and Ways and Means advances from the Bank of England.

Source: E. V. Morgan, *Studies in British Financial Policy, 1914–1925* (1952), 107, 321.

DOMESTIC FINANCIAL POLICY: THE ORIGINS OF INFLATION

The methods whereby funds were raised in Britain to finance the First World War have long been condemned. In the financial years 1914/15 to 1918/19 inclusive central government expenditure (including normal civil expenditure but excluding loans to the dominions and allies) was £7,912 million, while revenue amounted to only £2,628 million (see Table 3.1). Government borrowing at home and abroad raised the National Debt to £7,506.9 million by the end of 1918/19, almost twelve times what it had been five years earlier (see Table 3.2), and the servicing of the Debt (interest charges plus a limited amount of redemption) was to prove to be a serious burden on taxpayers after the war. In 1921 Philip Snowden, the future Labour Chancellor of the Exchequer, attributed the failure to raise more revenue by taxation during the war to 'the criminal folly or cowardice of our statesmen'.[21] The most authoritative study of financial policy in the period, by E. V. Morgan, has concluded that throughout the war fiscal policy was highly inflationary, showing, in his opinion, 'very little consciousness of the need to match the transfer of real resources to the Government by a reduction in private purchasing power'.[22]

The most obvious sign of wartime inflation was seen in the Board of Trade's price indices. Between July 1914 and July 1919 wholesale prices increased two-and-a-half times, and the working-class cost of living more than doubled. There can be little doubt that, had taxation been higher, inflation would have been lower, but, as we shall see, *pace* Morgan, officials were well aware of the need to transfer purchasing power from private individuals to the government, and even used primitive national income estimates to reach figures for taxable capacity and aggregate savings of the community. However, given the tax and credit structures of the day, it was difficult to achieve the required reduction in private purchasing power. Moreover, financial policy had to cope with considerable

[21] Philip Snowden, *Labour and the New World* (1921), 142.
[22] E. V. Morgan, *Studies in British Financial Policy, 1914–1925* (1952), 371.

uncertainty about the course of the war, and revenue tended to lag behind increases in expenditure.

Early action was required of the Treasury and Bank of England to resolve a financial crisis even before war was declared by Britain on 4 August. Most of the world's stock exchanges closed as the war clouds descended at the end of July, making it impossible for foreigners to meet their obligations to firms in the City of London, who were thereby threatened with ruin, while hoarding of gold coin by the joint stock banks led to a shortage of cash. At the prompting of the Treasury, Bank rate was raised briefly to 10 per cent, the traditional rate for a crisis, thereby justifying government intervention in the City. The London stock exchange was closed from 31 July to 4 January 1915, but, in Keynes's words, the financial system was saved by the 'good sense' of the Treasury and the 'courage' of the Bank of England.[23] Keynes himself was a participant from 2 August in Treasury discussions on what action to take.

That same day, a Sunday, conferences at the Treasury with representatives of the City resulted in a moratorium on debts, while the Bank was authorized to buy up frozen assets at a discount and the Government guaranteed the Bank against losses incurred in doing so. The moratorium, which lasted until 4 November, has been criticized by John Peters for favouring the City, while leaving industry with a major cash-flow problem. However, while there is no doubt that the Treasury gave first priority to dealing with the City's problems—a financial crash would not have been a good start to a war—Lloyd George and Montagu were concerned about reports that banks were failing to provide industry with necessary financial facilities. An Inland Revenue circular was sent out on 19 August and, of the 7,310 firms that responded, 6,341 reported that banking facilities then available were 'reasonably comparable with those available before the war'.[24]

The shortage of cash was overcome by the issue of currency notes of £1 or 10s. (50p) by the Treasury, to replace gold coins (sovereigns and half-sovereigns) of these values.[25] Keynes strongly backed the Treasury and the Bank against the

[23] J. M. Keynes, 'War and the Financial System, August 1914', *Econ. J.*, 24 (1914), 460–86. For a more recent account see Teresa Seabourne, 'The Summer of 1914', in Forrest Capie and Geoffrey E. Wood (eds.), *Financial Crises and the World Banking System* (New York, 1986), 77–116.

[24] Morgan, *Studies in British Financial Policy*, 24. John Peters, 'The British Government and the City–Industry Divide: The Case of the 1914 Financial Crisis', *20th Cent. Brit. Hist.*, 4 (1993), 126–48, argues that the way in which the crisis was handled is an example of the City's influence over government policy, but the stability of the financial system was a major asset in waging the war, besides being a direct responsibility of the Treasury.

[25] Bank of England notes were not used partly because they were not legal tender in Ireland or Scotland, and partly because the Bank's printing works lacked the capacity to produce enough notes in time. The author has been unable to find in the Treasury's papers any evidence to support Sir John Clapham's suggestion, quoted in K. Burk, 'The Treasury: From Impotence to Power', in id. (ed.), *War and the State: The Transformation of British Government, 1914–1919* (1982), 87, that 'perhaps a desire at the Treasury . . . for "financial self-assertion" in dealing with the Bank may have had some influence'. The currency notes were issued through the Bank.

bankers, who wished to be relieved of their obligations to make payments in gold coin. In a memorandum of 3 August he argued against suspending the gold standard before it was '*absolutely* necessary', on the grounds that to do so would lower international confidence in sterling, and would thereby impair Britain's purchasing power in international markets, while the suspension of international gold payments at the first sign of trouble would be a blow to London's profitable position as a financial centre. In particular, foreigners would cease to hold large balances in sterling. Accordingly he argued that only gold payments within the country should be restricted, a step made possible by issuing emergency paper currency.[26] Paish advised that the action taken by the authorities to rescue the credit structure of the country made it possible for City institutions to continue to finance the movement of food and raw materials from abroad to Britain, while the use of paper money made more gold available to the Bank of England for foreign exchange purposes.[27]

It was recognized from the outset that currency notes, unbacked by gold, were a danger to sound money, owing to the ease with which they could be issued. Bradbury's own view was that, once the danger of a collapse of credit was over, it would have been sound policy to withdraw the currency notes. However, Lloyd George, showing an unusual interest in technical financial matters, adopted the view of an earlier Chancellor, G. J. Goschen, who had suggested in 1891 that an issue of £1 notes would enable the Bank to mobilize for its reserves the gold used for coins. As soon as the crisis was past, Bradbury arranged with the Bank for gold to be set aside against the notes, some £27.5 million being transferred from the Issue Department of the Bank of England to a Currency Notes Redemption Account between September 1914 and March 1915, reducing the total currency by an equal amount, and leaving only £9.5 million of notes uncovered. Meanwhile, however, the government had borrowed £35 million on Ways and Means advances from the Bank between the outbreak of war and the end of November 1914. The government used these advances to pay its contractors and creditors by cheque. Once the cheques were cleared, the balances of the joint stock banks at the Bank of England increased. The action of transferring gold to the Currency Notes Redemption Account had the effect of reducing the 'proportion' between the Bank's reserve and its liabilities. The Bank then, in Bradbury's words, 'began to get nervous . . . and certain City pundits raised an outcry' about the adequacy of the Bank's reserves. As a result, the transfer of gold to the Currency Notes Redemption Account had to be abandoned, apart from the casual earmarking of £1 million of gold received from Russia in May 1915.[28]

[26] *JMK*, xvi. 7–15.   [27] Paish to Lloyd George, 1 Aug. 1914, T171/92.

[28] 'The Currency Note Gold Reserve and the Exchanges', unsigned, n.d., but internal evidence points to Bradbury's authorship, after May 1915, T170/73; 'Inflation and the Foreign Exchanges', by Bradbury, 23 Nov. 1915, T170/84. See also Morgan, *Studies in British Financial Policy*, esp. 166–9. For Goschen's proposal see Sir John Clapham, *The Bank of England: A History*, vol. ii (Cambridge, 1944), 344–8.

Bradbury believed that, if the practice of transferring gold had been continued until currency notes were matched pound for pound by gold, the full
rigour of the gold standard could have been maintained, checking and even
reversing the rise in prices, as the Bank sought to protect its reserve by restricting
credit with high interest rates. He would have been prepared to allow gold to be
exported and see Bank rate go back up to 10 per cent, or twice the rate prevailing from September 1914 to July 1916.[29] It is possible that such a rate might
have been effective in 1915 in bringing about enough bankruptcies to check
inflation, but Bradbury's advice was not accepted. As matters developed, the
risk of shipping gold abroad in wartime made the gold standard ineffective,
and the government was free to resort to inflationary finance.

The initial impetus to inflation came from budget deficits, which proved to be
much greater than officials thought wise. Lloyd George was advised in August
1914 to rely as much as possible upon taxation to finance the war. Blackett produced a memorandum, written by Bradbury at the time of the Boer War, which
stated that this was the traditional policy of Great Britain, and which pointed
out that 'even in the extreme case of the Great War of 1793 to 1815', 47 per cent
of the cost had been raised by taxation. Blackett added a memorandum of his
own, showing that only 28 per cent of the cost of the Boer War had been met by
taxation, and commented that there had been 'a good deal of contemporary
criticism of the inadequacy of such taxation'.[30] Bradbury's main argument in
1900 had been that a willingness to raise taxation in war maintained the credit
of the state, and thereby its ability to borrow at low interest. This traditional concern with the need to minimize the burden of the National Debt also formed the
main element in Lloyd George's budget speech of 17 November 1914, when he
introduced his proposals on how to pay for the war. In it Lloyd George gave figures, supplied by Bradbury, showing that Pitt's taxation measures (notably the
introduction of the income tax) had produced revenue at various stages of the
Napoleonic Wars equivalent to between a fifth and a third of national income.
The Chancellor commented: 'If we rise to the heroic level of our ancestors we
should be raising today a revenue of between £450 million and £700 million
and no borrowing would be necessary.'[31]

The autumn budget of 1914 seems to have been the first time that national
income estimates were used to estimate taxable capacity. As Bradbury noted,
data for estimating national income a century earlier were 'scanty': the only
official estimate which he could find was one for Great Britain given by Lord
Liverpool in 1822, and by some crude adjustments based on population
census returns, Bradbury arrived at a rather low figure of £250 million as the

---

[29] 'Inflation and the Foreign Exchanges', 23 Nov. 1915, T170/84.
[30] 'The Financing of Naval and Military Operations', by Bradbury, 12 Feb. 1900, and 'Additional
Taxation in Time of War', by Blackett, 21 Aug. 1914, T171/106.
[31] 68 HC Deb., 5s, 1914, cols. 351–5.

maximum for the United Kingdom (including Ireland) in 1801.[32] The data for estimating national income in 1914 were somewhat better, owing to the pioneering work of A. W. Flux of the Board of Trade. Flux had used the annual published returns by the Inland Revenue Commissioners and the first Census of Production to produce an estimate of £2,000 million for national income in 1907. Although Paish rightly regarded Flux's method as more scientific than the normal rule of thumb, which was to double the gross income declared to the Inland Revenue for income tax, Flux himself noted that his estimate had a margin of error plus or minus 10 per cent, besides being years out of date.[33] Using Flux's estimate, adjusted for population and price changes, Bradbury thought in 1914 that 'probably £2,200 million is a moderate estimate for the present time'. Paish had estimated national income in 1913 at £2,250 million, and Lloyd George gave a figure of £2,300 million when introducing his budget in November 1914.[34]

The use made by Lloyd George of national income estimates in relation to taxable capacity in his budget speech was purely illustrative, and the measures he proposed for financing the war were, as he admitted, a good deal less heroic than those that he had attributed to Pitt. They also fell a good deal short of what Bradbury and Blackett had suggested in August as the appropriate proportion of war expenditure to be met by taxation. Of the estimated total expenditure for 1914/15, £535 million, some £328 million was for waging war. The estimated deficit on the existing basis of taxation was £340 million, but new taxation was estimated to raise only £15.5 million. Far from pursuing Britain's traditional policy of paying for half the cost of the war through taxation, Lloyd George proposed to rely almost entirely upon borrowing. There seem to have been three reasons why he should do so: first, the outbreak of war had disrupted normal trading patterns, producing a temporary rise in unemployment and reducing taxable capacity; second, it was not yet clear that the gold standard would be ineffective; and, third, the City had not entirely recovered its confidence, and Lloyd George was anxious to make a success of the £350 million War Loan, which he announced in the speech.

[32] 'Total National Income', unsigned MS in Bradbury's hand, n.d., but 1914, T171/106. Lord Liverpool's statement is in 6 HL Deb., NS, 26 Feb. 1822, col. 704. The national income for Great Britain only in 1801 was estimated at £232 million on the basis of tax assessments by Phyllis Deane and W. A. Cole (British Economic Growth, 1688–1959 (Cambridge, 1962), Appendix II). Bradbury thought that the national income excluding Ireland in 1801 would have been between £180 million and £210 million. Neither he nor Deane and Cole knew of any satisfactory way to estimate the contribution of Ireland to the national income at that date, when Ireland accounted for about a third of the population of the United Kingdom, but had a much lower average income per capita than Great Britain.

[33] See A. W. Flux, 'Gleanings from the Census of Production Report', J. Royal Stat. Soc., 76 (1913), 580, 586, and Edgar Crammond, 'The Economic Relations of the British and German Empires', ibid., 77 (1914), 800, 811.

[34] 'Figures Obtained from the Board of Trade', and 'Total National Income', T171/106; 67 HC Deb., 5s, 1914, col. 351.

Certainly Bradbury, in framing his advice to the Chancellor, had taken account of increased unemployment and the consequent reduction in consumption of goods like beer and tea, which had traditionally been relied upon for indirect taxation. This had led him to consider a scheme for a direct tax on working-class incomes—which were then below the minimum level for income tax—using the national insurance system whereby employers deducted flat-rate contributions from employees' pay. The scheme had foundered on practicalities, however: complications brought about by casual work, piece-workers, and half-timers were believed by the National Health Insurance Commission to make it unworkable as an equitable means of raising revenue.[35] Consequently, the November budget provided for working-class incomes to be taxed in the traditional way, the duty on beer being more than doubled and the duty on tea being raised by 60 per cent. The greater part of war taxation was to be raised through the income tax: both income tax and supertax rates being doubled, although only in respect of the last four months of the financial year. It is worth noting that the *Economist*, which subsequently criticized the inadequacy of wartime taxation, expressed the view in November 1914 that the doubling of the income tax was 'a tremendous stroke' and 'heartily approved' the tax proposals. In 1914 the *Economist*, like Bradbury, looked to the maintenance of the gold standard to check inflation.[36]

Advice on taxation and the need to avoid discouraging subscriptions to the War Loan was also forthcoming from former Conservative Chancellors of the Exchequer, Lord St Aldwyn (formerly Sir Michael Hicks-Beach) and Austen Chamberlain, both of whom were consulted by Lloyd George. St Aldwyn, while recognizing that a Liberal government would not depart from free trade principles, and that the greater part of war taxation must be raised from incomes, noted that the Inland Revenue's proposals were 'much higher than have ever been known'.[37] Chamberlain, writing early in November, advised that heavy taxation might set back recovery from the economic disruption caused by the outbreak of war and, moreover: 'I assume you must at once take a really big loan. New taxation at the moment might adversely affect it.'[38]

The sum that the Treasury hoped to raise by the first War Loan, £350 million, was unprecedented for a single issue, and the Governor of the Bank of England was anxious that investors should be offered a rate generous enough to ensure a resounding success. The Treasury was less inclined to be generous, and the 3½ per cent offered was lower than the Governor would have preferred, even though the stock was issued at 95, repayable between 1925 and 1928, which

---

[35] 'Possible Increase of Existing Duties', by Sir Laurence B. Guillemard, chairman of the Board of Customs and Excise, 31 Aug. 1914, and 'Revenue Tax on Employed Persons' (National Health Insurance Commission minute), n.d., T170/12.

[36] The *Economist*, 21 Nov. 1914, 907–8.

[37] Lord St Aldwyn's memorandum on Sir M. Nathan's income tax proposals, n.d., T170/12.

[38] Chamberlain to Lloyd George, 9 Nov. 1914, Lloyd George papers C/3/14/5.

gave a yield of approximately 4 per cent.[39] Lloyd George claimed that the loan had been oversubscribed, when in fact only £200 million had been taken up—a deception that Hawtrey, nearly half a century later, described as 'the Treasury's blackest secret'.[40]

Hitherto money had been borrowed by Treasury bills for six months at $3\frac{1}{2}$–$3\frac{3}{4}$ per cent or by Ways and Means Advances at $2\frac{1}{2}$–3 per cent, and the immediate purpose of the War Loan was to repay this floating debt. Ways and Means Advances were the most inflationary form of borrowing, since they involved the creation by the Bank of England of new money, which found its way via the Government's contractors to the joint stock banks, who could lend to their customers or to the Government sums totalling four or five times the consequent increase in their cash reserves. Borrowing from the banks on Treasury bills had almost the same effect, since banks treated these short-dated securities as nearly as liquid as cash reserves. Even the War Loan itself did not necessarily absorb money from the hands of the non-bank public, who, according to calculations by Keynes in May 1915, subscribed only £154 million, the remainder, nearly £200 million, being taken up by the banks, including the Bank of England. Altogether Keynes estimated that in the first nine months of the war the Government had borrowed £500 million in one way or another, of which £200 million could fairly be described as 'inflation' borrowing, in the sense that the purchasing power of the community was increased by that amount without there being any increase in the amount of things to buy.[41]

In March 1915 Bradbury tried to educate ministers in what he saw as the fundamental principles of war finance. In a blunt memorandum, circulated to the Cabinet by Lloyd George, Bradbury explained that Britain's resources for meeting her requirements and those of her allies were threefold: stocks of commodities and munitions as at August 1914; plant and labour available for production; and her ability to purchase goods abroad. Of these three elements, he noted, stocks, although important in the early months of the war, were almost immaterial thereafter. Apart from borrowing for purchases abroad, what mattered in Bradbury's view was the possible margin between national income and non-government expenditure. The problem of war finance, as he saw it, was how to adjust production and consumption so as to maintain essential supplies for the civil population, while leaving the largest possible margin for waging the war. The Government could transfer to itself purchasing power from the community either by taxing or by borrowing. Borrowing on long-dated securities (other than from the Bank of England) would very largely have the same effect as taxation, Bradbury believed, since the amount of credit which the joint stock banks were prepared to create on the basis of such securities was very limited.

---

[39]   R. S. Sayers, *Bank of England, 1891–1944* (Cambridge, 1976), vol. i. 79.
[40]   Sir Alec Cairncross diary, 4 Feb. 1964, University of Glasgow Archive.
[41]   *JMK*, xvi. 102, 125–8.

Where, however, borrowing short term or from the Bank of England led to the creation of new credit, the transfer of purchasing power would be brought about by inflation.[42]

Down to March 1915 a very large part of the increase in legal tender had been absorbed, Bradbury believed, by hoarding on the part of the joint stock banks, who had been nervous about their reserves of legal tender. The real reason for the rise in prices since July 1914, in his view, was that the supply of commodities for sale on the home market had fallen but purchasing power, especially wages, had not. Indeed, if the claims of trade unionists for higher wages to compensate for higher prices were granted, Bradbury predicted, supply and demand would never be in equilibrium. The conclusion which Bradbury drew in his memorandum was that the rise in prices must be allowed to reduce consumption within Britain, which would mean 'a certain amount of privation' for the working classes. He added that, if 'the working man' was to submit to this, the necessity for sacrifice would have to be explained to him, and would also have to be demanded of the propertied classes, while profiteering by munitions contractors would have to be eliminated.[43]

Even while Bradbury's memorandum was being circulated to the Cabinet, Lloyd George, together with Runciman, the President of the Board of Trade, was meeting representatives of thirty-five trade unions at a conference in the Treasury. By the Treasury Agreement of March 1915 the union representatives agreed to recommend to their members engaged on war work both suspension of the right to strike (in return for compulsory arbitration) and a willingness to allow semi-skilled workers or women to do work hitherto reserved for skilled craftsmen. In return the trade unions were promised strict government controls on profits from munitions contracts. The 'Treasury Agreement', which may be regarded as the first modern incomes policy, was imperfectly implemented—on both sides—but one effect was that during the war there was a time lag between rising prices and wage rates of nearly a year. This, as Keynes observed later, meant that progressive inflation was an effective means of cutting real consumption, 'since prices could be continuously kept about 15 per cent above wages at the cost of a serious but not astronomical deterioration in the value of money'.[44]

It is not clear, however, that the Government was embarking on a deliberate policy of inflation early in 1915. When Bradbury wrote his memorandum in March he assumed that the gold standard ought to be maintained. He said that he very much doubted whether the Government would be able to borrow 'any further appreciable amount of genuine "savings" at anything like' current rates. This implied, in Bradbury's view, 'either the apparent collapse of our credit'—

---

[42] 'The War and Finance', by Bradbury, 17 Mar. 1915, CAB37/126/12 (also Asquith papers, vol. 27, and T171/110).
[43] Ibid.   [44] *JMK*, xxii. 259.

that is, borrowing at high interest rates—or 'the necessity for further inflation', which would undermine the gold standard.[45] This analysis did not, however, lead Bradbury to repeat earlier official advice that as much reliance as possible should be placed upon taxation, and, in the absence of evidence to the contrary, it seems that he looked to long-term borrowing in the first instance to transfer resources to the government, with further increases in taxation being held in reserve. Certainly a further big war loan was being contemplated early in 1915.

At all events, Lloyd George made no attempt in his budget of May 1915 to raise tax rates, except in respect of duties on alcoholic drinks, and then with the intention of reducing consumption rather than of raising revenue. The actual cost of the war to 31 March, £360 million, including loans to allies and dominions, had not greatly exceeded the estimate of £328 million made in November. Now Lloyd George claimed that it was impossible to foretell the duration of the war, which, he hoped, might be brought to a successful conclusion in five months. He therefore offered two estimates: £638 million (including £100 million in loans to allies and dominions) if the war ended by October, and £978 million for a full year (including £200 million in loans to allies and dominions). On the first estimate the budget deficit would be £516 million; on the second, £862 million. Nevertheless, Lloyd George proposed to wait upon events before resorting to levels of taxation equivalent as a proportion of national income to those raised in the Napoleonic War.[46]

Paish had earlier given Lloyd George a figure of £2,400 million for the nation's total income, and Lloyd George had observed that estimated cost of the war over twelve months represented over a third of that income.[47] Paish had also provided an estimate for the 'normal savings' of the country as £300 million to £400 million annually. However, the statement in the budget speech that these figures 'ought to be doubled', because war caused incomes to rise and the standard of living to fall,[48] is not to be found in Paish's brief, and may have been an imaginative addition by Lloyd George himself. Paish indeed had thought that 'erring on the larger rather than the smaller side . . . the saving power of the nation at the present time is somewhere between £400 million and £500 million per annum', but £75 million was needed for unavoidable capital expenditure at home, leaving only £375 million for war loans, of which allies and dominions would take at least £75 million. Paish had questioned whether the Government would be able to finance war expenditure on the scale envisaged without taking 'measures with respect to the civil population that would be exceedingly difficult to enforce'. He set the maximum sum which could be raised abroad annually by selling foreign securities at £300 million,[49] but even adding this sum to the savings available for war loans gave a total of only

[45] CAB37/126/12.   [46] 71 HC Deb., 1915, cols. 1001, 1008–9.

[47] 'The Finances of G.B.', by Paish, n.d., T171/110.

[48] 71 HC Deb., 1915, col. 1017.   [49] 'The Finances of G.B.', T171/110.

£675 million, which was far short of an estimated £862 million deficit for twelve months of war.

Paish's advice to Lloyd George before the budget had been to raise £300 million in tariffs, taxes, or forced loans, so as to compel the civil population to reduce consumption of resources needed by the armed services. Paish was particularly keen to levy a forced loan on all incomes, including those below the income tax limit, so that the poor might have savings which they might use after the war 'when unemployment may for a time be general'.[50] This idea, which anticipated a similar one by Keynes in the Second World War, was not, however, adopted in the First World War, presumably for the same administrative reasons as had been advanced in 1914 against direct taxation of small incomes. Tariffs and higher taxation were to come later in 1915, but a Liberal Government could not be expected to have any enthusiasm for the former, and Lloyd George procrastinated on the latter.

With so much money in the hands of the banks, Bank rate was ineffective at 5 per cent, but from mid-April 1915 the Treasury offered three-, six-, and nine-month Treasury bills on 'tap' (that is, in any amount at a fixed rate of interest), thereby stabilizing the market rate of discount at 3 per cent, and then raising it in July to 5 per cent. Meanwhile steps had been taken to discourage private investment from competing with Government requirements. In January 1915, after the reopening of the London stock exchange, the Treasury announced that Treasury approval was required for fresh issues of private stock and a Capital Issues Committee, headed by St Aldwyn, was set up to advise on applications. In principle, only domestic stock issues which were 'advisable in the national interest' and Empire issues of 'urgent necessity' should have been approved, but the rules were applied with some laxity until the summer.[51] On 1 July a Treasury circular was sent to all banks pointing out that it was undesirable that any large-scale building work should go ahead, unless required for the war, and asking them to exercise discrimination in making advances.[52]

In June a new War Loan was announced, unlimited in amount, at 4½ per cent at par, repayable between 1925 and 1945. For the first time an attempt was made to attract the small investor, the loan being issued in amounts as small as £5 bonds and 5s. (25p) vouchers through the Post Office. (Previously the Treasury had accepted the advice of the National Debt Office that a war loan which was made attractive to small investors would simply lead to a transfer of savings from Post Office Savings Banks, but Bradbury now thought it important to attract working-class subscribers, if only to encourage frugality.)[53] Keynes thought, in September 1915, that the immediate effect of the second War Loan was to cancel the 'inflationism' brought about by earlier borrowing of about

[50] Ibid.   [51] Morgan, *Studies in British Financial Policy*, 263.
[52] 'Building Operations and War Finance', 1 July 1915, T208/12B.
[53] 'War Loans', by W. G. Turpin, National Debt Office, 31 Aug. 1914, T171/106; 'War Loan', by Bradbury, 7 June 1915, T170/72.

£200 million short-term from the banks.[54] However, it was clear by September that the end of the war was not in sight and that new and more drastic steps would have to be taken to raise revenue in a supplementary budget.

The original estimates for 1915/16 had been based on average daily expenditure by the war departments (the Admiralty, War Office, and Ministry of Munitions) of about £2 million, but by August, mainly as a result of the efforts of the Ministry of Munitions, expenditure had reached £2.5 million a day. In addition, allies had been promised subsidies at a rate of nearly £1 million a day for the rest of 1915.[55] Probable total expenditure (civil and military) for 1915/16 was £1,590 million, but the revised estimate for revenue on the existing basis was only £272 million—a position which Morgan rightly described as 'almost fantastic'.[56]

In making proposals for the supplementary budget Withers was able to point out that even a deputation of bankers had asked the Prime Minister for additional taxation, not only to raise revenue but also to check personal consumption. Withers commented that it would not be taking a 'very high ideal of finance to maintain that at least one third' of war expenditure should be provided out of revenue, and suggested doubling all existing taxes as the simplest and boldest means to this end, with, as 'comic relief', special arrangements to get more taxation out of bachelors, spinsters, and childless couples.[57]

In the event, McKenna increased income tax rates by only 40 per cent, but, by reducing the exemption limit for income tax from £160 a year to £130, at a time when many wages were rising, he brought large numbers of lower middle- and working-class people within the ambit of direct taxation for the first time. He also imposed an excess profits duty (EPD) that was to be paid by all firms whose profits exceeded their 1914/15 assessment, which was based on the three years' profits before the war, by more than £100, the rate of the duty being 50 per cent. Most controversially of all, given the Liberal party's commitment to free trade, he introduced *ad valorem* duties on a range of 'luxury' imports, including cars, cinema films, and watches. McKenna still considered himself to be a free trader and, in private conversation, excused the duties on the grounds that their probable failure and consequent abolition would be 'a good object lesson as to the impossibility of tariffs in this country'.[58]

For various reasons, none of McKenna's measures in September was likely to produce much revenue in 1915/16; the increases in income tax were applied only to the second half of the year; EPD was necessarily collected in arrears, bringing in only £140,000 in 1915/16; and the primary purpose of the import duties was to save foreign exchange and shipping space. In consequence the

---

[54] *JMK*, xvi. 123.
[55] 'Average Rates of Expenditure, 1915/16' and 'Memo. by Mr Keynes', both 3 Sept. 1915, T171/116.
[56] Morgan, *Studies in British Financial Policy*, 91.
[57] 'Suggestions for Further Taxation', 11 Aug. 1915, T171/116.
[58] Alfred Mond to McKenna, 14 Oct. 1915, McKenna papers 5/10.

estimated budget deficit was reduced by only £65 million to £1,253 million. Lloyd George complained in Cabinet about the inadequacy of McKenna's pro-posals—suggesting that it would not be too much to ask people to contribute half their income to the cost of the war[59]—but such criticisms came ill from the man who had failed to raise any significant new revenue four months earlier.

As late as November 1915 Bradbury still had hopes that a more restrictive atti-tude by the Bank of England to the creation of credit and the issue of currency could reverse the rise in prices.[60] By January 1916, however, the financial situ-ation which McKenna and Bradbury had to report to the Cabinet's Finance Committee was such that there no longer seemed to be any prospect of avoiding some inflation. The anticipated deficit in the last three months of the financial year was £740 million. The Treasury optimistically hoped to realize £140 million from a new issue of five-year, 5 per cent Exchequer bonds (the actual sum realized by 31 March 1916 was £107 million), leaving an enormous sum of £600 million to be raised by short-term borrowing. On the optimistic assumption that war expenditure would continue at the existing rate, total expenditure in 1916/17 was estimated at £1,800 million, while revenue was esti-mated, somewhat pessimistically, at £400 million, giving an anticipated deficit of £1,400 million in 1916/17, or a grand total of £2,000 million to be raised by additional taxation or borrowing from 1 January 1916 to 31 March 1917.[61]

Bradbury advised that there was little to be gained by further taxation, since any increase in income tax would probably diminish to an almost equal extent the amount which could be raised by public loans. Some £470 million could be raised by the reissue of Treasury bills and other short-term borrowing, but it was unlikely that the balance—about £1,500 million—could be raised voluntarily from the non-bank public. He considered raising forced loans, but estimated that a levy on income tax payers of 5s. (25p) in the pound on taxable incomes would produce only £195 million, assuming the same allowances as for income tax, and three-quarters of this sum would be money diverted from a voluntary loan. Various taxes which had been suggested, for example on theatre tickets and dogs, would simply not produce sufficient revenue to make any significant impression in the deficit. The prospect Bradbury held out to ministers, there-fore, was a series of large loans with short-term borrowing in the intervals between them, with the best hope of avoiding financial disaster, including a collapse of the foreign exchange rate, being the fact that manufacturers were invariably behindhand with their contracts, so that the government's bills would not have to be paid on time.[62]

Keynes, for one, had no doubt that the potential inflation was very great. He regarded the increase in the deposits of the joint stock banks as the best index of

[59] *Lloyd George: A Diary by Frances Stevenson*, ed. A. J. P. Taylor (1971), 61.
[60] 'Inflation and the Foreign Exchanges', by Bradbury, 23 Nov. 1915, T170/84.
[61] 'The Financial Situation', by Bradbury, 6 Jan. 1916, ibid.   [62] Ibid.

inflation, and these he noted were almost as high in December 1915 as they had been before the funding operation represented by the big issue of War Loan in July.[63] All the Treasury could hope for, it seemed, was to carry out similar funding operations in future.

DOMESTIC FINANCIAL POLICY: THE MCKENNA RULE AND THE LIMITS OF TAXATION

It is against this background of loss of control over war expenditure that the 'McKenna rule' of the 1916 and subsequent wartime budgets has to be understood. McKenna claimed in his budget speech in April that the credit of the state was maintained by the fact that the government never borrowed without raising sufficient revenue from additional taxation to cover both interest and an ample sinking fund.[64] This statement has been described by one influential commentator as 'one of the strangest principles ever laid down in the history of public finance'.[65] However, in calculating the additional taxation required, the Treasury excluded special wartime levies on excess profits, and therefore the McKenna rule did at least provide a prospect of a return to balanced budgets and regular debt redemption once the emergency of war was over. The rule can be seen as an attempt to persuade potential lenders, abroad as well as at home, that British government bonds were a good investment, with a yield of 5 or 6 per cent, at a time when, according to the *Statist* index, wholesale prices were increasing at an annual rate of over 20 per cent.

The official *History of the Second World War* regretted that 'the illuminating idea' of using national income to guide financial policy 'flickered out' after Lloyd George's budget in 1915.[66] However, it would not have been possible in the First World War to do what was done from 1941, when, at Keynes's suggestion, national income data were compiled to enable the Treasury to work out how to transfer to the government, through taxation or borrowing, that part of the national income which was needed to wage the war without inflation. In 1916, and indeed for most of the inter-war period, economists and financial experts were not wholly agreed as to how national income should be defined or measured.[67] Bradbury commented in September 1915 on the difficulty of estimating national income given that, on the one hand, there had been a reduction in productive capacity owing to military recruitment of large numbers of workers,

[63] 'Deposits of Joint Stock Banks', by Keynes, 29 Jan. 1916, T171/129.
[64] 81 HC Deb., 5s, 1916, col. 1052.
[65] Morgan, *Studies in British Financial Policy*, 92–3.
[66] W. K. Hancock and M. M. Gowing, *British War Economy* (1949), 9.
[67] See Josiah Stamp, *British Incomes and Property: The Application of Official Statistics to Economic Problems* (1916), ch. 12. For inter-war period see A. L. Bowley, *Studies in the National Income, 1924–1938* (Cambridge, 1942).

and, on the other, prices had increased by 25 or 30 per cent since he had esti-mated national income at £2,200 million, on the basis of Flux's data, in 1914.[68] Figures of £2,500 million to £2,600 million were given by McKenna on 10 August 1916 in the House of Commons. Paish had earlier suggested £3,000 mil-lion, but Flux thought that that figure was too optimistic, and even in Novem-ber 1916 would not give a higher one than £2,800 million.[69] Subsequent research by Charles Feinstein suggests that Bradbury's estimate in 1914 had been approximately correct, but that Paish was nearer the mark in 1916 than Flux or McKenna.[70]

However, none of the estimates between 1914 and 1916 represented a serious attempt at national income analysis of the kind that was made in the Second World War, which required macroeconomic concepts that Keynes developed only in the 1930s. The use made of national income estimates in the First World War was bound to be unsophisticated. For example, McKenna used his figures in 1916 simply to support his claim that the National Debt being created during the war would not be an intolerable burden, since the Debt to be created by the end of 1916/17 would be approximately the same as a year's national income.

Failure to prevent inflation created problems with raising revenue. Indirect taxes were increased in every budget, totalling £161 million in 1918/19 com-pared with £69 million in 1913/14. However, as a proportion of total tax revenue, they fell from 42.5 per cent in 1913/14 to 20.5 per cent in 1918/19. Most indirect taxes were specific duties, that is they were related to quantity, as meas-ured by weight or otherwise, and were therefore unresponsive to increases in prices. The major sources of revenue were income tax and supertax (37 per cent of total tax revenue in 1918/19) and excess profits duty (36 per cent), but even they lagged behind inflation by about a year.[71]

In his 1916 budget McKenna raised the standard rate of income tax from 3s. (15p) to 5s. (25p) in the pound. In 1917 Bradbury advised that additional revenue amounting to some £90 million would be required to maintain the McKenna rule and suggested a graduated increase in supertax to a top rate of 5s. (25p), in place of the 3s. 6d. (17½p) top rate imposed in 1915/16, and, 'if political consid-erations' allowed, a 50 per cent increase in death duties. Law declined to accept

---

[68] 'Limits of Borrowing at Home and Abroad', by Bradbury, 9 Sept. 1915, T199/724.

[69] 85 HC Deb., 5s, 1916, col. 1289. H. P. Hamilton to Flux, and Flux to Hamilton, 23 Nov. 1916, T172/322.

[70] C. H. Feinstein, *National Income, Expenditure and Output of the United Kingdom, 1855–1965* (Cambridge, 1972), Table 4, gives the following figures for GDP at current prices (£m.):

	From expenditure data	From income data	Compromise estimate
1913	2,342	2,122	2,232
1914	2,382	2,157	2,270
1915	2,931	2,511	2,721
1916	3,366	2,976	3,171

[71] B. Mallet and C. O. George, *British Budgets, 1913/14 to 1920/21* (1929), tables 1 and 20.

either suggestion, but did increase excess profits duty (see below) to raise £60 million.[72] By 1918, however, the growth in the National Debt had apparently made him more amenable to official advice on taxes that would continue after the war: in his budget that year he increased the standard rate of income tax to 6s. (30p), and the top rate of supertax to 4s. 6d. (22.5p), in the pound, but death duties remained unchanged until Austen Chamberlain's budget in 1919.

TABLE 3.3. *Income Tax in Financial Years 1913/14–1918/19*

	Standard rate of income tax (Tax in £)	Top rate of income tax plus supertax	Number of income tax payers (000)
1913/14	1s. 2d. (5.8p)	1s. 8d. (8.3p)	1,130
1914/15	1s. 8d. (8.3p)	3s. 5¹/₃d. (17.2p)	1,140
1915/16	3s. (15p)	6s. 6d. (32.5p)	1,360
1916/17	5s. (25p)	8s. 6d. (42.5p)	2,184
1917/18	5s. (25p)	8s. 6d. (42.5p)	2,956
1918/19	6s. (30p)	10s. 6d. (52.5p)	3,547

Source: Bernard Mallet and C. O. George, *British Budgets, 1913/14 to 1920/21* (1929), 395, 398–9.

The McKenna rule recognized that the war would continue to be financed largely by borrowing. In 1916 the Bank of England formally represented to the Treasury its view that increasingly large Ways and Means advances were making it difficult to maintain the value of money. However, when Exchequer bonds were issued in October 1916 at 6 per cent the Bank deprecated what then seemed a high rate of interest. The major funding operation of the war came in January 1917, when 5 per cent War Loan 1929/47 was issued, £1,000 million being taken up by new subscriptions and another £1,000 million in conversions of previous issues, leaving post-war Chancellors with the awesome prospect of having to face the conversion or redemption of a single maturity of £2,000 million at some date after 1929.[73] The interest charge in 1918/19, £224 million, was about a quarter of the revenue in that year. The average rate of interest on the debt had been kept down to 4.65 per cent, compared with 3.25 per cent before the war, but this was partly because so much had been borrowed on short- or medium-term bills or bonds. The floating debt of £1,412 million allowed a huge expansion of bank credit to fuel an inflationary boom immediately after the war (see Chapter 4), while there were about £380 million of Exchequer bonds falling due to be repaid within four years of the end of the war.[74]

Financial policy from 1914 to 1918 thus failed to curb inflation. The chief element in demand was government expenditure, which rose from 7.5 per cent of gross domestic product in 1913 to about 45 per cent in each of the years 1916,

---

[72] 'Budget 1917/18', by Bradbury, 3 Apr. 1917, T171/138; Davidson, *Memoirs of a Conservative*, 52.
[73] Sayers, *Bank of England*, i. 95–7.
[74] Morgan, *Studies in British Financial Policy*, 114–15; Mallet and George, *British Budgets, 1913–1921*, tables 1 and 19.

1917, and 1918. Consumer expenditure, on the other hand, after rising about 2 per cent from 1914 to 1915, fell sharply thereafter to 13 or 14 per cent below the 1914 level in 1917 and 1918.[75] Much of this reduction was brought about indiscriminately by inflation—which, for example, halved the value of pre-war savings—with consequent complaints of injustice, and a general distrust of deficit finance that was to endure into the inter-war period. There was, however, a slackening in the rate of inflation in the last eighteen months of the war as the growth of government's direct controls over the economy reduced the scope for private expenditure, encouraging savings which were mopped up by selling medium-term bonds.

Doubtless more could have been done to control inflation earlier, but the Treasury was always perfectly aware of the need to reduce private purchasing power. The problem was how to raise revenue as fast as expenditure was rising. Total central government expenditure before the war had been £541,000 a day in 1913/14 but was over £2 million a day from 2 August 1914 to 31 March 1915; over £4.25 million a day in 1915/16; over £6 million a day in 1916/17; and over £7 million a day in 1917/18 and 1918/19.[76] Although the number of income tax payers increased from 1,130,000 in 1913/14 to 3,547,000 in 1918/19, the Inland Revenue found it difficult to levy direct taxation on the mass of workers, many of whom evaded taxes by failing to make returns to tax officers, or by moving house, and at the end of the war much working-class income tax had to be written off.[77]

Keynes estimated in September 1915 that, had it been possible to reduce by taxation or loans the working and lower-middle classes in Britain to the same standard of living that inflation had reduced their equivalents in Germany, the Exchequer would have benefited in that year to the extent of £400 million to £500 million, compared with not much more than £100 million if richer Britons had likewise been reduced to the position of the corresponding classes in Germany.[78] Additional revenue of, say, £450 million from the working and lower-middle classes would not have been insignificant in relation to actual revenue (£334 million). If one adds £784 million of hypothetical revenue to the figure of £300 million which Paish estimated as the limit in that year of borrowing from genuine savings within Britain (excluding £75 million for loans abroad), one arrives at a figure, £1,084 million, not far short of actual government expenditure (£1,229 million, excluding loans abroad) in 1915/16. It would seem, therefore, that a large part of the difference between inflation and no inflation, in 1915/16 at least, was the government's inability to curb the consumption of the mass of the population through direct taxation.

[75] Feinstein, *National Income, Expenditure and Output*, tables 4, 7, and 12.
[76] A. W. Kirkaldy (ed.), *British Finance During and After the War* (1921), 197–8.
[77] R. C. Whiting, 'Taxation and the Working Class, 1915–24', *Hist. J.*, 33 (1990), 895–916.
[78] *JMK*, xvi. 118.

There was another major deficiency in the tax system. Control of war profits had been the price demanded by the trade unions for the Treasury Agreement of 1915, and, under the Munitions of War Act of July that year, the profits of munitions firms were restricted to a standard rate—normally the average of the net profits of the last two pre-war years—plus one-fifth, the balance being paid into the Exchequer as munitions levy. The munitions levy was administered by the Ministry of Munitions, not the Inland Revenue, and assessment was very slow, since the Ministry was much more interested in production than taxation. Nevertheless, when excess profits duty (EPD) was introduced in September 1915, it was agreed that munitions firms should not be charged EPD until their liability for munitions levy had been assessed. As a result, most munitions firms did not begin to pay EPD until the Inland Revenue took over the administration of the munitions levy in August 1917.[79] Even Inland Revenue administration of EPD was largely ineffective in restricting profits, although it raised revenue. The Inland Revenue was denied powers to inspect firms' books, and businessmen usually regarded the duty as an expense and, where possible, would charge prices which left them with the same profits as they would have aimed at had it not existed.[80]

EPD was raised from 50 to 60 per cent by McKenna in his 1916 budget, and to 80 per cent by Bonar Law in 1917. The 1917 budget is unique in that ministerial deliberations on it were recorded in the minutes of the War Cabinet. What the minutes show is that ministers, including the Chancellor, were more concerned about hardship which might be caused by a tax of 80 per cent on excess profits than with the question of the adequacy of the proposals from the point of view of financing the war.[81] By 1918 there was political pressure to raise EPD to 100 per cent, on the analogy of conscription. Stamp wrote what he called a 'vehement' protest, which was circulated to the Cabinet, warning that such a step would remove all incentive to efficient production, and the rate was held at 80 per cent.[82] In the 1919 budget, which came after the Armistice but before the Peace Treaty, Austen Chamberlain reduced EPD to 40 per cent.

Although the difficulties of domestic war finance were in part administrative, they were also political. Attitudes to taxation were partly a matter of contemporary perceptions. The standard rate of income tax of 6s. (30p) in the pound, with a top marginal rate, combined with supertax, of 10s. 6d. (52½p), finally imposed in 1918, seemed incredibly high to a generation which had begun the war with a standard rate of 1s. 2d. (5.8p) and a top marginal rate of 1s. 8d. (8.3p). Allowance has to be made for the willingness, or otherwise, of the public to pay taxes, for unless there had been a huge increase in the number of tax inspectors, much direct taxation was in effect voluntary.

---

[79] Richard Hopkins, Inland Revenue, to Andrew McFadyean, 18 Oct. 1917, T1/12137/6199.
[80] Sir Josiah Stamp, *Taxation During the War* (Oxford, 1932), 216.
[81] War Cabinet minutes, 1 May 1917, CAB23/2.   [82] Stamp, *Taxation*, 215.

TABLE 3.4. *Money Supply*[a] *at End of Calendar Years in Britain and Germany, 1913–1918*

	Britain		Germany	
	£m	Percentage increase on previous year	m marks	Percentage increase on previous year
1913	1,154		17,233	
1914	1,329	(+15)	19,514	(+13)
1915	1,434	(+8)	23,175	(+19)
1916	1,655	(+15)	29,202	(+26)
1917	1,939	(+17)	43,801	(+50)
1918	2,429	(+25)	66,359	(+52)

[a] The money supply is defined to include all deposits with banks, other than savings banks or building societies.

Source: T. Balderston, 'War Finance in Britain and Germany, 1914–1918', *Econ. Hist. Rev.*, 2nd ser., 42 (1989), 237.

The Treasury's conduct of public finance in the First World War was far from perfect, but its shortcomings can be put in perspective by international comparisons. All combatants relied heavily upon borrowing to finance the war. It has been estimated that whereas 20 per cent of extra expenditure attributable to the war was paid for by extra taxation in Britain, the corresponding figure for Germany was only 6 per cent. However, the real difference between British and German war finance was the impact of government borrowing on the money supply (see Table 3.4). Britain's domestic money market was better able to absorb government debt than Germany's, and, crucially, Britain, unlike Germany, was able to place much of its government debt abroad, particularly in the United States.[83] Britain raised a higher proportion of its total expenditure from taxation during the war than any of its European allies, and consequently suffered less than they did from inflation after the war.[84] The McKenna rule, however inadequate it may have been from the point of view of preventing inflation, at least had the merit of indicating that there would be a return to fiscal orthodoxy after the war, thereby contributing to confidence in the financial system.

Lloyd George's policy of victory at any cost might have had greater financial repercussions than it did, had Britain not been able to borrow increasing large sums in the United States. These loans helped both to maintain the external value of the pound and to increase the flow of goods—foodstuffs, raw materials, and munitions—to Britain without creating any immediate demand upon Britain to produce exports to pay for them. It is to the Treasury's role in the external financing of the war that we now turn.

[83] T. Balderston, 'War Finance and Inflation in Britain and Germany, 1914–1918', *Econ. Hist. Rev.*, 2nd ser., 42 (1989), 222–44.

[84] Sir Josiah Stamp, *The Financial Aftermath of War* (1932), 42.

EXTERNAL FINANCIAL POLICY: PAYMASTER OF THE ALLIES

As a densely populated island, with few raw materials except coal, and unable even to feed her own population, Britain was more dependent upon imports than any other major belligerent. Britain could finance its imports by exporting goods and services, by shipping gold, by selling overseas assets, or by borrowing abroad. However, the demands of the army for manpower and for munitions quickly reduced the volume of goods available for export, and by the first half of 1918 exports by volume had fallen to 37 per cent of their 1913 level. Britain's gold reserves were small in 1914, but she could purchase newly mined gold in the Empire for sterling or obtain gold from allied countries in return for sterling loans. Altogether some £1,180 million in gold was entered into the Treasury account in New York between 1915/16 and 1918/19. Sales of British-owned foreign securities from 1915 were also substantial, but Britain's vast overseas investments, valued by Paish at around £4,000 million, could not be realized quickly, and in fact sales peaked in 1916 at £110 million, and totalled no more than £236 million in 1915–18. The principal means of raising overseas finance for the war was by borrowing abroad, an external debt of £1,365 million being incurred between 1915/16 and 1918/19, of which 75 per cent was in the form of American loans (all from private sources in 1915/16 and 1916/17 but mainly from the US Government in 1917/18 and 1918/19).[85] Britain herself lent £1,740 million to her allies and the dominions between August 1914 and 31 March 1919.[86]

Overseas borrowing represented 4.7 per cent of the British government's total expenditure (including loans to allies) in 1915/16; 18.3 per cent in 1916/17; 21.4 per cent in 1917/18; and 12.3 per cent in 1918/19, the reduction in 1918/19 being partly because of Russia's defection from the Allied cause and partly because the United States took over from Britain much of her lending to the remaining allies.[87] From these figures one may infer that the Allied war effort would have run out of steam in 1917 had it not been for the willingness of the United States to act as paymaster.

Closely linked to the problems of financing purchases abroad and handling loans was the question of the exchange rate. Unless this could be maintained at, or near, the 1914 level of $4.86, Britain would have to pay more for imports from America, while lacking the capacity to expand her exports. Although the decision was taken in August 1914 to maintain gold payments, the export of gold was discouraged by the fact that gold shipments were not covered by the government's war risks insurance scheme. The last withdrawals of gold from the Bank of England's reserves for gold on private account during the war took place in June 1916. Instead of being on a true gold standard, Britain came to be virtually

[85] Morgan, *Studies in British Financial Policy*, ch. 9, esp. tables 49 and 53. For the accuracy of Paish's valuation of British overseas estimates see Charles H. Feinstein, 'Britain's Overseas Investments in 1913', *Econ. Hist. Rev.*, 2nd ser., 43 (1990), 288–95.

[86] Kirkaldy, *British Finance*, 198–9.   [87] Morgan, op. cit, table 49.

on a dollar standard, the exchange rate being maintained at $4.76⁷⁄₁₆ by official sales of dollars in exchange for sterling.[88]

In 1914 London was the world's leading financial centre, with short-term credits overseas greatly in excess of short-term liabilities. Even the United States relied upon London to finance the movement of its exports, particularly its tobacco crop, and less advanced economies were much more dependent. Sterling was the principal medium of international exchange, a fact reflecting and reinforcing the ubiquity and strength of the City of London's financial services. When the question of the adequacy of Britain's gold reserves had been raised by some bankers six months before the war, Bradbury had felt confident that 'our position as a creditor nation gives us a call on foreign gold whenever we require it', adding that, if the demand for gold in the London market outran the inflow, 'foreign countries are too much interested in the stability of the London market not to come to our immediate assistance'.[89] In the short run this proved to be an accurate forecast: Britain's gold reserves increased in the last months of 1914 and sterling rose in August from its pre-war exchange rate of $4.86, briefly touching $7.00, and remained above par until mid-November. No one in 1914 could have foreseen that in three years Britain would be transformed into a short-term debtor, or that sterling would be pegged at $4.76⁷⁄₁₆ only with the aid of loans of dollars from the United States government.

The initial contact between the United States and British Treasuries was in fact brought about by a gold drain from America and by the withdrawal of British credit facilities from American exporters—both problems arising from the financial crisis of August 1914. The Secretary of the US Treasury, William Gibbs McAdoo, was anxious to discuss the situation with the British authorities. Lloyd George decided to send Paish and Blackett, the two Treasury representatives sailing early in October for a mission which lasted until late November. Market forces corrected the gold flow and the commercial situation before Paish could complete any agreement to extend British credit to the United States, and the mission accomplished little.[90] However, Paish found his visit to be of educational value. As he noted in his report, the exports of both France and Russia had fallen since the outbreak of war and both would need large credits to finance purchases abroad, as would the smaller Allied powers. 'Nor is it by any means improbable that we ourselves would require a certain amount of financial assistance in one way or another if the war were to be a protracted one', he added in what was to prove to be an understated prophecy. He expected

[88] 'Memorandum on the Probable Consequences of Abandoning the Gold Standard', by Keynes, 17 Jan. 1917, T172/643.

[89] 'Gold Reserves', memorandum by Bradbury, 28 Feb. 1914, T171/53. For full statement of the Treasury's position on gold reserves see memorandum by Blackett, 22 May 1914, reproduced in Sayers, *Bank of England*, iii. 3–30.

[90] Much of what follows on Anglo-American relations during the war is based on Kathleen Burk, *Britain, America and the Sinews of War, 1914–1918* (1985).

Britain's credit balances abroad to carry her over until 1916, but if by then Britain was maintaining an army of 3 million men and financing her allies, it was probable that British-owned American securities would have to be used to finance purchases in the United States. Only the United States among the neutrals would be able to supply the goods which the allies would need, to the value, Paish estimated, of upwards of £300 million a year, making American goodwill towards the Allied cause a factor of decisive importance.[91]

By October 1914 agents of British government departments were already actively purchasing all manner of stores in the United States, but in an uncoordinated way, bidding up prices. Blackett was concerned at the profits being made at the expense of the British taxpayer, and recommended that a single agency be established in New York to deal with all British government orders in America. The American banker H. P. Davison, a partner in J. P. Morgan & Co. of New York, had recommended to him that the American Supply Corporation act as agents, with Morgan's handling the financing, but in the event Morgan's were appointed in January 1915 as sole purchasing agent in the United States for the War Office and Admiralty, as well as acting as the Treasury's financial agent. The related London firm of Morgan Grenfell & Co. acted as a link between the New York firm and the Treasury, E. C. Grenfell, the senior partner, calling at the Treasury every day to discuss the financial position with Bradbury or Chalmers.[92]

Blackett also foresaw in November 1914 the role that Britain would come to play as a financial intermediary between the United States and Britain's allies. It was certain, he noted, that both France and Russia would have to purchase increasing amounts of supplies from America, which would lead to a gold drain from Europe to America. Since Britain was extending large sterling credits to her allies, and sterling could be exchanged freely for gold, London's gold reserves would bear the brunt of exchange operations. Blackett rightly anticipated that the American government would not prohibit the issue of long-term loans in the United States, and he suggested that consideration be given to one that would be sufficient to finance all the Allies' American orders.[93] Blackett, in conjunction with Keynes, developed these ideas further on January 1915, when he pointed out that Britain could raise loans in New York on more favourable terms than either France or Russia, and that Britain could then extend credits to France and Russia at a rate of interest which, while yielding Britain a profit, would still be less than France or Russia would have to pay in New York. Such a course of action would keep the control of exchange movements in British

[91] Memorandum from Paish, n.d., Asquith papers, vol. 26, fos. 188–193E.

[92] Blackett to Bradbury, 27 Nov. 1914, Asquith papers, vol. 26. The House of Morgan's links with the British Treasury went back to the Boer War, when the bank handled loans raised in the United States. See Kathleen Burk, 'Finance, Foreign Policy and the Anglo-American Bank: the House of Morgan, 1900–31', *Hist. Research*, 61 (1988), 199–211.

[93] Blackett to Bradbury, 27 Nov. 1914, Asquith papers, vol. 26.

hands, providing that France and Russia would agree to ship gold to London, in some proportion to British loans to them, to be earmarked for use to safeguard Britain's gold reserves if necessary.[94]

By the beginning of 1915, Britain had already lent about £33 million to her allies (excluding the dominions) with a further £40 million loan to Russia under discussion. By August 1915 the total had swollen to about £123.5 million, including £22 million raised by allies directly on the London market.[95] Over the same period movements in the sterling–dollar exchange rate indicated that sterling was under strain, falling from $4.85¾ at the end of January to $4.61 at the end of August. It is against this background that Treasury attitudes to inter-allied finance have to be understood.

The first joint financial conference of the Allies was held in Paris in February, Britain being represented by the Chancellor of the Exchequer, Lloyd George, accompanied by the Financial Secretary, Montagu, the Governor of the Bank of England, Lord Cunliffe, and two officials, Blackett and Keynes. The French and Russian representatives were anxious at the Paris Conference to secure the agreement of the British government to the issue of a loan for their domestic and international war expenses, with a joint guarantee by all three powers. The proposal was, however, rejected by the British. As Keynes pointed out, while it would have allowed the French and Russians to borrow more cheaply than on their own unsupported credit, a joint loan would have tended to depress the British government's credit and would make it harder to control the extent of French and Russian borrowing in the London market.[96]

The French and Russians agreed to transfer gold to the Bank of England, the gold to be shown on their balance sheets as cash held abroad, as Keynes had suggested. Britain and France also agreed to share equally in the financial support of Russia, and the Russians were to be allowed to raise loans in the London and Paris markets, in return for a promise to increase wheat exports once the route from the Black Sea had been cleared by Anglo-French operations at the Dardanelles. In the event, the Dardanelles expedition failed. Moreover the French did not fulfil their undertaking to bear half the cost of financial support to Russia, instead financing only Russia's expenditure in France, while Britain provided the Russians with funds for expenditure in the rest of the world. There was a second Inter-Allied conference, at Boulogne, in August 1915, by which time sterling was well below par in New York. On this occasion McKenna and Keynes persuaded the French and Russians to earmark more of their gold for use by the Bank of England and the French and British agreed to raise a joint loan in America.

[94] 'The United States of America' and 'The Gold Reserve and Loans to Foreign Governments', both 5 Jan. 1915, and 'British Loans to France and Russia', 6 Jan. 1915, all by Blackett, T171/107. This file also contains notes by Keynes, dated 30 Jan. 1915, which suggest that Blackett and Keynes were working together closely on these matters. Keynes's notes are reprinted in *JMK*, xvi. 67–72.
[95] 'The Gold Reserve and Loans to Foreign Governments', 5 Jan. 1915, T171/107, and 'Memo. by Mr Keynes', 3 Sept. 1915, T171/116.　　　　　　　　　　　　　　[96] *JMK*, xvi. 73–4.

By September 1915 Britain was committed to providing her allies collectively with loans at the rate of nearly a million pounds a day, compared with expenditure of about £2.5 million a day on her own armed forces.[97] It was inevitable that the Treasury should seek to control her allies' expenditure of sterling credits. As Bradbury, echoing earlier arguments by Blackett and Keynes, pointed out, even when allies spent the money in Britain, the effect was to increase imports by British manufacturers, without concomitant export earnings, and the consequence was that the sterling exchange rate tended to fall. It went without saying, Bradbury observed, that Britain must to her utmost ability provide her allies with the *things* necessary for waging the war, but it would merely cause financial and economic dislocation if allies were given the power to bid in British markets for things Britain could not readily produce or obtain.[98]

Effective control over allies' expenditure of sterling credits proved to be elusive. As early as August 1914 a conference arranged by the Foreign Office had agreed to the establishment of the *Commission Internationale de Revitaillement*, the purpose of which was to prevent the purchase by the French government of supplies in Britain leading to a bidding up of prices. The Commission was in fact a small consultative committee, based in London, with representatives of the French government, the Admiralty, the War Office, and the Board of Trade, with the last-named department providing the clerical staff. Russia and Belgium joined the Commission in September, and other powers joined later, and the Commission's functions were extended to all purchases in Britain and the Empire, and most purchases in Allied and neutral countries. Consultation was not, however, control. The Treasury exercised no supervision over French contracts, even after May 1916, when Britain had to take over the financing of French purchases in the United States. In the case of Italy, a country which was dependent on British finance for imports of munitions and food as early as September 1915, Keynes secured agreement that Italian representatives in the United States should act in consultation with British officials to avoid bidding against each other, and by 1917 the bulk of Italian orders in North America were placed through British government departments, after previous approval by the Treasury. From May 1915 Russian orders for munitions in the United States were placed through the British Ministry of Munitions, but this was not a department over which the Treasury possessed much influence. In September 1915 Keynes secured the agreement of the Russians to a procedure whereby all their orders made on British credit would first be examined and approved by British and Russian representatives in London, but in practice the Russians could and did place orders which the Treasury had rejected. Matters improved in this respect in the latter part of 1916 and by April 1917 Keynes was satisfied

[97] 'Average Rates of Expenditure, 1915/16', unsigned, 3 Sept. 1915, and 'Memo. by Mr. Keynes', same date, T171/116.
[98] 'Creation of Credits for Allies', by Bradbury, 16 Sept. 1915, T170/90.

that no British-financed Russian orders were being placed without the prior approval of the Treasury.

In 1914 Britain was herself the major industrial supplier of the Allies, but, as the shortage of shells in 1915 revealed, she had difficulty meeting the requirements of her own army. As Minister of Munitions, Lloyd George took steps to expedite supplies from North America, the United States accounting for 47 per cent of all direct imports of munitions in the first year of the war and Canada 41 per cent. The United States had far more potential as a supplier than Canada, and by the late summer and early autumn of 1915 the United States was the source of 65 per cent of all direct imports of munitions, and Canada only of 32 per cent.[99] The need to economize on shipping increased Britain's dependence upon imports from North America rather than more distant sources: before the war the United States and Canada had supplied only a little more than one-fifth of total imports, but by 1918 they were supplying nearly half.

As early as March 1915 Bradbury was noting that it might be necessary to stave off a fall in the exchange rate by borrowing abroad or by the sale of British-owned foreign securities.[100] During the summer unostentatious steps were taken by the Treasury to acquire dollar securities, but the comparative yield of British and dollar securities gave holders little inducement to sell the latter. Consequently, in December holders of dollar securities were formally invited to sell or lend them to the Treasury, and a penal tax followed in May 1916 on income from such securities which had not been transferred.

During 1915 there was growing awareness in the Treasury of the external payments problem. Prior to Lloyd George's budget in May, Paish warned that, on the basis of trade figures in March, and taking both government purchases and invisible earnings into account, Britain was already spending £300 million a year abroad more than she was earning, and the value of imports was rising month by month. This figure was the basis of the estimate of £350 million to £400 million in financing purchases abroad in 1915/16 given in the budget speech.[101] The connection between overseas and home finance was stressed by Bradbury in June, when he argued for an early issue of a new long-dated war loan in Britain. The rise in prices in Britain was stimulating imports and discouraging exports, and, unless inflation could be curbed, the country would be faced with the alternatives of saving its gold by restricting credit, and thereby purchasing power, or of suspending gold payments and allowing currency depreciation to restore the balance between purchasing power and commodities.[102] Bradbury certainly did not wish to suspend gold payments, an action which he had three months earlier warned would entail 'the loss of our financial

[99] Ministry of Munitions to S. D. Waley, Treasury, 26 Oct. 1915, T170/89.
[100] 'The War and Finance', 17 Mar. 1915, Asquith papers, vol. 27.
[101] 'The Finances of G.B.', by Paish, n.d., T171/110; 71 HC Deb., 5s, 1915, col. 1014.
[102] 'War Loan', by Bradbury, 7 June 1915, T170/72.

hegemony'.[103] As noted above, the second War Loan of June 1915 was used to mop up the supply of Treasury bills that had been fuelling bank credit, and McKenna's autumn budget was designed to curb both purchasing power through taxation and imports through tariffs.

Meanwhile, however, the supply of dollars available for purchases in the United States was running out. On 22 July the Chancellor told the Cabinet that a contract entered into by Britain for Russia could not be completed because Morgan's could not buy more dollars for sterling without forcing down the rate below $4.77. Temporary relief had to be sought by Morgan's arranging a loan for $50 million in New York, guaranteed by $40 million in American securities, provided, at McKenna's request, by the Prudential Assurance Company, and £5 million in gold shipped by the Bank of England. By mid-August most of the loan had been spent, and sterling had fallen to $4.67¼, forcing the Bank to ship gold and the British government to purchase American securities from their British owners for sale in New York. Subsequently, following the agreement between the British and French at Boulogne on 22 August to raise a joint loan in New York, an Anglo-French mission was dispatched, with Reading, the Lord Chief Justice, as its head, accompanied by Blackett and some bankers. The mission hoped to raise an unsecured loan of £200 million at 4½ or 4¾ per cent, but had to settle on 25 September for £100 million at 5 per cent, at a discount which gave a yield of nearly 6 per cent. Even so, the American public found the terms unattractive and about a third of the loan had to be taken up by the underwriters.[104]

It is against this background that the Cabinet battle from August 1915 to January 1916 between McKenna on the one hand, and Lloyd George and the conscriptionists on the other, over what kind of war Britain should wage has to be understood. The Treasury and Board of Trade argued that, if more men were taken from industry, Britain would be unable to supply her allies or to produce the exports needed to help pay for essential imports. McKenna believed that Britain could wage war for ten years, if industry were left alone, but that conscription would lead to national bankruptcy, whereas Lloyd George and his supporters believed that an enlarged British army of seventy divisions was necessary to avert defeat, and hoped that victory could be won by the end of 1916, before bankruptcy intervened.[105]

The arguments which McKenna used when presenting his case to a new Cabinet Committee on War Policy in August 1915 were those of Keynes. In a memorandum which served as McKenna's brief, Keynes tried to convey what the United Kingdom's financial contribution to the war—that is the aggregate cost of her armed forces and munitions plus subsidies to the Allies—meant in

[103] 'The War and Finance', 17 Mar. 1915, Asquith papers, vol. 27.

[104] Burk, *Britain, America and the Sinews of War*, 63–75.

[105] French, *British Strategy and War Aims*, 116–22, 129–31, 136, 158–9, 169–76; R. Skidelsky, *John Maynard Keynes: Hopes Betrayed, 1883–1920* (1983), 305–11.

terms of manpower. Taking the cost of each additional man in the army at about £200 a year, he estimated that the subsidies which Britain had promised to provide to France were equivalent to an army of 500,000 men, while those promised to Italy were equivalent to an army of another million men. Since the labour force of the United Kingdom was already fully employed, he argued, 'any considerable diversion of them to military uses is *alternative* and not *additional*' to the provision of subsidies, unless it should be possible to 'confiscate private power of consumption which is quite beyond normal methods of taxation'.[106] Ministers on the Committee on War Policy, however, were unconvinced. According to Roy Jenkins, who, as a former Chancellor of the Exchequer, should know how politicians' minds work, McKenna presented his argument in too intelligent a way: 'When he patiently explained that it was not so much money as the physical allocation of resources . . . which was the trouble,' men who might have accepted that the Chancellor could not find money for 70 divisions became mystified.[107]

In fact, as the New York exchange crisis in July and August showed, the problem was also one of money—the supply of dollars. That supply, however, again reflected real resources, and their allocation between different uses, in North America. Some ministers were inclined to think that overseas finance could not be a major constraint on war expenditure when Britain had overseas investments valued at £4,000 million. However, as Bradbury pointed out early in September, the ability of North America to make capital available abroad depended upon its ability to maintain a surplus of exports over imports. That surplus could be increased by diverting capital from domestic investment to external loans, and by increasing output in response to European orders, but it would not be unlimited.[108] The failure of the Anglo-French loan later in the month showed that American investors would not easily be diverted from investment at home.

In November 1915 the problems of overseas finance once more became pressing. Flux, of the Board of Trade, then estimated that Britain's positive balance on invisibles was still sufficient to cover the deficit in the balance of trade in merchandise, but that the whole of imports on government account, plus all subsidies to allies and dominions, would have to be paid for by exporting gold, selling securities, or borrowing abroad.[109] The view that Britain's financial resources were not inexhaustible was thus not limited to the Treasury, although the Treasury seems to have taken a slightly more pessimistic view than Flux about the prospects for the balance of trade.

[106] *JMK*, xvi. 110–15.   [107] Roy Jenkins, *Asquith* (1986), 371.
[108] 'Limits of Borrowing at Home and Abroad', by Bradbury, 9 Sept. 1915, T199/724.
[109] Note by Flux, 15 Nov. 1915, T170/73. A more recent estimate is that Britain had a deficit on her balance of payments on current account of £55 millions in 1915; surpluses of £90 millions and £50 millions in 1916 and 1917 respectively, and a deficit of £275 millions in 1918 (Feinstein, *National Income, Expenditure and Output*, table 37).

McKenna presented the Cabinet's Finance Committee in November with estimates of external liabilities and assets for the period from 13 October 1915 to 30 September 1916. These showed that Britain had entered into commitments totalling £743 million, to which £82 million was added for a trade deficit after allowing for invisible earnings. Against these liabilities of £825 million the Chancellor's immediate resources in gold and dollars amounted to about £116.5 million, including Britain's share of the Anglo-French Loan and £20 million of gold agreed to be shipped by Russia, with the possibility of further shipments of gold during the year from the Allies of up to £80 million. The additional amount which could be raised in the United States by selling British-owned securities, or by borrowing using these securities as collateral, was unknown, but a statement by Reading, stressing the difficulties of raising loans in New York, was attached, together with Reading's estimate that £400 million appeared to be the maximum which could be borrowed.[110] The sum of all of these methods of meeting external commitments, £596.5 million, thus fell short of what was required by £228.5 million, against which total British gold stocks, including gold deposited abroad, were estimated at the beginning of 1916 to be £186 million.

As Bradbury observed, however, any large inroad into these reserves would drive Britain off the gold standard. If this happened, sterling's exchange rate would fall and the price of essential imports would rise, and Britain would be able to import no more than she could export, implying either starvation or the collapse of her war effort. Indeed, Bradbury believed that the only chance of reaching the end of 1916/17 without financial disaster was that war material would be delivered late, so that the bills would not have to be met on the estimated dates.[111]

By May 1916 the Cabinet's Finance Committee (of which McKenna was, but Lloyd George was not, a member) was sufficiently alarmed at the gravity of the position to recommend to the Cabinet that future commitments abroad should be restricted within the narrowest possible limits. The external payments position had been much aggravated by the growing dependence of the French on British funds, but even if an optimistic view were taken of France's ability to raise funds on collateral security in New York, Britain's commitments to her allies were likely to total $315 million up to 30 September 1916. British government orders for military supplies indicated that $580 million fell due to be paid by that date, and even allowing for delays in deliveries, payments would be about $400 million, to which one had to add $80 million for sugar and other civil purchases. Total payments of $795 million by 30 September would leave Britain without reserves in sight by the last quarter of the calendar year.[112] Even this dire

[110] Finance Committee, 'Interim Report' and 'Statement by Lord Reading', Nov. 1915, T170/84.

[111] 'The Financial Situation', by Bradbury, 6 Jan. 1916, T170/84.

[112] Cabinet paper, circulated by McKenna, 19 May 1916, CAB37/148/6.

warning did not deflect the Cabinet from its war policy, with the consequence that Britain was extremely vulnerable to financial pressure by the United States.

EXTERNAL FINANCE: DEPENDENCE ON THE UNITED STATES GOVERNMENT

In the autumn of 1916 Britain's blockade of Germany, involving as it did a black-list of American firms dealing with Germany, led to Congress threatening reprisals. Although the Foreign Office doubted whether the Americans would act, it convened an interdepartmental committee to consider how far Britain was dependent commercially and financially on the United States, and how reprisals could be met. Keynes represented the Treasury and on 10 October warned that 'of the £5 million which the Treasury have to find daily for the prosecution of the war, about £2 million has to be found in North America'. Keynes's figure of about £2 million a day was no exaggeration since in 1917/18, despite reduced lending to allies on account of Russia's gradual withdrawal from the war, the British government was to raise about £700 million in the United States and Canada by borrowing, selling securities, and exporting gold. Keynes estimated that in future about four-fifths of this £2 million a day would have to be borrowed (in fact the proportion in 1917/18 was nearer 90 per cent) and warned that a statement by the United States executive deprecating Allied loans would make it impossible to borrow enough. The conclusion he drew was that Britain must 'conciliate and please' the Americans.[113] In a paper drafted by Keynes, McKenna warned the War Cabinet that 'by next June or earlier, the President of the American Republic will be in a position, if he wishes, to dictate his own terms to us.'[114]

In fact the danger Keynes feared materialized in November 1916 when, fol-lowing a statement by Morgan's that they intended to issue, without limit, short-term British Treasury bills to American banks, the Federal Reserve Board warned American investors to be careful about buying bonds issued by Britain and her allies. The Board had consulted the President, Woodrow Wilson, who stiffened the warning, as a means of bringing diplomatic pressure to bear on the British government at a time when the President was seeking to mediate between the Allies and the Central Powers. The warning led to a temporary fall in British credit in the United States, a run on the pound, and calls from Lon-don bankers to suspend gold payments. Bradbury and Chalmers were deter-mined to maintain payments and the exchange rate. Fearing that ministers might give way to the bankers' demands if the true position were known, Chalmers reported to the War Cabinet that the amounts of gold paid out to maintain the exchange rate had dropped in two days from $17 million to

[113] *JMK*, xvi. 197–8. For the accuracy of Keynes's estimate, see Morgan, *Studies in British Financial Pol-icy*, 320, 330, 335.   [114] *JMK*, xvi. 198–201.

$8 million and then to $4 million, without mentioning that $2 million would have been a very heavy loss, and that the reserves might be exhausted in a week.[115]

Keynes produced arguments in January 1917 why Britain should not abandon the gold standard, which by then took the form of the Bank of England being willing to sell dollars for sterling to all comers at $4.76⁷/₁₆. This arrangement had the effect of stabilizing exchanges throughout the world, but, Keynes warned, if dollars ceased to be sold for sterling, both sterling and the currencies of other Allied powers would fall heavily, causing commercial dislocation as bills of exchange denominated in sterling lost their value in terms of dollars. Britain would cease to be the banker of the world and foreign nations would no longer hold such large balances as they did in London, depriving Britain of an immediate financial asset, and threatening London's post-war position. Keynes also believed that abandonment of the gold standard would make loans abroad harder and more expensive to raise, while the blow to British prestige would also encourage Germany.[116]

The exchange crisis lasted until February 1917, when the Federal Reserve Board was persuaded to make an announcement modifying its November warning about holding British Treasury bills. Thereafter the sterling : dollar rate was maintained by the sale in New York of Treasury bills denominated in dollars. The crisis forced the Treasury to reorganize its arrangements for conducting overseas finance. The Foreign Office persuaded the Treasury that Britain could no longer rely on a private American bank as its financial representative in the United States. It was decided, therefore, to establish a small resident Treasury mission in New York, comprising Hardman Lever, the Financial Secretary, and one second-class clerk, Andrew McFadyean. (Later in 1917, after McFadyean had returned home, Lever was joined by Blackett.) Morgan's would continue to act as purchasing agent but Lever, who was given an office at Morgan's in February 1917, would be responsible for decisions about finance. It was at this time that 'A' division was hived off from the Treasury's finance division, to be responsible for overseas finance.

From 3 February 1917, when the United States broke off diplomatic relations with Germany on account of that country's policy of unlimited submarine warfare, the British government had hopes that America would enter the war on the Allied side. By mid-March, however, the Treasury had little more than a month's resources in New York to meet its payments in America. When the United States did enter the war, on 2 April, Britain had $490 million worth of securities in the United States and $87 million in gold in New York, but expenditure was at a rate of $75 million a week, and already the Treasury had an overdraft of $358 million at Morgan's, and the only other ready reserves were the £114 million in gold in the Bank of England and the joint stock banks. Nor did

---

[115]   Burk, *Britain, America and the Sinews of War*, 83–8.   [116]   *JMK*, xvi. 215–22.

the American declaration of war immediately solve the Treasury's external financial difficulties. Certainly the US Treasury took over the financing of the Allies' purchases in America, but Lever was at first able to secure American government loans for British purchases only on a hand-to-mouth basis, and the US Treasury was at first reluctant to allow its loans to be used for supporting the sterling : dollar exchange rate. Relations between Lever and the Secretary of the US Treasury, McAdoo, were poor, and eventually, in September 1917, Reading had to be sent to Washington, accompanied by Keynes, to secure long-term financing of Britain's needs.

Britain was still lending more to her allies (£194 million from 1 April to 14 July) than the United States was lending to her (£145 million over the same period). At the same time Britain was spending between £8 million and £9 million a week on maintaining sterling's parity with the dollar. By 23 July 1917 the strain on Britain's gold reserves was such that, despite the arguments which he had advanced six months earlier with regard to maintenance of the gold standard, Keynes recommended to Chalmers that Lever should now be instructed to suspend the purchase of sterling once the supply of dollars in the Treasury's account was exhausted. Chalmers agreed, and McAdoo was warned on 31 July that the consequences would be those which Keynes had listed in January: worldwide financial and commercial disorganization, and consequent encouragement to the enemy. The cost of maintaining the exchange by buying sterling was now given as $100 million a month, and, although McAdoo never actually promised to provide funds specifically for this purpose, from August additional advances were given 'for general purposes', and the exchange rate was pegged until the end of the war. Subsequently, in October, Reading persuaded the US Treasury to guarantee loans to Britain for three months ahead.[117]

The sterling crisis of July 1917 also brought to a head tensions between the Treasury and the Bank of England over the conduct of international monetary policy. Traditionally the gold standard was managed by the Bank alone, and the Governor, Cunliffe, was much given to independent action, often not troubling to consult his fellow directors on the Bank's governing body, rather confusingly called the Committee of Treasury, or the Treasury itself. As already noted, relations between Cunliffe and McKenna were bad. Neither the Chancellor nor his senior official advisers on overseas finance, Chalmers and Keynes, were disposed to be cyphers, and there was constant friction with the Bank from 1915.

In November 1915 McKenna had set up the American Exchange Committee, later known as the London Exchange Committee, with wide powers to ensure that payment for supplies from the United States could always be made consistently with maintenance of the exchange rate. Cunliffe was chairman of the committee, the other members also being bankers, but much of the detailed

---

[117] See Kathleen Burk, 'J. M. Keynes and the Exchange Rate Crisis of July 1917', *Econ. Hist. Rev.*, 2nd ser., 32 (1979), 405–16.

work fell to Keynes and Chalmers, along with the Committee's secretary, a Bank official. Cunliffe was in America from April to June 1917, and in his absence the Treasury officials, who were greatly overworked, neglected to keep the Bank fully informed of their actions. On 3 July a choleric Cunliffe complained to Lloyd George (now Prime Minister) of the 'absolute incivility' with which requests by the Bank for copies of telegrams were refused. Cunliffe claimed that the London Exchange Committee had been 'entirely superseded by Sir Robert Chalmers and Mr Keynes', in whose knowledge or experience in practical exchange or business problems he had no faith, and he predicted that 'short of a miracle, disaster must ensue', for which he would not be responsible.[118] Subsequently Cunliffe enraged the Chancellor, now Bonar Law, by demanding the dismissal of Chalmers and Keynes.

Bonar Law, who was determined to prove that he, and not Lloyd George, had the last word in Treasury affairs, stood by his officials, and he was ready to take any opportunity to assert his authority over the Governor. On 3 July Morgan's gave the Chancellor of the Exchequer formal notice that loans which that bank had extended to Britain before the United States entered the war would not be renewed. Some $85 million of the overdraft at Morgan's stood in the name of the Bank of England, and Cunliffe telegraphed to the Canadian Finance Minister to place at the disposal of Morgan's the equivalent amount of gold to liquidate that portion of the debt. The next day he learned that the Treasury's representative in America, Lever, was ordering other gold releases from Ottawa, and, without consulting the Chancellor, Treasury officials, or his own Committee of Treasury, Cunliffe telegraphed on 5 July to the Canadian authorities not to deliver any of the gold until the $85 million had been paid to Morgan's.

The challenge to Lever's authority was also a challenge to the Chancellor's, and Bonar Law gained Lloyd George's support for a demand that Cunliffe sign a statement, drafted by Bradbury, that 'during the War the Bank must in all things act on the directions of the Chancellor of the Exchequer whenever in the opinion of the Chancellor national interests are concerned and must not take any action likely to affect credit without previous consultation with the Chancellor'. This wording was too much for Cunliffe or the Bank's Committee of Treasury to swallow, even when Lloyd George threatened that, if the Governor would not sign the undertaking, the government would have to take over the Bank. The Deputy Governor, Brian Cokayne, produced a form of words whereby on 15 August Cunliffe gave Bonar Law an unreserved apology and an undertaking 'to work loyally and harmoniously with you and for you as Chancellor of the Exchequer and while I shall continue, if you will allow me, to tender you such advice as I consider it my duty to offer, I fully realise that I must not attempt to impose my views upon you'. The Joint Financial Secretary of the

[118] Cunliffe to Prime Minister, 3 July 1917, Bonar Law papers 65/2/26.

Treasury, Baldwin, became a member of the London Exchange Committee; Lever's authority in New York and Ottawa was clarified; and the account at Morgan's was transferred from the name of the Bank of England to that of the Treasury.[119] Relations between the Bank and Treasury improved when Cokayne replaced Cunliffe in April 1918.

The summer of 1917 also saw the Treasury run short of Canadian dollars. As early as June the purchase by Britain of Canadian cheese ceased for this reason, and on 5 July Chalmers appeared before the War Cabinet to explain that, as Canada had placed at Britain's disposal only 25 million Canadian dollars towards liabilities totalling 69 million Canadian dollars, and as American loans could only be used for purchases in the United States, all orders in Canada would cease unless the Canadians provided more dollars. Ministers agreed that Chalmers should draft a letter to the Canadian prime minister, Sir Robert Borden, making the situation clear to him, and Chalmers appeared again before the War Cabinet to warn that the Ministry of Munitions' order for gun ammunition in Canada in 1918 could not be financed, even though, at 33 million dollars a month, the programme was lower than the current rate of 40 million dollars. Once more, the United States had to be brought in as the *deus ex machina*. In late August, with the Canadian wheat crop coming on to the market, Lever tried, and failed, to secure the agreement of the US Treasury to allow American funds to be used to buy Canadian wheat. Nevertheless, he took the risk of using such funds for that purpose. It was not until 19 September that Reading secured McAdoo's acquiescence, and further Canadian loans were necessary both for part of the cost of the wheat and for other purchases.[120]

As paymasters of the anti-German coalition, the Americans faced tremendous demands for funds, and naturally tried to create administrative machinery for establishing the needs of the Allies. The US Secretary of Treasury wished in July 1917 to insist that all requests for loans be placed through an Inter-Allied Council to be established in London or Paris. However, with the War Cabinet's support, the British Treasury successfully insisted on the right to deal directly with the US Treasury, on the grounds that some of the most urgent financial problems, such as the maintenance of the exchange rate, would not be appropriately dealt with by the Inter-Allied Council, which would be concerned with military supplies.

American insistence that Allied demands should not be unlimited was not without value to the Treasury in controlling expenditure, in that it forced the British government to set up a committee under Austen Chamberlain to establish priorities. As a result, Churchill, now the Minister for Munitions, was

---

[119] See Robert Blake, *The Unknown Prime Minister: The Life and Times of Andrew Bonar Law, 1858–1923* (1955), 351–4, and Sayers, *Bank of England*, i. 99–108.

[120] War Cabinet minutes, 5 and 16 July 1917, CAB23/3; Burk, *Britain, America and the Sinews of War*, 172–4.

balked in the War Cabinet in January 1918 when he argued for priority for munitions orders, as against priority for food purchases, in the United States, and when he wished to continue to give the French 40,000 tons of shell steel a month. Chamberlain, speaking, as he said, in the position of a second Chancellor of the Exchequer, remarked that each demand for dollars could be justified on its merits if considered alone, but the Americans had offered credit for only $180 million against total orders by spending departments due to mature in January of $275 million. Britain, he said, could not agree to providing materials for France without obtaining compensating materials or dollars from the United States. The War Cabinet agreed that no further large orders, other than for food, should be placed in America until the total requirements had been brought within the expected level of US Treasury credits.[121]

Britain was in fact wholly dependent upon the US Treasury for dollars in 1918 and had to borrow on what terms it could. In order to repay maturing loans raised earlier in the war from the American public, the British Treasury had to agree to hand over to the US Treasury British-owned American securities which had been used as collateral for the loans, some of these securities not being returned until agreement was reached with the United States over the funding of Britain's war debt in 1923. Again the US Treasury was able to insist that a $24 million loan raised by Britain in Japan be used for current purchases and not to reduce the British overdraft with Morgan's. All this was regarded as humiliating in the British Treasury. As Keynes remarked: 'it almost looks as if they took a satisfaction in reducing us to a position of complete financial help-lessness and dependence.'[122]

Final evidence of Britain's dependence upon American assistance came with the collapse of the sterling : dollar exchange rate in 1919. In February that year the British were warned that American aid would be cut off, and on 20 March the decision was taken to unpeg sterling, the cost of supporting the rate being too great for Britain's gold reserves. Britain officially left the gold standard on 31 March, as the restrictive measures that would have been necessary to avoid a heavy drain of gold would have caused unemployment, just as the army was being demobilized, and ministers feared labour unrest. The exchange rate in fact held up quite well until the end of June, when it stood at $4.61¾, compared with the previous pegged rate of $4.76⁷⁄₁₆, but thereafter fell steadily, reaching $3.77¼ at the end of the year, and $3.40 in February 1920.

REPARATIONS AND WAR DEBTS

Towards the end of the war, overseas finance came to encompass the question of what reparations should be demanded from Germany and her allies, and

---

[121] War Cabinet minutes, 16 Jan. 1918, CAB23/5.   [122] *JMK*, xvi. 287.

how inter-allied debts should be settled. At the request of the Board of Trade, Keynes collaborated with another economist, Professor W. J. Ashley, to produce a memorandum in January 1917 on the effect of an indemnity. The memorandum dealt with the implications for British trade of requiring the enemy to make good damage in the territories which had been overrun, and with the possible ways in which payments could be made: by the transfer of property, such as ships or foreign securities, gold, or by the export of goods and services over a period of years.[123] As the war drew to a close, Keynes prepared notes on an indemnity, dated 31 October 1918, in which he estimated Germany's capacity to pay as £1,000 million, if she were not to be crushed, and £2,750 million if she were to be crushed. A subsequent Treasury memorandum, almost certainly drafted by Keynes, warned that an attempt to extract more than £2,000 million would damage British exports because Germany would only be able to pay if she built up a trade surplus.[124]

Under the terms of the Armistice of 11 November 1918 the Germans agreed to make good all damage done to the civilian population of the Allies, and Keynes was soon immersed, as Treasury representative, in preparations for the Peace Conference. He quickly found that there were business interests who wanted German rather than British industry to be taxed to service the huge National Debt which the financing of the war had created, and that Lloyd George was much more responsive to political pressure than to the Treasury's economic arguments. A committee, chaired by the Australian prime minister, William Hughes, with Cunliffe, the former Governor of the Bank of England, as a prominent member, recommended that Germany could and should not only pay reparations for damages but also an indemnity to meet the whole cost of the war, estimated at £24,000 million.

According to Lloyd George, both he and Bonar Law regarded the conclusions of the report as 'a wild and fantastic chimera'.[125] However, the Prime Minister appointed Hughes and Cunliffe to be members of the Reparations Committee of the Peace Conference, to the exclusion of any Treasury representative. Keynes was in attendance at Versailles, initially to handle the financial aspects of the transition to peace. In February, however, the new Chancellor of the Exchequer, Austen Chamberlain, appointed him, still aged only 36, to be his deputy on the Supreme Economic Council, and in March Keynes was included among the experts who were to agree the sum which Germany could pay.

Keynes could see that the Allies were bound to try to secure as much as they could from the enemy when they had war debts to Britain and the United States (these two countries had lent £1,451 million and £1,668 million respectively). In

---

[123] Ibid., 311–36, where the editor, Elizabeth Johnson, deals with Lloyd George's lie in *The Truth About the Peace Treaties* (1938), vol. i. 448, that this memorandum inspired extravagant ideas about Germany's ability to pay reparations. For the dating of the memorandum see Moggridge, *Maynard Keynes*, 289 n.
[124] *JMK*, xvi. 338–83.   [125] *Truth About the Peace Treaties*, i. 461.

March he suggested a cancellation of inter-allied indebtedness as a contribution to international concord and financial stability. However, this idea foundered on the natural reluctance of the Americans to forgo all their claims, especially as it could be argued that the British would make no real sacrifice. Britain owed £800 million to the United States, so that all-round cancellation would leave her with a net loss of only £651 million, most of which would in any case have to be written off as bad debts.[126]

Keynes therefore tried another tack, producing in April a 'Grand Scheme for the Rehabilitation of Europe', which Chamberlain recommended to Lloyd George as being 'marked by all Mr. Keynes's characteristic ability and fertility of resources'. In it Keynes suggested that Germany make an immediate issue of interest-bearing bonds, valued at £1,000 million, of which £724 million would be in payment of reparations and the remainder would be used to discharge debts or to purchase food and raw materials. The Allies would guarantee the interest on the bonds, which therefore would be marketable, mainly in the United States. The American government, however, did not see why Americans should provide working capital to Germany when the Allies were removing that capital in the form of reparations.[127]

As Skidelsky points out, Lloyd George used Keynes's expertise without Keynes having any influence on him.[128] The Prime Minister was determined that reparations should not be confined to physical damage, for then most of Germany's payments would go to the countries in which fighting took place, France and Belgium. By including war pensions and separation allowances as 'damages', he could hope to secure a larger share for Britain of Germany's payments, even if the final bill were to be beyond Germany's capacity to pay. In the end the Peace Treaty made Germany and her allies responsible for all the loss and damage caused in consequence of the war. Germany was required to pay £1,000 million in foreign exchange or commodities, such as coal and timber, to the Allies by May 1921, by which time an Inter-Allied Reparation Commission was to have compiled a list of payments that would be due to be paid over the following thirty years. Keynes's frustration at his failure to mitigate the terms of the treaty, particularly the reparation clauses, which he regarded as unworkable, led him to resign from the Treasury in June 1919.

CONTROL OF EXPENDITURE

Given the problems of paying for the war, the question arises: what steps did the Treasury take to control government expenditure to ensure that the best use was made of scarce resources? The Treasury was aware in 1914 that the

---

[126] Figures from *JMK*, xvi. 419–28.   [127] Ibid., 428–41.
[128] *J. M. Keynes: Hopes Betrayed*, 367.

slow-moving procedures of peace were not appropriate to war. Even before war was declared Montagu, the Financial Secretary, suggested that a standing emergency committee, with official representatives of the Admiralty, War Office, and Treasury, be established to deal with questions of expenditure promptly and to avoid the need for official correspondence. The Admiralty was willing to have such a committee set up as a channel of communication, provided that it was understood that the Admiralty would be free to take action on urgent matters in advance of committee meetings, Treasury sanction being obtained afterwards, and that questions of high policy would often be taken by the First Lord direct to the Cabinet, Prime Minister, or Chancellor of the Exchequer. The Admiralty also insisted that, while the emergency committee was intended to keep the Treasury informed, in order that it might co-ordinate work that was going on in different departments, there should be no inter-service discussion. Bradbury promised the Admiralty that he would not summon War Office representatives when Admiralty proposals were to be considered.

The War Office was even less enthusiastic about the proposed committee. It wished to be assured that it would not impinge on the usual procedure 'by which we have had a more or less free hand in war . . . subject to proper regard for general principles, periodic report [to the Treasury] and careful record of liabilities'. Bradbury urged that, while the War Office must have wide discretion 'there might even be some [matters] in which criticism or advice by the Treasury might be in the public interest'. The War Office, however, took the view that the Treasury would certainly not be asked to sanction expenditure from votes of credit. The committee was set up in August, with Montagu as chairman, Bradbury and Barstow as Treasury representatives, and a representative of the Admiralty, with whom the procedure for verbal sanction of expenditure in advance worked smoothly. Similar committees were set up later to consider proposed expenditure by the Ministry of Munitions and the Ministry of Shipping. However, the War Office refused to take part, preferring to obtain sanction in arrears by correspondence. Montagu complained to the Prime Minister early in September 1914 that 'we know absolutely nothing of any expenditure at the War Office until after it has been incurred'.[129]

Montagu, however, got scant support from the Chancellor, who believed that it was not possible to insist on Treasury control with regard to contracts, even though these often had abnormal financial terms, which might not stand up to scrutiny by the Public Accounts Committee. It was Lloyd George who suggested that throughout the war such contracts should be concluded without reference to the Treasury. Indeed, he subsequently claimed to have been more willing to provide funds to finance extensions of factories for munitions production than the War Office was to spend them.[130]

---

[129] The correspondence in this issue is in T1/11662/17287.
[130] Lloyd George, *War Memoirs*, i. 133–4.

Yet, while the Chancellor was willing to find £20 million for this purpose, Treasury officials were still making difficulties over additional payments to drill sergeants needed to train the huge numbers of new recruits.[131] Rates of pay, office staff, purchases of land, and construction of permanent buildings such as barracks, all continued to be subject to Treasury control practically as in peace-time. On the other hand, the need for accommodation for troops was such that there had to be substantial relaxation of Treasury control in respect of tempor-ary buildings. Moreover, despite complaints in the press of extravagance by the Army, the War Office resisted any control over expenditure considered by the Army Council to be necessary for the prosecution of the war.[132]

Treasury control was least effective over the Ministry of Munitions, where from May 1915 Lloyd George was a gamekeeper turned poacher. The Treasury had no control over the size of the ministry's staff, which after six months num-bered 2,000, and whose conception of their business seemed to be to order 'all of everything'. Barstow, the senior Treasury official responsible for supervising war expenditure, complained that the Ministry of Munitions would not even be guided by the War Office's own estimate of its requirements. For example, the Ministry ordered more big guns than the Army thought that it could man, making it difficult for industry to fulfil orders for allies who required guns of dif-ferent calibres. Barstow admitted that, in so far as these were matters of policy, the Treasury was not departmentally concerned, but the Treasury had the right to demand more information than the Ministry was giving it to enable the Treasury to finance the war.[133]

In November 1915, by which time the internal and external financial strains of the war were all too apparent, the Cabinet's Finance Committee, which included the Chancellor (McKenna); a former Chancellor (Austen Chamber-lain); and the Financial Secretary (Montagu), recommended that if the public were willingly to bear 'the immense burden of taxation', war departments must exercise 'much-needed economy in expenditure'. As examples, it suggested closer examination of contract prices, revision of the scale of Army rations, and the return to civil employment of men who would be unfit for active service for long periods.[134] McKenna was particularly concerned that the continual com-petition for scarce labour by the war departments, the Ministry of Munitions, and their contractors was leading to the bidding up of wages.[135] However, as we have seen, he lost his battles in Cabinet to limit the scale of war expenditure. As for the Ministry of Munitions, it continued to order guns in excess of War Office requirements.

[131]   C. Harris (War Office) to Bradbury, 8 Oct. 1914, T1/11662/17287.
[132]   H. W. Forster (War Office) to Prime Minister, 29 Nov. 1915, Asquith papers, vol. 28.
[133]   Barstow to Bradbury, Montagu, and Chancellor of the Exchequer, 6 Oct. 1915, T170/73.
[134]   Finance Committee, Interim Report, Nov. 1915, T170/84.
[135]   'Increase of Wages', by McKenna, Nov. 1915, T170/85.

The Treasury's case for more effective financial control received powerful reinforcement from the first and second reports of the Select Committee on National Expenditure in October and December 1917.[136] The Committee was critical of both accounting methods and control of expenditure in the War Office and the Ministry of Munitions, particularly the latter, and pointed out that 'full financial consideration of any proposal at the proper stage will not only tend to economy, but also, far from delaying the provision of munitions . . . will in fact accelerate it by preventing waste of effort material and labour'. The Committee recognized that the urgency of the need for munitions had militated against careful consideration of capital expenditure and contracts, when the Ministry was first set up, but considered that the government should have taken steps to establish effective Treasury control in these respects since 1915.[137] The Treasury itself did not escape criticism, in that its establishment of senior staff, on whom the burden of Treasury control fell, had only been increased by five to thirty-eight by 1917. 'Such limitation of staff might at first sight appear to be itself an example of economy to others', commented the Committee, 'but it is not really an example of economy to keep the forces that make for economy at a minimum.' It would have been better, the Committee thought, if the Treasury had recruited more people of ability and administrative experience outside the Civil Service. While the Committee recognized that normal procedures of detailed annual Estimates were inappropriate in war, there was still a need for active financial supervision, watching methods adopted by new departments, detecting mistakes and suggesting improvements, and preventing competition between departments for scarce sources of supply.[138]

Steps to strengthen Treasury control were taken slowly. A Treasury Committee on Contracts was set up in February 1918, with Lord Inchcape, the shipping magnate, as chairman, to enquire into the steps taken by the Admiralty, the Ministry of Munitions, and the War Office to control contract prices and to limit profits, and to consider how the practice of these departments could be co-ordinated and improved. The Treasury Committee's report in the following month drew attention to high prices resulting from the fact that departments sought to secure their own requirements irrespective of the needs of other departments, often buying the same or very similar articles independently, with duplication of inspecting and costing staffs, and lack of co-ordination as to wages. By mid-June 1918, the spending departments had agreed to the Treasury Committee's main proposal, the establishment of standing committees on contracts and stores, both to be chaired by Lord Colwyn, a businessman who had been a member of the Treasury Committee.[139] Clearly these changes were too

---

[136] What follows is based upon the *Special Report and Reports from the Select Committee on National Expenditure, with the Proceedings of the Committee*, PP 1917–18, iii. 591–655.

[137] *First Report*, ibid., 595–602, paras. 24, 34.   [138] *Second Report*, ibid., 603–23, paras. 9–10.

[139] The report is to be found in T1/12164/24215.

late to achieve significant economies in the First World War, but the practice of co-ordinating contracts and stores was developed in the inter-war period, so that Britain was better prepared in this respect for the Second World War.[140]

Regarding expenditure directly related to the war, however, the Treasury could do no more than suggest questions for ministers to ask in Cabinet. For example, Barstow, when reviewing the Naval Estimates for 1918, noted that it was possible to put pressure on the Admiralty not to order more ammunition than the navy could fire. He also wondered whether maintaining older, pre-dreadnought, battleships in commission was worth the expense. It was, he admitted, 'trenching very much on the prerogatives of the naval staff even to ask such a question', but it was the sort of subject which, if not raised by the Treasury, would not be raised at all. Chalmers, however, felt that the matter was one for the Chancellor, and not one that could be dealt with in correspondence by officials.[141] Barstow's question seems to have had little influence. Twelve of the pre-dreadnoughts had already been reduced to non-combatant roles or put in reserve by the beginning of 1918, but seventeen remained in service, with their large crews, although none had fired a shot in anger since the Dardanelles operation in 1915, and only three more were taken out of commission before the end of the war.

On the other hand, by 1918 the Treasury was able to take a firmer stand with regard to capital expenditure financed by the Ministry of Munitions. A case which had important implications for post-war reconstruction arose in February 1918, when the Minister of Munitions, Churchill, agreed with the Corporation of Birmingham and the Shropshire, Worcestershire and Staffordshire Electric Power Company to provide four electricity generating plants, costing a total of £3 million, to be financed by the Ministry, although smaller installations, each costing from £400,000 to £500,000, would have been sufficient for munitions purposes. Barstow commented to Bradbury:

this is another instance of what is becoming evidently the policy of the Ministry of Munitions, viz to exploit the Vote of Credit in order *not* to provide for War necessities but to equip the country for after-the-war trade. It is a form of 'State Capitalism'. The commercial gentlemen who have got a footing in the ministry—possibly with quite disinterested and patriotic motives—think that they will never get such another opportunity—with unlimited credits, Defence of the Realm Act powers and all the rest of it, to re-equip the country on the most modern lines at the risk of the general taxpayer.[142]

Although the Board of Trade thought that the electricity-generating scheme was flawed on technical grounds, Barstow recommended that the Treasury take its stand in the first instance on their own opinion that the scheme was not

[140] See G. A. H. Gordon, *British Seapower and Procurement between the Wars* (1988); William Ashworth, *Contracts and Finance* (1953).

[141] Memorandum by Barstow, 30 Mar. 1918, with comment by Chalmers, T1/12212/41087.

[142] Barstow to Bradbury, 21 Feb. 1918, T1/12207/39120.

within the terms of the vote of credit for war expenditure, and that it would be
necessary to ask Parliament for a separate vote of statutory powers. This view
was a great disappointment not only to the Ministry of Munitions but also to
Dr Christopher Addison, the Minister of Reconstruction, who seems to have
been very much in favour of the scheme. The Ministry of Munitions conceded
at the beginning of May that a less ambitious scheme could produce electricity
more quickly, perhaps by as much as six months. Bargaining followed, with the
Treasury being able to make use of the Board of Trade's technical arguments
against one of the proposed sites. By July Churchill was willing to settle for two
instead of four plants, but the Treasury would agree to sanction only one, with
a financial liability limited to guaranteeing only the difference between the
current and the post-war costs of construction.[143]

Strict Treasury control had continued to be exercised over the expenditure
and staffs of the old-established civil departments. At Hawtrey's suggestion,
the circular asking departments for their Estimates for 1915–16 stated that 'the
imperative necessity of making the resources of the country available to the
utmost to meet the heavy demands arising from the War will compel the exclusion from the Estimates of all civil expenditure which is not clearly indispensable
in the public interest'.[144] With regard to the new civil departments created by
Lloyd George in December 1916—the Ministries of Food, Labour, Pensions
and Shipping—Treasury control was less effective. The Treasury did exercise a
considerable measure of control over salary scales—a source of some complaint
in the departments concerned—but not the same measure of control over the
numbers of staff or organization.[145] As regards policy, the Treasury suffered a
defeat at the hands of Lord Rhondda, the Minister of Food, in September 1917
when he persuaded the War Cabinet to accept the introduction of a bread
subsidy in the face of Treasury opposition.[146]

In the last analysis, the effectiveness of Treasury control depended upon
the attitude of ministers, particularly the Prime Minister and Chancellor, but
also the Cabinet as a whole. During the war Lloyd George showed little interest
in Treasury control of expenditure, either as Chancellor or as Prime Minister.
Moreover, the normal procedure whereby financial aspects of questions of policy involving expenditure were discussed with the Treasury by the civil departments concerned before being brought before the Cabinet 'fell somewhat into
abeyance' during the war, owing to the pressure of business,[147] and was not
restored until August 1919. The fact that war expenditure was met out of votes
of credit, with no detailed Estimates and with no need to balance the budget,

[143] T1/12207/39120 *passim*.   [144] T1/11673/20244.
[145] *Second Report of the Select Committee on National Expenditure*, paras. 11–12.
[146] José Harris, 'Bureaucrats and Businessmen in British Food Control, 1916–19', in K. Burk (ed.),
War and the State, 141.
[147] Circular issued by Cabinet Office on instructions of Prime Minister, 12 Jan. 1920,
T160/639/F6064.

also much relaxed ministers' attitudes to approving new proposals for expenditure without any attempt to establish priorities, except when scarce dollars were
required in 1917–18. Many ministers seem to have remained unaware of the
extent to which Britain had exhausted herself in waging the war, particularly
her ability to finance essential purchases abroad,[148] and the Treasury had to
fight hard to curb ambitious plans for social reconstruction after the war.

RECONSTRUCTION PLANNING

Planning for the post-war period was directed partly to practical problems, such
as demobilization, which could be foreseen, and partly to the maintenance of
morale by offering the prospect of a better world once victory had been won.
Asquith set up a ministerial Reconstruction Committee in March 1916 with a
number of subcommittees, including the Whitley Committee on Relations
between Employers and Employed, which reported in 1917. The Whitley recommendations in favour of joint industrial councils representing both sides was
applied, reluctantly, by the Treasury to clerical as well as industrial civil servants
from 1919.[149] In March 1917 the ministerial Reconstruction Committee was
replaced by a second Reconstruction Committee, made up of experts, and
again a number of subcommittees were appointed, including Lord Haldane's
Committee on the Machinery of Government. In July 1917 a Ministry of
Reconstruction was established, under Dr Christopher Addison, but the
ministry's functions were mainly advisory, with responsibility for executing
policy being in the hands of other departments.

 The main questions over which the proponents of reconstruction clashed
with the Treasury were those relating to income support for demobilized soldiers and unemployed munitions workers at the end of the war, and what was to
be done about the housing shortage, which had been greatly exacerbated by
the war. The housing programme in particular threatened to be a heavy drain
upon the Exchequer. The Treasury was concerned, however, not only with the
merits of particular programmes but also with the possible total cost of all recommended programmes, which extended to such matters as the acquisition of
land for smallholdings and afforestation, as well as greatly improved health services. As early as October 1916 Blackett observed, in true Treasury style: 'As
might be expected, there is a natural tendency to believe that the Reconstruction period will be the Millennium when money will be available for everyone's

---

[148] There were, of course, no readily available statistics to measure the cost of the war, although
dependence upon the United States for dollar credits should have conveyed a sense of economic weakness. It has been estimated that the war brought about a decline of 15 per cent of total UK net capital
stock (domestic and overseas)—R. C. O. Matthews, C. H. Feinstein, and J. C. Odling-Smee, *British Economic Growth, 1856–1973* (Oxford, 1982), 523.

[149] See R. A. Chapman and J. R. Greenaway, *The Dynamics of Administrative Reform* (1980), 89–100.

pet scheme. Each of the Reconstruction Sub-Committees tends to assume that its own subject is of paramount importance.'[150] Given that only about 20 per cent of the cost of the war was being met out of taxation, and that there would be strong political pressures to reduce taxation after the war, it was by no means clear that there would be large funds available for reconstruction if, as the Treasury assumed, the budget was to be balanced as soon as possible after the war.

Treasury officials had their own views on reconstruction finance, and their priorities were very different from those of Addison. Early in 1918 the Treasury and the Ministry of Reconstruction set up two committees: a Committee on Currency and Foreign Exchanges after the War, to report on the steps required to restore 'normal conditions', and a Committee on Financial Facilities, to consider financial reconstruction. In November the Committee on Currency and Foreign Exchanges, under the chairmanship of Cunliffe, and with Bradbury as an influential member, published its *First Interim Report*, which made clear that an effective gold standard would require an end to government borrowing and a process of deflation, including high interest rates.[151] The Cunliffe Committee's recommendations were endorsed by the Committee on Financial Facilities, which Bradbury had been careful to ensure was dominated by bankers rather than industrialists.[152] It is true that Professor A. C. Pigou, the Cambridge economist, who was a member of the Cunliffe Committee, thought that it would be possible for a time to raise reconstruction loans, once government borrowing for war purposes had fallen, and both he and Bradbury saw that there might be political reasons for avoiding deflation immediately after the war. However, the implication of a return to a 'normal' gold standard was that long-term commitments for government expenditure should not exceed what could be raised from taxation—and in February 1919 Bradbury's speculative calculations for 1919/20 and 1920/1 showed substantial budget deficits on the existing basis of taxation, even before large new civil expenditures were included.[153]

Bradbury's own ideas about reconstruction finance were strongly influenced by his awareness that the National Debt had already been greatly expanded for war purposes and his expectations about future private demand for capital. By 1918 he anticipated that after the war there would be a private investment boom for 'a period of some years', owing to the exhaustion of stocks, and arrears of capital construction and maintenance, arising out of the war. During that

[150] Blackett to Waley, 6 Oct. 1916, T1/12205/38481.

[151] Committee on Currency and Foreign Exchanges after the War, *First Interim Report* (Cd. 9182), PP 1918, vii. 853–64, para. 47. For the committee's discussions see D. E. Moggridge, *British Monetary Policy, 1924–1931: The Norman Conquest of $4.86* (Cambridge, 1972), 17–22.

[152] Committee on Financial Facilities, *Report* (Cd. 9227), PP 1918, x. 25–34. Treasury papers relating to the establishment of the committee are in T1/12238/47228. For analysis of its composition see Robert W. D. Boyce, *British Capitalism at the Crossroads, 1919–1932* (Cambridge, 1987), 37–8.

[153] 'Note on the Commitments of the Exchequer for the Year 1919/20 and Subsequently', 10 Feb. 1919, T170/133.

period prices of fixed-interest-bearing securities would be depressed, and it would be relatively cheap to redeem government debt.[154]

However, although debt redemption would be to the advantage of the Exchequer, Bradbury's arguments about reconstruction finance were set out in terms of industry's prior claim on capital. Addison put forward a memorandum to the Cabinet in February 1918 asking for a general assurance that, once reconstruction measures were agreed upon as essential, they would not be delayed 'on the ground of expense'. In responding to the memorandum, Bradbury did not claim that everything should be subordinated to paying off of debt. Indeed, he claimed that it was common ground between Addison and the Treasury that it was desirable that production should be stimulated to the maximum degree possible, thereby creating the national wealth necessary to liquidate external and internal debts. However, Bradbury, unlike Addison, did not see this as a reason for incurring public capital expenditure on a large scale, and he rejected Addison's implied criticism that the repayment of internal debt involved the expenditure or absorption of capital. In Bradbury's view, internal debt redemption out of taxation involved no more than a transfer of purchasing power within the community. Indeed, in so far as taxation reduced consumption and the money paid to security holders was used for new investment, 'the capital fund of the nation' would actually be increased.[155]

Since the deposits of the joint stock banks were higher than ever before, Bradbury saw that there was a danger, which materialized in 1919, of bank credit forcing up prices. It followed, in Bradbury's view, that any new government borrowing for reconstruction must not be by way of creation of new credit but by diversion of existing credit from private hands. The fundamental problem, Bradbury argued, was that raw materials would be in short supply, and government schemes for social improvement would compete with industrial investment and exports, and the question resolved itself to one of how far desirable social improvement could be allowed to take up resources which, if market forces were allowed to operate freely, would be applied to economic necessities. It was not possible, Bradbury believed, to arrive at a firm answer to this question in advance of post-war developments, and therefore Addison could not be given the assurance he sought that there would be no financial restraints on his reconstruction programmes, even once they were agreed to by the Cabinet. This point was taken by the Chancellor, Austen Chamberlain, who argued successfully in Cabinet against any open-ended financial commitments.

Evidence that the Treasury was not implacably opposed to all forms of social expenditure can be found in the story of the 'out-of-work donation', an

---

[154] 'A Capital Levy for Repayment of Debt', n.d., but before the end of the war, T170/135. The document shows that Bradbury also anticipated a slump once the investment boom was over.

[155] 'Reconstruction Finance', 21 Feb. 1918, T170/125. Addison's memorandum, dated 10 Feb., is summarized in Paul B. Johnson, *Land Fit For Heroes: The Planning of British Reconstruction, 1916–1919* (Chicago, 1968), 107–9.

unemployment benefit originally intended for demobilized soldiers. Leith-Ross, the Treasury official dealing with the scheme, did, of course, seek to minimize its scope and to avoid firm commitment to rates of benefit greatly in excess of those available under unemployment insurance, not least because as early as November 1917 he could foresee that whatever rate was adopted for discharged soldiers would probably be extended, by some means or other, to munitions workers. There was an element of bargaining in the Treasury's attitude to rates of benefit, officials arguing that whatever rates were proposed to Parliament would be denounced as inadequate, and that it would be better to start with low rates so that the Government would have some leeway for concessions.[156]

Leith Ross's experience as Treasury representative on the Ministry of Reconstruction's Army Demobilisation Committee led him to recommend that steps should be taken to secure more adequate consideration of financial liabilities involved in such enquiries. The Ministry's committee had no responsibility for finance but, once the committee had reported, it was very difficult to turn down its proposals. Leith-Ross suggested in November 1917 that a strong Finance Committee with a Treasury minister as chairman and a 'financial-minded' MP and a businessman or financier as members, be added to the machinery of reconstruction. Bradbury, however, disagreed. He took the view that, while it would certainly be necessary to avoid firm commitments to capital expenditure after the war, the out-of-work donation was related to demobilization rather than reconstruction proper, and could be borne as part of the cost of the war. As he told the Financial Secretary, Baldwin: 'these charges are the last flicker (or perhaps rather the final blaze) of the fever itself and cannot be dealt with by the remedies appropriate to the period of convalescence'.[157]

In the event the out-of-work donation proved much more expensive than Demobilisation Committee discussions, which had centred on 5 million servicemen, had suggested. In October 1918, when it suddenly became apparent that the war would end soon, Addison realized that National Unemployment Insurance, although somewhat extended by an Act of 1916, covered fewer than 4 million workers, leaving about 10 million without any financial support if unemployed, other than the unpopular Poor Law. At his suggestion, the non-contributory out-of-work donation was extended to all workers until a comprehensive unemployment insurance scheme could be devised.[158]

The limited coverage of unemployment insurance reflected the opposition of many trade unionists to being included in compulsory state insurance. The Treasury itself, although it had resisted extension of unemployment insurance in 1914 (see Chapter 2), was actually prepared to go further than the Board of Trade felt wise in including as many workers as possible in the National Insurance Part II (Munitions Workers) Bill of 1916. The Treasury wished to have as

---

[156] Gilbert Upcott to Hewby, 12 June 1918 (approved by Barstow and Heath), T1/12205/38481.
[157] Memorandum by Leith-Ross, 8 Nov. 1917, and Bradbury to Baldwin, 17 Nov. 1917, ibid.
[158] Kenneth Morgan and Jane Morgan, *Portrait of a Progressive* (Oxford, 1980), 79.

many trades included as possible, to ensure that workers with a low risk of unemployment would contribute to the insurance fund, which otherwise would be left with only the bad risks, while trade unions, which believed that they could do better with their own schemes outside the fund successfully resisted inclusion. The resulting impasse was not resolved until 1920. The Unemployment Insurance Act of that year allowed industries to 'contract out' but, by adroit administrative manœuvring, the Treasury kept almost all the 'good risks' inside the national scheme.[159] Other provisions for the potentially unemployed went more smoothly: plans for the purchase of land for smallholdings for ex-servicemen were agreed by the Treasury in November 1917, and complete schedules of public works held back by the war had also been prepared by the Ministry of Reconstruction by 1918.

The really big item in reconstruction was housing, which would certainly require large-scale capital investment. The Treasury's most immediate concern was to limit the liability of the taxpayer. One problem facing private enterprise at the end of the war was that the value of houses and rents might well fall below costs of construction, once the initial shortage of houses had been met. To encourage local authorities to build, the Local Government Board proposed in February 1918 that the Treasury should pay 75 per cent of estimated abnormal building costs, or even 100 per cent in the case of poorer authorities. When the Board's proposed circular outlining the scheme to local authorities came before the Cabinet for its approval, the Treasury appended a cautionary note. Two clauses in the note provoked opposition from Addison, who believed that they would discourage local authorities from going ahead. The first clause stated that state assistance must be limited in amount as well as in time; the second warned that the date at which the scheme could begin depended on circumstances which could not yet be foreseen. Chamberlain offered to have the first of these clauses removed, but not the second, and it was clear that housing was not yet off the Treasury leash. In particular, the Chancellor still held the traditional Treasury view that it was bad finance to increase the taxpayer's share of local burdens, especially where there were rich ratepayers capable of bearing them.[160]

However, concerted lobbying by local authorities made it seem likely by the late summer that more generous terms would have to be offered to them. The Treasury—supported by the Local Government Board—resisted suggestions that local authorities should be given interest-free loans for housing, on the grounds, as one official put it, that 'so long as the burden of raising capital is not felt, the task of spending it is apt to be undertaken with a light heart'. The Treasury still hoped to encourage local authorities to borrow on their own credit, and

---

[159] Noelle Whiteside, 'Welfare Legislation and the Unions during the First World War', *Hist. J.*, 23 (1980), 857–74.

[160] Johnson, *Land Fit For Heroes*, 110–15; War Cabinet minutes, 12 Mar. 1918, CAB23/5.

also believed that, once the principle of interest-free loans had been applied to one form of public capital expenditure, it would be impossible to resist its application to other forms, such as smallholdings and forestry.[161] On the whole the resistance of the Treasury and the Local Government Board to pressure to limit the charge on the rates in connection with housing schemes to the produce of a penny rate in the pound has received little sympathy from historians, but much of the pressure came from the wealthier local authorities, who feared that they would receive less assistance than poorer authorities.[162]

In January 1919 Addison became President of the Local Government Board, and the Treasury could no longer look on the Board as an ally in resisting local authority pressure. Moreover, the Government had pledged itself in the election of December 1918 to build 'homes fit for heroes'. Addison's Housing and Town Planning Bill of March 1919 promised that the Treasury would meet local authorities' house-building costs in excess of revenue from rents plus the pro-ceeds of a penny rate—a very open-ended commitment. Such were the polit-ical pressures in favour of housing—Lloyd George even cited the dangers of Bolshevism if the confidence of the people was not won[163]—that no Treasury opposition at that stage was possible.

At ministerial conferences on unemployment and the state of trade in Feb-ruary, Sir Auckland Geddes, Addison's successor as Minister of Reconstruction, pointed out the incompatibility of the Treasury's financial policy—which he thought was 'undoubtedly sound', if the Cabinet's one aim was the earliest pos-sible return to an effective gold standard—and what he called the 'social (better Britain) policy' involving housing, land settlement, and education. When Lloyd George objected that he 'did not really see where the clash came in', Geddes explained that capital locked up in housing and other state schemes would be unavailable to trade and industry. The Chancellor, Austen Chamberlain, made the point that there was sufficient capital for the resumption of trade if capital was not required for other purposes, but that there was not enough capital for all the Government wished to do. However, Lloyd George refused to believe that the Government, which would have borrowed £2,000 million if the war had gone on another year, could not borrow £71 million for reconstruction in 1919/20. He recalled that McKenna, when Chancellor, had repeatedly warned that it would not be possible to borrow beyond a certain date, and had subse-quently had to move that date back by six months. Chamberlain then warned that continued borrowing and inflation would involve a fall in the dollar exchange, as happened a month later, but added that he agreed that the hous-ing problem was a danger to the stability of the state, and that it must be a first charge on public funds.[164]

[161] Memoranda by R. V. Vernon, 10 Sept. 1918, and M. G. Ramsay, 14 Sept. 1918, T1/12201/37399.
[162] 'Housing After the War: Government Assistance', by Noel Kershaw (Local Government Board), Sept. 1918, ibid.   [163] War Cabinet minutes, 3 and 4 Mar. 1919, CAB23/9.
[164] Minutes of conference on unemployment and the state of trade, 17 and 25 Feb. 1919, CAB24/75.

It is thus clear that at this stage even Conservative ministers were willing to sacrifice the gold standard on the altar of political necessity, and that, despite the Cunliffe Committee's *First Interim Report* in favour of the gold standard, the Cabinet had no clear view on financial policy and was certainly not prepared to jettison its electoral pledges in order to balance the budget. Indeed, in a report to the Cabinet in May 1919 Geddes recommended that the Treasury must delay deflation, and even permit a slight further inflation, and that the whole topic should be reviewed six months hence.[165]

While the prospects of a return to financial orthodoxy were being postponed, however, other developments were leading to a strengthening of the Treasury's position in the machinery of government. The Haldane Committee on the Machinery of Government reported in December 1918 in favour of the creation of a separate branch in the Treasury to specialize in 'establishment' work, that is studying all questions of staff, recruitment, and methods of conducting business.[166] Similar ideas emerged from a Treasury Committee of Inquiry into the Organisation and Staffing of Government Offices, chaired by Bradbury, which reported shortly after Haldane. The Bradbury Committee revealed widespread duplication and waste in Whitehall, and recommended that establishment work be concentrated in one division instead of being spread out among the divisions which dealt with control of expenditure.[167] An Establishments Division was duly set up in February 1919. Thus, even although the Treasury failed to curb plans for reconstruction expenditure in 1918/19, and had to defer hopes of re-establishing the gold standard, there was pressure in Westminster and Whitehall for the Treasury to curb extravagance and to promote efficiency. The Treasury's enhanced role in government and the Civil Service, the struggle to reimpose effective control of expenditure, and moves towards the return to the gold standard form the main themes of the next chapter.

SUMMARY

There is plenty of scope for argument as to the relative merits of the different approaches to war finance of Lloyd George on the one hand, and McKenna and the official Treasury (including Keynes) on the other. Lloyd George could claim that his pursuit of victory regardless of cost was justified by events, but these events included the entry of the United States into the war, something that was not anticipated while Lloyd George and McKenna were debating the limits to Britain's war effort in 1915–16. Had the Treasury prevailed in that

---

[165] Auckland Geddes' report, May 1919, CAB27/58, cited in Johnson, *Land Fit for Heroes*, 386–7.

[166] Ministry of Reconstruction, *Report of the Machinery of Government Committee* (Cd. 9230), PP 1918, xii. 1–80, para. 20.

[167] Chapman and Greenaway, *Dynamics of Administrative Reform*, 102–3.

debate, the government would have had to adopt a more selective approach to strategy and the use of scarce resources, including manpower. In the event the Treasury had almost no influence on the scale of expenditure related to the war, except where foreign exchange was concerned in 1917–18. At the end of the war, the Treasury's economic arguments in relation to post-war reconstruction were overwhelmed by political expediency. Even so, with tax rates much increased, in line with the McKenna rule, there was some prospect of balancing the budget once war-related expenditure had ceased.

With regard to the Treasury itself, the conduct of war finance enabled some officials to acquire greater competence in technical aspects of financial policy and greater confidence in dealing with the Bank of England, although the Treasury continued to rely on the Bank's expertise in money markets. Treasury control of Whitehall was weakened for the duration of the war, but waste and extravagance on the part of uncoordinated spending departments led to political pressure for a restoration of Treasury control of expenditure and for an extension of Treasury control over the Civil Service.

CHAPTER FOUR

Reorganization and Retrenchment, 1919–1924

INTRODUCTION

In understanding the formulation of policy it is important to remember that the term 'inter-war period' is an invention of historians. People at the time thought of the years from 1919 as a post-war period, and they could not foresee how attempts to reconstruct the pre-1914 economic order would founder in the post-1929 depression. Moreover, while unemployment is usually seen as the dominant problem of the inter-war period, the most marked characteristic of 1919–20 was inflation, with a post-war investment boom, fed by excess bank credit, and with a massive increase in labour costs. Unemployment, measured as an annual average of the insured labour force, was less than 4 per cent in 1920, but between April 1919 and April 1920 the Ministry of Labour's working-class cost-of-living index rose by 18 per cent, and wholesale prices rose by about 44 per cent. April 1920 marked the end of the upswing in wholesale prices, but retail prices continued to rise until October 1920, when they were 35 per cent above April 1919. Average hourly money wage rates increased by over 40 per cent between January 1919 and January 1921. However, in the winter of 1920/1 unemployment rose rapidly and prices and wage rates began to fall, the rise in wage rates between January 1919 and January 1921 being reversed by April 1922.[1] The rapid adjustment of prices and wages provided some grounds for hoping that unemployment would be cured by market forces. However, whereas in the twenty years before 1914 unemployment among trade unionists had averaged about 4.25 per cent and, measured as an annual average, had not exceeded 7.8 per cent,[2] unemployment almost never fell below 10 per cent of the insured labour force between 1921 and the Second World War (see Table 4.1).

There has been an influential Keynesian school of thought which has placed considerable importance on government policy as an explanation for high unemployment after 1920. On the other hand, there is no shortage of other explanations, such as wartime dislocation of trade, with consequent structural

---

[1] A. C. Pigou, *Aspects of British Economic History, 1918–1925* (1947), 161–3, 232. See also J. A. Dowie, '1919–20 is in Need of Attention', *Econ. Hist. Rev.*, 2nd ser., 28 (1975), 429–50.

[2] C. H. Feinstein, *National Income Expenditure and Output of the United Kingdom, 1855–1965* (Cambridge, 1972), 225 and table 57.

problems in industry, and rigidities in the labour market, both as regards wages (after 1923) and labour mobility, which slowed the process of adjustment to new conditions. In this context government financial policies are sometimes presented as having had neutral or, at worst, moderately unhelpful effects on economic growth and unemployment in the 1920s.[3]

TABLE 4.1. *Inter-war Unemployment*[a]

	Annual average percentage of insured workers unemployed	Annual average percentage of total workforce unemployed
1920	3.9	—
1921	16.9	12.2
1922	14.3	10.8
1923	11.7	8.9
1924	10.3	7.9
1925	11.3	8.6
1926	12.5	9.6
1927	9.7	7.4
1928	10.8	8.2
1929	10.4	8.0
1930	16.1	12.3
1931	21.3	16.4
1932	22.1	17.0
1933	19.9	15.4
1934	16.7	12.9
1935	15.5	12.0
1936	13.1	10.2
1937	10.8	8.5
1938	12.9	10.1
1939	10.5	—

[a] The National Insurance Act of 1920 extended the pre-war national insurance scheme to most industrial workers, but excluded groups less likely to be subject to cyclical unemployment, including domestic servants and non-manual workers earning over £250 a year. Consequently, the figures in column 1 are higher than those in column 2, but the figures in column 1 are the official statistics used at the time. A major inconsistency in column 1 arises from the application in 1924 of a 'genuinely seeking work' clause to insured as well as uninsured workers, with the result that many claims, particularly from married women, were disallowed. In 1930 the Labour government revoked the clause, but it was restored by the National Government in 1931.

Sources: Column 1: Department of Employment and Productivity, *British Labour Statistics: Historical Abstract, 1886–1968* (1971), table 160; column 2: C. H. Feinstein, *National Income, Expenditure and Output, of the United Kingdom, 1855–1965* (Cambridge, 1972), table 58.

The Treasury's first concern in 1919 was to re-establish its control over public expenditure and to halt inflation. As noted in the last chapter, the Treasury was at first unable to persuade the Cabinet to give a high priority to sound finance in the spring of 1919; ministers displayed much more concern about the prospect of unemployment, and the policy of pegging the exchange rate had to be abandoned in March. Although there was a large budget deficit for 1919/20,

[3] See contributions by Forrest Capie and Geoffrey Wood, Barry Eichengreen, Mark Thomas, and Tim Hatton, in Roderick Floud and Donald McCloskey (eds.), *The Economic History of Britain since 1700*, 2nd edn., vol. ii (Cambridge, 1994).

the Cabinet showed little inclination down to July 1919 to curb the growth in plans for new expenditure. As the Chancellor, Austen Chamberlain, warned on 26 July: 'The position grows daily more grave. No Estimates hold good, and the Cabinet sanctions increase after increase with, as it seems to me, an insufficient appreciation of the aggregate result.'[4]

However, even as the Chancellor appealed to his colleagues to have some thought for the consequences of their decisions for future taxation, the political imperatives which had persuaded ministers to accept inflation were weakening. Earlier in July the Cabinet had been informed by Sydney Chapman, the economist who was about to become Joint Permanent Secretary of the Board of Trade, that trade policy had been successful and employment was rapidly improving. Ministers' fears of unemployment and its political consequences were thus reduced even as public opinion was building up against high levels of government expenditure and alleged extravagance by officials. By the middle of July Lloyd George was as worried as his Chancellor about the situation. On 5 August a new Cabinet Finance Committee was convened to discuss Chamberlain's request for some measure of Treasury control over new proposals for expenditure, and eight days later the Cabinet agreed that it would not consider new proposals until the Treasury had approved them, or until the responsible minister had indicated his intention to appeal against a Treasury decision. On 20 August the Prime Minister circulated a letter to ministers stating that: 'the time has come when each Minister ought to make clear to those under his control that if they cannot reduce expenditure, they must make room for somebody who can.'[5]

It was against this political background that the Treasury was reorganized in the autumn of 1919 and the Permanent Secretary recognized as Head of the Civil Service. When the Cabinet's Finance Committee agreed to changes in the Treasury's organization in August 1919, Lloyd George welcomed them on the grounds that 'not only in view of the state of public opinion but because of the financial situation of the country, ruthless cutting down of expenditure was imperative'.[6] Austen Chamberlain likewise considered the changes, and the recognition of the Permanent Secretary as Head of the Civil Service, to be necessary for 'efficient control of expenditure'.[7] On 31 August, even before the reorganization of the Treasury was carried out, Lloyd George called for an immediate report on the progress made in cutting down expenditure, and Chamberlain had to ask him to allow Sir Warren Fisher, the Permanent Secretary designate, and Barstow, who was to be responsible for the control of Supply Services expenditure, to have a short holiday first in order to be fit for

[4] 'Note by the Chancellor of the Exchequer', 26 July 1919, CAB27/72.
[5] K. Burk, 'The Treasury: From Impotence to Power', in id. (ed.), *War and the State: The Transformation of British Government, 1914–1919* (1982), 101.
[6] Finance Committee minutes, 20 Aug. 1919, CAB27/71.
[7] Chamberlain to Fisher, 24 Aug. 1919, T199/351.

their work. Fisher's response to the Prime Minister's enquiry was a handwritten letter arguing that the scope for economy by reducing Civil Service staffs was insufficient, and that major economies could be won only if policies which led to expenditure were changed.[8]

The Treasury did not immediately prevail in all of its efforts to have policies changed to conform with the overall objective of economy: Chamberlain had to agree later in 1919 to a continuation of bread and coal subsidies, and increases in unemployment insurance scales and old-age pensions. However, the North-cliffe and Rothermere press continued to agitate for lower public expenditure and lower taxes. In response to this pressure, the Cabinet decided in December 1920 to instruct all spending departments to proceed no further with any scheme that had not yet begun, unless fresh Cabinet authority was granted.[9] In 1921 the economy campaign outside and inside Parliament reached a new pitch, with Rothermere's Anti-Waste League successfully putting up candidates against government supporters at by-elections. The Cabinet reacted by impos-ing restrictions on the housing programme and then, on Lloyd George's initia-tive, by appointing a committee of businessmen, under Sir Eric Geddes, to recommend cuts in public expenditure. Although the bulk of the cuts recom-mended by the committee were in defence expenditure, and although the gov-ernment endorsed only about 60 per cent of the recommendations, the Geddes 'axe' of early 1922 is usually seen as marking the end of the expansionary phase of post-war social reform.[10]

Reorganization of the Treasury and the assertion of its control over Whitehall thus coincided with, and mainly reflected, concern about lack of control over public expenditure. Politicians and their critics thought in terms of making the Treasury better able to count candle-ends, rather than of making it better able to conduct economic policy. The peacetime economic functions of government were still seen by ministers and officials as essentially the provision of a frame-work within which private individuals and companies would create wealth. Thus, the Treasury and the Bank of England were responsible for maintaining the value of the currency, and the Treasury was expected to keep government expenditure and taxation as low as possible. Certain social services, including the relief of unemployment, were provided, but government's relationship to the economy was still predominantly one of laissez-faire.[11] The gold standard, managed by an independent central bank, was seen by all political parties as

[8] Fisher to Lloyd George, 3 Sept. 1919, T171/170.
[9] Cabinet minutes, 8 Dec. 1920, CAB23/23.
[10] Andrew McDonald, 'The Geddes Committee and the Formulation of Public Expenditure Policy, 1921–22', *Hist. J.*, 32 (1989), 643–74.
[11] Since some historians have denied that there was ever an age of laissez-faire, it may be as well to note that the words 'predominantly one of laissez-faire' are those of Sir Donald Fergusson, who was private secretary to successive Chancellors of the Exchequer from 1920 to 1936 (Fergusson to Bridges, 28 June 1950, T273/188).

the best guarantee of sound money and a proper regulation of credit and the balance of trade.

It was this conception of the Treasury's function that made it possible for the Treasury and the Bank of England to pursue a consistent policy designed ultimately to facilitate a return to the gold standard, although there was a succession of governments of different political complexions: Lloyd George (a Liberal presiding over a Conservative-dominated coalition) 1918–22; Bonar Law (Conservative) 1922–3; Baldwin (Conservative) 1923–4; and Ramsay MacDonald (Labour) (1924). Such a policy required balanced budgets, and, therefore, given the political pressure for reductions in taxation, served to reinforce pressure for economy in public administration and expenditure. The policy was challenged within the Cabinet when unemployment rose in 1921 but the Treasury was able to defend fiscal and monetary orthodoxy.

REORGANIZATION, PERSONALITIES, AND ECONOMIC ADVICE

In July 1919 the Treasury still had two Joint Permanent Secretaries, Bradbury and Heath (Chalmers having departed in March). In the scheme put to the Cabinet's Finance Committee, however, there was to be only one Permanent Secretary, with the Treasury divided into three 'departments', each headed by a Controller, dealing respectively with finance, public expenditure, and the Civil Service. Each Controller would have the same status as the permanent head of a first-class department of state, although subordinate to the Permanent Secretary of the Treasury.

What evidence there is—and Fisher himself did not know who the author of the scheme was—suggests that Bradbury was responsible for the form the Treasury took after August 1919, although Lord Milner, who was a member of the Cabinet's Finance Committee, has also been given the credit.[12] In a letter to the Chancellor, Austen Chamberlain, on 19 August—the day before the scheme went to the Finance Committee—Bradbury wrote that while Chalmers, Heath, and he had worked together without friction—because of 'personal reasons and the fact that we had "grown up together" '—the arrangement of having two or three Joint Permanent Secretaries was not a suitable one. On the other hand, the work of the Treasury had increased enormously since 1913 and would probably increase even more in the near future, and it would be impossible for one Permanent Secretary 'to do justice to it without a very much larger amount of devolution than has existed in the past'.[13]

Bradbury expressed a willingness to stay on as Permanent Secretary, possibly

---

[12] Fisher to Chancellor of Exchequer, Lord President of the Council, and Prime Minister, 25 Nov. 1931, T199/50B. For Geddes's statement see 125 HL Deb., 5s, 1942–3, col. 286.
[13] Bradbury to Chamberlain, 19 Aug. 1919, Austen Chamberlain papers, AC 24/1/21.

combining his function with that of Controller of Finance. However, Lloyd George, with whom Bradbury had fallen out in 1915, had told Chamberlain that there should be changes in personnel at the top of the Treasury, to remove men who were 'powerfully obstructive' in their cleverness.[14] In the event, Bradbury was appointed to be principal British delegate on the Reparation Commission, at a higher salary than that offered to him as Permanent Secretary of the Treasury. Bradbury believed himself to have been seconded from the Treasury, and he continued to be listed in the *British Imperial Calendar* (the predecessor of the *Civil Service Year Book*) as 'Joint Permanent Secretary of the Treasury' until 1922. However, Fisher, who had obtained an assurance at the time of his appointment that he would be sole Permanent Secretary, had the title of Joint Permanent Secretary suppressed.[15] There was no doubt about the fate of Heath, who was notoriously out of touch with modern developments in administration, and who was removed from the Treasury in September 1919 and given the long-winded title of Comptroller-General and Secretary to the Commissioners for the Reduction of the National Debt.

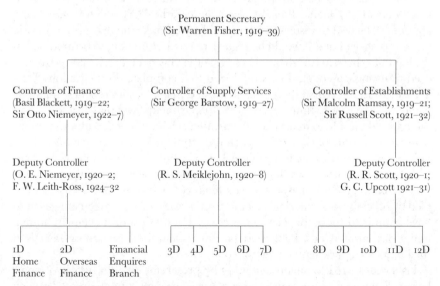

FIG. 4.1.   *Treasury Organization, 1919–1927*

Note: The number of divisions varied over time, and by 1927 the number of Supply Services divisions had been reduced to three, whereas Establishments divisions had increased to six.

The new threefold division of Treasury functions was as follows: the Finance Department was to handle revenue, loans, and the National Debt; the preparation

[14] A. Chamberlain, *Down the Years* (1935), 138.   [15] T162/56/E4508.

of the annual Estimates and the presentation of public accounts; financial relations with the dominions and foreign countries; and banking, currency, and foreign exchange questions (see Figure 4.1). The Establishments Department was concerned with the numbers and pay of civil servants and defence personnel; recruitment, superannuation, and pensions; and, following an Order in Council in July 1920, organization and staffing arrangements of every government department. The Supply Services Department dealt with all questions relating to public expenditure chargeable to money voted by Parliament and not dealt with by the other two departments. Both the Treasury minute allocating these functions and Bradbury's letter to Chamberlain of 19 August 1919 made plain that, while the Permanent Secretary would have general powers of supervision and co-ordination, he was not expected to concern himself with the detailed work of the Controllers, each of whom had the right of access to the Chancellor without going through the Permanent Secretary first.[16] Moreover, it was Bradbury, not Fisher, who nominated the first three Controllers: Blackett (Finance), Barstow (Supply Services), and Ramsay (Establishments).[17]

Fisher later described this organization as 'bizarre' and his own position in it as 'deliciously vague, floating somewhere rather Olympian'.[18] On being appointed, he told ministers that he would try to make the organization work, but it was agreed that it would be regarded as experimental, to be modified in the light of experience. Fisher believed that the new structure, if allowed to proceed to its logical conclusion, would lead to a complete disintegration of the Treasury. From the first, therefore, he insisted that Treasury officials should be liable to serve at any time in any of the departments, whereas Bradbury had thought it desirable to make each department self-contained, with promotions being made, *ceteris paribus*, within each department. Fisher's view reflected not only his concern with the unity of the Treasury but also his preference for generalist administrators. Bradbury, on the other hand, as a financial expert, was aware that the technical aspects of the Finance Division's work were best handled by officials with experience of these matters. Actual arrangements seem to have combined these two views: there was a good deal of movement among junior officials between the three departments, but the more senior officials in the Finance Department tended to remain there.

Fisher also tried to encourage unity by preserving the old system of numbering Treasury divisions consecutively, across the departments, instead of each department having its own 1st Division, 2nd Division, and so on. Despite his efforts, however, the enlarged post-1919 Treasury seemed 'ponderous and often uncoordinated' to at least one official who had served in the smaller, unified

---

[16] Treasury minute, 4 Sept. 1919, and 'Outline of Treasury organisation', by Fisher, 6 Apr. 1921, T199/50B.

[17] Bradbury to Chamberlain, 19 Aug. 1919, Austen Chamberlain papers, AC24/1/21.

[18] Fisher to Chancellor of the Exchequer, Lord President of the Council, and Prime Minister, 25 Nov. 1931, T199/50B; Fisher's evidence to Committee of Public Accounts, 30 Apr. 1936, PP 1935–6, v. 431.

department before the war.[19] On the other hand, Fisher encouraged the Chancellor's Principal Private Secretary, P. J. Grigg, to make sure that there had been no failures of co-ordination by the time any problem reached the Chancellor. Moreover, the annual Estimates cycle and the budget provided a focus for much of the Treasury's work: Finance Department worked out what aggregate level of expenditure was possible within a balanced budget; Supply Services Department and Establishments Department examined sketch Estimates from the point of view of what economies might be achieved; and Finance Department prepared the Estimates and the budget for presentation to Parliament. On the other hand, much of the detailed control exercised by Supply Services Department and Establishments Department throughout the year would have been concerned with the merits of spending departments' proposals, and whether they conformed to policy as agreed by the Cabinet, rather than with the relationship between expenditure and financial policy.[20]

Relations between officials and ministers were influenced by the volume and technical nature of the Treasury's work. The first Controller of Establishments, Ramsay, remarked that: 'it would be physically impossible for ministers in these times to deal personally with more than a small fraction of the total volume of Establishments business'; and the first Controller of Finance, Blackett, observed that, while he did his best to keep ministers informed of what he was doing and to obtain their approval of the broad lines of policy, he could not 'avoid committing ministers to all intents and purposes in advance on many even of the biggest questions'. These comments were included in briefs for the Chancellor (Austen Chamberlain) on the duties of the Controllers, and Fisher noted that caution should be taken lest the impression be given that officials had too great powers.[21]

Fisher himself had little influence over the work of the Controllers of Finance or Supply Services, preferring to concentrate his energies on reform of the Civil Service. On financial matters Blackett and his successor Niemeyer advised the Chancellor directly, as did Barstow on questions of Supply Services expenditure. The Finance Department was responsible for both home and overseas finance, the work being allocated between two divisions, 1D, which carried on the Treasury's pre-war financial functions, and 2D, which carried on the work of Keynes's wartime 'A' division. As Blackett remarked in 1921, 'the day-to-day work of the . . . Department . . . involves the assumption of responsibilities by the Controller of Finance which, when he makes the mistake of turning [his] mind to consider their magnitude are really staggering'.[22] All relations between the Treasury and the Bank of England and the money market were in his hands,

[19]   Maurice Headlam to Barstow, 23 June 1923, T162/89/E9964.
[20]   The work of the Treasury in relation to the control of public expenditure is described fully in Andrew McDonald, 'The Formulation of British Public Expenditure Policy, 1919–1925', Ph.D. (Bristol, 1988).
[21]   Note by Fisher, 17 Aug, and briefs by the Controllers, 16 and 17 Aug. 1921, T199/3.
[22]   'Controller of Finance', 17 Aug. 1921, T199/3.

and Blackett admitted that he could not possibly carry out that work were he not easily in personal contact with the Governor of the Bank. Even so, Blackett backed his own judgement in choosing the best moment to purchase dollars for Treasury purposes in America, at a time when sterling was floating against the dollar, and he conducted the whole of the negotiations for the repayment of a Canadian bankers' loan of $200 million and an Argentinian loan of $100 million. On the other hand, the settlement of the war debt to America, a sum involving $4,604 million of capital and interest, required direct participation by the Chancellor in the negotiations (see below). The Controller had also to keep in touch with the Foreign Office, particularly on questions relating to reparations and war debts, while himself seeing representatives of foreign or Empire countries almost daily.

Broadly speaking, the Supply Services Department exercised control over the whole field of central government expenditure, except for questions relating to numbers and rates of pay of the Civil Service, which were the province of the Establishments Department. One minor exception was expenditure by the Ministry of Transport, where there was a small Treasury outpost, headed by Hardman Lever, who had returned from his period as Treasury representative in the United States, and who acted in lieu of the Controller of Supply Services from 1919 to 1921. Another exception was expenditure in Ireland, for which Sir John Anderson, the Joint Permanent Under Secretary to the Lord Lieutenant of Ireland, exercised Treasury control in Dublin from 1920 to 1922.[23]

The Controller of Supply Services thus had a wide range of government activities to deal with: defence, housing, education, unemployment and health insurance, colonial development, and grants to local authorities, to take a few examples. Many of the items which landed on his desk represented small sums—such as the decision on the price of a ship to be sold to a colonial government—and not all could be placed before ministers. As a result the Controller sanctioned, rejected, or modified many proposals on his own authority. Likewise the Controller of Establishments rarely sought specific ministerial instructions when implementing general schemes of reorganization that had been approved by the Cabinet.[24] What this autonomy for the Controllers meant in practice was that officials had considerable independent influence so long as they were dealing with lesser questions in which ministers were not interested. However, as will be apparent from what follows, Treasury officials found it much harder to influence Cabinet decisions on policy.

[23] Fisher led an investigation of the Irish executive in May 1920 and produced a scathing report. As a result, Anderson, who had succeeded Fisher as chairman of the Board of Inland Revenue in Oct. 1919, was sent to Dublin with a team of British civil servants, to reform the executive according to the principles that Fisher was pushing through in Great Britain. Consequently, when the provisional government of the newly independent Ireland took over in Jan. 1922, it inherited what was considered to be the latest model of financial administration—see Ronan Fanning, *The Irish Department of Finance, 1922–58* (Dublin, 1978), 7–13.

[24] Memorandum by Barstow, 16 Aug., and 'Controller of Establishments', 17 Aug. 1921, T199/3.

None of the first five Chancellors after the war had much time in which to have much personal impact on policy. Austen Chamberlain lasted longest, from January 1919 to April 1921, but he showed signs of stress in 1919 and by June 1920 'was as tired as a man could be'.[25] His successor, Sir Robert Horne, found himself out of office after less than eighteen months, when the Lloyd George coalition fell in October 1922. Baldwin, who had been Financial Secretary of the Treasury from June 1917 to April 1921, became Chancellor in Bonar Law's Conservative government, combining that office with that of Prime Minister from May 1923, when Law resigned through ill health, until August of that year. Neville Chamberlain's first tenure as Chancellor, five months, until January 1924, was even briefer than Baldwin's. Philip Snowden likewise had less than a year as Chancellor, from January to November 1924, during Labour's first government.

Austen Chamberlain's interest in public finance focused on protection for British producers and imperial preference for imports from the Empire. His budget for 1919/20 was notable for the introduction of preferences of $33\frac{1}{3}$ per cent on cars, cameras, and clocks (in connection with the McKenna Duties); $16\frac{2}{3}$ per cent for tobacco, tea, and sugar, and a variety of rates for wines and spirits. Horne's interests were more eclectic, as befitted his meteoric career. He had been a university lecturer in philosophy and a member of the Faculty of Advocates, before gaining experience of administration with the railways and the Admiralty during the war. He was appointed Minister of Labour on entering the House of Commons in December 1918 and was President of the Board of Trade in 1920–1, before becoming Chancellor. Leith-Ross thought that Horne was really out of his depth in matters of public finance,[26] but an alternative interpretation would be that Horne was prepared to think out policy from first principles and to consider departing from orthodoxy in the recession of 1921–2 (see below).

Baldwin and Neville Chamberlain, like Neville's half-brother Austen, were protectionists, but the Conservatives' defeat in the election of 1923, when the extension of imperial preference was a prominent issue, made Baldwin wary of pressing for a general tariff thereafter. So far as other aspects of finance were concerned, Baldwin was thoroughly conventional in his attitude to balanced budgets and the reduction of the National Debt. Neville Chamberlain did not feel that he had any gifts for finance and would have preferred not to have been offered the post.[27] In the event, he was out of office before he could present a budget.

Snowden was in many ways an ideal Chancellor from the point of view of Treasury officials. He had written about public finance, and believed that

[25] David Dutton, *Austen Chamberlain: Gentleman in Politics* (Bolton, 1985), 157.
[26] Sir Frederick Leith-Ross, *Money Talks* (1968), 81.
[27] David Dilks, *Neville Chamberlain*, vol. i, *1869–1929* (Cambridge, 1984), 333–5.

'sound finance is the basis of national and commercial prosperity', and that 'a Labour Government must be the relentless foe of extravagance in national administration'.[28] He believed that the function of the Chancellor of the Exchequer was 'to resist all demands for expenditure made by his colleagues and, when he can no longer resist, to limit the concession to the barest point of acceptance'.[29] To his private secretary, Grigg, Snowden was the best type of Yorkshire nonconformist, and easily the most popular of all the ministers he had known, giving a clear lead on policy but interfering rarely in administration, and able to defend his decisions in Cabinet.[30] Like most of his officials, Snowden was a convinced free trader, and he abolished the McKenna duties in his budget in 1924. Perhaps his greatest achievement, however, was to demonstrate that a Labour government could be as financially sound as any other, and thereby assuage financiers' fears about 'socialism'.

Of the ministers who held the office of Financial Secretary in this period three may be mentioned. E. Hilton Young (April 1921–October 1922) was, most unusually, a financial expert, being the author of *The System of National Finance*, which ran to three editions between 1915 and 1936. Sir William Joynson-Hicks (May–October 1923) was a member of the Cabinet during the period when Baldwin was both Chancellor and Prime Minister, but does not seem to have enhanced his reputation thereby, for he was passed over when Neville Chamberlain was appointed Chancellor. The first Labour Financial Secretary, William Graham, was unusual at the Treasury in having a degree in economics (from Edinburgh University); he also had an outstanding memory and gave impressive performances in Parliament, quoting statistics and references without using notes.[31]

Personalities count for a good deal in explaining how Whitehall works. As his biographer makes clear,[32] Fisher was determinedly informal, in reaction to his Victorian upbringing, but he lacked balance in personal relationships, and gave offence by unguarded criticism of people of whom he did not have a high opinion. His appointment as Permanent Secretary at the age of 40 was unusual, but not unprecedented. Of his immediate predecessors, Hamilton, Murray, Chalmers, and Heath had all been over 50 at the time of their appointments, but Bradbury had been 41. Fisher had had personal connections with the departmental Treasury even while he was at the Board of Inland Revenue: Heath was his brother-in-law and Chalmers was godfather to Fisher's son. It was Lloyd George, however, who was more than anyone else responsible for Fisher's rise, the Prime Minister having been impressed by his outstanding work on the English National Insurance Commission before the war.

[28] Philip Snowden, *Labour and National Finance* (1920), 7, and id., *Labour and the New World* (1921), 138.
[29] Quoted in Colin Cross, *Philip Snowden* (1966), 207.
[30] P. J. Grigg, *Prejudice and Judgement* (1948), 136.   [31] Cross, *Philip Snowden*, 198–9.
[32] E. O'Halpin, *Head of the Civil Service: A Study of Sir Warren Fisher* (1989).

Despite being a protégé of Lloyd George, Fisher developed close links with Baldwin and Neville Chamberlain. He was one of Baldwin's regular dinner companions from 1923, and only Hankey could rival his influence even when Baldwin became Prime Minister.[33] Fisher's relations with Neville Chamberlain, at least until the late 1930s, were even closer, Fisher writing to the former Chancellor in 1924 that 'brief tho' our time together was, you had given me the hope that I might think of you as a friend—a word full of meaning'.[34] Fisher and Snowden had been on friendly terms for some years before the latter became Chancellor,[35] Fisher presumably having foreseen that Labour's spokesman on financial matters might one day be his minister. On the other hand, he does not seem to have been particularly close to Austen Chamberlain or Horne.

Fisher had no perceptible influence on financial policy. Indeed, remarkably few officials did. Whitehall suffered notable staff losses in 1919: Stamp left the Board of Inland Revenue for a career in business in March; Keynes resigned from the Treasury in June and returned to academic life in Cambridge; and Bradbury took up his post at the Reparation Commission in the autumn. Keynes was consulted by Austen Chamberlain about how to halt inflation in February 1920, but generally Chancellors relied upon advice from successive Controllers of Finance, Blackett (1919–22) and Sir Otto Niemeyer (1922–7), and the chairmen of the boards of Inland Revenue and Customs and Excise, on budgetary matters, and on the Controller of Finance and the Governor of the Bank of England, Montagu Norman, on monetary policy. Blackett and Niemeyer, like Fisher, had studied *literae humaniores* at Oxford. However, Blackett, who had worked with Keynes during the war, was an outstanding financial administrator, and become Finance Member of the Governor-General's Council of India. Niemeyer had come first in the Civil Service examination of 1906, the year that Keynes came second, and served as Blackett's deputy before succeeding him as Controller. Leith-Ross, who was Deputy Controller of Finance from 1924 to 1932, recalled that Niemeyer was, with Bradbury, one of the two outstanding officials of the period, but whereas Bradbury had an ingenious mind which could always be relied upon to prepare three alternative methods of dealing with a problem, Niemeyer would have only one solution.[36]

Relations between the Treasury and the Bank, although restricted to the highest level, were good. Visits from the Governor, Montagu Norman, were as normal after the war as they had been exceptional before 1914, occurring once or twice a week, when he would speak with the Chancellor and the Controller of Finance, rather than the Permanent Secretary. Snowden described Norman as a 'friend', who had an 'international mind', and 'the quality of inspiring

---

[33] Keith Middlemas and John Barnes, *Baldwin: A Biography* (1969), 177, 318, 496.
[34] Fisher to Chamberlain, 4 July 1924, Neville Chamberlain papers NC 7/11/17/7, Birmingham University Library.   [35] Philip Snowden, *An Autobiography*, 2 vols. (1934), ii. 613.
[36] Leith-Ross, *Money Talks*, 106. Leith-Ross was yet another product of Oxford's school of *literae humaniores*.

confidence'.[37] At the official level, Norman respected both Blackett and Niemeyer. Blackett embarked on a career in the City when he returned from India in 1928, and he became a director of the Bank of England the following year, on Norman's nomination. Norman also admired Niemeyer's work in international finance and recruited him to work for the Bank in 1927.

The reputation of economics had not yet reached the point where it was felt necessary to have a professional economist attached to the Treasury. Instead, in 1919 Ralph Hawtrey was released from administrative duties and put in charge of Financial Enquiries Branch, which comprised himself and an executive-grade assistant. In this post Hawtrey had leisure in which to study, and write books on, economics and economic problems. However, as a middle-ranking civil servant, he depended on the willingness of Blackett, Niemeyer, and their successors to use his ideas.

THE NATIONAL DEBT AND THE QUESTION OF A CAPITAL LEVY

The National Debt had increased from £650,000 in 1914 to £7,507,000 at the end of the financial year 1918/19. Continued borrowing in 1919/20 brought the Debt to a peak of £7,832,000, a twelvefold increase, in nominal terms, compared with before the war. Of particular concern to the Treasury and Bank of England was the 'floating debt': over £1,000 million held in the form of short-term Treasury bills, whose existence threatened the deflationary policy adopted by the monetary authorities in 1919, for banks could always find the money they wanted by not renewing Treasury bills when they reached maturity (see section on monetary policy below). The Debt also represented an uncertain burden on the taxpayer. Bradbury thought that about half of the increase in the Debt represented a fall in the value of money, but he shared the general expectation that prices would tend to fall after the restocking boom was over.[38] When prices did begin to fall after 1920, the burden of the debt, in terms of the flow of goods and services that had to be taxed in order to pay the interest, increased.[39]

In these circumstances it is not surprising that there should be proposals for some extraordinary measure to repay part of the National Debt. The question of whether there should be a capital levy for this purpose was a central issue in British politics at the end of the First World War.[40] A capital levy would have

[37]   *Autobiography*, ii. 614–15.

[38]   'A Capital Levy for Repayment of Debt', by Bradbury, n.d., but before end of war, T170/135.

[39]   Whereas the Debt interest/GDP ratio of 1913/14 had been 0.01, the average ratio for 1921/2 to 1932/3 was 0.07—see Roger Middleton, 'The Treasury in the 1930s: Political and Administrative Constraints to Acceptance of the "New" Economics', *Oxford Econ. Papers*, NS, 34 (1982), 54.

[40]   J. E. Cronin, *The Politics of State Expansion: War, State and Society in Twentieth-Century Britain* (1991), 82–7; M. J. Daunton, 'How to Pay for the War: State, Society, and Taxation in Britain, 1917–24', *Eng. Hist. Rev.*, 111 (1996),882–919; Mary Short, 'The Politics of Personal Taxation: Budget-making in Britain, 1917–31', Ph.D. (Cambridge, 1985), ch. 2; R. C. Whiting, 'The Labour Party, Capitalism and the

been a tax based on an assessment of individuals' net capital assets, and was described by its proponents as anticipated death duties.[41] The idea of a capital levy was particularly associated with the Labour party, but it was considered seriously by the Treasury. An alternative to a capital levy, which would been a tax on all capital assets, was the idea of a levy on increases in wealth that had resulted from the war. This 'war levy' had the political attraction of meeting popular resentment against fortunes made by 'profiteers' since 1914, and was more obviously a once-and-for-all tax than a capital levy would have been. However, in practice it would have been impossible to discriminate between wealth made out of the war and wealth that had increased for other reasons, such as inheritance or profits from activities unrelated to the war. Both levies were strongly opposed by the City and by the balance of opinion in the Conservative and Liberal parties, and much was made of the effect of a levy on ordinary people's savings and pensions. Even in the Labour party there was a growing realization that the net savings from a capital levy would be limited, as the surrender of assets would reduce revenue from income tax and death duties. By 1924, Snowden, who had been a leading advocate of a capital levy, thought that it had become an electoral millstone.[42]

Initial Treasury discussions of a capital levy took place in 1917, in the context of popular demands for conscription of wealth to match conscription of manpower. Treasury officials accepted the advice of the Board of Inland Revenue that conscription of wealth during the war was not practicable, owing to the difficulty of compiling a census of capital assets and to the likelihood that the sale of assets to raise cash to pay the levy would lead to a slump in values and disruption of financial markets. On the other hand, Bradbury was prepared to consider a post-war capital levy as a practical, and even prudent, way of dealing with the problem of the war-swollen National Debt.[43] Political opposition to a capital levy had not yet hardened. Indeed, Stamp, the Inland Revenue's leading expert on the size and distribution of the nation's capital, was impressed by an argument made by Sydney Arnold in favour of a capital levy during the debate on the 1918 budget. Arnold, a former member of the Manchester Stock Exchange who had been Principal Private Secretary to the Financial Secretary of the Treasury in 1914, put forward the levy as means of reducing the size of the Debt by £4,000 million, and thereby the cost of servicing it, before the expected post-war fall in prices, and thus make it possible to balance the budget without a crushing increase in income tax.[44]

National Debt, 1918–24', in P. J. Waller (ed.), *Politics and Social Change in Modern Britain: Essays Presented to A. F. Thompson* (Brighton, 1987), 140–60.

[41] Hugh Dalton, *Principles of Public Finance* (1923), 203.

[42] Snowden, *Autobiography*, ii. 595. For Snowden's arguments in favour of a capital levy see his *If Labour Rules* (1923), ch. 4.   [43] Daunton, 'How to Pay for the War', 890–3.

[44] Sir Josiah Stamp, *Taxation During the War* (Oxford, 1932), 128–9.

By 1919 the Board of Inland Revenue was arguing that a capital levy, with its need for intrusive assessments, would endanger the co-operation between officials and taxpayers necessary for the collection of income tax. Experience since 1909 of property owners' resistance to land valuation added force to the Board's argument that a levy was unlikely to be as effective a means of tapping wealth as the existing, accepted tax system. Even so, Treasury officials remained open to the idea of a levy as a means of reducing the number of Treasury bills in the hands of the banks, and thereby restoring the monetary authorities' control over credit. Although sensitive to City opposition to a capital levy, the Treasury wished to be able to assert its authority in money markets.[45]

Austen Chamberlain decided to appoint a Select Committee to investigate wartime increases of wealth and to report whether a tax on them would be practicable, and if so, what form it should take. Inflation was still a pressing problem when the Select Committee first met on 19 February 1920, and in his evidence before it in March Blackett stressed the advantage of 'some special method of raising the cash with which to pay off a considerable proportion of the floating debt'. The Board of Inland Revenue produced a scheme which was estimated to yield £900 million to £1,000 million, not far short of the floating debt of about £1,000 million Treasury bills and £200 million in Ways and Means advances. In his evidence before the Select Committee on 13 April Stamp supported the scheme as an emergency measure and described it as practicable, provided there was a reasonable measure of goodwill on the part of those affected. On 27 May, however, Richard Hopkins, the chairman of the Board of Inland Revenue, received a note from Blackett who now, despite his earlier support for the scheme, urged that a 'very early decision should be reached and that it should be against the proposal'. Blackett had changed his mind because he had learned that the banks were restricting credit because they were worried that some of their customers had over-committed themselves during the boom and would be unable to repay their loans. A levy, he believed, might create a financial panic. By June the Chancellor, explaining why the government had decided against a levy, could tell Parliament that Stamp too had changed his mind. In any case the Select Committee decided that, unless larger tax-free allowances were given than in the Inland Revenue scheme, much of the burden would fall, not on those who had made large profits, but upon ordinary people who had been brought above the proposed £5,000 exemption limit only by the fall in the value of money. With larger allowances, the estimated yield fell to £500 million, no more than the anticipated yield to be obtained from continuing the wartime duty on excess profits (EPD) for a further two or three years.[46]

[45] Cronin, *Politics of State Expansion*, 83–4; Daunton, 'How to Pay for the War', 894–5.

[46] J. Harry Jones, *Josiah Stamp, Public Servant: The Life of the First Baron Stamp of Shortlands* (1964), 116–18; *Memoranda submitted by the Board of Inland Revenue to the Select Committee of the House of Commons on Increases of Wealth (War)*, Cmd. 594, PP 1920, xxvii. 275; 130 HC Deb., 5s, 1920, col. 277.

When Labour took office, without a parliamentary majority, Snowden appointed a Committee on National Debt and Taxation under Lord Colwyn, on the understanding that, if the committee reported against a capital levy, the Labour party should drop the proposal.[47] When the committee finally reported in 1927 it concluded that the psychological moment for a levy had passed. Moreover, it estimated that the relief from debt which a scheme for raising £3,000 million offered, that is £60 million in annual taxation which would otherwise be necessary for interest and sinking fund payments, was equivalent to no more than 1s. (5p) in income tax, which the committee believed would be insufficient to justify the opposition that a levy would arouse.[48]

Decisions about the political disadvantages of a capital levy or a war levy were essentially matters for politicians. Treasury officials' own views about the relationship between the National Debt and private capital, however, were likely to lead them to favour debt redemption out of current taxation. As already noted, Bradbury had written in 1918 that internal debt redemption involved no more than a transfer of purchasing power, 'a process of compulsory thrift', which would increase the nation's fund of capital available for investment. Niemeyer made the same point in 1921, when he noted that 'debt repayment extracts money from those who are not likely to save and invest and makes it available for those who are likely to do so'. Treasury officials believed, like Hawtrey in 1913, that money that was saved would be spent, sooner or later, on fixed capital or invested abroad (and thereby provide a market for exports). As Blackett put this point in 1922: 'every penny devoted by Government to reducing debt goes straight back to help trade'. The limiting factor in this process was taxation of profits, which must not be carried to the point of 'strangling enterprise'.[49]

Bradbury considered it important that the state's demands on the nation's resources should not impinge upon the restoration of the capital stock of the private sector, engaged as it was on the restoration of Britain's export trade. For that reason he later frankly told the Committee on National Debt and Taxation that he regarded the debt-charge (interest plus sinking fund) as a most valuable incentive to economy in public expenditure for other purposes. Within a balanced budget, the debt-charge tended to squeeze out items which, he thought, were of lesser importance, given general economic conditions.[50]

With the benefit of hindsight, it can be argued that a golden opportunity to pay off debt through a capital levy was lost at the end of the war, for, as prices fell

[47] Snowden, *Autobiography*, ii. 595.

[48] *Report of the Committee on National Debt and Taxation* (Cmd. 2800), PP 1927, xi. 371, paras. 860–1, 875–6.

[49] 'Reconstruction Finance', by Bradbury, 21 Feb. 1918, T170/125; Niemeyer to Chancellor of the Exchequer, 5 Oct. 1921, T172/1208; R. G. Hawtrey, *Good and Bad Trade* (1913), 260–1; 'Budgeting for a Deficit', by Blackett, 24 Mar. 1922, T171/202.

[50] 'Reconstruction Finance', 21 Feb. 1918, T170/125; Cmd. 2800, para. 861.

after 1920, the burden of each pound of debt became greater. On the other hand, even with the benefit of hindsight, Stamp thought that rapid changes in prices would have made valuation of assets difficult.[51] What is certain is that the debt-charge made it difficult both to balance the budget and to reduce taxation.

BALANCING THE BUDGET

The proposals for a capital or war levy were related to a wider debate about what levels of taxation were politically and economically tolerable. Tax rates had reached levels during the war that would have been inconceivable in 1914; for example, the standard rate of income tax imposed from 1918/19, 6s. (30p) in the pound, was nearly five times the last peacetime rate, 1s. 3d. (6.25p). Moreover, the number of people paying income tax increased from 1,130,000 in 1913/14 to 3,900,000 in 1919/20. The number fell to 2,400,000 by 1922/3 because, on the recommendations of a Royal Commission on the Income Tax, Austen Chamberlain adjusted the burden of the tax in 1921 in favour of people with smaller incomes or family responsibilities, by providing extra allowances.[52] Even so, there remained twice as many income tax payers as before the war, many of whom might vote for a reduction in direct taxation. Moreover, the Federation of British Industries was very strongly represented in the House of Commons after the 1918 election, and agitation by these MPs could not readily be ignored, even if Austen Chamberlain described them as 'a selfish, swollen lot', who were mistaken if they thought that they could bully him.[53]

In June 1920 McKenna, the former Chancellor, put forward the argument that before the war government expenditure had amounted to £200 million and the savings of the community had been £400 million, making a surplus of production over consumption of £600 million, or £1,400 million at 1920 prices. On the assumption that output was lower in 1920 than in 1914, he suggested that a budget of £1,000 million would not leave a sufficient margin of savings for industrial investment. The figure of £1,000 million gained currency as a kind of axiom, at a time when revenue was estimated at £1,116 million. However, Stamp met this argument by pointing out in a public lecture that about half of the taxation was being devoted to the payment of interest on, or the repayment of, debt, and was therefore a contribution to, and not a diminution of, the savings of the community.[54]

The depression of 1921 increased the intensity of debate on taxable capacity, as businessmen found themselves faced with tax bills assessed on the average of the previous three years of good trade, at a time when prices and profits were

---

[51] Sir Josiah Stamp, *The Financial Aftermath of War* (1932), 37–9.

[52] B. Mallet and C. O. George, *British Budgets, 1913/14 to 1920/21* (1929), 398; Cd. 615, PP 1920, xviii. 97.

[53] Letter to his sister Ida, 25 Apr. 1920, Austen Chamberlain papers AC5/1/160.

[54] Sir Josiah Stamp, *Wealth and Taxable Capacity* (1922), 124–7.

falling. A Cabinet Committee on Taxation noted the continual references by MPs and in the press to the subject, and the Chancellor, Horne, asked the Board of Inland Revenue to report on the burden of taxation on industry. Its response was a paper which admitted that direct taxation, especially supertax, tended to discourage enterprise and limit the expansion of industry, but stated that it was not possible to remit arrears of EPD, or change the basis of assessment for income tax and supertax, if the budget was to be balanced. The paper added that the problem would ease with the ending of the temporary conjunction of assessments based on abnormally high profits in the past, with abnormally low profits in the post-war slump.[55] Horne's successor, Baldwin, returned to the subject in March 1923, when *The Times* claimed that trade was being 'strangled by taxation'. By that date the Exchequer's revenue was about £900 million, and Niemeyer was sceptical of an estimate by Board of Trade statisticians that a tax burden of that order was quite bearable. His advice was to reduce public expenditure to permit tax cuts.[56]

For Treasury officials, balancing the budget always had priority over tax cuts: for example, the standard rate of income tax remained at its wartime peak of 6s. (30p) in the pound down to 1921/2, and the top rate of income tax plus supertax was increased from 11s. 6d. (57.5p) to 12s. (60p) in the 1920 budget. Business opinion was disregarded to the extent that the 'temporary' wartime EPD, which had been reduced from 80 per cent to 40 per cent in 1919, was raised to 60 per cent in 1920, and supplemented by a corporation profits tax of 5 per cent of profits, after payment of any EPD. EPD was abandoned in 1921, but only in order to avoid future repayment of duty to firms whose profits fell below the pre-war standard.[57]

Alternatives to taxation of industry were not easily found. For example, the land value duties, on which Lloyd George had placed so much hope in 1909, were held by the Board of Inland Revenue to be unworkable as they stood, yielding very little—£140,000 in 1919/20—and that with the maximum of friction, injustice, and unpopularity. Austen Chamberlain was presented in 1919 with the choice of either wholly recasting them or abandoning them—and duly abandoned them in 1920.[58] As already noted, the Conservatives' preference for tariffs was rejected by the electorate. The McKenna duties of 1915 were renewed each year for revenue purposes down to 1924, but when Snowden abolished them that year the revenue forgone was only £3 million. The proportion of revenue from indirect taxation rose from its wartime nadir of 17.3 per cent in 1917/18 to 37.29 per cent in 1921/2, but thereafter Chancellors seem to have

[55] 'Industry and the Weight of Taxation', memorandum written by the Board of Inland Revenue in consultation with the Board of Customs and Excise, Jan 1922, T171/203.
[56] 'Trade Strangled by Taxation' (*The Times*, 14 Mar. 1923), 20 Mar. 1923, T171/214.
[57] Daunton, 'How to Pay for the War', 901, 909.
[58] Chamberlain to Ida, 16 Feb. 1919, Austen Chamberlain papers AC5/1/119; *Report of the Select Committee on Land Values* (Cmd. 556), PP 1920, xix. 753.

been reluctant to increase the proportion,[59] in deference to the principle of 'fairness' in the allocation of the tax burden between different classes of society.

Even with tax rates at or near wartime levels, balancing the budget was initially difficult because war-related expenditure did not end with the armistice on 11 November 1918. Peace with Germany was only signed on 28 June 1919, and the armed forces were involved in various 'policing' operations from Ireland to Iraq down to 1922. Moreover, in the first four months of 1919/20 ministers proved very ready to add to the budget deficit, which had been estimated at £250 million in Austen Chamberlain's budget speech of 30 April; by the end of June numerous increases in expenditure totalling £134 million had been approved, with more in prospect, while Exchequer receipts were falling, and the Chancellor had to warn his colleagues in July that they were on 'the road to ruin'. He warned that it was likely that the whole proceeds of the £450 million Victory Loan, originally intended to fund floating debt, would have to be used to cover the deficit for the year, leaving the public unwilling to support future loans.[60] In the event the realized deficit in 1919/20 was £326 million, but this was partly because the Cabinet took the cause of economy to heart as from August.

The Treasury made use of the concept of a 'normal year' to concentrate ministerial and other minds. This concept had its origin in the McKenna rule of 1916, whereby permanent tax revenue had to be sufficient to cover future normal expenditure, including interest and sinking fund on the debt being created during the war. A balance sheet for a 'normal year' was discussed in October 1919 by the Cabinet's Finance Committee, which decided to omit the Treasury estimate of £50 million for payment of the war debt to America, on the grounds that it was not possible to say how much might be received in war debt payments from allies or reparations from Germany. The balance sheet presented to Parliament by Austen Chamberlain thus focused on internal expenditure and revenue, the Chancellor commenting that 'the value of that paper is that the House may understand that every time they sanction fresh expenditure . . . they are rendering it necessary to impose additional taxation'.[61] Nevertheless, permanent commitments to future expenditure continued to be made, so that whereas expenditure in a future normal year was estimated at £808 million in October 1919, by June 1920 this figure had risen to £881 million, with a recommendation that a further £148 million be found for debt redemption.[62]

No particular year was specified as the future 'normal' year, and the budget was not balanced out of current revenue, as opposed to receipts from surplus war

[59] Mallet and George, *British Budgets, 1913–1921*, table 20; eid., *1921–33*, table 18.

[60] 'The Financial Situation', by Chamberlain, 18 July 1919, T171/170. By 7 Aug. a further £25 million of new items of expenditure had been approved.

[61] Finance Committee minutes, 22 Oct. 1919, CAB27/71; 120 HC Deb., 5s, 1919, col. 749.

[62] *Memorandum by the Chancellor of the Exchequer on the Future Exchequer Balance Sheet* (Cmd. 376), PP 1919, xxxii. 159; *Further Memorandum by the Chancellor of the Exchequer on the Future Exchequer Balance Sheet* (Cmd. 779), PP 1920, xxvii. 169.

TABLE 4.2. *Budget Balances With and Without War-related Revenue, 1919/20–1924/5(£m.)*

	Published deficit (−) or surplus (+)	Revenue included		Budget out-turn excluding columns 2 and 3 deficit (−) or surplus (+)	Debt redeemed out of revenue	Column 5 + or − Column 4
		Excess profits duty	Surplus stores etc.[a]			
	(1)	(2)	(3)	(4)	(5)	(6)
1919–20	−326.2	289.3	264.8	−880.3	—	−880.3
1920–1	+230.6	218.0	287.9	−275.3	21.3	−254.0
1921–2	+45.7	30.5	155.4	−140.2	25.0	−115.2
1922–3	+101.5	2.0	49.0	+50.5	24.7	+75.2
1923–4	+48.3	—	32.9	+15.4	40.0	+55.4
1924–5	+3.7	2.7	25.4	−24.4	45.0	+20.6

[a] Includes other special ex-war receipts (including reparations and allied debts).

Source: T171/371

stores, until 1922/3 (see Table 4.2). Revenue was buoyant in 1920/1, on account of high profits made before the slump, but even so the sum available for reduction of debt on the existing basis of taxation—£164 million—was only just enough to cover statutory sinking funds and maturing debt. Accordingly, increased taxation was imposed to bring the surplus up to £234 million, or £300 million in a full year, in order that the floating debt could be reduced. By 1921/2 revenue was adversely affected by the slump, and only £80 million was provided in the budget for debt redemption, and the realized surplus for the year was £46 million.

The slump led ministers to question the Treasury's fiscal doctrine. In June 1921, two months after he had become Chancellor, Horne asked Blackett what the probable effects would be of putting an extra £20 million of currency notes into circulation. Blackett replied that paying for £20 million of government expenditure by printing more money would revive home demand for goods and services. The immediate effect would be to increase prices, but, while that would stimulate increased production for sale within the country, prices would rise more quickly than production. As a result there would be increased imports and reduced exports, and a tendency for sterling to depreciate in terms of other currencies, setting off 'a new cycle of rising prices and rising wages and an increasing budget deficit'. Blackett believed that the only form of demand that would revive industry on a new basis of lower wages and prices was demand from abroad, and he advised that: 'an artificial stimulation of the home demand will merely mean encouraging people in this country to take in each other's washing and waste their energies in so doing.'[63]

[63] Blackett to Chancellor of the Exchequer, 8 June 1921, T176/5.

However, ministers continued to question financial orthodoxy. The idea of a deliberate policy of 'inflation' (meaning an increase in the money supply) was discussed as a solution to unemployment in September by a group of Liberal ministers, led by Lloyd George, while the Prime Minister was on holiday at Gairloch (see section on 'The Treasury view' below). Then in December Edwin Montagu, now Secretary of State for India, suggested to Lloyd George that the Chancellor should budget for a deficit, enabling him to reduce taxation, and thereby encourage enterprise and increase purchasing power. As a former Financial Secretary of the Treasury, Montagu could argue his case with some authority. Having consulted Treasury officials about tax yields, he proposed tax concessions, including a reduction in the standard rate of income tax from 6s. (30p) to 4s. (20p); a change in the assessment of supertax from gross to net income; and reliefs to the indirect taxpayer. Altogether these would cost £120 million on top of the anticipated deficit of £45 million at current tax rates. However, Montagu assumed that the efforts of the Geddes Committee, plus naval disarmament as a result of the Washington Conference (see below), could produce savings of £80 million, leaving £85 million to be borrowed. He believed that, even if £85 million were borrowed by increasing the floating debt, the effect on prices would be negligible. However, he suggested that, to satisfy orthodox financial opinion, it would be possible to borrow on a short-dated security, especially given that the taxpaying public would have more money to lend. Finally, he argued that the amount to be borrowed in future years would be reduced by rising tax yields as the initial tax cuts led to a revival of prosperity.[64]

Treasury officials did not accept what they came to call the 'act of faith theory' of public finance, although Niemeyer agreed that tax cuts would have been 'the most effective assistance to unemployment'.[65] Blackett and Niemeyer wished to protect the British financial system, whereby current expenditure was covered each year by current revenue, with a reasonable provision for amortization of debt, to maintain the government's credit. They accepted that the matching of revenue and expenditure required them to look further ahead than one year at a time, but they did so from the point of view of ensuring that the budget would always balance. In February 1923, for example, Niemeyer was already looking forward to the budgets of 1924/5 and 1925/6, pointing out that a likely drop in revenue in 1924/5 would make tax reductions in 1923/4 difficult to sustain, although he was more optimistic about 1925/6.[66]

However, in Horne, Blackett and Niemeyer found themselves confronted with a Chancellor who was determined, despite their advice, to reduce the burden of taxation in 1922. Faced with the prospect of an unbalanced budget,

[64] 'Memorandum by the Secretary of State for India', 9 Dec. 1921, Lloyd George papers, F/41/1/38.
[65] McDonald, 'Formulation of British Public Expenditure Policy', 193, 249.
[66] Niemeyer to Chancellor of the Exchequer, 16 Feb. 1923, T171/214.

Blackett did consider the possibility of treating war pensions as an exceptional capital charge, to be spread over a period of thirty to fifty years, with part of the cost being met by borrowing in the early part of the period. However, he dismissed the idea, on the grounds that:

The public as a whole objects not to State expenditure, but to the consequent taxation. It is dangerous for the State to have too easy a means for incurring expenditure without having to face the need for imposing taxes to meet it.[67]

Rather than do so, he opted to recommend suspension of the sinking fund. By suspending debt redemption and by borrowing to meet contractual sinking funds on particular loans, Horne was able to reduce income tax by 1s. (5p) to 5s. (25p), and still claim a nominal surplus of £706,000 on a budget of over £910 million. Niemeyer had thought that a 6d. (2½p) reduction would have had more than sufficient psychological effect on business. Horne's budget was a clear case of politics prevailing over the economics not only of the Treasury but also of the Bank of England, as Norman agreed with Niemeyer that suspension would be very unpopular in the City.[68]

In the event, the year 1922/3 ended with a surplus of £101.5 million, revenue having exceeded forecasts by £3.25 million, while expenditure fell below the estimates by about £98 million. The whole surplus was applied to debt redemption. Regular debt redemption was restored in Baldwin's budget in 1923 through the creation of a New Sinking Fund of £40 million, rising to £45 million in 1924/5 and £50 million thereafter, to meet statutory repayments, including the war debt to the United States. In addition to the usual Treasury argument that internal debt repaid increased the capital fund available to industry, Baldwin's speech noted that, whatever savings might be achieved in public expenditure, the big budget savings in future must come from the cost of servicing the National Debt. Some £1,300 million of debt would mature in the next seven years, in addition to the £2,100 million of War Loan that the government could redeem at its option in 1929. The New Sinking Fund was designed to improve the government's credit and make it possible to redeem existing debt by borrowing at lower rates of interest.[69] This strategy was congenial to the orthodox Snowden but, as will be related in the next chapter, was much less congenial to his successor, Churchill.

By 1923 trade and the revenue were beginning to recover from the slump and Baldwin was able, in addition to restoring orthodox finance, to reduce the standard rate of income tax by 6d. (2½p) to 4s. 6d. (22½p), and to halve corporation profits tax from 5 per cent to 2½ per cent. Over the period 1919/20–1922/3 as a whole, however, falling expenditure was the predominant reason why the budget was brought into balance: expenditure fell from £2,039 million in 1919/20 to

[67] 'Liquidation of Post-war Liabilities', Jan. 1922, T171/202.
[68] 153 HC Deb., 5s., 1922, cols. 1038–42; Short, 'Politics of Personal Taxation', 166–83.
[69] 162 HC Deb., 5s., 1923, cols. 1730–1.

£826 million in 1922/3, with 63 per cent of the reduction coming from the defence departments and the Ministry of Munitions, and most of the remainder from the elimination of war-related items such as loans to allies and dominions, or domestic subsidies.[70] On the other hand, there were strong political pressures from an expanded electorate for social expenditure, and the Treasury repeatedly had to accept compromises between its overall financial objectives and the totals which the spending departments and their ministers could be induced to accept (see sections on public expenditure below).

MONETARY POLICY: HALTING INFLATION

Monetary policy required closer co-operation between the Treasury and the Bank of England than before the war. As long as there was a large deficit that had to be covered by selling three-month Treasury bills, the Bank of England required the Treasury's co-operation before an increase in Bank rate could be effective. If the Bank tried to raise market rates above the Treasury bill rate by open-market sales of securities, the commercial banks could refuse to renew their large holdings of Treasury bills, forcing the government to borrow on Ways and Means from the Bank, and thereby increasing the money supply. However, as long as Treasury bill rates set the level of interest rates generally, there was likely to be political reluctance to impose the degree of deflation necessary to restore the gold standard to the pre-war parity. For example, in August 1920 the Chancellor, Austen Chamberlain, resisted advice from the Bank and Treasury officials to allow a rise in short-term interest rates, at a time when prices were still rising and the dollar : sterling rate falling.[71] There is some doubt about when, and to what extent, the Treasury and Bank restored the pre-1914 practice whereby the Chancellor either did not hear, or did not hear until about an hour before the public announcement, of a change in Bank rate, but apparently Chamberlain agreed to revert to this practice before he left the Treasury at the end of March 1921.[72] This step made the Bank of England more independent of political factors in its conduct of monetary policy, although regular personal contacts between the Governor and the Treasury meant that the Treasury continued to be aware of what was going on.

   Monetary policy had two related but distinct objectives: the first was to halt the credit boom and associated inflation in 1919 and 1920; the second was to bring British prices into line with prices in the United States, which had remained on the gold standard, thus preparing the way for a return to the gold standard at the pre-1914 sterling : dollar exchange rate. Treasury officials were

[70] Mallet and George, *British Budgets, 1913–1921*, 393; eid., *1921–33*, 558.
[71] Sir Henry Clay, *Lord Norman* (1957), 129.
[72] R. S. Sayers, *The Bank of England, 1891–1941*, 3 vols. (Cambridge, 1976), i. 119.

aware that, once monetary policy was linked to the maintenance of a fixed exchange rate, politicians would no longer be free to determine the supply of money or the level of interest rates. Under the gold standard the supply of legal tender was related to the supply of gold, all bank notes being backed by gold, apart from a certain amount, fixed by statute, known as the fiduciary issue. In theory, gold tended to move into or out of the country according to shifts in the balance of trade, and these gold movements raised or lowered commercial banks' reserves. In practice the Bank of England would normally vary its discount rate (Bank rate), the raising of which would not only check an outflow of gold, but would also raise the structure of interest rates in the country. Either way, an adverse balance of trade would lead to a restriction of credit, a postponement of new investment, a consequent reduction in employment and therefore of demand for goods, and a fall in prices, checking imports and stimulating exports until the balance of trade had been corrected.[73]

However, the gold standard had ceased to be effective during the war and the prospects for its restoration were uncertain following the unpegging of the sterling:dollar exchange on 20 March 1919. It was not until 15 December 1919 that Austen Chamberlain announced that the Government had accepted the Cunliffe Committee's recommendations, implying a regime of balanced budgets and a gradual but steady redemption of debt.[74] Meanwhile, monetary policy was primarily directed at controlling the domestic credit boom rather than the exchange rate, which was allowed to fall from $4.61¾ at the end of June to $3.40 in February 1920.

The course of monetary policy after the war has been fully described by Susan Howson,[75] and need only be summarized here. On Bradbury's recommendation, a meeting of ministers, including the Prime Minister, the Chancellor, and the President of the Board of Trade, agreed on 24 July 1919 to remove restrictions on the export of capital, other than control over new issues by the Capital Issues Committee. Bradbury reported that already most restrictions were ineffective in the absence of wartime cable and postal censorship, and even the Capital Issues Committee was approving most applications.[76] In theory, control over capital henceforth would be exercised through interest rates. In practice, to keep the market clear for government loans, the Bank imposed an informal embargo on the raising of loans on the London market by foreign countries, and sought the approval of the Treasury for any variation in its implementation.[77]

[73] Committee on Currency and Foreign Exchanges after the War, *First Interim Report* (Cd. 9182), PP 1918, vii. 853, paras. 2–7. For the economic and political constraints imposed by the gold standard see Barry Eichengreen, *Golden Fetters: The Gold Standard and the Great Depression, 1919–1939* (Oxford, 1992).

[74] 123 HC Deb., 5s., cols. 43–5.

[75] In her *Domestic Monetary Management in Britain, 1919–38* (Cambridge, 1975), ch. 2.

[76] Finance Committee minutes, 24 July 1919, with appendix, CAB27/71.

[77] John Atkin, 'Official Regulation of British Overseas Investment, 1914–1931', *Econ. Hist. Rev.*, 2nd ser., 23 (1970), 324–35.

Again on Bradbury's recommendation, the Bank of England adopted a policy from 6 August of earmarking Bank notes against any further increases in the currency note circulation and putting them in a Currency Note Reserve. Putting Bank notes aside in this way was intended to deplete the Bank's reserve in its Banking Department, making it necessary for the Bank to protect its reserve by raising Bank rate. By 6 November a reduction in the Bank's reserve had given the Chancellor grounds for accepting an increase in Bank rate from 5 to 6 per cent, despite earlier opposition from some of his Cabinet colleagues.

The Cunliffe Committee, in its *Final Report* in December, recommended the continuation of this practice, and also recommended the actual maximum fiduciary issue in any one year should be the legal maximum for the next.[78] Keynes was critical of this limitation, as it implied a progressive reduction of legal tender, but, according to Niemeyer, the limitation was intended to be simply a signal to the banks that the monetary authorities intended to restrict credit. In line with Hawtrey's belief that it would be fallacious to rely exclusively on regulation of the quantity of legal tender, Niemeyer noted that 'it is credit which governs the currency and not the currency which governs credit'.[79]

Despite the government's acceptance of the Cunliffe Committee's recommendations, there was pressure from Lloyd George in February 1920 for a return to lower interest rates, to help the issue of Housing Bonds as part of the Addison housing programme (see below). The Bank, on the other hand, wished to raise Bank rate by a further 1 percentage point to 7 per cent. Blackett, Niemeyer (then the principal assistant secretary in charge of the Home Finance Division), and Hawtrey all supplied the Chancellor, Austen Chamberlain, with memoranda in support of the Bank's argument, although Blackett urged that deflation must be very gradual and Hawtrey believed that a rise in Bank rate would be so effective, by changing expectations as regards future profits, that it should be lowered as soon as the boom was halted, which he expected to be almost immediately.[80]

Chamberlain also sought advice from Keynes, who said that credit inflation must be stopped and, in the absence of wartime controls over investment, which had been removed in March 1919, it might be necessary to push Bank rate up to the traditional crisis level of 10 per cent. Keynes did not believe that unemployment would result. Further professional economic advice was forthcoming from Pigou, whose letter of 1 March 1920 to *The Times* recommending Bank rate of 8 per cent was brought to the Chancellor's attention by Blackett.[81] It may fairly

[78] Committee on Currency and Foreign Exchange after the War, *Final Report* (Cmd. 464), PP 1919, xiii. 593.

[79] *JMK*, xix. 240–4; Niemeyer to Chancellor of the Exchequer, Mar. 1924, T176/5; Hawtrey, 'The Gold Standard', *Econ. J.*, 29 (1919), 439–40.   [80] The memoranda are in T172/1384.

[81] Susan Howson, ' "A Dear Money Man"?: Keynes on Monetary Policy, 1920', *Econ. J.*, 83 (1973), 456–64.

be said, therefore, that the deflationary step to a 7 per cent Bank rate on 15 April was taken on the best economic advice available at the time.

The rise in Bank rate coincided with the end of the post-war restocking boom in the spring of 1920. Exports held up well for some months longer but at the end of 1920 an international recession brought increased competition for shrinking markets. At the same time sterling rose on foreign exchange markets, partly in response to higher Bank rate, and partly reflecting continuing inflation in continental Europe. It has subsequently been estimated that, measured against a basket of the currencies of the United States, France, Germany, Japan, and Italy, weighted according to their importance in Britain's foreign trade, and taking into account changes in relative prices in these countries, sterling's real exchange rate rose more rapidly between 1920 and 1921 than between 1924 and 1925, and was higher in 1921 than in 1925.[82] While there are always problems in such calculations, relating to weights and base year, it is reasonable to infer that monetary policy was even more unhelpful to exporters in 1921 than it was to be when Britain did return to the gold standard in 1925. At all events, British exports collapsed in 1921 and by May no less than 23 per cent of the insured labour force was unemployed.

Some recession in 1921 was no doubt inevitable, but the deflationary policy that the Bank and the Finance Department of the Treasury urged on the Chancellor contributed to the severity and length of the slump. Hawtrey believed that once businessmen had been deterred from borrowing, a vicious circle of deflation was established, with dealers deterred from making purchases by the prospect of further reductions in prices, making it harder for producers to sell at existing prices.[83] Bank rate fell by stages to 5 per cent in November 1921 and 3 per cent in July 1922, but even economic historians who have disagreed about the extent to which businessmen were influenced by Bank rate in the 1920s can agree that in 1921 the combination of high Bank rate and falling prices, which raised real interest rates, was highly deflationary.[84] The fact that Bank rate was held at 7 per cent until April 1921 suggests that the Treasury and the Bank were more concerned with funding debt and controlling the money market than with checking inflation or encouraging exports. The floating debt was greatly reduced, the total of Treasury bills outstanding falling from a peak of £1,208,500 in July 1921 to £600,000 two years later.[85]

[82] S. N. Broadberry, *The British Economy Between the Wars: A Macroeconomic Survey* (Oxford, 1986), 120–1; id., 'The Emergence of Mass Unemployment: Explaining Macroeconomic Trends in Britain during the Trans-World War I Period', *Econ. Hist. Rev.*, 2nd ser., 43 (1990), 279–81.

[83] 'The Credit Situation' by Hawtrey, 19 Apr. 1921, T176/5.

[84] Derek Aldcroft, 'British Monetary Policy and Economic Activity in the 1920s', *Rev. Int. d'Hist. de la Banque*, 5 (1972), 277–304; Ross Catterall, 'Attitudes to and the Impact of British Monetary Policy in the 1920s', ibid., 12 (1976), 29–53.

[85] E. V. Morgan, *Studies in British Financial Policy 1914–1925* (1952), 147.

MONETARY POLICY: TOWARDS A RETURN TO GOLD

The monetary authorities' objective of restoring the gold standard at the pre-war parity did not imply a reduction of sterling prices to their pre-1914 level. As Blackett explained to a parliamentary Select Committee in March 1920, whole-sale prices in the United States had more than doubled since 1913 and, although there might be 'some fall' in prices, a return to 'anything near 1913 prices' was not likely, if only because that would make the burden of war debts intolerable. However, wholesale prices in the United Kingdom had risen faster than in the United States—taking 1913 as 100, the United Kingdom index stood at 270 compared with 220 in the United States—and the object of deflation in the United Kingdom was 'simply to bring back sterling prices to a level with gold [i.e. American] prices'.[86] Niemeyer made much the same point four years later when he briefed Snowden as follows:

The object of what is called 'deflation' is frequently stated to be a return to pre-war prices. This is not, however, the suggestion of the Cunliffe Report . . . Pre-war prices have never been the aim of any policy, nor, for that matter [would they be] within the realm of practical politics.[87]

However, in the same memorandum Niemeyer noted that American prices stood at about 150 to pre-war 100, indicating a fall of about 30 per cent in what Blackett had called 'gold' prices in 1920. In other words, returning to the gold standard would require a substantially greater degree of deflation than had been expected in 1920—a 44 per cent fall in prices compared with 18 per cent, on the basis of wholesale price indices.

Deflation was understood by the Treasury to involve a reduction in the money supply, a fall in prices, and some downward flexibility of wages. However, Hawtrey pointed out in July 1920 that wages had not kept pace with prices since 1914. Wage increases had been generally related to a cost-of-living index that had been kept down artificially during the war by subsidies and controls (for example, on rents), and which stood in mid-1920 at 150 (1914 = 100). Wholesale prices, on the other hand, had increased by 200 per cent. There seemed, there-fore, to be a large margin for a decrease in prices before wages need be affected.[88] In fact many wages did fall during the slump, particularly in indus-tries where wages were related to prices by sliding scales. It was possible, there-fore, for officials to believe in 1920 that deflation need not lead to unemployment, and when unemployment rose in the slump, it was possible to believe that wages and employment would adjust to a lower price level.

---

[86] 'Deflation and the Proposed Levy in War Time Increase of Wealth', memorandum by Blackett, Mar. 1920, included as an appendix to *Minutes of Evidence Taken Before the Select Committee on Increases of Wealth (War)*, PP 1920, vii. 370.

[87] Niemeyer to Chancellor of the Exchequer, Mar. 1924, T176/5.

[88] 'The Return to the Gold Standard', July 1920, Hawtrey papers, HTRY1/13.

Even so, Blackett was aware that 'anybody responsible . . . for a policy of deflation must guard with the most careful eye against doing more harm than good'. In March 1920 he still looked to an increase in production of goods and services to restore the 'proportion between purchasing power and purchasable things' and concluded that 'any policy of deflation must guard against being so precipitate as to interfere with production'. On the other hand, he believed that the 'continual process of rising prices and fresh inflation' had to be dealt with quickly: 'The longer you leave it alone the worse it will be. The vicious circle will go on spinning and the crash will come.'[89] Despite his hopes, there was to be no smooth transition from inflation to stable prices.

A return to the gold standard was expected, by the Board of Trade as well as the Treasury, to help employment by stabilizing exchange rates and thereby helping to restore international trade. Steps to stabilize exchange rates, by international agreement, were taken at a conference of European powers in Genoa in April 1922. Here a leading role was played by Hawtrey, who accompanied Blackett at the preparatory meetings and who wrote the draft financial resolutions which were later adopted by the conference. In setting out the basis for an international gold exchange standard Hawtrey identified two distinct problems: the large depreciations that some European currencies had undergone, which made a return to pre-war parities in these cases impossible; and the reduced purchasing power of gold itself. There could, therefore, be no simple return to the pre-1914 position regarding exchange rates and prices. Moreover, a general return to the gold standard would raise the monetary demand for gold and hence its value, increasing the amount of deflation required by countries which, like Britain, intended to return to pre-1914 parities. A deflationary increase in the monetary demand for gold could be avoided if countries were to include in their reserves currencies like the dollar and (after 1925) sterling which were freely convertible into gold. This gold exchange standard would ensure stability of exchange rates, but not prices, and therefore Hawtrey further recommended that central banks should co-operate to regulate credit with a view to preventing undue fluctuations in the purchasing power of gold.[90]

International monetary negotiations were, of course, at least as much a matter for the Bank of England as the Treasury, and Norman, while keen to return to gold, regarded stability of prices as a remote ideal. He showed his irritation with Hawtrey when, in a letter to Benjamin Strong, the Governor of the Federal Reserve Bank of New York, he described Hawtrey as 'a "leading light" of the Treasury [who] made it his particular business to quarrel with the policy of the

[89] *Minutes of Evidence Taken Before the Select Committee on Increases of Wealth (War)*, PP 1920, vii. 73–296, q. 1546–7; Blackett's memorandum, Mar. 1920, ibid., 370–2. Nor were these opinions for public consumption only. On 19 Feb. Blackett had advised the Chancellor that 'real wages must be kept up above pre-war levels and unemployment must be avoided to the utmost extent possible. Deflation must therefore be gradual and cautious' (T172/1384).

[90] R. G. Hawtrey, *Monetary Reconstruction* (1923), ch. 6.

Treasury and the Bank of England'.[91] Nevertheless, Blackett, as chairman of a committee of international experts, lent his support to Hawtrey's ideas, which were adopted with no essential modification by the Financial Commission of the Conference.[92]

Had the Genoa currency resolutions been universally applied, there would have been less pressure on Britain's gold reserves after 1925, and therefore lower interest rates, than proved to be the case. Moreover, the gold exchange standard would have expanded sterling's role as a reserve currency to Europe, where previously the franc, and to a lesser extent the mark, had been the major currencies. For that very reason, the gold exchange standard was bitterly opposed by the French, and viewed warily by the Americans. In the event, as will be discussed in Chapter 5, the accumulation of gold in Paris and New York in the later 1920s tended to force other countries, including Britain, to adopt deflationary policies to protect their reserves.

Hawtrey, very optimistically, believed in 1923 that fixed exchange rates involved no more than 'a slight departure from an exact stabilisation of internal prices', and need not, therefore, cause unemployment. The stabilization of prices, by management of credit through Bank rate, was, in his view:

not merely *a* remedy, but *the* remedy for the unemployment evil. Unemployment, not only since the war, but before it, has been directly caused by price fluctuations.[93]

Hawtrey's vision was a good deal more ambitious than that of the Cunliffe Committee, and indeed, as he admitted, might appear to be in conflict with that committee's recommendation of a return to a fixed fiduciary issue. If the purchasing power of the currency was to be stabilized, it might be necessary to increase or decrease the circulation of legal currency without regard to the Bank's gold reserve. However, such was Hawtrey's faith in the efficacy of the control of credit, if directed primarily to stabilizing prices, that he felt sure that it would be easier to maintain a fixed fiduciary issue than before the war.[94]

The problem facing the monetary authorities was that sterling still stood below its pre-war parity with the dollar (the surrogate for gold prices), and further deflation might cause levels of unemployment that would lead ministers to question the advisability of pursuing a policy of 'sound finance'. In April 1922 sterling stood at $4.43, and, although it reached $4.72 in February 1923, by June of that year it had fallen back to $4.59, and the Bank felt it necessary to defend it by raising Bank rate by 1 percentage point to 4 per cent, to keep in line with the New York rediscount rate. Niemeyer wrote to Norman opposing any upward change in Bank rate, because of the effects on unemployment, as well as on the

[91] R. W. D. Boyce, *British Capitalism at the Crossroads, 1919–1932* (Cambridge, 1987), 41.

[92] 'The Genoa Currency Resolutions', by Hawtrey, 4 Feb. 1923, T176/5; *International Conference Genoa: Resolutions of the Financial Commission* (Cmd. 1650), PP 1922, xxiii. 449.

[93] 'Genoa Currency Resolutions', 4 Feb. 1923, T176/5.

[94] 'The Return to Gold', by Hawtrey, Jan. 1923, T208/54.

cost of government borrowing. However, in line with the independence that the Bank had regained in monetary matters, Bank rate was nevertheless raised.[95]

Deflation was not without its critics even in the City. In January 1923 McKenna, the former Chancellor, who had become chairman of the Midland Bank, made a speech criticizing the policy adopted in 1921 of selling 5½ per cent Treasury bonds, redeemable in 1929, to the public and using the proceeds to pay off Treasury bills held by banks. He pointed out that the near liquid assets available to the banks were thereby reduced, with the result that the amount of bank deposits, and the purchasing power of the public, tended to fall. Niemeyer consulted the Deputy Governor of the Bank of England, who agreed with him that McKenna's argument only applied when banks lacked good customers to whom they could lend the cash they received for the Treasury bills. There was a lack of customers in the slump, but normally, Niemeyer believed, a gradual redemption of Treasury bills would provide the banks with cash that they could lend short term as working capital to trade and industry.[96] In any case, Niemeyer's first priority was to reduce the floating debt, and thereby avoid the possibility of a repetition of the credit boom of 1919–20. He wished therefore to fund Treasury bills in advance of economic recovery, on the grounds that, as trade expanded, and with it commercial demand for credit, it would be more difficult to renew Treasury bills.[97] 'Sound finance' had priority over the interests of both the banks and their customers.

Even so, given political concern about unemployment, it was natural that the Treasury should cast about for some means other than deflation for bringing sterling to parity with the dollar. One possibility, first canvassed by Hawtrey in 1921, was that of shipping gold to the United States, in the belief that a substantial consignment would hasten a relaxation of credit there, by increasing bank reserves, with the consequence that American prices would rise and, if a corresponding inflation could be avoided in Britain, the dollar would sink to the level of sterling.[98] Blackett had forwarded the suggestion to Norman, but seems to have received a discouraging answer, for no action was taken. Hawtrey returned to the idea in 1923 and Niemeyer suggested to Norman that gold from the Currency Note Account might be used for the purpose. Norman, however, doubted whether shipping gold would have the desired effect, since the Federal Reserve banks would find means to counteract the tendency which Niemeyer wished to produce, while the action of removing gold from the Currency Note Account might lower confidence in sterling.[99] Once more, the Bank's view prevailed.

In June 1924, at Norman's suggestion, the Chancellor, Snowden, set up an

[95] Howson, *Domestic Monetary Management*, 28.

[96] *The Times*, 25 Jan. 1923, 19; Niemeyer's notes and correspondence, 24 Jan. to 6 June 1923, T176/5; 'Debt Policy and Unemployment', by Hawtrey, 29 June 1929, T175/26.

[97] 'The Policy of Funding Debt', by Niemeyer, 6 June 1923, T176/5.

[98] 'The Credit Situation', 19 Apr. 1921, T176/5.

[99] 'Export of Gold to America', by Hawtrey, Mar. 1923, T208/54; Niemeyer to Norman, 20 Nov. 1923, and Norman to Niemeyer, 21 Nov. 1923, T176/5.

expert committee under Austen Chamberlain to consider whether the time had come to amalgamate the Treasury's currency note issue with the Bank of England note issue. Given that the Cunliffe Committee had recommended that amalgamation should await at least a year's experience of the gold standard, it was inevitable that the committee should also consider the question of when Britain should return to gold. By that date Hawtrey himself seems to have abandoned hope of raising American prices to ease the transition to the pre-war parity, and he advised that a rapid adjustment should be made to British prices, to avoid prolonging the inevitable depression and unemployment.[100] The final decision on the return to gold fell to Snowden's successor, Churchill, in 1925, and is considered in the next chapter. The point to be made here is that through-out the policy-making process from 1918 to 1925 Treasury officials seem to have been determined to keep manufacturing industry at arm's length from the for-mulation of monetary policy. The Federation of British Industries asked the Prime Minister for a new enquiry into monetary policy in 1921, but, on Treasury advice, Lloyd George denied the need for a new enquiry, on the grounds that the Cunliffe Committee's recommendations had been endorsed in November 1918 by the Committee on Financial Facilities, 'which was largely composed of busi-nessmen and widely representative of British industry'.[101] In fact, as noted in Chapter 3, Bradbury had been careful to ensure that the committee was not dominated by industrialists, its non-official membership comprising five bankers, a City accountant, the President of the Chamber of Commerce, but only four industrialists. A further request by the Federation of British Industries for a new enquiry into monetary policy in 1924 was rebuffed on the grounds that there was little to add to Lloyd George's reply three years earlier.[102]

It does not follow, however, that the Treasury favoured the interests of the City over those of industry. The Treasury's objective, which it shared with the Bank of England, was a return to 'sound finance', with firm control over money markets to avoid a repetition of the excessive bank lending that had fuelled the inflationary boom of 1919–20. Moreover, it cannot have escaped the notice of Treasury officials that the policy of returning to the gold standard, requiring as it did an end to government borrowing (except for renewing existing debt), was itself a powerful check on public expenditure, and would therefore strengthen Treasury control in Whitehall.

INTERNATIONAL FINANCE: REPARATIONS AND WAR DEBTS

Another great institution with which the Treasury had more dealings than before the war was the Foreign Office. Tension between the two departments

---

[100] 'Sterling and Gold', July 1924, T208/54.   [101] Boyce, *British Capitalism*, 37.
[102] Niemeyer to Chancellor of the Exchequer, Mar. 1924, T176/5.

arose over two issues: the relationship between the Foreign Office and the Home Civil Service, and the allocation of responsibility for policy with regard to reparations and war debts. During discussions between 1917 and 1919 on the reform of the Foreign Office and the Diplomatic Service, the Treasury had expressed a preference for interchange of staff between the Foreign Office and domestic departments, on the grounds that this would give Foreign Office staff wider experience than hitherto. However, the Foreign Office had stuck to the view that its work required specialist knowledge, and would agree to transfers only in exceptional cases. Controversy also arose over the terms of Fisher's appointment in 1919 as Head of the Civil Service, which made him responsible for advising the Prime Minister on the filling of senior posts in the Foreign Office as well as the Home Civil Service, although there is no evidence that Fisher was able to overrule a recommendation made by the Foreign Secretary.[103]

The Foreign Office and the Treasury both had claims to take the lead in financial diplomacy relating to reparations and war debts: the Foreign Office because such issues were central to international relations; the Treasury because the sums of money involved had implications for domestic taxation and financial policy generally. When in August 1919 the Finance Committee of the Cabinet discussed British representation on the Inter-Allied Reparations Commission, ministers were acutely conscious of Britain's financial difficulties, and the selection of the British delegate was left to the Chancellor of the Exchequer, Austen Chamberlain. As already noted, Bradbury was appointed. Moreover, it was Bradbury and Treasury officials who drafted the minute of 10 March 1920 that defined the relationship between the Treasury, the Foreign Office, and the British Delegation to the Reparation Commission. Bradbury, as the head of the delegation, was to be responsible to 'the Board of Treasury' (meaning the Prime Minister and the Chancellor), not the Foreign Secretary. In practice, according to McFadyean, the Treasury official who was appointed secretary to the British delegation to the commission, Bradbury regarded his functions as largely judicial and was unwilling to accept orders from the Treasury or even the Chancellor. While it was recognized that the Foreign Office should have the deciding voice in instructing the British Delegation on questions of general foreign policy, it was laid down that the Foreign Office should communicate its views through the Treasury.[104]

The Treasury minute emphasized the responsibility of all departments to consult the Treasury in advance in all cases where policy might have financial results, but the Treasury failed to reciprocate where policy might have diplomatic consequences. The Foreign Office frequently had cause to complain that the Treasury did not keep it informed on reparation questions, and in

[103] Ephraim Maisel, *The Foreign Office and Foreign Policy, 1919–1926* (Brighton, 1994), 14–21, 199–203; O'Halpin, *Head of the Civil Service*, 79–83.

[104] J. A. Hemery, 'The Emergence of Treasury Influence in British Foreign Policy, 1914–1921', Ph.D. (Cambridge, 1988), 268–76; A. McFadyean, *Recollected in Tranquillity* (1964), 75.

November 1921 the Treasury even published a White Paper on reparations, without consulting the Foreign Office, although it should have been clear that the White Paper would have an adverse affect on Anglo-French relations.[105] It would, however, be easy to exaggerate the Treasury's influence. Major negotiations were conducted by successive Prime Ministers rather than the Chancellor. Nevertheless, by the summer of 1923 Treasury involvement in reparations led Fisher to believe that, as Head of the Civil Service, he could offer advice to the Prime Minister, Baldwin, on wider aspects of foreign policy.

Officials in the Treasury and the British Delegation were strongly influenced by Keynes's book, *The Economic Consequences of the Peace*, which was published at the end of 1919.[106] Consequently, they were concerned not only with the budgetary implications of reparations payments but also with the implications for the German economy and British industry. The Reparation Commission assessed Germany's liability on 27 April 1921 at 132,000 million gold marks (£6,600 million). Under the London Schedule of Payments of 5 May 1921, which reflected British doubts about Germany's capacity to pay the full amount, Germany was to pay interest and a sinking fund on two series of bonds totalling 50,000 million gold marks (£2,500 million). However, the remaining series of 'C-bonds', totalling 82,000 gold marks (£4,100 million) would be issued by the Reparation Commission only when Germany had become sufficiently prosperous to service them in addition to first two series. Given the condition of the German economy, there was no foreseeable prospect of the C-bonds acquiring any tangible value. The immediate burden that Germany faced was a schedule of annual payments of 2,000 million gold marks (£100 million) plus, from November 1921, a variable sum equivalent to 26 per cent of exports. In 1921 Germany's exports were estimated to be worth about £200 million, so that the initial obligation was about £152 million, rising thereafter with the value of German exports.[107]

A number of historians have challenged Keynes's belief that reparations were an impossible burden for Germany.[108] Keynes's calculations in *The Economic Consequences of the Peace* had produced a figure of £2,000 million for Germany's capacity, or 80 per cent of the total for the A- and B-bond series, not a big difference given the margin of error in his calculations at a time when prices and exchange rates were changing rapidly. Schuker has argued that, had the Weimar

[105] Alan Sharp, 'The Foreign Office in Eclipse, 1919–22', *History*, 61 (1976), 216.

[106] *JMK*, ii; McFadyean, *Recollected in Tranquillity*, 71; id., *Reparation Reviewed* (1930), 11–18.

[107] Bruce Kent, *The Spoils of War: The Politics, Economics and Diplomacy of Reparations, 1918–1932* (Oxford, 1989), 132–8; *JMK*, xvii. 236–7.

[108] See, for example, Charles S. Maier, *Recasting Bourgeois Europe: Stabilization in France, Germany and Italy in the Decade after World War I* (Princeton, NJ, 1975), 250–4; Sally Marks, 'The Myths of Reparations', *Central Eur. Hist.*, 11 (1978), 231–55; Stephen A. Schuker, *American 'Reparations' to Germany, 1919–33: Implications for the Third-World Debt Crisis* (Princeton, NJ, 1988); Marc Trachtenberg, *Reparation in World Politics: France and European Economic Diplomacy, 1916–1923* (New York, 1980). For Keynes's views in 1921 see *JMK*, xvii. 231–56.

governments had the political resolve to reduce German living standards, and had there been good will on both sides regarding a willingness to deliver and receive both exports and payments in kind (for example, coal), it would have been possible for Germany to transfer the 5.4 to 7.2 per cent of national income implied by the 1921 schedule of payments. As an economist, Moggridge has produced a range of figures relating to the burden that reparations represented as a proportion of German national income and has concluded that, *in theory*, it would have been possible to transfer payments by a substantial net increase in exports, if the recipients had been willing to reallocate labour and capital away from industries that were in competition with German goods.[109]

The Treasury has been described as 'intensely pro-German' in relation to reparations.[110] In fact, it makes more sense to think in terms of Treasury officials being pro-British. Blackett had thought in June 1920 that £150 million was within Germany's capacity to pay, 'provided that she settled down to work'.[111] The considered Treasury view on reparations in November 1921 was that the total burden imposed by the 1921 schedule of payments might well be within Germany's capacity to pay, but only if Germany were given a breathing space in which to restore its working capital. If too much were demanded too soon, the effect would be to impoverish Germany, one of Britain's major trading partners, and therefore to make it impossible to keep British workers fully employed. German reparations would be largely paid by exporting goods that would compete with British electrical engineering, iron and steel, and chemical industries, but these exports need not be damaging to British interests, provided that world demand for such products expanded. Demand could be raised if development schemes, such as the electrification of railways, could be encouraged throughout the world, including Britain and the Empire. Reparations to Britain, however, should be paid in cash into the Exchequer and used to service Britain's war debt to the United States and to reduce the burden of taxation. (Typically, notwithstanding the benefits of development schemes as a solution to the transfer problem, the Treasury was concerned that reparation payments should not tempt the government to finance extravagant projects, and noted that 'it is obvious that government intervention . . . will have to be unusually enlightened'.) The essential point, however, was that the timing of payments was more important than the eventual total, and that the London Schedule should be readjusted to give the German economy time in which to recover, and the world economy time in which to absorb German products.[112]

[109] Schuker, *American 'Reparations'*, 11–19. D. E. Moggridge, *Maynard Keynes: An Economist's Biography* (1992), 340–5.
[110] Sally Marks, 'Reparations in 1922', in Carole Fink, Axel Frohn, and Jurgen Heideking (eds.), *Genoa, Rapallo and European Reconstruction in 1922* (Cambridge, 1991), 69.
[111] Conclusions of a meeting held in the Chancellor of the Exchequer's room, 18 June 1920, Worthington-Evans papers, Bodleian Library, Oxford.
[112] 'German Reparations: The Need for Readjustment of the Present Schedule of Payments' and 'Reparation in Kind', both 16 Nov. 1921, CAB27/72.

These views were set out in response to a suggestion by Bradbury that Germany should be granted a limited and provisional moratorium, to enable her to balance her budget and thereby restore her financial credit, as only then would she be able to raise loans abroad for reconstructing her economy. Horne accepted this advice, and told the Cabinet's Finance Committee that the City 'would certainly strongly support a moratorium for a period sufficient to enable Germany to recover'.[113] Despite the unwillingness of the French government to forgo early payment for damages suffered during the war, a partial moratorium was granted to Germany in January 1922. When the question of Germany's ability to pay was reopened in the autumn, Bradbury commented that the reparations total of £6,600 million was so absurd as not to be a serious factor in money markets. However, he told the Prime Minister, were the Allies to follow a French suggestion, and enforce payment of a reduced liability of £2,000 million, 'we should be passing from pure to applied lunacy'.[114]

Meanwhile, there had been developments in relation to Britain's war debt to the United States. Anglo-American negotiations on war debts in 1919 and 1920 had secured a postponement of interest payments for three years. Then, early in 1922, the US Congress created the World War Foreign Debt Commission to arrange the funding of debt, and the British Government was invited to renew negotiations. The Chancellor of the Exchequer, Horne, warned his Cabinet colleagues on 8 June that, given Congressional opinion, a decision to send a delegation to Washington would be a decision to pay the British debt in full, whatever might happen in respect of war debts or reparations due to Britain. Nevertheless, he advised that a delegation should be sent because, if the debt was going to be paid, the sooner the better, as the sterling exchange rate could then be stabilized. There was also the need to gain American support for the financial reconstruction of Europe, a problem that had become more pressing with Germany's inability to pay reparations and the depreciation of the mark.

However, the Cabinet did not accept the Chancellor's advice. Instead, at Churchill's instigation, it agreed in July to send a dispatch to countries owing war debts to Britain, explaining the seriousness of Britain's economic position, and the need for repayment of these debts in the light of the American demand. The dispatch, which became known as the Balfour note, pointed out that, exclusive of interest, Britain was owed a total of £1,300 million by its allies, £650 million by Russia, and £1,450 million by Germany, and owed in turn about £850 million to the United States. After making it clear that the British Government thought that the generous course was to write off the whole of the inter-allied debts, the note offered as a second-best solution to collect no more from Britain's debtors than what was required to pay its own debts.[115]

[113] Extract from Finance Committee minutes, 1 Dec. 1921, Worthington-Evans papers.

[114] Bradbury to Bonar Law, 23 Oct. 1922, *Documents on British Foreign Policy, 1919–1939* (hereafter cited as *DBFP*), 1st ser., vol. xx. 276.

[115] *Despatch to the Representatives of France, Italy, Serb–Croat–Slovene State, Roumania, Portugal and Greece at*

The Balfour note did not at all represent the views of the Treasury. Blackett attacked the policy adopted by the Cabinet as 'fundamentally insincere' and appealed to Horne to secure its reconsideration before the note was sent. It was 'entirely erroneous', Blackett argued, to suppose that Britain could really collect from its insolvent debtors what it owed to America, and the note really meant either that Britain was not sincere in professing to be willing to meet its obligations or that 'we mean to pay America and let off Europe in whole or in great part, but wish to grumble in public first'.[116] The note, 'pillorying American selfishness' (in Blackett's phrase) was none the less sent, causing great offence in the United States.

The fall of the Coalition delayed matters until January 1923, when Baldwin, as Chancellor in Bonar Law's Conservative government, led a delegation comprising himself, Norman, and Sir Auckland Geddes (the British ambassador in Washington), accompanied by two relatively junior Treasury officials, E. Rowe-Dutton, a principal in the Overseas Finance Division, and P. J. Grigg, the Chancellor's private secretary. Britain's war debt was theoretically payable on demand, and interest, at 5 per cent, was accruing at the rate of £50 million a year. The American Debt Funding Commission was authorized only to fund on a basis of not less that $4\frac{1}{4}$ per cent over twenty-five years, which would imply annual payments of $300 million (£61.7 million at the gold exchange rate of $4.86). Blackett thought that Britain could afford to settle on these terms, but Baldwin secured terms of 3 per cent for ten years, and $3\frac{1}{2}$ per cent for a further fifty-two years, requiring annual payments of $160 million (£33 million) for ten years and $184 million (£38 million) for the following fifty-two. Hawtrey did not think that such payments would require 'heroic measures' on Britain's part, but it was only with great difficulty that Baldwin managed to persuade Bonar Law to accept them.[117]

The Washington negotiations coincided with a declaration by the Reparations Commission (with Bradbury abstaining) that Germany was in partial default on reparations. Bradbury had tried to persuade the Allies to grant Germany a four-year moratorium and to agree to a general scaling down of reparations and inter-allied war debts. However, in the form known as the Bonar Law Plan, these proposals were rejected by the French, Belgians, and Italians in January 1923. Instead, French and Belgian troops occupied the Ruhr in an attempt to extract payment in kind and in cash. Some journalists wished to interview Baldwin, to discover his views, but Grigg tried to protect the Chancellor by giving them his own. Grigg predicted that the occupation would damage the

London respecting War Debts (Cmd. 1737), PP 1922, xxiii. 685–8. Neither Churchill nor Arthur Balfour had anything to do with the Treasury at the time, the former being Colonial Secretary and the latter being minister without portfolio with the title of Lord President of the Council.

[116] 'Inter-Government Debt', by Blackett, 12 July 1922, T176/8.
[117] 'British Debt to United States', by Blackett, 10 Oct. 1922, Bank of England papers C40/734/1707/5; 'Export of Gold to America', by Hawtrey, Mar. 1923, T208/54.

French more than the Germans, and, as he was the Chancellor's private secretary, his views were reported as being those of Baldwin. The French ambassador in Washington was directed to make enquiries of Baldwin, which he did, with what Grigg thought was undue *empressement* in the middle of a reception at the British Embassy. Baldwin, of course, was able to deny the reports, and it was only later that he discovered their source.[118]

Grigg had been naïve and indiscreet, but it was nevertheless true that the Treasury was hostile to the French action in the Ruhr. Bradbury thought that Germany's performance in meeting its reparations obligations was no worse in the latter half of 1922 than before. Budget deficits since the war had already fuelled hyperinflation, and the cost of passive resistance to the occupation of the Ruhr led the German government to print more and more money. To the Treasury it seemed clear that the restoration of stable financial conditions required a solution to the reparations problem. Fisher believed that the French were 'bullies' who had hit defenceless Germany 'below the belt', and advised Baldwin in July 1923 that Britain had an obligation as a signatory of the peace treaty to ensure 'fair play'.[119] Baldwin's biographers believed Fisher inspired the Prime Minister to take a firmer stand against the French action in the Ruhr than the Foreign Office wished.[120]

The French agreed that the question of what Germany could pay should be remitted to a fresh committee of experts, chaired by an American, Charles G. Dawes, who would calculate what maximum payments could be made if Germany's budget were to be balanced and the value of her currency stabilized. The two British members of the committee, Stamp and Sir Robert Kindersley, a director of the Bank of England, were well known to the Treasury, but were independent of it. Moreover, although the resulting Dawes Plan in April 1924 was largely drafted by Stamp, it had to present figures to which the French and Belgians would agree. Under the plan Germany was to pay £50 million for the first year (1924–5), rising in stages to £125 million by 1928–9, which was taken as the 'standard year'. However, annual payments would be adjusted if Germany's capacity to pay increased—an 'index of prosperity' was compiled for this purpose—or if the value of gold changed by 10 per cent or more from the 1928 value. The purpose of this last provision was to maintain a stable burden in terms of the goods and services that would have to be exported in order to effect transfers of reparations, which were to be paid in gold marks. Germany also undertook to return to a gold bullion standard, with the aid of an international loan.[121]

Treasury reactions to the Dawes Plan were unfavourable. Niemeyer called it the Americans' 'beastly plan' and took comfort from the thought that it was

[118] Grigg, *Prejudice and Judgement*, 98–9.   [119] O'Halpin, *Head of the Civil Service*, 125.
[120] Middlemas and Barnes, *Baldwin*, 184.
[121] For Stamp's part in drafting the report see Jones, *Josiah Stamp*, 209–31; McFadyean, *Recollected in Tranquillity*, 92–4.

'probably to a large extent a façade' and would not last.[122] Germany's payments still seemed to Treasury officials to be too high, and Stamp himself would have preferred them to be lower. Nevertheless, the new Labour government decided to accept the plan, as a means of achieving an end to the Ruhr occupation. Following an international conference in London, in which the Prime Minister, Ramsay MacDonald, and the Chancellor, Snowden, played a prominent part, the new reparations schedule was adopted in August.

Settlement of the reparations issue opened the way for a settlement of France's war debts, but negotiations were delayed by the British general election in October 1924. The point to be made here is that Treasury officials appear to have been decreasingly sympathetic towards France in the post-war period. Initially the Treasury had been understanding about French reluctance to discuss repayment of her war debt to Britain, and, like the Foreign Office, had regarded the debt as something to be held in reserve as a diplomatic bargaining counter. However, as Fisher's comments quoted above indicate, there was a less accommodating spirit in the Treasury from 1923. Tensions over the Ruhr provide some explanation for this change, but the fact that the French were paying no interest on their war debt, while they could find money for armaments and for loans to allies in Eastern Europe, also hardened Treasury attitudes. Snowden complained during the London conference on the Dawes Plan that he had to raise income tax of 8d. (3.3p) in the pound to pay interest on the French debt, and made no effort to disguise his contempt for French policy.[123] Labour's electoral defeat in 1924 denied him the immediate opportunity of expressing his feelings in diplomacy, but he was to have another chance in 1929 and 1930.

Germany was only one, although the most important, victim of the monetary chaos that prevailed in central and eastern Europe after the war. In some countries, notably Austria, starvation threatened. In November 1919, at a time when sterling was falling against the dollar, the Chancellor, Austen Chamberlain, noted that it would be inconsistent to extend credits to Europe while attempting to deflate sterling. Consequently, British aid to Austria in 1920 took the form of a scheme worked out by Bradbury and Treasury officials for a joint loan with the United States and other countries, with Britain's contribution being limited in 1920 to £10 million. In 1922 Britain provided a further loan of £2.25 million and participated in an international guarantee of a £22 million loan raised by the Austrian government. In both cases, Blackett was prepared to urge the Chancellors concerned, Chamberlain and Horne, to take what, from a Treasury point of view, was a generous attitude to Austria's needs. Moreover, Austria's currency reform, involving a return to the gold standard in 1923, owed much to

---

[122] Niemeyer memorandum, 14 Apr., and letter, 20 Aug. 1924, cited in Stephen A. Schuker, *The End of French Predominance in Europe: The Financial Crisis of 1924 and the Adoption of the Dawes Plan* (Chapel Hill, NC, 1976), 195, 379–80.

[123] See Arthur Turner, *The Cost of War: British Policy on French War Debts, 1919–1931* (Brighton, 1998), chs. 2–5.

advice from Blackett and Niemeyer, working closely with Norman at the Bank of England and with the League of Nations Financial Committee.[124]

The stabilization of the Austrian and German public finances and currencies represented important steps towards a restoration of the international gold standard. Sound finance included a regime of balanced budgets. Britain herself had balanced her budget only by a more rigorous economy in public expenditure than was common in Europe. It is to this aspect of the Treasury's work that we now turn.

THE CABINET AND TREASURY CONTROL OF EXPENDITURE

The Haldane Committee on the machinery of government had assigned to the Cabinet the function of 'continuous co-ordination and delimitation of the activities of the several Departments of State'.[125] This might have been possible if, as Haldane had wished, the Cabinet had been kept small, but instead of the five to seven ministers, mostly without portfolio, of the War Cabinet, post-war Cabinets numbered over twenty, with most ministers being concerned to fight their departmental corners rather than to have a broad overview of policy. Inevitably Cabinet was a forum for bargaining, particularly between spending ministers and the Chancellor.

During the war a Cabinet Secretariat had been created to prepare agenda, circulate memoranda, and record minutes and conclusions, and the conclusions, when issued to departments, had the force of instructions. The Cabinet Secretariat, therefore, had a claim to be called the Prime Minister's Department or the Cabinet Department—at least that was the opinion of Sir Maurice Hankey, the Cabinet Secretary.[126] However, it was the Treasury that was described in the Haldane Report as 'the Department of the Prime Minister', as well as of the Chancellor of the Exchequer, with responsibility for 'supervising and controlling all the operations of central government, in so far as these affected the financial position'.[127] Responsibility for co-ordinating policy was thus shared between the Cabinet Secretariat and the Treasury.

The survival of the Cabinet Secretariat as an independent entity was not a foregone conclusion. Its funding down to 1921/2 was provided on the 'Treasury and Subordinate Departments Vote' and, although the Cabinet Secretariat had its own vote from 1922, Lloyd George was succeeded in October of that year by Bonar Law, who regarded the Cabinet Secretariat as a wartime creation which could well be dispensed with. Fisher promptly offered Hankey

---

[124] Hemery, 'Emergence of Treasury Influence', 378–91; Anne Orde, *British Policy and European Reconstruction after the First World War* (Cambridge, 1990), 131, 136, 145.

[125] *Report of the Machinery of Government Committee* (Cd. 9230), PP 1918, xii. 1, part I, para. 6.

[126] J. Turner, *Lloyd George's Secretariat* (Cambridge, 1980), 197.

[127] Cd. 9230, part II, paras 1 and 3.

the position of a fourth controller in the Treasury, with as free a hand as before, but Hankey successfully resisted the Treasury's embrace. Even so, according to Hankey, Fisher did not hide his belief that the Cabinet Secretariat should ultimately be absorbed by the Treasury.[128] That did not happen, but the Cabinet Secretariat's establishment was kept small (about a dozen members, most of them working for the Cabinet's Committee of Imperial Defence) and, although Hankey's personal influence on ministers was great, Fisher could reasonably claim that the Treasury was the central department of government. Indeed, Hankey himself, speaking in the House of Lords in 1942, said that 'the Treasury is, and must remain, the central department of government because finance is the one link that runs right through government departments'.[129]

In Fisher's view the Treasury was charged 'with the responsibility of taking a bird's eye view of the position and with providing financial and economic advice and criticism'.[130] More succinctly, he claimed that the Treasury was 'concerned with everything'.[131] As already noted, the Cabinet agreed in August 1919 not to consider proposals involving expenditure until the Treasury had approved them or the minister concerned had given notice of his intention to appeal—the point being that the Treasury needed time in which to consider proposals from all angles and to brief the Chancellor. This decision had to be renewed several times and was made more comprehensive in April 1924, when, at Fisher's instigation, it was laid down that all memoranda, draft Bills, and other items of the Cabinet agenda would be sent to the Cabinet Secretariat for circulation only after their subject matter had been fully examined between the departments from which they originated and the Treasury, and any other department concerned.[132]

Given that the Haldane Committee included a former Financial Secretary of the Treasury, Montagu, who had experienced the breakdown of Treasury control over war-related expenditure in 1914, and a former Permanent Secretary of the Treasury, Murray, it is not surprising that the Haldane Report endorsed Treasury control with the words that 'on the whole, experience seems to show that the interests of the taxpayer cannot be left to the spending departments'. However, in passages apparently drafted by another member, Sir Robert Morant—whose experience as head of a spending department had led him to dislike the manner in which the Treasury exercised its control—the Haldane Report also stated that 'when once a particular policy has been adopted by the Government or by Parliament it is clearly the duty of the Chancellor of the Exchequer to provide the funds necessary for its execution'.[133] Unfortunately

[128] Stephen Roskill, *Hankey, Man of Secrets*, vol. ii (1972), 310–20.
[129] 125 HL Deb., 5s., 1942–3, col. 266.
[130] 'Proposals Involving Public Expenditure: Consultation with the Treasury before Submission to the Cabinet', by Fisher, 26 Mar. 1923, T160/639/F6064.
[131] Fisher to Chancellor of the Exchequer and Prime Minister, 7 Apr. 1924, ibid.
[132] T160/639/F6064.   [133] Cd. 9230, Part II, paras. 12–13.

the Report did not—and perhaps could not—say what the duty of the Chancellor was when the Cabinet adopted conflicting policies of economy in government expenditure and expensive schemes of social reconstruction. Ministers may have believed in 1919 that economies in administration alone would be enough, but Fisher made clear to Lloyd George that 'the big money is, of course, in policy'.[134] There were bound to be conflicts between spending departments and the Treasury so long as the Cabinet failed to reconcile contradictory policies.

Treasury control over expenditure could be achieved in three different ways: Finance Department could set limits within which spending departments' Estimates must be brought unless ministers were prepared to increase taxation; Supply Services Department could examine the Estimates in detail, suggest reductions, and brief the Chancellor if there were an interdepartmental dispute, and finally Establishments Department could limit a spending department's activities by controlling the numbers of its officials. Treasury officials had definite ideas in 1919 on where economies in expenditure might be achieved by changes in policy, but political circumstances made it impossible to achieve these economies immediately after the war.[135]

The largest economies that could be achieved lay in the area of defence, but it was not until 1922/3 that the international situation was sufficiently settled to allow expenditure to be brought down to the level suggested by the Treasury. The next most promising targets for economy were subsidies for railways (£60 million), coal (£26½ million), and bread (£50 million).[136] However, for political reasons, subsidies could not be eliminated at a stroke. Moreover, contrary to official forecasts, food prices remained high for over a year after the war and the bread subsidy was not eliminated until 1921. As regards the cost of administration, Fisher thought that departments like the Ministry of Munitions, which had been created during the war, should be wound up, with the exception of those engaged on an inevitably continuing service, like the Ministry of Pensions. The Ministry of Munitions, or the Ministry of Supply, as it had been renamed in January 1919, was wound up in 1921. On the other hand, the Ministry of Labour, which had seemed to the Treasury to be another candidate for abolition, was continued once it was realized that the extension of Unemployment Insurance in 1920, from covering 2 to 3 million workers in 1912 to over 12 million, provided enough work for an independent ministry.[137]

In general, decisions about major economies remained firmly in the hands of ministers, and Treasury officials exercised less influence than Whitehall

[134] Fisher to Lloyd George, 3 Sept. 1919, T171/170.

[135] These ideas are set out in Fisher to Lloyd George, 3 Sept. 1919, and 'Memorandum by the Treasury on National Expenditure', n.d., and 'Note by the Treasury on the National Balance Sheet', 14 Oct. 1919, all T171/170.

[136] 'Memorandum by the Treasury on National Expenditure', 20 Sept. 1919, CAB27/72.

[137] Rodney Lowe, *Adjusting to Democracy: The Role of the Ministry of Labour in British Politics, 1916–1939* (Oxford, 1986), 41; O'Halpin, *Head of the Civil Service*, 154.

demonology would suggest. Indeed, when Lloyd George decided to meet the political threat of the anti-waste campaign in 1921, he turned for suggestions on economies, not to the Treasury, but to a committee of businessmen, chosen by the Chancellor (Horne) and himself. This committee, known as the Geddes Committee, after its chairman, Sir Eric Geddes, a businessman whom Lloyd George had appointed as First Lord of the Admiralty during the war, was supplied with, and no doubt guided by, Treasury briefs. However, the Treasury was rightly suspicious that in the end politicians who had called for economy in general would oppose the detailed proposals for particular expenditure cuts. In the event, the Cabinet responded to the Geddes Committee's reports by fixing on compromise figures between the Committee's recommendations and the offers of spending departments, eventually endorsing only about £52 million of the recommended £87 million of cuts.[138]

TABLE 4.3. *Central Government Expenditure after the Geddes 'Axe' (£m.)*

	1921/2	1922/3	1923/4	1924/5
National debt (fixed charges, interest and 4.3 sinking funds)	332.3	324.0	347.3	357.2
Defence				
Army	95.1	45.4	43.6	44.8
Navy	80.8	56.2	52.6	55.6
Air Force	13.6	9.4	9.6	14.3
Total for defence	189.5	111.0	105.8	114.7
Social policy				
Education	53.7	47.4	46.3	46.6
Health				
(a) insurance	9.2	5.8	6.1	7.1
(b) services	4.4	3.6	3.2	3.2
Housing	9.1	8.0	8.3	9.1
Pensions				
(a) old-age	22.0	22.4	23.2	24.9
(b) war	95.8	80.6	72.6	69.9
Unemployment				
(a) insurance	7.8	12.0	12.8	13.1
(b) loans and grants for public works	3.8	2.3	3.0	3.5
Total for social policy	205.8	182.1	175.5	177.4

Source: Bernard Mallet and C. O. George, *British Budgets, 1921/22–1932/33* (1933), 556–9.

[138] McDonald, 'The Geddes Committee'. The committee's recommendations, which covered a multitude of items, both large and small, are to be found in its *First Interim Report* (Cmd. 1581), *Second Interim Report* (Cmd. 1582) and *Third Report of Committee on National Expenditure* (Cmd. 1589), PP 1922, ix. 1–456.

As Table 4.3 shows, the effects of the Geddes 'axe' of 1922 varied from department to department. It is, however, helpful to group policy into three areas: defence, social policy, and measures to deal with unemployment, including economic development of the Empire. In all three areas the Treasury had to question policy in order to achieve economies, or to prevent expenditure rising further.

DEFENCE POLICY

Fisher believed in 1919 that, if the success of the Allies in the war was to mark the end of militarism, it was not unreasonable to expect that the scale of Britain's defence services, both in personnel and equipment, should be less than before the war, even if the cost might be somewhat higher on account of higher prices and improved pay.[139] This general statement of principle was not easily interpreted, however: aircraft had developed dramatically since 1914, and, while there was some doubt about the continued independence of the Royal Air Force, which had been formed in 1918 out of the Royal Naval Air Service and the Army's Royal Flying Corps, there was no doubt about the continued need for a higher level of expenditure on aircraft than before the war. The scuttling of the German High Seas Fleet in 1919 reduced the Royal Navy's need for capital ships,[140] but technical developments during the war led the Admiralty to retain new types of warship, such as aircraft carriers, as well as more submarines in 1922 than in 1914. As for the army, Ireland and the Middle East required larger garrisons down to 1922 than before the war. In addition to these changes in circumstances, there was a natural tendency on the part of the defence services to retain part of their wartime increase in establishments, especially of officers, and the Geddes Committee had no doubt that both army and naval manpower was on a 'lavish scale' in 1922. In that year the manpower of all three services totalled 362,000, compared with 333,000 in 1914.[141]

The Geddes 'axe' fell with some severity on the armed forces, and total defence expenditure was reduced from £189.5 million in 1921/2 to £105.8 million in 1923/4. Even so, in 1923 the Air Ministry was able to persuade the Cabinet to approve an expansion programme, and the Admiralty had a similar success with its cruiser programme. Despite the advent of a Labour government committed to economy in 1924, the defence Estimates rose by £8.9 million to £114.7 million in 1924/5.

Historians for long commonly assumed that the Treasury held the 'whip hand' in disputes with the defence departments over proposals for expenditure,

---

[139] Fisher to Lloyd George, 3 Sept. 1919, T171/170.
[140] A category including battleships and equally large, but more lightly armoured, battle-cruisers.
[141] Cmd. 1581, ch. I, paras 1, 23; ch. II, para. 21.

as a result of a decision by the Cabinet in August 1919 that it should be assumed when preparing revised Estimates 'that the British Empire will not be engaged in any great war during the next ten years, and that no Expeditionary Force is required for this purpose'.[142] This 'Ten Year Rule', as it came to be called, was, in one form or another, to be the guiding principle of British defence policy until 1932, and gave the Treasury the opportunity to assert the primacy of financial policy. However, John Ferris has convincingly argued that, in the cases of the Admiralty and Air Ministry, it was only after 1924 that service policies came to be dominated by the Treasury.[143] As in other aspects of public expenditure, a general desire by the Cabinet for economy tended to be diminished when particular projects came to be discussed.

The Ten Year Rule itself was not drawn up by the Treasury, but was drafted by the Cabinet Secretary, Hankey, who was aware of Lloyd George's enthusiasm at the time for economy, and who was concerned that there should be a basis of policy upon which the service departments should work out their Estimates. The basis chosen was not very different from what had been suggested earlier by Churchill, who was both Secretary of State for War and Secretary of State for Air. Accepting the gravity of the financial situation, Churchill had proposed that the Cabinet give a ruling 'that the armed forces are not to prepare for war on a great scale within five years, and only to a limited extent for such a war within ten years'. He also suggested £200 million as a maximum for the defence services in 1920/1, at a time when the Treasury, as a 'pure guess', had pencilled in £350 million.[144] Later in August 1919 the Cabinet tentatively allotted £75 million to the post-war army and air force, and £60 million to the navy, but in the event it was not until 1922/3 that the services were brought within these limits.

Churchill himself was far from single-minded in the pursuit of economy. He devoted much of his time and energy in 1919 to promoting support for the Whites in the Russian civil war, and in September Lloyd George had to reprimand him for 'this obsession'. 'I again ask you to let Russia be', the Prime Minister wrote, 'and to concentrate your mind on the quite unjustifiable expenditure in France, at home and in the East, incurred by both the War Office and the Air Department. Some of the items could not possibly have been tolerated by you if you had given one-fifth of the thought to these matters which you devoted to Russia.'[145] Despite support from the Prime Minister, the Chancellor,

---

[142] War Cabinet 'A' Minutes, 15 Aug. 1919, cited in N. H. Gibbs, *Grand Strategy*, vol. i (1976), 3. The expression 'whiphand' is from Stephen Roskill, *Naval Policy between the Wars*, vol. i, *The Period of Anglo-American Antagonism, 1919–1929* (1968), 215.

[143] John Ferris, 'Treasury Control, the Ten Year Rule and British Service Policies, 1919–1924', *Hist. J.*, 30 (1987), 859–83, and id., *The Evolution of British Strategic Policy, 1919–26* (1989), ch. 2.

[144] W. S. Churchill, *Winston S. Churchill*, ed. M. Gilbert, vol. iv companion, part 2 (1977), 780, 784. Cf. 'Memorandum by the Treasury on the Financial Position and Future Prospects of this Country', 18 July 1919, appendix 2, T171/170.   [145] Churchill, op. cit., 869.

Austen Chamberlain, had for many months little success in curbing Churchill's policy of assisting the Whites by sending them 'surplus stores' with personnel to 'supervise' them or to give instruction, at a cost of about £100 million in 1919.

The War Office intended to reproduce the pre-war army, at a normal annual cost estimated in 1920 at £62 million.[146] The army had no obvious contingency to prepare for, however, apart from imperial policing, given the Cabinet's ruling that no expeditionary force would be required for a great war for ten years, and that there were ample stocks of munitions. It thus proved possible for the Treasury to bring War Office expenditure down to about £45 million in 1922/3, following a Cabinet decision at the end of 1920 to reduce overseas commitments by evacuating Persia and halving the garrisons for Egypt, Palestine, and Iraq.[147] The Cabinet accepted most of the Geddes Committee's recommendations in respect of army manpower: 22 infantry battalions were disbanded, against 28 recommended, and 7 battalions were withdrawn from overseas, against 9 recommended. Moreover, between 1922 and 1925 the War Office staff was reduced from 4,114 to 2,561 without, as Brian Bond has remarked, any marked decrease in efficiency.[148]

The Treasury's success in holding War Office expenditure below the 1922/3 level until 1936 reflected government policy. By way of contrast, Air Ministry expenditure began to recover in 1923 from the very low levels reached as a result of the Geddes axe, rising from £9.6 million in 1923/4 to £14.3 million in 1924/5. The Chief of Air Staff, Hugh Trenchard, was able to secure the Cabinet's support for the development of a strategic bombing force because of uncertainty about future relations with France, and because public opinion expected equality with French air power. Even Barstow had to advise Snowden not to challenge the RAF's 'home defence' programme in 1924, on the grounds that such action would inflame public opinion still further.[149] In 1922 Lloyd George's Government approved a plan for a Home Defence Air Force of 266 first-line and 302 second-line aircraft, and in 1923 Bonar Law's Cabinet increased the planned first-line strength to 600 first-line aircraft.

Fisher rightly believed that the French air threat was much exaggerated by the Air Ministry.[150] Even so, the Treasury was powerless to make an effective challenge to the Air Ministry's programme on its strategic merits, partly because in 1924 Trenchard withheld information which pointed to the fact that the French did not intend to create a strategic bombing force that could threaten Britain. It was not until 1925, once Anglo-French relations had improved, that the Treasury was able to slow down the rate of increase in Air Ministry

[146] Churchill, op. cit., 1030–1.   [147] Cabinet minutes, 8 Dec. 1920, CAB23/20.

[148] Brian Bond, *British Military Policy between the Two World Wars* (Oxford, 1980), 26–7.

[149] Barstow to Chancellor, 15 Feb. 1924, T161/228/S23285; John Ferris, 'The Theory of a "French Air Menace", Anglo-French Relations and the British Home Defence Air Force Programmes of 1921–25', *J. of Strategic Stud.*, 10 (1987), 62–83.

[150] Minute by Fisher, 20 Feb. 1923, T161/184/S16984.

expenditure. Until then the Treasury's only consolation was, as Barstow had predicted, the inevitable lags in the delivery of equipment, the construction of bases, and the training of men, which prevented the Air Ministry spending money as quickly as it had hoped to do.[151]

Reductions in Admiralty expenditure were the result of Cabinet policy and international diplomacy rather than of Treasury control. As before 1914, the Admiralty was self-confident in its dealings with the Treasury, or any other department. When, in 1923, a subcommittee of the Committee of Imperial Defence recommended that the Fleet Air Arm should be controlled by the Air Ministry, several members of the Board of Admiralty threatened to resign. The Admiralty produced a memorandum claiming sole authority for all things relating to the efficiency of the navy, leading Fisher, with typical exaggeration, to advise the Prime Minister (Baldwin) that the Admiralty was claiming to be independent of the authority of the Cabinet.[152] The Admiralty was, of course, bound by Cabinet decisions, and was unable to regain control of the Fleet Air Arm until 1937.

On the other hand, the Admiralty showed ingenuity in interpreting Cabinet decisions. In particular, in the course of 1919/20 the Cabinet laid down that the British navy should not be inferior to that of any other power, but this 'one-power standard' was interpreted six different ways between 1919 and 1925, each interpretation pointing towards a different naval policy.[153] The discussions between the Treasury and the Admiralty centred mainly, but not exclusively, on the new construction programme, and in the early 1920s a one-power standard implied a considerable programme of capital ships incorporating wartime experience, to match those under construction in the United States. In the absence of an agreement with the Americans on arms limitation, the Chancellor, Austen Chamberlain, was forced to agree to naval Estimates of just under £80 million for 1921/2, compared with the £60 million that the Cabinet's Finance Committee had proposed as a maximum. Matters went differently in 1922, because by then Britain, the United States, and Japan had agreed at the Washington Conference to limit their naval armaments, with Britain and the United States having equal numbers of capital ships, and Britain's new construction being limited to two such vessels. As a result, the Cabinet was able to accept the Geddes Committee's recommendations that the navy's Estimates be reduced from £81 million to £65 million.[154] Further economies and underspending during the year brought the navy's demands on the Exchequer down to £56 million.

[151] Ferris, op. cit., 71, 77–8.
[152] Fisher to Prime Minister, 30 July 1923, and Admiralty memorandum, 25 July 1923, Baldwin papers 2/237–8 and 2/243–4, Cambridge University Library.
[153] Ferris, 'Treasury Control', 861–2, 871.
[154] McDonald 'Formulation of British Public Expenditure Policy', 442, notes that the largest single cut, of about £10 million, was decided by the outcome of the Washington conference.

Normally the Treasury was unable to challenge naval policy effectively, and had to rely, as before 1914, on financial arguments and on piecemeal criticism for economies. Some success was achieved with the latter, notably a reduction in the Admiralty's plans for oil reserves and storage. The decision in March 1924 by the Labour government to cancel the Singapore naval base that had been approved in 1921, was a major defeat for the Admiralty but, like reductions in capital ships after the Washington treaty, it reflected foreign policy rather than Treasury influence. The defeat proved to be temporary as the Conservatives revived the scheme when they returned to power in November 1924.[155]

SOCIAL POLICY

In social policy the equivalent to the Ten Year Rule was the decision of the Cabinet in December 1920 that, except with fresh Cabinet authority, schemes involving expenditure not yet in operation were to remain in abeyance.[156] It will be noted that this decision came sixteen months after the Ten Year Rule, reflecting the reluctance of minsters to abandon pledges of a 'land fit for heroes'. Nor did the Cabinet's decision of December 1920 represent an unqualified success for the Treasury: existing schemes of social reconstruction were continued and actual reductions in expenditure did not take place until 1922/3, as a result of the 'Geddes axe'. Moreover, the cuts in housing expenditure had been made good by 1924/5, although it is true that central government expenditure on education and on health insurance remained below the 1921/2 level for the rest of the decade (see Table 4.3).

The Treasury warned the Cabinet in July 1919 that the raising of large sums, either by the state or by the local authorities, for housing would compete with the demands of trade and industry for capital, and thus tend to force up interest rates.[157] This view was shared by Keynes, who thought that:

it would be absolutely fatal to finance the Housing scheme on an inflationist basis. In present circumstances increased building can only take place by diverting labour and materials from other employments. It is foolish to suppose that a great housing scheme can be superimposed on the present industrial situation.[158]

In addition, the Chancellor, Austen Chamberlain, had party-political reasons for opposing the creation of a new class of tenant voter. Nevertheless, as noted in Chapter 3, political imperatives in favour of housing were overwhelmingly in favour of Addison, the Liberal Minister of Health, in 1919, and Treasury

[155] Roskill, *Naval Policy*, i. 290–1, 420–1, 448–9.

[156] Cabinet minutes, 8 Dec. 1920, CAB23/23.

[157] 'Memorandum by the Treasury on the Financial Position and Future Prospects of This Country', 18 July 1919, T171/170.

[158] Notes by Mr Keynes of interview with the Chancellor of the Exchequer on 4 Feb. 1920, T172/1384.

subsidies had been promised to enable local authorities to meet housing needs in their areas. In presenting his Housing and Town Planning Bill in April Addison told Parliament that the cessation of building during the war had resulted in a shortfall of 350,000 working-class houses, and in addition there were 370,000 houses that were either unfit for human habitation or seriously defective. A huge imbalance between demand for, and supply of, building materials and labour was thereby created, and, in the absence of controls, prices and wages both rose rapidly. In the summer of 1919 the average contract price of a local authority house was £740; by the autumn of 1920 this had increased to about £930.[159]

The only check that the Chancellor was able to apply was in his own field of finance. Backed by the Cabinet's Finance Committee, he frustrated Addison's proposal in December 1919 that local authorities be empowered to issue housing bonds paying interest of 6 per cent. Chamberlain successfully insisted on a rate of 5½ per cent, which, at a time when Bank rate had recently been raised to 6 per cent, held very little attraction to investors. Monetary policy, rather than detailed control of the Ministry of Health's Estimates, continued to be the Treasury's most effective weapon down to 1921. Chamberlain claimed that the housing programme would be best expedited not by making local authority borrowing easier but by bringing pressure to bear on trade unions to accept dilution of building labour, and to bring in large numbers of unskilled workers, particularly ex-servicemen.[160] Addison, however, was unsuccessful in reaching agreement with the unions.

Rising costs—brought about by contractors' price rings and trade unionists' restrictive practices—exposed Addison to increasing criticism from the anti-waste lobby, thereby strengthening the Treasury's hand. In November 1920 Chamberlain suggested to the Cabinet's Finance Committee that the number of subsidized houses to be built by local authorities should be strictly limited. At the time the Chancellor wished to allocate something between £250 million and £300 million for debt redemption in his budget for 1921/2, and he was seeking economies in all forms of expenditure. He pointed out that, if the Ministry of Health were to proceed with its programme, the annual cost of subsidies to local authorities would be £25 million a year for sixty years, and suggested a limit of 160,000 houses. Addison admitted that a figure of 800,000 houses, which had emerged from surveys by local authorities of housing needs in their areas, was a highly inflated one, and said he would prefer to work with his ministry's original figure, that is 300,000 houses. A compromise of 250,000 houses, to be sanctioned by June 1922, was agreed in early March 1921 shortly before Addison was removed by Lloyd George from the Ministry of Health.

[159] 114 HC Deb., 5s, 1919, cols. 1713–14, 1728–9; Marian Bowley, *Housing and the State, 1919–1944* (1945), 30.

[160] K. Morgan and J. Morgan, *Portrait of a Progressive: The Political Career of Christopher, Viscount Addison* (Oxford, 1980), 108–10, 113, 123, 125.

At the end of June, however, the question was reopened, and the Finance Committee agreed that, in view of the difficult financial position, the government's housing policy should be suspended, with an immediate end to subsidies to private builders, and a limit of 176,000 for local authority houses to be built under the 1919 Act. This decision, which was endorsed by the Cabinet, antedated the appointment of the Geddes Committee, and may fairly be described as a result of Treasury influence, but that influence was exercised through considerations of financial policy, and not detailed arguments by the Supply Services Department. The Finance Committee explicitly stated that its decision had been taken 'not on merits, but on financial considerations only'.[161]

The policy of subsidizing housing had indeed been only suspended and not terminated. In January 1923, when the Conservatives were in office, the Financial Secretary of the Treasury, John Hills, told a Cabinet Committee on Housing Policy that in the end the government would not get more houses by subsidizing local authorities and private enterprise than they would get without subsidies. Wage rates in the building industry, he believed, were higher than in comparable trades, and would only come down if there were no subsidy. This argument was weakened, however, by his admission that the Treasury could find money, and the Committee decided, on political grounds, that subsidies must be offered so long as there were rent controls that prevented landlords charging economic rents.[162] These controls could only gradually be removed as the shortage of working-class housing was reduced, and both the housing acts of Neville Chamberlain, the Conservative Minister of Health, in 1923 and John Wheatley, his Labour successor, in 1924 included subsidies, which were not finally terminated until 1934, and even thereafter there were Exchequer grants for slum clearance.

Education policy likewise suggests that the Treasury's arguments on the merits of spending proposals were not a decisive influence, and were certainly less important than arguments relating to financial policy.[163] Education was the largest single item of civil expenditure in the budget, after pensions, but it was difficult for the Treasury to exercise detailed control. Under the 1918 Education Act local education authorities in England and Wales were entitled to receive grants of not less than half their expenditure that was recognized by the Board of Education as within their statutory duties. In 1921/2 some 85 per cent of the Board of Education's vote was for such grants, which could only be reduced if ministers consented to changes in education policy or to reductions in teachers' salaries.

The Board was determined not to allow political pressures for economy in public expenditure to halt what it considered to be the normal growth of

[161] Finance Committee, 30 June 1921, CAB27/71.

[162] Cabinet Committee on Housing Policy minutes, 1 Jan. 1923, CAB27/208.

[163] What follows is based mainly upon McDonald, 'Formulation of British Public Expenditure Policy', 361–74, 382–96.

educational provision, and it was not until late 1922 that the teachers could be persuaded to accept a 5 per cent cut in salaries. Even so, owing to the fall in prices, teachers' salaries were still substantially higher in real terms after the cut than in 1920. The Treasury's suggestion in 1921 that the school entry age be raised from five to six years was not acted upon, almost certainly because such a move would be politically unpopular. There is no evidence of a reduction in existing educational services after the Geddes axe, the decline in the Board of Education's vote after 1921/2 being offset by the ending of temporary post-war provision for ex-servicemen, by a fall in prices, and by a reduction in the number of children of school age. The development of continuation schools which, under the 1918 Education Act, were to provide part-time education for 14- to 16-year-olds, was halted by the Cabinet's Finance Committee in December 1920, and this decision has been described as 'one of the most devastating mistakes of English twentieth-century education'.[164] However, the main opposition to continuation schools seems to have come from the powerful industrialists' lobby, and the money required for the scheme, £300,000 in 1921/2, could have been found had there been political pressure for it.[165] Even when the hunt for economies was at its height, political arguments could outweigh financial ones: for example, the Chancellor agreed in February 1921 to find extra money for university teachers, on the grounds that it would be dangerous to drive them 'into the ranks of Bolshevism'.[166]

The pattern of financial restrictions halting expansion of social services, but achieving no real reduction in existing provision in existing services, was repeated elsewhere. The approved societies which ran the National Health Insurance scheme were unable to resist reductions in Exchequer contributions, with the result that the development of the scheme was restricted.[167] Unemployment Insurance, however, was much harder to control. An Act of August 1920 expanded the scope of the original 1911 scheme to cover most industrial workers, just before the onset of the 1921/2 depression, and for political reasons unemployment benefit continued to be paid to workers who, if the scheme had been run on strict actuarial lines, would have been thrown upon the Poor Law. The shortfall in contributions had to be met by the Exchequer, which thus saw expenditure on unemployment increase even as depression was reducing the tax-base, thereby making it harder to balance the budget. For all that, in the early 1920s the Treasury saw that unemployment was the lesser of two evils—the other evil being the creation of employment through public expenditure. As the Chancellor of the Exchequer, Horne, explained to his ministerial colleagues in September 1921, unemployment insurance was much cheaper

---

[164] Michael Sanderson, 'Education and Economic Decline, 1890–1980s', *Oxford Rev. Econ. Policy*, 4/1 (1988), 43.   [165] L. Andrews, *The Education Act, 1918* (1976), 49–54, 72–3.
[166] Finance Committee minutes, 17 Feb. 1921, CAB27/71.
[167] Noelle Whiteside, 'Private Agencies for Public Purposes: Some New Perspectives on Policy Making in Health Insurance between the Wars', *J. Soc. Policy*, 12 (1983), 165–94.

than relief works even if the benefits were given without any previous contribution from the insured.[168]

High unemployment was believed by the Treasury in the early 1920s to be a temporary phenomenon, which would be cured by reductions in prices and wages, and by a restoration of international trade through a return to the gold standard. Nor was the Treasury alone in its optimism. An expansion in exports in the latter part of 1922 led the Board of Trade to assume at the beginning of 1923 that by the end of that year the number of unemployed workers would have fallen from an average of over 2 million in the years 1921–2 to 750,000, a figure which, as Niemeyer observed, was 'not so very much above the pre-war average'. In the event these hopes were disappointed, and the average number of workers unemployed in the years 1923–4 was about 1.5 million.[169]

Unemployment had been expected after the war. In the autumn of 1919 the Ministry of Labour proposed that government departments should consult it before placing large contracts, so that the ministry could advise on the state of unemployment in the areas where the firms invited to tender were situated. The idea was that contracts should be awarded for up to 10 per cent above the lowest tender, if a firm was in an area of high unemployment. Predictably, the Treasury opposed a departure from the existing rule of public finance, whereby an accounting officer must normally accept the lowest tender, on the grounds that otherwise there would be a danger of favouritism and corruption.[170]

When large-scale unemployment arose in the winter of 1920–1 the means of providing work were very similar to those of the Edwardian period: public works organized by local authorities; the Development Fund; and the Road Fund. In December 1920 a semi-official body, the Unemployment Grants Committee, was appointed to administer a fund, initially of £3 million, for works of 'public utility' in areas certified by the Ministry of Labour to have serious unemployment. Grants were not to exceed 30 per cent of the wages bill of additional men employed. Typical schemes were for drainage, reservoirs, sewage works, and dock or harbour improvements, and the total cost of such schemes approved between December 1920 and March 1922 was £26,574,000, with a further £15,874,000 between March 1922 and June 1923. In contrast, the Development Fund, which was administered by the Treasury, had assets of £1.5 million, and disbursed less than £400,000 in 1922/3. The Road Fund, which

---

[168] Cabinet Committee on Unemployment minutes, 13 Sept. 1921, CAB27/114.

[169] Note by Niemeyer, 14 Feb. 1923, T176/11. Figures are for totals of unemployed workers, including those in uninsured occupations—see W. R. Garside, *British Unemployment, 1919–1939: A Study in Public Policy* (Cambridge, 1990), 5.

[170] Frederick Phillips to Barstow, 18 Nov. 1919, T1/12414/49744.

had been suspended during the war, but which was reconstituted in January 1921 under the direction of the Ministry of Transport, enjoyed a growing revenue from motor vehicle licences, and its disbursements, mainly grants to local authorities who were responsible for the maintenance and improvement of roads, rose from £5,214,000 in 1920/1 to £15,203,000 in 1924/5.[171] All this activity was very modest in relation to the scale of unemployment,[172] but for the Treasury there was always the danger that the principles of sound finance would be subverted, or that capital might be diverted from industry's or the Exchequer's needs.

In September 1921, despite the fact that the Cabinet had decided only the previous month on the appointment of the Geddes Committee to enquire into possible economies in expenditure, the Chancellor, Horne, agreed with his colleagues on the Cabinet's Unemployment Committee that more finance should be provided for public works. Shortly afterwards a deputation of Labour mayors travelled from London to the remote Scottish village of Gairloch, where Lloyd George was on holiday, to complain about inadequate government assistance to local authorities. The Prime Minister summoned the chairman of the Unemployment Committee, Sir Alfred Mond, together with the Minister of Labour, Thomas Macnamara, and the Financial Secretary of the Treasury, Hilton Young, to discuss unemployment, and Churchill (the Colonial Secretary), who happened to be at Gairloch, also took part. Ministers questioned the Treasury's orthodox ideas and Lloyd George asked Hilton Young to investigate the reactions of City men and industrialists to different ways in which inflationary finance might be applied to create employment.[173]

Hilton Young's enquiries were confined to five days in London, but he sent Dudley Ward, a banker who had served as a temporary official in the Treasury during the war, to Glasgow to sound out industrial opinion. (As Hilton Young remarked, 'industrial men being mostly provincial take longer to get at than financial men'.[174]) As might be expected, City opinion was hostile to Lloyd George's ideas for spending £250 million on capital investment and land settlement. Hilton Young himself wanted to make available the minimum amount of new money necessary to feed the unemployed. He was advised by Stamp that an open policy of inflation would lead to an immediate increase in prices, making the settlement of wage levels more difficult, although a lower real wage was essential to restarting the economy. Stamp did say that 'gradual and

[171] Ministry of Labour, *Final Report of the Unemployment Grants Committee* (Cmd. 4354), PP 1932–3, xv. 963; 'Treasury: Method of Accounting', T162/102/E12604/030; McDonald, 'Formulation of British Public Expenditure Policy', 399–403.

[172] See Susan Howson, 'Slump and Unemployment', in Roderick Floud and Donald McCloskey (eds.), *The Economic History of Britain since 1700* (1981), vol. ii. 280–1.

[173] For a fuller account of the Gairloch discussions and their aftermath see G. C. Peden, 'The Road to and from Gairloch: Lloyd George, Unemployment, Inflation and the "Treasury View" in 1921', *20th Cent. Brit. Hist.*, 4 (1993), 224–49.

[174] Hilton Young to Lloyd George, 27 Sept. 1921, LG papers, F/28/8/4.

unannounced' inflation would be helpful in this context, but Hilton Young's own view was that workers' collective bargaining was now so strong that wages would keep pace with prices and the burden of inflation would fall on fixed incomes and people with capital.[175]

Hilton Young returned to Gairloch accompanied by Ward, Walter Layton, the director of the Economic Section of the League of Nations, and Sir James Hope Simpson, a banker. Together they drafted proposals for state assistance to keep as many workers as possible engaged in their normal occupations. They recommended that the Treasury should guarantee interest and sinking funds on loans raised by local authorities, public utilities, or private enterprise for capital works that would be of 'ultimate benefit' to the community and provide employment, the money to be raised by non-inflationary borrowing from the non-bank public.[176]

The Finance Department of the Treasury was thrown on to the defensive by these proposals. In a classic statement of what came to be called the 'Treasury view', Niemeyer argued that:

Government spending cannot permanently increase employment. If the spending were properly funded, i.e. covered by taxation or by genuine borrowing, it would merely diminish private spending and thus decrease employment elsewhere.[177]

'Genuine borrowing' meant borrowing that transferred loanable funds in private hands to the government; borrowing which simply involved the banks creating more money would be inflationary and would undermine the government's financial policy. Niemeyer believed that the nation's capital should not be squandered on uneconomic schemes and that the best assistance the government could give to the unemployed, 'apart from the minimum to prevent starvation', was to reduce its expenditure and to repay its debts.[178]

It should be noted that at this time Keynes agreed with the Treasury's views on real wages and state-financed expenditure. He thought in 1923 that, with real wages approximately the same as in 1913, but output lower on account of reduced working hours, it was doubtful if the whole labour force could be employed, except at the top of periodic booms, without great improvements in productivity.[179] In November 1924 he wrote that:

A supply of *new* capital . . . can only come into existence in so far as those who have claims on the community's flow of income are willing to *defer* their claims, i.e. out of savings . . . The expenditure, on the production of *fixed* capital, of public money which has been

[175] Stamp to Hilton Young, and Hilton Young to Lloyd George, 28 Sept. 1921, Lloyd George papers, F/28/8/6(a) and F/28/8/5.
[176] 'Draft Proposals of Commander Hilton Young's Committee', 2 Oct. 1921, T172/1208.
[177] Quoted in Robert Skidelsky, 'Keynes and the Treasury View: The Case For and Against an Active Unemployment Policy, 1920–1939', in Wolfgang Mommsen (ed.), *The Emergence of the Welfare State in Britain and Germany* (1981), 171–2.
[178] Niemeyer to Chancellor of the Exchequer, 5 Oct. 1921, T172/1208.
[179] *JMK*, xix (part 1), 78–9.

raised by borrowing, can do nothing of itself to improve matters; and it may do actual harm if it diverts existing working capital away from the production of goods . . . [180]

Notwithstanding the Treasury (and Keynes's) view, politicians felt that they had to be seen to be doing something about unemployment. As a result of the Gairloch deliberations Horne offered in October to find another £10 million for relief works for the unemployed, a sum which was increased to £13 million in December. The major innovation, however, was the Cabinet's decision, against Treasury advice, to make available £25 million under the Trade Facilities Act of November 1921 to guarantee the payment of interest and principal of public or private loans for projects such as railway extensions or electrification, if these were calculated to promote employment in the United Kingdom. Ministers had considered a sum of £50 million for this purpose, but accepted the advice of the Governor of the Bank of England that £25 million was the maximum capital sum that could be raised on the market.[181]

The Cabinet also decided in October to help export trades by amending the Overseas Trade Act, under which the Board of Trade was authorized to guarantee commercial trade bills drawn by British exporters to designated countries, up to a maximum of £26 million at any one time. The Treasury disliked the use of public funds to finance trade, on the grounds that it was likely that commercial banks would take all the good risks and leave the government with all the bad ones. Niemeyer thought that uncertainty about exchange rates, leading to uncertainty on the part of foreign importers as to the cost in local currencies of British goods, was a greater obstacle to trade than lack of credit, and was therefore extremely sceptical about the efficacy of the scheme.[182] Nevertheless, in October 1921 the Cabinet decided that the proportion of risk covered by the guarantees should be increased and that the scheme should be extended to all countries, including the Empire.

The Trade Facilities Act also seemed to offer the prospect of increasing trade with the Empire.[183] The Colonial Office had been making proposals for increased expenditure on the economic development of the Empire since Lord Milner had become Secretary of State in January 1919, with Leo Amery as his Under-Secretary, but the Treasury had severely limited the finance available, on the grounds that Britain's capital resources were required for reconstruction at home. Following the Gairloch discussions on unemployment, Churchill, who had replaced Milner in February 1921, argued that the Treasury should assist the Colonial Office to increase loans for colonial development, and the Cabinet agreed that colonies should be allowed to apply for assistance under the Trade Facilities Act. However, the Treasury laid down that no scheme should be

[180] *JMK*, xiii. 19–23.   [181] Cabinet minutes, 17 Oct. 1921, CAB23/27.
[182] Niemeyer to Chancellor of the Exchequer, 5 Oct. 1921, T172/1208.
[183] What follows is based mainly on Stephen Constantine, *The Making of British Colonial Development Policy, 1914–1940* (1984), 55–6, 64–71, 89–114.

accepted unless there was a reasonable prospect that the guarantee would not be needed, and none of the schemes put forward by the Colonial Office under the 1921 Act was successful.

Continued low levels of exports and high unemployment resulted in a new Cabinet Trade Policy Committee being set up in July 1922, with Amery as the Colonial Office representative, although he had been appointed Financial Secretary at the Admiralty three months earlier. Amery persuaded the committee to accept two ambitious schemes for consideration by Cabinet: that the British government should pay for three to five years the whole or part of the interest on loans to be raised for new works, and that, where raising a public loan would be difficult, the British government itself should lend the capital required. Horne blocked the latter suggestion in Cabinet in August, but agreement was reached on payment of the whole or part of the interest charges for three years on loans; on raising to £50 million the maximum amount of loans to be guaranteed under the Trade Facilities Act; and on extending the operations of the Act to November 1923. However, in the interests of economy, the provision for meeting interest charges for the first three years of a loan was deleted from the draft bill that became the Trade Facilities Act of 1922. The new Chancellor, Baldwin, had warned that reductions in expenditure were necessary if the budget were to be balanced without increased taxation, and had adopted the Treasury's dictum that 'money taken for Government purposes is money taken away from trade, and borrowing will thus tend to depress trade and increase unemployment'.[184]

Meanwhile, there had been a similar pattern of Treasury opposition and very limited concessions in relation to subsidized emigration. In December 1920 the Cabinet endorsed the recommendations of its Unemployment Committee that up to £150,000 should be spent to encourage emigration to the Empire as a means of relieving abnormal unemployment in the coming winter, and, for the longer term, that the Colonial Office should open negotiations with dominion governments to prepare a large-scale, jointly financed, scheme of assisted emigration. Amery had already supervised the drafting of an Empire Settlement Bill, which he planned as part of a long-term development strategy, and his ideas were discussed with dominion representatives in 1921. Treasury officials did not believe that subsidized land settlement in the Empire would do much to help the urban unemployed in Britain, and they feared that the Exchequer would be pressed to provide capital for settling emigrants, thereby reducing the funds available for domestic investment. They hoped the Geddes Committee would kill the idea, but the Colonial Office was strongly supported by the Board of Trade and the Ministry of Labour, as well as by political pressure from Australia, and the Chancellor, Horne, had to let the matter go to Cabinet in December 1921. When the Geddes Committee gave qualified approval to cautious

---

[184] Middlemas and Barnes, *Baldwin*, 127.

spending on Empire settlement the Treasury knew it had to concede the principle of a subsidy, but successfully reduced the amount to be provided under the
Empire Settlement Act of 1922 from £5 million a year to £1.5 million in the first
year and £3 million a year for fourteen further years. Moreover, the interests of
the British taxpayer were protected by the fact that the Colonial Office could
meet no more than half of the costs of grants or loans for migration, development or land settlement, and each grant or loan was to be subject to Treasury
consent.[185]

The Bonar Law and Baldwin governments of 1922–4 contained ministers,
Philip Lloyd-Greame (the President of the Board of Trade), and Amery, now
First Lord of the Admiralty, as well as the new Colonial Secretary, the Duke of
Devonshire, who saw the Empire as a long-term solution to Britain's loss of
overseas markets in Europe. In February 1923 the Cabinet was presented with a
plan whereby the Colonial Secretary should have up to £2 million a year for ten
years to use at his discretion to pay the whole or part of the interest on loans
raised by colonies, or to lend capital at cheap rates, for development projects.
Amery urged that the figure should be raised to £5 million. In response,
Niemeyer pointed out that half the money made available under the Empire
Settlement Act, and most of the money available for guarantees under the
Trade Facilities Act, remained unused for lack of good schemes. He advised that
the Colonial Office lacked 'City knowledge or connections', and would be 'at
the mercy of company promoters with bags of wild oats' if the Colonial Secretary were freed from Treasury control. His fundamental objection, however,
remained that colonial development would divert capital needed to make
British industry more competitive in world markets.[186] Thus advised, the Chancellor, Baldwin, offered to find £250,000 a year to pay half the interest charges
for five years on loans raised by colonies for purchases of equipment in Britain
over the next two years, but this offer was rejected by Devonshire on the
grounds that it was worthless for the poor colonies and unnecessary for the
richer ones.

Undeterred, Lloyd-Greame put forward a scheme in March 1923 for £2 million a year, to be made available to advance part or the whole of the interest on
capital for development projects, in the dominions as well as the colonies, for up
to ten years. Niemeyer advised the Chancellor to limit the scheme to £1 million
a year, to meet half the interest for five years on loans raised by the dominions
for purchases of capital goods in Britain, and to find the money by diverting
£3 million which had been voted under the Empire Settlement Act. Since
Baldwin was Prime Minister as well as Chancellor in the summer of 1923,
the Treasury was in a particularly strong position, and the scheme that was
approved by an Imperial Economic Conference in November followed

[185] Ian M. Drummond, *Imperial Economic Policy, 1917–1939: Studies in Expansion and Protection* (1974),
67–82.   [186] Niemeyer memorandum, 14 Feb. 1923, T176/11.

Niemeyer's proposals rather than Lloyd-Greame's, excepting only that the maximum grant was for three-quarters rather than half of the interest charges.

Hostility to colonial development did not imply that the Treasury took a more relaxed view of development schemes at home. In 1923 the Treasury rejected a suggestion that the Road Fund might borrow to support projects for the unemployed, pointing out that a loan for this purpose would compete with the needs of the Exchequer and industry. The Treasury was also concerned with value for money, and urged that road expenditure should be concentrated on small schemes, such as rounding off corners or widening bottlenecks, which would be of immediate benefit to road users, and which would provide work throughout the country, rather than, as the Ministry of Transport would have preferred, on relatively few ambitious major works which were remote from where the unemployed lived and which could not be completed for some years to come.[187]

The Treasury was even more concerned when confronted with a proposal for expenditure that would not produce an economic asset like a road or harbour. In October 1923 Amery, as First Lord of the Admiralty, suggested in Cabinet that the construction of cruisers and other warships should be accelerated to provide jobs in shipyards. Contrary to Cabinet procedures agreed in 1919, he did so without having the financial implications discussed first with the Treasury, and the Chancellor, Neville Chamberlain, seems to have given the idea his general approval. What particularly alarmed Treasury officials was Amery's intention that the construction programme should be financed by borrowing under a Naval Works Act of the kind that Asquith had denounced and discontinued in 1906. Barstow and Niemeyer pointed out that warships were not capital assets, or even permanent works, and that the repercussions on the government's credit would be serious if it did not pay for current expenditure out of revenue. Chamberlain himself noted how the ministers responsible for the Air Ministry and War Office had immediately claimed similar rights to finance expenditure out of loans, and accepted Niemeyer's advice that the only weapon the Chancellor had to secure economy was pressure from the taxpayer, a weapon that would be blunted if loans became available to finance every kind of expenditure.[188] It was agreed, therefore, that the naval construction should be included in the Admiralty's Estimates in the usual way, and in the event Amery's programme was reduced by Snowden when he became Chancellor.

Balanced budgets and the Treasury view about capital expenditure from loans were both ways of limiting politicians' scope for expenditure. Both served to preserve financial confidence in public finance. The Treasury view, although based upon orthodox economics, was very much an example of *political* economy.

[187] Treasury letter to Ministry of Transport, 16 Jan. 1923, and Alfred Hurst, 'Unemployment Road Schemes', 23 Jan. 1923, T161/202/S18957/1.

[188] Barstow to Chancellor, 23 Oct., Niemeyer to Chancellor, 26 Oct., Chamberlain to Amery, 26 Oct. 1923, T161/217/S21914.

THE TREASURY AND WHITEHALL

It remains to be considered how far Treasury control over the Civil Service was used to influence policy. Great controversy was aroused by the decision in 1919 to recognize the Permanent Secretary of the Treasury as Head of the Civil Service.[189] The Permanent Secretary of the Treasury had been referred to in semi-official documents in the 1870s and 1880s as 'Head of the Civil Service' but, as noted in Chapter 2, in 1913 a Treasury memorandum for the Royal Commission on the Civil Service referred to the Permanent Secretary only as 'ex officio the doyen of the permanent officials of the Civil Service'. Bradbury noted in August 1919 that the Permanent Secretary's function of advising the Prime Minister with regard to Civil Service patronage and honours had 'of late years fallen into desuetude' and advised that 'human nature . . . being what it is, it is vastly important to the prestige and influence of the Treasury that that function be restored'.[190] This advice was accepted by Austen Chamberlain and Lloyd George, and a Treasury circular of 15 September 1919 informed Whitehall that the Permanent Secretary of the Treasury would act as Head of the Civil Service and advise the Prime Minister on Civil Service appointments and decorations.

Questions were asked in Parliament about whether a civil servant should have as much influence as Fisher seemed to possess. Fisher's defence of his position was twofold: first, that the Treasury minute had been a 'public reaffirmation . . . of a status then [1919] at least 47 years old' and, second, that 'executive authority is vested solely in H.M. Government and officials, however high in rank, exercise no executive authority *of their own*'.[191] The first of these points seems to have rested upon the fallacy of ambiguity, in that there can be no doubt that Fisher exercised greater authority over the Civil Service than his predecessors had done, even if the title 'Head of the Civil Service' was not new. Fisher's second point was constitutionally correct and, as far as senior appointments were concerned, in practice he was unable to impose officials on unwilling ministers unless he had the Prime Minister's support.[192]

Fisher's influence was directed towards administrative reform.[193] In 1919 the chief finance officers of the major government departments, meeting under the

[189] For fuller accounts of what follows see E. Bridges, *The Treasury* (2nd edn., 1966), 173–6; O'Halpin, *Head of the Civil Service*; H. Roseveare, *The Treasury: The Evolution of a British Institution* (1969), 249–55.

[190] Bradbury to Austen Chamberlain, 19 Aug. 1919, Austen Chamberlain papers, AC 24/1/21.

[191] Note prepared for the Prime Minister, Mar. 1926, Sir Warren Fisher papers, British Library of Political and Economic Science, London.

[192] For example, Fisher's advice in 1925 as to who should be the next Permanent Under-Secretary of the Colonial Office was rejected by the minister in charge of that department, Leo Amery, and Fisher was dependent on support from the Prime Minister in relation to appointments at the War Office in 1920 and the Home Office in 1922. See O'Halpin, *Head of the Civil Service*, 69–73, 147–9.

[193] What follows is based on Sir H. P. Hamilton, 'Sir Warren Fisher and the Public Service', *Public Admin.*, 29 (1951), 3–38; A. W. Hurst, 'The Place of Finance Departments, Committees and Officers in Administrative Control', *Public Admin.*, 5 (1927), 418–30; O'Halpin, *Head of the Civil Service*, 47–55.

chairmanship of the Financial Secretary of the Treasury, Baldwin, produced a report which, as amended by Fisher, laid the basis of a new system of financial accountability. With a view to strengthening the position of chief finance officers, it was recommended that their selection or removal should require the consent of the Chancellor of the Exchequer and the Prime Minister; that the criticisms of finance officers should be allowed the fullest scope within departments; and that the chief financial officer should have the right of access to his minister. Fisher also recommended that the consent of the Prime Minister and Chancellor should be required for the appointment or removal of permanent heads of departments, their deputies and principal establishment officers. He feared that a permanent secretary's sense of financial responsibility might be diminished by the creation within his department of a more-or-less independent finance branch. Accordingly, he recommended that the permanent head of a department, or permanent civilian head in the case of the defence departments, should be ultimately responsible (under ministers) for economy in policy and management. These recommendations were accepted by the Cabinet's Finance Committee, and, after being noted by the Cabinet, were announced in a Treasury circular in March 1920.

Subsequently Fisher argued before the House of Commons' Public Accounts Committee that the permanent head of a department should also be the department's Accounting Officer, answerable to the Public Accounts Committee for financial matters. He preached a doctrine of joint responsibility for economy between the Treasury and spending departments, and believed that the idea of partnership should extend to the highest ranks of the Civil Service. The Public Accounts Committee agreed in 1920 to the permanent head of the defence departments and the smaller civil departments becoming Accounting Officers, with responsibility for giving evidence to itself, but hesitated to extend this principle to the larger civil departments, where the volume of work would make it difficult for the permanent head to have personal knowledge of the financial side of his department. It was not until 1925 that the Public Accounts Committee was persuaded that, in these cases, the permanent head and not the chief finance officer, should be the Accounting Officer.

The whole thrust of Fisher's recommendations was to link finance branches with their colleagues in spending departments, rather than to encourage finance branches to operate as independent outposts of the Treasury. Nevertheless, it has been suggested by Rodney Lowe, drawing upon his study of the Ministry of Labour, that the Baldwin–Fisher reforms concerning chief finance and establishment officers gave the Treasury 'the means to impose from within ministries the control which it had previously striven to impose from without'.[194] This thesis could only be disproved by studying the internal workings of every

---

[194] Rodney Lowe, 'The Erosion of State Intervention in Britain, 1917–24', *Econ. Hist. Rev.*, 2nd ser., 31 (1978), 282.

Whitehall department—a task beyond what any one researcher could achieve—but such evidence as is available lends little support to a belief that finance branches were a means of imposing Treasury control from within spending departments. Even in the case of the Ministry of Labour, where the chief finance officer, F. W. Bowers, was said to be 'very Treasury minded . . . and very useful for the Treasury interest', there is evidence of independence on Bowers's part, as regards Treasury views on such matters as the expansion of industrial training, or centralization of organized recreation or unemployment relief.[195]

Study of financial control within the Board of Education and the Ministry of Transport in the period 1919–25 has shown that the chief finance officers there were not obstructive, although naturally they urged financial prudence and warned colleagues when proposals were unlikely to receive Treasury sanction. It is also the case that the influence of finance officers varied from department to department, those in the Ministry of Agriculture and Fisheries, the Board of Trade, and the Home Office being comparatively junior compared with those in the Ministry of Labour, the Board of Education, or the Ministry of Transport. Generalization about the influence of finance officers is thus difficult. However, the Treasury's own files do not suggest that officials there intended finance officers in other departments to act as spies, and indeed a finance officer who had lost the trust of his departmental colleagues was of no value to the Treasury.[196]

Lowe has also charged the Treasury with using its administrative authority in defiance of government policy or parliamentary legislation. In particular, he has shown that between 1920 and 1922 the Establishments Department used its control over new appointments of staff to prevent the Ministry of Labour exercising its powers under the Trade Boards Act of 1918 to create joint boards of employers and employees to regulate minimum wages in industries where wages were inadequate. The Treasury saw such boards as likely to aggravate unemployment by restricting wage flexibility at a time of falling prices, and deliberately limited the number of investigating officers, who were necessary to establish an industry's need for a board.[197]

It is true that Hilton Young described control over establishments as the 'most close and efficient' way in which Treasury influence could be brought to bear on

---

[195] Ibid., 282, and id., *Adjusting to Democracy*, 58, 71–2, 160 n., 165–6.

[196] McDonald, 'Formulation of British Public Expenditure Policy', 376–8, 413–19, 453, 455–60. Steven Stacey, 'The Ministry of Health, 1919–1929: Ideas and Practice in a Government Department', D.Phil. (Oxford, 1984) contains no evidence of an obstructive finance branch, and notes (p. 83) that the Treasury did not think it necessary for the chief finance officer to be graded as more than an assistant secretary, that is no higher than the head of a division in the Treasury. Richard Roberts, 'The Board of Trade, 1925–1939', D.Phil. (Oxford, 1987) found (p. 244) that as late as 1938 the Board's chief finance officer was complaining that he had no role in policy formulation, contrary to Treasury guidelines.

[197] Lowe, *Adjusting to Democracy*, 61; id., 'The Erosion of State Intervention', 278–9.

spending departments,[198] but whether this influence was being used improperly is another matter. The Trade Boards Act of 1918 *enabled* but did not *require* the Minister of Labour to bring new trades under the original Trade Boards Act of 1909,[199] and therefore there was no defiance of parliamentary legislation involved in subjecting the implementation of the Act to general considerations of government policy. The 1918 Act had been passed before the Government had decided to give priority to economy in public expenditure, and by 1920 more than one policy originally adopted in 1918 was being questioned in the light of that priority. To have given each spending department a free hand to implement existing legislation as it saw fit would have meant government by departments, and an end to Cabinet government. The battle between the Treasury and the Ministry of Labour was fought out in Cabinet as well as at the administrative level, and Hilton Young was consulted by Treasury officials about the idea of limiting staff, since it was known that the matter might be taken to Cabinet.[200]

Lowe has also alleged that in its economy campaign the Treasury launched an attack on the 'thinkers and those who apply information and statistics to problems and indicate policy'. The Treasury file that he cites as evidence does not, however, support such a charge.[201] This is not to deny that the activities of the Ministry of Labour's Intelligence and Statistics Department were curbed by economies in staffing, but rather to question whether these economies can be represented as measures designed by the Treasury to hobble policy-making. It has been more convincingly argued that it was general concern to reduce government expenditure that led the Establishments Department to seek savings among officials 'not actually engaged in administration'—that is statistical, research, and publicity departments—and it was just such savings that ministers were enjoined to make in an economy circular issued from the Cabinet Office in November 1919.[202]

The Board of Trade also suffered from staffing economies, notably the closure by 1922 of its General Economic Department, which had been founded in 1917 to 'anticipate, watch and suggest means of dealing with, important questions and movements likely to arise in commerce and industry', but which fell a victim of the Geddes axe. The abandonment of the new advisory role in favour

[198] E. Hilton Young, *The System of National Finance* (2nd edn., 1924), 36.

[199] PP 1918, ii. 579, 599–612.

[200] Lowe, 'The Erosion of State Intervention', 279; McDonald, 'Formulation of British Public Expenditure Policy', 473–6.

[201] R. Lowe, 'The Failure of Consensus in Britain: The National Industrial Conference, 1919–1921', *Hist. J.*, 21 (1978), 661, citing T162/6/E372. The words given in quotation marks by Lowe do occur in the file, but only to distinguish the responsibilities of an administrative official (an assistant secretary) from staff clerks who would collate and interpret information and statistics. The file shows that the Treasury was seeking to curb increases in the establishment of staff clerks, *not* 'thinkers . . . who . . . indicate policy'. Moreover, the Treasury letter in the file actually states that the work of the staff authorized for the Ministry of Labour's Department of Intelligence and Statistics was to include the application to problems of the day of information and statistics collected by the Department.

[202] McDonald, 'The Formulation of British Public Expenditure', 470.

of a return to pre-war regulatory functions reflected not only the attitudes of businessmen in the Geddes Committee but also the views of leading Board of Trade officials.[203] The Treasury's attitude to research and statistical departments in Whitehall may have been unwise but it seems neither to have been unique to the Treasury nor out of line with Cabinet decisions and priorities.

There seems to be no convincing evidence that the Treasury made improper use of its influence in Whitehall. On the other hand, the fact that it was government policy to economize in expenditure and administration in the aftermath of war was bound to create tension between the Treasury and spending departments. Perhaps what is remarkable is that in 1933, after numerous battles over the naval Estimates, a newly retired Deputy Secretary of the Admiralty could write that Fisher had promoted 'team work throughout the Civil Service . . . with conspicuous success'.[204]

SUMMARY

In the aftermath of the First World War, Treasury officials found that they had to deal with a much wider range of activities than in 1914. In particular, they now collaborated, to a greater or lesser degree, with the Bank of England on monetary policy, and with the Foreign Office on reparations and war debts. Inflation in 1919–20 generated political pressure not only for a restoration of Treasury control over public expenditure but also for greater Treasury control over the Civil Service than had existed in 1914. The quest for major economies in public expenditure led the Treasury to play an active part in policy-making, both with regard to defence and social services, and the Permanent Secretary tried to make the Treasury the central department of government.

The Treasury and the Bank conducted a conscious policy of deflation to restore control over the monetary system and to move towards a restoration of the supposedly automatic gold standard. The Treasury was determined that the public sector should not crowd out productive private investment, and propounded the view that loan-financed public works would not reduce unemployment. At the same time, the need to curb governments' tendency to increase expenditure led Treasury officials to emphasize the importance of balancing the budget, although in 1922 they had to defer to Horne and give priority to cutting taxation. Over the period 1919–23 budgets were brought into balance largely by reducing public expenditure, and it is not surprising that Treasury control, including control over the Civil Service, should seem very negative, both at the time and subsequently to historians.

[203] S. Howson and D. Winch, *The Economic Advisory Council, 1930–1939: A Study in Economic Advice during Depression and Recovery* (Cambridge, 1977), 7; Roberts, 'Board of Trade', 35–40.
[204] Sir Charles Walker, *Thirty-six Years at the Admiralty* (1934), 216.

CHAPTER FIVE

The Gold Standard and Public Finance, 1924–1931

INTRODUCTION

By the mid-1920s the international financial system appeared to be recovering from the traumas brought on by the First World War, and it seemed to the Treasury that the time was ripe for implementing the Genoa resolutions for stabilizing national currencies on gold. By the time Britain returned to the gold standard in April 1925 a dozen other countries, including the United States, Germany, Austria, and Sweden, were already on it, and South Africa had given notice of her intention to return in July. However, although the gold standard was intended to promote financial stability by checking excessive expansion of credit and by stabilizing exchange rates, it was not designed to prevent a fall in prices, such as occurred in the two years after 1929, when the Board of Trade wholesale price index fell by 23 per cent and the Ministry of Labour working-class cost-of-living index by 10 per cent (see Figure 5.1). Indeed, the very rigidity of the gold standard was a principal cause of the depression. Even a decade after the war had ended, the balance-of-payments position of a number of countries, of which the most important was Germany, depended upon capital outflows from the United States. In 1928 a boom on the New York stock market, and a concomitant tightening of Federal Reserve monetary policy, led to a marked reduction in American investment abroad. Meanwhile, the stabilization of the franc on gold at the end of 1926 had been followed by a dramatic increase in the demand for money in France—a demand that the Banque de France could meet only by drawing in gold from abroad by offering high interest rates, because, with a view to preventing inflation, French currency regulations prohibited an expansion of the money supply in any other way. The reduction in American lending, together with the drain of gold to France, forced other countries to deflate in order to preserve the gold parities of their currencies. Export markets contracted, and with them opportunities for invisible earnings through financial services and shipping, with the result that Britain's balance of payments on current account deteriorated (see Table 5.1). Falling exports also meant rising unemployment, and the cost of cash benefits to the unemployed made it increasingly difficult to balance the budget. Consequently, confidence

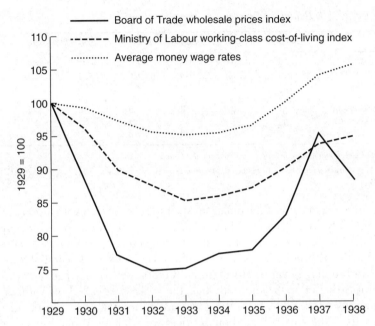

FIG. 5.1.   *Prices and Wages, 1929–1938*

Source: B. R. Mitchell and Phyllis Deane, *Abstract of British Historical Statistics* (Cambridge: University Press, 1971), 345, 477.

Note: Both the Board of Trade wholesale price index and the Ministry of Labour working-class cost of living index had serious shortcomings as measures of British domestic prices. The Board of Trade index was compiled from prices of food and industrial raw materials and semi-finished products, many of them imported. The Ministry of Labour index was based on an Edwardian standard of living, and was too heavily weighted towards food and rent to reflect consumption patterns in the 1930s.

in sterling weakened, and outflows of foreign capital during a European financial crisis forced the British monetary authorities to abandon the defence of the gold parity on 21 September 1931.[1]

None of these developments could have been foreseen by Treasury officials or the Bank of England when, between November 1924 and April 1925, the new Conservative Chancellor of the Exchequer, Winston Churchill, was being advised that the time was ripe for Britain to return to the gold standard at the pre-1914 parity. However, that parity represented a revaluation of sterling by

---

[1] The best account of the destabilizing effects of the gold standard is B. Eichengreen, *Golden Fetters: The Gold Standard and the Great Depression, 1919–1939* (Oxford, 1992). One of the earliest published analyses along the lines of this paragraph was Ralph Hawtrey's *Trade Depression and the Way Out* (1931).

TABLE 5.1. *UK Balance of Payments, 1925–1931 (£ m.)*

	1925	1926	1927	1928	1929	1930	1931
Imports (f.o.b.)	1,208	1,140	1,115	1,095	1,117	953	786
Exports (f.o.b.)	943	794	845	858	854	670	464
Visible balance	−265	−346	−270	−237	−263	−283	−322
Invisible balance	296	307	348	341	339	298	208
Current account	31	−39	78	104	76	15	−114
Capital account	−33	62	−60	−122	−84	−8	80ª
Currency flow	−2	23	18	−18	−8	7	−34

ª Including central bank credits of £50 million to support pound.

Source: Alec Cairncross and Barry Eichengreen, *Sterling in Decline: The Devaluations of 1931, 1949 and 1967* (Oxford, 1983), 35.

about 10 per cent against the dollar in April 1925 compared with a year earlier. Consequently, in order to retain market shares and profits, British exporters found themselves forced to reduce their sterling costs by cutting wage rates, or by rationalizing production, so as to employ fewer workers. The initial response of the trade union movement to attempts by employers to cut wage rates was the General Strike of 1926, and, although the strike was called off without extracting any concessions from the government, money wage rates tended to remain fixed thereafter, even though prices were falling. While it was known that there were a number of reasons why unemployment in Britain should be higher in the 1920s than before 1914, including increased tariff barriers abroad, the persistence of unemployment rates above 10 per cent of the insured labour force after 1925, compared with the pre-1914 pattern when unemployment among trade unionists had never been above 5 per cent for more than a year or two, was attributed by Treasury officials and pre-Keynesian economists to the failure of money wages rates to fall in line with prices.[2]

Churchill looked to reductions in the burdens of central and local government taxation on industry to offset the adverse effects of monetary policy (both the higher exchange rate, and the necessity to raise interest rates to defend it). However, at a time when revenue was far from buoyant, major reductions in taxation were possible, within the constraint of a balanced budget, only if there were economies in public expenditure. In the event, it proved to be hard to achieve adequate economies even before the onset of the slump raised the cost to the Exchequer of maintaining the unemployed.

The whole Treasury approach to economic recovery was challenged in 1929, when Lloyd George claimed that, if returned to power, he could reduce unemployment to 'normal' proportions within a year through a programme of loan-financed public expenditure. Even the Conservative Cabinet was tempted

---

[2] See Mark Casson, *Economics of Unemployment: An Historical Perspective* (Oxford, 1983), esp. 43–52; N. H. Dimsdale, 'Employment and Real Wages in the Inter-war Period', *Nat. Institute Econ. Rev.*, 110 (1984), 85–93.

to make some concession to Lloyd George's ideas, and the Treasury was forced to defend its orthodox view that government loans for public expenditure would crowd out private investment by competing for loanable funds and forcing up interest rates. The Treasury had to shift its ground somewhat after Labour took office in 1929 with a commitment to an active policy on unemployment, but Snowden, once more Chancellor, kept the level of expenditure well below what had been advocated by Lloyd George.

Snowden failed to balance his budgets in 1930 and 1931, but only because the world depression after 1929 tended to reduce revenue, while rapidly increasing the cost of unemployment relief. A growing sense of national crisis, and the failure of ministers to agree on cuts in unemployment benefits required to balance the budget, led to the resignation of the Labour government on 24 August 1931, and its replacement by a Conservative-dominated National Government.

PERSONALITIES, ORGANIZATION, AND ECONOMIC ADVICE

After the Conservatives had won the election in October 1924 Horne seems to have hoped that he would return to the Treasury. However, Baldwin believed that the City would not welcome Horne's reappointment as Chancellor. Horne had offended financial opinion by suspending the sinking fund in 1922, and the fact that he was leader of the industrial group in the House of Commons may have been taken in the City as a sign that he would favour the interests of industry rather than finance. Fisher expressed the hope that Austen or Neville Chamberlain would be appointed, rather than Horne, but Baldwin preferred to offer the Treasury to Churchill, apparently for the party-political reason that the Prime Minister wished to break up what he regarded as the threat of an alliance between Lloyd George and former Coalition ministers.[3]

Another factor influencing Baldwin may have been Churchill's reputation as an outspoken defender of free trade. Baldwin believed that the Conservatives' commitment to protection had cost them the 1923 election, and before the 1924 election he pledged that he would not introduce proposals for a general tariff until it was clear that the balance of electoral opinion had changed. With Churchill at the Treasury the pledge was secure. Churchill was delighted to take the office that had been held by his father, Lord Randolph, in 1886. When Churchill had been a young MP he had been instructed in Gladstonian principles on free trade and taxation by two Permanent Secretaries of the Treasury, Sir Francis Mowat and Sir Edward Hamilton, who had known his father.[4] He was prepared to question the wisdom of returning to the gold standard but,

[3] R. W. D. Boyce, *British Capitalism at the Crossroads, 1919–1932* (Cambridge, 1987), 72–3; David Dilks, *Neville Chamberlain*, vol. i, *1869–1929* (Cambridge, 1984), 398, 406.
[4] Paul Addison, *Churchill on the Home Front, 1900–1955* (1992), 20, 23–4, 36, 234.

given what he called his 'limited comprehension of these extremely technical matters', he acquiesced in the advice of Treasury officials and the Governor of the Bank of England.[5] On the other hand, although he tried to achieve a balanced budget through economies in public expenditure, he departed more than once from the orthodoxy that revenue and expenditure should balance year by year. As Peter Clarke has aptly summed up Churchill's chancellorship: 'he talked like Mr Gladstone but behaved like Mr Micawber.'[6]

Treasury officials did not find Churchill an easy Chancellor to work with. Some might smile at his eccentricities, as, for example, when he chose to dictate part of a budget speech while having a bath, with the result that his private secretary, Donald Fergusson, had to take notes in longhand, 'the normal ministrations of the lady shorthand writer' being obviously 'out of place'.[7] In other cases, however, Churchill's restless search for measures, often unorthodox, that would improve his reputation was felt to be more than tiresome. In 1925 Fisher told Neville Chamberlain, who had moved back to the Ministry of Health, that Churchill was 'an irresponsible child', and that officials never knew where they were with him or what hare he might start. Fisher warned both Baldwin and Chamberlain that Churchill would bring down the government unless removed from office.[8]

For his part, Churchill resented the way in which Fisher left the business of advising him largely to the Controllers of the Treasury departments.[9] Churchill may not have understood that in this respect Fisher was acting as the 1919 reorganization of the Treasury implied that he should, that is by allowing the Controllers to deal with finance or control of expenditure, while he concerned himself largely with his responsibilities as head of the Civil Service. According to Chamberlain (who was no doubt informed by Fisher), Churchill treated senior officials with such discourtesy that Barstow, the Controller of the Supply Services Department, resigned (to become government director of the

---

[5] D. E. Moggridge, *British Monetary Policy, 1924–1931: The Norman Conquest of $4.86* (Cambridge, 1972), 262.

[6] Peter Clarke, 'Churchill's Economic Ideas, 1900–1930', in Robert Blake and W. Roger Louis (eds.), *Churchill* (Oxford, 1993), 80.   [7] P. J. Grigg, *Prejudice and Judgement* (1948), 195.

[8] Chamberlain diary, 1 Nov. 1925, NC2/21.

[9] Churchill wrote to Fisher on 1 Dec. 1925: 'Sometimes as much as three months have passed without my even seeing you or receiving any official paper from you. . . . I am well aware that you do not regard yourself in any way responsible for assisting the Chancellor of the Exchequer and that you reserve your functions entirely for the First Lord of the Treasury . . . I cannot conceive that any of your distinguished predecessors have not been accustomed to give more constant and effective assistance to the Chancellor of the day, whether in regard to the controlling of expenditure or the framing of finance. . . . I record these facts only because I do not think that a Minute such as you have addressed to me is couched in a tone which should be used by an official, aloof from the labour and anxiety of financial business, to the Minister who, whatever his shortcomings, has actually to conduct it.' This memorandum is reproduced in full in W. S. Churchill, *Winston S. Churchill*, ed. M. Gilbert vol. v companion, part 1 (1979), 600–3, and is cited by E. O'Halpin, *Head of the Civil Service: A Study of Sir Warren Fisher* (1989), 145. Neither of these works mentions that, in the Treasury file (T199/415) in which the Treasury copy of the memorandum can be found, Fisher noted: 'Winston in fact never sent me this outpouring!! P. J. [Grigg] handed it to me for safekeeping on 14.11.30 when he ceased to be p.s. to Snowden.'

Anglo-American Oil Company) in August 1927. On the other hand, Leith-Ross thought that Churchill's habit of bombarding his officials with queries kept them on their toes.[10] It was doubtless with some relief that Treasury officials welcomed back Snowden as Chancellor in June 1929; Churchill commented that 'the Treasury mind and the Snowden mind embraced each other with the fervour of two long-separated kindred lizards'.[11]

Niemeyer, the Controller of the Finance Department, resigned at the same time as Barstow, in order to join the Bank of England. Fisher took the opportunity to appoint Sir Richard Hopkins, who had been chairman of the Board of Inland Revenue, to be Controller of both Finance and Supply Services departments, thereby creating a more unified structure for the Treasury. At the same time Fisher began to break down the rigid separation of Supply Services and Establishments questions by creating a new division to deal with both in relation to the Post Office, the Office of Works, and the Stationery Office.

These changes reflected an expectation that the Treasury would continue to be manned by generalists without specialized knowledge of economics apart from public finance. However, Treasury files show that Frederick Phillips, a rising star on the finance side of the department, was familiar with Keynes's *Treatise on Money* shortly after it appeared in 1930, as, of course, was Hawtrey.[12] Hopkins himself had studied classics and history at Cambridge but, on transferring to the Treasury, he read a wide range of books on economics, from basic texts to contemporary controversies. From 1927 to his retirement in 1945 he was to be the Chancellor's chief adviser on financial policy and control of public expenditure. He had a sceptical view of human motives and enlivened rigorous intellectual analysis with a quiet, often impish, good humour, which seems to have made him universally popular.[13]

The Treasury, in conjunction with the Board of Inland Revenue, could have contributed much more than it did to economic knowledge. For example, Churchill was indirectly responsible for a pioneering exercise in national income accounting. On becoming Chancellor he asked the boards of Inland Revenue and Customs and Excise whether it would be possible to calculate the ratio of production to consumption in the United Kingdom, so as to allow comparisons to be made pre-war and post-war. His officials decided that the only practicable method would be to calculate national income and savings, and the task was given to the Board of Inland Revenue. Hawtrey, who appears to have been the Treasury official most closely connected with the exercise, observed that there was no universally accepted definition of national income, but the resulting figures for 1913/14 and 1923/4 to 1925/6 made it possible to estimate that the ratio of savings to national income was lower in 1925/6 than it had been

[10] M. Gilbert, *Winston S. Churchill*, vol. v, *1922–39* (1976), 296; F. Leith-Ross, *Money Talks* (1968), 118.
[11] Winston S. Churchill, *Great Contemporaries* (1937), 255.
[12] See T171/287 and T208/153.
[13] Anon., 'Sir Richard Hopkins', *Public Admin.*, 34 (1956), 115–23.

in 1913/14. Hawtrey regarded the investigation as a very valuable one and thought that it should be published so that economists might use it and criticize it. Not for the last time, however, the Treasury declined to enter into debate with economists. Hopkins advised against publication, noting that the Inland Revenue calculations, 'like all calculations of national income, contain a large element of conjecture', and also happened to give a politically inconvenient figure for wage-earners' share of the national income that was lower than recently published unofficial estimates by Stamp and Bowley.[14]

The Treasury showed no enthusiasm for bringing economists into Whitehall on a permanent basis. In response to pressure for an economic general staff, on the analogy of the Committee of Imperial Defence for the fighting services, a Committee of Civil Research was established in 1925, but with its permanent staff limited to two officials in the Cabinet Office, of whom one, Tom Jones, was Deputy Secretary of the Cabinet. Fisher approved the creation of the Committee, but Jones thought that the Treasury Controllers were suspicious and hostile. Certainly the Committee's work was largely confined to technical matters with a low political content.[15]

Subsequently, during discussions that led to the creation of an Economic Advisory Council in 1930, Fisher opposed the recruitment of economists into the Civil Service, arguing that, insofar as it was necessary to have economic research done for the government, it would be better to enlist the co-operation of the best economists outside Whitehall. The Council owed its existence to the support of the Prime Minister, MacDonald, and was much more representative of practical experience than of academic economists, only two of its fifteen non-ministerial members, Keynes and G. D. H. Cole, coming into the latter category, compared with nine businessmen. The businessmen, however, included Stamp, who was also an economist, statistician, and taxation expert. Four more economists were taken on to the Council's secretariat, including Hubert Henderson, who had had experience of government service during the First World War as secretary of the Cotton Control Board, and Colin Clark, who was to be a pioneer compiler of national income estimates in the 1930s. However, the Treasury's priority as between economy in public expenditure and support for economic research was indicated by its refusal to buy an adding machine for Clark.[16]

The Bank of England's position as principal source of financial advice was untouched by these developments. Norman and Niemeyer worked together in harmony to persuade Churchill to take the decision to return to the gold standard, Niemeyer playing the decisive part through the greater clarity of his

[14] 'Inland Revenue Estimate of National Income', by Hawtrey, 13 Sept. 1928, and Hopkins to Phillips, 27 Sept. 1927, T208/127. The report is reproduced in Richard Stone (ed.), *Inland Revenue Report on National Income 1929* (Cambridge, 1977).
[15] S. Howson and D. Winch, *The Economic Advisory Council, 1930–1939* (Cambridge, 1977), 10–15; T. Jones, *Whitehall Diary*, 3 vols., ed. K. Middlemas, i. (1969), 319.
[16] Howson and Winch, op. cit., 22, 24–5.

advice.[17] The gold standard itself enhanced the Bank's autonomy in determining Bank rate, since decisions had to be taken on technical grounds with a view to maintaining the exchange rate. Churchill expected to be consulted in advance of changes in the rate, but disclaimed responsibility for settling it. Snowden likewise took the view that the control of credit must be kept free from party political influences, although, exceptionally, the Bank did agree to a request from him to defer a rise in Bank rate during negotiations on reparations in 1929.[18]

THE RETURN TO THE GOLD STANDARD

The decision announced by Churchill in his budget speech on 28 April 1925 to return forthwith to the gold standard at the pre-war parity thus marked a decisive step in the process of removing monetary policy from the hands of politicians. The story of how the decision was taken is a familiar one, but it is worth retelling from the point of view of the light that it casts on relations between officials and ministers.

As noted in Chapter 4, the process had begun in 1919, when the Coalition Government had accepted the Cunliffe Committee's *Final Report*, and had been carried forward in 1924 by the Labour Chancellor, Snowden, when he had appointed the Chamberlain Committee to consider whether the time had come to amalgamate the Treasury note issue with the Bank of England note issue, a technical question that was linked to the larger question of a restoration of the gold standard. Of Chamberlain's colleagues, three, Bradbury, Professor Pigou and Gaspard Farrer, a banker, had been members of the Cunliffe Committee, and the fourth, Niemeyer, was no less committed to the principles of that committee's report. There was also considerable pressure from the United States and the dominions for a British return to gold.[19] Even so, by the time Churchill became Chancellor in November, the Chamberlain Committee had gone no further than to produce a draft report, recommending waiting twelve months in the hope that American prices would rise, thereby avoiding the 'inconveniences' of the deflation that would otherwise be necessary to reduce British prices. The committee had estimated that, in the absence of a rise in American prices, sterling prices would have to fall by 10 to 12 per cent before equilibrium could be secured with the exchange rate at the pre-war parity of $4.86.[20]

[17] R. S. Sayers, *The Bank of England, 1891–1944* (Cambridge, 1976), vol. i. 134.

[18] Extracts from minutes of the Committee of Treasury, 9 Dec. 1925 and 28 Aug 1929, Bank of England papers, G15/7/1816/5; Donald Winch, *Economics and Policy: A Historical Study* (1969), 92–3.

[19] See Frank C. Costigliola, 'Anglo-American Financial Rivalry in the 1920s', *J. Econ. Hist.*, 37 (1977), 911–34; L. S. Pressnell, '1925: The Burden of Sterling', *Econ. Hist. Rev.*, 2nd ser., 31 (1978), 67–88; Kosmas Tsokhas, 'The Australian Role in Britain's Return to the Gold Standard', *Econ. Hist. Rev.*, 2nd ser., 47 (1994), 129–46.

[20] Committee on Currency and Bank of England Note Issues, Third Draft Report, 14 Sept. 1924, T160/197/F7528/01/2.

In view of evidence presented to the Chamberlain Committee, there were grounds for caution. Keynes, whose *Tract on Monetary Reform* (1923) had advocated a managed currency to ensure stability of domestic prices, had warned that a return to gold would require immediate deflation and yet risk inflation in the longer term if, as he thought likely, inflation occurred in America, for then Britain would be swamped with gold imports. (Hawtrey, correctly as it turned out, thought that the danger of inflation in America was 'probably quite remote'.) McKenna, the former Chancellor, had advised that to attempt to force down British prices through an increase in Bank rate at a time when there were a million workers unemployed was 'unthinkable'. The Federation of British Industries favoured a return to gold in principle—to stabilize exchange rates and thereby reduce uncertainty for exporters—but had nevertheless warned that an early return to the pre-war parity would involve industrial unrest and a 'severe check' to exports.[21]

On the other hand, the City and mercantile interests urging immediate action to restore the gold standard were much more confident and articulate than the Federation in making their case.[22] Moreover, the Conservatives' victory in the 1924 election raised speculators' hopes of an early return to the pre-war parity, and sterling rose from just under $4.50 in October to over $4.70 in December, tantalizingly close to $4.86. The former Chamberlain Committee, now chaired by Bradbury, as Austen Chamberlain had become Foreign Secretary, estimated in January 1925 that the restoration of the pre-war parity would require a reduction of only about 6 per cent in the general price level in Britain, or 1.5 percentage points more than would be necessary to maintain the existing rate of $4.79. Accordingly, on 5 February, in its final report, the committee recommended an early return to gold at the pre-war parity, specifically rejecting the alternatives of a 'devalued sovereign' or a managed currency.[23] The pre-war parity seemed to offer a more secure symbol to sustain financial confidence than either alternative, while devaluation would mean writing down the value of other countries' debts to Britain, in terms of gold, although Britain was a net creditor. Keynes's idea of managing the currency to stabilize prices in Britain appears to have been regarded as impracticable. In any case, Niemeyer was later to dismiss it as 'desert island stability', arguing that a trading country like Britain should aim at world price stability.[24]

Churchill's response to this advice is illustrative of the dilemmas of a politician when faced with expert advice that points to a course of action which he fears will have damaging consequences for the economy, and for his reputation.

[21] Moggridge, *British Monetary Policy*, 42–6; Hawtrey, 'The Gold Standard', 2 Feb. 1925, T172/1499B.

[22] See R. W. D. Boyce, 'Creating the Myth of Consensus: Public Opinion and Britain's Return to the Gold Standard in 1925', in P. L. Cottrell and D. E. Moggridge (eds.), *Money and Power: Essays in Honour of L. S. Pressnell* (1988).

[23] Moggridge, *British Monetary Policy*, 62; Cmd. 2393, PP 1924–5, ix. 435. The *Report* referred only to the 1.5 per cent figure.   [24] Niemeyer to Churchill, 4 Aug. 1925, T208/105.

Towards the end of January Churchill, accompanied by Niemeyer, discussed the dangers of returning to gold with Lord Beaverbrook, the financier and journalist, whom Churchill had known since before the war. Niemeyer brushed aside Beaverbrook's fears, with the consequence that Beaverbrook's *Daily Express* published an attack on the Treasury for favouring the City at the expense of industry, naming Niemeyer as the responsible official. The following day, 29 January, Churchill sent a memorandum to Niemeyer, Norman, Bradbury, and Hawtrey, observing that 'it is essential that we should be prepared to answer any criticism which may be subsequently made upon our policy', and setting out the arguments against the policy, asking for the counter-case. The arguments, as Bradbury remarked, were those of Keynes and McKenna. In particular, Churchill's memorandum pointed out that the existing 'managed' currency had brought about steadier prices than in the United States, although the latter was on the gold standard, and noted that, if a restored gold standard could only be maintained by raising Bank rate, the effects on trade, industry, and employment would be harmful, making it difficult to refute the charge that the Chancellor had favoured the interests of finance at the expense of industry.[25]

In response Niemeyer asserted that, apart from one or two theoretical advocates of a managed currency, there was no financial or industrial opinion that did not favour a return to gold, and that the only question was when to do so. A decision could not be avoided, as the legislation prohibiting the export of gold was due to expire on 31 December 1925. He thought that the current difference between British and American prices was probably $4\frac{1}{2}$ per cent or less, and that therefore 'no very heroic steps' would be necessary to maintain the pre-war parity. On the other hand, if the value of sterling continued to fluctuate against gold, the City would suffer as international traders would conduct their business in currencies that were on the gold standard, such as American dollars or German marks, rather than in sterling bills.[26]

Niemeyer admitted that the most serious argument against a return to gold was the fear of adverse effects of higher interest rates on industry and employment, but he believed that the benefits to trade of stable exchange rates would outweigh these effects in the long run. Niemeyer, Norman, and Bradbury all warned that the immediate result of disappointing currency markets' expectations that Britain would return to gold would be a heavy drop in the exchange rate. Bradbury spelled out the consequences of such a setback as a tendency for sterling prices to rise, and therefore a need for credit restriction which, in his opinion, was not unlikely to be more severe than that required to maintain sterling at $4.86. Hawtrey admitted that the current high level of foreign investment

---

[25]   Churchill's memorandum, known in the Treasury as 'Mr Churchill's Exercise', and the replies from Niemeyer, Norman, and Bradbury, are reprinted in Moggridge, *British Monetary Policy*, 260–76. The originals, and Hawtrey's reply, dated 2 Feb. 1925, are in T172/1499B.

[26]   Moggridge, op. cit., 262–7.

by Americans had tended to lower the dollar's exchange rate, and that a reduction in American lending abroad would tend to raise it, forcing the Bank of England to raise Bank rate to maintain sterling at $4.86. However, he did not foresee the falling off of American foreign investment from 1928, as he expected a high level of such investment to be a natural and permanent consequence of America's increased wealth and recent restrictions on immigration.[27]

Churchill refused to be rushed and called for further papers, including a historical note on the return to the gold standard after the Napoleonic wars. In the latter Hawtrey argued that, while the rapid fall in prices between 1814 and 1816 had caused distress, the delay in restoring parity with gold until 1819 had caused 'great unsettlement' to business.[28] The argument in favour of an early decision was reinforced by Snowden, who wrote to the *Observer* on 8 February that the difficulties of a return to gold would be small 'compared with the evils from which the world is suffering as a result of unstable and fluctuating currencies'. Within Whitehall, Board of Trade statisticians had produced figures that appeared to show that British exports had, if anything, risen as a proportion of total world exports since before the war, suggesting that the troubles of Britain's export industries were a result of a decline in the volume of world trade, itself partly a consequence of risks arising from fluctuating exchange rates.[29]

On the other hand, Churchill was impressed by Keynes's arguments, published in the *Nation* on 21 February, to the effect that in practice the gold standard would mean that British prices and interest rates would follow wide fluctuations in the United States, and also by what Keynes called 'the paradox of unemployment amidst dearth'. The Chancellor asked Niemeyer whether there was not a connection between 'the unique British phenomenon of chronic unemployment and the long, resolute consistency of a particular financial policy', and remarked that he would 'rather see Finance less proud and Industry more content'. On the other hand, he did not 'pretend to see even "through a glass darkly" how the financial and credit policy of the country could be handled so as to bridge the gap between a dearth of goods and a surplus of labour'.[30] Niemeyer, while admitting that Keynes was a 'serious critic of monetary policy', stuck to his own earlier views and, as regards unemployment, once more argued that inflation could not create permanent employment.[31]

---

[27] Moggridge, op. cit., 262–76, and 'The Gold Standard', by Hawtrey, 2 Feb. 1925, T172/1499B. Hawtrey believed that America's capital requirements had been reduced compared with before the restriction on immigration as it was no longer necessary to equip the country for the settlement and employment of a large annual increase in population.

[28] Churchill to Niemeyer, 6 Feb. 1925, and memorandum by Hawtrey, n.d., T172/1499B.

[29] R. S. Sayers, 'The Return to Gold, 1925', in S. Pollard (ed.), *The Gold Standard and Employment Policies between the Wars* (1970), 90–1.

[30] Gilbert, *Winston S. Churchill*, v. 96–8; Moggridge, *British Monetary Policy*, 75–6.

[31] Notes by Niemeyer, 21 Feb. 1925 and n.d., but 22 or 23 Feb., T172/1499B. In the latter, in a passage anticipating later monetarist arguments, Niemeyer noted: 'You can by inflation . . . enable, temporarily, spending power to cope with large quantities of products. But unless you increase the dose

In a last attempt to establish where the balance of the arguments lay, Churchill arranged a dinner party on 17 March with Keynes, McKenna, Niemeyer, and Bradbury present, together with Churchill's private secretary, P. J. Grigg. Grigg recalled that the symposium lasted until midnight or after, with Bradbury making much of the point that the gold standard was 'knave-proof', in that 'it could not be rigged for political or even more unworthy reasons'. Finally, reversing his earlier advice, McKenna admitted that Churchill would have to go back to gold, but it would be 'hell'.[32] Leith-Ross, the Deputy Controller in the Treasury's Finance Department, believed that Churchill finally decided on the return to gold partly because he knew that, if he did so, Niemeyer would give him irrefutable arguments in favour, whereas otherwise he would be exposed to criticism from the City, against which he would have no effective answer.[33]

Churchill may have avoided criticism from the City, but subsequent criticism from Keynes and Stamp, and the difficulties that the British economy experienced under the gold standard, led him to believe that the decision to return had been the greatest mistake of his life. In a widely read polemic, *The Economic Consequences of Mr Churchill* (1925), Keynes argued that comparisons of index numbers of the cost-of-living, wages, and prices of manufactured exports indicated that the sterling exchange rate was now 10 to 12 per cent too high in relation to the dollar, greatly adding to the difficulties faced by British exporters, who were bound to try to reduce costs by cutting money wages.[34] Niemeyer agreed in August 1925 that the immediate effect of monetary policy had been to increase real wages, by reducing prices while money wages remained unchanged, but he believed, wrongly as it turned out, that money wages would fall sufficiently to cancel the rise in real wages.[35] Keynes was prepared to admit that deflation could, in theory, reduce wages and prices, but he predicted, accurately, that the level of deflation required would be politically impossible.[36]

Keynes argued that Churchill's advisers had underestimated the degree of deflation necessary to adjust British wages and prices because they had compared wholesale prices in Britain and America, although wholesale price indices included a large element of internationally traded goods, such as raw cotton, which had a single world price.[37] Niemeyer and Hawtrey responded that the various American cost-of-living indices differed from each other too much to permit trustworthy comparisons with Britain, and even in retrospect

---

continually, there comes a time when having destroyed the credit of the country you can inflate no more, money having ceased to be acceptable as value. Even before this . . . you have had claims for increased wages, strikes, lock-outs, etc.'

[32] Grigg, *Prejudice and Judgement*, 182–4.   [33] Leith-Ross, *Money Talks*, 92.
[34] *JMK*, ix. 213, 220–3. Stamp supported Keynes's argument in an addendum to *The Report of the Court of Inquiry concerning the Coal Industry Dispute* (Cd. 2478), PP 1924–5, xiii. 935–58.
[35] Niemeyer to Chancellor, 4 Aug. 1925, T208/105.
[36] *JMK*, xix (part 1), 425–6.   [37] *JMK*, ix. 208–9, 212–13.

Hawtrey believed that, for international purposes, only wholesale prices were relevant.[38] Given that the Board of Trade wholesale price index was compiled from prices of food and industrial raw materials and semi-finished products, and not 'factory-gate' prices of British manufactures, it is difficult to agree with Hawtrey. Wholesale prices measured only part of British industry's costs and the other major element, money wages, did not fall as Niemeyer predicted; rather real wages rose as the Board of Trade's working-class cost-of-living index continued to fall until 1933. On the other hand, subsequent attempts by economic historians to measure the extent of sterling's overvaluation in 1925 have produced a wide variety of results, from no overvaluation at all to 14 per cent against the dollar, or 20 per cent to 25 per cent in terms of a 'basket' of foreign currencies weighted according to their importance in international trade.[39] On balance, Keynes may have overstated the extent of overvaluation against the dollar, but he seems to have understated the problem of overvaluation in relation to other currencies.

What is certain is that the return to gold was not a successful employment policy: British exports of merchandise fell between 1924 and 1927, whether measured by value in terms of dollars, or as a proportion of world exports, and unemployment in Britain was concentrated in regions which were dependent on export industries.[40] While there were other reasons why British export industries were in difficulty in the 1920s, including surplus world capacity in steel and shipbuilding, substitution of oil for coal, and loss of markets for cotton goods to Japan or on account of import substitution in India and elsewhere, a lower parity for sterling would have increased economic activity and lowered unemployment. From the Treasury's own point of view, such a policy would have had the merit of increasing the Chancellor's revenue and reducing expenditure on unemployment relief, thereby making it much easier for him to balance his budget.[41]

[38] Recorded conversation between Hawtrey and Sir Alec Cairncross, 1966, HTRY 13/5.

[39] See Moggridge, *British Monetary Policy*, 245–50; N. H. Dimsdale, 'British Monetary Policy and the Exchange Rate, 1920–38', *Oxford Econ. Papers*, NS, 33, supplement (1981), 306–42; J. Redmond, 'The Sterling Overvaluation in 1925: A Multilateral Approach', *Econ. Hist. Rev.*, 2nd ser., 37 (1984), 520–32; K. G. P. Matthews, 'Was Sterling Overvalued in 1925?', *Econ. Hist. Rev.*, 2nd ser., 39 (1986), 572–87; M. P. Taylor, 'The Dollar–Sterling Exchange Rate in the 1920s: Purchasing Power Parity and the Norman Conquest of $4.86', *Applied Econ.*, 24 (1992), 803–11; H. Barkai, 'Productivity Patterns, Exchange Rates and the Gold Standard Restoration Debate of the 1920s', *Hist. Pol. Econ.*, 25 (1993), 1–37; Susan Wolcott, 'Keynes Versus Churchill: Revaluation and British Unemployment in the 1920s', *J. Econ. Hist.*, 53 (1993), 601–22.

[40] Sayers, 'The Return to Gold', 322–3; M. E. F. Jones, 'The Regional Impact of an Overvalued Pound in the 1920s', *Econ. Hist. Rev.*, 2nd ser., 38 (1985), 393–401.

[41] See T. J. Hatton, 'The Outlines of a Keynesian Solution', in Sean Glynn and Alan Booth (eds.), *The Road to Full Employment* (1987), 83–6, where it is argued that a 10 per cent devaluation in 1928 would have permitted increased expenditure of well over £100 million within a balanced budget, at a time when total central government expenditure, excluding sinking fund, was £682 million.

MONETARY POLICY, 1925–1930

The policy of returning to the gold standard did not even succeed in restoring fully London's position as a financial centre. To avoid having to rely entirely on Bank rate to protect Britain's gold reserves, the Bank reimposed from November 1924 the informal embargo that had existed between 1919 and January 1924 on the raising of loans on the London market by foreign countries. In June 1925 Norman advised Churchill that the embargo should be extended to dominion and colonial loans for a period, which it was, in spite of protests from the Colonial Office. A subcommittee (chaired by Bradbury) of the Committee on Civil Research was asked by the Cabinet to examine Britain's capacity to meet demands for capital at home and abroad and reported in October that £100 to 120 million annually was as much as the country could spare for capital exports. Such a figure, Bradbury believed, might be exceeded if the embargo were removed, but, since the embargo was being successfully evaded by British investors purchasing securities in New York, the subcommittee recommended that embargo should be abolished. Churchill announced the removal of the embargo in November 1925, but Norman used informal persuasion within the City to restrict foreign loans when sterling came under pressure in 1929.[42]

Treasury officials were aware that high interest rates discouraged trade and industry, and therefore had an adverse effect on employment. Churchill protested vigorously against Norman's decision to raise Bank rate from 4 per cent to 5 per cent in December 1925, thereby prompting a Treasury enquiry into whether the Bank or the Treasury was responsible for monetary policy. Hawtrey, who thought that the raising of Bank rate to 5 per cent was 'nothing less than a national disaster', and that it would have been better for the Bank to acquiesce in the loss of some of its gold reserves, argued that ultimate responsibility for monetary policy rested with the Chancellor of the Exchequer. Niemeyer and Leith-Ross, however, who strongly disagreed with Hawtrey's economic analysis, consulted two former Joint Permanent Secretaries, Chalmers and Bradbury, who informed them that it was not the normal practice of the Bank either to consult the Treasury or to inform it beforehand of variations in Bank rate.[43] Bank rate stayed at 5 per cent until April 1927, when it was reduced to 4½ per cent. On the other hand, pressure from Churchill made Norman aware of the political constraint on monetary policy, the gold standard notwithstanding, and, despite the movement of speculative funds to New York from mid-1928, Bank rate was held at 4½ per cent until February 1929. At that point, however, faced with continued losses of its reserves, the Bank raised

[42] J. Atkin, 'Official Regulation of British Overseas Investment, 1914–1931', *Econ. Hist. Rev.*, 2nd ser., 23 (1970), 330–1; Sayers, *Bank of England*, iii. 289–93.

[43] 'The Credit Situation', by Hawtrey, 5 Dec. 1925, and testimony of Bradbury and Chalmers, 6 and 7 Dec. 1925, T176/13.

its rate to 5½ per cent, despite another strong protest from Churchill, with a further rise to 6½ per cent following in September.[44]

The Treasury's concern about high interest rates was not solely on account of the effects on trade and industry. High interest rates increased the cost of new government borrowing, the timing of which was determined by the maturing of old loans. A reduction in Bank rate was not possible until after the New York stock market crash in October 1929; but, beginning on 31 October, the Bank reduced its rate, in step with New York, from 6½ to 3 per cent by May 1930, and then to 2½ per cent in May 1931. Hopkins hoped in April 1930 that 'cheap money means that enterprise can be financed more easily and . . . prospective profits . . . increased',[45] but falling prices raised real interest rates even as nominal interest rates were reduced.

The Treasury did not attach any importance to the view, first put forward by McKenna in 1923, that its policy of funding Treasury bills reduced the banks' near liquid assets and therefore their willingness to lend (see page 157). Hawtrey argued in 1929 that, under the gold standard, any deflationary tendency such as McKenna described would lead to an improvement in the balance of payments on current account, which in turn would lead to importation of gold, a reduction in Bank rate and an expansion of credit until equilibrium had been restored.[46] The Treasury therefore continued to aim at a steady reduction in the floating debt. As Niemeyer told the Colwyn Committee on National Debt and Taxation in 1925, not only did reliance on Treasury bills leave the state at the mercy of the banks, as in 1919, but also large foreign holdings of Treasury bills increased the danger that a flight from sterling might take place in a European crisis (as was to happen in 1931).[47] The Colwyn Committee agreed with Niemeyer (who in turn seems to have derived his ideas on this point from Hawtrey) that a gradual but steady reduction in Treasury bills would tend to divert bank funds into commercial bills, thereby cheapening credit.[48] As Howson has pointed out, however, the crucial assumption in this analysis was that it was the behaviour of the short-term rate of interest that determined whether policy was deflationary. However, the Treasury's success in lengthening the maturity structure of the debt, by replacing bills and through conversions of maturing bonds, not only reduced the banks' liquidity, but also contributed to keeping up long-term interest rates for industrial borrowers.[49]

The final coping stone in the edifice of the restored gold standard was the Currency and Bank Notes Act of 1928, which amalgamated the Treasury's wartime currency note issue with that of the Bank of England. Keynes criticized

[44] Moggridge, *British Monetary Policy*, 162–3.
[45] S. Howson, *Domestic Monetary Management in Britain, 1919–38* (Cambridge, 1975), 68.
[46] Debt Policy and Unemployment', by Hawtrey, 29 June 1929, T175/26.
[47] Howson, op. cit., 37.
[48] Cmd. 2800, para 104, cited by Hawtrey, 29 June 1929, T175/26.
[49] Howson, op. cit., 41, 47–54.

the Act for setting the new fiduciary issue at £260 million at a time when the aggregate note issue varied between £370 million and £380 million according to the season of the year. The smaller the fiduciary issue—that is the fixed amount of notes not backed by gold—the more gold the Bank of England had to use to back its notes. Keynes thought that the Bank would have to lock up £110 million to £120 million of its gold reserves for this purpose, leaving only £50 million or less of the Bank's current gold reserves available to support the exchange rate. The last figure, he argued was much too small in relation to Britain's foreign trade (a one per cent variation in imports, he estimated, represented £11 million) or in relation to liquid foreign balances held in London (which, he thought, might be anything between £200 million and £300 million).[50] The likelihood was, therefore, that any pressure on sterling would force the Bank to deflate.

The Treasury's defence was that the figure of £260 million for the fiduciary issue was slightly in excess of the maximum requirement as shown by recent experience of the Bank's gold reserves, and that that figure 'had all the necessary rigidity to satisfy the world . . . that our gold standard remained a real gold standard and as good as any before'. The figure could be varied temporarily at the request of the Bank, if the Chancellor agreed, and any change could be made permanent by legislation—a procedure designed 'to make clear . . . that we were not providing easy means for a purely inflationary policy'.[51] The Act was thus designed to prevent a recurrence of inflation. However, recent experience was to be a poor guide as to what levels of gold reserves would be necessary to support sterling in the international financial crisis of 1931.

FISCAL POLICY, 1924–1930

It was in Churchill's nature to make his budgets as dramatic as possible. He used the occasion of his budget speech in 1925 not only to announce the return to the gold standard, but also to introduce a new scheme for widows', orphans', and old-age contributory pensions, although neither measure was strictly a budget proposal. In 1926, against his officials' advice, he imposed a novel tax on betting transactions, which predictably shocked people who did not approve of betting, and foundered on the opposition of the bookmakers. In 1928, at the cost of considerable administrative and legislative effort, he altered the structure of income tax and supertax (which he renamed surtax) so that taxpayers liable for what had hitherto been separate taxes would make a single return. He also reformed the budget accounts in 1928, by presenting net figures instead of gross

[50] *JMK*, xix (part 2), 742–9.
[51] 'The Currency and Bank Notes Bill', n.d., but in Hopkins's notes for his evidence before the Macmillan Committee in 1930, T175/46.

as hitherto: for example, only the Post Office's surplus was included, instead of all of that government department's revenue and expenditure. Churchill's own accounting, however, was opaque, for he adopted a series of devices of unprecedented ingenuity for at least giving the appearance of balancing the budget, although, as contemporary critics observed, it was doubtful if he ever balanced current revenue and expenditure according to the strict canons of the day.[52]

TABLE 5.2. *Churchill's Budgets, Out-turn (£ m.)*

	1925/6	*1926/7*	*1927/8*	*1928/9*	*1929/30*
Revenue					
Customs and Excise	238.0	240.5	250.8	253.0	247.4
Income tax	259.4	234.7	250.6	237.6	237.4
Supertax	68.5	65.9	60.6	56.1	56.4
Other tax revenue[a]	118.6	122.8	131.4	138.5	135.4
Non-tax revenue[b]	127.5	141.8	149.4	151.2	138.4
Total revenue	812.0	805.7	842.8	836.4	815.0
Expenditure					
Debt interest and management	308.2	318.6	313.8	311.5	307.3
Sinking funds	50.0	60.0	65.0	57.5	47.7
Defence	119.4	116.7	117.4	113.5	113.0
Civil votes	243.3	240.5	229.8	222.5	246.5
Other[c]	105.2	106.6	112.5	113.1	115.0
Total expenditure	826.1	842.4	838.6	818.0	829.5
Balance	–14.0	–36.7	+4.2	+18.4	–14.5

Note: Owing to rounding, totals do not always balance to final decimal place.
   [a] Including Road Fund.
   [b] Including all Post Office revenue.
   [c] Including all Road Fund and Post Office expenditure.

Source: Bernard Mallet and C. O. George, *British Budgets, 1921/22 to 1932/33* (1933), tables 1 & 2.

The new Chancellor clashed early with his officials over the question of sinking funds to reduce the National Debt. Churchill believed that the commitment that he had inherited from Baldwin to the New Sinking Fund of £50 million annually was excessive, and that budget surpluses should no longer be applied to the reduction of the National Debt (a convention known as the Old Sinking Fund). Niemeyer by no means agreed that £50 million was excessive, as it represented under two-thirds of 1 per cent of the National Debt, whereas before 1914 the then New Sinking Fund had represented more than 1 per cent of the Debt. Consequently, he advised against any raiding of the Old Sinking Fund. Churchill thought that budget surpluses in one year should be used to assist the

   [52] Grigg, *Prejudice and Judgement*, 194–9; M. Short, 'The Politics of Personal Taxation: Budget-making in Britain, 1917–31', Ph.D. (Cambridge, 1985), 211–34.

budget in the following year—a proposal that shocked Niemeyer, who pointed out that a windfall surplus carried forward might allow taxation to be reduced in one year, although taxation would have to be raised again the following year. Treasury officials felt so strongly about the convention that tax raised in a given year should be spent in that year, or be used for debt redemption, that Fisher informed the Prime Minister of what was going on, with the comment: 'When the time comes I am going to tell Winston in my own language what I think about it'.[53]

Both Treasury officials and Labour critics believed that it would be better to reduce the National Debt than to reduce taxation. For example, Hugh Dalton, a professional economist and future Labour Chancellor of the Exchequer, shared the Treasury's belief that repayment of debt released funds for investment in industry, and urged Churchill to increase the New Sinking Fund.[54] However, Churchill hoped to encourage enterprise and thrift through remission of direct taxation.[55] His first budget made a bold reduction in the standard rate of income tax, from 4s. 6d. (22.5p) to 4s. (20p), at the estimated cost of £32 million in a full year. He also sought to shift the burden of taxation from the active to the inactive members of the community by increasing the relief given to earned income, and by providing relief to supertax payers, and balancing the lost revenue by increasing death duties. As Fisher told Neville Chamberlain some months later, these budget proposals were modest compared with what Churchill had originally proposed, and the official Treasury advice had been that the income tax proposals could only be justified if no further expenditure were agreed to. In the event, in order to prevent a miners' strike, Churchill agreed to the coal industry receiving a subsidy which was greater than Fisher believed to be necessary.[56] Consequently, the financial year ended with a deficit of £14 million, which was equivalent to a reduction in the New Sinking Fund from £50 million to £36 million.

Churchill's taxation strategy depended upon economies in central government expenditure: indeed, in his budget speech in 1925 he set himself what proved to be an impossible target of a net reduction in Supply expenditure of not less than £10 million a year. Fisher wrote to Baldwin suggesting a new Geddes Committee, on the grounds that no Cabinet committee would be effective in identifying where major economies might be made.[57] However, it was a Cabinet Economy Committee that was set up, and the outcome was the Economy Bill of March 1926, which budgeted for savings of only £8 to £10 million in the

[53] Fisher to Baldwin, 13 Mar. 1925 and 'Old Sinking Fund', 6 Mar. 1925, Baldwin papers, 3/146–50. See also Churchill to Niemeyer, 28 Oct. 1926, reprinted in Churchill, *Winston S. Churchill*, vol. v companion, part 1, 859–61.

[54] 194 HC Deb., 5s, 1926, cols. 1724, 1770–1. For Dalton's arguments in favour of debt redemption, preferably through a capital levy, see also his *Principles of Public Finance* (1923), ch. 23.

[55] Churchill to Hopkins, 14 Dec. 1924, reprinted in Churchill, *Winston S. Churchill*, vol. v companion, part 1, 300–1.   [56] Neville Chamberlain's diary, 1 Nov. 1925, NC2/21.

[57] Fisher to Baldwin, 26 May 1925, Baldwin papers 3/154.

coming financial year, and £7 to £9 million in 1927/8, mainly through reductions in state contributions to health and unemployment insurance. The economy campaign had rather more success in 1927/8, £10.5 million being saved from Estimates that had already been scrutinized by the Treasury or from money voted by Parliament. Nevertheless, the principal intention and effect of these efforts was to create an atmosphere of parsimony that would constrain further growth of expenditure, rather than to make actual reductions.[58]

Whereas central government expenditure had fallen by 2.1 percentage points of GDP in the period 1921–5, it rose by 0.6 percentage points of GDP in 1925–9.[59] Government expenditure tended to be largely unresponsive to falling prices. In contrast, the nominal yield of tax revenue tended to fall as the purchasing power of the pound rose under the gold standard, with the result that revenue tended to fall below estimates. As Hawtrey pointed out in a paper connected with the 1928 budget, historical experience since 1867 showed that periods of falling prices were unfavourable to decreases in taxation.[60] The late 1920s, however, were particularly unfavourable: the General Strike and the seven months' stoppage in the coalfields in 1926 reduced revenue by £13.5 million in 1926/7, with a further £30 million lost in income tax and supertax or surtax in subsequent years, mainly 1927/8.[61]

In the circumstances, it is hardly surprising that Churchill had a deficit of £36.6 million in 1926/7, or that his declared surplus of £4.2 million in 1927/8 was achieved only by unrepeatable expedients yielding £32 million. The Road Fund reserve of £12 million was transferred to the Exchequer and used to balance current expenditure—a clear breach of the convention that such expenditure should be met out of current revenue; the collection of revenue from brewers was accelerated, bringing forwards £5 million from 1928/9 to 1927/8; and £15 million was found by similarly accelerating the collection of income tax under Schedule A. The last of these expedients was suggested by Hopkins, as chairman of the Board of Inland Revenue, and involved withdrawing the privilege granted in 1918 whereby income tax assessed on property was paid in two equal instalments at six monthly intervals, and instead collecting in January payments that otherwise would have fallen due in July of the following financial year.[62] Even so, the £4.2 million budget surplus included £9.5 million more than estimated from death duties, leading Churchill to remark that, in a year in which revenue had generally been below estimates, death had been almost the Treasury's only friend.[63]

Churchill's attempts at debt redemption were similarly less than they seemed in the published figures for sinking funds. In 1926/7 he abstained from any

[58] B. Mallet and C. O. George, *British Budgets, 1921/22 to 1932/33* (1933), 157, 215; R. Middleton, *Towards the Managed Economy: Keynes, the Treasury and the Fiscal Policy Debate of the 1930s* (1985), 44.
[59] Middleton, op. cit., 42.   [60] 'The Trade Cycle and the Budget', n.d., T208/136.
[61] 205 HC Deb., 5s, 1927, cols. 59–60.
[62] Hopkins to Chancellor, 11 Oct. 1926, T171/256.   [63] 216 HC Deb., 5s, 1928, cols. 59–60.

reduction in taxation in order to raise the New Sinking Fund from £50 million to £60 million, thereby compensating for the budget deficit of the previous year. However, the budget deficit of £36.7 million in 1926/7 reduced debt redemption in that year effectively to only £23.3 million. In 1927/8 he provisionally allocated £50 million to the New Sinking Fund, a sum which he increased during the financial year to £65 million. However, this £15 million increase did little more than balance the £12 million taken from the Road Fund. In 1928/9 and 1929/30 he substituted for the New Sinking Fund a fixed debt charge of £355 million to cover interest and the £51 million required to meet specific sinking funds on certain government stocks, but in the latter year the interest charges were underestimated, and the amount of debt redeemed was only £47.7 million.[64]

Churchill's willingness to depart from the convention of annual budgeting was not always directed at disguising a deficit. He was also prepared to raise taxation in advance of expenditure. When introducing the new pensions scheme in his 1925 budget, he observed that there would be no cost to the Exchequer for two years but that the cost would rise to £15 million in ten years. He therefore proposed to spread the cost evenly over the ten-year period, in instalments of £5¾ million a year from 1926/7.[65]

More controversially, in his 1928 budget, he carried forward the £4.2 million surplus from the preceding year, together with the anticipated £5.5 million surplus for 1928/9, to a 'Suspense Fund', or Account, instead of applying the surplus to debt redemption as he was required to do by budget convention. The Suspense Account was set up to help finance a favourite scheme of Churchill's for helping productive enterprises by relieving industry of 75 per cent of its liability for local government taxation (rates) and for completing the 'derating' of agriculture, which had already been relieved of 50 per cent of rates in 1896 and of 75 per cent in 1923. Rating relief was expected to reduce total local authority income by £22 million a year, and Churchill proposed to compensate local authorities through block grants from the Exchequer. These grants would be financed partly from the Suspense Account, partly from economies in central government expenditure, but mainly from a new fuel tax which was calculated to raise £14 million in 1928/9 and £17.8 million in 1929/30. The scheme was not to take effect until October 1929, six months after the end of the financial year in which the new tax was introduced.[66]

The preparation of the derating scheme required the Treasury to look further ahead than one year in making financial forecasts. In December 1927 Churchill asked his officials to prepare projections of budget prospects for the

[64] 'Notes on the New Sinking Fund', n.d., but 1930, Worthington-Evans papers.
[65] 183 HC Deb., 5s, cols. 1924–5, 79–80.
[66] Mallet and George, *British Budgets, 1921–33*, 222–3. Churchill's first thoughts on the subject are set out in a note to Alfred Hurst, 4 June 1927, Churchill papers, CHAR18/64, Churchill College, Cambridge.

financial years 1928/9 to 1932/3, so as to form a view whether there would be sufficient central government funds available to compensate local authorities for lost rate income. Fisher described the resulting figures as 'conjectures' which, among other things, assumed revenue based upon a net growth of profits over the period (the international depression after 1929 could not have been foreseen) as well as stable expenditure, although Fisher anticipated pressures for increased defence and civil expenditure in the 1930s. On this basis the estimated deficit in the future budgets arising from the derating scheme was £17 million annually—hence the new fuel tax referred to above.[67]

Rating relief also required co-operation with the Ministry of Health, to which Neville Chamberlain had returned in 1924 with his own agenda of Poor Law reform. Chamberlain's intention, achieved through the Local Government Act of 1929, was to abolish boards of guardians and to transfer their responsibilities to the borough and county councils. Rating relief was thus part of a major reform of local government finance, and was further complicated by differences in approach by the two ministers concerned. Whereas Chamberlain was aware of the detailed difficulties and the need for careful negotiations with local authorities, Churchill hoped to capture the imagination of the electorate by a great stroke of policy that would show that the government was able to help industry and agriculture, and save money into the bargain.[68] Treasury officials believed that the Exchequer's commitment to meet a percentage of the costs of many grant-aided services was an inducement to local authorities to spend, and certainly expenditure on these services had risen year by year since the war. Officials hoped that if percentage grants could be replaced by block grants, which would be fixed for three-year periods, starting in 1930/1, this upward trend would be limited. In the event, many local authorities reduced expenditure on grant-aided services after 1931 and received more from block grants than they would have done under the old system.[69] On the other hand, as a result of derating, roughly two-thirds of revenue raised from rates came from households, ensuring that even Labour-controlled local authorities would be reluctant to incur the ratepayers' wrath by spending extravagantly.[70]

Hopkins and Fisher feared that, with the new fuel tax, the Chancellor was pledging the last form of indirect taxation that might have been used to reduce the National Debt. As a result Fisher advised Chamberlain privately in December 1927 that the derating scheme was not thought in the Treasury to be financially watertight, and suggested that the Minister of Health should ask for a

---

[67] Fisher to Churchill, 20 Dec. 1927, T175/13.

[68] For differences between Churchill and Chamberlain see Addison, *Churchill*, 276–80; Dilks, *Neville Chamberlain*, i. 494, 502–3, 511–14, 534–57; Gilbert, *Winston S. Churchill*, v. 295–7.

[69] Jonathan Bradbury, 'The 1929 Local Government Act: The Formulation and Implementation of the Poor Law (Health Care) and Exchequer Grant Reforms for England and Wales', Ph.D. (Bristol, 1992), 167–8, 252–65.

[70] J. E. Cronin, *The Politics of State Expansion: War, State and Society in Twentieth-Century Britain* (1991), 96.

Cabinet committee to consider it, predicting that, if the Cabinet did not approve the scheme, the Chancellor would not resign.[71] In the event the dispute between Churchill and Chamberlain was argued out in full Cabinet on a number of occasions between December 1927 and April 1928, but the only major concession made by Churchill was to change his original proposal for a complete abolition of rates on industry, with a quarter of that concession being recouped through a new profits tax, to one for relief of 75 per cent of rates with no profits tax. Once again the Chancellor had prevailed in the face of opposition from Fisher. According to Chamberlain, Churchill had relied heavily upon a clever but relatively junior Treasury official, Alfred Hurst, for drafting his proposals for rating relief,[72] and Hurst seems to have had his reward in being promoted from the rank of assistant secretary to principal assistant secretary, a rank held by only two other Treasury officials in 1928.

Tariffs would have been a more direct means of assisting British industry. Indeed, Churchill's rating relief scheme was criticized by Lloyd George and Snowden precisely because it was a form of protection. Nevertheless, Churchill's defence of free trade, against considerable pressure from protectionists in the Cabinet, has been identified by one of his biographers as his principal achievement at the Treasury.[73] Free trade was a principle on which the Chancellor and his advisers were at one. Churchill did restore the McKenna Duties in his 1925 budget, but he did so only after Sir Horace Hamilton, chairman of the Board of Customs and Excise, had advised that the duties could be reintroduced for revenue purposes, as none of the protected goods could be described as necessities.[74] Snowden's abolition of the duties was calculated to have cost the Exchequer £2¾ million in a full year, and Churchill preferred to restore them to help to compensate for revenue lost through his reduction in the standard rate of income tax.

The Chancellor and his officials were agreed that proposals for a tariff on imported steel must be resisted, on the grounds that steel was a raw material for engineering and allied trades, which would suffer from increased costs if steel were protected, with detrimental effects on British exports.[75] In general, the Treasury line was that protection might give greater employment in the case of single trade, but the aggregate result of all such cases must be to increase costs, and to reduce production and the standard of living, with the result that there would be no greater employment on balance. Moreover, in 1927 Niemeyer optimistically believed that: 'the indications are turning against protection; and the excuses for it are diminished by . . . more stable currencies and general recovery. . . . For the greatest European exporting country to move in opposition

---

[71] Hopkins to Fisher, 15 Dec. 1927, T175/12; Neville Chamberlain's diary, 17 Dec. 1927, NC2/22.
[72] Gilbert, *Winston S. Churchill*, v. 296.   [73] Addison, *Churchill*, 250.
[74] 'The McKenna Duties', 27 Feb. 1925, T171/249.
[75] Leith-Ross to Chancellor, 12 June 1925, and Churchill to Hamilton, Fisher, and Hopkins (the last then being chairman of the Board of Inland Revenue), 10 Aug. 1925, T175/10.

to the dominant tendency in Europe would be a very serious matter.' Consequently, in his view, there should be no further meddling with import duties to raise revenue.[76]

In Snowden the Treasury had a Chancellor no less dedicated than Churchill to free trade, although the revenue position was such that he could not afford to do away with the McKenna duties in 1930, as he had done in 1924. Snowden also adopted a characteristically Gladstonian position with regard to budget deficits. When the out-turn for 1929/30 proved to be a deficit of £14.5 million, he proposed to pay it off out of revenue over three years, £5 million being provided for this purpose in the budget for 1930/1. Moreover, the 1930 Finance Bill terminated the practice, arising from legislation during the First World War, of covering budget deficits by borrowing without consulting Parliament. A prospective deficit of over £40 million in the 1930 budget on the 1929/30 basis of taxation was met principally by increasing income tax by 6d. (2½p) to 4s. 6d. (22.5p) and the top rate of surtax from 6s. (30p) to 7s. 6d. (37.5p) to raise £28.5 million. Reflecting Snowden's socialist principles, almost the whole of this sum came from the better-off taxpayers because the graduation of income tax was revised in a way that relieved three-quarters of income tax payers from any increase.

Notwithstanding his criticism of his predecessor's unorthodox budgetary practices, Snowden helped himself in 1930/1 to £16 million from one of Churchill's 'nest-eggs', the Rating Relief Suspense Account. He soon had to consider whether to follow Churchill's example further in the practice of fiscal window dressing. As early as July 1930 it was plain that a Supplementary Estimate for unemployment relief would result in a budget deficit for 1930/1, and Hopkins wondered whether the provision of £5 million to redeem part of the deficit for 1929/30 should not be diverted to reducing the deficit for 1930/1. 'It is a choice between less righteousness and a smaller deficit, and greater righteousness and a larger deficit', he noted wryly. He advised that the provision for redeeming part of the 1929/30 deficit should remain in the Finance Bill, as to do otherwise would raise doubts about the adequacy of existing taxation to meet expenditure and therefore would add to business pessimism.[77] In the event the budget out-turn for 1930/1 was a deficit of £23.2 million.

DEFENCE POLICY, 1924–1930

Churchill's attitude towards the armed forces, and particularly his old department, the Admiralty, can only be understood in the context of his budgetary difficulties. There was also a party-political dimension. Churchill was aware of the

---

[76] Niemeyer to Chancellor, 19 July 1927, T175/10.
[77] Hopkins to Grigg, 14 July 1930, T171/282.

need to maintain the Conservatives' electoral appeal in the face of Labour opposition. Consequently, in November 1924 he advised the Cabinet to 'concentrate on a few great issues in the social sphere', such as housing or national insurance, rather than fritter away revenue on a variety of services. With regard to defence, he recognized the need to spend more on the air force, in fulfilment of the expansion scheme agreed in 1923, and that there was little, if any, scope for reduction in the size of the army. His major hope for economy, therefore, lay in questioning the need for expenditure on the navy. Indeed, as he told Baldwin the following month, the Admiralty's new construction programme would raise the naval Estimates from £55 million for 1925/6 to £80 million by 1927/8, by which date the air Estimates were likely to have increased by £5 million. Churchill warned that this extra expenditure of £30 million would absorb all prospective reductions in expenditure or increases in revenue, leaving no scope for reductions in taxation or social reform, adding: 'I cannot conceive any more course more certain to result in a Socialist victory.'[78] Thus the combined logic of Treasury orthodoxy and party politics led Churchill, the great naval builder of 1911–15, back to his earlier position as an advocate of economy in naval expenditure.

Unlike most chancellors, Churchill had a passionate interest in grand strategy and he was prepared to challenge the Admiralty's arguments in support of higher Estimates. He insisted on having access to naval intelligence, in the form of intercepted telegrams between the Japanese embassy and Tokyo, to ensure that he would not be at a disadvantage in discussions with Admiralty representatives. In the absence of any serious threat from Germany, the Admiralty's case rested upon the strength of the Japanese navy. Churchill accepted that Japan could be a formidable enemy, but he did not believe that there was the 'slightest chance' of war with Japan 'in our lifetime'. The Admiralty's plans assumed that the main British fleet might have to move to the Far East to protect British interests there, and that therefore there should be a large, fortified, naval base at Singapore, together with adequate stocks of fuel along the route from Britain, as well as a submarine base at Hong Kong. Churchill, in contrast, did not think that the defences at Singapore need be completed for another fifteen to twenty years, and that no more than a floating dock and a 'gradual and discreet' provision of fuel supplies was required. Moreover, he challenged the scale of the Admiralty's war plans. The only war worth fighting in the Far East, he believed, would be to prevent an invasion of Australia; a war with Japan over Hong Kong would last for years, reducing Britain to bankruptcy and exposing the British Isles to threats from unfriendly powers. Instead of planning offensive operations in Japanese home waters, he said, the Admiralty should aim at securing trade routes in the Indian Ocean by arranging to send no more than a

---

[78] Cabinet minutes, 26 Nov. 1924, CAB23/49; Churchill, *Winston S. Churchill*, vol. v companion, part 1, 303–5.

squadron of fast capital ships to Singapore at the outbreak of a war with Japan, to take a defensive role until such time as the superior Japanese fleet had been reduced by submarines, mines, aircraft, or coastal guns.[79]

The Admiralty naturally did not care for this strategic analysis, especially when Churchill recommended in January 1925 that no major warships should be laid down by Britain in the coming year. Fisher sought to support Churchill's recommendation by sending Baldwin a memorandum by Barstow which argued that such a policy would allay fears aroused in Japan by the Conservative government's decision to restart work on the Singapore base.[80] As ever, however, the Admiralty was able to put up a stern defence against a challenge from the Treasury. The original naval Estimates for 1925/6 included the cost of laying down five cruisers, the same number as the Labour government had approved for 1924/5. When Churchill and the First Lord, William Bridgeman, failed to reach agreement, the Cabinet agreed to refer the matter to a Cabinet committee, which, to Bridgeman's amazement, found in favour of the Chancellor. However, faced with the threat of resignation by Bridgeman, and possibly by the whole Board of the Admiralty, the Cabinet reversed this decision and agreed in July to a compromise, suggested by Bridgeman, for four cruisers in 1925/6 and three in 1926/7. The Admiralty for its part secured some economies by scrapping older warships with high maintenance costs, and by closing dockyards.[81]

However, in March Churchill had secured a ruling from the Committee of Imperial Defence that the navy should not prepare for a campaign in the Far East before 1935. Churchill's next move was to have a Committee on Navy, Army, and Air Force Expenditure appointed, with a businessman, Lord Colwyn, as chairman, and two former permanent secretaries of the Treasury, Lords Bradbury and Chalmers, as the other members. The Committee's report in December 1925 castigated the Admiralty for having got 'completely out of touch with up-to-date civilian experience' in its administrative methods, leading Bridgeman to comment: 'I have seldom seen a more offensive document. . . . but what can you expect from 2 Treasury Clerks & a war millionaire?' Rather than act upon the advice of three civilians who had never been to sea, the Admiralty itself managed to produce sufficient economies from the 1926/7 sketch Estimates both to satisfy Churchill and to pay for the new construction agreed the previous July.[82]

Churchill pressed even harder thereafter, and in August 1927 called for a halt in cruiser construction pending a fresh enquiry by a Cabinet committee. He

[79] Churchill, op. cit., 300, 305–7, 361, 380, 451.

[80] Barstow to Fisher, 3 Feb. 1925, Baldwin papers, 2/47–9.

[81] Phillip Williamson (ed.), *The Modernisation of Conservative Politics: The Diaries and Letters of William Bridgeman, 1904–1935* (1988), 178–88.

[82] Ibid., 192; Lord Chatfield, *It Might Happen Again* (1947), 11. There is a copy of the report in the Churchill papers, CHAR18/14.

believed that it would be sufficient to lay down one cruiser in 1928 and two in 1929 in order to retain a predominance over Japan and America, and suggested that if either Japan or America were to lay down more cruisers meantime Britain could easily catch up in the 1930s. The Admiralty, on the other hand, argued that building should not be delayed, as many of the existing cruisers would be too old after 1935, when battleship building, suspended under the Washington Treaty, was expected to be resumed. Churchill's financial arguments prevailed: only one cruiser was built under the 1927/8 programme and only two cruisers were included in the 1928/9 Estimates—and both of these were subsequently cancelled by the Labour government in 1929.[83]

Meanwhile, Churchill also worked to slow down the rate of expansion of the air force and instructed Barstow in January 1925 to 'formulate a score or a dozen criticisms of detail' to show that the Air Ministry was asking for more than it needed.[84] Given improved relations with France, it was not difficult to get a Cabinet committee to agree by the end of the year that the scheme for the expansion of the Home Defence Air Force should not be completed until 1935 rather than 1929.

Taken together, the decisions in 1925 that the navy's and air force's plans need not be complete until 1935 amounted to a reaffirmation of the Ten Year Rule, formulated in 1919, that defence Estimates should be made on the assumption that the British Empire would not be engaged in any great war during the next ten years. However, as Hopkins pointed out in 1928, unless a new ruling were obtained, the defence departments would be able to increase their expenditure as the critical date 1935 came nearer. Accordingly, he suggested that the Cabinet should be asked to lay down an assumption that, at any given date, there would not be a major war for ten years from that date—the assumption to stand until, on the initiative of the Foreign Office, or one of the defence departments, the Cabinet decided to abrogate or alter it. Churchill took up the suggestion with his accustomed vigour and it was accepted by the Committee of Imperial Defence and the Cabinet. Although the pressure for this strengthening of the Ten Year Rule came from the Treasury, the decision was taken, as before, with the acquiescence of the Foreign Office.[85]

The Treasury had at last secured an effective means of controlling defence expenditure. Up to that point, however, despite Churchill's efforts, major *reductions* in defence expenditure had proved to be elusive. Total defence expenditure in 1927/8 (£117.4 million) was higher than in 1924/5 (£114.7 million), but in 1928/9 it was down to £113.5 million and in 1929/30 £113 million.

[83] Churchill to Bridgeman, 18 Aug. 1927, Baldwin papers 2/138–40 and 184–5; Neville Chamberlain diary, 4 Dec. 1927, NC2/22; Stephen Roskill, *Naval Policy between the Wars*, vol. i *The Period of Anglo-American Antagonism, 1919–1929* (1968), 555–9, 582.

[84] Churchill, *Winston S. Churchill*, vol. v companion, part 1, 345.

[85] Hopkins to Grigg, 1 May 1928, T175/35; N. H. Gibbs, *Grand Strategy*, vol. i (1976), 58.

The advent of a Labour government in 1929, and preparations for a naval disarmament conference in London in 1930, gave Treasury officials hopes of further major reductions in expenditure. A. P. Waterfield, the head of the Treasury's division dealing with the defence departments, drafted a paper in December 1929 suggesting that over £14 million could be saved from the naval Estimates if international agreement could be reached on the abolition of capital ships and submarines. The Prime Minister, MacDonald, was sufficiently impressed by the paper's contents to ask for a copy which he could take with him on holiday to Lossiemouth. Given public opinion, especially within the Labour party, on the subject of disarmament, Snowden was able to have two cruisers, four destroyers, and three submarines cut from the 1930 Estimates, as proof of political goodwill in advance of the conference, despite warnings from the Admiralty of the dangers incurred thereby for national and imperial security. A senior Treasury official, Gilbert Upcott, was attached to the British delegation to the conference, in an attempt to ensure that financial considerations would be taken into account. The conference's results fell short of the Treasury's hopes, but agreement was reached between Britain, the United States, and Japan to postpone replacement of capital ships until 1936, and to place limits on building cruisers, destroyers, and submarines. Construction of the Singapore naval base was too far advanced for the Labour government to abandon it altogether, but, at an Imperial Conference in 1930, the dominions were persuaded to accept a postponement of work on the docks and on the base's defences, pending a further review in 1935.[86] The net result of these major strategic decisions, and other less contentious economies, was to bring the defence Estimates down from £110.5 million in 1930/1 to £107.28 million in 1931/2.

SOCIAL POLICY, 1924–1930

Given that revenue in 1928/9 was only £24.4 million greater than in 1925/6, there was clearly little scope for major initiatives in social reform (see Tables 5.2 and 5.3). When Churchill urged the Cabinet in November 1924 to concentrate on a few social issues, the ones he had in mind were housing and national insurance. Both Churchill and the Minister of Health, Neville Chamberlain, were agreed on the need to build houses in quantity. Although housing subsidies, per house, were cut in 1927, central government expenditure on housing increased throughout Churchill's period at the Treasury, from £9.1 million in 1925/6 to £12.1 million in 1928/9. The latter figure represented a large real increase on the £9.1 million spent in 1925/6, as the average cost of local authority houses fell by 28 per cent between 1925 and 1929.[87]

---

[86] 'Naval Conference', by Waterfield, 17 Dec. 1929, T172/1693; Gibbs, *Grand Strategy*, i. 30–1, 63.
[87] M. Bowley, *Housing and the State, 1919–1944* (1945), 277.

TABLE 5.3. *Central Government Expenditure
on Social Services in 1925/6 and 1928/9 (£ m.)*

	1925/6	1928/9
Education (including		
teachers' pensions)	47.1	47.8
Health services	3.5	4.0
Housing	9.1	12.1
Pensions		
Old-age, non-contributory	27.0	34.1
Widows', etc., contributory,	—	4.0
War	67.3	57.1
National health insurance	6.9	6.3
Unemployment insurance	13.5	11.8

Source: Committee on National Expenditure, *Report* (Cmd. 3920),
PP 1930–1, xvi, 1, tables B and C.

Chamberlain was also responsible for the Widows, Orphans, and Old Age
Contributory Pensions Act of 1925, but Churchill worked closely with him and
announced the measure in his budget speech that year. Contributory pensioners were to receive 10s. a week, without means test, between the ages of 65 and
70, when they would qualify for the existing non-contributory pension, which
had been raised to 10s. a week in 1919. However, whereas non-contributory
pensioners were means-tested, with deductions made on account of earnings,
contributory pensioners would continue to receive the full pension after age 70.
Contributions would be linked to the existing National Health Insurance
scheme, with the same income limit for participants (£250 a year), and with an
Exchequer subsidy paid into a Treasury Pensions Account. Macnicol has
claimed that a contributory pensions system was a long-standing goal of the
Treasury, on the grounds that such a system would place less of a burden on the
taxpayer than non-contributory pensions. However, he cites no Treasury
records to support this claim. Indeed the evidence is that the 1925 Act represented a Whitehall consensus on provision for old age, being based on the work
of an interdepartmental committee of officials representing the Customs and
Excise (which had been responsible for means-testing old-age pensions since
1908), the Ministry of Health, the Ministry of Labour, and the Scottish Office,
together with the Government Actuary, under the chairmanship of Sir John
Anderson, the Permanent Under-Secretary of the Home Office. The Treasury was not directly represented on the Anderson Committee, although its
concerns about cost would have influenced its recommendations, as well as
the subsequent legislation. For example, budgetary constraints prevented
Chamberlain from fixing the contributory pension at a higher level than the
non-contributory one.[88]

[88] J. Macnicol, *Politics of Retirement in Britain, 1878–1948* (Cambridge, 1998), 186, 190–1, 200–2, 208–15.

Churchill favoured 'an "all-in" insurance scheme' as a possible objective,[89] but in fact health insurance, unemployment insurance, and the new widows', orphans', and old-age contributory pensions, were to remain separate until after the Second World War. The Chancellor resisted Chamberlain's ideas in 1925 for improving health insurance by providing dental treatment and more sophisticated medical care, with the remark: 'Is this the time to put forward such plans?' Chamberlain recognized the need to find economies, and agreed with Churchill's proposal in 1926 to cut the state's contribution to health insurance. However, the savings under this head were not large, the state's contribution in 1928/9 being £6.3 million compared with £6.9 million in 1925/6.[90]

From the Treasury's point of view, much larger savings might have been made in the state's contribution to unemployment insurance, which stood at £13.5 million in 1925/6, compared with £7.8 million as recently as 1921/2. Describing himself as 'the original author of the Unemployment Insurance Act' (of 1911), and therefore as having 'some qualification to speak on the subject', Churchill wrote to the Minister of Labour, Sir Arthur Steel-Maitland, to complain about the way in which the insurance principle had been undermined.[91] As noted in Chapter 4, successive governments since 1921 had allowed workers, who had been unable to maintain their contributions, to collect what was then called 'uncovenanted benefit' and was from 1924 called 'extended benefit'. Since large-scale unemployment had been expected to be temporary, it had been supposed that workers in receipt of uncovenanted benefit would pay contributions later. As unemployment persisted, the Unemployment Insurance Fund had to borrow more and more money from the Treasury. Churchill strongly favoured abolition of extended benefit and its replacement by discretionary payments, but had to be content with the withdrawal in 1926 of extended benefit from limited classes of workers, who were thus thrown back on the Poor Law. Moreover, the Blanesburgh Committee, which reviewed unemployment insurance, and whose report formed the basis of legislation in 1927, recommended that standard and extended benefit be merged, and claimed actuarial soundness on the basis of an unfulfilled expectation that unemployment would fall markedly by 1930.

The Treasury itself, however, has been blamed for all but £4 million of the Unemployment Insurance Fund's accumulated debt of £28 million in 1928. The Treasury had consistently tried to save money at the expense of the Fund and, in particular, in 1926 had refused to compensate it for a reduction in employers' contributions by increasing the state's contribution.[92] Despite his claims to paternity with regard to unemployment insurance, Churchill believed

---

[89] Cabinet minutes, 26 Nov. 1924, CAB23/49.   [90] Dilks, *Neville Chamberlain*, i. 428.

[91] Churchill to Steel-Maitland, 19 Sept. 1925, Baldwin papers, 7/378.

[92] R. Lowe, *Adjusting to Democracy: The Role of the Ministry of Labour in British Politics, 1916–1939* (Oxford, 1986), 143, 153.

that the state 'should so far as possible . . . disengage itself to an increasing extent from what is after all primarily a trade matter'.[93] However, savings in the state's annual contribution (down to £11.8 million in 1928/9 from £13.5 million in 1925/6) were won only at the cost of storing up trouble for the future, for the Fund could only continue to operate by borrowing from the Treasury, or by restricting benefits.

On taking office, the second Labour government relaxed the 'genuinely seeking work' condition for benefits under the unemployment insurance scheme, just as unemployment began to rise, with the result that borrowing for the Fund increased. In an attempt to maintain some semblance of actuarial soundness, the whole cost of continuing benefit ('transitional benefit') to workers whose entitlement to unemployment insurance had run out was transferred to the Exchequer in February 1930. By July Treasury officials were already concerned about the effects on the budget balance. They believed that transitional benefit should be replaced by 'discretionary payments measured by . . . individual or family necessities'. One senior official, Upcott, complained that many workers on transitional benefit were 'getting maintenance allowances . . . amounting to as much as, or more than, many miners, agricultural workers and others can earn by working', and added that many claimants were 'obviously married women and others who, but for the relaxed conditions, would not have applied for or obtained either benefit or poor relief'.[94] The rapid increase in the numbers of married women receiving transitional benefit was also criticized by the Opposition parties, but the Prime Minister delayed action by setting up a Royal Commission on Unemployment Insurance late in 1930.

THE 'TREASURY VIEW' CHALLENGED

One apparent success for the Treasury in its search for economies in public expenditure was the decision, taken by the Cabinet in November 1925, to restrict grants to local authorities for schemes of public works to relieve unemployment.[95] As Table 5.4 shows, the number and value of schemes approved by the Unemployment Grants Committee thereafter fell precipitately. The International Labour Office was subsequently informed that the decision 'was based mainly on the view that, the supply of capital in the country being limited, it was undesirable to divert any appreciable proportion of this supply from normal trade channels'.[96] However, contrary to Treasury hopes, normal trade

---

[93] Churchill to Steel-Maitland, 20 Mar. 1927, Baldwin papers, 7/388.
[94] Hopkins to Fisher and note by Upcott, 15 July 1930, T175/51.
[95] Cabinet minutes, 25 Nov. 1925, CAB23/51.
[96] Cited in P. Clarke, *The Keynesian Revolution in the Making, 1924–1936* (Oxford, 1988), 48.

TABLE 5.4. *Total Cost of Schemes Approved by Unemployment Grants Committee, 1923–1931 (£m.)*

Date	Cost
July 1923–June 1924	24.22
July 1924–June 1925	20.64
July 1925–June 1926	17.56
July 1926–June 1927	0.79
July 1927–June 1928	0.32
July 1928–June 1929	6.18
September 1929–August 1930	41.77
September 1930–December 1931	35.23

Source: *Final Report of the Unemployment Grants Committee, 20th December 1920 to 31st August 1932* (Cmd. 4354), PP 1932–3, xv, 963.

channels failed to reduce unemployment significantly after the return to the gold standard in 1925, the annual average level in 1928 being 10.8 per cent of the insured labour force, somewhat down on the 1925 figure (11.3 per cent) but above that of 1927 (9.7 per cent).

At the end of 1927 Baldwin asked Fisher to chair a new Industrial Transference Board, which was set up to consider how workers, especially miners, could be moved from decaying to expanding industries; then in October 1928 Baldwin set up a committee of permanent secretaries under Fisher to see what special measures, if any, could be taken to reduce unemployment in the coming winter. The chairmanship of these committees required Fisher to consider questions relating to unemployment that had not hitherto come the way of the Permanent Secretary of the Treasury. Even so, in November 1928 he recommended the spending of only £20 million over three years on roads and other public works.[97]

A general election was due to take place in 1929 and the Liberal Opposition, led by Lloyd George, hoped to revive their fortunes by advocating an active employment policy. Lloyd George's supporters included Keynes, who, on 31 July 1928, published an article in the London *Evening Standard* in which he called upon the Bank of England to ease credit conditions and the Chancellor of the Exchequer to 'reverse his pressure against public spending on capital account', so that 'good projects' for roads, ports, housing, electrification, telephones, etc. could proceed.[98] The borrowing for these purposes would be done by local authorities or public utilities outside the Chancellor's budget, so that no budget deficit, as then conventionally understood, was called for. All would produce a money return either directly, for example from telephone subscribers, or indirectly, for example through the growing revenues of the Road Fund.

---

[97] O'Halpin, *Head of the Civil Service*, 167–8; Jones, *Whitehall Diary*, ii. 2, 146, 155. The major recommendation of the Industrial Transference Board was the assistance of movement of workers by advancing fares and removal expenses, some 270,000 people being transferred between 1929 and 1938.See D. E. Pitfield, 'The Quest for an Effective Regional Policy, 1934–37', *Regional Studies*, 12 (1978), 429–43.

[98] *JMK*, xix (part 2), 761–6.

By February 1929 Conservative ministers' concern about the effects of unemployment on their party's electoral prospects led to discussion in the Cabinet about the advisability of attempting to steal Lloyd George's thunder, either by raising a government-guaranteed loan for development works in the British Empire or by building roads at home. The running battle between the Treasury and Amery, whom Niemeyer described as a 'mad Mullah Minister', over colonial development had been resumed when Amery was appointed Colonial Secretary in 1924. Helped perhaps by the fact that Churchill himself had been an advocate of colonial development to relieve unemployment, when he was Colonial Secretary, Amery was able to win the Chancellor's approval in 1925 for £10 million to be made available under what became the East Africa Loans Act of 1926. However, as always, the devil was in the detail. Niemeyer was able to arrange for the appointment of an independent advisory committee of people with business or engineering experience to vet applications, and while loans under the Act were guaranteed by the British government, there was no subsidizing of interest charges. By the end of 1929 only £3.5 million of the loan had been spent.[99]

Relations between the Treasury and Amery were not improved by a series of disputes over an annual grant of aid of £1 million for the Empire Marketing Board, which Amery chaired: with the approval of the Cabinet the Treasury reduced the grant to £500,000 in 1926/7, its first year, and clawed back £600,000 in 1927/8 and £500,000 in 1928/9. In 1929 the Treasury still believed that resources directed by government to colonial development would be taken from private enterprise, which was more likely than government to direct investment to the greatest economic advantage. However, sensing the political pressure for something to be seen to be done about unemployment, the Treasury took the lead in 1929 in making proposals for a colonial development fund that would conform to its ideas rather than Amery's, and, in particular, to argue that the fund should have a board made up predominantly of businessmen to ensure the efficient use of capital. In the event these proposals were overtaken by the general election.[100]

Churchill's own preference for dealing with unemployment was a development of the derating scheme that he had included in his budget in 1928. By the summer of that year he wished to anticipate the effect of removing local government rates in the case of two industries with high unemployment, coal and steel, by subsidizing rail freights for the carriage of coal for export and for the use of blast furnaces, at an estimated cost to the Exchequer of £4 million. Grigg, his principal private secretary, consulted Sir Horace Wilson, the Permanent

[99] I. M. Drummond, *Imperial Economic Policy, 1917–1939: Studies in Expansion and Protection* (1974), 26; S. Constantine, *The Making of British Colonial Development Policy, 1914–1940* (1984), 144, 151–4, 158.

[100] Robert Self, 'Treasury Control and the Empire Marketing Board: The Rise and Fall of Non-Tariff Preference in Britain, 1924–1933', *20th Cent. Brit. Hist.*, 5 (1994), 153–82; Constantine, op. cit., 176–83.

Secretary of the Ministry of Labour, and Niemeyer at the Bank of England, both of whom took the view that unemployment was due to the working out of a healthy process of reorganization by the industries concerned. Niemeyer was prepared to admit that Churchill's proposals might do something to help, but advised against the state becoming directly involved in industrial reorganization, since then the taxpayer's money would be used to preserve inefficient firms. Grigg passed on their views, and added the advice that state intervention in industry that was seen to fail would strengthen the case for protection. Churchill complained to Hopkins about 'the Niemeyer attitude of letting everything smash into bankruptcy and unemployment',[101] and, despite doubts expressed by the Board of Trade about the effectiveness of a freight subsidy, pressed on with his proposal. However, he appears to have accepted Grigg's warning that the subsidy might enable inefficient railway companies to milk the taxpayer, for when the scheme was announced in Parliament on 24 July it was made plain that the subsidy would only be paid once the government was satisfied that the companies were making genuine efforts to effect economies.

The major Cabinet debates relating to unemployment centred on financial policy and public investment at home. In February 1929 the Minister of Labour, Sir Arthur Steel-Maitland, raised the question of whether it was true that such schemes would divert capital from ordinary business, remarking: 'After eight years of financial orthodoxy and eight years of unabating unemployment, ought we not to ask for a reasoned proof, for some foundations of belief that the financial policy by which we guide our steps is right?'[102] However, Churchill was no supporter of unremunerative public works: recalling how Lloyd George had toyed with 'big national schemes of artificial employment' at Gairloch in 1921, only to abandon them, he urged that the government 'should not try to compete with L.G.' but should take its stand on 'sound finance'.[103] In a speech on 1 March Lloyd George claimed that the Liberal party, if elected, was ready with schemes of work that would reduce unemployment to 'normal proportions' within a year, a claim that implied the creation of 586,000 jobs. It was against this background, on 15 April, that Churchill made the best known statement of the 'Treasury view' that 'very little additional employment and no permanent additional employment can in fact and as a general rule be created by State borrowing and State expenditure'.[104]

The arguments with which officials defended the 'Treasury view' against its critics outside and within the government in 1928–9 have been carefully set out by Peter Clarke.[105] An article by Hawtrey in *Economica* was used by Leith-Ross

[101] Churchill to Hopkins, 22 July 1928, *Winston S. Churchill*, vol. v, companion, part 1, 1310; Wilson to Grigg, 12 July, Niemeyer to Grigg, 19 July, Grigg to Churchill, 20 July 1928, Churchill papers CHAR22/218.   [102] Lowe, *Adjusting to Democracy*, 202.

[103] Jones, *Whitehall Diary*, ii. 175–6.   [104] 227 HC Deb., 5s, 1928–9, col. 54.

[105] Clarke, *Keynesian Revolution*, ch. 3, and 'The Treasury's Analytical Model of the British Economy between the Wars', in Furner and Supple (eds.), *The State and Economic Knowledge: The American and British Experiences* (Cambridge, 1990), 171–207.

and Grigg to provide the theoretical basis of the Treasury's case, although Hawtrey himself was on leave teaching at Harvard. Hawtrey believed that normally government expenditure financed by borrowing from the public would merely crowd out an equivalent amount of private investment, by raising interest rates, unless additional bank credit were created (a process then commonly called 'inflation', in the sense of an increase in the supply of money greater than an increase in the supply of goods). He argued that, provided that business showed a normal degree of enterprise, the creation of bank credit alone would be sufficient to increase employment, and that public works would only be necessary if business refused to respond to a fall in Bank rate to 2 per cent.[106] The Cabinet was told in February 1929 that 'unless the government are prepared to take steps to bring about an inflation of banking credits', government spending could only create employment if the government were able to find ways of spending money that would create more employment than private enterprise would with the same money.[107]

Churchill responded in March to Lloyd George's claims by asking his officials what would happen if £100 million of new credit were to be created by government borrowing on Ways and Means. Leith-Ross replied that the result of an expansion of credit would be to increase prices in Britain, thereby encouraging imports and production for the home market, but discouraging exports. Some of the extra credit would be used for investment in New York. With the sterling : dollar exchange rate already hovering about the level at which it would be profitable to export gold from London in order to buy dollars, the Bank of England would then have to protect its reserves by raising Bank rate until 'the expansion of credit (and the improvement of industry) that had occurred had been nullified. We should therefore soon be precisely where we were, except that we should have lost some gold'. It might be possible to defer an increase in Bank rate by increasing the fiduciary issue, thereby releasing gold for supporting the exchange rate, but Hopkins thought that such action would frighten foreign holders of sterling and lead them to withdraw their balances from London. 'Inflation' was thus incompatible with maintenance of the gold standard.[108]

When Lloyd George's claims appeared in print in the middle of March as a pamphlet, *We Can Conquer Unemployment*, Churchill advocated the publication of a rebuttal. The latter appeared in May, shortly before the election, in the form of a white paper entitled *Memoranda on Certain Proposals Relating to Unemployment*,[109] incorporating comments on the Liberal proposals by the ministries of Labour, Transport, and Health, and the Post Office, as well as the Treasury. The general

[106] R. G. Hawtrey, 'Public Expenditure and the Demand for Labour', *Economica*, 5 (1925), 38–48.
[107] Cabinet paper (hereafter CP) 53(29), 23 Feb. 1929, CAB24/202.
[108] Churchill to Leith-Ross, n.d., and Leith-Ross to Chancellor, 12 Mar. 1929, T172/2095.
[109] Cmd. 3331, PP 1928–9, xvi. 873.

drift of these comments was that the Liberal schemes were impracticable in the time allotted to them and would not provide as much employment as had been claimed.

The Treasury's contribution to the white paper was based on arguments deployed earlier for use in Cabinet. The Liberal proposals for loan expenditure on roads, housing, telephone and electrical development, and London passenger transport were costed at £250 million over two years, compared with actual provision of £254 million for state capital expenditure in the previous four years. The Treasury agreed that the state was responsible for developing public services, but argued that, in the absence of the 'natural test of profit-making capacity', all schemes for state capital expenditure should be tested by the criterion of whether they were likely to increase the efficiency of industry and enable it to lower its costs. It was also noted that the Liberal pamphlet claimed that the necessary funds could be raised from idle savings or by diverting money from foreign investment. The Treasury conceded that not all savings were currently being invested, but believed that most balances that had accumulated in the banks were funds that firms wished to keep liquid while business was slack and which were not, therefore, available for long-term lending to the state. As for foreign investment, the Treasury, unlike Keynes, still believed that the movement of capital abroad encouraged exports. In any case, the Treasury doubted the efficacy of controls on foreign investment, and noted that an attempt to divert overseas investment by competing with high money rates in America would force up interest rates in Britain. In these circumstances, it argued, 'a very large proportion of any additional government borrowings can only be procured, without inflation, by diverting money which otherwise would have been taken soon by home industry'.[110]

Recognizing the downward inflexibility of money wages, the Treasury denied that reduction in the costs of production was any longer synonymous with wage reductions. Instead the memorandum referred to the need for 'rationalization'. This term, which was frequently used at the time by bankers and industrialists, lacked precise definition, but implied that industry must adapt to changes in demand by eliminating surplus capacity, by achieving greater economies of scale through mergers, and by making improvements in management and marketing. The Treasury argued that the Liberal proposals would

---

[110] Cmd. 3331, 43–54. There seems to have been some difference of opinion within the Treasury as to the relative advantage of overseas and home investment to British industry: Phillips, then a principal assist-ant secretary in the Finance Department, noted: 'If unemployment is extremely bad, I prefer to see the pendulum swinging a little in favour of capital investment at home. According to the Board of Trade people, the heightening of the slump in 1928 was *not* in connection with the export trade; relatively to internal trade the export trades were slightly improving their position.' Leith-Ross, however, continued to take the traditional view that British heavy industries had been built up on the basis of a flow of orders from abroad arising from overseas investment and that 'to shut down foreign loans would do exceedingly grave damage . . . to British industry' (Phillips to Leith-Ross, 11 Mar. 1929 and notes by Leith-Ross, 3 Apr. 1929, T172/2095).

tend to encourage false hopes among industrialists and workers, and thereby delay the necessary changes.[111] This analysis seems to have reflected the view, expressed a year earlier by Niemeyer and Wilson, that unemployment was a sign of a healthy process of industrial reorganization.

In promoting his active employment policy, Lloyd George was able to draw upon the services of Keynes and another economist then active in Liberal politics, Hubert Henderson. Keynes had not yet developed a theoretical rationale to support an active employment policy, but he believed intuitively that it must be possible to finance public capital expenditure at a time when there were unemployed resources and more savings than were being used for home investment, *'for it is with the unemployed men and unemployed plant, and with nothing else, that these things are done'* (emphasis in the original).[112] This rhetoric avoided the problem of how exports could be expanded to pay for imports of raw materials, either for the Liberal schemes or, more importantly, for the increasing industrial activity that they were designed to promote, a serious omission if, as Keynes believed, sterling was still overvalued. The most considered case for the Liberal pledge made before the election was a pamphlet by Keynes and Henderson, *Can Lloyd George Do It?* but, as Donald Moggridge has commented, its exposition of the effects of a reduction in foreign lending was unclear and no attention was paid to exports. Hawtrey found its treatment of idle bank balances 'extremely obscure'. Likewise, although Keynes and Henderson argued that the Liberal programme would provide employment not only directly on the schemes and indirectly on contracts for inputs (for example, in quarries or brickfields), but also through what they vaguely referred to as the 'cumulative force of trade activity', they had no means of calculating how much employment would be created.[113]

THE 'TREASURY VIEW' REVISED

In the event it was the Labour party, under Ramsay MacDonald, that formed the government after the election in June 1929, albeit without a parliamentary majority and dependent on Lloyd George's Liberals for support. Labour had made a commitment, which was deliberately kept vague, to do something about unemployment. Snowden, as chairman of a party committee on unemployment before the election, had said that he was 'prepared to suspend, if necessary, some of our financial orthodoxy', for example, by borrowing £100 million

[111] Cmd. 3331, 52–3. For an account of rationalization see W. R. Garside and J. J. Greaves, 'Rationalisation and Britain's Industrial Malaise: The Interwar Years Revisited', *J. Eur. Econ. Hist.*, 26 (1997), 37–68.   [112] *JMK*, xix (part 2), 765.

[113] 'The Liberal Unemployment Plan', by Hawtrey, 13 June 1929, T175/26; D. E. Moggridge, *Maynard Keynes: An Economist's Biography* (1992), 464. *Can Lloyd George Do It?* is reprinted in *JMK*, ix.

secured on Road Fund revenues.[114] In July 1929, despite his officials' reservations, he agreed to a Colonial Development Bill that empowered the Treasury,
with the agreement of the Colonial Office and on the recommendation of an
advisory committee, to advance money to any territory for agricultural or
industrial development that would promote trade or industry in Britain. A fund
of up to £1 million a year could be used for capital grants or meeting interest
charges.[115] Much larger sums were concerned in creating jobs directly in
Britain. By June 1930 the Labour government had approved public works programmes totalling £110.1 million, of which, however, only £44.3 million were in
operation, owing to the inevitable delays in starting new schemes.[116]

By December 1929 the Treasury had approved a £17.5 million extension to a
£37-million road programme approved five months earlier, although it was estimated that the cumulative deficit of the Road Fund would rise to £21.4 million
by 1933/4. Hopkins was far from happy about borrowing for constructing
roads, observing that:

A road, however useful it may be, produces no revenue to the State; it does not provide
the interest and Sinking Fund on any loan raised. Accordingly, therefore, according to
time-honoured principles of public finance it should be paid for out of revenue.[117]

Despite this advice, Snowden continued to favour roads, and in June 1930 he
approved an increase in the trunk road programme from £13.5 million to
£21 million, although Hopkins again complained that 'this is sheer borrowing
for current expenditure'.[118]

The Labour government was not, however, committed to the scale of expenditure set out in the Liberals' *We Can Conquer Unemployment*, which the minister
responsible for unemployment policy, J. H. Thomas, the Lord Privy Seal,
regarded as 'out of all proportion to what can be economically justified'. In
common with the Treasury, Thomas regarded the weakened position of the
export industries as the 'root cause' of unemployment and believed that 'unproductive expenditure at home can only add to this weakness'.[119]

On the other hand, Sir Oswald Mosley who, as Chancellor of the Duchy of
Lancaster, was Thomas's junior ministerial colleague with responsibility for
unemployment policy, doubted whether the export industries would ever be
able to reabsorb the unemployed. He therefore favoured a long-term strategy of
developing the home market with full employment, high wages, and easy credit.
Public works, financed by a national loan of £200 million, would, he claimed,

[114] Philip Williamson, *National Crisis and National Government: British Politics, the Economy and Empire,
1926–1932* (Cambridge, 1992), 40.
[115] Constantine, *Making of British Colonial Development Policy*, 184–7.
[116] Roger Middleton, 'The Treasury and Public Investment: A Perspective on Inter-war Economic
Management', *Public Admin.*, 61 (1983), 361.
[117] Hopkins to Fisher and Snowden, 3 Dec. 1929, T161/557/S34462/3, cited in W. H. Janeway, 'The
Economic Policy of the Second Labour Government, 1929–31', Ph.D. (Cambridge, 1971), 41.
[118] Janeway, op. cit., 51–2.   [119] CP345(29), 29 Nov. 1929, CAB24/207.

provide employment for 300,000 men for three years, during which time the rationalization of industry and adjustment to new markets would take place with government financial assistance. Changes to the machinery of government would be required to ensure that both the road programme and rationalization went ahead promptly, and Mosley envisaged that policy would be in the hands of a powerful executive committee of leading ministers concerned with economic policy, headed by the Prime Minister, and advised by economists and scientists. A memorandum setting out these ideas was submitted to the Cabinet in February 1930 but was referred to a Cabinet committee on unemployment policy, chaired by Snowden, who ensured that the Treasury had plenty of time in which to prepare counter arguments.[120]

Within the Treasury, Leith-Ross was prepared to admit that the Mosley memorandum contained an effective criticism of the way in which rationalization of British industries was proceeding very slowly, but, he argued, the solution was for the joint stock banks to support the efforts already being made by the Bank of England to promote rationalization. What Leith-Ross and Hopkins feared was political pressure for the government to organize rationalization, because then, as they pointed out to ministers, the government of the day would be responsible for writing down the value of private investors' shares or for closing down factories, at the risk of losing a constituency in the case of large undertakings. In such circumstances the temptation would be for government to provide financial assistance so that 'superfluous and wasteful organisations would be maintained for political reasons'. Officials had no difficulty in persuading Snowden to oppose this aspect of the Mosley memorandum.[121]

The Treasury also, predictably, opposed any reorganization of the machinery of government that would reduce the authority of the Chancellor of the Exchequer. In a striking phrase that survived into the Unemployment Policy Committee's report, Hopkins noted that Mosley's proposals implied that 'a committee of twelve paid whole-time economists, assisted by honorary committees of businessmen, etc., . . . will (if they can reach agreement) lay down the entire economic policy of the government'. The Prime Minister, according to the Treasury interpretation of the memorandum, would give executive effect to the decisions of the economists, presumably issuing instructions to the Chancellor and other ministers, contrary to the convention of individual ministerial and collective Cabinet responsibility for policy. Through the Unemployment Policy Committee's report, the Treasury also showed uncharacteristic concern 'to nurture the plant of local government', rejecting Mosley's plan to transfer responsibility for roads from local authorities to central government,

[120] Robert Skidelsky, *Oswald Mosley* (1975), 193–210. The Mosley memorandum is CP31(30) in CAB24/209.
[121] 'The Banks and Rationalization', by Leith-Ross, 5 Feb. 1930, T175/41; 'Sir O. Mosley on Unemployment', unsigned but almost certainly by Hopkins, 1 Feb. 1930, and 'Draft memorandum by Unemployment Policy Committee', drafted by Leith-Ross, 8 Mar. 1930, both in T175/42.

on the grounds that the machinery of central government would become hopelessly clogged thereby.[122]

With regard to Mosley's proposed road programme, the Unemployment Policy Committee's report pointed out the impracticality of carrying it out in the time suggested, drawing attention to underspending under previous, and much more modest, road programmes. Hopkins and Leith-Ross, however, had other objections to the whole idea of internal development: Hopkins believed that Mosley was a champion of 'inflation and protection appropriately disguised', and noted that the Chancellor had already ruled out protection. While drafting the committee's report Leith-Ross contrasted the situation of the United States, and its vast natural resources and high protective tariff, with Britain's need to engage in competitive international trade, and predicted that an attempt to imitate the United States would land Britain in the same situation as Australia (which, having borrowed extensively abroad for capital development in the 1920s, was struggling by 1930 to maintain its credit abroad as its income from exports fell). The Treasury warning was plain: a large national loan which investors believed to be for wasteful expenditure could only be raised by offering high interest rates, whereas, if money market conditions were left to themselves, interest rates would fall, to the benefit of ordinary (that is, private) industrial investment.[123] Confronted by all these arguments, the Cabinet committee rejected the Mosley memorandum in May, and Mosley resigned.

Meanwhile MacDonald had set up the Macmillan Committee on Finance and Industry to inquire into how the banking system affected the economy and, as already noted, had also established the Economic Advisory Council to act as an 'economic general staff'. Keynes was a member of both bodies, and was thus able to give advice directly to the Prime Minister. However, it is important not to exaggerate Keynes's influence. As Skidelsky notes, politicians rarely look to economists to tell them what to do; rather economists are expected to provide rationales for politicians' actions or inaction. Moreover, it was Henderson, not Keynes, who was MacDonald's favourite economist, and Henderson was becoming increasingly alarmed about the effects of unsound finance on business confidence.[124] Neither the Macmillan Committee nor the Economic Advisory Council was expected to produce a radicalization of policy. Indeed, the immediate political purpose of the Macmillan Committee was to appease the Labour party after Bank rate had been raised from 5½ to 6 per cent in September 1929 to prevent the loss of gold to New York. Nevertheless, Keynes was able to use his membership of the committee to debate economic issues with Hawtrey and Hopkins, who were invited to give evidence on financial policy

---

[122] 'Sir O. Mosley on Unemployment Policy', T175/42, and CP134(30), CAB24/211.
[123] 'Sir O. Mosley on Unemployment Policy' and 'Draft Memorandum by Unemployment Policy Committee', T175/42; CP134(30), CAB24/211.
[124] Robert Skidelsky, *John Maynard Keynes: The Economist as Saviour, 1920–1937* (1992), 344, 365.

and, in particular, the question of whether industry might be set going by a large programme of public works.

Hawtrey appeared before the committee in April 1930 in a personal capacity, rather than as a Treasury official, and indeed the views he expressed struck a balance between the Treasury view that investable funds could only come from existing savings, and support for Keynes's views on the advantages of diverting funds from overseas to home investment. Hawtrey believed that if 'genuine savings' (that is funds from the non-bank public) which currently found their way into overseas investment could be attracted to a government loan and used for some purpose other than overseas investment, the effect would be to strengthen Britain's gold reserves, which in turn would make possible an expansion of credit and a reduction in Bank rate. However, there was no support in the Treasury or the Bank of England for such a loan, even though Hawtrey expressed a preference for using the loan to fund Treasury bills, thereby, he believed, releasing short-term funds for investment in working capital for trade and industry, rather than using it, as Keynes wished, to pay for public works.[125]

The task of giving the Treasury's official evidence fell to Hopkins, who took exceptional care to prepare his brief, consulting Niemeyer at the Bank as well as Leith-Ross, Phillips, and Hawtrey, before he appeared before the committee in May. As Clarke has shown, Hopkins retreated from the Treasury view of 1929 relating to loanable funds and avoided debating the theoretical aspects of Keynes's ideas. Hopkins conceded that, on Keynes's assumptions, public works that did not produce a money return sufficient to pay the capital and interest on a loan might still pay for themselves, partly by diverting capital from abroad, partly by mobilizing idle balances, partly by diminishing the cost of unemployment relief, and partly by increased revenue arising from increased economic activity, but he doubted if these effects could be calculated. He took his stand on the practical objections that the 1929 white paper had raised to a rapid expansion of public works. In particular, he pointed out that, if a large public works programme seemed to investors to be wasteful, financial markets would expect the value of government stock to fall and investors would turn to overseas issues, thereby increasing pressure on the exchange rate, which in turn would lead to a rise in Bank rate.[126]

---

[125] See Clarke, *Keynesian Revolution*, 142–8. Clarke describes Hawtrey as being in favour of *redeeming* the National Debt. However, what Hawtrey was advocating was not a reduction in the National Debt, but a reduction in the floating debt, such as Niemeyer had recommended to the Colwyn Committee in 1925—'Debt Policy and Unemployment', by Hawtrey, 29 June 1929, T175/26. Niemeyer, when shown Hawtrey's plan, noted that he was all in favour of funding Treasury bills but that a loan such as Hawtrey envisaged would have to offer a high rate of interest to compete with overseas issues and moreover: 'the favourable results would take longer to arrive than politicians like and are . . . somewhat less certain than Hawtrey thinks.' Note by Niemeyer, 2 Oct. 1929, ibid.
[126] Clarke, *Keynesian Revolution*, 148–56. For debate between Keynes and Hopkins see *JMK*, xx. 166–79. Hopkins's brief is in T175/46.

Hopkins's considered view in June 1930 was that, while it was theoretically possible that government loan-financed expenditure on the scale envisaged by Keynes and Mosley might stimulate employment by increasing the velocity of circulation of money, it was much more likely, given the practical difficulties, to reduce business confidence, and would involve greater bureaucratic powers than the public would tolerate except in war. Subsequently, Hopkins and Henderson (now a civil servant and joint secretary of the Economic Advisory Council) drafted a white paper on unemployment policy, published in December 1930, which defended the increased scale of public works adopted by the Labour government. In the white paper public works were described as a 'short-range' policy, designed to provide immediate employment in an unprecedented world trade depression, while a 'long-range policy' (rationalization) increased the efficiency of British industry. However, just as Hopkins had freed himself from the economic theory underlying the Treasury view of the 1920s, so also had Henderson freed himself from what he now considered to be Keynes's irresponsible attitude to the practical problems of a larger programme public works than Labour had adopted.[127]

There has been some debate among economists and historians as to the relative importance of economic theory on the one hand, and practical administrative and political constraints on the other, in the formulation of the Treasury view on public works as an employment policy. Clarke's archival research has shown that the Treasury view of 1929 was based on an economic theory in which Hopkins at least had ceased to be confident by 1930.[128] However, the practical and administrative constraints remained. Public works were still confined to those which produced a money return sufficient to repay the interest and capital of a loan, or which would lower costs of production or distribution. Financial markets were assumed to be hostile to loans for uneconomic public works. The Treasury view was not dependent upon the existence of the gold standard (as Treasury resistance to the Gairloch proposals had shown) but the assumption that Britain would continue to adhere to the gold standard was a constraint on an expansion of credit. Likewise, the fact that Britain was dependent upon international trade for raw materials, and the associated Treasury assumption that Britain benefited from free trade, despite increasing tariffs abroad, likewise made the Treasury hostile to any solution to unemployment based upon development of the home market. These constraints, plus the Treasury's determination to steer the state clear of direct involvement in rationalization, left a reduction in interest rates as the Treasury's main hope for economic

---

[127] 'Note on Sir Oswald Mosley's Speech', by Hopkins, 16 June 1930, T175/42; *Statement of the Principal Measures Taken by H.M. Government in Connection with Unemployment* (Cmd. 3746), PP 1930–1, xviii. 769.

[128] Clarke, *Keynesian Revolution*, chs. 3 and 7. For review of the earlier literature see G. C. Peden, 'The "Treasury View" on Public Works and Employment in the Interwar Period', *Econ. Hist. Rev.*, 2nd ser., 37 (1984), 167–81. For a more recent comment see Donald Winch, 'Keynes, Keynesianism and State Intervention', in P. A. Hall (ed.), *The Political Power of Economic Ideas* (Princeton, NJ, 1989), 116–18.

recovery. That hope was unlikely to be fulfilled so long as world prices continued to fall, as they did until 1932, lowering expectations of profit and increasing the output of goods and services necessary to service debts. But how realistic was the alternative of public works?

COULD LLOYD GEORGE, OR LABOUR, HAVE DONE IT?

Economic historians have long debated whether Keynes was correct in claiming that Lloyd George's proposal to borrow £250 million for a two-year public works programme would have reduced unemployment to normal proportions. The assumption that such a programme would have been successful underlies the view of Margaret Weir and Theda Skocpol that the British Treasury's grip on public finance prevented the Labour government from establishing a full-employment, welfare state such as was to be established in Social Democratic Sweden in 1932–4.[129]

The argument about public works as an employment policy turns crucially upon the concept of the multiplier, which was developed by one of Keynes's associates, Richard Kahn, in the summer of 1930. The basic idea of the multiplier is that each person given employment by public expenditure will spend a proportion of his or her additional income, thereby generating further employment. In 1933 Keynes was to argue that every £200 of government capital expenditure, financed by borrowing, would provide employment for one man either directly, or indirectly in producing the materials used. Part of the £200 would be spent on imports, or would be saved, or would otherwise not be a net increase in income (for example, wages paid to workers previously unemployed would be offset by the fact that these workers would no longer collect unemployment benefit), but part would take the form of net additional expenditure on goods and services produced in Britain. If the latter proportion were one-half of the original capital expenditure of £200, then the equivalent of another half of a job would be created. This additional employment would itself, after an interval, generate further repercussions of additional expenditure and employment. If at each stage half of the additional expenditure were spent on goods and services produced in Britain, then the employment multiplier would be 2, since arithmetically $1 + \frac{1}{2} + \frac{1}{4}$, etc. $= 2$. Kahn thought in 1931 that 1.88 was the most realistic estimate of the multiplier but subsequent research has suggested that 1.5 would be closer to the mark, and then only after an interval of time.[130]

---

[129] Margaret Weir and Theda Skocpol, 'State Structures and the Possibilities for "Keynesian" Responses to the Great Depression in Sweden, Britain, and the United States', in Peter B. Evans, Dietrich Rueschemeyer, and Theda Skocpol (eds.), *Bringing the State Back In* (Cambridge, 1985), 107–63.

[130] R. F. Kahn, 'The Relation of Home Investment to Unemployment', *Econ. J.*, 41 (1931), 173–98; *JMK*, ix. 335–66; T. Thomas, 'Aggregate Demand in the United Kingdom, 1918–45', in R. Floud and D. McCloskey (eds.), *The Economic History of Britain since 1700*, vol. ii (Cambridge, 1981), 332–46.

Using an employment multiplier of 2, Howson calculated that, if the Labour government's expanded public works programme of 1930/1 had been carried out as planned, and if all of its potential impact on employment had been felt within twelve months, 865,000 jobs would have been created by 1932. With a multiplier of 1.5, the effect would have been 648,750 jobs. However, as Howson pointed out, the assumptions that the programme could have been implemented, and that its effects would have been felt so quickly, are unrealistic. In a similar exercise, Middleton estimated that the Labour government's programmes actually begun by June 1931, amounting to £107.7 million, would have created a total of 299,000 jobs, on the (optimistic) assumption that the employment multiplier would have been 1.5 and would not have been subject to significant lags in its effects. In 1929 unemployment among insured workers had stood at 1.25 million; by 1931 it had reached 2.7 million as the world depression deepened.[131] Labour's public works policy, like the Treasury's cheap money policy, was overwhelmed by the scale of the depression.

Econometric studies of the employment debate by T. Thomas and Tim Hatton, using Keynesian models of the inter-war economy, concluded that a programme on the scale advocated by Lloyd George would have created balance-of-payments problems, and that 500,000 jobs could have been created only by preventing an increase in imports by allowing sterling to depreciate or by imposing tariffs (although Lloyd George, like the Treasury, was committed to both the gold standard and free trade). Even so, given contemporary views on the requirements of sound finance, there would probably have been a flight of private capital from Britain.[132] Curiously, one of the more optimistic analyses of Lloyd George's programme, by K. G. P. Matthews, used a 'monetarist' model of the inter-war economy to argue that a temporary expansion in government expenditure, financed by what contemporaries would have called inflation, would have reduced unemployment permanently by about 500,000. However, this calculation also assumed that the gold standard would have had to be abandoned, and also that real wages could have been reduced, and the competitiveness of British goods in international trade increased, by allowing the exchange rate to decline, although devaluation by other countries was partially to offset the effects of sterling depreciation after Britain suspended the gold standard in 1931. Matthews's work also gives support to the Treasury view on public works, in that he suggests that public expenditure financed by selling bonds would have produced very little in terms of output gain and that there would have been strong crowding out even in the short term.[133] Middleton has argued that

    [131] S. Howson, 'Slump and Unemployment', in Floud and McCloskey, op. cit., 280; Roger Middleton, 'The Treasury and Public Investment', 360–1.
    [132] Thomas, 'Aggregate Demand', and Hatton, 'The Outlines of a Keynesian Solution'.
    [133] K. G. P. Matthews, 'Could Lloyd George Have Done It?', Oxford Econ. Papers, NS, 41 (1989), 374–407.

contemporary financial markets' perceptions of public finance, and the balance-of-payments implications of a major public works programme, both give substance to the Treasury view.[134]

On balance, given shared assumptions of a fixed exchange rate and free trade, the Treasury had reason to be sceptical about claims made by Lloyd George and Keynes in 1929. On the other hand, as the Treasury itself recognized, public works designed to lower costs of production had a role to play in employment policy, and the position adopted by Hopkins and Henderson in 1930 in support of the actual Labour programme was more balanced than earlier Treasury doctrine.

INTERNATIONAL FINANCE

On the eve of the slump the Treasury focused on the need to expand exports, and therefore on the need for stability in the international monetary system, rather than on domestic public works, as a cure for unemployment. The United States and France were accumulating gold, but these countries had banking systems which made it difficult for them to expand domestic credit to an extent that would encourage imports and halt the gold inflow. As a result, other countries were short of gold, and prices fell, because the world's supply of marketable goods grew more rapidly than the amount of monetary gold available to finance the expansion of production and trade at current prices.[135] Hopkins had been made aware by Keynes as early as February 1929 that 'a gold hunger might develop'.[136] By 1930 Treasury officials believed that there was a need for more central bank co-operation to economize in the use of gold, but they were determined to keep such matters out of the hands of politicians.[137] Similar views prevailed in the United States, with the result that financial diplomacy remained largely in the hands of bankers. However, the scope for international co-operation, even between experts, was restricted as long as the United States insisted that such co-operation should not involve any further sacrifice of American claims on other countries for war debts or any plan to encourage an outflow of loans from the United States and France. It was not until June 1931 that President Hoover of the United States felt able to initiate a one-year moratorium on all intergovernment debt transfers, but by then the world was deep in depression and the moratorium came too late to stave off a European financial crisis.[138]

[134] Middleton, *Towards the Managed Economy*, 149–65.
[135] See Eichengreen, *Golden Fetters*, 194–207.
[136] *JMK*, xix (part 2), 775–80, and Hopkins to Grigg, 31 Feb. 1929, T172/2095.
[137] 'Note on Sir Oswald Mosley's Speech', by Hopkins, 16 June 1930, T175/42; 'Possibilities of Government Action in Regard to the Recent Fall in World Prices', by Leith-Ross, 1 July, 1930, Lothian papers, GD40/17/137, National Archives of Scotland, Edinburgh.
[138] See Kathleen Burk, 'The House of Morgan in Financial Diplomacy' in B. J. C. McKercher (ed.),

According to the Balfour note of 1922, British policy was to try to collect from reparations and war debts due to her enough to balance payments on her war debt to the United States. Churchill tried to fulfil this policy when he negotiated agreements with France and Italy for repayment of their war debts, but, as Leith-Ross remarked, the Chancellor had too generous a heart to be a hard debt collector. Both the French and Italian negotiators were able to settle with Churchill for smaller sums than they had been authorized by their governments to offer. The Italians agreed in January 1926 to pay £4 million a year; the Franco-British agreement of July 1926 was more complex: £4 million in 1926–7, £6 million in 1927–8, £8 million in 1928–9, £10 million in 1929–30, and then £12.5 million annually until 1956–7 and £14 million annually until 1987–8. Churchill claimed that these sums, together with the British share of reparations, would enable Britain over time to receive the equivalent of £33.5 million a year, more than Britain's current payments of £33 million a year to the United States, but, as his critics pointed out, less than the £38 million that Britain would have to pay from 1933. Moreover, Leith-Ross recalled that Treasury officials regarded the figures for twenty to twenty-five years hence as 'pure eye-wash' and would have preferred slightly larger payments than were agreed for the first ten years to doubtful promises for the future. Indeed, the French made plain that they would ask for reconsideration of the terms if their receipts under the Dawes plan fell by more than half, and thus reparations continued to be the key to a satisfactory resolution of the problem of inter-allied war debts.[139]

An international committee of financial experts, chaired by an American businessman, Owen D. Young, was set up at the end of 1928 to devise a final reparations plan. The Treasury had little direct influence on its deliberations as the British members of the committee, originally Stamp and Lord Revelstoke (of Barings Bank), and then Sir Charles Addis (a director of the Bank of England), who replaced Revelstoke when the latter died, regarded themselves as independent of the government. In its report in June 1929 the committee recommended that Germany's annual payment be fixed at about £90 million initially, rising to £121 million, or an average of £102.5 million, compared with the standard Dawes Plan payment of £125 million. However, whereas the Dawes Plan had made provision for payments to be adjusted if the value of gold varied by 10 per cent or more from the 1928 value, no such provision to ensure that payments had a steady value in terms of prices of goods and services was included in the Young Plan. This omission proved to be unfortunate, for the price of gold rose in terms of other commodities during the world depression after 1929, with the consequence that the volume of goods that had to be

Anglo-American Relations in the 1920s: The Struggle for Supremacy (1991), 146–50; Melvyn P. Leffler, *The Elusive Quest: America's Pursuit of European Stability and French Security, 1919–1933* (Chapel Hill, NC, 1979), chs. 5–7.

[139] 198 HC Deb., 5s, 1926, cols. 234–5, 923, 930; Leith-Ross, *Money Talks*, 94–5; A. Turner, *The Cost of War: British Policy on French War Debts, 1919–1931* (Brighton, 1998), chs. 6–8.

exported to repay debts increased. Moreover, under the Young Plan, Germany agreed that one-third of each annual instalment was unconditional, although the balance might be postponed if its transfer would threaten the mark's gold exchange rate. Germany's reparation liabilities were intended to cover Allied liabilities for war debts, but the report reduced Britain's annual share of receipts from Germany by £2.4 million and gave France and Italy a prior claim on most of the unconditional annuities, so that about 90 per cent of British receipts would depend on that part of reparation payments that the German government could suspend to protect the mark.[140]

Thus, on taking office as Chancellor of the Exchequer, Snowden faced the prospect of a budgetary problem arising from a German failure to maintain reparation payments, a point that the London press did not fail to emphasize. The Young Plan was the subject of heated negotiations at an international conference at the Hague in August 1929, when Snowden was the chief British delegate, although he was accompanied by the Foreign Secretary, Arthur Henderson. Snowden refused to accept Foreign Office advice that the sums involved did not justify putting the political goals of the conference—conciliation of Germany and French agreement to evacuate the Rhineland—at risk. Grigg recalled that Snowden, Henderson, and the third minister in the delegation, William Graham, now President of the Board of Trade, used to have discussions every day, with Graham invariably supporting Snowden. One evening Henderson, hoping to make the Chancellor less obstinate, remarked: 'Well, Philip, you and Willie seem to pay no regard to my views; I might as well go home.' However, Snowden's reply—'That's about it, Arthur!'—was not what Henderson hoped for. Snowden likewise did not consult the Governor of the Bank of England, although Norman evidently expected him to do so.[141]

Assisted by Leith-Ross, the Chancellor treated the representatives of France, Italy, and Belgium in much the same manner as the Treasury was accustomed to dealing with spending departments in Whitehall. For twenty days Snowden insisted that the full amount of £2.4 million should be restored to Britain. When an official of the Banque de France, in the presence of Belgian and Italian financial experts, threatened to put pressure on sterling by converting the Banque's sterling assets into gold if Snowden did not give way, Leith-Ross curtly had all three men shown the door. In the end, Snowden settled for £2 million, together with an increase in Britain's share of Germany's unconditional liabilities.[142]

---

[140] Roberta A. Dayer, *Finance and Empire: Sir Charles Addis, 1861–1945* (1988); *JMK*, xviii. 329–40; Leith-Ross, *Money Talks*, 113, 119–20; A. McFadyean, *Reparation Reviewed* (1930), ch. 9.

[141] Grigg, *Prejudice and Judgement*, 229.

[142] Leith-Ross, *Money Talks*, 120–7; David Carlton, *MacDonald versus Henderson: The Foreign Policy of the Second Labour Government* (1970), 37–49. As another example of Treasury intransigence in diplomacy about this time, Lord Sherfield recalled that, when he was a very junior 'bag-carrier' in the Foreign Office (he joined the FO in 1928), he was present at a League of Nations conference where Hawtrey was the chief British delegate. Hawtrey maintained his position, without making any concessions, for a week, when the matter in question could have been solved in three days. René Massigli, a French diplomat, came to

Snowden gained immense popularity with the British public by his stand, but the amended Young Plan was not to endure for long and the budgetary problems that the Chancellor was to face in 1930 and 1931 were to be of a magnitude that dwarfed the sums at issue at the Hague.

The Young Plan provided for the establishment of the Bank for International Settlements to supervise the collection and distribution of the reparation annuities. This supranational institution was also intended to regularize co-operation between central banks through monthly meetings at its headquarters in Basel, and to facilitate international capital transfers, prevent exchange instability, and promote trade. Its founders hoped to remove intergovernmental debt from politics, but in practice, as Norman complained in September 1930, there were frequent discussions between Bank and Treasury officials, which eroded the hitherto total control of central banks over foreign transfer payments. The Treasury also became involved in direct negotiations with France over the tendency of the Banque de France to absorb gold from the Bank of England and the London market. Following inconclusive discussions between Norman and his opposite number at the Banque, Clement Moret, inter-treasury talks were held first in Paris and then in London in January 1931, with Leith-Ross heading the British delegation. The British were inclined to blame technical weaknesses in French money markets for the drain of gold, while the French, with some justice, implied that the British should look to their adverse trade balance and consider raising Bank rate. Despite continuing differences of outlook, however, Leith-Ross detected an improvement in Anglo-French relations, and the Banque de France seems generally to have been helpful with regard to the Bank of England's growing difficulties in 1931.[143]

Another avenue for international co-operation was the Financial Committee of the League of Nations, which in 1929 had set up an enquiry, entitled the Gold Delegation, to examine the causes and effects of changes in the purchasing power of gold. Leith-Ross was kept in touch with the work of the Delegation through the London financier Sir Henry Strakosch, who took a leading part in its work, but initiatives for redistribution of gold reserves remained with central banks. In February 1931, following an interim report from the Gold Delegation that discussed the distribution of gold reserves, Norman put to the Bank of International Settlements a scheme for an international corporation whose main function would be to redistribute gold from France and the United States to debtor countries through international loans. However, Norman, who was becoming increasingly pessimistic, told Treasury officials that the scheme, variously known as the Norman Plan or the Kindersley Plan (after its architect, Sir Robert Kindersley, a director of the Bank of England), would not work.

see Hawtrey privately, but could not budge him. At length, in exasperation, Massigli exclaimed: 'Monsieur Hawtrey, vous êtes le logic même!' (conversation with author, 26 July 1990).

[143] Diane B. Kunz, *The Battle for Britain's Gold Standard in 1931* (1987), 24–32, 36.

Time was running out for international monetary co-operation as Europe moved towards a financial crisis whose immediate cause was the failure in May 1931 of the Creditanstalt, a leading Austrian bank that had been caught out by its policy of borrowing short term abroad and lending long term to industry at home. International creditors sought to protect themselves by withdrawing short-term funds from German banks and Germany's desperate financial position raised the question of a moratorium on intergovernmental debts. Officially the Treasury's position, while briefing the Foreign Office before a visit by German ministers to London, was that the reduction in foreign lending to Germany was largely due to a lack of confidence and that the solution was for the German government to restore confidence by achieving budget equilibrium. In practice Leith-Ross recognized the danger that continuation of reparations would lead to extremists taking over the German government, and he urged that Britain should use its influence to secure a complete cancellation of both reparations and war debts, even though a moratorium would involve an annual loss to the Chancellor's budget of about £11 million.[144] Despite the Hoover moratorium, for which French support was finally obtained on 5 July, a financial crisis broke in Germany on 13 July, leading to an international scramble for liquidity as foreign credits were frozen. On 15 July there were large-scale withdrawals of gold from London and sterling fell sharply towards the point where it would be profitable to export gold. The international financial crisis had reached Britain.

THE 1931 CRISIS

The main landmarks in the 1931 crisis are well known. The publication of the Macmillan Report on 13 July alerted financial markets to London's short-term vulnerability; City institutions had borrowed short term to make long-term investments, and foreign holders of the government's floating debt could let their holdings run off, forcing the Bank of England to take up Treasury bills for which there were no bidders in the market. Distrust of sterling assets was heightened by the Labour government's budgetary difficulties brought about by the depression. Public awareness of the rising cost of unemployment benefits had been raised when the Royal Commission on Unemployment Insurance reported early in June 1931 that the Unemployment Insurance Fund was actuarially unsound, and that its deficit should be reduced by cutting cash benefits in line with the cost of living and by other measures, including preventing married women making claims.[145]

---

[144] Treasury to Foreign Office, 22 May 1931, and 'Future Settlement of Reparations', n.d., Leith-Ross papers, T188/16.

[145] (Macmillan) Committee on Finance and Industry, *Report* (Cmd. 3897), PP 1930–1, xiii. 219; Royal Commission on Unemployment Insurance, *First Report* (Cmd. 3872), PP 1930–1, xvii. 885.

Then, on 31 July, came the report of the May Committee, which had been asked by Snowden to make recommendations on all possible reductions in government expenditure. The committee's chairman, Sir George May, had formerly been secretary of the Prudential Assurance Company, and his report expressed the views of City men on public finance: government accounts were strictly calculated to include not only expenditure in the budget as conventionally defined, but also borrowing for the Unemployment Insurance Fund and the Road Fund, which had hitherto been excluded. On the other hand, in estimating future revenue, various non-recurrent 'nest eggs' with which Snowden had balanced his budget in 1931 were excluded. On this basis the budget deficit for 1932/3 was estimated at £120 million. The committee recommended economies of £96.6 million, with the balance of £23.4 million to be met from increased taxation. Of the economies, no less than £66.5 million were on unemployment insurance, including a reduction in the levels of benefits by 20 per cent, in line with the decline in the Ministry of Labour's working-class cost-of-living index since 1925.[146]

TABLE 5.5. *Snowden's Budgets, 1930 and 1931, and May Report Forecast for 1932 (£ m.)*

	1930/1 out-turn	1931/2 April forecast	1932/3 May Report forecast
Revenue	857.8	885.1[a]	828.1[b]
Expenditure	881.0	884.9	896.9
Balance	−23.2	+0.1	−68.8
Borrowing for Unemployment Insurance Fund	36.4	40.0	40.0
Road Fund	—	9.0	10.0
Estimated deficiency			−120.0

[a] Including a total of £37 million of non-recurrent 'nest-eggs' in the form of £23 million from Exchange Account; £10 million by acceleration of payment of income tax; and £4 million from Rating Relief Suspense Account.

[b] On existing basis of taxation, excluding £37 million non-recurrent 'nest-eggs' in 1931/2 budget, and assuming a decline of £20 million in income tax owing to effects of depression.

Sources: Roger Middleton, *Towards the Managed Economy: Keynes, the Treasury and the Fiscal Policy Debate of the 1930s* (1985), 98–9; Committee on National Expenditure, *Report* (Cmd. 3920), paras. 26–30.

The May Report turned a financial crisis into a political crisis. Snowden, together with the Conservative and Liberal opposition, insisted on attempting to balance the budget by making larger cuts in expenditure than the majority of the Labour Cabinet would agree to. There was a proposal to raise a government loan in New York to supplement central bank credits which the Bank of England had already secured to support the gold value of sterling. However,

[146] (May) Committee on National Expenditure, *Report* (Cmd. 3920), PP 1930–1, xvi. 1.

Morgan's, the government's bankers in New York, advised that a loan would only be successful if the government's financial measures had the approval of the Bank of England and the City of London. The Labour Cabinet resigned on 24 August and MacDonald formed the National Government with the Conservatives and Liberals plus a few Labour ministers. During these events the government's principal source of advice on financial markets and international loans was the Bank of England—despite the fact that Montagu Norman had had a nervous breakdown earlier in the summer—but the advice of Treasury officials also played an important part, the more so because of the centrality of the budget in the crisis and because Snowden, although weakened by ill health, was still the leading minister in the Labour government after MacDonald.

The government had been warned by the Treasury as early as 7 January 1931 that there were signs of a lack of confidence in sterling, with a 'steady trickle' of gold being transferred from London, a movement that would be increased by 'unsound State finance', especially increased borrowing for the Unemployment Insurance Fund.[147] Unemployment had risen rapidly after Labour had come to power, from an annual average of 10.4 per cent of the insured labour force in 1929 to 16.1 per cent in 1930, and was still rising (the annual average for 1931 was to be 21.3 per cent). The Treasury's message to the government was reinforced when Hopkins gave evidence to the Royal Commission on Unemployment Insurance on 29 January to the effect that continued borrowing to pay for unemployment benefits 'on the present vast scale . . . would quickly call into question the stability of the British financial system'.[148] The crisis in August should not have surprised ministers.

The Treasury's attitude to the budget problem can only be understood in the context of monetary policy. A balanced budget with adequate sinking funds was seen as essential if the public were to be willing to continue to subscribe to government loans at 'reasonable' interest rates, and any loss of confidence in the government's finances would postpone all prospects for a successful conversion of 5 per cent War Loan. Interest rates had been falling since 1929, and the prospects of a successful conversion of 5 per cent War Loan to a lower rate was seen by Treasury officials both as one of the few ways in which government expenditure could be reduced in future, and as a means of maintaining the trend to a lower long-term rate of interest, which was the Treasury's chief hope for economic recovery.

The Treasury and the Bank of England had been aware of the possibility of a sterling crisis since the end of 1930, but the prospect of devaluation was not welcomed, even though it would tend to check the fall in domestic prices. While assisting with the preparation of the 1931 budget, Phillips showed awareness that falling prices exacerbated the country's economic difficulties by

---

[147] 'The Financial Situation', CP3(31), T171/287.
[148] Royal Commission on Unemployment Insurance, *Evidence* (1932), i. 384.

penalizing entrepreneurs who had borrowed capital, while rewarding rentiers and increasing the burden of the National Debt. Even so, the Cabinet was told in January 1931 that: 'prices cannot go on falling for ever, and sooner or later, perhaps quite soon, the fall will be checked and there will be a substantial recovery of trade and industry.'[149] The Treasury was not alone in fearing the international consequences of going off gold: the Macmillan Report, which was largely drafted by Keynes in May 1931, stated that 'it would be an immense shock to the financial world if Britain were deliberately to devalue'.[150]

Nor was the Treasury alone in seeing a balanced budget as the key to the situation. Keynes wrote to MacDonald on 5 March that a crisis of financial confidence was 'very near', and advised that the only way in which the budget could be balanced was by the introduction of a revenue tariff. The idea of a revenue tariff had been gaining support even from people who, like Keynes, had previously been free traders. As it happened, Snowden's principal private secretary, Donald Fergusson, had already written on 4 March to the Chairman of the Board of Customs and Excise, E. R. Forber, asking for 'some ammunition' in opposition to a revenue tariff, noting that the higher the administrative and other difficulties could be put the better from the Chancellor's point of view. Snowden was, in fact, absent from the Treasury on account of illness, but on 9 March MacDonald replied to Keynes that 'the Treasury people' had said that it would be impossible to impose revenue duties as the necessary administrative machinery could not be organized in time for an April budget.[151] Fergusson was acting in the knowledge that the Chancellor remained the most important advocate within the Labour government of free trade. Budgetary difficulties had forced Snowden to retain the McKenna duties, contrary to Labour's election pledges, but the Chancellor continued to believe that protection would be a burden on the working class, who would have to pay higher prices for imports.[152]

Snowden was encouraged in his stand by his officials. For example, Hopkins, when briefing him with arguments against Mosley's protectionist ideas in 1930, had warned that any interference with free trade would provoke retaliation, ruining the industrial areas of Scotland and northern England, with their dependence on exports. The prospective additional revenue from a 10 per cent ad valorem duty on manufactured imports was estimated by the Board of Customs and Excise in March 1931 at between £14 million and £17 million in a full year, assuming that imports already taxed would be excluded from the new

---

[149] CP3(31), 7 Jan. 1931; 'Effect of Price Changes on Burden of the National Debt', 2 Dec. 1930, T171/287.   [150] Cmd. 3897, paras. 255–7.

[151] David Marquand, *Ramsay MacDonald* (1977), 590–1; Fergusson to Forber, 4 Mar. 1931, T175/52 and Fergusson to Chancellor of the Exchequer, n.d., T171/286.

[152] See Philip Snowden, *The Truth about Protection: The Worker Pays* (1930). For Snowden's part in preserving free trade in 1930–1 see Tim Routh, 'The Political Economy of Protectionism in Britain, 1919–1932', *J. Eur. Econ. Hist.*, 21 (1992), esp. 70–1, 74–5, 81–5.

tariff. The Board also estimated that Keynes's proposal for a 15 per cent duty on all manufactured and semi-manufactured goods, and a 5 per cent duty on food and 'certain raw materials', might raise between £50 million and £60 million in a full year, but again, if all imports already taxed were exempted, the additional revenue might be no more than £40 million (a figure with which Keynes agreed). There was, however, a political aspect to the question: Keynes had suggested that free traders could support a revenue tariff as an emergency measure, to be dispensed with in the event of world prices recovering to the level of 1929, but, in notes forwarded to Hopkins, Forber commented that 'nobody . . . can seriously believe that a tariff can be put on and taken off like a cloak' and that the Conservative party 'would find nothing easier than to convert a revenue tariff into a protective one'.[153]

Snowden, like Lloyd George in 1909, favoured land taxation as an alternative source of revenue. However, in the short term, land taxation had its limitations. The Board of Inland Revenue estimated in March 1931 that the gross yield of the proposals which it had prepared, under the guidance of Sir Stafford Cripps, the Solicitor General, for an annual tax on the value of land would be only £6.25 million in a full year. Moreover, the cost of the first valuation of land would be between £1.5 million and £2 million, and the subsequent cost of assessment and collection would be £800,000 or £1 million. Drawing upon the experience of Lloyd George's land values duties, which had raised less revenue than they had cost to assess and collect, Snowden decided not to levy any tax until the valuation had been substantially completed, a process expected to take two years from the passing of the Finance Bill. Thus, although the principles of land taxation occupied a good deal of attention during the passage of the 1931 Finance Act, the proposals before the House could make no immediate contribution to the solution of the budget problem.[154]

Snowden's difficulties in preparing his budget in 1931 were worsened by ill health. He had to rest for seven weeks after an operation in March for inflammation of the bladder and, although he managed to rise from his sickbed to open his budget on 27 April, he had to rely heavily on the assistance of Cripps and Graham, as well as on the Financial Secretary to the Treasury, F. W. Pethick-Lawrence, to conduct the Finance Bill through the House. On 14 June the Chancellor offered his resignation but it was rejected by MacDonald. As a consequence of the Chancellor's frequent absences from Cabinet, some ministers may have been less well informed about the economic crisis than they might otherwise have been.[155]

---

[153] 'Note for Chancellor', by Hopkins, 16 June 1930, T175/42; 'Some Notes on "Revenue Tariff" ', unsigned, but forwarded by Forber, 26 Mar. 1931 T175/52; Fergusson to Chancellor, n.d., T171/286. For Keynes's arguments see *JMK*, ix. 231–8 and xx. 493–7.

[154] 'Land Values Taxation', by Grigg (Chairman of the Board of Inland Revenue), 20 Mar. 1931, T171/284; Grigg, *Prejudice and Judgement*, 246–52.

[155] Keith Laybourn, *Philip Snowden: A Biography* (Aldershot, 1988), 125–6.

The anticipated deficit for 1931/2 on the existing basis of taxation, even on the optimistic assumption of economic recovery, was forecast in April to be £37.4 million. Only £7.5 million of the prospective deficit was met by an increase in the petrol tax. To balance his budget Snowden drew on various non-recurrent 'nest-eggs' (see Table 5.5), including £23 million from the Exchange Account, which had been used to manage the American debt until that function was taken over by the Bank for International Settlements in 1930. Raids on funds like the Exchange Account and the Rating Relief Suspense Account were no more than paper devices to make budgets look better, since these funds had long since been invested in Treasury bills or similar assets, which had to be sold, thereby increasing the size of the floating debt, before the government could have the use of the money.

On the other hand, Treasury officials advised against any curtailment of the sinking fund, the one form of fiscal window dressing that could have made possible a balanced budget without something drastic being done about expenditure on unemployment relief. Had the sinking fund been reduced, it would have been possible to turn the deficit for 1930/1 into a surplus, and greatly to have eased Snowden's task in 1931. However, Treasury officials pointed out in January 1931 that the inclusion of a sinking fund of £52 million in the 1931 budget was offset by the exclusion from the budget of Treasury loans to the Unemployment Insurance Fund, although the Fund was estimated at that date to be borrowing at a rate of £40 million a year with little or no prospect of the money being repaid. No Cabinet minister felt able to refute Snowden's claim that any curtailment of statutory sinking funds would have such an adverse effect on financial confidence as to raise the cost of government borrowing and put the gold standard at risk. Hopkins advised Snowden that 'we are endeavouring to overcome a radical lack of confidence abroad in our financial position', and that any reduction in sinking fund provision could only be justified if it were 'part of a scheme which commanded the respect of the world'. Snowden himself was in no doubt that such a scheme would have to include curbs on expenditure on unemployment relief.[156]

Why did Treasury attention focus on unemployment relief in 1931 rather than other forms of expenditure—defence expenditure for example? Part of the answer lies in the fact that the Treasury had already squeezed other forms of expenditure in successive battles over the Estimates. Moreover, the sums involved in unemployment relief were not only very large in relation to other items in the budget (for example, £17.7 million for the air force), but also there was no obvious upper limit to what unemployment relief might cost. In January 1931 Snowden warned his Cabinet colleagues that transitional benefit was likely

---

[156] 'The Financial Situation', CP3(31), 7 Jan. 1931, T171/287; 'Forecast of the Budget position in 1931 and 1932', n.d., but for Cabinet Committee on May Report, and Hopkins to Chancellor, 20 Aug. 1931, T171/288; Williamson, *National Crisis*, 218–21, 294–6, 318.

to cost £22 million in 1930/1, as against a forecast of £10.5, and was estimated to cost at least £30 million in 1931/2.[157] The apparently unchecked growth in expenditure on transitional benefit, in addition to borrowing for the Unemployment Insurance Fund, was bound to have an adverse effect on financial opinion.

However, the Cabinet was reluctant to tackle the problem of unemployment relief except as part of an all-round reduction in incomes in the community. Ministers were conscious of the fact that the fall in prices had benefited holders of government bonds as well as the unemployed. Treasury and Inland Revenue officials did not directly oppose ministers' ideas for spreading financial sacrifice through taxation as well as retrenchment in unemployment insurance, but advised that a separate 'rentier' tax on investment incomes was impracticable, and suggested instead an adjustment of income tax. Snowden himself admitted that his budget in April was no more than a 'stopgap', pending the report of the May Committee, which would give him authority for proposing reductions in expenditure, and he claimed to have anticipated that a second budget would be necessary in the autumn.[158]

Hopkins's initial reaction to the May Report was that it 'show[ed] no mercy', exaggerating the budget position by insisting that there should be no borrowing for unproductive purposes, that is for the Unemployment Insurance Fund or for the Road Fund (the latter being used to provide work for the unemployed). On 24 July Hopkins's own estimate of the prospective deficit for 1932/3 on the existing basis of taxation was £70 million (excluding borrowing at least £50 million for the Unemployment Insurance Fund or the Road Fund) and thus differed from the May Committee mainly in presentation. He also had no doubt that it would be the May Committee's figure of £120 million that would be 'flashed round the world' and urged that publication of the report be accompanied by an announcement that a Cabinet committee headed by the Prime Minister would sit through the holidays to formulate proposals to put the budget on a sound basis.[159]

By August, however, the boards of Inland Revenue and Customs and Excise were estimating that, as a result of the depression, revenue would be down by £39 million in 1932/3 as against 1931/2, compared with the shortfall of £20 million assumed by the May Committee. Moreover, the May Committee had not taken account of the £11 million lost as a result of the Hoover moratorium on inter-government debts. On the expenditure side, with unemployment still rising, it seemed that the scale of borrowing for the Unemployment Insurance Fund and expenditure on transitional benefit would have to be revised upwards. The position was thus markedly worse than that set out in the May Report, and the Cabinet committee, which met four times before the full Cabinet met on

[157] CP3(31), CAB24/219
[158] Williamson, *National Crisis*, 221; Philip Snowden, *Autobiography*, vol. ii (1934), 904.
[159] Hopkins to Chancellor, 24 July 1931, T175/51.

19 August, was advised that the prospective shortfall for 1932/3 was £173 to £178 million, including anticipated borrowing for the Unemployment Insurance Fund and the Road Fund, as against the May Committee's estimate of £120 million. For the current year, 1931/2, the budget deficit was now estimated at £35 million, or £99 million including borrowing for the Unemployment Insurance Fund and the Road Fund. These figures may well have been deliberately pessimistic, to reinforce the Chancellor's bargaining position in Cabinet. In particular, the assumption of the April 1931 budget that the depression would soon be over was replaced by one that it would continue to deepen into 1932. On the other hand, the new assumption about future economic prospects was in fact more realistic than the old one. The Cabinet committee approved Snowden's taxation proposals for an additional £37 million in the current year and £88.5 million in a full year, but neither the committee nor the full Cabinet could agree on economies that would balance the budget and the government resigned.[160]

Reappointed Chancellor in the National Government, Snowden attempted to restore confidence in public finance by presenting an emergency budget on 10 September, when he announced that borrowing for the Unemployment Insurance Fund would cease. In Cabinet discussions with his new Conservative colleagues he had ruled out a revenue tariff. In an attempt to spread the tax burden fairly, 70 per cent of the increased taxation was direct, and 30 per cent indirect. The Board of Inland Revenue had warned against additional surtax, on the grounds that further taxation of higher incomes would encourage tax avoidance, but Snowden increased surtax by 10 per cent. On the other hand, there was no taxation aimed specifically at rentiers who had benefited from the fall in prices; in addition to administrative difficulties raised by the Board, there had been evidence, via the Bank of England, that rumours of discrimination against any particular form of security had an adverse effect on the value of government stocks, and therefore on the prospects of converting existing debt to a lower rate of interest.[161]

The standard rate of income tax was raised from 4s. 6d. (22.5p) to 5s. (25p), and personal allowances were reduced, thereby increasing the number of people paying income tax by 1.5 million. Altogether, revenue was increased in the current year by £40.5 million and £81.5 million in a full year. Twenty million pounds were saved in a full year by reducing the sinking fund to £32.5 million, the minimum required to meet specific sinking funds set up under the terms of the prospectuses of various loans. In order to balance the budget, there were to be cuts in public expenditure totalling £22 million in the current year, and £70 million in a full year. A related National Economy Bill imposed reductions in

[160] 'Forecast of the Budget Position in 1931 and 1932', n.d., T171/288. Williamson, *National Crisis*, 304–6, 317.
[161] Middleton, *Towards the Managed Economy*, 60–1; 'Notes of a Conversation between Sir Ernest Harvey and Mr Peacock and Members of the Cabinet', 3 Sept. 1931, T172/1756.

unemployment benefit (by 10 per cent, rather than the 20 per cent proposed by the May Committee) and in many public sector salaries and wages.[162]

Even a balanced budget did not save the gold standard, the final run on sterling being set off, ironically, by rumours of a naval 'mutiny' at Invergordon over pay cuts. By September, moreover, the Bank of England was aware that there was concern abroad about Britain's increasing adverse balance of trade—although the trade figures were uncertain. However, although it is now known that Britain moved between 1930 and 1931 from a balance of payments surplus on current account of £15 million to a deficit of £114 million (see Table 5.1), the evidence does not support the view that the financial crisis of 1931 is explicable mainly in terms of the balance of payments. The fundamental issue seems to have been a lack of confidence in sterling at a time of a scramble for liquidity in Europe, following the Austrian and German banking failures, and when the Bank of England lacked the gold reserves to ride out the storm. The experience of central European countries suggested that the psychology of the money markets was such that raising Bank rate would only have added to fears that Britain would be forced off the gold standard, and a prolonged defence of the exchange rate would have allowed withdrawals of short-term deposits from London to continue, leading potentially to a banking crisis.[163] On 21 September a Bill was rushed through Parliament to suspend the gold standard.

From a Keynesian perspective there would seem to have been little justification for a deflationary budget in 1931. On the other hand, even in the high noon of Keynesian economics, Ursula Hicks could still praise Snowden's September budget on the grounds that, as a result of his prompt action, no further deflationary measures were necessary even after sterling was devalued. It may well be, as she suggested, that the total amount of deflation required to restore confidence in British public finance was minimized thereby.[164] Certainly there was no collapse of confidence in public finance such as occurred in Weimar Germany in 1931 and 1932.[165] The British Treasury used its grip on public finance to restore confidence, partly because it was the Treasury's job to restore 'sound finance', but also because officials believed that the confidence of financial markets had to be won before there could be a successful conversion of War Loan to a lower rate of interest in 1932. That conversion itself would both ease

---

[162] Snowden, *Autobiography*, ii. 964–70.

[163] Alec Cairncross and Barry Eichengreen, *Sterling in Decline: The Devaluations of 1931, 1949 and 1967* (Oxford, 1983), 35, 72–83; Forrest Capie, Terence Mills, and Geoffrey Wood, 'What Happened in 1931?', in Forrest Capie and Geoffrey Wood (eds.), *Financial Crises and the World Banking System* (New York, 1986), 120–48; Harold James, 'Financial Flows Across Frontiers During the Interwar Depression', *Econ. Hist. Rev.*, 2nd ser., 45 (1992), 594–613.

[164] Ursula Hicks, *The Finance of British Government, 1920–1936* (Oxford, 1970), pp. xxxi–xxxii. On the other hand, as Middleton (*Towards the Managed Economy*, 137–8) points out, the reduction in public investment, much of it outside the Chancellor's budget, in 1932–3 was destabilizing, in contrast to the expansion of such investment under Labour in 1929–31.

[165] See Harold James, *The German Slump: Politics and Economics, 1924–1936* (Oxford, 1986), chs. 3 and 8.

the burden of debt on the budget and make possible the cheap money policy that they believed would promote private investment and economic recovery.

SUMMARY

Treasury officials successfully guided ministers to complete the post-war return to fiscal and monetary orthodoxy by restoring the gold standard. On the other hand, questions must be asked about the utility of attempts to impose rigid doctrines on public finance. Both Churchill and Snowden resorted to fiscal window dressing in order to achieve the appearance of a balanced budget, although the budget constraint on spending departments was real enough. The gold standard was 'knave-proof', up to a point, in that it drew politicians' attention to the need for public finance to retain the confidence of international money markets. The 'Treasury view' on borrowing for public works also served to rein in politicians' propensity to spend money, by restricting the categories of expenditure that might be financed out of loans. However, the problem of unemployment refused to go away, and the cost of unemployment relief increased rapidly as the world moved into a massive depression after 1929. The confidence of international money markets in British public finance was shaken in 1931 when it became apparent that the cost of unemployment relief was unbalancing the budget to an unknown extent. The very rigidity of the doctrines that the Treasury had imposed on monetary policy and public finance made it difficult in 1931 to absorb shocks from the international economy.

The period 1924–31 further broadened the experience of those Treasury officials who had to deal with economic theory in relation to unemployment, or international finance, as the world moved into a depression. All that experience and more would be needed to deal with the uncertainties of the rest of the 1930s.

CHAPTER SIX

Recovery and Rearmament, 1931–1939

INTRODUCTION

In October 1931, having failed to carry out the purpose for which it had been formed, that is the preservation of the gold standard, the National Government called and won a general election, asking for a free hand to deal with the crisis. Led initially by MacDonald, until his retirement in June 1935, then by Baldwin, until his retirement in May 1937, and finally by Neville Chamberlain, the National Government held power throughout the 1930s, Baldwin winning a further general election in 1935.

Economic historians still disagree about the nature of Britain's economic recovery in the 1930s. The depression bottomed out in 1932, in which year unemployment, measured as a national average, stood at 22.1 per cent of workers covered by the unemployment insurance scheme (the figure used by contemporaries), or 17 per cent of the total labour force. By 1937 unemployment had fallen to 10.8 per cent of the insured labour force, broadly the same level as in 1929. It has been argued that there was a strong cyclical element in the recovery that took place after 1932,[1] but recovery was not inevitable: both France and the United States had lower GDPs in 1937 than in 1929, whereas Britain's GDP in 1937 was 17 per cent higher than in 1929.[2] In 1937 and 1938 there was a recession, originating in the United States, and in 1938 unemployment in Britain averaged 12.9 per cent of the insured labour force.

The suspension of the gold standard in September 1931, and the subsequent depreciation of sterling, help to explain why industrial production in Britain did not fall as far in the slump as in countries that stayed on the gold standard; the fall in wholesale and retail prices was arrested in 1932 and 1933, and then reversed, helping to restore businesses to profitability.[3] The National

---

[1] Forrest H. Capie and Michael Collins, 'The Extent of British Economic Recovery in the 1930s', *Econ. and Hist.*, 23 (1980), 40–60.

[2] Angus Maddison, *Dynamic Forces in Capitalist Development* (Oxford, 1991), 214–15. Growth rates are measured from peak to peak of the trade cycle to eliminate distorting effects of the slump.

[3] Barry Eichengreen, 'The Origins and Nature of the Great Slump Revisited', *Econ. Hist. Rev.*, 2nd ser., 45 (1992), 227, 232–3. Real wages rose during the depression and then fell from 1934, but both slump and recovery appear to have been caused by changes in demand rather than movements in real

Government was also willing to take a more active role in managing the economy than hitherto in peacetime, through a low exchange rate, low interest rates, protective tariffs, and the encouragement of price-fixing and rationalization. Although such policies might appear to be *ad hoc*, all tended to increase profits through higher prices relative to wages, or to encourage investors to move from holding money assets to fixed assets.[4] The Treasury tried to uphold fiscal orthodoxy, but balanced budgets were not necessarily in conflict with other aspects of economic policy since financial markets then associated balanced budgets with lower interest rates. As Cairncross has pointed out, if private investment is highly sensitive to changes in interest rates, and if interest rates are highly sensitive to changes in the money supply, it may be possible to increase economic activity more through a policy of cheap money than through a policy of deficit spending.[5] Since the 1980s economic historians have doubted whether budget deficits to stimulate aggregate demand would have cured unemployment, although many continue to believe that an expansionary fiscal policy would have helped. More recently criticism has focused on the National Government's policies to protect British firms from competition, either through tariffs or by price-fixing agreements, which have been seen as strengthening resistance to modernization.[6]

For the Treasury the period contained two major challenges: first, how to encourage economic recovery, and second, how to finance rearmament, without undermining confidence in British public finance in either case. Rearmament was financed by borrowing from 1937, but was not seen as a means to economic recovery until the effects of the 1938 recession had been felt, and even then reflation was not seen as an unmixed blessing. Additional defence orders did produce jobs—about a million man years of employment between 1935 and 1938 according to one subsequent estimate (compared with an overall level of

wages—see N. H. Dimsdale, S. J. Nickell, and N. Horsewood, 'Real Wages and Unemployment in Britain during the 1930s', *Econ. J.*, 99 (1989), 271–92.

[4] Donald Winch, 'Britain in the 'Thirties: A Managed Economy?', in Charles H. Feinstein (ed.), *The Managed Economy: Essays in British Economic Policy and Performance since 1929* (Oxford, 1983), 47–67; G. C. Peden, *British Economic and Social Policy: Lloyd George to Margaret Thatcher* (Deddington, 1985), 92–110, 118–19; Alan Booth, 'Britain in the 1930s: A Managed Economy?', *Econ. Hist. Rev.*, 2nd ser., 40 (1987), 499–522 (but see comments by Middleton and Peden, ibid., 42 (1989), 538–47).

[5] Alec Cairncross, *Economics and Economic Policy* (Oxford, 1986), 161.

[6] Doubts on the efficacy of an expansionary fiscal policy arise from administrative constraints on initiating public works; from Britain's dependence upon international trade; from the structural and regional nature of unemployment; and from the probable effects of rising long-term unemployment on the non-accelerating inflation rate of unemployment (NAIRU). For useful surveys of the shift from the predominantly Keynesian interpretation of the period see Patrick K. O'Brien, 'Britain's Economy between the Wars: A Survey of a Counter-revolution in Economic History', *Past and Present*, 115 (1987), 107–30, and Michael Collins, 'Did Keynes Have the Answer to Unemployment in the 1930s?', in John Hillard (ed.), *J. M. Keynes in Retrospect: The Legacy of the Keynesian Revolution* (Aldershot, 1988), 64–87. For NAIRU see N. F. R. Crafts, 'Long-term Unemployment and the Wage Equation in Britain, 1925–1939', *Economica*, NS, 56 (1989), 247–54. For negative effects of protective policies on modernization see S. N. Broadberry and N. F. R. Crafts, 'The Implications of British Macroeconomic Policy in the 1930s for Long Run Growth Performance', *Riv. Storia Econ.*, NS, 7 (1990), 1–19.

unemployment of 2.4 million in 1935).[7] On the other hand, rearmament was also associated with growing problems with the balance of payments and with loss of confidence in sterling, raising fears in the Treasury of another 1931. The Treasury continued to be concerned with the loss of control over expenditure, civil as well as military, associated with budget deficits, and to be sceptical about the value of public works as an employment policy. Its preferred means of countering a downturn in the economy was still a lowering of interest rates to encourage private investment.

The Treasury's claims with regard to the extent of its functions as the central department of government were particularly wide in the 1930s. From 1933 Fisher tried to influence defence policy and offended the Foreign Office by his belief that the Treasury must concern itself with 'foreign . . . affairs (which are now-a-days largely economics, finance and armaments).'[8] The Treasury was to emerge from the 1930s tainted not only with failure (in the eyes of liberal opinion) to adopt Keynes's ideas to solve economic problems, but also by association with Neville Chamberlain's policy of appeasement of Germany.

PERSONALITIES, ORGANIZATION, AND ECONOMIC ADVICE

From November 1931 the Treasury had an exceptionally strong Chancellor in Neville Chamberlain. Treasury officials regarded him as the most competent Chancellor since Gladstone. Moreover, Chamberlain could also speak in Cabinet with the authority of the heir apparent to the leadership of the Conservative party and the premiership. Neither MacDonald nor Baldwin provided dynamic leadership in their last years as prime ministers, and Chamberlain, being self-confident and prone to seek his own solutions to political problems, did not hesitate to concern himself with such issues as defence and foreign policy.

On becoming Prime Minister in May 1937 Chamberlain chose Sir John Simon, the leader of the Liberal National group within the National Government, as his successor at the Treasury. As usual, the appointment reflected political priorities: Simon was ambitious for high office, and would not be content with anything less than his previous posts as Foreign Secretary and Home Secretary, and his presence in the government helped to give it a 'National' appearance. Simon said that, having no special knowledge of national finance, he approached his new office with humbleness, to which Chamberlain replied: 'not a bad qualification to start with'.[9] However, Simon lacked Chamberlain's

[7] Mark Thomas, 'Rearmament and Economic Recovery in the Late 1930s', *Econ. Hist. Rev.*, 2nd ser., 36 (1983), 552–79.
[8] Minutes of Treasury Organization Committee, 2 Nov. 1936, T199/50c.
[9] J. Simon, *Retrospect* (1952), 227.

decisiveness. As a barrister, the new Chancellor could express ideas clearly, but Chamberlain himself had once described Simon as 'temperamentally unable to make up his mind when a difficult situation arose'.[10]

Fisher and Chamberlain had been on close terms since the latter had been Chancellor, 1923–4, but Fisher fell out with Chamberlain in the autumn of 1938 over the policy of appeasement. Chamberlain's closest adviser once he became Prime Minister was Sir Horace Wilson, the Chief Industrial Adviser to His Majesty's Government, whom Fisher had sent to the Prime Minister's Office to be Baldwin's adviser in 1935. Wilson and Fisher had long enjoyed a relationship of mutual confidence and affection but, once Wilson became Chamberlain's confidential adviser in 1937, he was in no way dependent on Fisher. When Fisher realized that he no longer enjoyed Chamberlain's confidence, he decided to make way for Wilson, whom Chamberlain had chosen in February 1939 to be the next Permanent Secretary of the Treasury. Fisher went on extended leave from mid-May 1939, although he was not due to retire until 31 October, and Wilson began what proved to be an unhappy dual existence as Permanent Secretary and the Prime Minister's confidential adviser, spending only half his time in the Treasury, until Chamberlain's resignation in 1940.

There was a major reorganization of the Treasury in 1932 after the then Controller of the Establishments Department, Sir R. Russell Scott, was appointed Permanent Under-Secretary of the Home Office (see Figure 6.1). Fisher took the opportunity to abolish the rank of Controller and to unify the Treasury's three 'departments' into one. Hopkins, hitherto Controller of both the Finance and the Supply Services departments, retained his existing responsibilities and status, but with the new title of Second Secretary. The work formerly done by the Controller of the Establishments Department, and by the Deputy Controllers of the Finance and Supply Services departments, was given to a new rank of Treasury officials, Under-Secretaries, who had lower salaries than the Controllers had, and did not have the status of heads of departments.

The most prominent of the new Under-Secretaries was Frederick Phillips, who had had long experience of the work of the Finance Department, and who now oversaw the work of the Overseas Finance and Home Finance divisions. Phillips was a Treasury 'character'. He had come first in the Civil Service examination in 1908, after reading Mathematics and Natural Sciences at Cambridge, with Firsts in both. The son of a teacher in an obscure secondary school, he was socially reserved and inarticulate in conversation, but lucid on paper. Lord Trend, who was a junior official working in the Overseas Finance Division in 1937 and 1938, recalled that Phillips lived in a gruff, brusque world of his own, and thought best while listening to loud music in an over-heated room. Blunt and taciturn, Phillips won the admiration of his colleagues, including Keynes,

---

[10] Chamberlain's diary, Jan. 1934, NC2/23A.

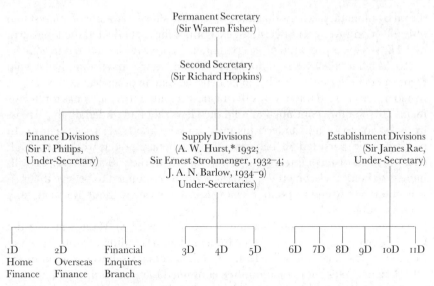

FIG. 6.1.   *Treasury Organization, 1932–1939*

* Seconded to Import Duties Advisory Committee

on account of his ability to express incisive criticism and constructive judgement, and those who penetrated his shyness found that he had wide intellectual interests and a quizzical sense of humour.[11]

Leith-Ross, who had not enjoyed being Hopkins's deputy in the Finance Department, was given the title of Chief Economic Adviser to His Majesty's Government, with an office in the Board of Trade as well as the Treasury, and from March 1932 he took little part in intra-Treasury discussions on policy. He regarded his new title as a misnomer, since his principal duties involved representing Britain in international financial negotiations. He was certainly no economist; he had resigned from the Tuesday Club because he found discussions with Keynes and others too exhausting after a day's work at the Treasury.[12] It is perhaps symptomatic of Fisher's attitude to economics that he should have replaced the previous Chief Economic Adviser, Sir Sydney Chapman, who was a professional economist, with an administrative civil servant, Leith-Ross, who had studied classics at Oxford.

Hawtrey, as Director of Financial Enquiries, continued to be the Treasury's only economist. Keynes engaged in lengthy correspondence with him over the *General Theory*, but was unable to persuade him that unemployment could not be

[11] Memorandum by W. W. Butterworth, US Embassy, London, 4 Sept. 1937, Country files: Great Britain 100, box 108, Records of the Bureau of Accounts, Record Group 39 (hereafter RG39), National Archives, Washington, DC; *JMK*, x (1972), 330–1; conversations with Sir Thomas Padmore, 15 Mar. 1975, and Lord Trend, 26 June 1975.

[12] F. Leith-Ross, *Money Talks* (1968), 144–8.

solved by monetary expansion alone, or that the short-term rate of interest had little effect on investment decisions, except insofar as it affected the long-term rate. Hawtrey was prepared to accept that, in theory, the long-term rate of interest could fall to a level where no one would any longer have a motive to hold securities in preference to cash, but he believed that, in practice, new inventions would offset such a tendency by offering new remunerative openings for investment. He therefore continued to hold the views that had underlain the 'Treasury view' of 1929, and indeed his own work on the trade cycle in 1913. In particular, he persisted in believing that monetary policy worked through changes in short-term interest rates, particularly as they affected traders' willingness to hold stocks on credit, and therefore he continued to believe that private enterprise would respond to changes in Bank rate without, normally, any need for public works.[13]

The main source of professional economic advice in Whitehall was the Committee on Economic Advisory Information, a standing committee of the Economic Advisory Council. Meetings of the Council itself were discontinued after January 1932 but the Committee continued to meet until 1939. Its membership included academic economists, such as Henderson, Keynes, and (from 1936) Dennis Robertson, and the fact that Leith-Ross attended meetings from 1932, and Phillips from 1935, gave Keynes the opportunity to discuss economics with them. The Committee reported to the Cabinet through the Cabinet Secretariat, but had no ministerial sponsor, and by 1937 Henderson doubted if ministers read them. The Committee's secretaries were not always successful at reconciling opposing opinions in its reports—Keynes complaining in one instance of 'confused verbosity' that very few people would read to the end— but Leith-Ross and Phillips produced summaries for Hopkins. The differences of opinion were not confined to the well-known theoretical disputes between economists: Henderson noted that whereas Leith-Ross was an internationalist, Phillips was an 'isolationist', in the sense that he was more prepared to look for domestic solutions to Britain's economic problems.[14]

Treasury officials did not concede that economists had a greater competence than themselves in advising ministers on economic policy. Indeed, with reference to the opposing views regarding the economic effects of private saving, represented by Friedrich von Hayek and Lionel Robbins on the one hand, and Keynes and Stamp on the other, Hopkins commented to Chamberlain in 1932 that:

It seems useless to endeavour to follow professional economic teaching, for there is no criterion for determining the proper economists to follow, and whoever one chooses,

---

[13] 'Mr Keynes's "General Theory of Employment, Interest and Money" ', by Hawtrey, 14 Mar. 1936, T208/195; R. G. Hawtrey, *A Century of Bank Rate* (1938). The Keynes–Hawtrey correspondence is in *JMK*, xiii. 565–633, and xiv. 3–55.

[14] *JMK*, xxi. 421–5; S. Howson and D. Winch, *The Economic Advisory Council, 1930–1939: A Study in Economic Advice during Depression and Recovery* (Cambridge, 1977), chs. 5–6.

one is apt to find oneself led into actions which are either repugnant to commonsense or incapable of practical achievement.[15]

The Treasury preferred economic advisers who had practical experience of government. When it was suggested in May 1939 that there should be an 'economic general staff' to prepare for war, Hopkins commented that such a staff should not be made up of 'a lot of economists operating *in vacuo*'; to which Fisher added: 'what is *not* wanted is a panel of economists and doctrinaires'.[16] No such staff was set up before the war. Instead, Stamp was invited in July to conduct a survey of Britain's war plans, on a part-time basis, assisted by Henry Clay, the Bank of England's in-house economist, and Henderson, who had served on the Cotton Control Board during the First World War as well as with the Economic Advisory Council in the 1930s. The most important source of advice on monetary policy continued to be the Bank of England, but it was not immune from the influence of professional economists. According to Sayers, Clay persuaded Norman at some point between 1933 and the spring of 1935 that it might be possible to promote economic recovery through internationally co-ordinated programmes of public works along the lines advocated by Keynes. However, public works were not the Bank's business, and in its own sphere of controlling credit the Bank was unwilling to put at risk confidence in sterling or in London's position as a financial centre.[17]

Although the Bank remained the major link between the Treasury and financial markets, the effect of the suspension of the gold standard was to restore the Treasury to the dominant position with regard to monetary policy that it had held from 1917 into the early 1920s. In particular, Treasury officials largely determined policy on both Bank rate and sterling's exchange rate. 'I am an instrument of the Treasury,' Norman told a gathering of Commonwealth central bankers in 1937.[18] On the other hand, he was careful to maintain the independence of the Bank, confining discussions of policy with the Treasury to the Deputy Governor and himself. When in 1935 and again in 1939 the Treasury asked if it would be possible to borrow a member of the Bank's staff to assist in the hard-pressed Overseas Finance Division, Norman refused on the grounds that such a transfer would suggest an interchangeability between the staff of the Treasury and the Bank, and thereby set up a 'dangerous precedent'; he also thought that the member of staff involved 'might be in a difficult position because of his divided allegiance'.[19]

[15] Memorandum to Chancellor of the Exchequer, 20 Oct. 1932, T175/70, cited in S. Howson, *Domestic Monetary Management in Britain, 1919–38* (Cambridge, 1975), 91.
[16] Hopkins to Fisher, 17 May 1939, T160/885/F17545.
[17] R. S. Sayers, *The Bank of England, 1891–1944* (Cambridge, 1976), vol. ii. 461–3.
[18] H. Clay, *Lord Norman* (1957), 437.
[19] Extracts from minutes of the Committee of Treasury, 25 Sept. 1935 and 3 May 1939, Bank of England papers G15/7/1816/5.

MONETARY POLICY AND ECONOMIC RECOVERY, 1931–1937

The course of monetary policy in the 1930s has been fully described by Drummond and Howson,[20] and is considered here from the point of view of how the Treasury used it as its major policy instrument to achieve economic recovery. Once the gold standard had been suspended, the Treasury and the Bank had to formulate a new policy with regard to the sterling exchange rate. It was realized that instability in exchange rates would cause disruption in the international system of payments, and therefore trade. As early as 26 September 1931 Niemeyer, at the Bank, suggested the formation of a sterling block, that is a group of countries pegging their currencies to sterling. India, the colonies, and some semi-independent countries like Egypt and Iraq, could be required to link their currencies to sterling and, within a short period, all the dominions, except Canada, had chosen to do so, as had some foreign countries, like Portugal, which had close trading links with Britain. However, with sterling floating between $3.90 and $3.24 in the last three months of 1931, traders dealing with countries outside the sterling area faced major exchange problems.

By late September only Leith-Ross among senior Treasury officials was wholeheartedly in favour of an early return to the gold standard. Phillips argued that the gold standard, by linking the value of sterling to gold, had lowered wholesale prices by 25 per cent and the cost of living by 10 per cent since 1929, to the benefit of rentiers, but at the expense of business profits, while 'the working classes were losing as much from unemployment as they were gaining from an increase in real wages'.[21] During the course of 1932 the Treasury made clear that there would be no return to the gold standard until such time as the international monetary system had been reformed to make it less deflationary, and until there was a new equilibrium in world prices.[22] Even the Bank of England, which regarded anything short of a full international gold standard as a temporary arrangement, recognized that the gold standard would have to be reformed before it could be restored.[23]

The question of the level at which the floating pound should be pegged was discussed in the Treasury from September 1931 to February 1932. The Economic Advisory Council's Committee on Economic information had reported on 25 September that a 25 per cent depreciation would not be excessive,[24] and further advice was taken from Hawtrey, Henderson, and Keynes. There was agreement that, while depreciation benefited exporters, too great a depreciation would have

[20] I. M. Drummond, *The Floating Pound and the Sterling Area, 1931–1939* (Cambridge, 1981); Howson, *Domestic Monetary Management*; id., *Sterling's Managed Float: The Operations of the Exchange Equalisation Account* (Princeton, NJ, 1980).   [21] Howson, *Domestic Monetary Management*, 83.

[22] 'Report of the Committee on Monetary and Financial Questions to Imperial Conference at Ottawa, July–August 1932', reprinted in Sayers, *Bank of England*, iii. 273–5; 'The Foreign Demand for the Return of the United Kingdom to Gold', 29 Oct. 1932, T175/70.

[23] Sayers, *Bank of England*, ii. 451, 455.

[24] Howson and Winch, *Economic Advisory Council*, 243–54.

an adverse effect on the balance of payments, as shipping receipts and overseas investments were mostly denominated in sterling. Depreciation would also increase the burden of Britain's war debt to America, which was denominated in dollars, while reducing the value of inter-allied debts due to Britain, which were mainly denominated in sterling. The key factor in fixing the target level for the exchange rate, however, was the likely effect on prices in Britain.[25]

Moggridge credits Keynes with having influenced Phillips and Hopkins in favour of a target rate of $3.40 to $3.60, rather than the $3.90 rate advocated by Henderson,[26] but the evidence of the Treasury files suggests that Hawtrey's influence was no less important, and perhaps more so. Keynes let the Treasury have his views in November, but by then Hawtrey had already argued for a 30 per cent depreciation, to $3.40, to compensate for world prices being about 30 per cent below their 1925 level. Hawtrey thought that a 30 per cent depreciation would be enough at current price levels to secure full employment and adequate profits for industry, with some increases in wages in export industries where wage reductions had been exceptionally severe.[27] Norman told the Chancellor at a meeting on 8 December that fluctuations in the exchange were more serious for trade than the actual exchange rate, but the Bank lacked the gold and foreign exchange reserves with which to stabilize sterling. When asked by Chamberlain whether trade recovery depended on a rise in wholesale prices, Norman agreed, but thought that there was nothing the Bank and the Treasury could do to bring about a rise in prices.[28]

In February 1932 Treasury officials settled on $3.40 as the best level for the pound and advised the Cabinet accordingly. The Treasury wanted prices to rise to their pre-depression levels and, Phillips noted, 'the only method seems to be to hold sterling down until a rise in world gold prices takes us there'.[29] Such a policy would reduce the burden of the National Debt, and help businessmen, particularly exporters. In future, if world prices fell further, the exchange rate might have to be lowered further still, and it should not be allowed to rise until sterling prices had risen at least 25 per cent over the September 1931 level. Phillips, whose views seem to have carried most weight, argued that:

The size of our national debt and the rigidity of wages and other costs in this country make a falling price level peculiarly dangerous to us. It is not merely that falling prices, unaccompanied by falling wages, affect the manufacturer directly—they have also important psychological reactions tending to damp down business activity.[30]

[25] At least this was so for Phillips, if not Leith-Ross. Phillips apparently still felt he had to persuade the latter that 'the question of our own price level is fundamental' in Mar. 1932 (T188/48).

[26] D. E. Moggridge, *Maynard Keynes: An Economist's Biography* (1992), 537–8.

[27] 'Pegging the Pound I', 28 Sept. 1931, and 'Pegging the Pound II', 2 Oct. 1931, T175/56.

[28] Howson, *Domestic Monetary Management*, 81–3. Howson points out that the Bank did not inform the Treasury of the level of gold and foreign exchange reserves held by the Bank but, at £28 million in December, these were indeed too low to combat speculators.

[29] 'The Mond-Strakosch Memorandum', by Phillips, 4 Mar. 1932, T175/57.

[30] Phillips to Leith-Ross, 31 Mar. 1932, T188/48, cited in Howson, op. cit., 86.

By March 1932 Treasury officials, while advising the Chancellor on future budgets, were assuming that over the next three years prices would rise to about the 1929 level, while it was hoped that wage rates would remain stable.[31] In the event, even in 1937, at the top of the upswing from the slump, the Board of Trade's wholesale price index stood at 95 (1929 = 100); the Ministry of Labour's working-class cost-of-living index at 94; and the Ministry of Labour's index of average money wage rates at 104 (see Figure 5.1).

If sterling was to continue to be an international currency, some means had to be found of reducing fluctuations in its exchange rate. At the same time, if the adverse balance of trade was to be improved, and if prices were to be increased, some means had to be found of holding the sterling exchange rate down. The Bank's ability to manage the exchange rate was limited by its lack of sterling assets and, as a private institution, by the possibility of loss on foreign exchange holdings if the sterling exchange rate were to rise. To meet these difficulties, Phillips devised the Exchange Equalisation Account (EEA). The EEA was under the ultimate control of the Treasury, but was managed on a day-to-day basis by the Bank. The EEA took over the assets, totalling £20 million, left in the old Exchange Account after Snowden's raid on it in 1931, and was given power in the 1932 budget to borrow up to £150 million. The Bank sold Treasury bills from the EEA when it needed sterling to pay for gold or foreign exchange, and bought Treasury bills for the EEA when it acquired sterling by selling gold and foreign exchange. The purpose of balancing transactions in gold and foreign exchange with transactions in Treasury bills was to enable the monetary authorities to reduce the impact on the domestic monetary supply of movements in foreign speculative funds. Moreover, any losses incurred in exchange dealings to stabilize sterling would be borne by the EEA rather than by the Bank.

Phillips and Waley, the principal assistant secretary in charge of the Overseas Finance Division, were the officials responsible for overseeing the operations of the EEA for the rest of the decade, and they consistently countered any tendency of the Bank to allow the exchange rate to rise, although it did not prove to be possible to hold sterling at the level chosen by the Treasury. As early as February 1933 Phillips noted that there were 'very definite and ominous signs' of opposition abroad to any further depreciation of sterling, and he warned that Britain must avoid provoking countermeasures: 'We have everything to lose from tempting our manufacturing competitors to leave the gold standard themselves.'[32] Japan had already done so, and the depreciation of the yen by 57 per cent, compared with sterling's 30 per cent, enabled Japanese goods to undercut British goods in international markets. In the event, as part of his 'New Deal', President Roosevelt floated the dollar in March 1933, and stabilized it in January 1934 at 59 per cent of its former gold content, in an attempt to raise

---

[31] 'Speculative Forecast of 1935 on the Basis of "Old Moore's Almanac" ', 21 Mar. 1932, T171/296.
[32] Phillips to Hopkins, 28 Feb. 1933, T175/17.

prices in the United States and to help American exporters. Thereafter sterling was generally above $4.86 until the prospect of war in Europe, and balance-of-payments problems associated with British rearmament, caused confidence in sterling to decline in 1938 and 1939. On the other hand, other countries, notably France, remained on the gold standard and Redmond has calculated that sterling's effective exchange rate, that is a weighted average of its movements against all other currencies, was still 4 to 5 per cent below the 1929–30 level from 1934 to the devaluation of the franc in 1936, and that it was not until the period from 1937 to 1939 that British exporters had to cope with a higher effective exchange rate than in 1929–30.[33]

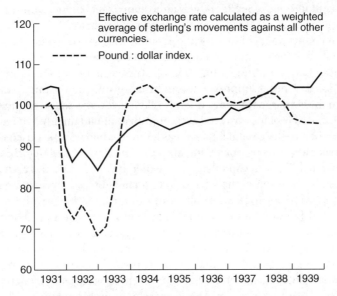

FIG. 6.2.   *Indices of the Sterling Exchange Rate in the 1930s*

Source: J. Redmond, 'An Indicator of the Effective Exchange Rate of the Pound in the Nineteen-thirties', *Econ. Hist. Rev.*, 2nd ser., 33 (1980), 87.

Initially, with the suspension of the gold standard on 21 September 1931, sterling had been defended by raising Bank rate from 2½ per cent to 6 per cent. However, once the Bank had attracted enough gold and foreign exchange to repay debts incurred to central banks during the crisis, and once it was decided that sterling should be kept down at about $3.40, Bank rate was reduced to 5 per cent on 18 February, and then by stages to 2 per cent on 30 June 1932. On that

---

[33] John Redmond, 'An Indicator of the Effective Exchange Rate of the Pound in the Nineteen-thirties', *Econ. Hist. Rev.*, 2nd ser., 33 (1980), 83–91.

day the long-awaited conversion of the massive 5 per cent War Loan, which represented 28 per cent of the National Debt, was announced to Parliament, the Bank of England having advised the Treasury that market conditions were favourable. Investors at home and abroad had confidence in the financial policies of the National Government, and a worldwide fall in interest rates made the conversion offer of 3½ per cent to holders of War Loan attractive.[34] The reduction in interest rates itself made it easier to balance the budget, which in turn reinforced confidence in government finance.

Despite a flexible exchange rate, and the introduction of a general tariff in 1932 (see below), Britain had a persistent balance-of-payments problem throughout the 1930s. There was a deficit on current account every year from 1931, except in 1933 (when there was almost an exact balance) and 1935 (when there was a small surplus), whereas previously deficits had been unknown, except in connection with war, or the general strike in 1926. The changed situation regarding the balance of payments forced a change in the Treasury's attitude to the City's traditional function of overseas lending. The conversion of War Loan had been supported by an embargo on new capital issues and, although the embargo was subsequently relaxed, foreign issues remained under restriction. As Hopkins observed, now that Britain had an adverse balance on current account, the capital for overseas lending could only be raised by realizing overseas assets or by borrowing abroad. The danger was that Britain's net short-term liabilities on capital account would be increased, in return for what would usually be assets in the form of long-term debt, thereby inviting a repetition of the events of 1931, when short-term funds had been withdrawn from London, but London had been unable to realize, or even draw income from, some of its long-term assets.[35] The dominions and colonies, unlike foreign countries, could borrow freely on the London market, and one consequence may have been to strengthen the links between the City and the Empire. On the other hand, the embargo on foreign issues represented some recognition that there should be priority for productive investment in Britain.

The Treasury had had hopes since 1930 that cheap money would stimulate industry, and it was at the insistence of the Treasury that Bank rate was kept at 2 per cent until August 1939.[36] However, bank overdraft rates and building society lending rates were slow to respond to the fall in Bank rate. The Treasury

[34] F. H. Capie, T. C Mills, and G. E. Wood, 'Debt Management and Interest Rates: The British Stock Conversion of 1932', *Applied Econ.*, 18 (1986), 1111–26.

[35] Hopkins to Fisher, 6 Feb. 1933, T175/17. Sayers, *Bank of England*, ii. 440, 466, 491–2.

[36] Howson, *Domestic Monetary Management*, 89. A. Booth, *British Economic Policy, 1931–1949: Was There a Keynesian Revolution?* (1989), 24, states that Howson argues that budgetary rather than employment considerations were of primary importance to the Treasury, but in fact she argues the reverse: 'Cheap money . . . was desired by the Treasury from at least the onset of the slump . . . and it was desired as an aid to recovery. In 1931 with the growing budgetary difficulties a large conversion . . . was also desired as a means of reducing expenditure . . .[but] cheap money was still wanted primarily as an aid to industry' (loc. cit.).

had meagre information about the lending policies of the banks, particularly with regard to overdraft rates, and Hopkins was surprised in the autumn of 1932 to learn that the aggregate amount of overdrafts had declined since Bank rate had been reduced. He advised Chamberlain that the banks would resent any Treasury intervention but that the Chancellor might raise the issue informally with the principal bankers. By April 1933, however, Hopkins had been assured by the Deputy Governor of the Bank of England that overdraft rates had been reduced to an average of 4 or 4⅛ per cent and that it was the general policy of the banks to give advances freely to sound new borrowers.[37]

Despite the Treasury's hopes that money would be abundant as well as cheap, neither it nor the Bank wished to abandon the policy of funding the short-term and floating debt, especially Treasury bills. Indeed, Norman regarded the loss of the automatic mechanism of the gold standard as an additional reason to keep tight control of domestic credit. By 1934 Hopkins and Phillips were sensitive to criticism from what Hopkins called the 'small school' of thought which claimed that reduction of the floating debt was intrinsically deflationary, but they believed that the Bank could always offset the effect of funding by increasing the monetary base. As Nevin and Howson have pointed out, this 'funding complex' tended to slow down the growth in the money supply and from the end of 1936 longer-term interest rates began to rise. Even so, the cost to British industry for new funds in the capital market had declined noticeably since 1932, and it was not until early 1939 that longer-term interest rates regained the level of 1933 (the yield on 2½ per cent undated Consols in both years being about 3½ per cent, compared with 4½ per cent in 1930). There was a substantial increase in capital issues for industry between 1932 and 1937. There was also an unprecedented housing boom, and although that boom reflected other factors, including increased family formation, rising real incomes, and lower construction costs, it has been calculated that cheap money accounted for about half of the rise in housing investment, which itself, directly and indirectly, accounted for about 30 per cent of the increase in employment between 1932 and 1935.[38]

Whatever its shortcomings, monetary policy contributed substantially to economic recovery down to 1937. Indeed it can be argued that the (enforced) devaluation of sterling may have been a more effective response to the slump than any conceivable demand stimulus through fiscal policy.[39] It is true that manufacturers did not benefit from a more competitive exchange rate for long,

[37] Hopkins to Chancellor of the Exchequer, 13 Oct. 1932, T175/70; Hopkins to Fergusson, 21 Apr. 1933, T175/17.

[38] E. Nevin: *The Mechanism of Cheap Money: A Study of British Monetary Policy, 1931–1939* (Cardiff, 1955); Howson, op. cit., 90–1, 95–106; S. N. Broadberry, 'Cheap Money and the Housing Boom in Interwar Britain: An Economic Appraisal', *Manchester School*, 55 (1987), 378–91; G. D. N. Worswick, 'The Sources of Recovery in the UK in the 1930s', *Nat. Institute Econ. Rev.*, Nov. 1984, 85–93.

[39] Barry Eichengreen and Jeffrey Sachs, 'Exchange Rates and Economic Recovery in the 1930s', *J. Econ. Hist.*, 45 (1985), 925–46.

and that exporters could not benefit fully owing to the spread of barriers to international trade. More importantly, however, sterling depreciation in 1931 and 1932 helped to reverse the downward trend in prices. As a result, real interest rates fell from 1932 to 1937, in contrast to the period 1929 to 1931, when real interest rates had risen even as nominal interest rates had fallen. Whereas falling prices had benefited rentiers at the expense of business profits between 1929 and 1932, the reverse was true between 1932 and 1937.

Treasury officials were certainly pleased with the results of cheap money, but they were not committed to a 2 per cent Bank rate indefinitely. At the end of 1936 Phillips noted that prices were rising with some rapidity, which was all to the good for the moment, but that it was probable that the price level would be as high as the Treasury wished to see it within twelve months; moreover, he thought, the best precaution that could be taken against a future slump would be to ensure that the current boom was not allowed to reach a dangerous level. Following Hawtrey's theory that Bank rate could be regulated to moderate the growth of economic activity to any desired extent, Phillips advised that some increase in Bank rate would be necessary in the autumn of 1937, with $3\frac{1}{2}$ to 4 per cent being the likely level for 1938. At the beginning of 1937 Keynes, with support from the Committee on Economic Information, advised against a rise in interest rates and recommended that the level of economic activity should be regulated by holding back public investment. This suggestion was investigated by an interdepartmental committee, chaired by Phillips, which reported in favour of postponing some public works schemes (see below). Bank rate remained at 2 per cent until August 1939, but this seems to have been because Hawtrey advised that recovery was not yet complete, and because the economy moved into recession from the end of 1937, rather than because of Keynes's ideas.[40]

THE TREASURY AND TARIFFS

The Treasury's role in the introduction of protection in 1931 and 1932 provides a striking example of the importance of party politics, and the personality of the Chancellor, in the shaping of policy. Under Snowden the Treasury had been a bastion of free trade, as it had been since Gladstone had been Chancellor. Neville Chamberlain, however, was the leading proponent of protection in the National Government and, with his return to the Treasury in November 1931, officials were required to draft arguments in favour of tariffs. Although some

---

[40] 'How to Avoid a Slump', *JMK*, xxi. 384–95; 22nd Report of Committee on Economic Information, 19 Feb. 1937, reproduced in Howson and Winch, *Economic Advisory Council*, 343–53; Howson, *Domestic Monetary Management*, 128–31; G. C. Peden, 'Keynes, the Treasury and Unemployment in the later Nineteen-thirties', *Oxford Econ. Papers*, NS, 32 (1980), 10.

officials were doubtless less than happy in this new role, others may have felt that the 1931 crisis had changed the balance of the argument in favour of protection. As is often the case, the nature of the evidence from Treasury and Cabinet Office papers makes it difficult to know when officials were writing from conviction and when they were writing to order.

The emergence of a balance-of-payments deficit on current account in 1931 reflected the decline in income from financial services and shipping, and income from abroad, rather than a shift in the balance of trade in goods. Nevertheless, there was some (although not much) evidence early in November that the election of a Conservative-dominated government was encouraging importers to increase their inventories in anticipation of possible future import duties. Although Chamberlain would have supported protection anyway, he was able to convince the President of the Board of Trade, Walter Runciman who, as a Liberal, had strong free-trade credentials, and even Snowden, that something should be done to correct the trade deficit, and thereby prevent an excessive depreciation of sterling. As a result, the Abnormal Importations Act was rushed through Parliament, giving the Board of Trade temporary power to impose duties of up to 100 per cent *ad valorem* on imports judged to be entering the country in abnormal quantities, even before a Cabinet Committee on the Balance of Trade was set up under Chamberlain's chairmanship on 11 December.

Chamberlain rejected a Liberal proposal that economists should be consulted by the committee, while his own officials provided him with arguments why the sterling exchange rate should not be allowed to fall too far. The committee duly reported that the current account deficit was likely to be between £90 million and £120 million in 1931, and would be worse in 1932 if remedial action were not taken. A revenue tariff of 10 per cent was expected to reduce the deficit by only £34 million in a full year, on the assumption that there would be an average preferential rate of 6⅔ per cent for the dominions and India, and free entry for some foodstuffs, raw materials, and colonial produce. It was hoped that the lower exchange rate would lead eventually to a substantial increase in exports, perhaps by as much as £106 million a year, but only if other countries could be persuaded to reduce their tariffs against British manufactures.[41]

The battle between protectionists and free traders was fought out in two meetings of the full Cabinet on 21 January 1932. Chamberlain stressed the seriousness of the position of the pound, and when Snowden suggested that the proposed tariff might raise the cost of living by 15 per cent, and thereby cause industrial unrest, Chamberlain said that the Treasury had calculated that nothing in the proposals would bring the country near the danger point. He thought that the tariff could be used as a bargaining counter, both with other countries,

[41] Committee on the Balance of Trade, 'Report', 19 Jan. 1932, CP25(32), CAB24/227; T. Routh, *British Protectionism and the International Economy: Overseas Commercial Policy in the 1930s* (Cambridge, 1993), 63–6.

to reduce barriers to British exports, and with the British iron and steel industry, by making protection conditional on reorganization of the industry. At a further meeting on 29 January the Cabinet went through the draft Import Duties Bill clause by clause, with Chamberlain giving an explanation of each item. It was also Chamberlain who introduced the Bill in the House of Commons on 4 February, having been furnished by Donald Fergusson, his principal private secretary, with a brief which described the general tariff as part of the government's 'flexible and many-sided policy' to deal with the consequences of the 1931 crisis. The Treasury brief emphasized the importance of improving the balance of trade by checking imports, thereby providing an insurance against the risk of a serious rise in the cost of living due to an unchecked depreciation of currency, the influence of the tariff on the value of sterling being 'the essential consideration'. Chamberlain's speech in Parliament added the objectives of improving employment, raising revenue, improving Britain's bargaining position with other countries, and, 'last but not least', strengthening the Empire through imperial preference.[42]

The Act established an Import Duties Advisory Committee under Sir George May (the author of the May Report in 1931) to advise the Treasury and the Board of Trade on the progress of protected industries. This Committee soon recommended that the base rate for the general tariff should be raised from the initial 10 per cent to 20 per cent, and in some cases, including steel, to 30 per cent. Treasury officials did not share Chamberlain's optimism that reorganization of the steel industry would be eased by the tariff; instead they believed that, unless the tariff was explicitly temporary and conditional, it would hinder reorganization. This pessimism proved to be justified. Despite the urging of May and Alfred Hurst, the leading Treasury official with special responsibility for the Import Duties Advisory Committee, the representatives of the steel industry proved to be much more interested in lobbying for higher tariffs than in reorganization. In practice, however, it was politically impossible not to renew the tariff, even though the body set up to promote reorganization of the industry, the British Iron and Steel Federation, was regarded by Treasury officials as likely to be 'rather ineffective'.[43]

Treasury officials continued to worry about the possibly distorting effects of tariffs on the structure and costs of British industry and agriculture. As Phillips noted in 1934, the tariff could wisely be 'pushed up to the point at which we have secured as much of the home market as we think can be permanently held in all circumstances', but to go beyond that point in order to secure a temporary improvement in employment would not be worth the expense of reversing the

[42] CAB23/70; 'Import Duties Bill', 30 Jan. 1932, T172/1514; 261 HC Deb., 5s, 1931–2, col. 287.
[43] 'Re-organization of the Iron and Steel Industry. An Analysis of the Present Position', by Hurst, 8 Feb. 1933, T172/1773; Steven Tolliday, *Business, Banking and Politics: The Case of British Steel, 1918–1939* (Cambridge, Mass., 1987), esp. 299 and 305.

changes in structure later on.[44] These worries did not prevent the Import Duties Advisory Committee recommending further increases in import duties in 1934 and 1935. In 1939 Leith-Ross, noting how the pricing policy of iron and steel had adversely affected a range of export industries, especially shipbuilding, industrial machinery, and engineering generally, called for changes that would encourage rationalization rather than price-fixing,[45] but the war intervened before anything could be done.

Power was reserved to the Treasury under the 1932 Act to direct that the duty on goods from the dominions might be reduced or waived. Chamberlain had hopes that this power could be used to strengthen trade (and political) links within the Empire, but the Ottawa conference later that year proved to be a disillusioning experience, in that none of the dominions would sign Chamberlain's draft 'principles of imperial trade policy', each dominion preferring to put its own interests first. The fundamental economic obstacles to making the Empire a closed economic system were that Britain was not a large enough market to absorb all the food and raw materials produced in the dominions, while the dominions were unwilling to expose their infant industries to British competition. Thus the Ottawa Agreements tended to provide imperial preference by increasing duties, or introducing quotas, on non-Empire goods, rather than by making large-scale mutual tariff concessions. British exports to the Empire did increase, but the impact on the British economy was modest. Drummond, assuming a high multiplier of 2, has suggested that the Ottawa agreements increased total United Kingdom output by 0.5 per cent in 1933 and 1 per cent in 1937.[46]

The overall impact of tariffs on the British economy from 1932 is a matter of controversy among economic historians.[47] It is difficult to distinguish between the effects of the tariff and the effects of lower sterling exchange rates in improving the trade balance after 1931, although it can be said that the protection given by the tariff lasted longer, given the effects of the devaluation of the dollar and the franc on sterling's effective exchange rate after 1933. On the other hand, although tariffs were not applied to raw materials, they were applied to pig iron, which was an input for the steel industry; steel, which was an input for a wide range of industries; and bricks and builders' woodwork, which were inputs for the construction industry. It is by no means easy to measure the net effect of this

---

[44] 'Note on Paragraph 36' (of 12th Report of Committee on Economic Information), 27 July 1934, T175/93.   [45] 'Prices and Exports', n.d., but Jan. 1939, T175/104.
[46] I. M. Drummond, *Imperial Economic Policy, 1917–1939: Studies in Expansion and Protection* (1974), 286.
[47] See F. H. Capie, 'The British Tariff and Industrial Protection in the 1930s', *Econ. Hist. Rev*, 2nd ser., 31 (1978), 399–409; James Foreman-Peck, 'The British Tariff and Industrial Protection in the 1930s: An Alternative Model', with rejoinder by Capie, ibid., 34 (1981), 140–2; Michael Kitson, Solomos Solomou, and Martin Weale, 'Effective Protection and Economic Recovery in the United Kingdom during the 1930s' (with rejoinder by Capie), ibid., 44 (1991), 328–42. The strongest case for the tariff's beneficial effects is made in Kitson and Solomou, *Protectionism and Economic Revival: The British Interwar Economy* (Cambridge, 1990).

'negative protection'. Industries handicapped by higher costs of inputs would have benefited indirectly from tariffs, in so far as tariffs, by improving the trade balance, increased economic activity in Britain and thereby raised demand for new factories and housing. Generally speaking, one would expect the effects of the tariff to have been most favourable to industries where it was possible to achieve economies of scale through increased output, such as iron and steel, or where the cost of inputs was low in relation to value added by labour, as in textiles. On the other hand, in so far as improved industrial performance was dependent upon protection, it was likely to be short-lived unless British industry as a whole was more interested in rationalization that steel seems to have been, especially given the effects which Leith-Ross observed of steel prices on export prices. British industry may have benefited from import substitution and imperial preference in the short run, but adverse effects on competitiveness in the longer term may have justified the Treasury's long-standing bias towards free trade.

FISCAL POLICY AND ECONOMIC RECOVERY, 1932–1937

Down to 1935 fiscal policy was designed to restore confidence in the soundness of public finance, and thereby to support the cheap money policy, while also encouraging private enterprise through tax concessions, when these could be made without deliberately incurring a deficit. From 1936/7 budgets were increasingly concerned with raising finance for rearmament without inflation.

Inland Revenue and Treasury officials continued to reject the 'act of faith theory', whose proponents claimed that revenue lost through a reduction in income tax would be recovered through improved trade. In February 1933 Horne returned to the case that he had made when he had been Chancellor in 1922, and advocated through the *Daily Express* a reduction in taxation at the expense of the sinking fund, on the grounds that the psychological boost to business would stimulate trade, but his arguments were rejected by Grigg and Phillips.[48] The following month Keynes published an article in *The Times* also advocating reducing taxation by suspending the sinking fund, and by renewing borrowing for the Road Fund to finance new roads, and again reaction in the Treasury was negative (see section on employment policy below). Treasury officials did not believe that a budget deficit would automatically be inflationary, since as long as the government could borrow from the public, and not from the banks, there would be no increase in the supply of money. However, they did believe that repeated government borrowing from the non-bank public would force up interest rates, making it harder to balance the budget, and eventually,

---

[48] Grigg (Inland Revenue) to Fergusson, 11 Apr. 1932, T171/296; Phillips's comment on 'Daily Express', 28 Feb. 1933, T171/309.

when the non-bank public lost confidence in the government and would lend no more, the government would have to resort to borrowing from the banks, still equated with 'inflation'.[49]

Moreover, like Blackett before him, Hopkins saw the political danger of unbridled public expenditure if the convention of balanced budgets were relaxed. With reference to Keynes's proposal, he noted:

It would be impossible once we had abandoned the principle of paying our way to stop a rising tide of expenditure. Within a year or two (i.e. very near the next General Election) there would be the same sort of situation we had in 1931, i.e. the need for new cuts and new taxes.[50]

The best starting point for a study of fiscal policy under Neville Chamberlain is an exercise in forecasting in 1932, known whimsically in the Treasury as 'Old Moore's Almanac', after a popular compilation of astrological forecasts. Chamberlain wished to know what scope he would have for tax cuts or increases in expenditure over the next three or four years, and Hopkins responded by calculating the budget out-turn for 1935 on the existing basis of taxation and on assumed economic data for that year. The spirit in which these forecasts were prepared is indicated by Hopkins's remark that some of the assumed data 'might possibly prove to have some relation to the facts when ascertained, but more probably will not'.[51]

Hopkins noted that 'if we are to recover prosperity at all it must be on prices much higher than those of 1931'. Higher prices and economic recovery were estimated to increase revenue by £87.6 million. However, it was assumed that rationalization in industry and the distributive trades would prevent unemployment falling below the 1929 level. Moreover, the hoped-for savings of £11 million on unemployment relief were expected to be largely offset by what Hopkins called 'the onward march (even under a severe economy policy)' of expenditure on education, widows' pensions, housing, and other social services. In the light of a Cabinet decision in March 1932 to abandon the assumption that there would be no major war for ten years, Chamberlain instructed his officials to assume that defence expenditure would rise from £104.4 million to £115 million. Hopkins (optimistically, from his point of view, as it turned out) assumed

[49] *JMK*, ix. 348; R. Middleton, 'The Treasury in the 1930s: Political and Administrative Constraints to Acceptance of the "New" Economics', *Oxford Econ. Papers*, NS, 34 (1982), 56–7.

[50] 'Arguments Against Unbalancing the Budget', n.d., but Apr. 1933, T171/309, cited in Middleton, op. cit., 60.

[51] Hopkins to Chamberlain, 11 Mar. 1932, T171/296. It is easy to exaggerate the significance of this exercise. As noted above, Churchill had initiated a similar exercise in 1927 and therefore Chamberlain was not responsible for what Middleton has called 'a completely new departure in forward planning' (*Towards the Managed Economy: Keynes, the Treasury and the Fiscal Policy Debate of the 1930s* (1985), 104). Likewise, given Hopkins's diffidence about the likelihood of the forecast being fulfilled, it would seem that Booth goes too far when he says that with the 1932 exercise the Treasury 'began to establish medium-term goals for policy' (A. Booth, 'The British Reaction to the Economic Crisis': in W. R. Garside (ed.), *Capitalism in Crisis: International Responses to the Great Depression* (1993), 45).

that savings on the conversion of War Loan would be used to increase the sinking fund. On this basis, he estimated that there would be an £80 million surplus in 1935 on the existing basis of taxation—a figure that he described as 'mournfully small' compared with almost £150 million of economies in expenditure or increases in taxation imposed in Snowden's last budget in September 1931.[52]

Despite the emergency measures in the autumn, the budget out-turn for 1931/2 was a meagre surplus of £400,000. On the existing basis of taxation there would be a deficit in 1932/3 as the yield of direct taxation (most of it lagging by one to two years behind the slump) declined. Inland Revenue forecasts made in connection with 'Old Moore' showed that 1933 was expected to be no better than 1932. Major new sources of revenue were not available. Whereas in discussions in the Cabinet Committee on the Balance of Trade, the original 10 per cent tariff was described as being for revenue purposes, the additional duties imposed on the recommendation of the Import Duties Advisory Committee were intended to provide protection, and it was rightly anticipated in the Treasury in 1932 that tariffs would not be a buoyant source of revenue.[53] Moreover, abolition of Snowden's land values tax, in response to pressure from Conservative MPs, was foreseen in 1933, although it did not take place until 1934.[54] Further major economies in public expenditure were expected to encounter serious political problems. In particular, one Treasury official noted in 1932 that it was very doubtful whether either Parliament or the public would tolerate a cut in old-age pensions, unless it were accompanied by a cut in the income of holders of the National Debt. The latter action would mean repudiation of the government's contractual obligations, which would be a blow to financial confidence. The best hope of avoiding a budget 'catastrophe', therefore, was to secure a rise in the price level.[55]

Meanwhile, the Treasury had to continue to disguise the true budget position. Non-recurrent receipts were used to balance current expenditure, and estimates of both revenue and expenditure were manipulated to cover potential deficits. The Ministry of Labour was asked to trim 10 per cent from its Estimate for expenditure on unemployment relief in 1932/3 and, despite the fact that the Ministry then required a politically embarrassing Supplementary Estimate to cover the shortfall, the same expedient was resorted to in the following year. In 1935 Chamberlain was forced to raid the Road Fund. Even with the Treasury's window dressing, there was a deficit of £32.3 million in 1932/3, but thereafter there was no visible deficit until rearmament began in earnest in 1936/7.[56]

[52] 'Speculative Forecast of 1935 on the Basis of "Old Moore's Almanac" ', 21 Mar. 1932, T171/296.

[53] 'The Estimated Yield of the Additional Duties', unsigned, 3 May 1932, T172/1514.

[54] Grigg (Inland Revenue) to Fergusson, and Douglas Newton (Chairman of the Conservative Parliamentary Agricultural Committee) to Chancellor, both 15 Mar. 1933, T171/310.

[55] Note for Hopkins, attached to 'Memorandum on National Expenditure', May 1932, T175/67. The official was Bernard Gilbert, then an assistant secretary, who was to be one of the most senior officials responsible for managing the economy in the 1950s.

[56] Middleton, *Towards the Managed Economy*, 81–3, 101, 104.

TABLE 6.1. *Out-turns of Budgets, September 1931–April 1938, and Original Estimates for April 1939 (£ m.)*

	Revenue	Expenditure	Sinking fund	Published balance	Defence loans[a]
1931/2	851.5	851.1	32.5	+0.4	—
1932/3	827.0	859.3	26.3	−32.3	—
1933/4	809.4	778.2[b]	7.7	+31.2	—
1934/5	804.6	797.1	12.3	+7.5	—
1935/6	844.8	841.8	12.5	+3.0	—
1936/7	896.6	902.2	13.1	−5.6	—
1937/8	948.7	919.9	10.5	+28.8	64.9
1938/9	1,006.2	1,018.9	13.2	−12.7	128.1
1939/40 (Estimates)	1,026.0	1,025.8	7.2	+0.2	380.0

[a] Authorized under Defence Loans Act of 1937, and treated as revenue.
[b] Fixed Debt Charge reduced from £308.5 million to £224 million: £49.3 million on account of lower interest and management expenses, £18.6 million on account of reduced sinking fund, and £16.3 on account of cancellation of US War Debt payments.

Source: Roger Middleton, *Towards the Managed Economy: Keynes, the Treasury and the Fiscal Policy Debate of the 1930s* (1985), ch. 6.

In these circumstances Chamberlain could not hope to match the standards of orthodoxy in relation to debt redemption to which earlier Chancellors had aspired. The War Loan conversion of 1932 reduced interest on the National Debt down from £274 million in 1931/2 to £260.2 million in 1932/3 and £211.9 million in 1933/4. Even so, rather than use the savings, as Hopkins had originally hoped, for debt redemption, powers were taken to borrow for the statutory sinking funds in 1933. The reasons were frankly political. As the head of the Home Finance Division, Waterfield, advised Hopkins in May 1932, both Parliament and the taxpayer regarded current levels of taxation as well-nigh intolerable, and, with government expenditure more likely to increase than to fall, it was 'too much to ask of human nature that the whole of the savings on debt interest should be added to the sinking fund'.[57] Hopkins was prepared to reduce the sinking fund as preferable to a return to borrowing for payments to the unemployed. The Fixed Debt Charge, which had already been reduced in the 1932 budget from the £322 million set in September 1931 to £308.5 million, was further reduced in the 1933 budget to £224 million. As interest rates remained low, Fixed Debt Charges of this order permitted sinking funds averaging about £12 million a year down to the outbreak of war, compared with £26.3 million in 1932/3 (see Table 6.1), which itself was far below Snowden's £66.8 million in 1930/1.[58]

On the other hand, the economy cuts and tax increases made in September 1931 remained in force until April 1934, and were only partially reversed then.

[57] Waterfield to Hopkins, 3 May 1932, T175/67.
[58] Note by Hopkins on 5th report of the Committee on Economic Information, T175/93; B. E. V. Sabine, *British Budgets in Peace and War, 1932–1945* (1970), 16, 34, 56, 120–1.

Unemployment benefit was fully restored in the 1934 budget but the pay of civil servants was restored only in two equal stages in 1934 and 1935. Chamberlain reduced the standard rate of income tax in 1934 to 4s. 6d. (22.5p), the level at which it had stood before September 1931, rather than make concessions on indirect taxation, on the grounds that income tax relief would have 'the greatest psychological effect' and would 'impart the most immediate and vigorous stimulus to the expansion of trade and employment'.[59] Tax allowances were raised in 1935, but the need to balance the budget limited the scope for what would now be called supply-side economics, and the standard rate remained at 6d. (2.5p) above the level it had been under Churchill.

By autumn 1935 there was a new threat to balanced budgets: the Permanent Secretary of the Treasury, Fisher, himself advocated borrowing for rearmament, in the light of intelligence reports that Germany and Italy were doing so, and in the belief that the British taxpayer was not sufficiently alerted to the country's danger to provide all the funds that were necessary. Accordingly, the rearmament programme approved by the Cabinet for the five financial years from 1936/7 assumed that part of the cost would be met by borrowing. At a time when Lloyd George had recently been again proposing public works financed by loans as a solution to unemployment (see below), Hopkins advised Chamberlain in October that 'it would be unfortunate if the country began to think of a Defence Loan as a comfortable Lloyd-Georgian device for securing not only larger forces but also lower Estimates, budget surpluses and diminishing taxation'. Hopkins thought that there should be no borrowing until the country was taxed to full capacity, and he suggested that the 1936 budget should be 'optimistically constructed' to pay for increased defence Estimates without a deficit, although borrowing might be necessary at the end of the financial year to meet the cost of Supplementary Estimates from the defence departments.[60] The 1936 budget accordingly provided for the barest of surpluses (less than £0.5 million), despite a raid on the Road Fund for £5.2 million, and the period of tax cuts was brought to an end with the raising of the standard rate of income tax by 3d. (1.25p) to 4s. 9d. (23.75p).

From a Keynesian point of view, Chamberlain's attempts to balance his budgets made little sense, since they involved raising taxes to a higher level in relation to national income in 1932/3 and 1933/4 than before or after the depression. Moreover, although subsequent balanced budgets did much less to restrict aggregate demand, the changes in fiscal stance reflected what economic recovery was doing to the budget rather than the impact of budgetary changes on aggregate demand. On balance, the effect of year-to-year changes in fiscal stance in Snowden's and Chamberlain's budgets seems to have been broadly

[59] 288 HC Deb., 5s, 1933–4, cols. 925–6.
[60] G. C. Peden, *British Rearmament and the Treasury, 1932–1939* (Edinburgh, 1979), 73–4.

neutral from 1930/1 to 1933/4, and actually expansionary after 1934/5.[61] There was, however, no deliberate attempt by the Treasury to use the budget to manage demand during the economic recovery down to 1937. The Treasury's objectives were the restoration of financial and business confidence, and the preservation of balanced budgets as a means of controlling public expenditure. Prior to rearmament, these objectives were achieved.

EMPLOYMENT POLICY

Proposals for public expenditure as a means of creating employment continued to present a challenge to traditional public finance. Accounts of the Treasury's responses to these proposals have often focused on the Treasury's willingness or otherwise to be convinced by Keynes's economic theory. What follows suggests that officials were more responsive to political pressures than to theoretical arguments.

The change from a Labour to a Conservative-dominated government in August 1931 reduced the pressure within Whitehall for public works as an employment policy. Following the suspension of the gold standard, even Keynes switched his emphasis from public works to the need to reduce the rate of interest, and letters to *The Times* in July and October 1932, which he signed along with other economists, were designed to encourage 'wise spending' by private enterprise as well as by local authorities.[62] In fact, although the Unemployment Grants Committee was wound up in 1932, neither the government nor the Treasury was wholly hostile to the use of public expenditure to reduce unemployment. A Ministry of Health circular in September 1931 did instruct local authorities to pay special regard to whether any new expenditure would produce a money return, or provide employment for local workers and thereby reduce the cost of unemployment relief. Partly as a result, new loans for non-remunerative services did decline from a total of £41.75 million in the twelve months to March 1931 to £23 million in the twelve months to October 1932. However, there was, Hopkins insisted, no ban on 'wise spending' (for example, on public health services).[63]

In December 1931 the Cabinet set up an Employment Policy Committee under the chairmanship of Walter Elliot, the Financial Secretary to the Treasury, and in February 1932 the Cabinet approved its recommendations, including an extension for three years of the Development (Loan Guarantees and

[61] Roger Middleton, 'The Constant Employment Budget Balance and British Budgetary Policy, 1929–39', *Econ. Hist. Rev.*, 2nd ser., 34 (1981), 266–86; S. N. Broadberry, 'Fiscal Policy in Britain during the 1930s', with reply by Middleton, ibid., 37 (1984), 95–106; Paul Turner, 'Wealth Effects and Fiscal Policy in the 1930s', ibid., 44 (1991), 515–22.

[62] Moggridge, *Maynard Keynes*, 529, 544–5.

[63] Hopkins to Fergusson, 16 Feb. 1933, T175/93.

Grants) Act to finance 'developments calculated to increase national income', but there was to be no more borrowing by the Road Fund.[64] The Treasury was hostile to additional expenditure on roads—Phillips advising Chamberlain in October 1932 that road works had been 'so desperately overdone for the last ten years' that all schemes of real economic value had been carried out or were in hand, and that heavy borrowing for roads would have a serious depressing effect on industry. On the other hand, Phillips and Hopkins disclaimed any wish to obstruct 'reasonably profitable' schemes from local authorities for trams, gas works, or water works, or from the London Passenger Traffic Board for underground railways, or from the Central Electricity Board for extensions to the national grid.[65] All this amounted to a continuation of the 'Treasury view' of 1930.

Political pressure for a more active employment policy came in March 1933, when *The Times* published a series of articles by Keynes entitled 'The Means to Prosperity'.[66] Keynes hoped to influence both the budget in April and the World Economic Conference which was due to meet in London in June. Chamberlain responded by meeting Keynes, after being briefed by Treasury officials. The Chancellor was particularly interested in Keynes's suggestion that he should reduce taxation by £50 million by suspending the sinking fund and by borrowing for the cost of new roads and unemployment benefits, and that there should also be additional loan-expenditure outside the budget of £60 million. Deploying the concept of the multiplier explicitly for the first time (at a high figure of 2), Keynes predicted that not only would unemployment fall substantially but also that the Chancellor's budget would benefit by over £50 million, while admitting that there would be a time lag before national income, and thereby revenue would rise. How long the lag would be was not made clear, but Hopkins noted that the lag between income being earned and tax being paid was, on average, twenty months in the case of income tax and thirty-two months in the case of surtax, during which period the budget would remain unbalanced.[67]

Keynes's argument no longer relied, as it had done in 1929, on the existence of idle savings. Instead, he believed that expenditure financed by borrowing would create most of the savings required to finance the public works. Phillips was unimpressed. 'It is no good saying that the works will produce the savings for investment', he noted, 'for *ex hypothesi* the borrowing precedes the works.'[68] As Keynes was subsequently to admit, the bridging of the time lag between investment and the subsequent flow of funds available for investment was a

[64] Employment Policy Committee, 'Report', CP36(32), CAB24/227.

[65] Phillips to Chancellor of the Exchequer, 19 Oct., and Hopkins to Chancellor of the Exchequer, 20 Oct. 1932, T175/70.

[66] *The Times*, 13, 14, 15, and 16 Mar. 1933. An extended version, which was published in pamphlet form, is reproduced in *JMK*, ix. 335–66.

[67] Note by Hopkins, 13 Mar. 1933, T175/17.

[68] 'Questions for Keynes', 20 Mar. 1933, T175/17.

function of the credit system[69]—but this brought one back to Hawtrey's point that creation of credit alone would normally be sufficient to stimulate private enterprise. Meanwhile, the Treasury was not yet ready for 'an act of faith' in regard to unbalancing the budget, especially as borrowing for unemployment benefits had helped to undermine confidence in public finance in 1931, and Chamberlain used his budget speech to stress the virtues of sound finance and low interest rates for industry.[70]

Treasury officials were quite unmoved in their attitude to public works as an employment policy. When briefing Chamberlain before his meeting with Keynes, attention was drawn to the difficulty in finding remunerative works, especially given that many public works had been brought forward in the past, and to the delays of about a year before they could be started and of about three years before they showed a money return. It was pointed out that Keynes's calculations based on the multiplier took no account of the fact that much of the work done in a public works programme would not really be additional work, but would be in substitution for work that would otherwise have been done without additional subsidies (for example, local authority housing). It was agreed that public works financed by 'inflation' would provide employment, but present policy was to avoid any form of borrowing that would depress the exchange rate severely. Phillips particularly objected to Keynes's procedure whereby the first 'Means to Prosperity' article in *The Times* implied that there was a domestic solution to unemployment, only for Keynes to state in a later article that it would be necessary to increase loan-financed public works throughout the world simultaneously to avoid balance-of-payments problems.[71] The Treasury intended to urge a general reflation of prices at the forthcoming World Economic Conference, but, as we shall see, officials had good grounds for pessimism regarding international co-operation.

In 1935, as unemployment persisted, despite cheap money, Lloyd George once more called for public works and land settlement schemes financed in a separate capital budget out of a 'great prosperity loan'.[72] On this occasion Phillips took advice from Henry Clay, the Bank of England's economist, who did not share Phillips's theoretical perspective regarding savings, in that he believed that there was a case for the government doing something to induce holders of idle deposits to invest them. Nevertheless, Clay not only accepted Phillips's arguments based on the practical obstacles to increased public capital expenditure, but he also advised that the mere issue of a loan for the purposes advocated by Lloyd George would cause a drop in gilt-edged values.[73] On the

[69] *JMK*, xiv. 284. For discussion of this point see J. A. Trevithick, 'The Monetary Prerequisites for the Multiplier: An Adumbration of the Crowding Out Hypothesis', *Cambridge J. Econ.*, 18 (1994), 77–90.
[70] 277 HC Deb., 5s, 1932–3, cols. 57–61.
[71] 'Questions for Keynes', 20 Mar. 1933, and 'Mr Keynes' Articles', 21 Mar. 1933, both by Phillips, T175/17.   [72] *The Times*, 18 Jan. 1935.
[73] Memorandum by Phillips, 31 Jan. 1935, and Clay to Phillips, 1 Feb. and 21 March 1935, T175/89.

other hand, by this date it was clear to Hopkins and Phillips that the response of private enterprise to cheap money had, apart from housing and some industries, been slower than expected. They still believed that public works were futile as a cure for unemployment, in that any programme that could be got going within a reasonable period would provide only temporary work for about 3 per cent of the unemployed for a year or two, but they also thought that some expansion of public borrowing would be useful for keeping up the impetus of recovery.[74] Such a conclusion was in line not only with Clay's advice but also with Hawtrey's belief since 1925 that public works might be necessary if private enterprise did not respond to a reduction in Bank rate to 2 per cent.

Even so, the Treasury had not forgotten the Asquith doctrine on borrowing for purposes that would not produce a financial return. Asquith's denunciation in 1906 of the Naval and Military Works Acts was mentioned in 1935 in a Treasury memorandum for ministers on public works with the comment that to return to the practice of paying for barracks and other 'permanent works' out of loans 'would be widely held to have far too bad precedents to be consistent with sound credit.' The same argument applied to civil construction, such as public offices, for which there was a recurrent demand, although exceptions could be made for large public buildings. Roads were in a category of their own because the Road Fund's revenue from motor vehicle licences covered the cost of construction and maintenance. Otherwise, acceptable projects continued to be those, like Post Office telephones, that produced a money return to repay capital with interest.[75]

Meanwhile it had also become apparent that such recovery as had taken place was very uneven geographically. Despite the government's industrial transference scheme, unemployment among insured workers in 1934 varied from 8.7 per cent in the South-East of England to 22.1 per cent in the North-East, and 32.3 per cent in Wales. An avowedly experimental and temporary Special Areas Act was passed that year to facilitate the economic and social improvement of designated areas of high unemployment and, at Chamberlain's suggestion, two Commissioners were appointed, one for England and Wales and one for Scotland, to carry out the Act with an initial grant of £2 million. The Commissioners were not, however, empowered to provide money for profit-making enterprises, and the Treasury even prevented the Commissioner for England and Wales from financing any public works undertaken as unemployment relief schemes. The Commissioner, Malcolm Stewart, drew attention to the limitations to his powers in his first report, which was debated in Parliament in July 1935, when it became clear that more would have to be done to satisfy public opinion that the government was doing all it could for the Special Areas, especially as 1935 was an election year.

[74] Fergusson to Chancellor of the Exchequer, 26 Jan. 1935, T172/1828.
[75] 'Public Works', n.d., but position in file and internal evidence indicate late Mar. 1935, T175/89.

Hopkins regarded the prospect of financing assistance for business in the Special Areas as 'pretty horrible, tho' it may be unavoidable'[76] and, immediately before the general election, the Cabinet approved Stewart's proposal to set up non profit-making companies to create trading estates. In 1936 Hopkins reviewed possible financial inducements for firms to move to the Special Areas, but concluded that income tax exemptions would have little effect, since firms would not expect to make much profit, while relief from rates would reduce costs of production by only 2 per cent or less. However, again parliamentary debates convinced Chamberlain that the government must be seen to be doing more than current policy allowed. The Special Areas (Amendment Act) of 1937 provided two kinds of inducements: the Commissioners could make contributions toward rent, rates, and income tax, while the Treasury could make loans, subject to the recommendations of an advisory committee, up to a total of £2 million.[77] The Treasury's reluctance to interfere with the market economy is indicated by the fact that, although it accepted that special inducements might be needed in the early years, such as especially low rates of interest on loans, it reserved the right to call in loans made under the Act if the borrower became able to secure a loan elsewhere on reasonable terms.[78]

Initially the government's own expenditure made only a limited contribution to regional policy. In 1936 Fisher drew Chamberlain's attention to the paradox that public works, such as roads and bridges, were required on economic grounds in the prosperous areas rather than in the Special Areas. However, by this date rearmament was providing an alternative way in which to assist areas of high unemployment, by placing defence contracts or setting up munitions factories in these areas, and the Treasury urged defence departments to do so. Such a policy made good sense in that the Ministry of Labour believed that there was a national shortage of skilled labour for rearmament work. It was also a policy that enjoyed Keynes's support, as Keynes believed by 1937 that national economic recovery had reached a point where there was more need for 'a rightly distributed demand than of greater aggregate demand', although $12\frac{1}{2}$ per cent of the insured labour force was unemployed.[79]

This context, plus the deterioration of the overall budget position from 1937/8 (see below), helps to explain the Treasury's continuing belief that the Special Areas policy should be temporary. Hopkins thought in June 1938 that the expenditure to which the Treasury was committed under the Special Areas Acts was 'chiefly for public works and factory development, much of it, I think,

[76] Hopkins to Phillips, 30 Oct. 1935, T175/90.
[77] Treasury discussions on regional policy can be found T172/1828. See also Herbert Loebl, *Government Factories and the Origins of British Regional Policy* (Aldershot, 1988).
[78] Minutes of preliminary meeting of the Special Areas Loans Advisory Committee, 27 Apr. 1937, T187/1.
[79] *JMK*, xxi. 385. For discussion of this aspect of regional policy see Peden, 'Keynes, the Treasury and Unemployment', 14–17.

of doubtful utility', and advised the Chancellor that, if the legislation, which was due to expire in March 1939, were not renewed, the savings to the budget would be £4 million in 1940 and about £8 million by 1943.[80] A Cabinet Committee on the Reports of the Investigators and Commissioners for the Special Areas did decide later in June 1938 that the Special Areas Acts should be allowed to lapse. However, by November a number of ministers, including the Minister for Labour, Ernest Brown, had changed their minds, for what Simon described as political reasons. Simon tried to secure Brown's agreement to limit further financial commitments by administrative action, but Brown refused unless there were to be a public announcement of a reversal of policy—which the Chancellor knew to be impossible at a time when unemployment was higher than it had been a year earlier.[81]

The Treasury also had to make concessions with regard to the use of public capital expenditure to counter the trade cycle. In February of 1937 the Committee on Economic Information anticipated a downturn in investment in Britain as demand for housing was satisfied, and as expenditure on industrial equipment, induced by recovery from the depression and by rearmament, came to an end. The Committee accepted Keynes's view that, at the stage of the trade cycle reached in early 1937, an attempt to increase investment outside the special areas would raise profits rather than employment, and that public works should be postponed, except in areas of high unemployment, and held in reserve for when the total amount of investment in the economy fell. An Inter-departmental Committee on Public Capital Expenditure, chaired by Phillips or, during his frequent absences, by the Ministry of Labour's representative, Humbert Wolfe, reported in August that it might be possible to reduce by £20 million the 'normal' annual capital expenditure of £250 million controlled by public authorities (including local authorities). Together with schemes prepared in advance, the work so postponed might make it possible to increase public capital expenditure by £30 million above 'normal'. Thus the difference between a year of maximum reduction and a year of maximum acceleration was £50 million, with a transition of at least a year between these stages while new projects got under way.[82]

The figure of £50 million was a far cry from Lloyd George's scheme for increased public capital expenditure of £250 million over two years. Moreover, as Lowe has pointed out, the parts of the report supporting counter-cyclical public works owed more to Wolfe's drafting than to Phillips's. The report made plain that Treasury attitudes had not changed by much. It argued that any programme that forced the government to borrow repeatedly in the market would

[80] Unsigned note to Fisher and Chancellor of the Exchequer, n.d., but position in file indicates June 1938, T273/322.

[81] Loebl, *Government Factories*, 142; Lowe, *Adjusting to Democracy: The Role of the Ministry of Labour in British Politics, 1916–1939* (Oxford, 1986), 227.

[82] The papers of the Interdepartmental Committee are in CAB27/640.

give rise to 'serious apprehension' in financial markets, which would make it difficult 'to produce that lowering of the rate of interest which must always remain the principal weapon in the hands of the authorities during times of trade depression'. It would be impossible, Phillips warned, for government to resist a demand for economy if it arose in circumstances like 1931, and to abandon a public works programme in a depression would retard recovery. Phillips may have been open to new ideas, as Howson and Winch have argued, but political factors seem to have been what influenced him most with regard to public works and employment policy. In 1938 Phillips remarked to Hopkins that in the next depression—which might be in 1941—the pressure for extended road works could be expected to be irresistible, not because roads were a good form of unemployment measure, but because the supply of other unemployment relief works would be too small. The position of the budget then would be such that they would have to be financed by borrowing, whatever their economic value.[83]

Treasury officials tended to take a qualitative approach to public works and to have a sceptical attitude to their wider repercussions through the multiplier. Likewise they were sceptical of the value of regional policy. However, the need to make concessions to public opinion, and for government to have at least the appearance of an active policy towards unemployment, was recognized. Treasury officials hoped that cheap money would spread its benefits throughout the United Kingdom, but Phillips was aware that cheap money was not sufficient. In 1934 he commented that there was a definite limit to the downward progress of unemployment figures that could be achieved through a restoration of internal trade, and that, except for London and the South-East, low levels of unemployment could only be achieved through a marked revival of exports.[84] It is to the Treasury's part in efforts to restore world trade that we now turn.

ECONOMIC DIPLOMACY: THE FAILURE OF INTERNATIONAL
COLLABORATION, 1932–1934

From the Treasury's standpoint, the principal problem with the international economy in 1931 was that world prices had fallen, raising the burden of debts in terms of the goods and services that had to be sold in order to service them. However, the suspension of the gold standard, while a precondition for reversing the decline in prices, itself disrupted world trade by upsetting the international system of payments, encouraging bilateral clearing agreements, which

[83] Howson and Winch, *Economic Advisory Council*, 141–2, 147; Lowe, *Adjusting to Democracy*, 221–2; G. C. Peden, 'The "Treasury View" on Public Works and Employment in the Interwar Period', *Econ. Hist. Rev.*, 2nd ser., 37 (1984), 177–8.

[84] 'Notes on Cheap Money', by Phillips, n.d., but position in file indicates February 1933, T175/17; note by Phillips on para. 27 of 11th Report of the Committee on Economic Information, Mar. 1934, T175/93.

tended to reduce the total volume of trade and to reduce the amount of business conducted through London. Britain was able to incorporate most of the Empire, and some foreign countries too, into the sterling area, but this development could only be a partial substitute for a worldwide, multilateral financial system. There were thus three broad, interrelated areas where the Treasury sought international agreement: (1) reduction or elimination of the burden of intergovernmental debts, (2) the need to raise world prices to pre-depression levels, and (3) the restoration of an international monetary system with stable exchange rates. Other matters, such as negotiation of reductions in tariffs, were the province of the Board of Trade.

The collapse of international confidence in the German banking system in July 1931 had forced German bankers and their foreign creditors to negotiate a 'standstill' agreement, whereby Germany's foreign creditors would not withdraw their short-term credits for a period of six months, and a further standstill agreement, this time for one year, was concluded in January 1932. The Hoover moratorium on intergovernmental debts was due to end in July 1932. The Treasury position on intergovernmental debts, as formulated by Leith-Ross in the autumn of 1931, and subsequently accepted by the Foreign Office, was that Britain's first objective must be the cancellation of its debt to America. In view of the political difficulties of the United States and France, Leith-Ross expected that the only way to bring matters to a head would be to refuse to pay more than was received from France, Italy and other former allies, and from Germany. He expected that Germany would default on her obligations under the Young Plan, and that the only question was how to ensure that Britain received compensation for cancellation equivalent to any received by France.[85] Leith-Ross's expectation regarding Germany's default was fulfilled when the German Chancellor, Brüning, announced in January 1932 that Germany would be unable to resume reparation payments after the end of the Hoover moratorium. The British response, as announced by Chamberlain in Parliament, was to call for a comprehensive settlement of reparations as soon as possible, and, ignoring the United States' long-standing insistence that war debts were a separate issue from reparations, Chamberlain openly advocated a general cancellation of both reparations and war debts.[86]

The Treasury position in 1931 and 1932 was influenced by a belief that Germany could not recover economically unless reparations were ended, and a fear that, unless they were, Germany might declare a total moratorium on private as well as intergovernmental debts. Such a moratorium would be damaging to City institutions with credits caught up in the standstill agreement, and might cause a run on sterling, as in 1931. At an international conference on reparations

[85] 'British Policy on Debts and Reparations', n.d., but position in file suggests Oct. 1931, T188/16. For Treasury and Foreign Office agreement in May 1932 that reparations and war debts should end see T188/47.   [86] 261 HC Deb., 5s, 1931–2, cols. 25–6.

at Lausanne in June 1932, Britain and France agreed to scale down Germany's total obligations to 3,000 million gold marks, with a three-year moratorium, and with payments thereafter being dependent on economic conditions (which, in the circumstances, effectively meant an end to reparations).[87] France tried to link the Lausanne agreement with a scaling down of war debts and, when the United States insisted on payment of the instalments due in December, France defaulted. Hopkins advised that, following sterling's devaluation, payments on Britain's war debt (in dollars) would be a heavier burden on the budget and would cause maladjustments to the balance of payments. On the other hand, Norman advised that failure to pay the December instalment in full would damage British credit, causing further depreciation of sterling, at a time when it had fallen to $3.14½, and would also encourage default by Britain's debtors. Chamberlain accepted Norman's advice, but it was made clear that the level of repayments would have to be renegotiated at an early date.[88]

A World Economic Conference was due to be held in London in June 1933 to try to establish a measure of international co-operation to deal with the depression. There was a wide division of opinion between France, which was determined to maintain the gold parity of the franc by deflation, and which thought that Britain's return to the gold standard at some unspecified parity was essential to stabilize exchange rates, and Britain, whose objective of raising world prices had been proclaimed at the Ottawa Conference, an objective that precluded any linkage of sterling to gold in the absence of an international commitment by central banks to reflation. The new American President, Franklin D. Roosevelt, was an unknown quantity. However, he quickly made exclusion of any discussion of war debts a condition of American participation in the conference, and then in April gave priority to monetary reflation in the United States, by taking the dollar off gold, rather than seeking international co-operation on exchange rates. There were good reasons, therefore, for the British Treasury to expect that the conference would achieve nothing, as indeed turned out to be the case. Leith-Ross thought that there was no prospect of progress if a satisfactory settlement of war debts were not secured, and Phillips noted that there was no prospect of continental central bankers agreeing to reflation.[89]

Nevertheless, Treasury officials took an interest in plans to raise world prices. In May 1932, in connection with the Lausanne conference, Henderson had prepared a plan for what was in effect an international currency, in the form of gold

[87] The proceedings of the Lausanne conference are in *DBFP*, 2nd ser., vol. iii, with statements of the Treasury's position at pp. 207–9, 219, 323–6.

[88] 'American Debt', unsigned draft by Hopkins, 24 Nov. 1932, T175/70; H. Clay, *Lord Norman* (1957), 447; Leith-Ross, *Money Talks*, 154–5.

[89] Note by Hopkins, n.d., but June 1932, fos. 28–31, T175/70; Leith-Ross to Hopkins, 27 Mar. 1933, T175/79; Phillips on 'EAC Apologia for Henderson Plan', 27 Mar. 1933, T175/17. For the economic and political divisions at the conference see Patricia Clavin, 'The World Economic Conference 1933: The Failure of British Internationalism', *J. European Econ. Hist.*, 20 (1991), 489–527.

certificates to be issued by the Bank for International Settlements, the certificates to be accepted as equivalent of gold for all purposes by the countries participating in the scheme. This new currency was intended to have two purposes: (1) to provide an additional means whereby debtor countries could pay liabilities denominated in gold or gold-backed currencies, and (2) to inflate the currencies of the creditor countries, thereby tending to raise prices. The distribution of the notes was to be according to some economic criterion—for example, the value of each country's export trade. To qualify for participation, countries would have to fix their exchange rates, remove exchange restrictions, and agree to repay advances to the Bank of International Settlements as prices rose towards their 1928 level. Interest would be payable on the certificates only if a country failed to fulfil this last condition.[90] Henderson showed his plan to Hopkins, who passed it on to Phillips, who in turn asked Hawtrey for comments. Hawtrey thought that the Henderson plan for gold certificates had no technical advantage over other methods of expanding the money supply, such as the purchase of government securities by central banks or increases in fiduciary issues, and he thought that the plan's international aspects had the disadvantage of stabilizing parities at a time when conditions regarding relative prices were very uncertain, and would not in themselves rectify balance-of-payments deficits on current account.[91] Neither Hawtrey nor Phillips thought that the plan was practical politics and it was not submitted to the Lausanne conference.

As part of the preparations for the 1933 World Economic Conference, MacDonald set up an Economic Advisory Council Committee on International Economic Policy, and this committee adopted a revised version of the Henderson plan written by Blackett (now a director of the Bank of England), Keynes, and Henderson. Under this version only governments or central banks of countries requiring help would receive certificates, which would be interest-bearing from the outset. Treasury officials could see the advantage of having a counterproposal to French demands that Britain return to the gold standard, especially a proposal that did not commit Britain to an international programme of public works as outlined in Keynes's 'Means to Prosperity'. Nevertheless, they preferred to focus attention on maldistribution of the world's monetary gold rather than to create a new currency. In November 1932, after discussion with Phillips, Leith-Ross, Hawtrey, and Niemeyer, Sir Cecil Kisch, the Financial Adviser to the India Office, produced a plan for an International Credit Corporation. Governments of countries with surplus gold stocks would borrow gold from their central banks and use it to subscribe to the corporation, which would lend the gold at a low rate of interest to the governments of debtor countries, who

---

[90] The plan is reproduced in H. D. Henderson, *The Inter-War Years and Other Papers*, ed. Henry Clay (Oxford, 1955), 103–6.

[91] 'Mr Henderson's Monetary Proposal', 19 May 1932, and 'Further Note', 7 June 1932, both by Hawtrey, HTRY 1/49.

would in turn sell the gold to their central banks, thereby reducing the governments' indebtedness and improving the central banks' positions as regards their
reserves. The idea was to enable debtor countries to resume normal relations
with creditor countries. In the event, preliminary discussions with the French
and Americans led the Treasury to abandon hope of putting forward even the
Kisch plan at the conference.[92]

By May 1933, a month before the conference was due to open in London,
Phillips identified Britain's first objective as keeping the Americans from doing
anything rash in relation to devaluation of the dollar. Phillips believed that the
dollar had been in roughly the right relation to the pound and the franc prior to
Roosevelt's action in taking it off the gold standard. While there was uncertainty
as to the dollar's future gold value, capital was leaving the United States, but
once the dollar was once again fixed in terms of gold, and undervalued, Phillips
thought there would be a movement of capital into the United States, 'perhaps
on a scale we have not yet seen'.[93] In the event, although Britain did introduce a
resolution at the conference in favour of central bank co-operation to raise
prices through cheap and plentiful credit, exchange-stabilization negotiations
dominated the proceedings. In the face of pressure from the French delegation,
Chamberlain said that he had no intention of pegging sterling to the franc and
other currencies that remained on an unreformed gold standard. What he was
prepared to do was to accept temporary *de facto* stabilization of sterling, the dollar, and the franc as a means of securing international agreement on tariffs,
quotas, and other barriers to trade.[94] However, Roosevelt made clear on 2 July
that the United States must be free to manage its domestic price level. Subsequently, although the dollar appeared to be stabilizing at about $4.60 to the
pound in September and October 1933, the Roosevelt administration fulfilled
Phillips's fears by deliberately depreciating the dollar before fixing it in terms
of gold in January 1934 at $35 dollars an ounce. With sterling still floating,
the sterling:dollar exchange rate varied between $4.94 and $5.15 in 1934,
compared with $3.28 to $3.75 in 1932.

The year 1933 also saw the failure of Anglo-American attempts to find a new
settlement for payment of Britain's war debt that would be acceptable to public
opinion in both countries. Leith-Ross conducted technical discussions with
American experts in Washington in April and May 1933, as part of the preparations for the World Economic Conference. The upshot was an American
scheme whereby annual instalments would be reduced in return for immediate
payments in gold to the United States, which could use the money to pay for
public works. In Britain's case the immediate payment would be $500 million

---

[92] For fuller accounts of the discussions on the Henderson and Kisch plans see Howson and Winch,
Economic Advisory Council, 114–21, and Drummond, *Floating Pound*, 133–9.

[93] 'The Question of Raising Prices', by Phillips, 17 May 1933, T175/17.

[94] For negotiations see Stephen V. O. Clarke, *The Reconstruction of the International Monetary System: The
Attempts of 1922 and 1933* (Princeton, NJ, 1973), 30–9; Drummond, *Floating Pound*, 162–73.

(or about £125 million), which, as Leith-Ross pointed out, would denude the Bank of England's reserves, and the annual instalments would be $16.6 million (or about £4 million) for fifty years. Hopkins observed that although the scheme had been presented as a skilful camouflage for American opinion, 'it reads to me like the work of an economist in full cry'. The American experts apparently still believed that Britain could secure gold from her debtors, but Fisher stressed that no attempt should be made to overturn the Lausanne agreement.[95] It was agreed that Leith-Ross could not continue to discuss the American proposals at a distance from ministers, and, as already noted, the Americans refused to discuss intergovernmental debts at the World Economic Conference.

In June the British government made a token payment of $10,000 in silver, as an acknowledgement of the debt, compared with annual instalments of $161 million in gold previously; and in the autumn Leith-Ross was dispatched to Washington by Chamberlain with instructions to try to reach a permanent settlement on the basis of annual payments of $20 million, if the preferred British solution of outright cancellation was not available. The Americans, however, were not prepared to go below a figure of $60 million for annual payments. Leith-Ross admitted privately that such a sum (£13 million at the current rate of exchange) was within Britain's ability to pay and that the British Treasury's objections to the American offer were fundamentally political.[96] A further 'token' payment was made in December 1933, but Congress refused to allow Roosevelt to accept any more token payments. As a result Britain was included in the provisions of the Johnson Act of 1934, which prohibited new loans to any government that was in default. The full significance of this outcome only became apparent when the threat of war loomed in the late 1930s and the Treasury wondered how (in view of Britain's experience in 1916–18) it would be possible to finance a war without American loans.

ECONOMIC DIPLOMACY: THE LIMITS OF INTER-TREASURY
COLLABORATION

Despite the breach over war debts, Henry Morgenthau, the Secretary of the US Treasury, was anxious from 1935 to form contacts with his counterpart, Chamberlain, with a view to establishing a degree of international monetary cooperation between treasuries such as had previously only existed between central banks. The Belgian currency had been devalued in March and thereafter speculation against the French franc raised doubts as to how long its parity against gold could be maintained. France's adherence to the gold standard gave the British Exchange Equalisation Account a convenient means of managing

---

[95] Telegrams 291 and 292 from Washington Embassy (from Leith-Ross), 2 and 3 May 1933, and comments by Hopkins and Fisher, T175/79.   [96] Leith-Ross, *Money Talks*, 171–7.

the sterling exchange rate. Under the provisions of the French monetary law of 1928, the Banque de France bought and sold gold without limit at a fixed price, whereas American policy since 1934 had been to make the dollar freely convertible into gold only for countries that were on the gold standard. The Exchange Equalisation Account could not, therefore, operate effectively in New York, but it could do so in Paris. Britain, France, and the United States shared a common interest in ensuring that any French devaluation did not disrupt the *de facto* arrangements for stabilizing exchange rates, but there was plenty of scope for disagreement about what exchange rates would represent equilibrium, especially given the changes in relative prices brought about by different policies of deflation and reflation in the three countries since 1931.

The first contact between the US and British Treasuries regarding co-operation on continental European devaluations occurred in March 1935, when Harry Dexter White, then an obscure economic analyst working on the US Treasury's equivalent of the Exchange Equalisation Account, called on Leith-Ross in London. White said he had been studying the financial situation in Europe and had come to the conclusion that the continental countries still on gold were bound to devalue sooner or later and that, unless the United States and Britain came to some general arrangement with them, the devaluations would almost certainly be too great, creating new maladjustments. He argued that such an arrangement would allow Britain to retain some of the competitive advantage that she had enjoyed since 1931, while also encouraging international trade and discouraging speculative movements of capital. Leith-Ross was not impressed, commenting: 'Mr White struck me as a pretty sharp fellow, but I would not place much confidence in him'. What White proposed would involve a willingness on the part of central banks in New York, Paris, and London to make short-term credits available to each other, and Phillips thought that this would give foreign central bankers the opportunity to question Bank rate policy in Britain.[97] There was thus no positive response from the British Treasury at this stage.

In November 1935 Morgenthau took the opportunity of an enquiry by Thomas Bewley, the Treasury official seconded to be financial counsellor at the British embassy in Washington, about the future sale of China's silver reserve, to press for co-operation between Britain, France, and the United States on currency stabilization. Morgenthau suggested an exchange of information between the British and US Treasuries as the first basis for co-operation, but the exiguous and tardy financial information reaching him through Bewley over the next six or seven months led him to believe that the British Treasury was not interested in co-operation.[98] However, perhaps because of the mounting

[97] 'Note of Interview with Mr White', by Leith-Ross, and attached note by Phillips, both 8 Mar. 1935, T188/116.
[98] Morgenthau diaries, vol. 11, 7 Nov. 1935; vol. 23, 5 May 1936, and vol. 24, 18 May 1936, Franklin D. Roosevelt Library, Hyde Park, New York.

speculative pressure against the franc following the Popular Front's electoral success in France in 1936, Chamberlain decided to respond to Morgenthau's approaches by sending him a personal letter on 1 June expressing the desire for the 'closest and most friendly contact' between the American and British treasuries, together with a more formal message setting out the British position regarding exchange rate stabilization.[99]

The British government hoped that sterling could continue to be held steady in terms of gold, whatever happened to the franc, and that therefore the sterling: dollar rate would remain unchanged (that is, at about $5.00), but Britain reserved the right to review its policy if there was a big drop in commodity prices or a large-scale outflow of gold from London. In the complicated negotiations in Washington, Paris, and London that followed, the British Treasury was careful not to enter into any commitment regarding exchange rates that might imperil its domestic policy of cheap money. The eventual Tripartite Agreement of 25 September 1936 amounted to no more than a declaration of good intentions by Britain, France, and the United States to avoid, as far as possible, any disturbance resulting from the devaluation of the franc, and to consult together to this end. Other countries were invited to express support for the agreement, and the hope was expressed that no country would try to obtain an unreasonable competitive advantage through devaluation and thereby hamper efforts to restore more stable economic relations. Despite, or perhaps because of, its lack of binding commitments, and despite the spasmodic nature of inter-Treasury consultation, the Tripartite Agreement appears to have brought some stability to international financial markets. Information was exchanged daily regarding the price at which each of the three countries' exchange equalization funds would buy gold, thereby reducing the risk of support operations by the others, and from October 1936 the US Treasury agreed that the British and French funds could buy gold in New York, although neither sterling nor the franc was fixed in terms of gold, thereby facilitating the funds' operations and making the dollar (the value of which was fixed in terms of gold) the point of reference for international finance. Notwithstanding a further decline of the franc in 1937 and 1938, and of sterling in 1938 and 1939, the three years following the Agreement were marked by more stable exchange rates than in the previous three years, making it possible to begin to re-establish normal relations between financial centres.[100]

Morgenthau was encouraged to pursue inter-Treasury diplomacy on an issue that was not purely financial. In February 1937 he sent a message to Chamberlain, via Bewley, expressing concern about the effects of armaments expenditure on the credit of major countries, and about the concomitant risk of

---

[99] John Morton Blum, *From the Morgenthau Diaries* (Boston, Mass., 1959, 1965, and 1967), i. 143.

[100] See Stephen V. O. Clarke, *Exchange-Rate Stabilization in the Mid-1930s* (Princeton, NJ, 1977); Ian M. Drummond, *London, Washington, and the Management of the Franc, 1936–39* (Princeton, NJ, 1979).

devaluations and exchange controls, and hinted that Roosevelt would be willing to take a lead in calling a disarmament conference. After consulting Baldwin and the Foreign Secretary, Eden, Chamberlain replied that the major cause of armaments expenditure in Europe was fear of German aggression. Germany, Chamberlain noted, appeared to wish to make itself so strong that no one would refuse whatever demands it might make for European or colonial territory, and therefore Germany was unlikely to agree to any disarmament. The greatest contribution that the United States could make to world peace, he said, would be to amend its Neutrality Act of 1935 whereby, in the event of war, there would be an embargo on the export of munitions from America to all combatants, regardless of which country was the aggressor.[101] Chamberlain's belief that it was better not to rely upon the Americans can only have been confirmed when, shortly afterwards, Roosevelt signed another neutrality act, extending the provisions of the 1935 Act.

The year 1937 did, however, see a tentative move towards closer contacts between the British and US Treasuries. Phillips took the opportunity of a private visit to Canada in September to go to Washington to discuss the future price of gold and other matters of mutual interest with Morgenthau. Rather unexpectedly, the unpolished and taciturn Phillips turned out to be a successful diplomat, establishing a good relationship with Morgenthau that was to stand him in good stead when he returned to Washington in 1940 as the Treasury's representative in search of dollars to finance British imports of munitions (see Chapter 7). More immediately, Phillips and Morgenthau also agreed that it would be better to respond to depreciation of the franc by keeping France within the Tripartite Agreement rather than have the franc defended by exchange controls, as the latter would stimulate the imposition of exchange controls elsewhere.[102]

There were, however, strict limits to contacts between the two Treasuries. Morgenthau tried some telephone diplomacy in December 1937, ringing up Simon—apparently on impulse—as the Chancellor and his wife were having dinner at their house in the country. Simon, however, had good reason to know the value of having conversations with American politicians properly minuted, as he had had a notorious misunderstanding with Stimson, the US Secretary of State, over Anglo-American responses to Japanese aggression in 1932, when he had been Foreign Secretary. Accordingly he persuaded Morgenthau not to call him again on the telephone.[103] Although Morgenthau was alarmed by the policies of Nazi Germany, as regards both armaments and autarky, and hoped to

---

[101] *DBFP*, 2nd ser., xviii. 279–82, 348–52, 381–5, 415–16, 428, 543–5.

[102] Records of Phillips's meetings with Morgenthau are in the Morgenthau diaries, vol. 89, 20 Sept.–24 Sept. 1937.

[103] The Morgenthau–Simon telephone conversation is recorded verbatim in the Morgenthau diary, vol. 103, 17 Dec. 1937. Simon's record of the conversation and his response are in *DBFP*, 2nd ser., xxi. 597 and 607–8. For the Simon–Stimson misunderstanding, see *DBFP*, 2nd ser., xx. 1034–41.

promote co-operation between the western powers within his sphere of finance, he failed to convince the British Treasury that he had much to offer.

A major issue that might have been negotiated between the two treasuries was a war debt settlement that would have released Britain from the restrictions of the Johnson Act. Fisher (very optimistically) had hopes in July 1937 that it might be possible to make a final settlement in about eighteen months' time. However, gossip in London in the summer of 1938 about a settlement provoked unfriendly comment in the American press, which rightly attributed British anxiety to settle war debts to a wish to be able to borrow again if war broke out with Germany. Hopkins's view that it would be impossible to reach a settlement that would be acceptable to both British and American public opinion prevailed, and the matter was allowed to rest.[104]

TABLE 6.2. *External Finance, 1935–1939*

	Current balance of payments, excluding gold (£m.)	Gold and foreign exchange reserves (£m. in March)	Exchange rate against US dollar	
			High	Low
1935	+13	430	4.971	4.776
1936	−40	522	5.041	4.888
1937	−57	706	4.997	4.885
1938	−65	833	5.018	4.671
1939	−250	582	4.687	4.030

Sources: Column 1: for 1935–8: R. G. Ware, 'The Balance of Payments in the Inter-War Period: Further Details', *Bank of England Quart. Bull.*, 14 (Mar. 1974), 49; for 1939: London and Cambridge Economic Service, *The British Economy Key Statistics, 1900–1970* (1971), 17; column 2: S. Howson, *Sterling's Managed Float* (Princeton, NJ, 1980), 62; column 3: LCES, *British Economy: Key Statistics*, 15.

The most pressing problems concerning overseas finance in 1938 and 1939 were sterling's exchange rate and the level of gold and foreign exchange reserves (see Table 6.2). Contemporary Board of Trade estimates for the balance of payments on current account showed that the deficits in 1937 and 1938 (about £55 million in each year) were higher than in 1932 (£51 million). As defence expenditure surged ahead in 1937, sucking in imports and diverting British industry from export markets, it seemed not unlikely that the deficit would reach a level comparable to 1931 (£104 million). Initially it was possible for Treasury officials to take a fairly relaxed view of the balance of payments because Britain's gold and foreign exchange reserves rose from £430 million in March 1935 to £833 million in March 1938, largely, it would seem, because political instability in continental Europe, especially in France during the years of the 'Popular Front', made London seem a relatively attractive haven for 'hot money'. However,

[104] G. C. Peden, 'A Matter of Timing: The Economic Background to British Foreign Policy, 1937–1939', *History*, 69 (1984), 18.

in 1938 a change of government in France encouraged the repatriation of French funds, while British budget deficits, on account of rearmament, and the growing danger of war in Europe, also encouraged an outflow of foreign funds from London. By December 1938 Britain's gold and foreign exchange reserves had fallen by 25 per cent in nine months, while the resources of the Exchange Equalisation Account were being strained to hold sterling above $4.60 compared with $5.00 earlier in the year. In January 1939 Simon warned the Cabinet that 'it must be said that recent conditions have been painfully reminiscent of those which obtained in this country immediately prior to the financial crisis of 1931'.[105]

A lower exchange rate was a mixed blessing. On the one hand it helped export industries with spare capacity, although the Committee on Economic Information thought that the effects of sterling depreciation on exports would be limited, as a large number of currencies were based on sterling. On the other hand, sterling depreciation would raise the cost of essential imports, many of them from the dollar area, at a time when it was estimated that one-sixth of the cost of rearmament represented the price of imports. As for the loss of gold and foreign exchange, the Treasury and the Bank agreed with the Committee on Economic Information in December 1938 that Britain might be better off without the large liquid assets held by nervous foreigners in London, and that withdrawals of such money could not justify exchange controls.[106]

Parker has argued that a sharp reduction in the exchange rate to a level that could definitely have been defended would have deterred foreign holders of sterling from moving their capital elsewhere, thereby enabling Britain to retain the accumulated gold reserves as a 'war chest' with which to finance imports after the outbreak of hostilities. There was, however, a political factor in that the United States Treasury had to be convinced that sterling was not being allowed to depreciate to give British (and sterling area) producers a competitive advantage in world markets. Britain was not in a strong position to resist American pressure at a time when the appearance of American goodwill, symbolized by the Anglo-American Trade Agreement of November 1938, was seen by Chamberlain as being of great psychological importance. Accordingly, in order to convince the Americans that everything possible was being done to peg sterling at $4.67, it was decided in January 1939 to transfer all the gold that had been put into the Issue Department of the Bank of England since 1932 to the Exchange Equalisation Account, giving the operators of the Account the maximum resources with which to combat speculation against sterling. After the German occupation of Prague in March 1939, fear of war put inexorable

[105] 'Statement by the Chancellor of the Exchequer', 18 Jan. 1939, CAB23/97; Peden, *British Rearmament*, 96.
[106] 26th Report of the Committee on Economic Information, CAB58/23; 'Views of Treasury and Bank of England on Suggestions Made in Paragraph 23 of Economic Advisory Committee Report of 16 Dec. 1938', T175/104.

pressure on sterling and over a quarter of Britain's gold and foreign exchange reserves were lost between 31 March and 22 August, when Hitler's non-aggression pact with Stalin became known. Over the next two days over £30 million was lost and on 24 August the pound was unpegged, Bank rate being raised from 2 to 4 per cent to check its fall. On 3 September the rate was fixed at $4.03. Britain thus ended up with the worst of both worlds: a diminished 'war chest' and higher costs for essential imports from the dollar area.[107]

TOWARDS THE MANAGED ECONOMY? FINANCING
REARMAMENT, 1937–1939

From 1937 the Treasury had to respond to the danger that rearmament, partly financed by borrowing, superimposed upon new civil investment, could result in what Chamberlain described as 'a sharp steepening of costs due to wage increases, leading to the loss of our export trade, a feverish and partly artificial boom followed by a disastrous slump, and finally the defeat of the Government'.[108] Initially, the Treasury tried to keep defence expenditure at a level that would not weaken financial confidence. By 1939, however, financial policy had to be adapted to the needs of a rapidly accelerating rearmament programme.

As already noted, the rearmament programme approved by the Cabinet for the five years from 1936/7 assumed that part of the cost would be met by borrowing. Before introducing his Defence Loans Bill in February 1937 Chamberlain consulted his officials about Asquith's 'classic' statement in 1906 condemning the practice of borrowing under the Naval and Military Works Acts. He evidently decided that it would be better to deny that the Acts provided an appropriate precedent for his Bill, and instead justified it with reference to the unprecedented circumstances with which the country was faced. Neverthe-less, he promised Parliament that the 'vices' that Asquith had identified with these Acts would be avoided: the Treasury would try to preserve the distinction between capital and revenue expenditure; a tendency to extravagance would be prevented by maintaining strict Treasury control of expenditure; and all money, whether borrowed or raised from taxes, would be voted by Parliament.[109] The Defence Loans Bill was designed to persuade financial markets that borrowing was according to a definite plan, unlike the hand-to-mouth borrowing for the Unemployment Insurance Fund that had helped to undermine confidence in the Labour government's finances in 1931. Thus the maximum, total sum to be borrowed over the next five years was given as £400 million, and annual votes

[107] R. A. C. Parker, 'The Pound Sterling, the American Treasury and British Preparations for War, 1938–1939', *Eng. Hist. Rev.*, 98 (1983), 261–79.
[108] Chamberlain to his sister Hilda, 25 Apr. 1937, NC18/1/1003.
[109] MSS note by Chamberlain, n.d., T172/1853; 320 HC Deb., 5s, 1936–7, cols. 1206–7.

of the defence departments were to include interest on the debt incurred to date and also a sinking fund to pay off the debt over thirty years from April 1942.[110]

Fisher was initially reluctant to advocate higher taxation, in case support in the country for rearmament was reduced thereby. However, Hopkins insisted that tax revenue must be sufficient to pay, not only for all non-defence items in the budget, but also for the cost of the enlarged forces once the period of borrowing was over. This policy, which resembled the McKenna rule of 1916, entailed increases in taxation, including income tax, the standard rate of which was raised from 4s. 6d. (22.5p) to 4s. 9d. (23.75p) in 1936, then to 5s. (25p) in 1937 and 5s. 6d. (27.5p) in 1938. In 1937 Chamberlain also proposed to pay for part of the cost of rearmament by introducing an avowedly temporary tax, national defence contribution, which was to be graduated according to the growth of profits that could be expected as a result of increased government expenditure. However, the City and business organizations were so hostile to such a 'socialist' measure, and discontent in the Conservative party was so great, that Chamberlain thought that he had 'risked the premiership'. Business interests offered to find his successor, Simon, the same revenue from an alternative tax, which turned out to be a straight 5 per cent tax on profits.[111]

The limit of £400 million set for borrowing seems to have been reached by subtracting estimated revenue from the total of the defence departments' programmes over the five years 1937/8–1941/2. The Labour spokesman on economic matters, F. W. Pethick-Lawrence, predicted that borrowing would lead to an inflationary boom followed by a slump, but Hopkins and Phillips, with support from Keynes, believed that, with the annual savings of the country at about £400 to £500 million, it would be possible to avoid borrowing from the banks, and therefore repeating the experience of 1914–18. Norman thought that the figure of £400 million would be a shock to money markets and would have a depressing effect on the government's credit, but was not alarmed. In the event, an issue of £100 million of 2½ per cent National Defence Bonds in April 1937 was a complete fiasco, and £86.5 million had to be taken up by the Issue Department of the Bank of England, a then secret procedure for underwriting government loans. These bonds had to be sold at a discount, as and when possible, and by the end of 1937 it seemed that the Treasury would be forced to increase its reliance on Treasury bills for future borrowing. However, the recession of 1938 reduced alternative investment opportunities for the non-bank public, and in April 1939 Phillips could report that over £200 million had been borrowed for rearmament to date and the investments of the clearing banks were slightly lower than in 1936.[112]

At one level, borrowing eased the budgetary problem, for sums voted under the Defence Loans Act were treated as revenue, and thus the budget accounts showed an apparently respectable surplus (£28.8 million) for 1937/8, followed

[110] Peden, *British Rearmament*, 78.
[111] Ibid., 87; Simon's 'diary', 15 Jan. 1938, Simon papers, vol. 7, Bodleian Library, Oxford.
[112] Peden, *British Rearmament*, 72, 75–9, 81.

by a deficit of £12.7 million in 1938/9, even though some £193 million were borrowed for defence in these years (see Table 6.1). However, as Phillips noted, the pretence of producing a balanced budget was a 'fiction'.[113] Moreover, the Defence Loans threatened both the short-term and long-term budget positions. In the short term, the absence of the constraint of a genuine balanced budget made it difficult to control expenditure by the defence departments; in the longer term, there was a danger that the rearmament programme would create larger defence forces than could be maintained out of any politically acceptable level of taxation, once the five-year period covered by the Defence Loans Act was over.

Although defence programmes and Chancellor's budgets were presented in purely financial terms, the Treasury thought in terms of what it called 'real resources . . . our manpower and productive capacity, our power to maintain our credit, and the general balance of our trade'. The last of these was particularly important, given Britain's dependence on imports for food and raw materials, and it was the external balance that ultimately determined how much could be borrowed for defence. In a passage drafted in 1937 for the Minister for the Co-ordination of Defence, Sir Thomas Inskip, the Treasury stated:

> The amount of money which we can borrow without inflation is mainly dependent on two factors: the savings of the country as a whole which are available for investment, and the maintenance of confidence in our financial stability. But these savings would be reduced and confidence would at once be weakened by any substantial disturbance to the general balance of trade. While if we were to raise sums in excess of the sums available in the market, the result would be inflation, i.e., a general rise in prices which would have an immediate effect upon our export trade.[114]

At the Treasury's prompting, Inskip argued that rearmament should strike a balance between, on the one hand, making the country secure from attack and, on the other, maintaining the country's financial stability, for the latter would be essential to support the conduct of a war, and was therefore a 'fourth arm of defence'.[115]

The problem of financing rearmament was made more difficult by the recession in 1938, which threatened to reduce revenue in 1939/40. Yet, at the same time, the recession released manpower and productive capacity from civil work, and as industrial capacity planned at the beginning of the rearmament programme came on stream, defence expenditure could be expected to surge ahead in 1939. Middleton has shown that the Treasury responded to this situation by making 'the first attempts to actively manage demand—in a Keynesian sense—using the budget as an instrument of economic policy'. Tax increases to pay for rearmament were withheld in the 1939 budget because the Treasury was

---

[113] Phillips to W. R. Fraser (Treasury), 27 Nov. 1936, T177/25.

[114] 'Defence Expenditure in Future Years', CP316(37), CAB24/273.

[115] For the Treasury's part in the preparation of Inskip's report see Peden, *British Rearmament*, 10, 19–20, 41–2, 64–5.

waiting for rearmament to bring the economy to a state of full employment. At full employment the yield of taxation would be significantly increased, and a higher level of savings would make it easier for the government to borrow without resorting to the banks.[116]

There is certainly evidence of a change in fiscal policy in 1939, but, as Middleton himself points out, the change was a pragmatic response to the political and economic problems generated by rearmament, rather than the result of changes in the Treasury's theoretical approach to fiscal policy.[117] By December 1938, when the shape of the budget for 1939/40 was being discussed, it was estimated that the revenue available for defence expenditure on the existing basis of taxation was £230 million, £70 million less than the estimated future annual maintenance costs of the defence services then planned. If the Treasury had continued its policy since 1936 of raising revenue in line with future maintenance costs, taxation would have had to be increased by £70 million in the 1939 budget. Fisher thought that an increase in the standard rate of income tax by 6d. (2.5p) to 6s. (30p), the peak rate reached in the First World War, was desirable to alert the country to the danger from Germany. However, on the advice of Phillips and Hopkins, the budget in April 1939 provided for additional revenue of only £24 million, mainly from indirect taxation designed to check consumers' expenditure on imports of cars, tobacco, and sugar, and with the increase in direct taxation confined to surtax (10 per cent on the top rate, and 5 per cent on incomes up to £8,000) and death duties (10 per cent on the largest estates). Of the £630 million forecast to be spent on defence in 1939/40, no less than £380 million would be met by borrowing, requiring an upward revision of the limit set by the Defence Loans Act from £400 million to £800 million, which was itself a deliberate understatement.[118]

Phillips argued that the effect of raising an additional £70 million in taxation would be to depress general trade and with it the yield of the income tax and surtax. At a time when unemployment stood at 1,800,000 and was still rising, Hopkins agreed with Phillips that there was no great danger of inflation (in the sense of a general increase in prices).[119] The idea that a rise in prices and an increase in production were to a great extent alternatives was not new to the Treasury—Hawtrey, after all, had made that point in the 1928 edition of his book *Currency and Credit*.[120] In connection with the April 1939 budget Hawtrey explained to Phillips:

When the productive power of the community is under-employed, such an expansion of demand as is required to bring it to full employment is not inflation (that is what has been called 'reflation'). Nevertheless, it is possible that a vicious circle of rising wages and rising prices might be started even before full employment is reached. In that case the

[116] Middleton, *Towards the Managed Economy*, 119.   [117] Ibid., 120–1.

[118] Ibid., 118–9; Peden, *British Rearmament*, 100–1.

[119] Phillips to Hopkins, 15 Dec. 1938, T171/341, and Hopkins to Chancellor of the Exchequer, 23 Dec. 1938, T175/104.   [120] R. G. Hawtrey, *Currency and Credit* (1928), 50.

expansion will be excessive and therefore inflationary even although some unemployment remained.[121]

As with his theory in relation to public works in the 1920s, Hawtrey believed that rearmament created employment only in so far as it was financed by an increase in credit, and not by borrowing funds that would otherwise have been invested in private enterprise. Phillips agreed that 'if there were no reflationary finance, the government works would tend merely to replace private works without much effect on employment'. However, he counselled against making a statement in Parliament along these lines, on the grounds that: 'this is the famous or infamous "Treasury view", still a most bitter subject of controversy which it would be a great mistake to raise.'[122]

The 1939 budget did conform to the 'act of faith' school of thought in being based on the hope that, by withholding a tax increase, economic recovery would be encouraged, to the ultimate benefit of the revenue. However, revenue was still calculated on the basis of what the taxpayer could be persuaded to pay, with the difference between that sum and the sum that the government proposed to spend being met by borrowing. No attempt was made to calculate national income or how the savings which the government hoped to borrow might be affected by changes in national income, and there is no evidence of Treasury officials using the analytical framework of national income accounting that Keynes was to persuade them to adopt for the 1941 budget. Keynes's subsequent reputation may have led economists and historians to exaggerate his influence in the 1930s and to have underestimated that of Hawtrey.[123]

In April 1939 Keynes published two articles in *The Times* in which he advised the Chancellor to frame his budget on the assumption that additional defence expenditure to be financed by borrowing would eliminate abnormal unemployment. Keynes predicted that government expenditure would increase primary demand by £200 million, which should mean an increase in total demand of 'perhaps twice this amount', or about 8 per cent of national income, of which half would be saved, making an additional £200 million available for government loans. Hawtrey commented that this was a '*possible* calculation', but warned that, if the whole of the government's loan expenditure were to be financed from additional savings; reduced private investment; and sales of securities, gold, or other capital assets abroad, there would not necessarily be any increase in economic activity, employment, or national income.[124] The considered Treasury position on Keynes's ideas, as given to the Cabinet in May, was that there was

---

[121] 'Borrowing and Inflation', 29 Apr. 1939, T208/201.

[122] Note by Phillips, 29 Apr. 1939, T208/201.

[123] In particular, Phillips's use of Hawtrey's ideas in Apr. 1939 suggests that the latter had more influence in the Treasury in the 1930s than suggested by Susan Howson in her paper on 'Hawtrey and the Real World' in G. C. Harcourt (ed.), *Keynes and His Contemporaries* (1985), 142–88, although she is correct when she says that he had none at all during the Second World War.

[124] *JMK*, xxi. 509–18; 'Mr Keynes on Crisis Finance', by Hawtrey, 20 Apr. 1939, T208/201.

'no action which the government could take to increase the total volume of savings of the country as a whole'. The annual savings were taken to be about £450 million and, while there was, 'of course, an element of truth' in Keynes's theory, in so far as government expenditure increased prosperity, and that in turn increased revenue and national savings, the latter were normally required for civil investment. If the government borrowed savings that would normally have been used for building or industrial equipment, the country would be worse off, and not better off, in that its capital stock would be depleted.[125]

Nevertheless, at the time of the April budget, Phillips at least was not pessimistic either about preventing inflation or maintaining full employment. He advised Hopkins:

if and when we reach a stage of full employment and prices continue to rise without labour being absorbed into work we must be ready to revert to all the usual controls, including heavier taxation, heavier customs duties, higher bank rate, a strong loan policy, reduction in floating debt and so on.

However:

once full employment has been reached, the country can very well stand increased financial pressure *without* going back to a state of unemployment, and there will be no reversion to deflation unless the monetary authorities are ignorant of their job.[126]

In other words, a range of policy instruments could be used to manage the economy, but the principal one was monetary policy. The experience of the ever-increasing rearmament programme confirmed the difficulty of controlling expenditure outside a balanced budget, and the Treasury remained committed to a return to balanced budgets from 1942/3, when it was expected that the rearmament programme would have been completed.

The decisive advice on borrowing for defence came from the Bank of England. On 17 May Norman told the Treasury that about £150 to £200 million could be borrowed on Treasury bills, without inflation, because receipts of sterling by the Exchange Equalisation Account, as a result of foreign withdrawals of gold, had made it possible to reduce the normal volume of Treasury bills in the hands of the market. However, he advised, any further borrowing should be long-term, which, given the increase in the defence programmes, would amount to £200 to £250 million in 1939/40, and £400 million or more annually thereafter. Borrowing on such a scale, he warned, would be impossible without legal compulsion. The Governor recommended a series of draconian policies: all capital investment not required for armaments should be prohibited; recipients of increased incomes from government expenditure must be prevented by taxation or other means from spending it; and unemployed workers should be given

---

[125] Cabinet minutes, 23 May 1939, CAB23/99.
[126] Phillips to Hopkins, 24 Apr. 1939, T177/47. For further discussion of Phillips's views, see Middleton, *Towards the Managed Economy*, 118–20, 181.

special training to mobilize them for the kinds of production that the government required. On 5 July Hopkins appeared before the Cabinet to warn that the usual methods of preventing inflation would have to be supplemented by new powers to prohibit new issues on the Stock Exchange; to control companies' dividends and investment of their reserves; and to control building society loans as well as bank advances, once the economy reached full employment. An autumn budget, with large increases in taxation, was already under consideration.[127]

Rearmament was leading the Treasury, advised by the Bank of England, towards policies associated with war finance, even although Chamberlain still hoped in the summer of 1939 to maintain peace with Germany. It is possible in retrospect, as Middleton suggests, to see the budget of April 1939 as a step towards a Keynesian managed economy. At the time, however, financial policy from 1937 to the outbreak of war was regarded as a series of emergency measures to deal with an unprecedented external danger.

CONTROL OF EXPENDITURE, 1931–1939

Given the National Government's commitment to restore confidence in British public finance, and the strong support in the dominant Conservative party for reductions in direct taxation, one might have expected that the Treasury would be in a good position to reduce central government expenditure after 1931. However, although *The Times* was calling in May 1932 for 'a progressive reduction of expenditure measured not in millions but in tens of millions', it was not easy to identify areas where there could be further reductions to follow those of September 1931. Defence expenditure could be expected to rise, with the cancellation of the Ten Year Rule in March 1932, leaving the social services and grants to local authorities as the only likely targets. Even there reductions of 'tens of millions' could only be achieved if there were a radical change in the scope of these services.[128]

It is in this context that the Treasury's battles with the Ministry of Labour over the relief of the unemployed between 1932 and 1934 have to be understood.[129] In 1932 the Unemployment Insurance Fund was brought into balance by drastic rates of increase in the rates of contribution and the reduction of benefits, but it still had a substantial debt to repay to the Treasury, and the Treasury still had to provide the finance for the maintenance of the million or so workers who had run out of entitlement to unemployment insurance and who received transitional benefit instead. Treasury officials opposed Ministry of Labour

---

[127] Norman to Wilson, 17 May 1939, quoted by Hawtrey, 'Financial History of the War', ch. 1, p. 5, T208/204; Peden, *British Rearmament*, 102–3.

[128] 'Memorandum on National Expenditure', with notes by Gilbert, n.d., and by E. J. Strohmenger, then the Under-Secretary in charge of the Supply Services divisions, 2 May 1932, T175/67.

[129] See Lowe, *Adjusting to Democracy*, 154–67.

proposals in 1932 for easing the means test for transitional benefit, arguing that to treat that category of the unemployed differently from ordinary applicants for public assistance would jeopardize a comprehensive scheme of relief for all the unemployed. The Treasury preferred to keep concessions on the means test in reserve, to be announced at the same time as the creation of a new statutory commission for the unemployed, thereby making the commission more accept-able to the unemployed.[130] Nevertheless, the Cabinet came down on the side of the Ministry of Labour on the means test.

Chamberlain himself, as a former Minister of Health, took an active role in preparing the Treasury's proposals for a new statutory commission to take con-trol of all relief for the able-bodied unemployed, with a national, means-tested benefit replacing the existing means-tested benefits administered by local authorities. He believed that there was a danger of relief being 'put up for auc-tion' at local and national elections, and wanted to take unemployment out of party politics by removing the commission as far as possible from parliamentary scrutiny. Administrative duplication, whereby the insured unemployed and the non-insured were dealt with by different bodies, would be removed by having the commission cover both. Hopkins also hoped that, once the Unemployment Insurance Fund's finances had been restored, it would be possible to extend the period during which benefit could be drawn from the fund, thereby reducing the number of workers on transitional benefit and saving money for the Treas-ury.[131] (Whereas the Treasury bore the whole cost of transitional benefit, two-thirds of the cost of unemployment insurance was borne by the insured workers and their employers.)

However, despite support from Hilton Young, the Minister of Health, Cham-berlain lost most of his battles with Sir Henry Betterton, the Minister of Labour, in the preparation of the Unemployment Act of 1934. Two separate statutory commissions were created, the Unemployment Insurance Statutory Commit-tee to deal with benefits for the insured, and the Unemployment Assistance Board to deal with means-tested assistance for the uninsured, and the prospects of savings for the Treasury, other than those brought about by the reduction in the total number of the unemployed, receded. As a result, Hopkins, when con-sidering in 1937 the level of defence expenditure that could be afforded once rearmament was over, had to accept that a major consideration in future budget prospects was the cost of maintaining the unemployed, which could not be expected to fall below £55 to £65 million, compared with £20 million in 1929, and which might rise to £100 million.[132]

---

[130] Strohmenger to Hopkins, 13 Oct. 1932, and Fergusson to Chancellor, 18 Oct. 1932, T172/1769.
[131] 'Royal Commission on Unemployment Insurance: The Insurance Scheme', by Hopkins, 16 Jan. 1933, T175/69; Alan Booth, 'An Administrative Experiment in Unemployment Policy in the Thirties', *Public Admin.*, 56 (1978), 139–57.
[132] Minutes of Inskip Review, 25 Nov. 1937, T161/855/S48431/04.

When the Ten Year Rule was abrogated in March 1932, at the instigation of the Chiefs of Staff Committee,[133] the Cabinet agreed with Chamberlain that its decision must not be taken to justify higher defence expenditure without regard to the risk to the country's financial stability. In the event, the 1929/30 level of defence expenditure, £113 million, was not reached again until 1934/5. Meanwhile, Fisher and Chamberlain had taken active parts in a review of the deficiencies in the country's armed forces in 1933 and 1934, and Chamberlain was successful in persuading his fellow ministers to give priority to Great Britain's air defences, with the rate of re-equipment of the Army still being subject to severe financial limits. However, once it had been agreed in 1935 that defence expenditure could be paid for from loans, it was much harder for the Treasury to impose financial restraint, and the forecasts of the defence departments' requirements under the five-year rearmament programme for 1936/7 to 1941/2 were greatly exceeded (see Table 6.3). The Admiralty, Air Ministry, and War Office were naturally more concerned to press ahead with their programmes than they were to keep within their Estimates for any particular year, and it was impossible for the Chancellor to refuse Supplementary Estimates. Lack of industrial capacity was the real constraint on expenditure, leading to voted funds remaining unspent, but in March 1938 the Cabinet agreed to a demand by the Chiefs of Staff that industry should be asked to give priority to rearmament work, thereby reversing the earlier policy of not allowing rearmament to disrupt normal trade, and defence expenditure surged ahead.

TABLE 6.3. *Growth and Distribution of Expenditure by Defence Departments, 1932/3–1938/9*

	Planned expenditure	Actual expenditure	Shares of actual expenditure		
			Air Force	Army	Navy
	(£m.)		(per cent)		
1932/3	—	103.0	16.6	34.9	48.5
1933/4	—	107.9	15.6	34.8	49.6
1934/5	118.5	113.9	15.5	34.9	49.7
1935/6	124.6	137.0	20.0	32.6	47.3
1936/7	173.9	186.1	26.9	29.5	43.6
1937/8	211.0	262.1	31.4	29.7	38.9
1938/9	226.7	382.5	35.0	31.7	33.3

Note: Because of rounding up or down, the percentage figures do not always add up to 100.

Sources: Column 1: for 1934/5 and 1935/6: First Defence Requirements Report, 28 Feb. 1934, CAB16/109; from 1936/7: Third Defence Requirements Report, 21 Nov. 1935, CAB16/112; column 2: *Statistical Abstract for the United Kingdom for Each of the Fifteen Years 1924 to 1938* (Cmd. 6232), PP 1939–40, x, 367.

---

[133] A standing committee comprising the heads of the three defence services, the First Sea Lord and Chief of the Naval Staff, the Chief of the Imperial General Staff, and the Chief of the Air Staff.

In contrast to 1914, however, effective interdepartmental machinery was set up to ensure that there was an orderly flow of contracts. A Treasury Emergency Expenditure Committee was established in September 1935, with representatives of the three defence departments, and a Treasury official in the chair, to expedite Treasury sanction of expenditure at a time when war with Italy seemed likely; the same body, renamed the Treasury Inter-Service Committee, dealt with rearmament orders from February 1936, ensuring that the proposals of the different defence departments were considered promptly together.

The Treasury division, 5D, dealing with defence expenditure was headed by an exceptionally able principal assistant secretary, Edward Bridges, until August 1938, when he succeeded Sir Maurice Hankey as Cabinet Secretary. Notwithstanding a shy, donnish manner, Bridges 'went down well with the soldiery', on account of having been awarded the Military Cross, while serving as an infantry officer on the Western Front. In his work Bridges reflected Fisher's philosophy of acting as a candid friend of the defence departments, questioning their methods, and encouraging his subordinates to think in terms of having a co-ordinating role.[134] Officials in 5D examined new proposals for expenditure on their merits but it was difficult for laymen, however intelligent, to match defence experts in technical arguments. Bridges believed that it was impossible for the Treasury to refuse to sanction expenditure for new projects that the defence experts declared to be necessary, except on the ground that money was not available—and that argument could not be used when Supplementary Estimates were readily granted. In order to apply a brake to the growth in the defence departments' programmes, Hopkins and Bridges advised Chamberlain in January 1937 that Treasury control should be restored by naming for each defence department an aggregate 'ration' of finance which could not be exceeded over the next five years. In that way the defence departments would themselves have to establish priorities and leave out the less essential items from their programmes. After lengthy negotiation, financial rations totalling £1,570 million for the three departments over the next five years were agreed by the Cabinet in February 1938. However, it proved to be impossible to confine defence expenditure in this way as the threat of war increased. In December 1938 it was estimated that £300 million would be required annually to maintain the armed forces being created by the rearmament programme, but this figure had to be revised to £450 million in June 1939 after the Cabinet had decided that the army should be ready to fight a major war in Europe.

In the absence of a ministry of defence, the Treasury used its position in the Cabinet and the Committee of Imperial Defence, and their subcommittees, to try to persuade ministers and the defence departments to adhere to the Cabinet's decision to give priority to the air defence of Great Britain. In 1937 Chamberlain took the lead in a review of defence policy, which was completed after he

---

[134] Conversation with Sir John Winnifrith, who worked under Bridges in 5D.

became Prime Minister. Chamberlain favoured a policy of 'limited liability' with regard to military assistance to France, and the Cabinet agreed that preparation of the Army for warfare on the continent of Europe should only take place once three other priorities—air defence, defence of trade routes, and defence of overseas territories and interests—had been secured. In practice, Treasury control was less than completely successful in ensuring that the defence departments' programmes reflected priorities as agreed in Cabinet. In particular, the Air Ministry continued to give a high priority to building up a large bomber force, even after the Cabinet had agreed that fighters should have priority; the Admiralty continued to plan to send a fleet to Singapore in the event of war with Japan, even though the Cabinet had decided that Germany was the main threat; and the War Office was reluctant to use scarce gun-making capacity for anti-aircraft guns rather than field guns, even though the Cabinet had decided that air defence was to have priority over continental warfare. Nevertheless, by relaxing Treasury control on Air Ministry expenditure, the Treasury was able to ensure that the Air Ministry gained an increasing share of the available funds and industrial capacity, and therefore the air force's programme proceeded more quickly than those of army or navy (see Table 6.3).

Given the rapid rise in defence expenditure, it is hardly surprising that the Treasury tried to hold back civil expenditure. Between 1932/3 and 1938/9 civil expenditure that had to be paid out of the Chancellor's budget increased by £70 million, or 20 per cent. While Hopkins accepted that some increase was inevitable as the economy cuts of 1931 were restored, he warned Simon and Fisher in 1938 that: 'We cannot forever borrow what we please but the upward march of civil expenditure shows little sign of abating.' The cost of old-age and widows' pensions and education could be expected to increase steadily; expenditure on roads was increasing rapidly as the five-year programme initiated just before the general election of 1935 got ahead; unemployment could be a crippling charge in some years (and could be expected to rise in a post-rearmament slump), and new proposals for expenditure on housing could be expected in connection with a new standard for overcrowding.[135]

Thus prompted, Simon warned the Cabinet in July that there were signs that civil expenditure would rise by £20 million in 1939/40 and that it might be necessary to impose a ration on it, as had been done in the case of the defence departments.[136] Ten months later, with defence expenditure free of effective rationing and civil expenditure as yet unrationed, and with the Cabinet considering new proposals on their merits rather than in relation to the overall financial position, the Chancellor and Chamberlain persuaded the Cabinet to set up a subcommittee to examine substantial new spending proposals from the latter point of view. This step has been seen as a forerunner of the changes

---

[135] Unsigned memorandum, n.d., but by Hopkins, and position in file indicates June 1938, T273/322.
[136] Cabinet minutes, 20 July 1938, CAB23/94.

suggested by the Plowden Report in 1961 to ensure that the Chancellor was not alone responsible in Cabinet for restraining expenditure, but it had no chance to prove its utility before its fate was sealed by the outbreak of war.[137]

The difficulties of financing rearmament provide a sufficient explanation of why the Treasury officials resisted pressure from the Labour opposition, the TUC, and the National Federation of Old Age Pensions Associations from 1935 to 1939 to improve pensions, yet the fact that rearmament was financed led proponents of improved pensions to claim that the government could find money if it wanted to. Nineteen-forty was expected to be an election year, and in July 1939 Chamberlain admitted that 10s. a week was not enough to live on (over 10 per cent of pensioners were claiming public assistance) and announced that an official enquiry would be undertaken by the Treasury. The enquiry was suspended on the outbreak of war, but the need to make concessions led to the Old Age and Widows' Pensions Bill of January 1940, which lowered the qualifying age for women for contributory pensions to 60, and provided means-tested supplementary allowances of up to 5s. a week.[138]

There has been some debate among historians of social policy whether there was in fact what Hopkins in 1932 had forecast would be an 'onward march' of social services in the 1930s. A large part of social welfare expenditure was related to unemployment relief, but the effects of the depression can be excluded by comparing two years in which unemployment was at much the same level, 1928 and 1937. Over the period 1928–37 central government expenditure on social services rose from 9.6 per cent of gross national product to 10.9 per cent—figures that suggest that the Treasury may have slowed down, but certainly failed to halt, the 'onward march' of education, pensions, housing, and health services. Indeed José Harris has pointed out that social welfare expenditure grew at a faster rate in the 1930s than in any other peacetime period before the late 1960s.[139] The continued willingness of ministers to sanction new expenditure on social services, as well as greatly increased defence expenditure, from 1937, when there was no longer a need to balance the whole of current central government expenditure out of taxation, suggests that the Treasury's grip was slipping.

THE SHADOW OF APPEASEMENT

It was while Chamberlain was Chancellor and Prime Minister that the Treasury came closest to carrying out Fisher's conception of a central department of

---

[137] H. Heclo and A. Wildavsky, *The Private Government of Public Money: Community and Policy inside British Politics* (1974), 185–6.

[138] J. Macnicol, *The Politics of Retirement in Britain, 1878–1948* (Cambridge, 1998), chs. 13 and 14.

[139] Anne Crowther, *British Social Policy, 1914–1939* (1988), 14–16, 20; G. C. Peden, *British Economic and Social Policy: Lloyd George to Margaret Thatcher* (Hemel Hempstead, 1991), 105; José Harris, 'War and Social History: Britain and the Home Front during the Second World War', *Contemp. Eur. Hist.*, 1 (1992), 30.

government concerning itself with defence and foreign policy. Indeed it was claimed by Fisher's enemies that he had used his influence, both over Chamberlain and the Civil Service, to shape British defence policy and to promote the appeasement of Germany.[140] An alternative version of Fisher as an appeaser was provided in Ian Colvin's biography of Lord Vansittart, the Permanent Under-Secretary of the Foreign Office from 1930 to 1937. According to Colvin, Fisher's influence suffered something of an eclipse in late 1935, and he found it expedient to link his fortunes with those of the rising man among senior civil servants, the Chief Industrial Adviser, Sir Horace Wilson; and the two men worked to establish friendly contact with the dictator states, in spite of Vansittart's warnings.[141] Subsequent research has put Fisher's role into a very different perspective from that provided by political controversy of the 1930s and 1940s, but there is no doubt that the Treasury under his leadership encroached upon what the Foreign Office regarded as its functions.[142]

Even with the range of documentation now available, it is difficult to assess Fisher's (or Wilson's) influence on Chamberlain. It is possible in the Treasury papers to detect occasional differences of opinion between Chamberlain and Fisher, but the fact that they usually agreed does not necessarily indicate that Fisher was influencing Chamberlain. Chamberlain had a mind of his own. He was, of course, influenced by Treasury advice on how much money could be safely spent on rearmament. Indeed, the strongest defence of his policies with regard to appeasement draws heavily upon the economic limits of British power in relation to its responsibilities.[143] Even so, there was room for disagreement on how far to go with concessions to Germany.

Fisher was passionately interested in foreign policy after 1933—even telling Chamberlain in 1936 that he would take a step down in rank and a cut in pay to become Permanent Under-Secretary of the Foreign Office rather than see Vansittart succeeded by Sir Alexander Cadogan. (As it happened, despite Fisher's poor opinion of Cadogan, the latter did take over from Vansittart from 1 January 1938.[144]) Fisher's concern with the threat posed by Nazi Germany antedated the financial problems associated with rearmament. By his own account, he was on sick leave in 1933 until September, but on his return to Whitehall he urged a review of Britain's defences.[145] A defence requirements committee (DRC) of the

---

[140] See D. C. Watt, *Personalities and Policies: Studies in the Formulation of British Foreign Policy in the 20th Century* (1965), 100–16, and sources cited therein. Watt showed that Fisher was obsessively anti-German and that his concern to meet the German menace shaped his views on defence policy.

[141] Ian Colvin, *Vansittart in Office* (1965), 145–8.

[142] See E. O'Halpin, *Head of the Civil Service: A Study of Sir Warren Fisher* (1989); G. C. Peden, 'Sir Warren Fisher and British Rearmament Against Germany', *Eng. Hist. Rev.*, 94 (1979), 29–41; Gaines Post, jnr., *Dilemmas of Appeasement: British Deterrence and Defence, 1934–1937* (Ithaca, NY, 1993).

[143] See David Dilks, ' "We Must Hope for the Best and Prepare for the Worst": The Prime Minister, the Cabinet and Hitler's Germany, 1937–1939', *Proc. Brit. Acad.*, 73 (1987), 309–52.

[144] Peden, 'Sir Warren Fisher', 42.

[145] Fisher to Chamberlain, 1 Oct. 1938, PREM1/252; *The Times*, 3 Mar. 1942, 5.

Committee of Imperial Defence was set up with the Chiefs of Staff of the three defence departments plus Fisher and Vansittart as members, and with Hankey as chairman. It became apparent to Fisher that the Chiefs of Staff had failed to come to a collective view on the relative importance of the threats from Japan and Germany, and he and Vansittart persuaded the DRC to report in February 1934 that Germany, although not yet rearmed, must be regarded as the ultimate danger, against whom the bulk of Britain's defence preparations must be made. Fisher went further than his colleagues, however, in arguing that Britain must not become involved in a war with Japan, for to commit scarce resources to the Far East would be to invite defeat by Germany. Fisher believed that Japan would respect strength more than weakness and, therefore, he urged that Britain should go ahead with the Singapore base, but he also argued that Britain should try to restore good relations with Japan, if necessary at the expense of good relations with the United States.[146]

Chamberlain, although less inclined than Fisher to discount the danger of Japanese aggression, agreed with his general analysis. The Foreign Office, however, with the support of the Prime Minister, MacDonald, made clear its opposition to any move that might offend American opinion, and Chamberlain and Fisher thereupon attempted to conduct foreign policy independently. Fisher believed that Britain must avoid offending Japanese pride by combining with the United States in attempting to set a lower limit of naval tonnage for Japan than for Britain or the United States, and, with the Chancellor's support, he became a member of the British delegation for the London naval conference of 1935. On 24 October 1934, the day after preliminary Anglo-Japanese naval talks began, Fisher had what he called 'a very frank talk' with the Japanese ambassador in London, Matsudaira Tsuneo, and told him of the Treasury's views on the need to improve Anglo-Japanese relations. Fisher was undeterred by the failure of the naval talks and the subsequent abrogation by Japan of the Washington treaties. In 1935 Leith-Ross was sent to the Far East to advise the Chinese government on its currency problems and to try to bring about a 'treaty of peace and good understanding' between China, Japan, and Manchukuou, the Japanese satellite state carved out of China's north-eastern provinces in 1931 and 1932. However, although he stayed in the Far East for twelve months, Leith-Ross was unable to establish a basis for an Anglo-Japanese rapprochement, and Chamberlain's and Fisher's belief that they could conduct Far Eastern policy better than the Foreign Office proved to be an illusion.[147]

---

[146] Memorandum by Fisher, 19 Apr. 1934, *DBFP*, 2nd ser., xiii, 924–30.

[147] Gill Bennett, 'British Policy in the Far East, 1933–1936: Treasury and Foreign Office', *Mod. Asian Stud.*, 26 (1992), 545–68. Ironically, at much the same time as he was promoting independent Treasury diplomacy, Fisher was using Treasury control over the Civil Service to insist that the Foreign Office's efforts to incorporate economic aspects of international relations into its work should be done on the basis of interdepartmental co-operation, rather than by building up its own economic relations section—see D. G. Boadle, 'The Formation of the Foreign Office Economic Relations Section, 1930–1937', *Hist. J.*, 20 (1977), 919–36.

Fisher's overriding concern with Germany also led him to advise Baldwin and Chamberlain to avoid any threat of force against Italy in 1935, when Mussolini was threatening to invade Ethiopia. Fisher believed that tripartite talks between Britain, France, and Italy should precede any referral of the dispute to the Council of the League of Nations, and that any action by the League should be confined to the kind of protest made when Japan had seized Manchuria.[148] The government nevertheless imposed economic sanctions on Italy after Ethiopia had been attacked, and in due course Italy became a potentially hostile power, as well as Germany and Japan.

Revealingly, while advising Baldwin and Chamberlain against the use of force in support of Ethiopia, Fisher asked rhetorically: 'if Germany were to seize Memel or other areas beyond her eastern frontier, would England intervene?'[149] Fisher supported the policy of appeasement down to September 1938. As he wrote to Hankey at the time of negotiations leading to the Anglo-German naval treaty of 1935, he disliked and distrusted Germany—he was well aware of the contents of *Mein Kampf*—but 'that would never imply a refusal to parley'.[150] In 1937 he warmly approved an internal Treasury memorandum by Edward Hale, the head of a new Treasury division dealing with Foreign Office matters, which argued that it was possible that Germany was a 'beast of prey waiting for an opportunity to pounce', but it was also possible that the Nazi struggle was primarily one for self-respect, and that Germany was appealing to Britain as 'the least unfriendly boy in the school to release him from the Coventry to which he was sent after the war'.[151] Thus, while Fisher urged ministers to build up Britain's defences against Germany, he also opposed Vansittart's plans in May 1938 for a bigger propaganda department for the Foreign Office, agreeing with Hale that it was not possible to combine a policy of appeasement with a forward policy in propaganda.[152]

Down to 1939 the Treasury broadly supported what has been called 'economic appeasement', that is, attempts to secure peace by removing the economic imperatives for war—for example, by improving Germany's access to raw materials by restoring some of her colonies, or by lowering tariffs and encouraging multilateral trade. Britain, of course, stood to gain from a reintegration of Germany into the world economy, not only on account of German markets for British goods, but also because of the boost to multilateral world trade, and therefore demand for British shipping and the City's financial services.[153] Waley

---

[148]   Fisher to Baldwin and Chamberlain, 5 July 1935, Fisher Papers, 2/2.   [149]   Ibid.
[150]   Fisher to Hankey, 24 May 1935, CAB21/540.
[151]   Memorandum by Hale for Chancellor of the Exchequer, 10 Aug. 1937, on memorandum by the Foreign Secretary, Anthony Eden, on Anglo-German relations, T172/1801.
[152]   Ian Colvin, *The Chamberlain Cabinet* (1971), 133. Vansittart had been 'kicked upstairs' in 1938 as Chief Diplomatic Adviser at the Foreign Office.
[153]   See C. A. MacDonald, 'Economic Appeasement and the German "Moderates", 1937–1939: An Introductory Essay', *Past and Present*, 56 (1972), 105–35; Bernd-Jurgen Wendt, ' "Economic

commented in 1936 that the problem was to get Germany 'out of her lunatic asylum' (of autarky) 'into the fresh air'.[154] The Treasury took an active part, with the Bank of England, in annual negotiations down to 1939 to renew the Stand-still Agreement of 1931 on German debts, thereby making it possible to maintain lines of short-term credits issued to German banks, industry, and merchants by British banks to be used, at least in theory, to finance trade. However, although these negotiations reveal close links between the Treasury and City institutions, there is no evidence that there was anything conspiratorial in the nature of that relationship, or that policy was shaped by anything other than the Treasury's perception of the national interest (although that perception certainly included concern that no London acceptance house should fail as a result of German default).[155] When the colonial question was discussed in Cabinet in January 1938 Simon was one of the ministers who argued that there should be no settlement except as part of a comprehensive agreement with Germany.[156]

For Fisher, the sticking point in the policy of appeasement came when at Berchtesgaden, prior to the Munich Agreement, Chamberlain agreed to the transfer of German-speaking areas of Czechoslovakia to Germany. As Fisher told Wilson (and through him Chamberlain), Britain had won the approval of world opinion by trying to secure a settlement of the Sudeten Germans' dispute with the Czechs without territorial transfers, and it was vital not to jeopardize that approval by becoming '*particeps criminis* with the Germans' by even appearing to surrender to force. He called for the transfer of territory to be conditional on the basis of 'a *real* plebiscite in contrast to the farcical one engineered in the case of Austria'—which would require, *inter alia*, prior demobilization of the German armed forces; careful demarcation of the areas to be subject to the plebiscite; and time during which the 'hysteria' of the inhabitants would have cooled.[157] These were hardly the terms that Chamberlain secured at Munich.

On the other hand, Wilson continued to be associated with foreign policy after he took over from Fisher at the Treasury in mid-May 1939, being involved in informal contacts with Germany down to the outbreak of war.[158] It would seem that critics who associated the Treasury with Chamberlain's foreign policy were not wide of the mark, but it should be noted that Wilson, like Fisher, was a

Appeasement"—A Crisis Strategy', in Wolfgang J. Mommsen and Lothar A. Kettenacker (eds.), *The Fascist Challenge and the Policy of Appeasement* (1983), 157–72.

[154] Waley to Leith-Ross, 23 Oct. 1936, T160/729/F12829/2.

[155] Neil Forbes, 'London Banks, the German Standstill Agreements, and "Economic Appeasement" in the 1930s', *Econ. Hist. Rev.*, 2nd ser., 40 (1987), 571–87; Scott Newton, *Profits of Peace: The Political Economy of Anglo-German Appeasement* (Oxford, 1996), 60–5, 91.

[156] *DBFP*, 2nd ser., xix. 777–91.

[157] Fisher to Wilson ('for N.C.'), 17 Sept. 1938, Fisher papers, 2/7.

[158] Donald Cameron Watt, *How War Came: The Immediate Origins of the Second World War, 1938–1939* (1989), 247, 399–400, 403, 407.

supporter of rearmament.[159] Neither he nor Fisher regarded appeasement as a policy of weakness.

SUMMARY

The Treasury had to respond to severe challenges in the 1930s: first, an international depression of unprecedented severity, and then a world drift to war. So long as Chamberlain was Chancellor the Treasury had the advantage of a powerful ministerial head, but events were to force a relaxation of the Treasury's grip on policy and expenditure. Now that a simple Keynesian answer to the problems of unemployment or defence expenditure can no longer be assumed, the responses of the Treasury to the challenges that it faced do not seem to be so inadequate as they did when Keynes's ideas dominated historians' as well as economists' ideas. There was innovation in monetary policy after Britain had been forced off the gold standard, and, in the special circumstances of rearmament, even in fiscal policy. The pessimism that had marked much of the Treasury's thinking about unemployment for most of the decade was absent from Phillips's memoranda in the spring of 1939, as defence expenditure promised to bring the economy to full employment. However, the Treasury always thought in terms of government being about making choices as to the best use of scarce resources, and tried its hardest to maintain a tight grip on the purse-strings. As late as 1935 Treasury officials would have liked to have held to the Asquith doctrine, whereby central government borrowed only for revenue-producing purposes, and only the exigencies of the international situation persuaded them to borrow for defence expenditure from 1937. The fact that the Treasury found it hard thereafter to contain civil as well as military expenditure must have confirmed officials' worst fears about the propensity of politicians to spend when it was no longer necessary to balance the budget.

[159] Sir Thomas Padmore to Sir Edward Playfair, 4 Oct. 1974. Sir Thomas, who was Wilson's private secretary in 1939–41, gave a copy of the letter to the author.

CHAPTER SEVEN

The Second World War,
1939–1945

INTRODUCTION

Britain and France declared war on Germany on 3 September 1939, following Hitler's invasion of Poland. The National Government (long since indistinguishable from a Conservative one) remained in office for the first eight months of the war. At first, apart from the war at sea, there was little direct contact between British armed forces and the enemy, but then in April 1940 the Germans invaded Denmark and Norway and British forces sent to Norway were defeated. Following a debate on the conduct of the Norwegian campaign, Chamberlain resigned, and Churchill formed a coalition government of Conservatives, Labour, and the Liberals on 10 May. On the same day, the Germans invaded the Netherlands and Belgium. By 4 June the main British army had been evacuated from Dunkirk, leaving behind all its heavy equipment, and on 10 June Italy entered the war on Germany's side, extending the war to the Mediterranean and Africa. By 25 June France had fallen and, until Hitler invaded the Soviet Union on 22 June 1941, and the Japanese brought the United States into the war by attacking the American fleet at Pearl Harbor on 7 December 1941, the British Empire stood almost alone. It was not until late 1942 that the tide of war turned against Germany and its allies.

The dramatic events of 1940 were not without their consequences for the Treasury. Under Chamberlain the Treasury had continued to act as the central department of government, and strategy assumed that financial resources should be husbanded to enable Britain and France to wage war for three years, during which time, it was hoped, Germany would be weakened by blockade. The Allies wished to supplement their own war production by importing from the United States, and in November 1939 Roosevelt amended American neutrality legislation to the extent of allowing exports of munitions to the Allies, but only on a strict 'cash and carry' basis. On taking office Churchill, like Lloyd George in the First World War, rejected financial prudence and Britain's reserves were spent freely, in the hope that some arrangement could be made with the Americans for the continuation of supplies even after Britain had run out of dollars. In the event it was not until March 1941 that Congress passed the

Lend-Lease Act, which enabled President Roosevelt to provide war supplies for Britain without any cash payment.

Churchill's determination to wage war regardless of the cost was indicated by the fact that he did not at first include the Chancellor of the Exchequer in his War Cabinet. The allocation of physical resources, especially manpower, replaced financial budgeting as the means of establishing priorities between different defence programmes. Non-military aspects of policy, including economic policy, were co-ordinated by a Cabinet committee presided over by the Lord President of the Council. The reputation of the Treasury was not helped by the antipathy that Churchill felt towards its Permanent Secretary, Wilson, whom he did not forgive for his role as an 'appeaser', or by Labour ministers' belief that the Treasury was an obstacle to innovative social and economic policies and should be reformed.[1]

The fact that finance was no longer a determinant of strategy after May 1940 did not mean that the Treasury had no role to play in the war. Within Britain, financial policy aimed to assist in the transfer of resources without resorting to inflation. As Table 7.1 shows, a much higher proportion of central government expenditure was met from taxation than in the First World War. It was also easier to raise loans from the non-bank public because the early introduction of

TABLE 7.1. *Central Government Revenue*[a] *as a Percentage of Current Expenditure, 1913–1919 and 1938–1946*

Date	Revenue as percentage of expenditure
1913	99.4
1914	56.9
1915	23.3
1916	30.6
1917	35.6
1918	38.4
1919	69.7
1938	86.3
1939	69.2
1940	43.5
1941	48.3
1942	51.9
1943	56.1
1944	57.8
1945	64.2
1946	88.2

[a] Including national insurance contributions.

Source: C. H. Feinstein, *National Income, Expenditure and Output of the United Kingdom, 1855–1965* (Cambridge, 1972), table 12.

[1] John Colville, *The Fringes of Power: Downing Street Diaries, 1939–1955* (1985), 36, 124, 147, 226, 773.

direct controls and rationing limited opportunities for civil investment or consumption, and thereby the alternatives to lending to the government. Britain was more successful in suppressing inflation than any other major, non-communist, belligerent in the Second World War.[2]

TABLE 7.2. *UK Balance of Payments and Net Imports, 1938–1945*

	Balance of payments on current account (£000 m.)	*Lend-lease and mutual aid, less reciprocal aid (£000 m.)*	*Net imports (percentage of net national product)*
1938	−0.05	—	5
1939	−0.25	—	8
1940	−0.8	—	17
1941	−1.1	0.3	14
1942	−1.7	1.1	11
1943	−2.1	1.4	10
1944	−2.5	1.8	9
1945	−1.6	0.8	11

Sources: Columns 1 and 2: R. S. Sayers, *The Bank of England, 1891–1944*, 3 vols. (Cambridge, 1976), iii. 309, and id., *Financial Policy, 1939–1945* (1956), 499; column 3: Mark Harrison, 'Resource Mobilization for World War II: The USA, UK, USSR, and Germany, 1938–1945', *Econ. Hist. Rev.*, 2nd ser., 41 (1988), 189.

External financial policy aimed to ensure that Britain secured the supply of goods from overseas on the best possible terms, and this involved the Treasury in complex negotiations in the United States and other countries. As Table 7.2 shows, it was possible, as a result of external financcng, to wage war on a scale far beyond what could have been done from Britain's own output. The Lend-Lease Act of 1941, followed by the Mutual Aid Agreement of 1942 with the United States (and a similar agreement with Canada in 1943), provided munitions and supplies which were vital for the British war economy. While Britain supplied military stores to American forces under what was called 'reciprocal aid', the balance of goods supplied without cash payment was heavily in Britain's favour. Even so, Britain paid a high price for Churchill's policy of victory at any cost. Overseas investments valued at £1,118 million had to be sold or otherwise disposed of during the war, reducing Britain's money income from abroad from £168 million in 1938 to £50 million in 1945, during which period wholesale prices had increased by 75 per cent. Overseas debt increased from £476 million in August 1939 to £3,355 million in June 1945, while over the same period Britain's gold and dollar reserves fell from £605 million to £453 million.[3]

[2] Gyorgy Ranki, *The Economics of the Second World War* (Vienna, Cologne, and Weimar, 1993), ch. 5.
[3] Central Statistical Office, *Statistical Digest of the War* (1951), table 180; *Statistical Material Presented During the Washington Negotiations* (Cmd. 6707), PP 1945–6, xxi. 1.

Britain's position as the world's largest debtor cast a shadow over planning for post-war reconstruction.

Like war finance, reconstruction had international and domestic aspects. In August 1941 Churchill and Roosevelt signed the Atlantic Charter promising, *inter alia*, to collaborate to secure improved labour standards, economic advancement, and social security, and much effort was subsequently spent on Anglo-American plans to promote international trade and to reform the international monetary system. Planning for domestic post-war reconstruction began in late 1940, partly with a view to maintaining morale, with a distinct quickening of the pace after publication of the Beveridge Report on *Social Insurance and Allied Services* in November 1942. In 1944 the government issued white papers on post-war social insurance, health services, and employment policy, as well as passing a major education Act. The Treasury naturally tried to ensure that such planning took proper account of Britain's economic difficulties and did not undermine sound public finance. Within its own sphere, the Treasury had to give thought to the future management of the war-swollen National Debt.

PERSONALITIES, ORGANIZATION, AND ECONOMIC ADVICE

Even in the period down to May 1940 the Treasury suffered from having a Chancellor who found it increasingly difficult to cope with the responsibilities of his office. Simon had always had a tendency to be indecisive, and on the eve of war Wilson and Bridges told Hankey that the Chancellor had very much deteriorated.[4] The government was under pressure from October 1939 to appoint a Minister of War Economy, but Chamberlain rejected the idea, on the grounds that such an appointment would undermine his own authority as well as that of the Treasury.[5] Instead, Stamp, who was already surveying Britain's war plans from the economic point of view, was appointed (part-time) adviser on economic co-ordination; Wilson, as Permanent Secretary of the Treasury, chaired a committee, which included Stamp and permanent heads of departments concerned with economic affairs; and Simon chaired a Ministerial Committee on Economic Policy.

About the end of the year, doubts about Simon's adequacy for his job led the Governor of the Bank of England to advise the Prime Minister that there would have to be a change of Chancellor. On 2 January 1940 Chamberlain asked Stamp whether he would consider becoming Chancellor, an appointment that would have required an Act of Parliament to remove Stamp's peerage, to enable him to stand for election to the House of Commons. However, having consulted

[4]   S. Roskill, *Hankey Man of Secrets*, vol. iii (1974), 413.
[5]   356 HC Deb., 5s, 1939–40, col. 1336.

Norman and Wilson, Stamp declined, on the grounds that he was innocent of party politics and that his position as a director of the Bank of England would involve the Bank in party controversy. Simon, who had expected his budget in September to be his last, seems to have been unaware that Wilson and Hopkins hoped that he could be replaced, although by May 1940 he was looking forward to a change of ministerial office.[6]

Simon's successor, Kingsley Wood, seems to have owed his position to party politics. Like Simon, he was a lawyer and not a financial expert. However, Wood had helped Churchill to become Prime Minister, and, as someone who had been close to Chamberlain, his appointment could be seen as a concession to Chamberlain's supporters in the Conservative party. As Postmaster-General (1931–5), Minister of Health (1935–8), and Secretary of State for Air (1938–40), Wood had established a reputation for getting things done, and his capacity for hard work and his willingness to act upon the best advice were to be useful characteristics in a Chancellor. He was initially excluded from Churchill's War Cabinet, then became a member from October 1940, only to be excluded again in February 1942. He died suddenly in September 1943 at the age of 62.[7]

Wood's replacement, John Anderson, was one of the leading members of the War Cabinet. Born in modest circumstances, Anderson had advanced his career through sheer intellectual power, graduating with first-class honours in mathematics and natural philosophy from Edinburgh University, where he also attended lectures in economics, and taking first place in the Civil Service exam-ination in 1905. In the course of a brilliant career in the Civil Service he suc-ceeded Sir Warren Fisher as chairman of the Board of Inland Revenue in October 1919, served as the Treasury's representative in Ireland for twenty months from May 1920, and was appointed Permanent Under-Secretary at the Home Office in March 1922, all before his fortieth birthday. Entering politics in March 1938 as Independent MP for the Scottish universities, he held minister-ial office from November that year, being responsible for civil defence in Cham-berlain's government. Then, as Lord President of the Council in Churchill's government, he chaired the Lord President's Committee, which was the key Cabinet committee for home and economic policy from 1941. When Anderson became Chancellor of the Exchequer on 24 September 1943, Clement Attlee, the Labour party leader, became Lord President, but Anderson retained the chairmanship of the important Manpower Committee. Thereafter, he took a leading part in Cabinet discussions on both manpower and financial budgeting. However, these were in effect two separate jobs, and Treasury officials did not become involved in manpower planning. As a minister, Anderson retained the characteristics of a civil servant. Hopkins once said that, of all the Chancellors he had known, Anderson alone, when faced with the need to take a decision,

[6] J. H. Jones, *Josiah Stamp Public Servant* (1964), 335–9; Simon's diary, 28 Sept. 1939 and 8 May 1940, Sir John Simon papers, vol. 11.   [7] *The Times*, 22 Sept. 1943, 5.

was unconcerned with how it would affect his party or himself politically, being only concerned to find the right answer.[8] When the wartime coalition broke up on 23 May 1945, after the end of the war in Europe, Anderson remained at the Exchequer in Churchill's caretaker government until, following defeat in a general election, Churchill resigned to make way for a Labour Government on 26 July.

While Chamberlain was Prime Minister, the Permanent Secretary of the Treasury, Wilson, enjoyed great influence. He was regularly in attendance at Cabinet meetings and he had an office at 10 Downing Street. All this ceased as soon as Churchill became Prime Minister. Thereafter Wilson concentrated on his duties as Head of the Civil Service, directing the adaptation of the machinery of government to its wartime functions, and he retired at the earliest possible age, 60, in August 1942, although he would have been entitled to remain until he was 65. Wilson was unusual among senior civil servants in not having a public school or Oxbridge background—he had attended a Board school before entering the Patent Office as a boy clerk in 1898—and he was also the first Permanent Secretary of the Treasury to have a formal qualification in economics, having taken a B.Sc. (Econ.) by part-time study at the London School of Economics in 1908. He was described by one official of the period as 'a delightful man; a wise and good head of the Treasury'.[9] However, even officials who were very fond of him recalled that, so great was his confidence in his own intellectual processes, that he could not conceive that he could be—or could have been—wrong on any issue, even Munich.[10] Moreover, in the opinion of one official with considerable experience on the establishments side of the Treasury, Wilson lacked experience of the Treasury prior to May 1939, and did not know enough about the Civil Service as a whole for his job as its Head.[11]

Wilson's impending retirement led to a reopening of the old controversy over the Permanent Secretary's position as official head of the Civil Service, and in April 1942 some Cabinet ministers apparently favoured dropping the title 'Head of the Civil Service'. Wilson responded with a defence of the Treasury's position as the central department of government, with responsibility, not only for finance, but also for ensuring that the machinery of government was efficient. He claimed that a unified Civil Service had been created, as regards standards, and promotions and transfers between departments, without impairing civil servants' responsibility to their ministers. Ministers reconsidered the matter and decided not to change the existing arrangements.[12]

---

[8] John Wheeler-Bennett, *John Anderson, Viscount Waverley* (1962), esp. 300–1. For role of the Lord President's Committee in the machinery of government see D. N. Chester (ed.), *Lessons of the British War Economy* (Cambridge, 1951), 5, 8–13.   [9] Conversation with Sir Edward Playfair.
[10] Conversation with Sir Thomas and Lady Padmore, 15 March 1975.
[11] Conversation with Sir John Winnifrith.
[12] Manuscript note, n.d., covering Churchill to Lord President, 19 Apr. 1942, and 'The Official Head of the Civil Service', by Wilson, 22 Apr. 1942, T199/351.

Churchill and Wood agreed in April that Wilson's successor should be Sir Arthur Street, Permanent Under-Secretary of State at the Air Ministry, but in June the Prime Minister and the Chancellor decided that Hopkins should take over from Wilson. Hopkins's appointment was not uncontroversial. It was said to have caused 'some discontent' among members of the Labour party, who accused him of giving bad advice to Snowden in 1931. On the other hand, the 1922 Committee of Conservative backbenchers was said to have had pressed for Hopkins to be appointed instead of Street.[13] Hopkins was two years older than Wilson and, although widely admired for his financial expertise, he was described by Keynes as 'old and tired' by the time of his retirement on his 65th birthday, 28 February 1945.[14] Hopkins was succeeded as Permanent Secretary by Bridges, but Churchill wanted Bridges to continue to be Cabinet Secretary for as long as the war and peace negotiations should last, and it was not until after Attlee became Prime minister in July that Bridges could concentrate on his duties at the Treasury.

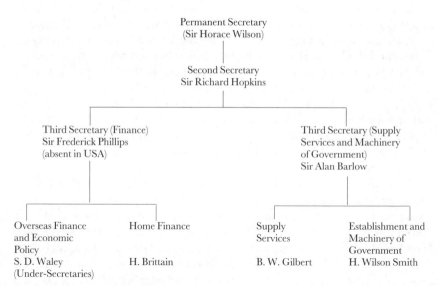

FIG. 7.1.   *Senior Treasury Officials, April 1942*

Life and work in the Treasury was not easy during the war: the Treasury building was hit by a bomb during the blitz in 1940, and ministers and officials shared with Londoners the inconvenience of disrupted transport services. The senior establishment of the Treasury was very overworked. Down to 1942

[13] Wood to Churchill, 7 Apr. and 16 June 1942, and 'Change of Heart at the Treasury', cutting from *Financial Times*, 22 June 1942, T199/351.

[14] J. Meade, *Collected Papers*, vol. iv, ed. Susan Howson and Donald Moggridge, *The Cabinet Office Diary, 1944–46* (1990), 26.

Hopkins was the sole Second Secretary, and much of the burden of running the department fell on him, particularly while Wilson was still acting as Chamberlain's confidential adviser. On the eve of the war, in an attempt to relieve Hopkins of part of his workload, Phillips had been promoted to a new rank of Third Secretary in charge of the finance side of the Treasury, and another of the Under-Secretaries, Sir Alan Barlow, had been promoted to be Third Secretary with responsibility for Supply Services (later extended to include machinery of government questions). From 1940, however, Phillips was the Treasury's representative in the United States, where he died in 1943 at the age of 59, and the most senior officials in London under Hopkins on the finance side were two Under-Secretaries: Waley, who dealt with overseas finance and economic policy, and Herbert Brittain, who dealt with home finance, including the budget (see Figure 7.1). When Hopkins was promoted to Permanent Secretary, Sir Wilfrid Eady, the Chairman of the Board of Customs and Excise, was brought into the Treasury as Second Secretary in charge of the finance side. Most of Eady's career had been in the Ministry of Labour or with the Unemployment Assistance Board, and he lacked Hopkins's grasp of economic issues, and failed to convince the Bank of England that he had a command of monetary issues.[15] Barlow and Phillips were also given the rank of Second Secretary in 1942, as was Bernard Gilbert in 1944, after he took over Barlow's responsibility for Supply Services.

As in the First World War, there was considerable delegation of financial authority to the service departments and those involved in war production. The Supply Services and establishment divisions tried to maintain at least the forms of Treasury control, but in the crisis of 1940 decisions were often required to be taken hastily. For example, one Saturday afternoon, on returning home from the Treasury (civil servants then still worked on Saturday mornings), Gilbert found himself being asked to authorize, on the telephone, expenditure of £100,000 to buy up all the aluminium pots and pans in the shops to be melted down for aircraft production. The caller, a temporary civil servant called Edwin Plowden, told him, 'somewhat untruthfully', as he later admitted, that Lord Beaverbrook, the Minister for Aircraft Production, wanted the authorization personally, and without enquiry into the technical problems of turning pots and pans into aircraft, Gilbert replied: 'Oh, very well, you can have it.'[16] Twenty-one years later Plowden was to give his name to a major report on how to reform the control of public expenditure by surveying planned expenditure several years ahead.

Even when there was no immediate threat of invasion, the Treasury's financial approval often merely confirmed decisions taken elsewhere on the allocation of manpower or raw materials. However, the Treasury was able to

[15] J. Fforde, *The Bank of England and Public Policy, 1941–1958* (Cambridge, 1992), 50.
[16] E. Plowden, *An Industrialist in the Treasury: The Post-War Years* (1989), p. xviii.

co-ordinate contract policy to ensure that there was much less scope for profiteering than had been the case in the First World War.[17] In contrast to 1914–18, the relaxation of Treasury control over expenditure extended to civil departments because, with the whole population experiencing the rigours of war, the need to maintain morale outweighed arguments based on financial prudence: thus, for example, from the summer of 1940 there were greatly enlarged Exchequer subsidies for school meals and for free or subsidized milk to children under five years of age and their mothers, with the level of expenditure determined by consumption.

The defeats of 1940 aroused criticism of the established machinery of government. In response, the Anderson Committee on the Machinery of Government was set up in 1942, with the Chancellor of the Exchequer (Kingsley Wood) as a member, imposing a substantial workload on the establishments divisions in the form of a wide-ranging review of existing practice and possible changes. Anderson's committee in general supported the role of the Treasury in Whitehall, but one important change was secured by the Foreign Secretary, Eden, in that it was decided to separate a reformed Foreign Service from the Home Civil Service.[18]

As regards economic advice, the nominal Chief Economic Adviser, Leith-Ross, had lost his link with the Treasury when he had been appointed Director-General of the Ministry of Economic Warfare on 30 August 1939. On the other hand, the Treasury recruited professional economists who had served on the Economic Advisory Council's Committee on Economic Information. Robertson was brought in by Phillips in August 1939 to help to manage the balance of payments, and by September Henderson was also working in the Treasury as an economic adviser. Then, at the end of June 1940, Keynes, who had been in poor health, accepted an invitation to become a member of a new Consultative Council that was to advise the Chancellor. Hawtrey's influence underwent a complete eclipse, his main employment during the war being the compilation of the Treasury's chronicle of wartime financial policy.[19]

Keynes had not expected that membership of the Consultative Council would require much effort on his part, but he was drawn increasingly into the work of the department. He was given his own room and secretary on 12 August, and he was asked to join the Chancellor's Budget Committee in October 1940. Subsequently he was much involved in negotiations with the United States, both as regards war finance and post-war reconstruction. He became a director of the Bank of England in September 1941, filling the vacancy brought about by Stamp's death in an air raid five months earlier, but was not

[17] See W. Ashworth, *Contracts and Finance* (1953).

[18] J. E. Cronin, *The Politics of State Expansion: War, State and Society in Twentieth-Century Britain* (1991), 143–4, 146–51.

[19] There are copies of Hawtrey's unpublished 'Financial History of the War' in the Public Record Office, London (T208/204) and at Churchill College, Cambridge (HTRY 2/1 and 2/2).

very active at the Bank, being more than sufficiently occupied at the Treasury. With no formal position in the Treasury hierarchy, he was free to pursue enquiries into any question in which the Treasury was involved, or in which he thought it should be involved, arousing admiration for his intellectual powers, even when he got his facts wrong. In particular, he got on extremely well with Hopkins, whose opinions he respected. Keynes's role as a economic statesman was recognized by his elevation to the peerage in June 1942 as Baron Keynes of Tilton.[20]

Neither Henderson nor Robertson could match Keynes's personality. More-over, as Henderson had grudgingly to admit, 'the currents of abstract economic thought' had been 'flowing in recent years in the direction of sympathy with the doctrines to which Lord Keynes is attached'.[21] On the other hand, Henderson's distrust of abstract reasoning, when it seemed to him to lose contact with common sense, was an attitude shared by administrative officials, who seem to have used his ideas to counter the Keynesian doctrines emanating from the Eco-nomic Section of the War Cabinet Office. Both Henderson and Robertson left the Treasury at the end of 1944, to take up chairs in Oxford and Cambridge respectively, but Keynes stayed on until his death in 1946.

The Second World War saw economists establish themselves elsewhere in Whitehall. The Stamp Survey team of Stamp, Clay, and Henderson, like the Economic Advisory Council's Committee on Economic Information (which was wound up at the outbreak of war), reported through the Cabinet Office, and it was to the staff of the War Cabinet Office that economists or statisticians were recruited from December 1939 to a new Central Economic Information Service. A year later the Central Economic Information Service was split into the Economic Section, headed first by John Jewkes and then (from 1941) Lionel Robbins, with about nine economists, and the Central Statistical Office, with a staff of about eight. The Economic Section was helped by the fact that it reported to the Lord President of the Council, who, as already noted, had dis-placed the Chancellor of the Exchequer as the senior minister dealing with eco-nomic policy. In addition Churchill established his own Statistical Section, first in the Admiralty and then in the Prime Minister's Office, under his personal adviser, Professor Lindemann (from 1941 Lord Cherwell), a physicist, with about half a dozen young economists on its staff. Economists were also recruited to the Board of Trade and to ministries dealing with the production of aircraft or munitions. Most of the economists who entered Whitehall during the war were young academics, who shared the same approach to economic analysis as Keynes. Among the more senior economists, even Robbins, who had held views opposed to those of Keynes during the slump, became a great admirer of him.

---

[20] D. E. Moggridge, *Maynard Keynes: An Economist's Biography* (1992), esp. 636–44, 650–7, 662–3. Con-versation with Sir Thomas and Lady Padmore, 13 Feb. 1978.

[21] H. D. Henderson, *Inter-War Years and Other Papers*, ed. Henry Clay (Oxford, 1955), 316.

From the point of view of a history of the Treasury, the significance of these developments was that ministers could obtain expert advice from diverse quarters, and it was therefore harder for the Treasury to impose its views on economic policy.[22]

However, it would be misleading to imply that economists established an unchallenged authority in economic policy. Administrative civil servants did not regard their own experience of public finance as irrelevant in discussions on policy. Moreover, the Treasury wished to draw upon practical experience as well as theory. Of the nine original members of the Chancellor's Consultative Council, only two, Henderson and Keynes, were economists, the others having financial, business, or Labour-movement backgrounds.[23] The Council does not seem to have been very active, but its composition indicates the range of economic knowledge which the Chancellor might wish to draw upon. The influence of the City was brought inside the Treasury through the appointment, on the advice of the Governor of the Bank of England, of Lord Catto, a director of the merchant banking firm of Morgan Grenfell, as Financial Adviser to the Chancellor, until Catto succeeded Norman as Governor in 1944.

Relations between the Treasury and the Bank of England were markedly better than in the First World War, but inevitably there were tensions, given the personalities concerned. For example, on 12 July 1940 the American Ambassador in London, Joseph Kennedy, reported to the Secretary of the US Treasury, Morgenthau, a conversation with Norman in which the Governor had told him that Phillips, the British Treasury's Third Secretary dealing with finance, knew nothing about a particular question relating to payments in dollars. Kennedy continued: 'very confidentially, for your information, he [Norman] added that he did not expect to live long enough to be able to explain it to him. This indicates that between the Bank of England and the Treasury good will is running high.'[24] It is unlikely that Phillips, who had been invited to talks with Morgenthau, would have regarded Norman's remark as helpful.

DOMESTIC MONETARY POLICY

The experience of the First World War had shown how government borrowing could be inflationary, contributing to industrial strife and political discontent, while burdening post-war budgets with high interest charges. At the request of

[22] See Alan Booth, 'Economic Advice at the Centre of British Government, 1939–41', *Hist. J.*, 29 (1986), 655–75; Alec Cairncross, 'Economists in Wartime', *Contemp. Eur. Hist.*, 4 (1995), 19–36; id. and N. Watts, *The Economic Section, 1939–1961* (1989); D. MacDougall, *Don and Mandarin: Memoirs of an Economist* (1987), ch. 2; Lord Robbins, *Autobiography of an Economist* (1971); E. A. G. Robinson, 'The Beginning of the Economic Section of the Cabinet Office', *Cambridge J. Econ.*, 15 (1991), 95–100; T. Wilson, *Churchill and the Prof.* (1995).   [23] For the appointment of the Council see T273/137.

[24] Morgenthau diary, vol. 282.

the Manpower Sub-Committee of the Committee of Imperial Defence, a memorandum on 'The Course of Prices in a Great War' had been prepared by Fisher, Hopkins, Leith-Ross, Phillips, and Hawtrey in 1928 and 1929, in consultation with the government's Chief Economic Adviser, Sir Sydney Chapman, and the statistician A. W. Flux (both at the Board of Trade), and Norman and Niemeyer, of the Bank of England. The memorandum stated:

The problem is to reduce the volume of money in circulation so as to correspond to a decreased supply of commodities at the same time as we increase the amount of employment and services called for from the nation.[25]

The officials believed that it would be necessary to control prices, profits, and wages, so as to reduce as far as possible the demand for bank credit; there would have to be import controls and rationing so as to reduce consumer expenditure and increase savings; and interest rates should be raised to the point where they produced 'pessimism in the country', thereby making savings available for government borrowing. Some increase in prices was inevitable but the Treasury would seek to 'bridge the gap' between revenue plus savings on the one hand, and war expenditure on the other, by increasing taxation and borrowing without creation of credit by banks.[26]

As noted in Chapter 6, it had proved to be possible, down to 1939, to finance rearmament by borrowing from the non-bank public, but by May that year the Bank of England was advising that drastic measures would soon be necessary, if resources were to be diverted from civil to military purposes. On the outbreak of war the Stock Exchange was closed for a week and steps were taken to restrict the use of capital for private purposes, thereby making funds available to the government. As Simon told the Cabinet on 8 September, all bodies collecting savings, such as insurance companies and building societies, were to be asked to invest a stated proportion of the money collected in government stocks, as were businesses in respect of undistributed profits, except where these were required for armaments work, and compulsory powers would be introduced if voluntary agreement failed. He advocated the speedy restriction of civil demand for capital goods and materials, such as steel, by direct methods of control. From 4 September application for new issues of securities had to be made to the Treasury, which was advised by the Capital Issues Committee, chaired by Lord Kennet (formerly Hilton Young), and, although government control of materials proved to be the principal means of diverting investment to war use, the Treasury and Bank of England were able to use the committee to ensure that the terms of new issues did not affect the desired price structure of gilt-edged loans.[27]

[25] 'The Course of Prices in a Great War', 15 May 1929, CAB57/2. The Treasury papers relating to the preparation of this memorandum are in T175/27.   [26] Ibid.
[27] 'The Exchange Position: Inflation', CAB66/1; R. S. Sayers, *Financial Policy, 1939–1945* (1956), 163–8.

In contrast to the First World War, and to the Treasury's expectations in 1929, there was to be no tendency for the rate of interest for war loans to rise. The Bank of England recommended in April 1939 that the maximum rates of interest for medium- and long-term issues should be fixed at the beginning of the war and adhered to thereafter.[28] Phillips's initial reaction was that such a course of action would be:

just bluff. In the last resort we have got to get the money. We cannot be sure of raising all we want by taxation and forced loans. Thus if the saver prefers to give up saving rather than accept a low rate of interest we can do nothing but raise the rate of interest.[29]

A Treasury Committee on the Control of Savings and Investment was appointed on 30 June, comprising two economists, Clay (from the Bank of England) and Robertson, Cornelius Gregg of the Board of Inland Revenue, and Phillips as chairman. At its meetings in July, Robertson explained how, under certain circumstances, Keynes's idea that government expenditure would create the savings necessary to finance the war without inflation could be made to work. Steps should be taken to ensure that, as far as possible, the rise in money national income reflected a rise in physical output. Both direct controls, such as rationing structural materials, and monetary controls, such as compulsory borrowing of undistributed profits, should be used to ensure that increased savings were placed at the disposal of the government. Even so, Robertson did not rule out some hardening of interest rates, whereas Keynes argued in the Economic Advisory Council's Committee on Economic Information and in the columns of *The Times* against any rise in interest rates.[30]

The Phillips Committee recommended that the authorities should offer a range of short- and medium-term securities designed to meet different needs and preferences of potential purchasers. As Howson has pointed out, in doing so the committee was drawing upon Keynes's liquidity preference theory.[31] This differed from earlier theories of the rate of interest by seeing it, not as the price that brought the demand for resources to invest into equilibrium with the readiness to abstain from consumption, but as the reward for parting with control over money for a stated period of time. According to Keynes, people held cash or assets, like Treasury bills, that could quickly be turned into cash, partly for current business transactions, partly for security, and partly because of uncertainty over future rates of interest. From this proposition he developed a theory of the term structure of interest rates. On the basis of this theory he argued that

[28] 'Borrowing in Wartime', note by the Bank of England, 14 Apr. 1939, Sir Henry Clay papers, box 66, Nuffield College, Oxford.

[29] 'Borrowing in Wartime', by Sir Frederick Phillips, 12 May 1939, ibid.

[30] 'The Problem of "Pre-War" Finance', by Robertson, 7 July 1939; draft 27th Report of the E.A.C. Committee on Economic Information, 17 July 1939, and 'Borrowing by the State', by Keynes, cuttings from *The Times*, 24 and 25 July 1939, all in Clay papers, box 66.

[31] Susan Howson, 'Cheap Money and Debt Management in Britain, 1932–51', in P. L. Cottrell and D. E. Moggridge (eds.), *Money and Power: Essays in Honour of L. S. Pressnell* (1988), 250–1.

it was possible for the monetary authorities to control interest rates by supplying demand for different types and maturities of securities, and by influencing expectations about long-term interest rates, if the monetary authorities were prepared to allow the quantity of money to increase to meet requirements for current business transactions, and to give up attempts to control the money market by funding the National Debt.[32]

The Phillips Committee agreed that high interest rates would not be very effective in curbing inflation, when firms would have large, undistributed profits to finance investment, and yet high interest rates would raise the cost of government borrowing. However, in its report the Committee avoided any recommendation as to what rates of interest should be, as these would depend, not only on monetary conditions, but also on controls over capital issues and physical controls over building materials.[33] As Robertson had said, the application of Keynes's theory depended upon circumstances.

Once reasonably effective exchange controls were in place in wartime, there was no need to use interest rates to defend the exchange rate. Bank rate, which had been raised from 2 per cent to 4 per cent on 24 August to help to stem a flight from sterling, came down to 3 per cent on 28 September and to 2 per cent on 26 October, more slowly than Norman thought to be necessary, but Hopkins and Phillips had preferred to wait until after the budget on 27 September. Likewise, interest rates had no function to play in regulating bank credit. Instead the Chancellor wrote to the Governor on 26 September to request the banks to restrict advances to the needs of defence production, exports, coal-mining, and agriculture, and the Treasury relied upon the co-operation of the banks rather than on detailed control from Whitehall, which would, indeed have been impossible.[34]

Meanwhile the Treasury and the Bank were discussing the terms on which to raise a long-term war loan. The gilt-edged market was very inactive in the first weeks of the war, partly on account of fears of inflation. Phillips remarked on 11 October that 'the Bank seem to be exceedingly pessimistic about the future, and I think that the time has come to shake them up'. Phillips and Hopkins wished to aim at raising £400 million in December, but, at a meeting with the Chancellor on 20 October, Norman said that it would be difficult to raise any large sum before government expenditure had increased the money in the hands of the market, and that a loan issued in December might be a failure. In subsequent discussions Norman said that the real question was whether the war was to be financed by cheap money or by dear money. He thought that for political reasons—presumably Labour opposition to bondholders receiving returns

---

[32] *JMK*, vii. 165–72, 194–207.

[33] Committee on Control of Savings and Investment, Report, paras. 15–16, 11 Aug. 1939, Clay papers, box 66.

[34] R. S. Sayers, *Bank of England, 1891–1944* (Cambridge, 1976), vol. ii. 573–5; id., *Financial Policy*, 184–6.

comparable to those in the First World War—there was no alternative to 3 per cent for a long-term loan, although on purely financial grounds he would have preferred 3½ per cent. At a meeting with the Chancellor and the Prime Minister on 26 October, Phillips dissented from Norman's advice that the announcement of the loan should be accompanied by a statement that subsequent loans would not be given more favourable terms. Notwithstanding the instruction he had received in July from Robertson on Keynes's monetary theory, Phillips still thought that, apart from forced loans, the monetary authorities would have to persuade the investor by offering terms that were just attractive enough. However, both Simon and Chamberlain agreed with Norman that it would be very difficult politically to justify a higher rate than 3 per cent, and the Governor's advice was accepted.[35]

Despite the failure of the public to take up all of a £300 million issue of 3 per cent War Loan 1955–9 in March 1940, the principle of a '3 per cent war' was adhered to, with 2½ per cent for medium-term issues (five to ten years). The monetary authorities set about attracting accumulating depreciation funds and undistributed profits from June 1940 by the tap method of issue, offering a variety of terms relating to yields and maturities, in line with the Phillips Committee's recommendations, and with a tendency for the terms to become slightly less generous with successive new issues, to persuade the public that interest rates would not rise. As an alternative to the sale of three-month Treasury bills yielding about 1 per cent, the cash reserves of the clearing banks were mopped up from July 1940 with the issue of non-negotiable, six-month Treasury deposit receipts on which 1⅛ per cent was paid. From the end of 1941 firms were encouraged to use idle funds to take up tax reserve certificates (in readiness for tax liability), so as to reduce government borrowing from the banks. Efforts were made throughout the war to mobilize small savings through the National Savings Movement, and altogether small savings amounted to almost 10 per cent of government debt in 1945.

However, the price to be paid for a 3 per cent war was that firms and financial institutions could not easily be persuaded to part with their money for long periods: overall, of the £14,800 million borrowed by the government within Britain during the war, £4,273 was represented by Treasury deposit receipts or Treasury bills, and £770 million by an increase in the fiduciary issue arising from Ways and Means advances from the Bank of England.[36] The money stock (measured as M1, comprising notes and coin in circulation plus sterling current accounts held by the private sector) increased by 149 per cent between 1939 and 1945, while total output of goods and services (GDP) at current prices increased by 67 per cent,[37] indicating a considerable overhang of spending power, with a

[35] Hawtrey, 'Financial History of the War', ch. 3(b), 3–5, T208/204.
[36] Sayers, *Financial Policy*, 223.
[37] Forest H. Capie and Alan Webber (eds.), *A Monetary History of the United Kingdom, 1870–1982*, vol. i

concomitant danger of an inflationary boom if direct controls were to be relaxed too quickly after the war, as they had been in 1919.

FISCAL POLICY

Starting with Simon's budget in September 1939, taxation was increased to keep borrowing to a minimum, and to reduce civil consumption so as to release resources for the war. However, it was only during the preparation of Kingsley Wood's budget of April 1941 that Keynes was able to persuade the Treasury to think in terms of a national income accounting framework. The problem of war finance can be presented in terms of the familiar identity:

$$Y = C + I + G + X - M$$

(where Y is total output of goods and services; C is total private consumption; I is total private investment; G is total government expenditure; X is total exports, and M is total imports). If total expenditure tended to exceed total output, prices of goods and services would rise until the nominal value of Y was equal to the sum of items on the right hand side. During the war, the imbalance between imports and exports was offset by disinvestment of gold reserves and overseas assets, by borrowing and (from 1941) by lend-lease supplies from the United States. Within Britain, if government expenditure increased by more than total output could be increased, the inflationary gap between total expenditure and output must be closed by a reduction in civil consumption and investment. Increasingly civil expenditure was restricted by direct controls, but it was not possible to ration all goods and services, and surplus purchasing power was absorbed by taxation, or by attracting funds to government loans, or as a result of rising prices.

Although taxation played a vital part in restricting wartime inflation, the Treasury's Budget Committee had to take other considerations into account: in particular, the distribution of the burden of taxation between social classes, and the effects of direct taxation on incentives. As always, party politics were another factor. Although Churchill's coalition government, with its strong Labour element, was not formed until 10 May 1940, Labour's influence on taxation had been felt since the spring of 1939. When a Bill for compulsory military training was introduced in April 1939, demands were made by the Opposition for 'conscription of wealth'. Chamberlain responded on 27 April by saying that proposals for a tax on profits arising from armament contracts were being prepared, and promising that, if war came, taxes on the very wealthy would be substantially increased; measures would be taken to deal with all profits arising

(1985), table 1(2); C. H. Feinstein, *National Income, Expenditure and Output of the United Kingdom, 1855–1965* (Cambridge, 1972), table 4.

from the war; and the possibility of a post-war levy on wartime increases in wealth would be studied.[38]

An armaments profits duty was enacted a few weeks before the war, but was merged with a new excess profits tax (EPT) in Simon's budget of 27 September. Both the duty and EPT were levied at 60 per cent on profits in excess of a standard based on pre-1938 profits. The first war budget also provided for an immediate increase in the standard rate of income tax from 5s. 6d. (27.5p) to 7s. (35p)—with a further increase to 7s. 6d. (37.5p) announced for 1940/1—while the top rate of surtax was fixed at 9s. 6d. (47.5p), making a marginal rate of 16s. 6d. (82.5p) on the highest earnings. Increases in indirect taxation, on the other hand, were restricted to the usual duties on alcohol, tobacco, and sugar. In the event, the vote of credit of £500 million for war expenditure was underspent, and revenue was higher than expected, but the resulting deficit of £768 million was only partially financed by the net increase in National Savings certificates and Defence Bonds (£109 million) and the immediate proceeds of 3 per cent War Loan (£99 million).[39]

Keynes's first attempt to influence future budgets was to publish articles on 'Paying for the War' in *The Times* on 14 and 15 November 1939. In them he advocated reducing consumption for the duration of the war, including consumption by the working class (who, he said, were responsible for three-fifths of all consumption), by means of higher taxation and a novel scheme for compulsory savings, as an alternative to inflation. Keynes discussed the material with Hopkins beforehand and subsequently sent him 'the statistical background out of which the particular magnitude of my proposals emerges'. There being then no official figures for national income, Keynes had had to compile his own data, in collaboration with Erwin Rothbarth, a statistical assistant in the Cambridge Faculty of Economics, the data being drawn mainly from earlier published estimates by Colin Clark.[40]

Hopkins was prepared to think in macroeconomic terms—as noted in Chapter 6, he and Phillips had decided in the spring of 1939 to wait for the economy to move towards full employment before increasing taxation—but as yet he saw no need for more precise national income data. His first concern was to meet opposition from the Labour movement to steps designed to reduce working-class living standards for the duration of the war. In December, when drafting a statement to the National Joint Advisory Council, in which representatives of employers, trade unions, and government considered problems of labour, Hopkins took up Keynes's ideas as follows:

The problem of war finance is . . . how to make at least one half of the total national output available for Government needs. In terms of money it may be said that the national

[38]   340 HC Deb., 5s, 1938–9, cols. 1349–51.
[39]   351 HC Deb., 5s, 1938–9, cols. 1365–73, 1377–9; 360 HC Deb., 5s, 1939–40, cols. 54–5.
[40]   *JMK*, xxii. 41–66;

income is perhaps £5,000 million a year and the national expenditure required for the war something like £2,500 million a year.[41]

The problem of war finance, he said, was not 'really a problem of inventing ingenious devices' (a reference to Keynes's scheme for compulsory loans). Rather the problem was one of persuading people of all classes to do without things they wanted, although 'justice demands that the first step should be heavy taxation of the rich'. Appealing to the trade union element in the Council, Hopkins closed his statement as follows:

an intimate acquaintance of the outlook on life of the ordinary man, and still more of the ordinary woman, is essential if we are to obtain that immense degree of willing sacrifice and of civilian courage which are likely to be the decisive factor in winning or losing the war.[42]

In late 1939, and for some months thereafter, however, the Labour movement was hostile to any deliberate reduction in working-class living standards. It was with a view to educating public opinion as well as influencing the Treasury that Keynes published a pamphlet, *How to Pay for the War*,[43] in February 1940. In it he used a national income accounting framework to set out where resources might be found for increased government requirements: £825 million from increased output compared with 1938/9; £450 million by diverting depreciation funds or normal new investment to government use; and £350 million from the sale of gold and foreign investment. Any government expenditure above the total for these sources (£1,625 million), he argued, must be at the expense of civilian consumption. Moreover, the £825 million earned by increasing output would increase demand for a limited supply of civilian goods and services. Given that government was likely to spend about £1,850 million more than in 1938/9, Keynes thought that about £1,000 million should be withdrawn from private consumption, through taxation or savings, a larger sum than he believed could be achieved through taxing the rich or through voluntary savings. He thus continued to advocate compulsory savings that could be repaid after the war, although in the name of social justice he now sought to counterbalance compulsory savings with universal family allowances of 5s. (25p) a week per child, payable to the mother.

Simon asked his officials to investigate Keynes's plan, but the budget on 23 April did not deviate from the classical formula based on central government accounts. The major innovation was a wide-ranging purchase tax on the sale of non-essential goods. A report on sales taxation by a joint committee of the boards of Inland Revenue and Customs and Excise had noted that such taxation was regressive, provoking Hopkins to comment:

[41] 'Draft Statement on War Finance for the National Joint Advisory Council', 6 Dec. 1939, T175/117 Feinstein subsequently estimated GDP in 1939 at current prices as £5,132 million on income data and £5,318 on expenditure data (*National Income, Expenditure and Output*, table 4).
[42] 'Draft Statement', by Hopkins, 6 Dec. 1939, T175/117.   [43] Reproduced in *JMK*, ix.

Of course it is; that is what we want. We have carried taxation of the rich and the middle classes to a point where further increases are exceedingly difficult to make. It is essential for war purposes to prevent consumption increasing further, and if possible to reduce it below its present level. The classes whom we have taxed account perhaps for one third of this consumption, and the remaining two-thirds is consumed by classes who are not affected or scarcely affected at all by our direct taxation. How in the name of wonder could one hope to find any solution in the form of taxation if such taxation were not regressive?[44]

Such blunt speaking did not find its way into the budget speech. On Hopkins's advice, the Chancellor avoided changes in indirect taxation that would increase the cost-of-living index, which was used by trade unions as a guide to wage demands (see next section). Total tax revenue for 1940/1 was estimated at £1,234, only £185 million more than in 1939/40, leaving an estimated £1,433 million to be met by borrowing. Rejecting Keynes's scheme for compulsory savings, the Chancellor said that compulsion would 'kill' the voluntary method of the National Savings Movement.[45]

Working-class sentiment also affected policy on profits. To meet criticism that increased profits were reaching shareholders, at a time when workmen were being asked to forgo wage increases, a Bill was introduced on 9 May to give the Chancellor power to limit the dividends of public companies. Hopkins had remarked that the alternative of raising EPT from 60 to 100 per cent was not really practical politics, because it would take away all incentive from businessmen to economize on resources or to take risks in new investment.[46] Nevertheless, when the Emergency Powers (Defence) Bill was introduced on 22 May, requiring all persons to place themselves and their property at the government's disposal, it was announced that there was to be no profit from the national emergency, and EPT was raised to 100 per cent during the Second Reading of the Finance Act.

The new balance of politics also affected income tax and surtax. On 5 July Kingsley Wood told Wilson, Hopkins, and Lord Catto, the new financial adviser to the Chancellor, that he hoped to reduce Labour's opposition to purchase tax by introducing as soon as possible a supplementary budget in which he would make substantial increases in direct taxation. The budget which followed on 23 July raised the standard rate of income tax by 1s. (5p) to 8s. 6d. (42.5p) in the pound, which with a top rate of surtax of 9s. 6d. (47.5p) in the pound, gave a marginal tax rate for the highest earners of 18s. (90p). Together with 100 per cent EPT and further increases in indirect taxation, the Chancellor's proposals were intended to raise additional revenue of £239 million, but they were not enough to save him from contemporary criticism, or subsequent

[44] Hopkins's comment on report sent by Sir Gerald Canny (chairman of the Board of Inland Revenue), 27 Nov. 1939, cited in Hawtrey, 'Financial History', ch. 3(c), 1, T208/204.

[45] 360 HC Deb., 5s, 1939–40, cols. 51, 78–81.

[46] Hopkins to Chancellor, 19 Mar. 1940, cited in Hawtrey, 'Financial History', ch. 3(c), 5, T208/204.

criticism by the official historian of financial policy, that his budget was inadequate from the point of view of preventing an inflationary expansion of the floating debt.[47]

In fact £239 million was rather more than Keynes, who was now a member of the Chancellor's Consultative Council, had estimated was required to curb inflation. On 11 July he had produced a list of sources of finance for the year from 1 July 1940, similar to what he had published in *How to Pay for the War*, and estimated that new revenue of £200 million must be raised if the government's expenditure (now forecast to be £3,500 million, compared with the April forecast of £2,667 million) was to be financed without inflation. Robertson, however, pointed out that Keynes's calculations depended upon a series of estimates or guesses, plausible alternatives to which could be combined to give a 'gap' to be filled by new taxation of £700 million, rather than £200 million. Accordingly, Hopkins observed that 'a doubt suggests itself whether his [Keynes's] method of approach is as useful as might appear'.[48] Keynes's national income analysis certainly found no place in the budget speech, which was again traditional in its approach.

Robertson's criticism highlighted the need to have more accurate data. Fortunately, the Central Economic Information Service had already persuaded the Cabinet Secretary, Bridges, to recruit two economists to compile official estimates of national income, the work being begun in the summer of 1940 by James Meade and Richard Stone. In the autumn the Central Economic Information Service proposed that it should make a thorough investigation of the country's financial potential, the budgetary gap, and various methods of restricting consumption. The Treasury's first response was to defend its own pre-eminence in financial policy, Hopkins apparently going so far as to say that he had strong objections to any investigation of the size of national income.[49] Keynes, however, persuaded Hopkins to support the exercise, and in January 1941 the Budget Committee had before it data that were later reworked as the white paper, *An Analysis of the Sources of War Finance and an Estimate of the National Income and Expenditure in 1938 and 1940*,[50] which was published in connection with the budget in April.

Keynes considered the budget for 1941/2 to be 'a revolution in public finance', in that for the first time a Chancellor used a national income accounting framework to estimate the additional revenue that must be raised if there was to be no inflation. Overseas expenditure was excluded, as was 'overseas disinvestment' (the latter including increases in sterling balances due to overseas

[47] Sayers, *Financial Policy*, 56–7.

[48] *JMK*, xxii. 202; 'Mr Keynes' "Notes on the Budget" ', by Robertson, 15 July, and 'Mr Keynes on the Budget Problem', by Hopkins, 17 July, 1940, T171/354.

[49] Robbins to Keynes, Oct. or Nov. 1940, printed in *JMK*, xxii. 326–7.

[50] Cmd. 6261, PP 1940–1, viii. 387.

suppliers, as well loans raised abroad and sales of overseas assets). Calculation of the inflationary gap was thus confined to the amount of expenditure requiring domestic finance. Using the national income data, the amounts of voluntary saving and of revenue at existing tax rates were estimated, and the difference between total money demand and the value of all goods and services available was taken as the inflationary gap that would have to be filled with increased taxation or increased savings. Keynes found that Wood, Wilson, and Hopkins were ready to be persuaded about the value of this approach, and that Catto was also helpful. However, Wilson also noted Henderson's advice that there was a danger that too steep an increase in direct or indirect taxation in an attempt to close the inflationary gap might stimulate demands for higher wages, and that it was better to impose only such taxes as the public would accept without such a reaction, and to rely on rationing and controls to stabilize prices.[51]

While the 1941 budget did mark a new departure, the statistical basis of the national income accounts was rough and ready. Moreover, the national income data were compiled in money terms on the basis of calendar years, but were used for the coming financial year without adjustment for rising prices.[52] There was the usual uncertainty as to what government expenditure would be in wartime. In the words of the official historian, 'the exact burdens placed upon the taxpayers continued to be the outcome of the collective judgement of a handful of men depending in quite large measure upon common sense and the "hunch" that eludes analysis'. What was new was the acceptance by the Budget Committee of the Keynesian arithmetic 'as one weighty element—but only one element—in the emergence of the decisive hunches'.[53] The inflationary gap was estimated to be £500 million, but Keynes thought that 'if upwards of £300 million' were raised in additional taxation, the remainder of the gap could be left to disinvestment of stocks, higher prices outside the cost-of-living index, and some increased voluntary saving.[54] However, confronted by Churchill's hostility to what the Prime Minister considered to be severe tax proposals, the Chancellor decided to aim at £250 million rather than 'upwards of £300 million' in new taxation.[55] Even the sum of £250 million was the additional yield for a full year from the time the tax changes would be implemented, that is the autumn of 1941, by which time the inflationary gap might well have increased; the additional yield of tax changes in the financial year 1941/2 was estimated to be only £150 million.[56]

[51] *JMK*, xxii. 289–92, 354; 'Notes on the Budget', by Henderson, n.d., and 'The Next Budget', by Wilson, 10 Jan. 1941, T171/355.
[52] Nicholas Kaldor, 'The White Paper on National Income and Expenditure', *Econ. J.*, 51 (1941), 181–91.   [53] Sayers, *Financial Policy*, 69.
[54] *JMK*, xxii. 293–4.
[55] Sayers, op. cit., 78; Wood's amendments to 'Budget Policy Peptonised and Predigested for the P.M.', T171/356.
[56] Michal Kalecki, 'The Budget and Inflation', in Oxford University Institute of Statistics, *Studies in War Economics* (Oxford, 1947), 86–7.

The 1941 budget increased the standard rate of income tax from 8s. 6d. (42.5p) to 10s. (50p) in the pound, while the earned income and personal allowances were reduced so as to widen the number of people liable to income tax. Tax paid as a result of the reduction in earned income and personal allowances was to be treated as a credit to be repaid at a time of the government's choosing after the war. The amount involved in the 1941 budget was £125 million, and the annual average actually raised in this way during the war was £121 million, far short of the figure of £600 million a year that Keynes had envisaged for compulsory savings in *How to Pay for the War*.[57]

The scope for fiscal policy for the rest of the war was limited by the disincentive effects of high rates of direct taxation. Before the war liability to direct taxation had been largely confined to the middle and upper classes, but the reduction of allowances, and wartime increases in wages, brought many workers within the ambit of income tax. Six months after the first 'Keynesian' budget in 1941 the Ministry of Information was seriously concerned that the increase in income tax rates was reducing the willingness of workers to undertake overtime. Inland Revenue and Treasury officials were united in opposing any further increase in income tax, and even Keynes appears to have admitted that, with regard to major financial measures, the Chancellor had shot his bolt.[58] Arguments relating to disincentives also applied to the top marginal rate of direct taxation (income tax plus surtax) of 19s. 6d. (97.5p) in the pound and 100 per cent EPT. The latter removed any financial incentive to make efficient use of resources or to take risks, and the 1941 budget recognized the need to restore incentives by promising that 20 per cent of EPT paid during the war would be repaid afterwards, on condition that the refund was ploughed back into a business.

Although the marginal rates on high earning were much higher during the Second World War than the First, the major contrast between the two wars was the extent to which taxation was imposed on the working class. Down to 1939 most employees had paid their income tax in two half-yearly instalments, but the extension of the tax to people unaccustomed to accumulating bank balances made it necessary to develop some means of deducting tax at source. As a result, the pay-as-you-earn system (PAYE), which had been introduced in embryo in 1940, was extended to all incomes under £600 in 1944. The limits of direct taxation having already been reached, new sources of revenue had to be found from 1942 in indirect taxation, including increases in purchase tax and entertainments duty, as means of absorbing what Hopkins in 1943 called the 'surplus purchasing power which obstinately persists in finding its outlet in consumption goods of a luxury or semi-luxury character instead of in personal savings'.[59]

[57] Sayers, *Financial Policy*, 84.
[58] *JMK*, xxii. 355–7; 'The Budget 1942', by H. Wilson Smith, 5 Nov. 1941, and 'Notes by the Board of Inland Revenue', n.d., T171/360.
[59] 'The Next Budget', by Hopkins, 13 Feb. 1943, T171/363.

PRICES AND WAGES POLICY

The war also saw the Treasury becoming directly involved in prices and incomes policy. Government's concern with prices focused on two issues: (1) a rise in the Ministry of Labour's cost-of-living index was liable to be used by trade unions as a reason for wage increases, which, if granted, would raise costs; (2) higher prices would lead to claims of profiteering, with consequent social and political unrest. Some rise in prices of imported goods early in the war was inevitable, given that sterling had been devalued against the dollar by 14 per cent in August 1939, and given wartime shipping shortages. Indeed, Phillips argued that some rise in prices was justifiable, as most wage rates in 1939 had been fixed when prices had been higher than those then prevailing.[60] The important question was, how could a vicious spiral of rising prices and wages be avoided?

The 1929 memorandum on 'The Course of Prices in a Great War' had referred to the possibility of a 'fixation of wages', but by 1939 the Ministry of Labour had persuaded planners in the Committee of Imperial Defence's Man-power Sub-Committee that wage control by government was unthinkable, and that reliance must be placed on the moderation of the trade unions. A standing interdepartmental committee, with representatives of the Treasury, the Board of Trade, and the ministries of Food, Labour, Supply, and Transport, was set up in September 1939 to keep prices under review. Price controls were operated by the Board of Trade, but prices could not be fixed when costs rose, unless subsid-ies were available. By January 1940 Hopkins accepted that the rise in the cost of living had become the chief influence in stimulating claims for higher wages, and that the cost of stabilizing the cost-of-living index (currently £70 million a year in food subsidies) would be worth bearing for some fixed period in return for a standstill agreement on wage claims. Phillips emphasized that a vicious inflationary spiral could also be brought about by a failure to finance the war from taxation and loans from the non-bank public, and that the cost of food sub-sidies might be the last straw. Hopkins, however, was less apprehensive about the burden on future budgets, believing that, with war generating increased employment, national income would grow substantially, and with it the Chancellor's revenue. On the other hand, Phillips was correct when he pointed out that artificially low prices stimulated demand and that price stabilization through subsidies must be restricted to items which were subject to rationing, or where, as with bread, demand was largely independent of price.[61]

By the summer of 1940 a policy of subsidizing rationed goods that were within the cost-of-living index, and taxing those outside it, had emerged, but it was not until rationing was firmly in place that the Chancellor committed the

---

[60] 'Cost of Living', MSS note for Wilson, 18 Oct. 1939, T273/297.
[61] Phillips to Hopkins, 30 Dec. 1939 and Hopkins to Wilson, 2 Jan. 1940, T175/117.

government in his 1941 budget to stabilizing the index at its existing level of 25 to 30 per cent above the September 1939 level. Even then no explicit concessions were sought from the trade unions, although Wood made clear that if wage rates continued to rise the government would have to abandon its price stabilization policy.[62] The fact that food accounted for 60 per cent of the index placed particular importance on subsidies administered by the Ministry of Food, and there was ample scope for disagreement between that ministry and the Treasury on the scale of subsidies and how they should be distributed; on the other hand, the Ministry of Food and the Treasury were allies in interdepartmental battles to keep the guaranteed prices offered to farmers by the Ministry of Agriculture within bounds.[63]

The policy of price stabilization was not a complete success, in that the Ministry of Labour's index of wage rates rose by 23 per cent between 1941 and 1945, whereas the cost-of-living index rose by 2.3 per cent over the same period (see Figure 7.2). However, given that the economy was at full employment from 1941, perhaps all that could be expected was some moderation in claims for higher wages, compared with what might otherwise have been expected. The policy of price stabilization was only possible because the cost-of-living index was based on Edwardian working-class patterns of expenditure, leaving out, or giving little weight to, a wide range of goods and services that could be subject to indirect taxation. While the official cost-of-living index remained stable for the rest of the war, a more complete index covering all items of consumers' expenditure rose by 17 per cent between 1941 and 1945.[64]

The cost of subsidies caused continuing concern at the Treasury. In April 1944 the Chancellor, Anderson, noted the upward trend in successive budgets, from £70 million in 1940, to £140 million in 1941, and to £190 million in 1943, and warned that a cost-of-living figure of 25 to 30 per cent above pre-war could no longer be regarded as sacrosanct. The cost of living must be allowed to rise where increases in wages had raised the cost of goods, as in the case of coal. Anderson told Parliament that the index should be allowed to rise to 30 to 35 per cent above pre-war, which would offset only about a quarter of the increase in wage rates over the same period.[65] Within the Treasury officials calculated in December 1944 that the effect of removing all subsidies would be to increase the cost-of-living index to about 55 per cent of pre-war, and that this might set in motion an inflationary spiral of wages chasing costs. The upshot was a decision to maintain subsidies into the post-war period until the supply and manpower position became easier, with a view to holding the index at 35 per cent above pre-war, although something like 50 per cent might be the eventual

[62] 370 HC Deb., 5s, 1940–1, cols. 1321–2.
[63] See R. J. Hammond, *Food*, vol. i (1951).
[64] Feinstein, *National Income, Expenditure and Output*, table 61.
[65] 399 HC Deb., 5s, 1943–4, cols. 659–63.

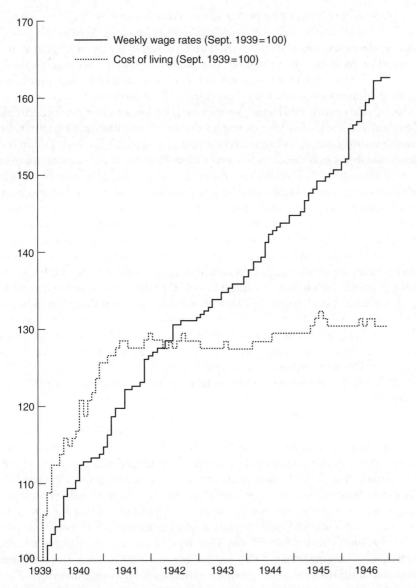

Fig. 7.2. *The Treasury's Record of Wage Rates and the Cost of Living, 1939–1946*
Source: T171/389.

figure.[66] The problem was one that was to continue to exercise Treasury officials into the 1950s.

[66] Hawtrey, 'Financial History', ch. 14, pp. 63–4, T208/204.

EXTERNAL FINANCE: PREPARING FOR A THREE-YEAR WAR

As the Treasury had warned in the 1930s, Britain's ability to wage war was limited by its ability to finance the purchase of raw materials and munitions overseas. There were three ways in which Britain could pay for such purchases: with gold and foreign exchange; by sales of British-owned foreign securities which could be acquired by the government; and by borrowing. In 1914 Britain had had a balance-of-payments surplus on current account, and had been able to divert this balance to war purposes. In the late 1930s, in contrast, Britain had had a balance-of-payments deficit on current account, and measures had to be taken immediately to restrict non-essential imports and to stimulate exports. Providing Britain could maintain financial confidence abroad, other countries, particularly those in the sterling area, would be willing to accumulate sterling balances instead of requiring immediate payment for goods and services. However, Britain was prohibited from borrowing in the United States by the Johnson Act, and Britain's ability to draw upon American resources appeared to be restricted to its gold and dollar reserves (about £450 million in September 1939), securities in British hands that could be sold for US dollars (estimated at about £250 million), plus exports.[67] Chamberlain himself hoped that, if the war did last three years, the United States would provide some financial aid, and that 'the only thing that matters is to win the war, even though we go bankrupt in the process'.[68] The advice from Lord Lothian, the ambassador in Washington, to Simon in February 1940 was that it would take time to educate American public opinion and that there would probably be prolonged resistance to a repeal of the Johnson Act.[69]

It is with these factors in mind that one has to view the Treasury-inspired decision by the Cabinet in February 1940 to order a review of the possibility of scaling down armament programmes. In the official history of the Second World War, this move is discussed in terms of curtailing dollar expenditure, with the remark that 'it might be equally effective as a way of losing the war'.[70] In fact, even from the Treasury's point of view, the issues were not purely financial. For most of the pre-war period of rearmament, priority had been given to the air force and navy, and until the spring of 1939 the army's rearmament programme had provided for only five divisions. In February 1939, however, the Cabinet had approved a ten-division programme and in April this had been raised to thirty-two divisions. From the outbreak of war some members of the War Cabinet, notably the First Lord of the Admiralty, Churchill, wished to commit Britain to supporting France with fifty-five divisions, and it was clearly

[67] 'The Exchange Position: Inflation', memorandum by the Chancellor of the Exchequer, 8 Sept. 1939, CAB66/1.   [68] Simon diary, 23 Sept. 1939, Simon papers, vol. 11.
[69] Lothian to Simon, 3 Feb. 1940, Simon papers, vol. 86.
[70] W. K. Hancock and M. M. Gowing, *British War Economy* (1949), 116.

important to consider whether the plans, actual and prospective, of three defence departments could be met from the available resources, financial and otherwise.

Already in December 1939 the Stamp survey of Britain's resources in relation to the scale of the war effort had indicated provisionally that the existing programmes, if carried out, would lead to greater expenditure abroad than would be justifiable under a policy of husbanding foreign exchange resources over a three-year war. Moreover, as Hopkins warned the Ministerial Committee on Economic Policy, the Treasury expected that the strain on foreign exchange resources would increase in the second and third years of the war, by which time productive capacity would be fully occupied and, as a recent manpower report showed, additional service demands would have to be supplemented by importing armaments.[71]

By 13 February 1940, when the question of relating programmes to resources was discussed by the Cabinet, it was hoped that £100 million might be raised in loans from the Empire or sales of overseas assets (other than dollar securities), and that a further £50 million might be raised from a net increase in exports. However, the net adverse balance of payments on current account was likely to be £400 million, which implied a reduction of £250 million in the foreign exchange reserves, whereas Stamp and the Treasury had agreed that the reserves should not be run down by more than £150 million in the first year of a three-year war. Wilson, who was present at the Cabinet meeting, warned ministers that the consequence of current levels of expenditure abroad would be a reduction in foreign exchange reserves below what was regarded as a margin of safety. Simon drew attention to Stamp's warning that the adoption of armaments programmes that were greater than the country's resources of industrial manpower could fulfil would interfere with the orderly execution of war plans, and he suggested that the fifty-five-division programme should be met either by adopting a lower standard of equipment or by delaying its completion. As Churchill, probably advised by Lindemann, had pointed out four days earlier at the Military Co-ordination Committee of the War Cabinet, the army's planned scales for artillery and wastage of ammunition were well above what was likely to be needed in war, and the Secretary of State for War had accordingly initiated an investigation into the scales of initial equipment and wastage rates. All the Cabinet did on 13 February was to invite the Air Ministry and Admiralty to do likewise. At the same time the Ministry of Supply was authorized to proceed with factories necessary for the fifty-five-division programme.[72] As always, the Treasury was concerned to persuade ministers to decide upon priorities in relation to available resources. In the event, the Churchill government did make a fifty-five-division army its basis for planning in May 1940, but

---

[71] 12th conclusions, 15 Dec. 1939, CAB72/1.
[72] War Cabinet minutes, 13 Feb. 1940, CAB65/5; M. M. Postan, *British War Production* (1952), 134.

that decision was made in the hope that somehow the necessary supplies from the United States would be available.

The shortage of foreign exchange made it necessary to impose exchange controls to ensure that no foreign currency was wasted on unnecessary imports or used for unauthorized capital exports, and from the outbreak of war all payments to non-residents were subject to approval by the Treasury. However, this restriction was not applied to countries that agreed to keep their currency reserves in London and to enforce exchange control in common with the United Kingdom. Within this sterling area all private residents were required to surrender foreign exchange earned from their transactions with non-sterling area countries, in return for balances in their national currency. Any excess foreign exchange was sold by the monetary authorities in the rest of the sterling area to the Bank of England, in return for Treasury bills or British government securities. The Bank thereby came to hold the foreign exchange reserves of the sterling area as a whole, and the monetary authorities of the rest of the sterling area could draw upon the central reserves by selling their sterling assets to the Bank for foreign exchange.

The whole issue of exchange controls was complex and technical, and the Treasury relied heavily upon the expertise of the Bank of England, although Keynes was valued as an independent source of advice. In September 1939 Phillips asked him for suggestions on exchange control, and Keynes, drawing upon his experience in the First World War, recommended controls only over the most important transactions, leaving the less important to the free market, as long as this policy did not cost too much foreign exchange. By February 1940, however, as a result of his own activities as an investor, Keynes had become aware of loopholes in the exchange controls as they were then operated and, in consultation with Bank of England officials, he prepared memoranda for Phillips in May and June on how they might be extended and tightened. He estimated in July 1940 that the delay in imposing the strictest possible controls might have cost £50 million in gold and dollar resources, but the Bank seems to have regarded this figure as doubtful and highly controversial.[73] Such a sum, representing as it did about 7 per cent of Britain's gold and dollar resources plus marketable US securities, would not have been insignificant, but it was to be dwarfed by the outflow arising from purchases of munitions in the United States in the summer of 1940.

EXTERNAL FINANCE: DEPENDENCE ON THE UNITED STATES

As early as 28 February 1940 Waley warned that, with Britain's gold and dollar reserves being expended at a rate of £200 million a year, the prospect was that

---

[73] *JMK*, xxiii. 2–3. Phillips's correspondence from Sept. 1939 to May 1940 is in the Keynes papers W/3, King's College, Cambridge.

Britain would have to capitulate before the end of the fourth year of the war, because she could no longer buy food and raw materials, unless, of course, the Allies had been victorious by then.[74] Initially the United States had been regarded only as a marginal source of supply for aircraft and munitions, in order to conserve dollars for food, raw materials, and machine tools. However, from May 1940 financial prudence was thrown to the winds. Substantial orders for aircraft had already begun to be placed in the United States in the spring of 1940, and the loss of most of the army's heavy equipment at Dunkirk led to large orders in the United States for replacements. When France fell, French orders for aircraft and munitions were taken over, placing a sudden and enormous burden on Britain's gold and dollar reserves.

The British and US treasuries had been in contact about the marketing of British-owned securities, and the financing of British government purchases, in America since October 1939. The Secretary of the US Treasury, Morgenthau, wished to be kept informed about these transactions, and the Chancellor of the Exchequer had agreed to open a special account with the Federal Reserve Bank of New York, to which Morgenthau should have confidential access. On 13 May Morgenthau invited Phillips to come to Washington to discuss matters that needed 'smoothing out' between the two treasuries,[75] and Phillips eventually sailed on 2 July. Morgenthau was anxious to have much fuller information than he had so far been given about Britain's resources to finance her purchases in the United States, and Phillips presented him and President Roosevelt with figures for Britain's prospective dollar requirements on the one hand, and her gold, dollars, dollar securities, and prospective export earnings on the other. The figures left no doubt that Britain would need massive financial assistance in the first half of 1941, but Phillips realized that no change in the American policy of 'cash and carry' could be expected until after the presidential election in November 1940. The conclusion he drew was that dollar expenditure must be kept within limits that would ensure that Britain's resources would not run out before the President could act.[76]

Consequently, on 21 August the Treasury warned the War Cabinet that Britain's gold and dollar reserves had fallen from £380 million at the beginning of July to £292 million in mid-August, at which rate Britain would run out of gold by the end of December. Further US dollar resources represented by British holdings of American securities (about £200 million altogether) could be marketed only gradually and with difficulty. 'Scraping the pot', by selling British-owned direct investments in the United States (which Morgenthau thought were worth about another £200 million) or even works of art, and the

[74] Waley to Phillips, 28 Feb. 1940, T177/52.
[75] Morgenthau diary, vol. 220, 30 Oct. 1939, and vol. 262, 13 May 1940.
[76] Telegram from Phillips; 'Conjectural Balance of Payments between the United Kingdom & USA', and 'Dollar Requirements of the United Kingdom Exchange Control', all 17 July 1940, and report by Phillips on his visit, n.d., Foreign Office papers (hereafter FO) 371/25209.

transfer to Britain of gold owned by Empire or foreign countries, might stave off bankruptcy, but the prospect was one of complete financial dependence on the United States.[77]

Members of the Roosevelt administration, especially Morgenthau, wished to prevent Britain's defeat by Germany, but they also wished to promote the interests of the United States. Morgenthau was suspicious of the way in which the sterling area operated to Britain's advantage in trade, and hoped to secure for the United States a dominant voice in international monetary relations. For that reason the US Treasury wanted to ensure British financial dependence by severely limiting the level of British gold and dollar reserves. On the other hand, the US State Department hoped to pressurize Britain into abandoning imperial preference and any other form of discrimination against American goods, and therefore wanted Britain to be left with sufficient reserves to be able to adopt freer trade policies after the war. At the highest level, political relations were of course a matter for Churchill and Roosevelt, but the British Treasury was involved throughout the war in economic diplomacy with a view not only to securing supplies from the United States but also to minimizing the political price that would have to be paid for them.[78]

Following Roosevelt's electoral victory in November 1940, Morgenthau invited Phillips to return to Washington to discuss financial assistance. Phillips's instructions were to seek a direct grant from the American government to pay for aircraft and munitions, on the grounds that Britain was the United States' advanced defence line against the fascist powers. Mere repeal of the Johnson Act was no longer sufficient, since the sums that Britain would be able to borrow on its own credit in the United States would be too small to finance Britain's expanded war effort for more than a brief period. It was realized in the British Treasury that Congress was bound to object to giving a blank cheque, and that the price of a grant would be some measure of American control on how it was spent. At Keynes's suggestion, however, Phillips was to point out that any repayments for financial assistance could only be in kind, which would require some rigid control on trade at the cost of disruption of normal trade. It was also known in London that, to forestall criticism in Congress, the American government would require Britain to show that it had exhausted its available resources. Keynes, drawing upon his experience of 1917–18, argued that Britain should not be so stripped of its dollar resources that it could not be self-supporting in respect of purchases of food and raw materials, financial assistance for which would be harder to justify to American opinion.[79]

[77] 'Gold and Exchange Resources', 21 Aug. 1940, CAB66/11; J. M. Blum, *From the Morgenthau Diaries*, (Boston, Mass., 1959, 1965, and 1967), ii. 169–71.
[78] For a critical account of Anglo-American economic relations during the war see Alan P. Dobson, *US Wartime Aid to Britain, 1940–1946* (1986).
[79] The drafts of Phillips's instructions are in T175/121.

On arrival in Washington in December, Phillips found his talks with Morgenthau 'pretty heavy going', leading him to observe that: 'I regret that some of the gentlemen who thought that the more we asked for the more we were certain to get were not here to try their hands at it.'[80] Morgenthau insisted that the British should turn their 'pockets inside out', giving him full details of their remaining assets in the United States and Latin America, and what price they were prepared to take for them.[81] On 17 December Roosevelt himself came up with the idea of lend-lease, whereby the United States would 'eliminate the dollar sign' from aid to Britain. Material and equipment would be handed over to Britain, if the President thought that this was the best way of employing them for the 'defense of the United States', as the Lend-Lease Act of March 1941 put it. In return the United States would receive, not money, but some 'consideration' to be negotiated. In order to persuade Congress that Britain had really exhausted its own resources, however, Morgenthau insisted on a political gesture, which took the form of the sale of a direct British investment, the Viscose Corporation of America, which was owned 97 per cent by Courtaulds. Courtaulds valued its investment at $120 million; American bankers advised that $75 million was the current market value, but the sale, which was rushed through within a week, realized only $54 million.[82] Wilson objected to this 'disorderly procedure', whereby valuable investments were sold at 'jumble prices', making the Treasury look 'ridiculous',[83] but political considerations outweighed such objections.

There remained the problems of how British purchases were to be financed until Congress voted the first lend-lease appropriation on 27 March, and what 'consideration' the United States should receive. The first issue was urgent; the latter less so, but was ultimately more important, as it would indicate what use the United States would make of its power of the purse. Sales of assets, a transfer to the United States of South African gold, and a loan from the exiled Belgian government were not enough to cover British purchases before lend-lease became law. Consequently, Morgenthau had to arrange for the American government's Reconstruction Finance Corporation, which had originally been set up to promote the New Deal, to extend a loan to Britain on the security of British-owned assets in the United States. Even so Britain was left without what the Treasury regarded as the minimum gold and dollar reserves necessary for a working balance, given that Britain's reserves were those of the sterling area as a whole. The Treasury thought that the minimum amount was $600 million (£150 million), but the actual figure in June 1941 was $150 million (£37.5 million).[84]

One way in which the financial strain on Britain could be eased was for the American government to take over contracts already placed by Britain ('the old

[80] Phillips to Hopkins, 13 Dec. 1940, ibid.   [81] Blum, *From the Morgenthau Diaries*, ii. 204.
[82] Sayers, *Financial Policy*, 373–4, 388–90.
[83] 'Direct Investments in U.S.A.', 20 Feb. 1941, T273/297.   [84] Dobson, *US Wartime Aid*, 127–8.

commitments'). The wording of the Lend-Lease Act did not prevent this action, but there were political difficulties, especially after the Director of the Budget assured the Congressional Appropriations Committee on 15 March that none of the $7 billion[85] then being asked for lend-lease would be used to pay for material delivered under old contracts. Contrary to British assumptions, the Director of the Budget was not a US Treasury official, and Morgenthau did not feel bound by his pledge. Instead, he was able to tell Phillips on 19 March that he had persuaded Roosevelt that Britain should be relieved of $300 to $400 million of old commitments.

Keynes was sent to Washington in May to discuss the desirable future level of Britain's gold and dollar reserves, and the extent to which these could be increased by the Americans taking over old commitments. On this visit, which lasted until the end of July, Keynes was not altogether successful as a diplomat. He aroused Morgenthau's suspicions that he would make him appear to be a 'sucker' in American eyes. Whereas Keynes suggested that Britain should pay cash for items that could not readily be included in lend-lease, and that the Americans should take over $1,300 million of old commitments and refund $700 million of advances already paid, Morgenthau would agree to no more than to try to relieve Britain of between $400 and $600 million of old commitments. In the event, lengthy negotiations by Phillips resulted in relief of only $290 million of old commitments in May 1942.[86] Britain was, in effect, deliberately kept in a state of financial dependence.[87]

The Treasury, which Keynes described as 'the guardian of the future',[88] had to work hard to resist American demands for a 'consideration' that would restrict Britain's freedom of action after the war. Under the Lend-Lease Act, Britain had to provide the United States with 'direct or indirect' benefits in return for supplies. In July 1941 the State Department, in collaboration with Keynes, prepared a draft mutual aid agreement, in which the Americans inserted a clause whereby both countries would agree not to discriminate against imports from each other. This clause, inserted in Article VII of the agreement, was intended to abolish the system of imperial preference between countries in the British Empire, and was therefore unacceptable to several ministers who saw imperial preference as a means of strengthening links between

[85] American billions, meaning one thousand millions.

[86] Moggridge, *Maynard Keynes*, 655–8; Dobson, op. cit., 129.

[87] The desperate financial position in the spring of 1941 helps to explain why the Treasury began to press for gold and currency assets held in Britain by residents of enemy countries or enemy-occupied territories to be used for the British war effort—see Foreign and Commonwealth Office Historians (Gill Bennett), *British Policy Towards Enemy Property during and after the Second World War* (FCO History Notes, no. 13, Apr. 1998), 10–13. Many of these assets were held by Jewish victims of the Nazi regime, a fact that led to controversy half a century after the war was over. Britain's subordinate position during the war is indicated by the manner in which the Treasury deferred to American views on policy towards Jewish and other assets seized by the Germans—see FCO Historians (Gill Bennett), *Nazi Gold: Information from the British Archives* (History Notes, no. 11, Sept. 1996), 4–11.

[88] Keynes to Catto, Hopkins and Wilson, 7 Jan. 1941, T175/121.

Empire countries. The Treasury's position on Article VII, however, was based on a desire to retain the right to use any policy instrument, including import controls and exchange controls, that might be necessary to cope with the balance-of-payments problems that Britain could expect to face at the end of the war. Keynes, with the Chancellor's approval, aimed at an agreement to the effect that the United States and Britain would act jointly to promote multi-lateral trade, but he wanted any concessions by Britain on preferences or controls to be balanced by reductions in the United States' high tariffs, and to be conditional upon economic circumstances.

Suspicion that the United States was less than consistent in its conception of non-discriminatory, multilateral trade was aroused in Whitehall by concurrent American attempts to impose a wheat trade agreement, whereby Britain would be required to reduce its own production of wheat after the war, and to import American wheat surpluses at high, fixed prices, to the exclusion of other coun-tries which might wish to sell wheat at lower prices. The Treasury was not directly involved in the wheat talks, but Wood was one of the leading ministers in the Cabinet opposing either the abolition of imperial preference or acceptance of the proposed wheat agreement. These ministers' case seemed to be strength-ened when, following the Japanese attack on Pearl Harbor on 7 December, the United States entered the war as Britain's co-belligerent. Wood and others hoped that the original conception of lend-lease could be replaced by a pooling of resources, making Article VII redundant. The State Department did drop the proposals for a wheat agreement, but remained committed to Article VII as the basis for lend-lease.

The Treasury, aware of the need to retain autonomy in economic policy after the war, was more determined than the Foreign Office to resist American pres-sure, but the only concession that the British were able to secure before signing the Mutual Aid Agreement in 1942 was a letter from Roosevelt to Churchill stat-ing that the Americans did not want a commitment in advance that imperial preference would be abolished. However, the final form of Article VII still com-mitted Britain and the United States to 'agreed action', albeit 'in the light of governing economic conditions', to 'the elimination of all forms of discrimin-atory treatment in international commerce, and to the reduction of tariffs and other trade barriers'. Talks were to begin 'at an early convenient date' on how to achieve an expansion of production, employment, and trade.[89]

The progress of these talks, which did not in fact begin in earnest until Sep-tember 1943, will be followed below in the section dealing with planning the reconstruction of the international economy. The point to be made here is that the implementation of the lend-lease agreement prevented Britain negotiating from a position of strength, and was intended to do so. As had been anticipated

---

[89] Sayers, *Financial Policy*, 413. For detailed account of role of Treasury in these negotiations see L. S. Pressnell, *External Economic Policy since the War*, vol. i, *The Post-War Financial Settlement* (1986), ch. 3.

in November 1940, the Americans expected to exercise control over how material provided by the American taxpayer was used. Britain received food, raw materials, and industrial equipment, as well as munitions, and pressure was brought on the British government to agree in September 1941 not to allow lend-lease materials to be used to enable Britain to export goods at the expense of American commercial interests, a restriction that was removed only when Germany was defeated in May 1945. Partly for this reason, but also because lend-lease made possible a greater conversion of the British economy to war production than would otherwise have been possible, British exports fell to 29 per cent of their 1938 volume in 1943,[90] raising the prospect of a huge balance-of-payments problem after the war.

There was the related question, which Keynes and Morgenthau had not resolved in 1941, of what level of gold and foreign exchange reserves would be needed by Britain to cover 'old commitments' in the United States, to finance trade with third countries, and to maintain international confidence in sterling when Britain was incurring huge debts in sterling area countries as a result of war expenditure. The stationing of American servicemen in Britain and elsewhere in the sterling area from 1942 had the unanticipated effect of improving Britain's dollar reserves, since the servicemen had to convert their pay in dollars into sterling before they could purchase goods and services locally. Moreover, although Britain provided the Americans with military stores free under reciprocal aid, other goods and raw materials were paid for on a commercial basis. The effect was to enable the sterling area to earn a substantial dollar income, and under arrangements for pooling reserves, most of these dollars came to be held in London. In June 1941 Britain's gold and dollar reserves had stood at only $150 million; by the end of 1942, however, the reserves were approaching $1,000 million. Thereafter, whenever Britain's reserves tended to rise, it was American policy to reduce the range of civil goods covered by lend-lease, thereby forcing Britain to use its dollars, despite protests from the British Treasury that the ratio of Britain's reserves to her rapidly increasing debts was falling.

The importance that the Treasury attached to Anglo-American relations is indicated by the fact that it was represented in Washington by its most senior official on the Finance side of the department, Phillips, from the end of 1940 until his death in the summer of 1943. Thereafter the most senior official dealing with overseas finance, Waley, took over in Washington, and then Robert Brand, the eminent banker and public servant, who had been head of the British Food Mission in Washington, became the Treasury's resident representative in Washington in 1944 and 1945. Perhaps the most surprising aspect of the Treasury's wartime diplomacy was that the inarticulate Phillips was much more successful than the highly articulate Keynes in winning Morgenthau's trust. Morgenthau believed that he and Phillips had achieved a mutual

[90] Central Statistical Office, *Statistical Digest of the War*, table 142.

understanding since they had first met in 1937.[91] In contrast, Keynes felt that he 'got on' with Morgenthau for the first time in July 1944, over three years after their first encounter, and even then he avoided difficult subjects rather than risk spoiling the atmosphere.[92]

EXTERNAL FINANCE: THE COMMONWEALTH AND THE STERLING AREA

The War Cabinet's decision to wage war regardless of the financial consequences had effects on Britain's relations with countries other than the United States. Canada was second in importance only to the United States as a source of munitions.[93] However, about one-third of the cost of munitions produced in Canada represented imports of components and raw materials from the United States, and, as Canada had a trade deficit with the United States, she required payment for supplies for Britain to be partly in US dollars. This problem was eased from 1941 when the necessary American supplies could be obtained by Britain on lend-lease terms and transferred to Canada. The rest of the cost of supplies from Canada (including food and raw materials) had to be paid for in Canadian dollars, obtained partly by selling British assets in Canada, and partly through loans from the Canadian government.

The largest loan was known as the Billion Dollar Gift, which was part of a package proposed by the Canadian government in 1942, whereby Britain's existing overdraft with it should be converted to an interest-free loan, to be secured on the remaining British-owned securities in Canada. Hopkins had to point out that there was 'a very big snag' in this last aspect of an otherwise generous offer: if Britain offered collateral security for a Canadian loan, a precedent would be set that would seriously damage the conception of a Commonwealth in which relations were not the same as with foreign countries, while the apparent need for collateral would seriously damage Britain's credit, affecting the terms on which she would be able to borrow during and after the war.[94] The Canadians agreed to forgo collateral security as long as none was offered for loans raised elsewhere in the Empire. Eventually, after months of discussions, these arrangements were superseded in 1943 by an Anglo-Canadian mutual aid agreement, which, in the event, did not prevent Canada from acquiring substantial sterling balances by mid-1944. The Treasury successfully curbed this development by instructing purchasing departments to

---

[91] Note dated 21 May 1941, General Records of the Department of the Treasury, Aid to Britain files, AB/31, vol. 4, RG56, National Archives, Washington, DC.   [92] *JMK*, xxvi. 81.

[93] Canada produced 7.9 per cent of the British Empire's munitions during the war, compared with 69.5 per cent in the UK; 21 per cent from the United States, and 1.6 per cent in the rest of the Empire (mainly Australia and India)—Hancock and Gowing, *British War Economy*, 373.

[94] Sayers, *Financial Policy*, 344.

seek alternative sources of supply, and by sending Keynes and Eady to re-negotiate the agreement.

Relations with the other dominions were less complicated because, unlike Canada, they were members of the sterling area, conducting all their international transactions in sterling and being generally willing to accumulate sterling balances as an important part of their currency reserves. For its part, the British government was willing to purchase wool from Australia, New Zealand, and South Africa on what was regarded in the Treasury as unduly expensive terms. South Africa required special attention, for it was the major source of new gold within the Empire, and it was not always willing to part with the gold in return for additional sterling balances. As a result, the Chancellor of the Exchequer had to agree to the sale of British-owned securities in return for gold from June 1941. There was also opposition in South Africa to participation in the war outside what was regarded as South Africa's sphere of interest (Africa south of the Sahara), and negotiations between the Chancellor of the Exchequer and the South African Prime Minister, General Smuts, in November 1943 resulted in a Treasury commitment to subsidize South African forces outside that sphere, although the other dominions paid for all the maintenance of their own forces.

The biggest problem relating to the payment of imperial forces, however, concerned the Indian Army. Here again politics outweighed finance. India had achieved a measure of internal self-government before the war, with Britain retaining responsibility for India's external affairs. In February 1940 the Chancellor agreed with the Secretary of State for India a formula for sharing the cost of Indian defence expenditure, whereby India's share would be related to its pre-war defence budget, and the remainder would be borne by the British Exchequer. The implications of the agreement changed markedly when the outbreak of war in the Far East led to an expansion of the Indian Army and the scope of its operations, while inflation raised Indian prices. The Treasury tried repeatedly from 1942 to revise the financial arrangements for cost-sharing, but political unrest in India prevented any major adjustment. Despite the repatriation of India's pre-war sterling debt, India's sterling balances rose rapidly from £295 million in mid-1942 to £1,138 million by mid-1945. Sterling balances also accumulated rapidly in Middle Eastern countries, reaching a total of £500 million by the end of the war, largely on account of purchases of goods and services by British armed forces stationed there.[95] India and the Middle East's sterling balances accounted for over half of the increase in Britain's overseas debts (£2,879 million) during the war, and the Treasury was left with the problem of how to control the release of the balances after the war, when continued balance-of-payments difficulties could be expected.

[95] Sayers, *Financial Policy*, 259, 283.

PLANNING THE POST-WAR INTERNATIONAL ECONOMY

The story of Anglo-American negotiations leading to the establishment of the International Monetary Fund (IMF) and the World Bank, and, in particular, of Keynes's part in these negotiations, has been told at length elsewhere.[96] What follows is an attempt to relate these negotiations to the overall picture of the Treasury's work during the war, including planning for the post-war period. A prime object of Treasury policy was to prevent post-war arrangements for the international economy putting Britain at the mercy of the United States. As noted above, Article VII of the Mutual Aid Agreement committed Britain to talks on the elimination of all forms of discriminatory restraints on international trade. In these talks the Treasury's direct responsibility lay with plans to reform the international monetary system, but it also had to take account of the likely outcome of trade talks for Britain's post-war balance of payments.

In January 1943 an interdepartmental committee chaired by the Permanent Secretary of the Board of Trade, Sir Arnold Overton, reported in favour of a British initiative to promote international trade. In particular, the Overton Report suggested multilateral negotiation for an international 'Commercial Union', with drastic all-round tariff cuts; the dismantling of quantitative restrictions on trade by the fifth year after the war; and cuts in imperial preferences, with no new preferences without international agreement. The Overton Report was supported by the Board of Trade, the Foreign Office, the Department of Overseas Trade, the Dominions Office, and the Economic Section of the War Cabinet Offices, and within the Treasury, Waley, and Robertson thought that it would make the Americans more sympathetic to Britain's balance-of-payments difficulties. However, other members of the Treasury were sceptical or hostile to the Report. Henderson argued that Britain's first priority should be to correct its own adverse balance of payments, and for that purpose quantitative controls and preferences might be necessary. Phillips thought that the ending of bilateral trade agreements with Argentina and Denmark, and preferences with the colonies, would be a real loss, the extent of which the Overton Committee had failed to estimate. Even Keynes, who favoured a reduction in barriers to multilateral trade, thought that the committee had given scarcely any thought to Britain's self-interest.[97]

In the event, the Cabinet decided that the Overton Report should provide the basis for discussions with the Americans on post-war commercial policy, subject to Britain retaining freedom to impose quantitative import controls

[96] Moggridge, *Maynard Keynes*; Pressnell, *External Economic Policy since the War*, vol. i; Armand Van Dormael, *Bretton Woods: Birth of a Monetary System* (1978).

[97] 'The Overton Report', by Waley, 5 Jan. 1943, 'Post-War Commercial Policy', by Robertson, n.d., Phillips to Hopkins, 30 Jan. 1943, Henderson papers, Box 3, Nuffield College, Oxford; 'Great Britain's Post-War Commercial Policy—a Positive Statement', 6 Jan. 1943, in Henderson, *Inter-War Years*, 209–19; *JMK*, xxvi. 254.

without obtaining the permission of an international monetary authority, if the country had an adverse balance of payments. Subsequent progress on trade policy was slow, partly because of Commonwealth concern to retain imperial preference and partly because of the political importance of protecting British agriculture. The American and British positions were still far apart when the war ended.

The Treasury had been formulating proposals for post-war financial policy since the autumn of 1941. Britain would end the war with a well developed network of bilateral payments agreements, in addition to the sterling area and exchange controls. Together with continuing controls on trade, these arrangements seemed likely to be necessary to carry Britain through the difficult transition to a peacetime economy with balance-of-payments equilibrium. Indeed, the Bank of England thought that, even in the longer term, exchange controls and trade controls would be less harmful alternatives than fluctuating exchange rates and speculative movements of funds. As regards exchange rates, the Bank would have preferred to build on the Tripartite Agreement of 1936, in which Britain, the United States, and France had undertaken to co-operate to stabilize exchange rates. The Bank wished to maximize the international use of sterling, free from American interference, and to preserve the principal features of the sterling area, and consequently was hostile to proposals from Keynes or the Americans for international institutions to regulate monetary policies. Thus, although the Bank's advice was necessarily listened to regarding measures that might be necessary during the transition to permanent peacetime arrangements, it played no constructive part in drafting the Treasury's plans for reforming the international monetary system.[98]

Keynes's first draft for what he then called an International Currency Union, and what was later called a Clearing Union, appeared in September 1941. His objective was to make exchange rates stable but adjustable. He assumed that exchange controls would continue, giving central banks effective control of all international payments, including capital movements, and he suggested that the transactions between central banks should be conducted through the Clearing Union. Each member of the Union would be given an account, in proportion to its international trade. Countries whose deficits exceeded their accounts would be required to adjust their currencies downwards; those with persistent surpluses would be required to adjust their exchange rates upwards, by up to 5 per cent a year in both cases.[99] The latter requirement was designed to remove the deflationary bias that had marked the operation of the gold standard in the inter-war period, when deficit countries had had to deflate to protect their gold reserves, but the United States' monetary and tariff policies had acted to prevent gold inflows from increasing imports.

---

[98] For the Bank's views on financial policy after the war see Fforde, *Bank of England*, 36–61.
[99] *JMK*, xxv. 21–40.

In subsequent drafts, made in response to criticisms from the Economic Section and within the Treasury, Keynes left more room for discretion in managing the Clearing Union, and he developed his ideas about international bank money, which he suggested should be called 'bancor', which would be accepted by members of the Union as the equivalent of gold, and the supply of which, unlike gold, would be 'absolutely elastic'.[100] His main purpose, however, remained the same, to place responsibility for international equilibrium on creditor nations as well as debtor nations, and to replace gold as the major form of international reserve currency by bank money. He wanted bancor to be an acceptable substitute for gold, but he also wanted creditor nations to aim at zero balances, and even considered the merits of interest charges on credit as well as debit balances, leading Robertson to ask him:

> Are we to love, honour, cherish and thank or
> To kick in the bottom the blokes who hold bancor?[101]

Britain had exiguous gold reserves, but, as the world's leading trading nation before the war, she would be credited with a large account with the Clearing Union. The appeal of Keynes's ideas to the British Treasury was thus more than intellectual. However, their appeal was much less obvious in the United States, which held the bulk of the world's reserves of monetary gold, and therefore saw no reason why it should agree to proposals designed to replace gold as the major form of international reserve currency. Thus, although the British government published Keynes's proposals as a white paper in April 1943,[102] in practice Anglo-American discussions focused on the alternative plan developed by Harry White of the US Treasury for an international monetary fund to stabilize exchange rates. Keynes recognized that the principal virtue of his own proposals was that they encouraged the United States to commit itself to some kind of arrangement that would favour an expanding international economy.

The White Plan underwent considerable revision between the time when it was first presented to Phillips in draft in July 1942 and when it was published in April 1943. There was to be a Stabilization Fund and a Bank for Reconstruction. Members of the Fund would subscribe according to a complex formula related to gold holdings, gold production, national income, foreign trade, population, foreign investments, and foreign debts. The White Plan included an international unit of account, called 'unitas', but, unlike bancor, unitas was not intended to be an international currency created on banking principles. Members' quotas of drawing rights from the Fund would be restricted to some proportion of their subscriptions made up of gold and their own currencies, further drawing rights being dependent upon Fund approval of measures to correct balance-of-payments disequilibrium. Conditions of membership

---

[100] Ibid., 72–3, 140.   [101] Ibid., 215.
[102] *Proposals for an International Clearing Union* (Cmd. 6437), PP 1942–3, xi. 129.

included abandonment of all restrictions on exchange transactions with other members of the Fund, other than those approved by the Fund, and maintenance of an exchange rate which could be altered only when the Fund agreed that there was 'fundamental disequilibrium' in the balance of payments. Votes were to be allocated according to size of subscription, thereby giving the United States a veto on Fund decisions, as these would require a four-fifths majority. British hopes centred on encouraging the Americans to modify their proposals so as to make it possible for countries to correct balance-of-payments equilibrium without resort to deflation.[103]

Early in September 1943 a British delegation was sent to Washington to discuss international monetary and commercial policies, together with related topics such as international investment and commodity prices. The delegation, drawn from the Foreign Office, the Board of Trade, the Colonial Office, the Ministry of Food, the Bank of England, and the Economic Section, as well as the Treasury, was led by Richard Law, minister of state at the Foreign Office. The Treasury members, Keynes, Waley, and Frank Lee, were joined by Dennis Robertson, who was already in Washington. The talks were informal and non-committal. James Meade, who was present as a member of the Economic Section, described the Anglo-American currency discussions as 'absolute Bedlam', with Keynes and White confronting each other without any agenda. White was a difficult character but, in Meade's opinion, Keynes's bad manners made him 'a menace in international negotiations'.[104] On the other hand, careful preparation in London and aboard ship, together with considerable common ground between the British and Americans regarding the principles and aims of postwar monetary policy, ensured that progress was made. The Americans agreed to increase the size of the Stabilization Fund from $5 billion to $8.5 billion, or about the size sought by the British, and also to a clause whereby members of the Fund could discriminate against a currency declared to be scarce within the Fund.

The Washington talks of September–October 1943 were followed by debate in the British Treasury in which Henderson was determined not to allow what Waley called 'Utopia-builders' to promise more than could be performed, given Britain's balance-of-payments position.[105] Henderson's belief that the experience of the 1920s showed that an international economic system based on the free play of market forces would be unable to correct large maladjustments in the international balance of payments, and that therefore powers developed in

[103] The original White Plan and a note on 'British Treasury Questions on the White Proposals for a Stabilization Fund', 12 Mar. 1943, are in Records of the Bretton Woods Agreements, General Records of the Department of the Treasury, RG56, National Archives, Washington, DC.

[104] L. Robbins and J. Meade, *The Wartime Diaries of Lionel Robbins and James Meade, 1943–45*, ed. S. Howson and D. Moggridge (1990), 127, 135, 139.

[105] Sir David Waley, 'The Treasury during World War II', *Oxford Econ. Papers*, NS (1953), supplement on Sir Hubert Henderson, 47–54.

the 1930s to regulate trade should be retained, was endorsed by Catto and Eady.[106] It was common ground between Henderson and Keynes that the efficacy of devaluation as a means of restoring equilibrium must not be over-estimated, given Britain's dependence on imports of food and raw materials, and given that wages were linked to the cost of living. They also agreed that there were strong reasons for aiming at exchange stability, including London's position as an international financial centre, and as the centre of the sterling area.[107] The question was whether a currency scheme based on the Keynes and White Plans would be workable. There was considerable opposition in the Cabinet and from the Bank of England to the White Plan, which was represented by hostile opinion as a restoration of the gold standard that would expose Britain to the effects of an American slump, as in 1929. Keynes described the debate in Whitehall as 'complete bedlam, which only Hoppy's calm hand keeps in any sort of order', and even Hopkins wondered whether Britain could commit itself to an international currency scheme unless there were some assurance of an American loan that would spare Britain from having to apply for assistance from the Fund 'prematurely'.[108]

Keynes himself had no doubt that the Bank's alternative of a sterling currency bloc was not practical politics, for an American loan would be conditional on British co-operation in an international currency scheme. Without such a loan the British people would face extreme austerity, and it would be difficult to persuade countries in the sterling area to pool their dollar earnings rather than use them to import from the United States. Britain, Keynes advised the Chancellor, would end the war owing far more than it could pay, and would be in no position to restore London as a financial centre, as the Bank hoped, unless American financial assistance were forthcoming.[109] These arguments, plus the assurance that what was being proposed was much more flexible than the gold standard, persuaded Anderson, and the Cabinet, to endorse Keynes's ideas on an international currency scheme, subject to three conditions: (1) there should be some international investment institution, outside the proposed monetary fund, to provide reconstruction and long-term finance; (2) the provisions of the monetary fund should be introduced gradually after the war; and (3) acceptance by Britain of these provisions should be subject to experience during the transition.[110]

By April 1944 there was sufficient agreement between the American and British monetary experts for them to publish a joint plan for an international

---

[106] 'International Economic History of the Inter-War Period', 3 Dec. 1943, printed in Henderson, *Inter-War Years*, 236–95; Catto to Henderson, 20 Dec. 1943, Henderson papers, box 23A; Eady to Hopkins, 26 Feb. 1944, T273/336.

[107] 'Extract from Treasury paper on External Monetary and Economic Policy', and memorandum by Henderson, 9 Feb. 1944, T273/336.

[108] *JMK*, xxv. 409; 'The Washington Conversations on Article VII', by Hopkins, 10 Feb. 1944, T273/336.

[109] *JMK*, xxv. 410–13.   [110] Pressnell, *External Economic Policy*, i. 146.

monetary fund,[111] and in June and July Keynes, Brand, Eady, and Robertson, together with Robbins from the Economic Section, negotiated the Bretton Woods agreements establishing both the IMF and the World Bank. Keynes was very much in the ascendant, even the Americans, according to Robbins, being entranced by his genius.[112] Even so, it was clear that American views had prevailed in that the IMF and World Bank would provide a much less expansionary bias to the post-war international economy than Keynes had hoped for. The idea of new international bank money, whether bancor or unitas, was dropped in favour of the IMF holding quotas of gold and currencies of the members, an arrangement which would provide a much less elastic supply of international bank money than under Keynes's proposals for the Clearing Union. There was no obligation placed on countries with a balance-of-payments surplus to revalue, and, apart from the scarce currency clause, the strain of disequilibrium was left, as under the gold standard, to countries in deficit. On the other hand, it could be argued that Keynes was justified in advocating acceptance of the Bretton Woods agreements, in that the thinking behind them was based upon the intellectual position which he had developed in the inter-war years in favour of rules that would allow short-run departures from external balance.[113]

The agreements were not altogether unsatisfactory from the point of view of retention of British sovereignty in international finance. The Americans agreed to a clause, which had been suggested by Catto, that members of the Fund would retain the right to vary their exchange rates, although they must consult the Fund, which could suspend a member's drawing rights if a devaluation was held not to be justified by 'fundamental disequilibrium' in the balance of payments. There was, on the other hand, lengthy disagreement over the meaning of Article VIII, relating to convertibility, the wording of which was ambiguous. Keynes had successfully excluded sterling balances accumulated in wartime from any commitment to convertibility, but there remained the question of how far Britain was committed, as a member of the Fund, to make sterling convertible for current payments and transfers. Keynes had assumed during the Conference that, if a member ceased to be eligible to draw on the Fund, the obligation regarding current payments and transfers would lapse, but Robertson pointed out that the wording of Article VIII suggested otherwise. The US Treasury was reluctant to clarify the issue, since to do so would reveal to a critical Congress that the drafting of the plan for the IMF was deficient, and preferred to leave the matter unresolved.[114]

It may well be asked why Keynes urged Britain to enter a system for stabilizing exchange rates without some prior adjustment of sterling's exchange rate to

---

[111] *Joint Statement by Experts on the Establishment of an International Monetary Fund* (Cmd. 6519), PP 1943–4, viii. 263.   [112] Robbins, *Wartime Diaries*, 158–9.

[113] See John Williamson, 'Keynes and the International Economic Order', in David Worswick and James Trevithick (eds.), *Keynes and the Modern World* (Cambridge, 1983), 87–113.

[114] Pressnell, *External Economic Policy*, i. 160, 166, 168–82.

take account of changes in Britain's competitive position and the need to expand exports to correct its adverse balance of payments. A then relatively junior official in the Overseas Finance Division, Richard Clarke, did argue in May 1945 that Britain was unlikely to achieve balance-of-payments equilibrium without improving its competitive power, and that it was vitally important therefore to enter the proposed multilateral world of Bretton Woods with an exchange rate that at least gave Britain the benefit of the doubt, and which did not leave the Americans under the illusion that the rate of $4.03 to the pound was immutable. Clarke suggested $3.50, but Keynes took the view that $4.03 was a competitive rate of exchange. He believed that, thanks to successful stabilization of domestic prices, Britain had retained most of the benefit of the 20 per cent depreciation against the dollar in 1939.[115] It is not clear, however, that Keynes took sufficient account of the way in which mass production for the war in the United States had increased the gap between American and British industrial productivity, and devaluation was to prove to be inevitable in 1949, once the post-war sellers' market for British goods was over.

Congress did not approve the Bretton Woods agreements until July 1945, and British ratification was delayed until the position about American financial assistance in the post-war period was clearer as a result of the Anglo-American Loan Agreement of December 1945. There was uncertainty about when the war would end, and with it the flow of lend-lease supplies. There was likewise uncertainty as to what agreements could be reached regarding the scaling down or blocking of sterling balances. Keynes tried to concentrate ministerial minds with a memorandum which was circulated to the War Cabinet on 15 May, a week after Germany's surrender, but at a time when the length of the war with Japan (a period known as Stage II) was unknown, and overseas financial policy in the transitional period after the war (Stage III) was still undecided. Keynes characterized the alternative to American financial assistance in Stage III as 'Starvation Corner', with austerity at home on a scale likely to lead to serious political and social disruption, and a withdrawal, for the time being, from the position of a first-class power abroad. The time to approach the United States would be after the Bretton Woods agreements had been approved by Congress.[116] This timetable meant that the problem of securing an American loan was left to the incoming Labour government in July (see Chapter 8).

PLANNING POST-WAR SOCIAL POLICY

The uncertainty surrounding Britain's external financial position was bound to reinforce traditional Treasury reserve towards plans for better social services.

---

[115] Sir Richard Clarke, *Anglo-American Economic Collaboration in War and Peace, 1942–1949*, ed. A. Cairncross (Oxford, 1982), 108–9, 122; *JMK*, xxiv. 261–2.   [116] *JMK*, xxiv. 256–95.

Planning was also complicated by the fact that civil servants had to draft proposals that could win the assent of both Conservative and Labour ministers, and the party truce for the duration of the war did not always extend to post-war issues. Nevertheless, the need to maintain morale and to counter Nazi propaganda about a New Order in Europe forced ministers and civil servants to give attention to issues such as poverty, housing, education, and unemployment.[117]

Planning post-war reconstruction began in late 1940 under Arthur Greenwood, a Labour minister without portfolio in the War Cabinet, who had taken part in the reconstruction discussions of 1917–19. Greenwood naturally wished to draw upon previous experience, and a proposal was made that an economic historian, R. H. Tawney, and an economist, G. D. H. Cole, should write a factual analysis of economic demobilization at the end of the First World War. Both Tawney and Cole had been members of the Economic Advisory Council, and Cole had been a member of its Committee on Economic Information, but both were linked to the Labour movement. Bridges doubted if such an enquiry would be unbiased, and Wilson vetoed Cole's appointment. However, the conclusion which Tawney drew, that direct controls should not be done away with precipitately after the war, when an inflationary reconstruction boom akin to 1919–20 was expected, seems to have been generally regarded, even in the Treasury, as uncontroversial.[118]

Greater controversy attended measures relating to social policy. Family allowances had been suggested in 1939 and 1940 by Stamp and Keynes as part of a policy to encourage restraint in demands for higher wages. The Treasury collected information and sought advice from interested parties, only to discover that a family allowance scheme was likely to place a substantial burden on the Exchequer, even if partly financed by insurance contributions. Moreover, long-standing trade union opposition to family allowances made it seem likely that food subsidies and wider provision of school meals and milk would be more effective ways in which to encourage wage restraint. However, from mid-1940 there was growing pressure in Parliament for family allowances, to relieve family poverty rather than to restrict wages. In June 1941 the Chancellor gave the cost of a 5s. (25p) allowance for each child under 15 as £130 million, or £60 million if existing child allowances in income tax and the social services were to be abolished. There would, however, obviously be more public support for the introduction of new allowances than for the abolition of existing ones, and the Treasury adopted delaying tactics, to ensure that any scheme would not be introduced until after the war. An internal Whitehall enquiry conducted by a middle-ranking Treasury official, Edward Hale, resulted in a non-committal

[117] See Rodney Lowe, 'The Second World War, Consensus and the Foundation of the Welfare State', *20th Cent. Brit. Hist.*, 1 (1990), 152–82.

[118] Bridges to Wilson, 19 Feb. 1941, and 20 Mar. 1941, T273/274; R. H. Tawney, 'The Abolition of Economic Controls, 1918–21', *Econ. Hist. Rev.*, 13 (1943), 1–30.

white paper in May 1942, and any decision was put off until an interdepartmental committee, chaired by Sir William Beveridge, had reviewed social
insurance as a whole.[119]

The Beveridge Committee had been set up in 1941 to enquire into anomalies
that had arisen as a result of the piecemeal growth of the social security system
since before the First World War, and to make recommendations. Hale was the
Treasury representative on the committee, and he is credited with having
played an important part in focusing Beveridge's attention on administrative
and financial reality.[120] Even so, Beveridge was responsible for the general principles set out in the report—so much so that the Chancellor insisted that it
should be signed by Beveridge alone, thereby relieving the departmental representatives of any responsibility for its recommendations. Beveridge's plan, as
published on 1 December 1942, was for a compulsory social insurance scheme
against all interruptions of earnings, including unemployment, sickness, and
industrial injury to cover the whole population of working age, offering flat-rate,
subsistence benefits, without means test, in return for flat-rate contributions,
and with benefits to meet the special needs of housewives. To limit the size of
contributions and the burden on the Chancellor's budget, Beveridge recommended that initially old-age pensions should not be paid at the same rate as
other benefits, but should be raised to that level at gradually increasing rates
over twenty years, during which period means-tested assistance pensions would
be available to ensure that no old person was in want. The whole plan was based
on three assumptions: (a) there would be a separate scheme of family
allowances; (b) there would be comprehensive health and rehabilitation services; and (c) unemployment would not average more than about 8½ per cent
of the labour force (approximately the level in 1937—the best year in the
1930s).[121]

The Treasury's influence had been felt on Beveridge's proposals even before
they were published. Beveridge had approached Keynes as early as March 1942
for advice on the financial aspects of the plan, and Keynes subsequently served
as an intermediary between Beveridge and Treasury officials, who were worried about the implications of Beveridge's proposals for the budget. It had been
Keynes who had encouraged Beveridge to phase in old-age pensions on
reduced scales, and to limit family allowances to the second and subsequent
children in a family. In the 'social security budget' included in the Beveridge
Report the estimated additional cost to the taxpayer and ratepayer, compared
to existing schemes, was limited to £86 million initially and £254 million after
twenty years. On the other hand, Keynes rightly expressed scepticism about
Beveridge's belief that the cost of health services included in this social security

[119] 372 HC Deb., 5s, 1940–1, col. 364; *Family Allowances: Memorandum by the Chancellor of the Exchequer* (Cmd. 6354), PP 1941–2, ix. 51. See also John Macnicol, *The Movement for Family Allowances* (1980), 170–82.
[120] See Harris, *William Beveridge, a Biography* (Oxford, 1977), ch. 16.
[121] Sir William Beveridge, *Social Insurance and Allied Services* (Cmd. 6404), PP 1942–3, vi. 119–417.

budget could be held at a constant level by preventive medicine, accurately predicting that the standards of medical treatment, and therefore their cost, would rise.[122]

Keynes was generally supportive of Beveridge's proposals. In contrast, Henderson offered a root-and-branch critique of the principles underlying the report. Henderson pointed out that the lack of a means test, and the extension of national insurance to all social classes, would mean that Beveridge's flat-rate benefits would not be targeted at the people who needed them most, and must therefore be more expensive than what would be strictly necessary to abolish poverty. Eady took up this point and recommended that the Beveridge scheme should be applied only to the existing, largely industrial working-class, insured labour force. Gilbert opposed Beveridge's proposal to make unemployment benefit at full rate of indefinite duration, subject to attendance at a work or training centre after a limited period of unemployment, arguing that the pro- posal would be practicable only if it were possible to eliminate structural un- employment and to reduce other unemployment to low levels. Even Keynes thought that Beveridge's final figure for family allowances of 8s. (40p) a week for each child, except the first, in a family was extravagant. Eady, echoing the opin- ions of an interdepartmental committee chaired by Sir Thomas Phillips of the Ministry of Labour, noted that a reduction to 5s. (25p) would reduce the cost from £113 million to £58 million, thereby leaving room in the budget for an expansion of services in kind for children. Both Keynes and Eady saw a danger to the budget in tying the level of benefits to current doctrines of subsistence minima, since any revision of the latter would mean an automatic revision of benefits.[123]

These and other criticisms of Beveridge's proposals were conveyed to Churchill in a memorandum from the Chancellor on 17 November, a fortnight before the Report was published.[124] However, Treasury officials realized that, in setting their objectives for what should be done about social insurance, they must take account of what was politically possible, and they seem to have adopted a strategy of accepting Beveridge's recommendations as an ultimate objective, to be implemented piecemeal as the future budgetary position became less uncertain.

There was strong support among the general public and the Labour party for Beveridge's proposals. However, as the Treasury pointed out, acceptance of the complete plan would involve a contract with millions of beneficiaries, which would probably have to be a first charge on the government's finances, in good times and bad. (Although it was tactful not to mention 1931, given Labour

[122] *JMK*, xxvii. 204, 216–17, 221–2, 228–30, 237–9, 249.
[123] 'The Principles of the Beveridge Plan', by Henderson, 4 Aug. 1942 (printed in Henderson, *Inter- War Years*, 191–208), Eady to Hopkins, 22 Oct. 1942, Gilbert to Hopkins, 6 Nov. 1942, and 'Beveridge', unsigned but probably by Hopkins, n.d., but position in file indicates early Dec. 1942, T273/57; *JMK*, xxvii. 245, 247.   [124] Prime Minister's Office papers (hereafter PREM) 4/89/2.

sensibilities, ministers can hardly have forgotten the political difficulties arising from an actuarially unsound unemployment insurance scheme that year.) On the basis of a conservative estimate of taxable income after the war (£7,150 million), and on the assumption that EPT and that part of income tax which was returnable as a post-war credit, both of which were avowedly temporary, would cease, the Treasury estimated that revenue in a post-war year would be £2,050 million, plus or minus £125 million. Against this must be set:

For existing policy commitments (exclusive of defence)	£1,125 million
Defence	£500 million
Sinking fund on enlarged National Debt	£100 million

On this basis, only £325 million would be left to cover a possible shortfall in revenue, or tax cuts, or the cost of new policy commitments. Regarding taxation and employers' contributions to national insurance, the Treasury advanced the supply-side argument that a heavy burden on industry would tend to depress enterprise at a time when an increase in exports of 50 per cent over the pre-war level would be necessary to correct an adverse balance of payments. The Treasury also thought it possible that unemployment in a post-war slump could exceed Beveridge's figure of 8½ per cent. The Chancellor, Wood, successfully urged his Cabinet colleagues not to commit the government to the full implementation of the Beveridge report without first reviewing together all the claims that might be made on the budget for additional expenditure other than on social insurance, such as housing, education, agriculture, and colonial development, and relating these claims to the financial situation when the time came for legislation. The Cabinet also agreed that family allowances should be restricted to 5s. (25p), and that cash allowances should be supplemented by developing child welfare services, as the Phillips Committee had recommended. On the other hand, ministers thought that Beveridge's recommendation that full rates for old-age pensions should be phased in over twenty years was politically impracticable.[125]

The government's guarded response in Parliament to the Beveridge Report, with Anderson, then Lord President, and Wood dwelling on the problems it presented rather than the opportunities that it offered, went down badly with Labour and Liberal MPs, and even some Conservatives, making it harder for the Beveridge Plan to be challenged openly.[126] The strength of the Treasury's arguments depended on what assumptions were made about post-war levels of unemployment and national income. The (ministerial) Reconstruction Priorities Committee asked the Treasury, the Economic Section, and the Central

---

[125] 'The Social Insurance Plan: Memorandum prepared in the Treasury', 1 Jan. 1943, 'The Financial Aspects of the Social Security Plan: Memorandum by the Chancellor of the Exchequer', 11 Jan. 1943, and War Cabinet conclusions, 14 Jan., and 12 and 15 Feb., 1943, CAB65/33.

[126] 386 HC Deb., 5s, 1942–3, cols. 1655–78, 1825–38.

Statistical Office to come up with agreed figures. Keynes and the Economic Section wished to assume that unemployment would be 5 per cent, but, as a concession to Treasury views, agreed to assume 7½ per cent. On this basis, taxable income in 1948 was estimated in June 1943 at £7,710 million, but Keynes persuaded the Chancellor to accept a figure of £7,825 million. Either figure greatly eased the Treasury's earlier Procrustean limits, which had been based on a taxable income of £7,150 million. A month later an examination of the 1948 budgetary position by Norman Chester, of the Economic Section, showed that full implementation of Beveridge's proposals in addition to agreed future civil and military expenditure, would allow the standard rate of income tax to be reduced from 10s. (50p) to 7s. 6d. (37.5p) in the pound, with a corresponding reduction in indirect taxation.[127]

The significance of Chester's work depended upon whether one regarded a rate of 7s. 6d. as acceptable, when the standard rate had been 5s. 6d. (27.5p) in 1938—and only 4s. 6d. (22.5p) in 1935. Moreover, Hopkins pointed out, employers' contributions, which under the Beveridge plan would be almost doubled from 1s. 10d. (9p) to 3s. 3d. (16.25p) per adult male worker, might be easily bearable in some industries, but very hard on some others.[128] Chester's exercise thus tended to confirm the Treasury in its belief that the cost of the Beveridge plan was too high.

Moreover, the Cabinet continued to agree to new items of expenditure, such as reconstruction of war-damaged areas, increases in pensions, and training and rehabilitation, so that by June 1944, even on an estimate of taxable income of £7,825 million, and making no provision for a sinking fund, the margin left for any shortfall in revenue, the post-war cost of the armed forces and tax remissions was only £800 million.[129] It was thus not too difficult for the Treasury to persuade the Cabinet to be cautious about commitments in its social security plan as set out in the 1944 white paper on *Social Insurance*. In particular, the white paper rejected the principle of subsistence benefits, and promised only 'reasonable insurance against want'.[130] This change from the Beveridge Report foreshadowed an end to Beveridge's hopes of doing away with the means test for people covered by national insurance. Benefits based on 'reasonable insurance' after the war turned out to be so low that claimants without savings or other sources of income had to apply for means-tested national assistance to supplement their benefits. The Treasury had thus largely got its way: the level of national insurance benefits was to be determined by the budgetary position rather than by changes in the cost of living or the opinions of experts as to what amounted to subsistence.

[127] Cairncross and Watts, *Economic Section*, 91–4.
[128] Note by Hopkins, 22 Oct. 1943, T273/57.
[129] 'Post-War Financial Commitments: Memorandum by the Chancellor of the Exchequer', 28 June 1944, CAB66/52.
[130] *Social Insurance, Part I* (Cmd. 6550), paras. 12–13, PP 1943–4, viii. 463.

The Treasury's view that definite post-war commitments should be avoided until the financial position was clearer was in line with the Prime Minister's belief that reconstruction decisions should be kept to the minimum possible until the war was over. Indeed, when the 1944 budget alerted Churchill to the extent of commitments already entered into by the government, his enquiry about how this situation had arisen implied criticism of the Treasury for not being restrictive enough![131] However, the politics of coalition government could make it difficult for the Treasury to be restrictive. For example, Treasury officials were concerned in early 1944 about the unqualified nature of the commitment to 'a comprehensive service to all' in the 1944 white paper on *A National Health Service*, but the Cabinet's Reconstruction Committee ignored this criticism, and, in the interests of securing Labour's acquiescence to the white paper, Anderson agreed to the removal of a proposal for a 'hotel charge' to be imposed on hospital patients. One major piece of legislation which had the blessing of Wood and Anderson was the Butler Education Act of 1944. However, this support reflected a recognition that some social reform was necessary to deflect public attention from Beveridge, and also the fact that the Board of Education drew up its proposals in a way that meant that it would be a generation before the Exchequer had to bear the full cost of implementing the Act.[132]

PLANNING POST-WAR EMPLOYMENT POLICY

The Beveridge Report had served to raise ministerial interest in post-war employment policy. Contributions to the enlarged social insurance fund were calculated to ensure actuarial soundness if unemployment averaged $8^{1}/_{2}$ per cent, but unemployment had been higher than that in most years between 1921 and 1939. Ministers naturally wished to know if it would be possible to prevent a return to inter-war levels once the period of post-war reconstruction was over.

As noted above, there were Anglo-American discussions during 1943 and 1944 on international monetary and commercial policies, which held out the prospect of a more stable international economy. Keynes was much involved in these discussions, and it has been suggested that Treasury officials may have deliberately sought to channel his energies away from domestic aspects of employment policy.[133] If so, they were unsuccessful. Moreover, from 1941 Keynes's macroeconomic approach was shared by members of the Economic Section, especially James Meade, who advocated measures to maintain expenditure in the community at a sufficiently high level to ensure that any decline in

[131] Kevin Jeffreys, *The Churchill Coalition and Wartime Politics, 1940–1945* (Manchester, 1991), 175.
[132] Frank Honigsbaum, *Health, Happiness and Security: The Creation of the National Health Service* (1989), 200–1; Paul Addison, *The Road to 1945: British Politics and the Second World War* (1975), 238.
[133] Moggridge, *Maynard Keynes*, 662, 695.

demand for labour in particular occupations would be offset by a corresponding increase in demand for goods and services of other kinds. Keynes himself
had no doubt that theoretical economic analysis had reached a point where it
could be applied to policy, if adequate national income data could be compiled.
It was not easy, however, for busy administrators to keep up with developments
in economic theory—Eady complained in 1943 to Keynes that a note from him
on employment policy was 'a voyage in the stratosphere for most of us'.[134]

Keynes's note had been written in support of an Economic Section paper,
drafted mainly by Meade, on 'The Maintenance of Employment', in which it
was suggested that the level of public investment and the balance between
expenditure and revenue in the Chancellor's budget should be varied to maintain a high level of aggregate demand.[135] Within the Treasury, Henderson was
highly critical of a macroeconomic approach to employment policy, partly
because he believed that it was too abstract and neglected the indeterminate
nature of lags before the multiplier effect of deficit finance would be felt on
employment, and partly because he believed that experience in the inter-war
period showed that the principal dangers to employment were a loss of export
trade or penetration of the home market by foreign competitors.[136] The Chancellor, Wood, did not allow Meade's paper to go unchallenged in the (ministerial) Committee on Reconstruction Priorities. Consequently, the Lord President,
Anderson, asked all interested departments, including the Board of Trade and
the Ministry of Labour, as well as the Treasury, to study employment policy, with
an official Steering Committee on Post-War Employment being set up under
Hopkins's chairmanship to produce a comprehensive report.

Whereas the Economic Section's memorandum on the maintenance of
employment had described the problem as 'essentially' one of maintaining
aggregate demand, and assumed 'an effective mobility of labour', to prevent
'the so-called structural unemployment of the inter-war period', members of
the Treasury, especially Eady and Henderson, regarded structural unemployment as equally important as unemployment arising from a general deficiency
of demand. They argued that the decline of particular industries would reduce
purchasing power in the regions in which these industries were located. The
Economic Section thought that it would be worth while incurring 'some deficit'
in the Chancellor's budget to offset a depression, and suggested that the appropriate period for balancing the budget should be regarded as 'longer than the
traditional year'. Treasury officials denied that it was the traditional practice to
balance expenditure and revenue every year, since in the past the sinking fund
had been suspended, or various nest-eggs used, instead of raising taxation in a

---

[134] *JMK*, xxvii. 325, 371.

[135] PR(43)26, 18 May 1943, CAB87/13. Keynes's note is in *JMK*, xxvii. 320–5.

[136] 'Lord Keynes and Employment Policy', 1 Mar. 1944, printed in Henderson, *Inter-War Years*,
316–25.

depression. However, they argued that financial confidence would be under-mined if the principle of deficit financing were to be applied over an indefinite period, and that, if the causes of unemployment were structural, deficit finance would have serious repercussions on economic stability and ultimately on employment.[137]

While Keynes and the Economic Section shared a concern about a long-term problem of unemployment arising from a saturation of investment after the transition from war to peace, Keynes was not wholly in agreement with the Economic Section's ideas. Keynes was more inclined that the Economic Section stress the importance of structural unemployment. He also placed less emphasis than the Economic Section did on devices to vary consumption, partly because he was aware of the political difficulties of reversing tax cuts, but mainly because he believed they would have little effect on middle-class con-sumption in the short run; while the consumption of the working classes, with their lower propensity to save, could be more effectively managed through a scheme devised by Meade to vary national insurance contributions inversely with the level of unemployment. Keynes thought that, if the bulk of investment were to be under public or semi-public control, a stable, long-term programme would prevent sharp fluctuations in the economy. Whereas the Economic Section was relatively indifferent to the distinction between public current and capital expenditure, Keynes wanted the budget to be divided into an ordinary budget, which would normally be balanced out of revenue at all times, and a capital budget, covering all forms of public capital expenditure and the social insurance fund, which would be used to stabilize aggregate demand. Even he, however, accepted that deficits in the ordinary budget would be 'a means of attempting to cure disequilibrium' should serious unemployment occur.[138]

As chairman of the Steering Committee, Hopkins tried to steer a middle course between the views of the Economic Section on the one hand, and Eady and Henderson on the other, by dividing the possible causes of high unemploy-ment into two categories. In category A he placed a low general level of invest-ment or consumption; in category B he placed a major loss of export trade or a major decline in employment in particular industries, owing to changes in demand, or to lack of competitiveness, or to the introduction of labour-saving methods. He also placed in category B the problem of major changes in the levels of investment in different industries at different times as each made up for a lack of investment during the war. In Hopkins's opinion, the Steering Committee's terms of reference directed its attention primarily to category A, in that ministers wanted to know what could be done about unemployment in the long run, before committing themselves to the Beveridge Report, and this

[137] 'Memoranda prepared in the Treasury', 16 Oct. 1943, and 'Maintenance of Employment', note by the Economic Section, 18 Oct. 1943, CAB87/63.

[138] *JMK*, xxvii. 225, 319–20, 326, 352–7, 360.

interpretation ensured that the Economic Section's views on the importance of measures to maintain aggregate demand occupied a prominent place in the Steering Committee's report. Even so, Hopkins made sure that the report contained the 'essential qualifications to the aggregate demand theory', including statements that an expansion of demand in Britain would not do much in the short run to alleviate unemployment in export trades hit by an international depression, and that public works did not provide permanent employment.[139]

Early in 1944 the government was anxious to 'scoop' Beveridge, who was known to be publishing a private 'report' on full employment, by bringing out its own white paper on employment policy.[140] Norman Brook, Permanent Secretary of the Office of the Minister of Reconstruction, used the Steering Committee's report as the basis for the white paper, but Hopkins insisted on changes that would avoid commitments to unsound finance. Consequently, the white paper stated that 'none of the main proposals . . . involves deliberate planning for a deficit in the National Budget in years of sub-normal trade activity'. As before the war, most public investment would be by local authorities or public utilities, and would therefore be largely outside the Chancellor's budget, and the only concession to Keynes's ideas on a capital budget was to provide for a more complete analysis of savings and investment in the annual white paper on national income and expenditure.[141] A claim by the Economic Section that the technique of varying public capital expenditure was familiar and certain provoked Gilbert, now in charge of the Supply Services divisions, to remark that the technique was novel and far from certain. In deference to the Treasury's views, the white paper stated that 'there are . . . practical limits to the extent to which Government action can produce swings in public investment'. Likewise, reflecting Hopkins's fears that Meade's scheme for varying national insurance contributions might fall a victim to political expediency, replicating the difficulties over the unemployment insurance fund in 1931, it was made clear that the fund was still expected to balance its outgoings over a period of years.[142] The white paper, therefore, was a compromise that embodied the views of orthodox Treasury officials as well as those of professional economists.

The government's commitment to maintaining a high and stable level of employment as one of its objectives had implications for the role of the Treasury. Bridges, Brook, and Robbins agreed in September 1944 that the final responsibility for advising ministers about the timing of action to expand or contract expenditure must lie with the highest Treasury official concerned with internal financial and economic policy—'the Sir Richard Hopkins of the day'. It was also agreed that the Treasury would have a new division to supervise the

---

[139] G. C. Peden, 'Sir Richard Hopkins and the "Keynesian Revolution" in Employment Policy, 1929–45', *Econ. Hist. Rev.*, 2nd ser., 36 (1983), 289.

[140] *Employment Policy* (Cmd. 6527), PP 1943–4, viii. 119. Beveridge's report appeared after the white paper as *Full Employment in a Free Society* (1944).

[141] Cmd. 6527, paras. 74, 84.   [142] Peden, 'Sir Richard Hopkins', 292.

acceleration or retardation of public capital expenditure. Bridges, who was still Cabinet Secretary, thought that government economists working on employment policy should 'owe allegiance to the Chancellor of the Exchequer', whether the Economic Section remained in the Cabinet Office or was placed in the Treasury.[143] In short, employment policy seemed likely to restore the position of the Treasury as the central department of government.

PLANNING FOR POST-WAR DOMESTIC FINANCIAL POLICY

In addition to planning undertaken in connection with external financial policy and employment policy, the Treasury had to decide what should be done about the National Debt, domestic monetary policy, and the future role of the budget. These were related questions. Eady remarked that the chief novelty of the white paper on employment policy lay in the technique of national income accounting. This technique, he thought, could be used to raise the revenue necessary to deal with the greatly enlarged National Debt.[144] As after the First World War, the Labour party was attracted to the idea of a capital levy, and in July 1944 Attlee suggested to Meade that the Economic Section should prepare a note on the subject. Meade thought that there should be an enquiry into what could be done to lighten the charge for National Debt interest on post-war budgets. Hopkins took up the idea, and established a National Debt Enquiry Committee drawn from the Treasury, the Board of Inland Revenue and the Economic Section. Somewhat surprisingly, the Bank of England was not represented on the committee, but Hopkins made plain that the question of future gilt-edged interest rates should not be decided without prior consultation with the Bank.[145]

Hopkins himself chaired the first meeting of the enquiry in February 1945; thereafter his successor as Permanent Secretary, Bridges, took over, with Hopkins continuing as a member of the committee. The subject of a capital levy was soon disposed of. Hopkins was very familiar with the difficulties from his time at the Inland Revenue during and after the First World War. He thought that a levy would be practicable, if the state became a gigantic investment trust, taking over assets rather than collecting money, and if all private valuers were taken over as temporary civil servants for the duration of the levy, but neither he nor any other members of the Enquiry seems to have taken Meade's arguments for a levy seriously. Even Meade recognized that it would have too small a yield to be worth while when interest rates were low and income taxes were high.[146]

[143] Bridges to Brook, 31 July 1944, Brook to Bridges, 11 Aug. 1944, and 'Note for Record', 7 Sept. 1944, T273/318.   [144] Eady to Brook, 26 Apr. 1944, CAB124/215.
[145] Draft prepared by Sir R. Hopkins of an interim report, n.d., T233/157.
[146] Hopkins to Chancellor of the Exchequer, 18 July 1944, T273/389; National Debt Enquiry (hereafter NDE), 1st meeting, 19 Feb. 1945, T233/158; Meade, Collected Papers, iv. 65, 91.

Thereafter the committee focused on how to maintain a cheap money policy after the war. The theoretical aspects of monetary management were expounded by Keynes, and debated by Robbins and Meade, with the most senior Treasury and Board of Inland Revenue officials responsible for home finance doing their best to relate theory to practice. Meade remarked that 'it must have been very difficult for the layman'. He characterized Bridges as 'very able and competent without much technical knowledge'; Hopkins as 'very wise and learned', but Eady as 'muddled and uncertain'. Meade, however, thought that it was quite indefensible for Keynes at one meeting to describe the remaining Treasury representative, Brittain, who was in charge of the Home Finance Division, as 'intellectually contemptible'.[147]

Using his liquidity preference theory, Keynes emphasized the need to continue the wartime practice of issuing gilt-edged stock on tap. He argued that, if the monetary authorities refrained from funding the National Debt, they could have whatever level of interest they liked. He thought that it was desirable to issue long-term gilts at about 3 per cent as a reward for thrift, but that moderate variations in the rate of interest at around that level would have no effect on investment, and that therefore interest rates should be held steady even during the short inflationary transitional period to be expected at the end of the war. He believed that Bank rate should be reduced from 2 per cent to 1 per cent, and the rate on 3-month Treasury bills from 1 per cent to 1/2 per cent. With about £2,000 million of the floating debt held overseas, such a reduction would help the balance of payments. Meade shared Keynes's theoretical approach, but argued that some flexibility in interest rates might be necessary to check inflation or deflation.[148]

Hopkins took pains to follow the economic arguments, and, in the course of writing a paper for submission to the Chancellor on the basis of Keynes's proposals, he read the *General Theory* twice and Robertson's *Essays in Monetary Theory*.[149] He used Keynes's arguments and agreed that there should be no return to the pre-war preoccupation with funding debt. However, Hopkins, like Keynes in 1945, assumed that there would be permanent control on external movements of capital, which would substantially insulate Britain from the effects of higher interest rates abroad. Hopkins also believed that it would be possible to continue to control investment through the Capital Issues Committee, and to ration the volume of credit by influencing the volume of bank advances. In other words, as in wartime, monetary policy would depend upon what controls were available as well as on theory. Indeed, Hopkins was decidedly

[147] Meade, *Collected Papers*, iv. 46, 48, 61. For accounts of the enquiry and the economic theories underlying the debate on monetary policy see Susan Howson, *British Monetary Policy, 1945–51* (Oxford, 1993), 18–25, 45–61, 329–31, and Moggridge, *Maynard Keynes*, 714–17.

[148] NDE minutes, 8, 22, and 27 Mar., and 5 Apr., 1945, and 'Summary by Lord Keynes of his Proposals', NDE paper 7, T233/158; Meade, *Collected Papers*, iv. 48, 61.

[149] Meade, *Collected Papers*, iv. 70.

ambivalent in his references to the *General Theory*. He referred to the importance of low interest rates, if the burden of the National Debt was to be
minimized, and he noted that members of the enquiry knew of no other theory
that 'began to hold out the same prospect' of achieving that objective. He also
quoted the white paper on employment policy to the effect that 'theory can be
applied to practical issues with confidence and certainty only as experience
accumulates and experiment extends over untried ground'.[150] Keynes's theory
thus legitimized the continuation of the wartime cheap money policy into the
post-war period, which was a great departure from what had happened after
the First World War, but the policy was the product of circumstances as much as
of theory, and was not to survive the relaxation of controls after 1951.

The same cautious pragmatism characterized Hopkins's views on post-war
budgetary policy. He accepted that what he called the 'structure of the modern
budget' included not only the traditional review of receipts into and payments
out of the Exchequer, but also the use of national income analysis to identify
whether the scale of government borrowing was likely to be inflationary. The
budget continued to be for the financial year (from April), whereas the national
income estimates prepared by the Central Statistical Office were for the calendar year, but Hopkins argued that this was necessary to ensure that reasonably
up-to-date figures were available when the budget was being prepared.[151] He
agreed with Robbins at the end of 1944 that there should be closer contact
between the Treasury and Economic Section in the course of preparing
national income figures.[152]

However, Hopkins was firmly opposed to Keynes's idea, put to the National
Debt Enquiry, that there should be a capital budget as well as a revenue budget
in the post-war period. Hopkins argued that the Chancellor's budget contained
very little capital expenditure that was charged to revenue—only £12 million
on civil votes in 1936. Most capital items were treated as being 'below the line';
that is the government was authorized by Parliament to borrow under such
legislation as the Telegraph (Money) Acts and the Trade Facilities Acts. Hopkins
believed that it was wrong to disturb traditional public finance when there was
so little point in doing so.[153]

Meade was surprised at Hopkins's attitude, but in fact Hopkins was being
consistent with views that he had expressed a year earlier in connection with
employment policy. He was very reluctant to give up the traditional doctrine

---

[150] Draft prepared by Sir R. Hopkins of an interim report, n.d., T233/157, and 'National
Debt Enquiry—First Report: The Question of Future Gilt-edged Interest Rates', 15 May 1945,
T233/158.
[151] 'The 1944 Budget', by Hopkins, 3 Feb. 1944, T171/367.
[152] Note by Hopkins, 21 Dec. 1944, T273/260; Meade, *Collected Papers*, iv. 21.
[153] *JMK*, xxvii. 405–13; Meade, *Collected Papers*, iv. 101; 'Proposals for a "Capital Budget" and a
"Capital Survey" ', unsigned, n.d., but position in file indicates June 1945, and 'Lord Keynes' Proposal
for an "Exchequer Capital Budget" ', by Brittain, 26 June 1945, T233/159.

that Asquith had restated in 1906: central government expenditure of a non-self-liquidating nature should be met out of revenue. Hopkins had asked rhetorically in July 1944: 'if one treats army barracks as capital because they are enduring, why not also battleships and, if so, why not also cruisers?' Keynes did in fact think that borrowing for defence expenditure might prove to be one of the methods of achieving full employment, a view which can only have reinforced Hopkins's determination to resist any form of budget that would be 'merely an invitation to gloss over the facts of a difficult situation by putting into that budget, on one pretext or another, anything that should be, but cannot be . . . currently paid for'.[154] For Hopkins the budget was still a means of protecting politicians from temptation, and he preferred surveys of public capital expenditure and analyses of national income to be conducted outside the budget.

There was plenty of evidence that politicians needed to be protected from temptation. For example, in the summer of 1944 some ministers, including Lord Beaverbrook and Leo Amery, had been reluctant to accept Keynes's dire warnings about Britain's external financial position. Robbins remarked to Hopkins in February 1945 that the very success of wartime economic measures had led nearly everyone to come to the conclusion that finance, even external finance, did not matter, and the Director of the Economic Section expressed the hope that 'the great weight of the Treasury will succeed in reversing this disastrous tendency'.[155]

In March 1945 Eady, while accepting that Britain must maintain strong defence forces after the war, argued that these should not be allowed to exceed what resources of finance, manpower, and productive capacity could reasonably be expected to maintain over a given period. 'No defence', he remarked, 'is weaker than one that seems to be stronger than it is, e.g. France and Italy in this war.' The defence departments' plans might well exceed what was physically possible: for example, the War Office was planning on the basis of a Regular Army of 275,000, in addition to an annual intake of 156,000 conscripts for 1½ to 2 years training, compared with a Regular Army of 176,000 in 1939 (exclusive of 47,000 British troops in India). Keynes agreed that it would be a waste of resources to embark upon policies that could not be maintained, and drew particular attention, as he had done several times before, to the strain that British forces stationed in the Middle East and Africa were placing on Britain's external financial situation.[156]

---

[154] Note by Hopkins on 'The General Form of the Budget', n.d., but position in file indicates July 1944, T273/389; Keynes to Bridges, 23 Mar. 1945, T273/327.

[155] Robbins to Hopkins, 8 Feb. 1945, T273/260.

[156] 'Cost of Defence', by Eady, 14 Mar. 1945, with Keynes's comments, 23 Mar. 1945, T273/327. For Keynes's earlier criticisms of British armed forces' projected overseas expenditure of £550 million in 1945, most of which would be unconnected with operations against Germany or Japan, see JMK, xxiv. 119–22, 166–71, 263–4.

When Churchill was told by Anderson that military expenditure in the Middle East and Africa was as high in 1944 as in 1942, he agreed that all departments should submit plans to the Treasury for reductions of wartime activities, but he also felt that political circumstances precluded immediate decisions on the strength of the services. Meanwhile Bridges set in train measures to restore Treasury control over expenditure following the defeat of Germany, withdrawing delegations from the Treasury of financial authority except where they related to immediate operational needs against Japan, and preparing to restore the traditional system of annual Estimates.[157] As after the First World War, it seemed likely to be some time before the Treasury could restore its grip on public expenditure, and this circumstance was unlikely to encourage experiments in public finance which might allow ministers to expand the National Debt even further for unproductive purposes.

SUMMARY

The Treasury lost much of its authority between 1940 and 1945, as far as the conduct of the war was concerned, but it played an important role in financial diplomacy and in planning post-war reconstruction. It had some success in limiting financial commitments to post-war social services. The successful use of a national income accounting framework in domestic war finance, and the commitment to maintaining a high level of employment after the war, pointed the way to the Treasury becoming more than ever the central department for economic policy. However, that development was not to take place immediately, owing to the incoming Labour government's preference for economic planning that relied upon maintaining wartime direct controls rather than financial measures.

Moreover, the Treasury was not well-placed, as regards its personnel, to become the central department for economic policy. Its permanent officials were largely brought up in the generalist tradition favoured by Warren Fisher, and the death of Phillips and the retirement of Hopkins were severe losses among the small group of officials who had experience of dealing with broad economic issues. For a short time this deficiency was made up by Keynes's willingness to stay on as the Chancellor's economic adviser, but it was clear that the Treasury would have to rely more on the advice of the Economic Section of the Cabinet Office than it had done on the advice of the Economic Advisory Council's Committee on Economic Information before the war. Indeed, the wartime expansion of the Cabinet Office had created an alternative focus for the central co-ordination of government.

[157] Anderson to Churchill, 13 Apr. 1945, and Churchill to Anderson, 21 May 1945; Treasury Circular No. 9/45: 'Control of Expenditure after the Defeat of Germany', 14 May 1945, T273/325.

CHAPTER EIGHT

The Treasury Under Labour, 1945–1951

INTRODUCTION

When the Labour government took office on 26 July 1945 it was confronted with the prospect of what Keynes called 'a financial Dunkirk'. By this expression he meant that Britain's external financial position was so weak that, unless further American aid were forthcoming, it would be necessary to concentrate resources on expanding exports, to withdraw quickly from overseas responsibilities, with great loss of prestige, and to postpone Labour's programme of social reform.[1] Lend-lease was terminated abruptly in August, following the unexpectedly early end of the war in the Far East, and Keynes was sent to the United States to negotiate what became the Anglo-American Loan Agreement of December 1945. He hoped to obtain $5 billion from the United States to help to cover the deficit that was expected in Britain's balance of payments in 1946, 1947, and 1948, while exports recovered and overseas expenditure was reduced. In the event, the United States granted a line of credit of only $3,750 million, on terms that included a commitment to making sterling convertible for current transactions a year after Congress had ratified the agreement.

An acute dollar shortage developed in 1947, as prices in the United States rose, and as Britain, the rest of the sterling area, and western Europe imported more from the United States than their current dollar earnings could pay for. Normally Britain would have been able to earn sufficient dollars by having a balance-of-payments surplus with countries, such as Malaya, that had a trade surplus with the United States. However, this triangular pattern had been interrupted by the war, and had not yet been restored. A flight from sterling in the summer led to the suspension, after five weeks, of the convertibility promised in the Loan Agreement. However, the developing Cold War between Russia and the West made the United States willing to provide the dollars necessary for a European Recovery Programme (better known as Marshall Aid), Britain receiving $2,693 million in 1948–51. In 1949 a recession in the United States made it harder to earn dollars and the consequent sharp drop in Britain's reserves led to a devaluation of sterling from $4.03 to $2.80. Devaluation was successful in that

---

[1] *JMK*, xxiv. 410.

there was a large surplus in the balance of payments on current account in 1950. However, in 1951 there was a dramatic change in the terms of trade as American or American-inspired rearmament and stockpiling raised raw material prices at the time of the Korean War, and Labour's period in office ended as it had begun, with a severe balance-of-payments problem.[2]

Labour had won a parliamentary majority for the first time with promises to provide more and better social services; to build large numbers of houses of a high standard; to maintain full employment; and to nationalize the Bank of England, the coal, gas, electricity, and steel industries, and air, rail, and road transport. At the same time, Ernest Bevin, the Foreign Secretary, was determined that Britain should continue to act as a great power, maintaining larger armed forces than before the war. At first the Cabinet was reluctant to heed Treasury warnings about high levels of expenditure. Labour ministers tended to believe that planning, especially manpower planning, and the use of direct controls, such as the allocation of steel, could counteract market forces. The Treasury was not at first given overall responsibility for economic policy. Ministers apparently expected it to act simply as a ministry of finance—dealing with the budget and monetary policy, conducting financial negotiations with other countries, and controlling expenditure and co-ordinating spending departments' policies—and as the supervisor of the Civil Service.[3] The wartime pattern of interdepartmental committees was continued, and Herbert Morrison, as Lord President, was put in charge of economic planning—but not overseas economic policy, which was dealt with in a separate committee chaired by the Prime Minister, Clement Attlee.

The economic crises of 1947 exposed the weakness of these arrangements, and on 29 September Sir Stafford Cripps was given the new post of Minister of Economic Affairs, with responsibility for co-ordinating policy, while Morrison, who was already deeply involved with implementing Labour's nationalization programme, was left in charge of parliamentary legislation. Attlee was chairman of a new Cabinet committee, the Economic Policy Committee, but it seemed likely that Cripps's new ministry would be the central authority for economic planning and policy. However, on 13 November the Chancellor of the Exchequer, Hugh Dalton, resigned, having inadvertently let slip details of tax changes to a journalist immediately before introducing an autumn budget to Parliament. Cripps was appointed Chancellor and took with him to the Treasury the responsibility and staff that he had had as Minister of Economic Affairs. The Treasury thus, by chance, found itself leading and co-ordinating economic policy as a whole, as well as carrying out its traditional functions in relation to

[2] Alec Cairncross, *Years of Recovery: British Economic Policy, 1945-51* (1985), esp. 36, 79, 116, 154, 366; E. A. G. Robinson, 'The Economic Problems of the Transition from War to Peace', *Cambridge J. Econ.*, 10 (1986), 165-85.
[3] 'The Functions of the Treasury as a Department of State', n.d., Dalton papers, part II, section 9, file 2, British Library of Political and Economic Science, London.

finance and the civil service. By 1949 a Treasury Organisation Committee felt able to assume that this situation would continue under future Chancellors, although it was known that this assumption might very well not commend itself to a number of ministers, and that, in particular, it would be frowned upon by the Foreign Office.[4]

Between 1945 and 1951 Britain moved from a wartime economy, with widespread controls on consumption (through rationing), investment (principally through the allocation of materials), imports, and prices, to one where there was increasing reliance on managing aggregate demand through budgetary policy. However, the transition to Keynesian techniques was neither complete nor intended to be so by Labour Chancellors of the Exchequer. Even in 1950 Hugh Gaitskell believed that it would not be practicable to maintain full employment without a slight excess of money incomes, which would make it necessary to retain direct controls in order to prevent inflation, because monetary and budgetary instruments would not be sufficient for that purpose.[5] There has been considerable academic debate about whether or when the Treasury became converted to Keynesian techniques to manage the economy.[6] It is perhaps more useful to think in terms of Keynesian techniques being integrated into Treasury thinking in the late 1940s without displacing Labour Chancellors' concern for planning or direct controls over the economy as a whole, or officials' concern for maintenance of effective control over public expenditure.

PERSONALITIES AND ORGANIZATION

Dalton was the first Chancellor of the Exchequer to be a professional economist. He had taught at the London School of Economics from 1919 to 1935 and was the author of *The Principles of Public Finance* (1923), a standard text on the subject.[7] Moreover, he had had experience of being in charge of two economic ministries, the Ministry of Economic Warfare and the Board of Trade, during the war. Even so, he would have preferred to be Foreign Secretary in 1945. When Attlee asked him to be Chancellor, Dalton said that he was much less confident that he could do a good job at the Treasury than he would have done at

[4] 'Treasury Organisation Committee: Interim Report', 17 Feb. 1949, and Sir John Woods (chairman) to Bridges, 22 Feb. 1949, T273/309.

[5] Economic Policy Committee minutes, 19 Jan. 1950, CAB134/224.

[6] See, for example, Alan Booth, 'The "Keynesian Revolution" in Economic Policy-making', *Econ. Hist. Rev.*, 2nd ser., 36 (1983), 103–23; id., *British Economic Policy, 1931–49: Was There a Keynesian Revolution?* (1989); Neil Rollings, 'The "Keynesian Revolution" and Economic Policy-making: A Comment', *Econ. Hist. Rev.*, 2nd ser., 38 (1985), 95–100; id., 'British Budgetary Policy, 1945–1954: A "Keynesian Revolution"?', *Econ. Hist. Rev.*, 2nd ser., 41 (1988), 283–98; J. Tomlinson, *Democratic Socialism and Economic Policy: The Attlee Years, 1945–1951* (Cambridge, 1997), ch. 10.

[7] Dalton had been trained at Cambridge and the London School of Economics. At LSE he was lecturer in economics, 1919–20, and Cassel Reader in Commerce, 1920–35. His *Principles of Public Finance* ran to four editions between 1923 and 1954.

the Foreign Office.[8] In his memoirs Dalton speculated on why Bevin had been appointed Foreign Secretary instead of Chancellor, as Attlee had apparently first intended, but Dalton seems to have been unaware that his own Permanent Secretary, Sir Edward Bridges, had advised Attlee not to appoint Bevin to the Treasury, on the grounds that Bevin would be unable to work amicably with Morrison, who, as Lord President, would have responsibility for co-ordinating domestic economic policy.[9] Dalton's appointment thus owed as much to personalities as it did to his expertise in economics.

Dalton had played a major role in preparing economic and financial policies for a future Labour government. In the 1930s he had recruited younger economists, Colin Clark, Evan Durbin, and Hugh Gaitskell, together with Douglas Jay, a financial journalist who had studied economics as a fellow of All Souls College, to the party's influential Finance and Trade Subcommittee. With their help he had taken a leading part in drafting *Labour's Immediate Programme* (1937), which set out the main items of Labour's nationalization programme. Using drafts by Durbin, Gaitskell, and Jay, he had also produced the party's policy statement, *Full Employment and Financial Policy* (1944), in advance of the Coalition Government's white paper on employment policy. Dalton himself described *Full Employment and Financial Policy* as 'largely Keynesian', and it certainly accepted Keynes's ideas on macroeconomic policy, but it was also based upon a belief in the efficacy of socialist planning, using physical controls developed in the war economy. As President of the Board of Trade, Dalton had been concerned with regional policy. He also had a long-standing academic and political interest in the inequality of incomes, which led him to favour progressive taxation. He was thus interested in much more than Keynesian macroeconomic management.[10]

Dalton later listed the urgent problems he faced as Chancellor in 1945 as: first, the reconversion of industry, manpower, and expenditure to peaceful purposes; second, a smooth transition, maintaining full employment and avoiding strikes or any sharp rise in the cost of living (a boom and slump on the pattern of 1919–21 were widely feared); third, fulfilment of Labour's promises to extend social services; fourth, a reduction in the total of taxation, but also the use of taxation to reduce the gap between rich and poor; fifth, the carrying out of nationalization pledges; and sixth, most difficult and pressing of all, finding the means to pay for essential imports of raw materials and food.[11] This was a formidable list and it is not surprising that the strain of work should lead to a decline in his health from 1946. Moreover, he did not carry enough weight in Cabinet

[8] Diary, 27 July 1945, Dalton papers, part 1, vol. 33.
[9] Hugh Dalton, *High Tide and After: Memoirs, 1945–1960* (1962), 8–13; Douglas Jay, *Change and Fortune* (1980), 129–30.
[10] Elizabeth Durbin, *New Jerusalems: The Labour Party and the Economics of Democratic Socialism* (1985), 156, 244–8; Ben Pimlott, *Hugh Dalton* (1985), esp. 138–42, 237–8, 395–407.
[11] Dalton, *Principles of Public Finance* (1954), 229.

to secure the reductions in overseas expenditure that his officials thought were necessary.

Cripps had no training in economics, but he had a barrister's skill in exposition, which he used with effect in Cabinet. He was not without experience of economic problems, having helped to prepare Snowden's budget in the spring of 1931, and as Minister for Aircraft Production during the war, and President of the Board of Trade from 1945 until he become Minister of Economic Affairs in 1947. In the 1930s he had believed that a socialist programme could only be carried out by changing the machinery of government, with the Treasury being absorbed into a new department of finance, of which it might form a sub-department, and with the annual budget incorporated into an annual planning and finance bill.[12] He may well have felt that the Treasury, as enlarged by the inclusion of his staff from the Ministry of Economic Affairs, and advised by the Economic Section, approximated to this earlier conception. Certainly, he was committed to the idea of socialist planning and, like the rest of the Cabinet, he was reluctant to be guided by market forces. He was interested in microeconomic questions that extended beyond the normal brief for a Chancellor of the Exchequer: for example, he played a leading role in the creation of the British Institute of Management and the Anglo-American Council on Productivity, which were intended to increase productivity by respectively raising the quality of managers and facilitating the transfer of American know-how.[13]

Lord Jay, who was Economic Secretary from 1947 to 1950, and Financial Secretary 1950–1, thought that Cripps made the most of an exceptionally able group of advisers in the Treasury. He held an informal meeting with them every morning and, such was his passion for punctuality, the Permanent Secretary, Bridges, who travelled by train from Epsom, could sometimes be seen running down the pavement of Great George Street so as to reach the Chancellor's room by 9.30. Cripps would also hold at least one working weekend in the country before his budgets, the most favoured rendezvous being a home for rehabilitating nervous invalids. He himself worked such long hours that his health suffered and he had to retire in October 1950.[14]

Cripps's successor, Gaitskell, was a professional economist, having been a lecturer, and then reader, in political economy at University College London, between 1928 and 1945. He had gained practical experience of economic affairs as a temporary official in the Board of Trade during the war, and as Minister of Fuel and Power from 1947 to 1950. He moved to the Treasury after the general election of February 1950 as Minister of State for Economic Affairs, to assist the

[12] Stafford Cripps, 'Can Socialism Come by Constitutional Methods?', in Christopher Addison, et al., *Problems of a Socialist Government* (1933), 61–2.
[13] Nick Tiratsoo and Jim Tomlinson, *Industrial Efficiency and State Intervention: Labour, 1939–51* (1993), 111–12, 132.
[14] Jay, *Change and Fortune*, 170–80; E. Plowden, *An Industrialist in the Treasury: The Post-War Years* (1989), 19–22.

ailing Chancellor. Although only a junior minister, Gaitskell was a member of the Cabinet's Economic Policy Committee, and, when Cripps went on leave for three months in August, he moved into the Chancellor's office and took over his duties. Robert Hall, the Director of the Economic Section, noted that Gaitskell liked to talk about economics, and indeed took up a lot of time doing so, but had two great defects as a Chancellor: he went into too much detail instead of relying on his staff, and he tended to antagonize senior civil servants by adopting a critical or imperative tone. Gaitskell also tended to be unpunctual for meetings with his senior advisers, in contrast to Cripps. The new Chancellor, for his part, did not care for Treasury officials' sense of their own independent, departmental position as apart from serving him.[15]

There were inevitably differences between traditional Treasury views and those of Labour ministers. Dalton, for example, thought he had to go against the 'foolish, unpolitical' advice of his officials in 1945 when they attempted to discourage him from raising surtax and exempting two million people from income tax.[16] Likewise officials and ministers tended to differ over the utility of direct or price controls. Dalton, Cripps, and Gaitskell all believed that there were positive advantages in using such controls to allocate resources, whereas officials tended to assume that controls should be used only where there were shortages, and that otherwise it was desirable to interfere with the market economy as little as possible. At a meeting in 1950, in which Dalton, Cripps, and Gaitskell all took part, there was, in the words of an official who was present, 'a lot of talk about civil servants reared in poor but honest Liberal homes, who gave misguided advice . . . because of their background and upbringing'; Dalton adding that officials were bound also to be influenced by the tone of the *Economist* and the speeches of bank chairmen.[17] However, the Permanent Secretary, Bridges, denied that he and other officials were incapable of giving unprejudiced service to Labour ministers. Jay thought, in retrospect, that the only example of Treasury officials' resistance to what Labour ministers were trying to do was when officials tried to persuade Dalton and Cripps to restrict food subsidies, although cheap food was essential for the government's incomes policy.[18] On balance, the experience of 1945–51 provides very little evidence in support of claims by Tony Benn and Richard Crossman that civil servants deliberately obstruct Labour programmes.[19]

Bridges occupied an extraordinary position in 1945 and 1946, being Cabinet Secretary as well as Permanent Secretary of the Treasury and head of the Civil

[15] *The Robert Hall Diaries, 1947–1953*, ed. Alec Cairncross (1989), 133, 162; *The Diary of Hugh Gaitskell, 1945–1956*, ed. Phillip Williams (1983), 220–1.

[16] Dalton Diary, vol. 33, 1 Nov. 1945.

[17] Alexander Johnston to Sir Bernard Gilbert, 20 Jan. 1950, T273/311. In 1949 Cripps complained to Gaitskell that 'my official advisers are all "liberals" '—Gaitskell, *Diary*, 130.

[18] Bridges to T. L. Rowan, 19 Nov. 1946, Dalton papers, part II, section 9, file 2; conversation with Lord Jay, 11 Nov. 1988.

[19] See Kevin Theakston, *The Labour Party and Whitehall* (1992), esp. 1–3, 25–31.

Service. It is true that his position as Cabinet Secretary was largely nominal, with his future successor, Norman Brook, doing all the effective work of arranging and recording the Cabinet's business, while Bridges oversaw the transfer of the Cabinet Office's war-related work to the new Ministry of Defence. Bridges was in many ways a model civil servant. He thought and wrote clearly, even elegantly, as might be expected of the son of a Poet Laureate. Like so many other senior officials, he had read *literae humaniores* at Oxford, but he was unusually distinguished academically in being a fellow of All Souls College. Gaitskell described him as a 'shy, rather dry, academic person', but Bridges' fellow civil servant, Sir John Winnifrith, described him as someone who could describe a long session of drafting as 'great fun', and who inspired affection as well as respect. Bridges had served in Establishment or Supply divisions of the Treasury prior to becoming Cabinet Secretary in 1938, and had no experience of the financial side of the department. As late as 1948 he could describe aspects of monetary policy, or wages and prices policy, as 'unfamiliar', 'difficult', or 'elusive'. Nevertheless, as chairman of the Treasury's Budget Committee from 1945, he mastered the complexities of public finance and persuaded his more traditionally minded colleagues to accept the continuation of the budget's wartime role in economic management. He also supported the government's commitment to employment policy, although some sceptical senior colleagues did not.[20]

Bridges regarded himself as carrying on Warren Fisher's work as head of a unified Civil Service, but avoided using the title lest it stir up unnecessary controversy. It was typical of his quiet, informal approach that he should strengthen his contact with the rest of Whitehall by founding a dining club for permanent secretaries. He did not seek to accumulate power. It was at his own suggestion that, having completed the changeover of the Cabinet Office to a peacetime basis, he gave up the title of Cabinet Secretary. It was also at his suggestion that he should not be a regular attender at Cabinet meetings as Permanent Secretary of the Treasury, lest it be said, as had been said of Sir Horace Wilson, that he was seeking to exercise more influence than was right for a civil servant.[21]

Below the level of Permanent Secretary the Treasury had three Second Secretaries in 1945, Sir Wilfrid Eady, Bernard Gilbert, and Sir Alan Barlow, each with the status equivalent to the official head of any other Whitehall Department, and each with direct access to the Chancellor (see Figure 8.1). When Cripps became Chancellor he brought with him two more officials of this status: Leslie Rowan, who had been Permanent Secretary of the Office of the Minister of Economic Affairs, and who was given the rank of Second Secretary in the Treasury, and Sir Edwin Plowden, the Chief Planning Officer and head

[20] Gaitskell, *Diary*, 248; J. Meade, *Collected Papers*, vol. iv, ed. S. Howson and D. Moggridge, *The Cabinet Office Diary, 1944–46* (1990), 85; Neil Rollings, 'Keynesian Revolution', 98; Sir John Winnifrith, 'Edward Ettingdean Bridges—Baron Bridges', *Biographical Memoirs of Fellows of the Royal Society*, 16 (1970), 37–56.
[21] Bridges to Prime Minister, 5 Nov. 1946, T273/74.

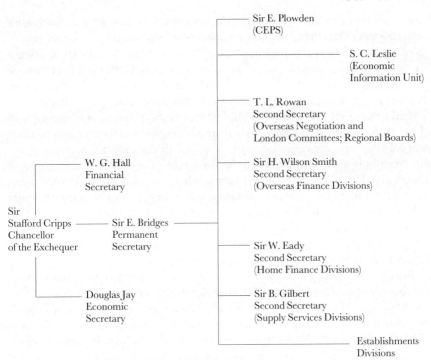

FIG. 8.1.   *Treasury Organization at July 1948*
Source: T199/702.

of the Central Economic Planning Staff (CEPS). Barlow retired in 1948, leaving the Treasury with no Second Secretary responsible for establishment and machinery of government questions, but in the same year Sir Henry Wilson Smith, who had been Permanent Secretary of the Ministry of Defence, returned to the Treasury as a Second Secretary, initially (January) to share Eady's responsibility for overseas finance and then (from June) to take over responsibility, leaving Eady to supervise home finance. The Treasury thus continued to have four Second Secretaries, whereas until 1942 there had only been one (Sir Richard Hopkins). In 1948 Bridges instituted regular meetings, which he chaired, of the four Second Secretaries, plus Plowden, and the Permanent Secretary of the Board of Trade, Sir John Woods, to ensure proper co-ordination of the various aspects of economic policy.[22]

There was also an increase in the number of Third Secretaries from three in 1945 to seven by 1949. It is not surprising that the chairman of a committee

---

[22] Bridges to Trend, 17 June 1948, T273/391.

enquiring into the Treasury's organization remarked in 1950 that the higher organization of the department 'certainly looks to be on the top-heavy side'.[23] Even so, many heads of departments outside the Treasury believed that Bridges carried too great a burden, given that his duties as head of the Civil Service were particularly onerous as Whitehall adapted from war to peace. It was suggested during the enquiry into the Treasury's organization that either Bridges' job should be divided between two Joint Permanent Secretaries, one dealing with the Civil Service and the other with the rest of his duties—the solution adopted when Bridges finally retired in 1956—or that Bridges should have a deputy. Bridges did not, in fact, attempt to be the Chancellor's chief adviser on every aspect of policy, although he liked to know what was going on, and would intervene if he thought that advice to ministers was wrong, or had been insufficiently discussed either within the Treasury or with other departments. Nevertheless, Bridges was certainly feeling the strain. He developed a mysterious muscular nervous complaint, and it seems likely that by 1951 he was looking forward to retirement on his sixtieth birthday in the following year.[24]

Bridges was slow to carry out his intention of developing better central machinery of government in which the relationship between the Treasury and the Cabinet Office would be clearer. He himself believed in Warren Fisher's doctrine that 'the Treasury is the central department of government, of which the Prime Minister is First Lord'. However, he had also overseen the development of the Cabinet Office's civil side, which had hardly existed when he had become Cabinet Secretary in 1938, but which during the war had come to include the Economic Section and the Central Statistical Office. As he told Attlee in 1946, 'no-one today would think of describing the central organisation of the Government machine without describing the role played by the Cabinet Office'. Bridges said he preferred to wait upon 'practical experience' before making formal changes, but it seems likely that he was also inhibited by the division of ministerial responsibility for economic policy between the Lord President, Morrison, the Chancellor, Dalton, and, from 1947, the Minister of Economic Affairs, Cripps. Although the Economic Section and the Central Statistical Office were to 'carry out special duties for the Treasury', they remained in the Cabinet Office.[25]

The Treasury's own organization was untidy with regard to external economic policy. Until his death in April 1946, Keynes largely determined policy and conducted the major negotiations, but dependence on Keynes inhibited officials from developing their own technique and ideas.[26] Moreover, until 1948,

---

[23] Informal report on 'Higher Organisation of the Treasury', sent by Woods to Bridges, 28 July 1950, T273/202. Woods had served in the much smaller Treasury of 1920–43 before becoming Permanent Secretary of the Board of Trade.   [24] Winnifrith, op. cit., 49, 53.

[25] Bridges to Prime Minister, 5 Nov. 1946, with 'Suggested Draft Announcement', T273/74.

[26] R. Clarke, *Anglo-American Economic Collaboration in War and Peace, 1942–1949*, ed. A. Cairncross (Oxford, 1982), 71.

the same Second Secretary, Eady, had oversight of both the overseas finance and home finance divisions. Dalton was dissatisfied with the quality of advice given with regard to the convertibility of sterling in 1947, and he asked Bridges to redistribute the work so as to spread the burden more evenly—hence Wilson Smith's appointment as Second Secretary in charge of overseas finance.

The arrival of Plowden and Rowan in 1948 increased the number of senior officials with an interest in, or responsibility for, external economic policy. The CEPS, which Plowden headed, had originally been set up in March 1947, with the function of developing a long-term plan to utilize Britain's manpower and other resources, but the planners could not ignore external economic policy in doing so; indeed the Economic Survey for 1948–52 was largely concerned with how Britain could achieve balance-of-payments equilibrium, a question that also impinged on the Marshall Aid negotiations. Rowan, while Permanent Secretary at the Office of the Minister of Economic Affairs, had been put in charge of the interdepartmental committees handling the balance of payments, and continued to do so as a Treasury official.

These committees were the Overseas Negotiation Committee, chaired by Rowan, which met almost daily to manage Britain's trading and financial dealings with other countries; the London Committee, chaired originally by a Treasury Under-Secretary, Richard ('Otto') Clarke, and then, from mid-1948, by Rowan, which advised on the European Recovery Programme; the Programmes Committee, chaired by Clarke, which prepared all balance-of-payments programmes; and the Export Committee, chaired by an official from the Board of Trade. Rowan's success in co-ordinating balance-of-payments policy reflected his own ability and energy as an administrator, and was in spite of, rather than because of, the division of responsibility between overseas finance, the CEPS, and himself. Although he had neither the training of an economist nor long experience of economic matters, he was appointed Economic Minister at the Washington Embassy in 1949. Responsibility for co-ordinating external economic policy thereafter lay with a working group chaired by Plowden, with representatives of the Cabinet Office, Board of Trade, Foreign Office, and Commonwealth Relations Office, as well as the different sections of the Treasury.[27]

The shortcomings of the Treasury with regard to overseas finance were not confined to organization. There was also a shortage of officials with the necessary experience and knowledge. As already noted, Eady seems to have had an uncertain grasp of the technical aspects of financial policy. His successor at the Second Secretary level from 1948, Wilson Smith, had previously been Third Secretary in charge of supervising the Civil Service—not obviously relevant

[27] Plowden to Woods, 29 Nov. 1948, CAB21/2220; 'Treasury Organisation Committee: Interim Report', 17 Feb. 1949, and Bridges to Chancellor, 29 Mar. 1949, T273/309; Jay, *Change and Fortune*, 171; Hall, *Diaries, 1947–1953*, 117.

experience for handling the dollar shortage. Gaitskell thought that Wilson Smith was no expert, in that the latter did not understand economics as well as he did.[28] However, when Wilson Smith left the Civil Service for a career in business in August 1951, he was succeeded by another generalist, Rowan.

The Third Secretary dealing with overseas finance work down to March 1947, Sir David Waley, had served on that side of the Treasury since the First World War, and when he retired it proved to be hard to fill the gap that he left. His immediate successor, Ernest Rowe-Dutton, had also first experienced overseas finance work during the First World War, and had been financial adviser at the embassy in Berlin from 1928 to 1932 and in Paris from 1934 to 1939, but he suffered from ill health. The pressure of work was such that in August 1948 Sir Sydney Caine was brought in from the Colonial Office as a second Third Secretary on the overseas finance side of the Treasury. Unlike most of his new colleagues, Caine had studied economics at university, graduating from the London School of Economics with first-class honours. He had at one time been Financial Adviser to the Secretary of State for the Colonies, and was described by Hall as 'very wise and sensible'.[29] However, in December 1948 Caine was appointed head of the UK Treasury and Supply Delegation in Washington. It became apparent in 1949 that Rowe-Dutton could not carry a heavy load, and in May Sir Herbert Brittain, a Third Secretary on the home finance side of the Treasury, was transferred to help out the overseas finance side, only to be taken away again four months later to lead 'a Treasury blitz' on government expenditure. Wilson Smith deplored this last move, on the grounds that someone with Brittain's qualities had been invaluable 'in the somewhat untidy and temperamental O.F. menage'.[30]

Otto Clarke was one of the more temperamental members of the overseas-finance menage, but, although ranking below the Second and Third Secretaries, he was perhaps the most influential, providing drive and flair, and playing a crucial part in working out British policy towards the Marshall Plan. Clarke, who had come to the Treasury in 1945 after wartime experience as a temporary civil servant in the ministries of Information, Economic Warfare, Supply, and Production, had studied economics as well as mathematics at Cambridge. As a financial journalist before the war, he had devised what became the *Financial Times* Index and it was said that he could do anything with figures.[31] The other overseas finance official with a firm grasp of economics was Denis Rickett, a fellow of All Souls College, who had studied economics privately after taking a First in *literae humaniores*, and who had served on the staff of the Economic Advisory Council before the war.[32]

---

[28] Gaitskell, *Diary*, 186.   [29] Hall, *Diaries, 1947–1953*, 117.

[30] Wilson Smith to Bridges, 14 Sept. 1949, T273/138, and other papers in that file; J. Fforde, *The Bank of England and Public Policy, 1941–1958* (Cambridge, 1992), 107, 159.

[31] David Hubback, 'Sir Richard Clarke—1910–1975: A Most Unusual Civil Servant', *Public Policy and Admin.*, 3 (1988), 19–34.   [32] Conversation with Lord Jay.

There was no senior official on the home finance or the Supply Services side of the Treasury with any flair for general economic policy. Bridges, who was a good judge of other people's arguments, ensured that discussions of the Treasury's Budget Committee were informed by professional economic analysis by inviting the Director of the Economic Section to attend, even though the Economic Section was not formally a part of the Treasury until 1953. The old school of administrative officials continued to be influential, however: Gilbert, the Second Secretary in charge of the Supply Services divisions, was described by Dalton as 'the wisest of my advisers'. A Cambridge wrangler in mathematics, Gilbert could summarize complex issues in a one-page memorandum and translate technical jargon into plain English. At a more junior level, Dennis Proctor, the principal assistant secretary in charge of the Treasury's division responsible for co-ordinating employment policy, understood applied economics. He was promoted to Third Secretary in 1948 but left the Civil Service in 1950 to go into business.[33]

Most Treasury officials continued to be occupied in the department's traditional roles of controlling expenditure or supervising the Civil Service. However, the control of expenditure involved taking a close interest in the policies of other departments. In 1950 Gilbert noted that in recent years Supply Services divisions had extended their field of interest to questions that did not directly involve expenditure of voted money. For example, they were consulted on wage and cost-of-living policies, and agricultural price policy.[34] Cripps stressed that economic policy needed public opinion behind it, if it were to be effective, and he brought into the Treasury the Economic Information Unit under Clem Leslie, in an attempt to explain to the public the need for austerity and for increased exports and productivity.[35]

As head of the Civil Service, Bridges seems to have assumed that Whitehall would return to its pre-war shape and functions, once the transition to a peacetime economy was complete. Along with permanent heads of other departments he discouraged Dalton and Attlee from setting up a parliamentary inquiry into whether the Civil Service was capable of implementing Labour's legislation. Most senior officials recognized that they had something to learn from the industrialists with whom they had worked during the war, if the Civil Service was to be able to carry out the managerial functions required under a planned economy, but men brought up in the pre-war tradition were unlikely to favour change from a service of generalists to one where a premium was placed on technical knowledge. Bridges set up a number of interdepartmental working parties of officials in 1946 to consider such questions as recruitment, training, and organization and business efficiency. Thereafter he chaired a Government

[33] Pimlott, *Hugh Dalton*, 426. Conversation with Lord Jay.
[34] Treasury Organisation Committee, 6th meeting, 23 Mar. 1950, T273/203.
[35] Hall, *Diaries, 1954–1961*, 193; Jay, *Change and Fortune*, 175–6.

Organisation Committee, which, in consultation with all permanent heads of departments, promoted a number of modest measures designed to improve organization and methods of departments, but it could hardly be claimed that any of these measures amounted to a major break from the past.[36]

Even so, there was change so far as Treasury control of the Civil Service was concerned. The Treasury recognized that the pressure of government business precluded a return to the close control of establishments in other departments that had been exercised down to 1939. On the recommendation of a committee of establishments officers chaired by John Winnifrith, a Treasury Under-Secretary, Bridges accepted in 1949 that the Treasury should no longer require departments to put up a case for its consideration for each new post; instead more responsibility should be taken by establishments officers in the spending departments, and Treasury time should be devoted instead to carrying out systematic surveys of the staff of each department as a whole.[37]

ECONOMIC ADVICE

Although the generalist tradition prevailed in the Civil Service, the Treasury's extended responsibilities for economic policy required professional advice. Down to his death in April 1946 Keynes continued in his wartime role of adviser to the Chancellor, but his relations with Dalton were uneasy. Keynes had been Dalton's tutor at Cambridge before the First World War and the latter was aware that he had not been regarded as an outstanding student. According to Sir Alec Cairncross, Dalton felt that, as an economist, he was not in need of professional advice, yet it was Dalton who arranged that Keynes should stay on at the Treasury as his adviser, along with Sir Richard Hopkins.[38] Hopkins was not, of course, a professional economist—he was an expert on public finance—but the fact that Dalton appointed an adviser in his own academic field does not suggest that he felt too proud to take advice. Indeed, as already noted, Dalton had freely drawn upon the ideas of younger economists in the 1930s, and he appointed one of them, Evan Durbin, as his parliamentary private secretary in 1945.

James Meade, who was actively in charge of the Economic Section from the autumn of 1945 until April 1947, was a member of the Treasury's Budget Committee. However, although he was an outstanding economist—he was awarded

---

[36] R. A. Chapman, *Ethics in the British Civil Service* (1988), 197–204; P. Hennessy, *Whitehall* (1989), 122–7; J. M. Lee, 'Reviewing the Machinery of Government, 1942–1952: An Essay on the Anderson Committee and its Successors' (Civil Service Department, 1977). I am grateful to Professor Lee for supplying me with a copy.

[37] 'Treasury Control of Establishments Business', 2 Mar. 1948, and Bridges to Financial Secretary and Chancellor of the Exchequer, 28 June 1949, T273/201.

[38] Cairncross, *Years of Recovery*, 55; id. and N. Watts, *The Economic Section, 1939–1961: A Study in Economic Advising* (1989), 133; Dalton diary, vol. 33, 3 Aug. 1945; Pimlott, *Hugh Dalton*, 426, 428–9.

the Nobel Prize in Economics in 1977—Meade had his failings as an economic *adviser*. According to Otto Clarke, Meade was 'ridiculously academic and perfectionist',[39] and certainly he produced some very long and technical papers. Moreover, the pressure of Whitehall life gave him stomach ulcers, forcing him to resign. Meade was also handicapped by the difficulty he experienced in recruiting good economists, most of the best ones in the Economic Section having returned to academic life at the end of the war, and Sir Robert Hall, Meade's successor, thought that the staff in 1947 was 'very mediocre'.[40] There was, too, as Pimlott has pointed out, a fundamental difference between Meade's conception of what he called the Liberal-Socialist state and Dalton's conception of socialist economic policy: whereas Meade believed that fiscal policy must be the main instrument, Dalton preferred physical controls and physical planning because they seemed to enable the government to allocate resources and to reduce the gap between rich and poor. There was also the problem that, until Cripps took over from Dalton as Chancellor, the Economic Section had to serve more than one ministerial master. For all these reasons, the Economic Section was at its least effective in the period 1945–7.[41]

Hall, who became Director in September 1947, was a rather taciturn Australian, who had been a fellow in economics at Trinity College, Oxford, since 1927. More significantly, perhaps, in the context of Whitehall, he had had several years of administrative experience in the Ministry of Supply and the Board of Trade. Before the war he had published a book on *The Economic System in a Socialist State*, in which he had advocated controls over dressmakers to prevent them competing through changes in fashion, permitting only those changes originating with consumers, 'who would be compelled to make their own dresses'.[42] This idea suggests that he must have found Cripps's advocacy of austerity congenial. Hall was not in the same class as Meade as a theoretician but was much more successful as an economic adviser. Unlike Meade, he understood that 'in general administrators find that a balanced view from an economist is no use at all. . . . In my experience it is not much good giving advice to Ministers unless it is very loud and clear.'[43] Hall also had the advantage, following Dalton's resignation in November 1947, of having to deal only with Cripps. Like Meade, Hall became a member of the Budget Committee, and was soon treated by the Treasury as if he were a member of the department. He was able to recruit some able young economists, partly through the innovation of secondments from universities for two years, and it was the Economic Section's

[39] Clarke's diary, Jan. 1946, cited in Hubback, 'Sir Richard Clarke', 25.
[40] Hall, *Diaries, 1947–1953*, 23.
[41] Pimlott, *Hugh Dalton*, 470–5; E. A. G. Robinson, 'The Beginning of the Economic Section of the Cabinet Office', *Cambridge J. Econ.*, 15 (1991), 96.
[42] R. Hall, *The Economic System in a Socialist State* (1937), 185–6.
[43] Hall to J. Downie, 26 Oct. 1949, T230/163. For Hall's background and career see Kit Jones, *An Economist Among Mandarins: A Biography of Robert Hall, 1901–1988* (Cambridge, 1994).

assessment of the economic situation, as presented by him, that formed the basis of budget discussions from 1948. He also played an important part in advising on other aspects of policy, notably devaluation in 1949.[44]

There was clearly some overlap between the work of the Economic Section and that of the CEPS, which had its own economists, notably Austin Robinson. Plowden had studied economics at Cambridge, but he regarded himself as an industrialist with experience of administration and planning in the Ministry of Aircraft Production, rather than as an economist. Insofar as there was a distinction between the CEPS and the Economic Section, the former tended to be concerned primarily with the use of physical resources—for example, making studies of coal, electricity, steel, and transport, whereas the Economic Section tended to have a macroeconomic approach to economic problems. Fortunately Plowden and Hall collaborated very well with each other, and the potential overlap was reduced by the decision not to replace Robinson when he left the CEPS in 1948. Thereafter Plowden relied upon the Economic Section for specialist economic advice, while the CEPS concentrated on the administrative aspects of planning and co-ordination. Plowden described his partnership with Hall as follows: Hall 'would most often provide an idea or piece of analysis, we would discuss it, and then I would present it to the relevant committee or to the Chancellor as best I could. As such, he loaded the gun and I fired the bullets.'[45]

On monetary policy Dalton particularly valued the advice of Keynes and Hopkins,[46] but the Treasury continued to rely on the Bank of England's expertise in managing the National Debt and the banking system. Nationalization of the Bank in 1946 made very little practical difference to relations between it and the Treasury, or to the Bank itself. Indeed, the Bank welcomed the Act of 1946, which it had helped to draft, because the Act reinforced the *status quo*. The Governor continued to give advice in person to the Chancellor, with very little consultation between Treasury and Bank officials. Neither Lord Catto, who had succeeded Norman as Governor of the Bank in 1944, nor his successor from February 1949, Cameron Cobbold, made any major changes to the way the Bank worked. The Bank's official historian has criticized its failure to make use of professional economists or to compile adequate statistics. Constitutional subordination to the Chancellor of the Exchequer allowed the Bank to avoid direct responsibility for the consequences of its actions or advice, the latter being confidential and narrowly technical, based on expertise in managing money markets. On the other hand, when Treasury officials asked the Treasury Solicitor in 1951 about the Chancellor's power to issue directions to banks under the Bank of England Act, they were told that he had none. The power to give

---

[44]   Cairncross and Watts, *Economic Section*, ch. 9.

[45]   Plowden, *Industrialist at the Treasury*, 25. See also Cairncross and Watts, *Economic Section*, 157–60, 170–2, 179–80, 184.

[46]   S. Howson, *British Monetary Policy, 1945–51* (Oxford, 1993), 128–31, 326–9; Trend to Bridges, 8 Sept. 1947, T171/392.

directions to the banks lay with the Bank, which could not, for example, be forced to tell them to hold a specified amount of government debt.[47]

ECONOMIC PLANNING

According to the Public Record Office's guide to documents relating to economic planning, the Treasury was concerned in 1945 to regain its predominant position in Whitehall and 'there is much to suggest' that senior officials 'judged it useful to employ the rhetoric of planning even if they did not subscribe to its principles'.[48] Much, of course, depends upon what one means by planning, and it is certainly the case that Treasury officials do not seem to have subscribed to the same principles of planning as the authors of the introduction to the guide, where it is stated that planning requires predetermination of consumer choices as well as the specification of targets for output, with central allocation of resources between different industries.[49] On the other hand, Treasury officials did not favour a swift return to a free market in the circumstances of 1945. There was no question that a smooth transition from war to peace would require some central allocation of scarce resources using direct controls; no one in Whitehall wished to see a repetition of the inflationary boom followed by a slump, which had followed the First World War. Officials' support for planning in the immediate post-1945 period should not, therefore, be dismissed as mere rhetoric. Rather than impose an abstract definition on 'planning', it is perhaps better to regard that term as an ambiguous, omnibus concept, that might mean different things to different people, rather like 'rationalization' in the inter-war period. There is little evidence that Labour ministers collectively had a clear conception of what they meant by the term. As it happened, however, two members of the Cabinet who had clear ideas about macroeconomic planning, Cripps and Gaitskell,[50] were, somewhat fortuitously, successive Chancellors of the Exchequer between 1947 and 1951, and they tended to strengthen the Treasury's position at the centre of government.

As Rollings has pointed out, Treasury officials sought to protect the department's prerogatives by maintaining a clear distinction between financial and

---

[47] Fforde, Bank of England, 2–10, 318–20, 345–6; Howson, British Monetary Policy, 110–17, 297.

[48] B. W. E. Alford, Rodney Lowe, and Neil Rollings, Economic Planning, 1943–1951 (1992), 6.

[49] Ibid., 4. For discussion of the nature of planning in 1945–51 in relation to other periods and conceptions of planning see Alan Budd, The Politics of Economic Planning (1978).

[50] According to Sir Richard Clarke, in relation to the Economic Survey for 1947, only Cripps thought in terms of economic planning, rather than in terms of nationalization (Morrison) or fiscal policy (Dalton)—Clarke, Anglo-American Economic Collaboration, 78–9. Gaitskell was the moving spirit behind planning for full employment, with some permanent economic controls, in 1950–1—see Neil Rollings, ' "The Reichstag Method of Governing"? The Attlee Governments and Permanent Economic Controls', in Helen Mercer, Neil Rollings, and Jim Tomlinson (eds.), Labour Governments and Private Industry: The Experience of 1945–1951 (Edinburgh, 1992), 15–36, and Jim Tomlinson, 'Planning: Debate and Policy in the 1940s', 20th Cent. Brit. Hist., 3 (1992), 154–74.

direct controls, and thereby avoiding interference from other departments in financial matters.[51] For example, the Investment (Controls and Guarantees) Act of 1946 made permanent the wartime Capital Issues Committee, which advised the Chancellor of the Exchequer, and which could prevent the issue of shares, but the committee's functions were kept quite separate from the direct controls operated by the Board of Trade. The 1946 Act also created a National Investment Council (NIC) under the chairmanship of the Chancellor of the Exchequer, as a very limited concession to long-standing support in the Labour party for a national investment board that would license the issuing of new capital and would have the power to issue funds itself. However, the NIC was dominated by people with a City background, and was purely advisory. Dalton recalled that Treasury officials never liked the NIC, because they thought that the advice it gave the Chancellor might conflict with their own, and it was wound up by Cripps in December 1948.[52]

Even so, the position which Bridges envisaged for the Treasury in Whitehall does not seem to have been identical to what had existed before the war. In conjunction with Norman Brook at the Cabinet Office, Bridges reformed the central organization of government to make maximum use of interdepartmental committees, and no more was heard of Warren Fisher's belief that the Treasury should, of itself, act as Whitehall's 'general staff'. In understanding Bridges' role in reforming the central organization of government, one has to remember that he had considerable experience of interdepartmental committees as a means of co-ordinating policy, both as a Treasury official dealing with defence problems from 1935 to 1938 and thereafter as Cabinet Secretary. Interdepartmental committees, either of ministers or officials, made it possible to consult interested parties and to resolve differences without overburdening the Cabinet, while the fact that they reported through the Cabinet Office, which circulated their papers, provided a flow of information to all ministers. Bridges and Brook worked harmoniously together to make the machinery of government efficient, and, although the Treasury (including the CEPS) provided the chairmen of most of the committees relating to economic policy, the convention was that chairmen should undertake their tasks in a spirit that would be accepted by all concerned as 'interdepartmental'.[53]

---

[51] What follows is based on Neil Rollings, 'The Control of Inflation in the Managed Economy: Britain, 1945–53', Ph.D. (Bristol, 1990), 222–34.

[52] Hugh Dalton, *High Tide and After*, 98. Eady and other officials sat in on meetings of the NIC, the members of which included the Governor of the Bank of England; the chairmen of the Finance Corporation for Industry, which had been established in 1945 to improve the provision of capital for industry, and of the Industrial and Commercial Finance Corporation, which had been established at the same time to provide capital for small and medium-sized companies; the chairman of the Capital Issues Committee; the chairman of the Public Works Loan Board; the chairman of the Stock Exchange; the President of the Federation of British Industries, and a representative of the Co-operative movement.

[53] Peter Hennessy, *Cabinet* (Oxford, 1986), 38–45; Economic Organisation Working Group, 'The Major Activities of Government', 16 June 1950, T236/2598.

As Chief Planning Officer, Plowden was invited to be a member of the Budget Committee, even while the CEPS was still part of the Office of the Minister of Economic Affairs, just as Meade and Hall had been as successive directors of the Economic Section. The Economic Section, the CEPS, and Treasury officials all contributed to the drafting of the government's annual *Economic Survey*, which was supposed to provide a basis for planning. When Bridges and Brook had agreed in 1944 that the most senior Treasury official dealing with financial policy should be responsible for advising ministers on macroeconomic policy, Brook had used a telling phrase when he had referred to 'the central Department—which, for historical reasons we shall go on calling the Treasury'.[54] What happened after 1945 was not so much a restoration of the Treasury's pre-war power as an enlargement of its functions and a transformation of its relationship with the rest of Whitehall.

Bridges' conception of economic planning in 1945 reflected traditional Treasury concern with enabling ministers to judge proposals in relation to other aspects of policy, rather than solely on the individual merits of the proposals. Whereas before the war proposals for government expenditure had been aggregated in the annual Estimates and compared with likely revenue in the Chancellor's budget, now proposals would ideally be measured against a single national plan that would take account of competing demands on scarce resources. In particular, Bridges thought that it would be necessary to ensure that exports, industrial investment and development, housing, and other essential civilian needs received their proper shares, and that consideration be given to the timing of major projects from the point of view of employment policy. No single department could advise on all these issues, and he established a Steering Committee on Economic Development of senior officials from Treasury, Board of Trade, Ministry of Labour, Ministry of Supply, and the Office of the Lord President, and the Director of the Economic Section, to give general advice to ministers, with the detailed work of the Steering Committee being done through working parties on investment, balance of payments, manpower, economic survey, and statistics. The Treasury was to have a key co-ordinating role, however, in that, although the Steering Committee reported to the Lord President's Committee, detailed directions to implement decisions taken by ministers on proposals made by the Steering Committee were to be transmitted through the Treasury.[55] In the event, the Steering Committee became a rubber stamp that met infrequently. In October 1950 its functions were take over by a new official Economic Steering Committee, which was also to advise ministers on the economic implications of defence policy. Bridges was once more in the chair, and the membership included Brook, Plowden, Hall, and senior officials from the same departments as the earlier Steering Committee.[56]

[54] Brook to Bridges, 11 Aug. 1944, T273/318.
[55] 'Planning of Economic Development', by Bridges, 19 Sept. 1945, T273/298.
[56] Economic Steering Committee, 1st meeting, 26 Oct. 1950, CAB134/263.

The presence of Plowden on these committees, and of his staff on innumerable subcommittees and working parties, provided a hitherto much needed co-ordinating link between domestic and international policy. The CEPS might have developed within the Office of the Minister of Economic Affairs as a rival to the Treasury, as regards the co-ordination and direction of economic policy. Even after Cripps took it into the Treasury the CEPS was said by the Treasury Organisation Committee in 1949 to be 'a separate entity' within the department,[57] and it continued to be so until 1954. However, co-operation rather than rivalry marked relations between Plowden and the Treasury from the start. Moreover, Plowden found it difficult to recruit first-class personnel, his staff never numbering more than sixteen, and the CEPS could thus hope to do no more than supplement, rather than replace, the work of the Treasury's finance and Supply Services divisions in co-ordinating policy. Although it was intended that the CEPS should be concerned with long-term planning, the greater part of the staff's energies from 1947 to 1951 were devoted to relatively short-term issues regarding the allocation of materials and the operation of controls, and to 'trouble shooting'.[58]

Bridges' conception of planning indicated broad agreement with Meade, who saw planning as a macroeconomic exercise, involving a review of the resources likely to be available, and a forecast of the extent to which these resources would be employed on the basis of current programmes and policies, with suggestions for adjustments to programmes and policies to 'ensure that the total claims on the community's resources are neither excessive nor deficient'.[59] Both Meade and Hall saw long-term planning in terms of national-income analysis, and it is tempting to see Keynesian macroeconomic management as something that emerged from 1947 as an alternative to planning through the physical allocation of resources such as steel or manpower. However, there is little evidence that such a change in official thinking occurred as early as 1947. It was in August 1947 that the Investment Programmes Committee was set up under Plowden to establish more effective control over investment than had hitherto existed, and, in particular, to curtail all capital investment projects other than those contributing to exports or to import-saving.[60] Moreover, far from seeking to make the annual budget the centrepiece of Keynesian macroeconomic management, Treasury officials resisted proposals, even when these were supported by Cripps and Gaitskell, for alterations to the system of budget accounts that would have allowed the economic impact of the budget to be measured on a national-income accounting basis; instead Bridges, Gilbert, and others preferred to retain the traditional system of cash accounts, which had

[57] Treasury Organisation Committee, 'Interim Report', 17 Feb. 1949, T273/309.
[58] 'Work of the Central Economic Planning Staff', by Plowden, 20 June 1947, and 'Work of the Central Economic Planning Staff', unsigned, 1 May 1951, T229/417.
[59] Cairncross and Watts, *Economic Section*, 121.
[60] See Martin Chick, *Industrial Policy in Britain, 1945–1951* (Cambridge, 1998), esp. chs. 2–3.

been designed for the purposes of parliamentary control of expenditure and taxation. The budget accounts were kept apart from the national income accounts
in the annual *Economic Survey*, by being prepared for the forthcoming fiscal year,
ending in March, whereas the latter were on the basis of the calendar year.[61]

Budgets were not intended as an alternative to planning; rather fiscal policy
was intended, as in the war, to remove excess demand once the prior claims of
exports and investment had been met. Nor should it be assumed that Treasury
officials wished to abandon planning and to rely solely upon financial policy,
certainly so long as there was a danger of inflation. Proctor, as head of the Treasury's division dealing with employment policy, actually argued in July 1947 that
the planners working on the government's long-term plan for 1948–52 were too
inclined to think in terms of the amount of savings needed for a given level of
investment, rather than thinking in terms of what real resources would be available once essential consumer needs had been met; and Gilbert remarked tren-
chantly: 'What we want to avoid is the revival of the idea which we have met in
the past that, if only the money is got right, everything else then will follow automatically.'[62] The Treasury was aware that, without direct controls over investment, there would be a scramble to borrow, leading to a rise in interest rates and
the cost of government borrowing, as in 1919–20. Treasury officials had no love
of direct controls for their own sake; indeed, Gilbert, as chairman of a Controls and Efficiency Committee in 1948, was to contribute to the policy, associated with the President of the Board of Trade, Harold Wilson, of making a
'bonfire' of controls that were no longer effective because the resources that they
were intended to allocate were no longer in short supply. Nevertheless, reasonably effective controls were retained over imports, investment, and the allocation of raw materials.[63]

The long-term economic survey for 1948–52 conformed to Bridges' conception of economic planning. A draft 'Long-Term Survey' was prepared by the
CEPS and the Economic Section on certain assumptions about the balance of
payments, including a somewhat pessimistic prediction that, on the evidence of
the 1930s, British exports should not be expected to increase by 1952 to more
than about 145 per cent of the volume of 1938, and that therefore imports should
be restricted to about 75 per cent of 1938. Austin Robinson later recalled that the
survey was an exercise in indicative planning, being partly an attempt to identify the future pattern of consumption and exports, together with requirements
for additional productive capacity.[64] The implication was that industry would

[61] Rollings, 'British Budgetary Policy', and id., 'The Control of Inflation in the Managed Economy',
179–94.

[62] 'The Function of the Treasury in the 1948–51 Plan', by Proctor, and Gilbert to Eady and Bridges,
both 8 July 1947, T273/304.

[63] J. C. R. Dow, *The Management of the British Economy, 1945–1960* (Cambridge, 1964), ch. 6.

[64] Cairncross and Watts, *Economic Section*, 181; E. A. G. Robinson, *Economic Planning in the United
Kingdom: Some Lessons* (Cambridge, 1967), 15.

have to have first call on materials and manpower, particularly where exports could be expanded or imports replaced. The work on the survey was given fresh impetus by the need to submit to the Organisation for European Economic Co-operation (OEEC), the international organization that was to co-ordinate national plans for Marshall Aid, a long-term plan showing how Britain could overcome its dollar problem in four years. As Cripps told his colleagues in the Cabinet's Economic Policy Committee in July 1948, the balance of payments was 'the central problem of our economic difficulties'.[65] Consequently a 'Long-Term Programme' was prepared by the Treasury (including the CEPS) and the Economic Section, in conjunction with other interested departments, on the basis of the earlier draft long-term economic survey, for submission in October 1948.[66] The effect of the Marshall Plan was thus to reinforce the pattern of economic planning and co-ordination on an interdepartmental basis.

The Treasury has been criticized for a lack of conviction in this kind of planning, Sir Sydney Caine being quoted as commenting that the programmes submitted to the OEEC were 'nearer to estimates than intentions', and that recipients of aid were not to be dragooned into complying with them.[67] However, in view of the comment by Eric Roll, a professional economist in the CEPS at the time, that the 'Long-Term Programme' was 'primitive in regard to the means (conceptual and statistical) at its disposal, and was essentially a diplomatic document designed to secure American aid,[68] Caine's comment seems to be based on sound scepticism as to what could then be achieved through long-term planning. The targets in the 'Long-Term Programme' were indicative of broad priorities, given the goal of making Britain independent of American aid, and there is no reason to dispute Dow's judgement that the 'Long-Term Programme' dominated policy with regard to investment, exports, imports, and home consumption during the Marshall Plan period.[69]

The Treasury was also much involved in planning for full employment between 1945 and 1951. Although unemployment averaged 2 per cent over that period, the Labour government was concerned with the possibility of a slump, which might result from a general decline in domestic demand as reconstruction was completed, or from an inability to finance sufficient imports of raw materials and capital equipment to maintain industrial activity (the danger that the Marshall Plan was designed to avert), or from a decline in demand for British exports as a result of an American recession (the danger that led to

[65] '1948/52 Balance of Payments Programmes', EPC(48)66, 9 July 1948, T229/258.
[66] Published in *European Co-operation: Memoranda submitted to the Organisation for European Economic Co-operation relating to Economic Affairs in the Period 1949 to 1953* (Cmd. 7572), PP 1948–9, xxxiv. 139. In the version submitted to the OEEC, exports in 1952/3 were estimated at 150 per cent of 1938 (or 38 per cent above 1947), and imports at 85 per cent of 1938.
[67] Caine to Hall, 9 Nov. 1948, T230/109, cited in Adrian Ham, *Treasury Rules* (1981), 79.
[68] Eric Roll, *The World After Keynes* (1968), 59.
[69] Dow, *Management of the British Economy*, 31–2.

devaluation in 1949). It was not until 1951 that the government adopted a target unemployment figure of 3 per cent—a figure proposed by Gaitskell, despite the recommendation of Bridges and other members of the official Economic Steering Committee that the target be 4 per cent, the latter figure being designed to accommodate the effects of a recession abroad.[70]

The Treasury's scepticism about the domestic instruments favoured by the Economic Section for maintaining aggregate demand, evident in discussions leading to the 1944 white paper on employment policy, continued into the post-war period. In particular, Gilbert, through whom Proctor's employment policy division reported to Bridges, objected strongly to a claim by the Economic Section that it had been decided that the main instrument of control over aggregate demand should be variations in public investment. In Gilbert's view, such a claim took no account of the difficulties of controlling variations in local authority investment.[71] Likewise, Dalton was able to use the lack of an agreed target for 'normal' unemployment to delay (*sine die*, as it turned out) the implementation of Meade's scheme for varying national insurance contributions according to a sliding scale of unemployment.[72]

It did not follow that Gilbert thought that there was no value in planning in relation to employment policy. Anticipating a period of excess demand, he noted in March 1945: 'For some years it is likely that the policy will involve keeping the brake on with varying degrees of pressure, on both capital and consumer expenditure. I see no difficulty in that, it is in harmony with all our past training and experience, and the constitution of government is well fitted for the exercise of negative controls'.[73] Initially most work on employment policy took place through sub-panels of the interdepartmental Investment Working Party—chaired by Gilbert—the terms of reference of which included drawing up general priorities for investment. Attempts were made to encourage local authorities to build up a reserve of plans for public works, and, although local authorities were too preoccupied with urgent work to undertake long-term planning, the backlog of projects held up for want of materials or labour could, for the time being, be regarded as such a reserve. Labour's nationalization programme greatly expanded the range of public investment, but the Treasury was opposed to any general system of subsidies to enable the nationalized industries to bring investment forward during some future recession, since such subsidies would undermine the principle that nationalized industries should pay their way. Moreover, the Treasury argued that the private sector must be included in a policy of stabilizing aggregate demand, otherwise an intolerable strain would

[70] Economic Steering Committee, 8th meeting, 7 Dec. 1950, and 'The Full Employment Standard', 26 Oct. 1950, CAB134/263; J. Tomlinson, *Employment Policy: The Crucial Years, 1939–1955* (Oxford, 1987), 129–30.

[71] Gilbert to Bridges, 6 June, and Eady to Bridges, 7 June, 1945, T273/319.

[72] Tomlinson, op. cit., 99–100.   [73] Quoted in Rollings, 'The Keynesian Revolution', 99.

be placed upon the public sector; and, for the time being, existing building and raw material controls, essentially negative controls, were applied to both sectors.[74]

In 1950 Gaitskell took the lead in discussions on a draft Economic Planning and Full Employment Bill, arguing that powers ought to be taken to stimulate private investment, but even he accepted that government powers to manufacture or purchase goods might lead the private sector to defer investment. Gaitskell, Jay, and their officials agreed that fiscal instruments, including reductions in tax rates and national insurance contributions, and repayment of post-war credits, would be major weapons in a depression, but that, as budget matters, these should not be included in the Bill. The Treasury also placed such stringent conditions on subsidies to private industry in the Bill that their scale was unlikely to be sufficient to avert a major decline in private investment. In any case, by that date it was clear that the main danger of unemployment lay in a fall in demand for British exports, and, at a time when excess demand arising from rearmament pointed to a need to continue with negative controls, the Full Employment Bill was not proceeded with.[75]

Economic planning brought a flow of information into the Treasury about the 'real economy' of production, such as the hours worked by coal miners or the physical constraints on investment. Cripps came to the Treasury with an active interest in improving productivity by providing information to encourage workers to make greater efforts, and in 1948 the Treasury was represented on an official Productivity Committee by Leslie, of the Economic Information Unit.[76] However, the Treasury was principally concerned with the guidance of political choices in the allocation of scarce resources. The extreme weakness of Britain's external financial position after the war led the Treasury to give priority to planning how to achieve a sound balance of payments, which was seen as essential both for full employment and for the government's plans for social improvement. The Treasury had no reason immediately after the war to wish to substitute financial controls for direct controls. Even Labour ministers' preference for planning in terms of manpower rather than money raised no problem for the Treasury. Bridges was chairman of the official Steering Committee on the annual economic surveys which incorporated manpower planning, and he was careful to draw ministers' attention to the general shortage of labour and the need to scale down departmental requirements for it.[77] Longer-term planning

---

[74] F. J. Atkinson (Economic Section), 'Full Employment and the Level of Demand', 1 June 1951, T229/323; Sir Norman Chester, *The Nationalisation of British Industry, 1945–51* (1975), 1045–6.

[75] Tomlinson, *Employment Policy*, 130–8.

[76] Cripps to Morrison, 13 Oct. 1947, T172/2029. The Productivity (Official) Committee's papers are in T228/214.

[77] Ministerial Committee on Economic Planning: Note by the Chairman of the Official Steering Committee on Economic Survey, 11 July 1946, CAB134/503. For manpower planning in 1945–51 see Cairncross, *Years of Recovery*, 385–99.

in relation to the Chancellor's budget also indicated a continuing need for restraint. In 1949, a CEPS paper reviewed the existing trend of government expenditure in relation to the burden of taxation and future levels of investment, in the light of forecasts of national income and assumptions about the dollar balance once Marshall Aid had ended, and concluded prophetically that: 'present indications are . . . that the economy may still be under inflationary strain in 1955.'[78]

EXTERNAL ECONOMIC POLICY, 1945–1947

External economic policy involved much more than external finance, and was not a matter for the Treasury alone: the Foreign Office, the Board of Trade, the Dominions Office (from 1947 the Commonwealth Relations Office), and the Colonial Office were all involved. In 1944 a Treasury official, Edmund Hall-Patch, had been transferred to the Foreign Office to direct its economic work.[79] At one level external economic policy was concerned with Britain's relations with the United States, the Commonwealth and the sterling area, and western Europe. Britain needed not only dollars to finance imports of food, raw materials, and capital equipment from North America during the transition from a war economy, but also American co-operation in creating a stable, expanding world economy, in which British exporters and City of London services could hope to prosper, and restore Britain's external financial position. Furthermore, on political grounds, the Foreign Office believed that the wartime 'special relationship' with the United States should be maintained, even at the price of accepting the occasionally irksome role of junior partner.[80]

However, between the end of the Second World War and the emergence of a perceived Soviet threat to American interests in Europe in 1947, the United States saw no reason to treat Britain as a partner, junior or otherwise. For example, at the inaugural meeting of the Governors of the International Monetary Fund and the International Bank for Reconstruction and Development in Savannah in March 1946, British views on where these institutions should be located and on other matters were ignored, leading Keynes to complain that Americans like Fred Vinson, the Secretary of the US Treasury, seemed to have no conception of international co-operation. (Keynes had favoured New York, where the Fund and Bank would be in close contact with the world of

---

[78] 'A First Look at 1955', 10 Mar. 1949, T229/154.

[79] Hall-Patch had had an unusual career, including spells as a musician in Paris and America. He was an assistant secretary at the Treasury from 1935 to 1944, serving as financial commissioner in the Far East in 1940–1.

[80] The Foreign Office views are set out in 'The Effect of our External Financial Position on Foreign Policy', 30 Mar. 1945, and circular by the Foreign Secretary, 12 Feb. 1947, enclosing a memorandum with the same title, FO371/62420.

international finance, rather than Washington, where they would be in close contact with the politics of Congress.[81])

The British were partly responsible for their own difficulties. Military expenditure overseas in 1946 and 1947 accounted for about 15 per cent of total current debits in the balance of payments. While the bulk of this expenditure was incurred in the sterling area, and thus did not add directly to Britain's dollar problem, pounds spent in the sterling area generated purchasing power in recipient countries, and thereby indirectly led to increased demand for dollar goods. The sterling area was maintained in its Second World War form, with external exchange control, but with no controls on overseas investment within the area, resulting in an unplanned, and at the time unquantified, capital outflow from Britain to the dominions. Moreover, whereas the colonies were collectively net contributors to the sterling area's dollar pool, the dominions were collectively in heavy deficit with the dollar area in every year except 1948. Finally, defence expenditure, whether overseas or in Britain, diverted manpower from the production of exports or goods that were substitutes for imports.[82]

As noted in Chapter 7, the war had resulted in a very serious deterioration in Britain's external balance: exports in 1945 were only 46 per cent of the 1938 volume; the sale of overseas investments had reduced income from abroad; shipping losses and trade dislocation reduced 'invisible' exports, and the terms of trade with North America had moved against Britain. Taking these changes into account, Austin Robinson advised Keynes during the Washington loan negotiations in 1945 that British exports would have to be increased by 75 per cent by volume above the pre-war level to pay for the 1938 volume of imports, an estimate that must have confirmed Keynes in his belief that it would be to Britain's advantage to liberalize international trade.[83]

For reasons explained in Chapter 7, Britain's overseas debts had increased from £476 million in 1939 to £3,355 million in mid-1945, most of the increase being in the form of sterling balances with members of the Empire and Commonwealth, or associated states like Egypt. Keynes believed that justice demanded that about a third of the sterling balances should be cancelled voluntarily, as part of a general redistribution of the cost of the war. However, it would clearly be very difficult to negotiate such a redistribution with Britain's creditors, especially as the main holders of sterling balances, India and Egypt, were poor countries, with whom political difficulties could be expected. Moreover, as Eady and Waley pointed out, Britain could not afford to impair its credit by imposing unacceptable terms, while at the same time negotiating overseas for long-term food contracts denominated in sterling. In the event, even

[81] D. E. Moggridge, *Maynard Keynes: An Economist's Biography* (1992), 831–3.

[82] For effects of military expenditure and sterling area links see Jim Tomlinson, 'The Attlee Government and the Balance of Payments, 1945–51', *20th Cent. Brit. Hist.*, 2 (1991), 47–66.

[83] Robinson, 'Economic Problems of the Transition', 170.

Australia and New Zealand, with whom there were no political difficulties, would not go beyond making gifts totalling £38 million, equivalent to 15 per cent of their sterling balances. There was no other scaling down, and Eady had to conduct difficult negotiations in Argentina, India, and Egypt in 1946 and 1947 in order to persuade these countries to accept phased releases of their sterling balances.[84]

In contrast to the 1920s, there was no prospect of substantial reparations to offset Britain's war debts. The Treasury supported steps to reduce Germany's industrial capacity to wage war but, in the light of Keynes's advice, it was opposed to any attempt to do more than to collect some reparations in kind over a limited period, since otherwise Germany would have to expand its exports, to the detriment of British trade. In the event, after the war Britain had to use some of its scarce dollar reserves to buy food for the population of its zone of occupied Germany, leading Dalton to complain that Britain was paying reparations.[85]

Following the end of lend-lease in August 1945, there was no doubt in the Treasury that it would be necessary to ask the Americans for further assistance to finance Britain's immediate balance-of-payments deficit on current account. The question was: how much assistance, and on what terms? Estimates of Britain's prospective deficit on current account in the first three years after the war (after which the economy might break even) were necessarily speculative. Keynes, who (with Lord Halifax, the British ambassador) was to conduct the negotiations in Washington, suggested at a meeting of ministers on 23 August that Britain should seek a grant of $4,000 million or $5,000 million, which would neither be repayable nor bear interest. Contrary to some accounts, notably Dalton's, however, Keynes was not confident that a free grant would be forthcoming; indeed, the proposal was little more than a negotiating tactic.[86]

Officials on the overseas finance side of the Treasury, notably Eady and Clarke, were less optimistic than Keynes about the terms on which American assistance would be forthcoming, and suggested that only $1,000 million should be borrowed, without strings, to meet immediate needs, with a further sum to be borrowed in 1947 in the light of developments. Meantime, Britain would sign the Bretton Woods agreement and promote multilateral trade by combining the sterling area with France, Belgium, and the Netherlands, with their colonies,

[84] Fforde, *Bank of England*, ch. 3; L. S. Pressnell, *External Economic Policy since the War*, vol. i, *The Post-War Financial Settlement* (1986), 230, 240, 247, 366; B. R. Tomlinson, 'Indo-British Relations in the Post-Colonial Era: The Sterling Balances Negotiations, 1947–49', *J. Imperial and Commonwealth Hist.*, 13 (1985), 142–62.

[85] *Documents on British Policy Overseas* (hereafter *DBPO*), series 1, vol. i. 751–6; R. H. Brand to Keynes, 17 May 1945, R. H. Brand papers, file 195, Bodleian Library, Oxford; Alec Cairncross, *The Price of War: British Policy on German Reparations, 1941–1949* (Oxford, 1986), 18–21, 151.

[86] Dalton, *High Tide and After*, 73–4 (see also Richard N. Gardner, *Sterling-Dollar Diplomacy* (New York, 1969), 189–90, and R. F. Harrod, *The Life of John Maynard Keynes* (1951), 596–7). For accurate accounts of Keynes's views on eve of the negotiations, see Moggridge, *Maynard Keynes*, 797–8, and Pressnell, *External Economic Policy*, i. 264–7, 271–2. For record of the meeting on 23 Aug. see *DBPO*, series 1, iii. 72–7.

and possibly other countries, much as was to happen with the European Payments Union in 1950.[87] However, even to Eady and Clarke, it seemed to be worth while exploring the more optimistic course of seeking generous terms from the United States. In the event, the negotiations from September to December did not go well, partly because of Keynes's tactless manner,[88] but also because the Americans were aware that there would be other supplicants for aid, many of them with economies in a worse state than Britain's, and the generosity of Congress could not be expected to be boundless.

The State Department and the US Treasury recognized that something would have to be done to ease Britain's external financial position, if Britain were to be expected to make rapid progress towards free multilateral payments and a relaxation of barriers to trade, and the Americans also feared that Britain might use the sterling balances to bind a large part of the world to buying British goods. Consequently they hoped that Britain would secure partial cancellation of the wartime accumulation of sterling balances, and they also insisted that sterling should become convertible at an early date, and that imperial preference should be reduced, if not eliminated. At the end of November, with Keynes evidently exhausted, it seemed to Dalton that the negotiations might break down, and he dispatched Bridges to Washington, at three hours' notice, on 1 December to see what could be done. Bridges admitted that he was 'not versed' in the technicalities of exchange arrangements or accumulated sterling balances, but he was able to clarify issues sufficiently to persuade a reluctant Cabinet to accept the Americans' terms.[89]

Under the Loan Agreement there was a final settlement of wartime claims under Mutual Aid, Britain becoming liable for $650 million for lend-lease supplies unconsumed or in transit at the date of Japan's surrender. Both this sum and the line of credit of $3,750 million made available under the agreement were to be paid off in fifty annual instalments of $140 million, beginning on 31 December 1951, with the 2 per cent interest to be charged from that date being waived in years in which Britain could not afford to buy its pre-war volume of imports. More important, the agreement included commitments to make

[87] Clarke, *Anglo-American Economic Collaboration*, 57–8.

[88] In particular, Keynes failed to establish a rapport with Vinson, Morgenthau's successor as Secretary of the US Treasury. Clarke (op. cit., 63) preserved the following story by Frank Lee, who was a Treasury official in attendance in the negotiations. Keynes was seeking a waiver clause whereby Britain would not have to pay interest in years in which such payments would place a strain on its balance of payments on current account:

> VINSON. I'm not clear what happens to the waiver if something entirely unexpected happens to you . . . suppose you found a billion dollars in a cave?
>
> KEYNES. [*like lightning*]. Mr Secretary, I am willing right now to include a clause providing that the Waiver clause is immediately cancelled if we find a billion dollars in a cave.

[89] Dalton diary, vol. 33, 7 Dec. 1945; *DBPO*, series 1, iii. 422–3; Corinna Balfour, 'The Anglo-American Loan Negotiations: The US Viewpoint', in Fforde, *Bank of England*, 807–22; Pressnell, *External Economic Policy*, i. 319–25.

sterling convertible for current transactions a year after ratification by Congress (which turned out to mean one year from 15 July 1946); to remove discrimination against imports from the United States from the end of 1946; and to adhere to the Bretton Woods agreements on stable exchange rates. Britain would thus not be able to use exchange controls to prevent other countries' current receipts of sterling, or any sterling balances that had been released, from being converted into dollars, and demand for dollars could not be reduced by discriminatory tariffs or quotas. Britain thus gave up one of the main safeguards of the Bretton Woods agreements, the right to a full, five-year, transitional period before sterling became convertible. The American counter-argument was that the loan should be sufficient to enable Britain to abandon discrimination against American exporters more quickly that otherwise. Britain also agreed to support proposals to be put by the United States to an international conference on trade and employment, whereby there would be no increase in imperial preferences, which would ultimately be eliminated as part of a general reduction of tariffs.[90] Even at the time there seems to have been no responsible person in the Treasury, from the Chancellor downwards, who thought that it would be possible to fulfil the Loan Agreement in its entirety, and the only question seems to have been how long the credit could be made to last before seeking some revision of its terms.[91]

Although Canada generously extended to Britain a line of credit of $1,250 million, the Anglo-American Loan Agreement would only have been workable if Keynes and the experts of the US Federal Reserve Board had been correct in their belief that the world shortage of dollars would not persist beyond 1946.[92] In the event, the slow recovery of the world economy undermined this assumption. Moreover, forecasts made in 1945 of the amount of credit needed by Britain were falsified by post-war inflation in the United States, which reduced the purchasing power of dollars by about a quarter by 1947. From the end of 1946 the drain upon British dollar resources accelerated rapidly, and by mid-1947 over half the American and Canadian credits had been used, with

---

[90]   *Financial Agreement between the Government of the United States and the United Kingdom dated 6th December 1945, together with a Joint Statement regarding Settlement for Lend-Lease, Reciprocal Aid, Surplus War Property and Claims* (Cmd. 6708), PP 1945–6, xxv. 787. For Eady's reactions see *DBPO*, series 1, iv. 11–16. For a useful commentary see H. D. Henderson, 'The Anglo-American Financial Agreement', *Bull. Oxford Univ. Institute Stat.*, 8 (1946), 1–13. In the event, at a conference in 1947–8 called to establish an International Trade Organisation, American proposals for a speedy move to end discriminatory practices in trade encountered opposition from European countries and Britain refused to end imperial preferences. Congress refused to ratify the Havana Charter, which incorporated a whole series of exceptions to the original American proposals, and the General Agreement on Trade and Tariffs (GATT), signed by 23 countries in 1947, became the focus for negotiating mutual tariff concessions.

[91]   Dalton, *High Tide and After*, 89; Sir Hugh Ellis-Rees, 'The Convertibility Crisis of 1947', Treasury historical memorandum, 24 Feb. 1961, T267/3. Ellis-Rees had been an assistant secretary on the overseas finance side of the Treasury in 1947.

[92]   See J. M. Keynes, 'The Balance of Payments of the United States', *Econ. J.*, 56 (1946), 171–87; Gardner, *Sterling-Dollar Diplomacy*, 291–2.

every prospect that the drain would continue. The Americans were told that convertibility, added to non-discrimination under the Loan Agreement, would place a heavy burden on the British people, since the only way to reduce the dollar drain would be to cut all imports, not just imports from the United States, but no concessions had been made on non-discrimination by the time sterling was made convertible on 15 July.

Dalton later claimed that he had been given mistakenly optimistic advice with respect to convertibility, the suspension of which he regarded as a personal humiliation.[93] Yet as early as November 1946, while on a visit to Washington, Waley had warned that Britain might have to ask for a postponement of convertibility. Dalton himself told the American ambassador in London, Lew Douglas, in May 1947 that at the present rate of drawing the dollar line of credit would be exhausted early in 1948. However, the Americans were slow to respond to such warnings, perhaps partly because British Treasury officials admitted that estimates about the future rate of drawing were very uncertain, owing not only to the lack of control over capital transactions between the United Kingdom and the rest of the sterling area, but also to the speculative nature of estimates of future government expenditure abroad, which would depend, in part, on world events.[94] Treasury officials tried to secure Cabinet agreement to reductions in imports in May 1947, in the hope that Britain would be able to carry on without additional credit until after the presidential elections in 1948, but the ministries of Food and Health argued successfully that large-scale cuts would adversely affect health and morale, and the reductions made were much less than the Treasury had hoped for. Clarke recalled that, at a meeting to discuss the health and nutritional implications of import cuts, the Chief Medical Officer at the Ministry of Health, Sir Wilson Jameson, carried all before him. Clarke had some doubts that Jameson's nutrition figures were wholly consistent with the import figures, but found that a mere Treasury official could not match a Scottish pipe-smoking doctor on matters relating to health.[95] Likewise, as will be noted below, Dalton was unsuccessful in persuading his Cabinet colleagues to agree to a rapid reduction of military expenditure overseas.

What seems to have surprised Treasury officials was the speed with which dollars drained away after 15 July. There had been a gradual extension of convertibility before then through a series of bilateral monetary agreements

---

[93] Dalton, *High Tide and After*, 257–8, 262.

[94] 'Progress under Anglo-American Financial Agreement', by H. T. Ness, Department of State, 21 Nov. 1946, RG59, 611.4131/11-2146, box 2727; Douglas to Secretary of State, 16 May 1947, RG59, 841.51/5-1647; Douglas to Secretary of State, 25 June 1947, RG59, 841.51/6-2647; and Avery F. Petersen, London embassy, to Secretary of State, 30 June 1947, RG59, 841.51/6-3046 (all box 5943), National Archives, Washington, DC.

[95] Minutes of interdepartmental meetings of officials, 12 May and 16 May, 1947, CAB130/19; Clarke, *Anglo-American Economic Collaboration*, 85.

whereby sterling held by central banks was made convertible for current requirements, but should not be used to finance capital transactions, and there was thus some reason not to expect rapid change in the rate at which sterling was converted into dollars after 15 July.[96] The Treasury depended on the Bank of England for information derived from exchange controls, but the Bank itself was dependent on confidential information from overseas central banks, and seems to have imparted this information sparingly to the Treasury.[97] Indeed, one outcome of the convertibility crisis was the creation of overseas finance's own statistical division in September 1947 under Sam Goldman, who had only recently joined the Central Statistical Office from the Bank of England.[98] Thereafter the Treasury became better able to handle balance-of-payments forecasts.

Eady's own account of the crisis stressed the failure of ministers to respond adequately to the Treasury's warnings from April that expenditure abroad must be cut. The scale of the reductions sought by the Treasury in May somehow became known outside Whitehall, so that the government measures prior to convertibility were seen to be inadequate, and the subsequent debate in the House of Commons on 8 July had an adverse effect on confidence in sterling. The result was that, whereas in the second quarter of 1947, sterling was being converted into dollars at the rate of $77 million a week, of which about $60 million was British dollar expenditure, the weekly rate rose to $115 million from the beginning of July. Then came a further parliamentary debate on 7 August, with a statement by Dalton on the seriousness of the position, but without any further measures to cut back dollar expenditure. In the absence of such measures, it was clear that there must be restriction on the external use of sterling, or devaluation, or both, and there was a speculative run on sterling, with the loss of $237 million in six working days from 11 August.[99] On 20 August the Americans agreed to the suspension of convertibility.

In theory convertibility should have made little difference to the amount of sterling that was converted into dollars after 15 July, since sterling was convertible only for current purposes. However, on the basis of figures that have become available since the 1940s, there is evidence of an outflow of capital from

[96] Dalton told Parliament on 8 July that: 'In large measure 15 July has already been discounted and the additional burden of assuming these new obligations under the Anglo-American Loan Agreement will be noticeably less than many people suppose' (439 HC Deb., 5s, col. 2150).

[97] With the wisdom of hindsight, Rowan observed that 'the Bank should have given us day-to-day information about the [dollar] drain rather than holding it up until a rather longer interval' (Rowan to Bridges, 11 Sept. 1947, T273/241).

[98] Goldman had graduated with first-class honours in economics from the London School of Economics in 1931 and an M.Sc. in 1933, before embarking on a City career, followed by service in the Bank of England 1940–7. He became Chief Statistician in the Treasury in 1948 and Second Permanent Secretary in 1968–72.

[99] Eady to Bridges, 28 Aug. 1947, T273/241; 439 HC Deb., 5s, 1946–7, cols. 2041–58, and 441 HC Deb., 5s, 1946–7, cols. 1654–89.

Britain in 1947 equal to about 8 per cent of net national income, or nearly equal to total net domestic capital formation, for the year. This outflow was facilitated by the absence of controls over capital movements within the sterling area, and had little to do with convertibility directly, although it did finance the rest of the sterling area's deficit with the dollar area. The sharp deterioration in the situation in July and August seems to have been brought about by the speculative device of 'leads and lags', that is the making of prompt payments in sterling but slow payments in foreign currencies, a device that was little understood in official circles at the time.[100] While Dalton had some reason to be dissatisfied with the statistical basis of the Treasury's advice, the fundamental problems in 1947 were: (a) inadequate controls over capital movements, and (b) a lack of confidence in sterling arising from his own failure to persuade the Cabinet to agree to stricter limits on government expenditure overseas, this lack of confidence itself encouraging a flight of capital.

The crisis was probably a necessary one, in that only a clear demonstration of Britain's inability to carry out the terms of the Anglo-American Loan Agreement could have persuaded Congress to agree to relax the terms, as it did by the end of the year, by which time Britain was openly using state purchasing and exchange controls to economize on dollars by discriminating against American products. However, in the short run, even though Eady visited the United States at the time of suspension of convertibility to explain the situation, the Secretary of the US Treasury, John Snyder, felt obliged, in view of congressional opinion about Britain's non-compliance with the terms of the Loan Agreement, to freeze the $400 million remaining of the line of credit under the 1945 agreement.

EXTERNAL ECONOMIC POLICY: MARSHALL AID AND ATTITUDES
TOWARDS EUROPE, 1947–1950

From the summer of 1947 there was the prospect of Marshall Aid, first suggested on 5 June by the Secretary of State, George C. Marshall, whereby the United States would provide financial support for a recovery programme to be jointly agreed by European countries. However, the timing and scale of such aid remained uncertain until Congress had approved the necessary appropriations in June 1948. Meanwhile, there was a need to find the dollars necessary to finance British imports. In the light of his visit to the United States at the time of suspension of convertibility, Eady advised Bridges that the IMF would not allow Britain to draw the whole of its annual quota of $325 million, as the IMF would be unlikely to regard Britain's balance-of-payments difficulties as a temporary dislocation, such as the Fund had been designed to deal with. It would be

---

[100] Cairncross, *Years of Recovery*, 145–64.

difficult to raise a loan exceeding $100 million from New York banks on reasonable terms, leaving the frozen credit of $400 million as the best immediate source of dollars.[101] Bridges held up an approach to the American government for a release of the $400 million until November, by which time ministers had agreed on cuts in the investment and import programmes, an autumn budget, and an acceleration of exports. At the same time the US Treasury was advised that Britain was negotiating a series of bilateral trade and payments agreements with western European countries, to minimize the drain on Britain's reserves. Snyder and the Secretary of State, James Forrestal, took the question of the release of the $400 million to congressional leaders, who were persuaded to agree early in December, partly because British economic recovery was in America's own interest, as a necessary precondition for achieving a high level of world trade on a multilateral, non-discriminatory basis, and partly as a gesture of support for the United States' most important ally against the Soviet Union.[102]

There was no doubt in the Treasury that Britain must accept Marshall Aid. The Cabinet was told in June 1948 that, on current trends, London's gold and dollar reserves would fall to about £270 million by April 1949, or less than half the level to which they had fallen in August 1947, and well below the £500 million that the Treasury considered to be the minimum, given that the reserves were those of the sterling area as a whole. If that minimum balance were to be preserved, without a fresh influx of dollars, there would have to be drastic restrictions on imports from the dollar area, particularly food, but extending also to oil and raw materials. Total raw material imports would have to be cut by 12 per cent, with consequent dislocation of industry, causing unemployment of perhaps as much as 1.5 million. The figure of 1.5 million appears to have been drawn from an earlier paper by Clarke, in which he wrote of 'having say 1,500,000 unemployed as a regular thing' (in addition to reduced food rations), and was not intended to be on the high side. A year earlier Austin Robinson had estimated that restrictions on imports could raise unemployment to 3 million.[103]

The principal problem with Marshall's offer of aid, from a British perspective, was the Americans' insistence that they would not deal with the United Kingdom separately from the rest of western Europe. Congress would vote

[101] Eady to Bridges, 'Raising the Wind', 29 Aug. 1947, T236/1667.
[102] 'Further American Aid', unsigned, undated carbon, but rest of file indicates memorandum is by Bridges, 15 Oct. 1947, T273/242. 'Memorandum of Conversation with British Treasury official [Ellis-Rees] showing current trend in UK financial and trade policy', by John W. Gunter, US Treasury representative in London, 20 Nov. 1947, RG59, 641.0031/11-2047, box 2810; 'Availability to the British of the Frozen $400 million Balance of the Loan', by Acting Director, Office of European Affairs, Department of State, 19 Nov. 1947, RG59, 841.51/11-1947, and Snyder to Cripps, 5 Dec. 1947, RG59, 841.5/12-447, both box 5943, National Archives, Washington, DC.
[103] 'Economic Consequences of Receiving No European Recovery Aid', 23 June 1948, CP(48)161, CAB129/28; 'The Future of Sterling', 25 Feb. 1948, by Clarke, T236/2398. Robinson, *Economic Planning*, 16.

funds for what came to be called the European Recovery Programme (ERP) only if there were economic co-operation between European states, and only if it could be shown that Europe would no longer need dollar aid after three years.[104] Treasury officials subsequently took a major part in planning ERP; in particular, Clarke drafted the report of the international Committee on European Economic Co-operation in September 1947, which formed the basis of the programme which was submitted to Congress. Nevertheless, there seemed to Treasury and Board of Trade officials to be good reason to resist American pressure on Britain to co-operate with other European countries, if such co-operation were to take the form of a customs union, at the expense of links with the Commonwealth.

Clarke pointed out that Britain had twice as much trade with the Commonwealth as with Europe, and, moreover, most intra-Commonwealth trade was conducted in sterling, and was thus multilateral, whereas most intra-European trade before 1950 was subject to restrictive, bilateral clearing agreements. When the function and structure of the Organization for European Economic Co-operation (OEEC), which came into existence in March 1948, was being discussed, he advised that its principal purpose should be to develop ways of earning and saving dollars through co-operation between European countries (for example, by planning the most economical way to increase steel production), and to develop improved payments arrangements. A customs union, he argued, would contribute nothing to reducing Europe's collective dollar deficit; indeed, by encouraging production for the European market, it could actually divert capacity from dollar earning. Clarke thought that it was conceivable that the United Kingdom, with access to Commonwealth natural resources, especially oil, rubber, and gold, would soon be able to earn enough dollars to be independent of American aid, but that there were no such prospects for much of western Europe. According to American calculations, less than two-thirds of OEEC imports from the dollar area would be paid for by exports even in 1951/2. There thus seemed to be good economic reasons to avoid any moves towards a federal Europe that would weaken Commonwealth links, and Clarke advocated that effective control of the OEEC should be in the hands of the national delegations and not the OEEC secretariat.[105]

Although Bevin, as Foreign Secretary, was aware of the political advantages of closer links with western Europe through a customs union, he was unable to override opposition in the Cabinet's Economic Policy Committee in the autumn of 1947 not only from Dalton (as Chancellor of the Exchequer), but also from Cripps (as Minister of Economic Affairs) and Harold Wilson (President of the Board of Trade). Dalton was also at one with Cripps and Wilson about the value of Commonwealth links. Indeed Labour ministers were very keen to

---

[104] Note of meeting in the Chancellor of the Exchequer's room, 24 June 1947, CAB130/19.
[105] Clarke, *Anglo-American Economic Collaboration*, 190–201, 204.

develop Britain's colonies as sources of dollar earnings or dollar savings.[106] The considered view in early 1949 of the senior Whitehall officials involved, including not only Bridges, Plowden, and Wilson Smith of the Treasury, but also Roger Makins of the Foreign Office, and Sir Percivale Liesching and Frank Lee of the Board of Trade, was that Britain must secure a special relationship with the United States, for political, military, and economic reasons, independently of the rest of Europe. Britain did have a major interest in Europe's economic recovery, and should seek to promote it, but, the officials believed, long-term co-operation held no attraction. Europe would be a drain on Britain's resources, and therefore, in a phrase echoing military thinking in the 1930s, 'the concept must be one of limited liability'.[107] Thus, although Bevin presided over the development of closer security links with western Europe through the Brussels Treaty (1948) and the North Atlantic Treaty (1949), to meet the apparently growing Soviet threat, he accepted the economic departments' view that steps towards economic integration in western Europe should be designed to deal with the dollar shortage and stop short of supranationalism, as indeed, despite American hopes, the OEEC did.[108]

The Treasury also took part in forming Britain's response to the Schuman Plan for a European coal and steel community centred on France and Germany. The plan was launched on 9 May 1950 and the British government was asked by the French to commit itself to the principle of a supranational authority by 1 June, as a precondition for entering into negotiations. Attlee set up a committee of permanent secretaries or senior officials from the Foreign Office, Board of Trade, and the ministries of Defence, Fuel and Power, and Supply, with Bridges as chairman, and Plowden as a member, to advise on the possible effects of the plan on the British economy, the Commonwealth, and the sterling area, and to provide an appreciation of the implications for defence policy. Detailed study was delegated to a working under W. Strath of the CEPS, the members of the working party being drawn from the same departments as the official committee, with the addition of a representative of the Ministry of Labour, as Bridges thought that matters affecting labour were sure to arise.[109]

In conjunction with the other departments, the Treasury prepared a paper in which the economic effects of the French proposals on the British economy were described as likely to be negligible in the short term, but disadvantageous in the longer term, owing to the natural advantages of the Ruhr/Saar/Luxembourg area. However, the key issue, as Jean Monnet, the progenitor of the plan, made plain to Makins and Plowden, was whether Britain would be prepared to surrender national sovereignty over important economic and strategic matters in

[106] Economic Policy Committee minutes, 9 Oct. and 7 Nov. 1947, CAB134/215.

[107] 'Policy Towards Europe', record of informal discussion between officials, 5 Jan. 1949, T273/351.

[108] See Michael J. Hogan, *The Marshall Plan: America, Britain and the Reconstruction of Western Europe* (Cambridge, 1987), 109–18, 125–7; Alan S. Milward, *The Reconstruction of Western Europe, 1945–51* (1984), ch. 5.

[109] Papers relating to the establishment of the committee and working party are in T273/254.

the interest of furthering European unity. The considered advice of the official committee was that no such commitment should be made until the implications of the French proposals, which were very vague, could be explored through participation in Franco-German discussions on them. Cripps was personally in favour of entering negotiations, on condition that there would be no capitalist cartel, and he would also have liked to explore the possibility of joint production programmes in specific industries, military as well as civil, as an alternative to the Schuman Plan, but his worsening illness prevented him from pursuing this idea. In his absence, and indeed in the absence of Attlee and Bevin, the Cabinet decided not to go ahead with negotiations on the French terms, as to do so would mean a reduction in British sovereignty so far as coal and steel were concerned.[110]

Although hurried, the process by which the decision on the Schuman Plan was reached was a classic example of Bridges' conception of interdepartmental committee work, and it cannot be said that the Treasury's voice was any more important than that of other departments. After the Cabinet had taken its decision Bridges, Wilson Smith, Sir John Woods (Permanent Secretary of the Board of Trade), and Sir Edmund Hall-Patch and Eric Roll (both of the British delegation to the OEEC) all agreed at a meeting on 14 July that Britain must not adopt a hostile attitude to moves towards economic unification in western Europe, especially if these moves brought about a rapprochement of France and Germany, but Britain must use all its influence to ensure that the continental countries did not form an exclusive trading system with high protective barriers.[111] The economic dangers to Britain of exclusion from the movement towards European unity were not unforeseen, but political considerations of sovereignty were paramount.

EXTERNAL ECONOMIC POLICY: DEVALUATION, THE EUROPEAN
PAYMENTS UNION, AND THE KOREAN WAR, 1949–1951

Meanwhile, Marshall Aid had given Britain a breathing space in which to improve its external financial position. Roll, as one of the OEEC's 'Committee of Four' which made recommendations on the distribution of aid in August 1948, was able to win Britain the largest allocation,[112] and, although this allocation was subsequently adjusted by the Americans, Britain's receipts under ERP greatly eased the strain on Britain's gold and dollar reserves, as Table 8.1 shows.

However, a renewed dollar problem in 1949 suggested that Treasury officials had been right to be sceptical about the ability of ERP alone to close western

---

[110] *DBPO*, series 2, i. 35–45, 69–71, 137–44. See also Plowden *Industrialist in the Treasury*, ch. 9; Eric Roll, *Crowded Hours* (1985), 83.

[111] *DBPO*, series 2, i. 261–3, 267–71.   [112] Roll, *Crowded Hours*, 63.

TABLE 8.1. *UK Balance of Payments with Dollar Area, 1947–1951 (Calender Years, £m.)*

	1947	1948	1949	1950	1951
Current balance, excluding grants	−506	−241	−291	−79	−427
Marshall Aid (European Recovery Programme)	—	+144	+244	+239	+54
Change in gold and dollar reserves	−152	−55	−3	+575	−344

Source: S. Howson, *British Monetary Policy, 1945–51* (Oxford, 1993), 213.

Europe's gap. A recession in the United States in 1949 made it harder than ever to earn dollars, and British policy was to reinforce existing measures to curb imports from the dollar area by negotiating bilateral commercial agreements in favour of non-dollar sources of imports, while urging OEEC countries to do like-wise. When Hall and Wilson Smith visited Washington in June they were asked by the US Treasury whether there had been a change in British policy away from working towards free convertibility and non-discrimination, and from the spring there was pressure in the American-dominated IMF for a devaluation of sterling. Devaluation would make British goods more price-competitive in dollar markets, encouraging British producers to expand exports there, and thus make discrimination against imports from America less necessary.

Within the British Treasury, Clarke had pointed out as early as February 1948 that foreigners expected a devaluation of sterling sooner or later, and that devaluation would discourage imports from the dollar area and encourage exports, thereby tending to solve Britain's dollar shortage. Indeed, Clarke argued, what was really required was an appreciation of the dollar in terms of all other currencies, thereby tending to solve the world dollar shortage. However, at that date, Rowe-Dutton, Clarke's superior in overseas finance, thought that the first priority was to rehabilitate sterling's international functions as a medium of exchange and a store of value, which, he thought, could be done through bilateral agreements with non-dollar countries to encourage the use of sterling in international trade, together with 'some measure of deflation' at home.[113]

It was only from March 1949, when Hall persuaded Bridges to set up an enquiry into the case for devaluation,[114] that senior officials began seriously to contemplate devaluation, and it was not until June, after Hall and Wilson Smith had visited Washington, that official opinion in the Treasury was agreed that some measure of devaluation at some future date was inevitable. Hall could see no alternative way in which British export prices could be reduced. On the other

[113] 'The Future of Sterling', by Clarke, 25 Feb., Clarke to Rowe-Dutton, 2 Mar., and 'The Pressure on Sterling', by Rowe-Dutton, 30 Mar. (all 1948), T236/3940.
[114] For detailed accounts of how devaluation was decided see A. Cairncross and B. Eichengreen, *Sterling in Decline: The Devaluations of 1931, 1949 and 1967* (Oxford, 1983), 111–42; Howson, *British Monetary Policy*, 239–50; Jones, *Economist among Mandarins*, 89–97. See also Jay, *Change and Fortune*, 187–91; Hall, *Diaries, 1947–1953*, 60, 63–84.

hand, Bridges, who regarded devaluation as unsavoury and underhand, was anxious that it should not be seen as an alternative to immediate reductions in public expenditure, for such cuts would be necessary to release capacity to increase exports in the event of devaluation. In the absence of Cabinet agreement on expenditure cuts, Bridges gave no firm advice on when devaluation should occur.

Cripps, as a socialist planner, did not readily think in terms of adjustments through the price mechanism. Although he recognized that, on current trends, the dollar reserves would be exhausted early in 1950, he thought both devaluation and deflation wrong in principle, preferring reductions in dollar expenditure and tighter controls. It was only while Cripps was recuperating in a Swiss sanatorium in July that there was a change in ministerial thinking. Three economically literate ministers, Gaitskell (Fuel and Power), Wilson (Board of Trade), and Jay (Economic Secretary), who were jointly in charge of economic policy in the Chancellor's absence, convinced the Cabinet that devaluation was necessary (although Wilson seems to have been uncertain of his position). Even then, Cripps delayed action until it had been decided that there would be no election in the autumn and until after he had been to Washington in September for the annual IMF meeting, so that devaluation could be linked to views expressed there, thereby saving the Chancellor's face after he had publicly stated in July that there would be no devaluation. As always, devaluation was not simply a technical question, even when delay resulted in greater losses of reserves than would otherwise have occurred.

The decision on the extent of devaluation, from $4.03 to $2.80, was taken in Washington by Cripps and Bevin, on the advice of Hall, Plowden, Wilson Smith, and George Bolton, the last named being an executive director of both the Bank of England and the IMF. The figure of $2.80, rather than $3.00, was selected on the basis of the Economic Section's advice that $2.80 would remove the possibility of a second devaluation. The associated cuts in public expenditure and the investment programme predictably fell short of what Hall advised was necessary to avoid inflation. Hall had thought a total of £300 million to be a minimum; Cripps forced a figure of £280 million through the Cabinet in October, but only £122.5 million of the target of £140 million for public expenditure took effect, and the investment programme, which was supposed to be cut by £140 million, actually increased in 1950.

There followed a general realignment of currencies, almost the entire sterling area following Britain by devaluing 30 per cent against the dollar, while European devaluations varied from 20 per cent for the French franc and the German mark to 8 per cent for the Italian lira. On a trade-weighted basis the devaluation of sterling was about 9 per cent. The cost of living rose by only 2 per cent in the year following devaluation, partly on account of the General Council of the Trades Union Congress's support for a government appeal for a wages standstill, on condition that the retail price index rose by less than 5 per cent. There was a definite easing of the dollar problem: British trade with the dollar area increased from £195 million in 1949 to £324 million in 1950, while imports from the dollar area remained steady (£442 million in 1949; £439 million in 1950). The gold and dollar reserves increased by 70 per cent in the first nine months after devaluation.[115] Against such a background it could be expected that there would be pressure from the United States for Britain to make some progress towards a world of freely convertible currencies and multilateral trade.

The Economic Co-operation Administration (ECA), the American agency which was responsible for Marshall Aid, was impatient for liberalization of trade within the OEEC and pressed hard from late 1949 for the creation of a European Payments Union (EPU) to replace the temporary, and largely bilateral, payments agreements that had been negotiated in western Europe since 1947.[116] Indeed the pressure brought to bear on Britain was such that Cripps had to ask Paul Hoffman, the US Administrator of ECA 'not to hustle us unduly in this matter'.[117] The ECA was willing to provide extra Marshall Aid to help to cover settlements between creditors and debtors within the union. The idea of a European clearing union was discussed by the Treasury, the Economic Section, and, reluctantly, by the Bank of England on 1 December 1949. The Bank would have preferred to make sterling freely transferable within Europe as an alternative to such a union, but had to admit that such an arrangement could not be extended to include Belgium, Switzerland, and, perhaps, also western Germany, all of which were on a dollar standard. The Bank and the Treasury were agreed, however, that it was desirable to get away from the idea of an artificial currency unit (the term 'ecu' had already been suggested), and that 'most of all, we wish to avoid anything like a European version of the IMF', such as was believed to be favoured by Robert Marjolin, Secretary-General of the OEEC. In the event, the idea of a European version of the IMF was killed by opposition from European central bankers, the US Treasury, and the IMF itself, and payments within the Union were organized by the existing Bank for International Settlements.[118]

The British monetary authorities' position in negotiations leading to the creation of the EPU shows how they were opposed to anything that might weaken the position of sterling, or their independence in managing it. In the circumstances of 1949–50, they were particularly concerned about the risk that sterling earned outside the Union by a member of the EPU would be used in

---

[115] Cairncross, *Years of Recovery*, 201, 207–11.

[116] Norway, Sweden, the Netherlands, and Spain had undertaken to accept sterling in payment for goods and services. All other British trade with OEEC countries prior to 1950 was covered by bilateral agreements that tended to lead to trade restrictions when the bilateral balance was such that gold or dollars had to be used in settlement. The EPU allowed all surpluses and deficits between member countries, including surpluses and deficits with the sterling area, to be offset against each other, leaving the net balance to be settled with the Union. Settlement was partly in gold and partly in credit from the Union, with debtors being more liable than creditors to pay gold, to put pressure on the former to correct a persistent deficit.   [117] Cripps to Hoffman, 7 Mar. 1950, T172/2040.

[118] 'Future of Intra-European Payments', by Bridges, 1 Dec. 1949, T273/310; Cairncross and Watts, *Economic Section*, 298–301; Fforde, *Bank of England*, 193–219.

settlement of a bilateral deficit with Britain, while Britain itself would have to settle its bilateral deficits within the Union partly in gold or dollars. Gaitskell, who effectively took over ministerial responsibility for overseas finance from March 1950, was aware of the political case for economic integration between allies in the North Atlantic Treaty Organization (NATO), which had been formed in 1949. However, he was only prepared to accept membership of the EPU after an Economic Section exercise had shown that there would have been no net loss of gold or dollars had a payments union been in operation in the eighteen months to 31 March 1950. The ECA and prospective members of the EPU also agreed that Britain could maintain existing arrangements for the use of sterling, thereby preserving sterling's world role, and enabling Britain to reconcile membership of both the sterling area and the EPU. Finally, on 4 June, Gaitskell, who believed that his experience as an economist enabled him to take charge of the negotiations, worked out a compromise with Milton Katz, the deputy to the US Special Representative in Europe, regarding the settlement of EPU imbalances that limited the risk to Britain's gold and dollar reserves. In the event, the EPU was very successful in accommodating a rapid increase in intra-European trade down to 1958, when a general resumption of convertibility between European currencies and the dollar made the mechanism of the Union unnecessary.[119]

Gaitskell's willingness to come to terms on the EPU was probably helped by the fact that he also took charge of preparation for fundamental discussions with the United States about future financial and economic policy. Intra-Treasury discussion began with a note by overseas finance on 9 March 1950, and reached the Cabinet's Economic Policy Committee on 27 April. As the Chancellor's memorandum to the latter explained: 'evidence is accumulating that the United States Administration is engaged in a stock-taking of its basic financial and economic policy'. In particular, the Secretary of the US Treasury, Snyder, had written on 5 February asking Cripps for information on how Britain proposed to deal with the sterling balances, and on 11 April Snyder wrote again, asking for the Chancellor's views on the significance of the sterling balances for Britain's ultimate objectives in international trade and currency arrangements, and what steps Britain proposed to take towards these goals in the light of the recent improvement in its dollar reserves. In the event, the discussions with the Americans on fundamentals, which began on 21 June, did not lead anywhere, as the outbreak of the Korean War four days later diverted attention to more immediate problems, but preparation for the discussions seems to have clarified and resolved differences between official and ministerial thinking in the Treasury on external economic policy and related issues.[120]

---

[119] Gaitskell, *Diary*, 175–82, 185–6, 189–91; Jacob J. Kaplan and Gunther Schleiminger, *The European Payments Union: Financial Diplomacy in the 1950s* (Oxford, 1989), esp. 70–9, 342–52.

[120] 'Fundamental Discussions with the United States', memorandum by the Chancellor of the Exchequer, 27 Apr. 1950, EPC(50)44, CAB132/225. Treasury papers relating to these discussions are in

It was agreed that external financial policy must be based on the government's general economic objectives: full employment, an improved standard of living, and a stable balance of payments, particularly with the dollar area. The first two objectives had been achieved only behind a protective barrier of discrimination against dollar imports and strict limits on the convertibility of sterling. However, the Americans had always insisted on, and Britain was committed to, progress towards an ultimate objective of a world without discriminatory restrictions and where currencies were freely convertible with each other. Ministers and officials shared a concern about the implications of American depressions for full employment in Britain, and for that reason were willing to compare notes with the Americans on internal economic policy in their respective countries, while preserving the principle that there should be no interference by either country in the other's decisions on internal policy. Ministers and officials were also agreed that Britain could not even begin to contemplate full sterling-dollar convertibility, even for current transactions, or the abandonment of discrimination against dollar imports, until (1) Britain's gold and dollar reserves were greatly increased and (2) the United States' balance of payments was no longer in surplus with the rest of the world. The United States should be willing to make dollars more plentiful by pursuing internal policies that tended to be inflationary rather than deflationary, and should be more willing to import goods and services (for example, shipping) from other countries, even during an American depression. On the other hand, Britain should prevent inflation at home, deal with the sterling balances, and maintain an adequate balance-of-payments surplus, particularly where gold could be earned (principally South Africa) or where countries were in surplus with the dollar area (for example, Malaya or Nigeria).[121]

On the other hand, Bridges and Hall had had to dissuade Cripps from including in his budget speech a statement that employment policy had an absolute priority (as this would be taken by external opinion to mean that the government had abandoned the objective of convertibility and non-discrimination). Hall was also concerned about Gaitskell's belief, revealed in discussions on EPU, that Britain should never return to completely free convertibility of sterling, or at least not until it had been proved that there would be no slump in the United States. Wilson Smith, Hall, and Clarke thought that such a negative attitude would be an almost impossible starting point for talks with the Americans, who would expect some concessions on convertibility. Much of the improvement in Britain's gold and dollar reserves since devaluation (see Table 8.1) had resulted from a willingness on the part of the Americans to let

T232/199. Snyder's correspondence with Cripps is in T172/2034. Gaitskell noted that he had had 'rows' with Wilson Smith over 'fundamentals' (and EPU) but that Cripps had ruled in favour of arguments put forward by Gaitskell and Jay (Gaitskell, *Diary*, 185).

[121] 'Fundamentals: Gold and European Payments', suggested redraft of 'Summary' and 'Supplementary Thoughts', all by Gaitskell, Apr. 1950, T232/199.

the British put the whole of their allocation of Marshall Aid into the reserves, and it would be difficult to persuade the American taxpayer to contribute another $750 million to bring Britain's reserves up to $3,000 million, simply because the British feared the effects of an American slump. If further American aid were to be forthcoming, Britain would have to show how it proposed to develop its policy in a manner consistent with the objectives that it had agreed in connection with Bretton Woods, the Anglo-American Loan Agreement, and ERP. Britain would have to continue to discriminate against dollar imports, in order to build up the reserves, and therefore the only area in which concessions could be made was currency convertibility. Americans and Canadians already had full convertibility of sterling acquired by current transactions, as did those sterling area countries which pooled their dollars, subject to agreements on import policy, and EPU would provide the opportunity to encourage other countries to use sterling as much as possible in trade with each other and the rest of the world.[122]

The 'fundamental' discussions within the Treasury also confirm that it was simply taken for granted that there would be no abandonment of sterling as an international currency. It was realized that it was important to distinguish between the pre-war conception of the sterling area as a group of countries trading in sterling and holding reserves in sterling, and the current practice of also forming a discriminatory group with a common import policy designed to protect common reserves of dollars. Overseas finance officials favoured a continuation of the latter conception, while recognizing that a greater degree of co-operation between the Britain and the rest of the sterling area might be necessary, and that some of 'the weaker brethren' ought to be excluded from it (as Egypt had been in 1947).[123]

By 1949 the Bank of England and the official Treasury had come to the view that it would be greatly to Britain's advantage if the United States could be persuaded to take on part of the burden of the sterling balances, because political pressures from India, Pakistan, Egypt, and Argentina made it impossible to keep releases of sterling balances as low as had been contemplated when the first agreements with these countries had been signed in 1946 and 1947. In November 1949 a Treasury working party reported in favour of an approach to the Americans which would educate the latter in the facts of the situation, and suggest that one solution might be for the United States to take over some of the balances, converting them from sterling assets to dollar assets, on condition that they were written down.

However, a US Treasury study of the sterling balances had concluded that, although a settlement of the sterling balances was a necessary condition for a

---

[122] Hall, *Diaries, 1947–1953*, 109–12; 'Fundamentals—some Comments', by Clarke (representing the views of Wilson Smith, Hall, and himself), 13 Apr. 1950, T232/199.

[123] Note by Overseas Finance Division, 10 Mar. 1950, T232/199.

move by Britain to multilateral trade and convertibility, it would not be a sufficient condition. (Other necessary conditions included more competitive British
exports.) The US Treasury and other interested parties in Washington (including the State Department, the Federal Reserve, the Export-Import Bank, the
ECA, and the IMF) therefore saw no reason why the United States should provide the *quid pro quo* required to persuade Britain's creditors to change present
arrangements, as the British would still not be ready to proceed to convertibility. Consequently, as Wilson Smith remarked in May 1950, Britain was left to
continue, under the terms of the Anglo-American Loan Agreement, to endeavour to reach an agreement with its creditors, but, without a 'dollar sweetener',
no such agreement was likely to be reached.[124] It was politically impossible by
1950 for a Commonwealth, let alone a foreign, government to accept cancellation of part of its sterling balances; moreover, Cripps believed, the balances
could be used to preserve British export markets in a future depression, and
therefore there was a need for caution in negotiating funding arrangements.[125]

In the summer and autumn of 1950 Britain's external financial position
appeared to be buoyant, at least to the United States administration. An internal State Department study suggested that Britain could be expected to
achieve dollar balance independent of external aid by the American fiscal year
1952/3, providing that the rest of the sterling area continued to export to the
United States more than it imported. Thereafter the sterling area's contribution
to the gold and dollar reserves increased as the United States stockpiled raw
materials in connection with the Korean War, and in October there was a heavy
inflow of foreign funds to London in response to rumours of an upward revaluation of sterling. It therefore came as no great surprise to the Treasury when it
was warned by the Americans in November that Marshall Aid to Britain would
shortly cease, as it did early in 1951.[126]

The Treasury and the Economic Section considered the pros and cons of an
upward revaluation of sterling from time to time during the first half of 1951, and
agreed that the cons outweighed the pros: frequent changes in the rate would
encourage speculation and capital movements, and, while revaluation would
reduce the cost of imports, it would also impede the growth of exports to the
dollar area at a time when the balance of payments on current account was
expected to deteriorate in the second half of the year. There was, further, the
political consideration that the United States would object to the strengthening

[124] (US) National Advisory Council on International and Financial Problems, minutes, 5 Apr. 1950,
RG56: Office of the Secretary of the Treasury, box 2; memorandum of a conversation with Sir Roger
Makins and Sir Henry Wilson Smith, by Henry R. Labouisse (State Department), 17 May 1950, RG59,
841.10/6-1550, National Archives, Washington, DC.
[125] Economic Policy Committee minutes, 28 Mar. 1950, CAB134/224.
[126] 'The Long-term Economic Outlook for the United Kingdom', by Samuel Katz, for (State)
Departmental Dollar Gap Working Group, 21 July 1950, RG353, lot 122, file DDG D-10/3, box 19;
'Monthly Financial Report for October 1950', 14 Nov. 1950, RG59, 841.10/11-1450, box 4779, National
Archives, Washington, DC; EPC minutes, 10 Nov. 1950, CAB134/224.

of the reserves being used to revalue sterling against the dollar, rather than to move towards full convertibility and an end to discrimination against imports from America.[127]

Britain's balance-of-payments problem in 1951 arose from international tension brought about by the Korean War: worldwide rearmament raised the cost of imports, especially raw materials, producing a 9 per cent shift in the terms of trade against Britain, and Britain's own rearmament diverted some industrial capacity away from exports. When deciding on a rearmament programme at the beginning of August 1950 the Cabinet had assumed, on the basis of informal discussion between the Prime Minister and the American ambassador in London, that the United States would provide aid to offset the balance-of-payments effects, but no written commitment was secured from the Americans. Cripps proposed to ask for financial assistance amounting to £550 million, but in September it became apparent that American aid would primarily be in the form of munitions and materials. The Americans suggested there should be a formula for the equitable sharing of the burden of rearmament between all countries in NATO, including the United States, and Gaitskell, who was handling questions relating to rearmament even before he succeeded Cripps as Chancellor, thought that such a formula would be the best way to avoid political difficulties with Congress.[128]

It came as a surprise to the Treasury when the United States administration warned at the end of March 1951 that, when Congress was asked to approve the necessary foreign aid appropriation, it would be told that Britain was not expected to need any help under the formula in the coming year. The American view was that no aid, other than finished military equipment, was necessary if Britain's gold and dollar reserves rose. However, as Hall pointed out, these reserves might rise on account of increased dollar earnings by the rest of the sterling area, or speculative movements of capital, and might not reflect the damage being done by rearmament to the British economy. In Hall's view, had ministers known that the burden-sharing exercise was to be subject to this limitation, they would not have agreed, at American urging, to increase the rearmament programme in January 1951.[129] In the event, the amount of aid received by Britain for rearmament in 1951 amounted to a paltry £4 million, despite a deterioration in the balance of payments on current account from a surplus of £307 million in 1950 to a deficit of £369 million in 1951.

There was thus no period when economic policy was free from external constraints. Even in the years when there was no acute balance-of-payments problem, there was a continuing need to build up the reserves to a level that would

---

[127] Cairncross, *Years of Recovery*, 235–7; EPC(51)65, 22 June 1951, CAB134/230.

[128] For Gaitskell's views see *DBPO*, series 2, iii. 123–6. The best account of the economic aspects of rearmament in 1950–1 is Cairncross, *Years of Recovery*, ch. 8.

[129] 'American Aid and Nitze Exercise', by Hall, 10 Apr. 1951, T273/290.

make Britain independent of American aid. External economic policy was linked to domestic economic policy, in that the extent to which government controls could be used to limit imports, and to give exports priority in the allocation of materials or building licences, depended on political judgment as to what would be acceptable to the electorate. Cripps played a leading role in exhorting the public to accept austerity, and manufacturers to give priority to exports.

DOMESTIC MONETARY POLICY

The continuation of wartime controls made it seem unnecessary to use monetary policy to defend the exchange rate or to regulate investment. Wartime experience suggested that a cheap money policy was possible when it was backed by exchange controls and direct controls over materials, and the National Debt Enquiry of 1945 had converted Treasury officials to the idea of continuing low interest rates to minimize the burden of the National Debt. As noted in Chapter 7, Hopkins in particular was willing to be persuaded that Keynes's liquidity preference theory showed that the monetary authorities could keep nominal long-term interest rates at historically low levels. On the other hand, the Bank of England, which had been excluded from the Enquiry, was not so persuaded and believed that a policy of reducing the rate for government's long-term borrowing below the wartime level of 3 per cent would be misjudged and unsustainable.[130]

Dalton came to the Treasury with firm ideas on monetary policy, a subject in which he had taken an active interest since the 1930s. In Labour party circles low interest rates were favoured partly as a means of minimizing the reward of the rentier, and partly as a means of facilitating future borrowing for employment policy. Deflation through high interest rates was associated with high unemployment, and Dalton believed that planning and direct controls offered a better way of avoiding an inflationary boom followed by a slump. In 1942 he had been attracted to a proposal, made by the Cambridge economist Joan Robinson, to the Labour Party's Post-war Finance Subcommittee, that long-term interest rates should be deliberately lowered after the war, by reducing short-term interest rates and selling longer-term government bonds on tap at progressively lower rates, aiming in the first instance to get undated Consols to par at 2½ per cent. The National Debt Enquiry Report pointed in the same direction, and Dalton could claim that his cheaper money policy had Keynes's strong support up to the latter's death in April 1946.[131]

---

[130] See Fforde, *Bank of England*, 335–8, where trenchant comments by Niemeyer on the National Debt Enquiry Report are reproduced.

[131] Susan Howson, 'The Origins of Cheaper Money, 1945–7', *Econ. Hist. Rev.*, 2nd ser., 40 (1987), 437; Dalton, *High Tide and After*, 124.

The conduct of monetary policy in 1945–51 has been very fully described by Susan Howson, and need only be summarized here.[132] After halving interest rates on the floating debt, returning Treasury bill rate to its pre-war ½ of 1 per cent, in October 1945, the government offered two long-term bond issues in 1946, each at 2½ per cent. The first, in May, had a twenty-year maturity; the second, in October, was, like Consols, irredeemable. In both cases the monetary authorities used the methods developed during the war: the bonds were available on tap, and the Bank of England and the National Debt Commissioners supported the market by buying up long-term gilt-edged securities before and after each issue. The Bank warned that the effect of the May issue would be to lead the market to think that interest rates had gone as low as possible, and to expect any further move to be in an upward direction, but Dalton believed that Post Office and Trustee Savings Bank funds, which were administered by the National Debt Commissioners, gave the monetary authorities the resources with which to support the market for long-term issues in the face of such fears. The October irredeemable issue was so identified with him that the bonds were known as 'Daltons'. However, large-scale purchases of long-term gilt-edged securities by the Bank of England and the National Debt Commissioners had the effect of rapidly increasing bank deposits, leading commentators in the financial press to warn investors that interest rates would rise sooner or later, thereby reducing the price of gilt-edged securities. With private investors holding off, the monetary authorities had to take up most of the issue of 'Daltons', and the price of government bonds fell after the authorities' support ceased early in 1947. Dalton was much criticized in the financial press, but the Bank of England's official history has criticized the Bank for not giving the Chancellor stronger warnings about the risks that he was taking with the market.[133]

Treasury officials themselves bore some responsibility for Dalton's policy. Even when it was clear that there was inflationary pressure in the economy, Eady thought in July 1947 that the traditional check to investment of raising Bank rate would be 'a crude instrument', unless the government provided low-interest funds for essentials, such as housing, which would otherwise be curbed as much as investment in non-essentials, such as greyhound racing tracks. Moreover, to be effective in checking inflation, Bank rate would have to be raised from 2 per cent to 5 or 6 per cent, which Eady regarded as 'terribly dear' money.[134] Officials were aware that over £1,500 million of government-guaranteed stock would have to be issued in 1948 to compensate shareholders for nationalization of the railways, Cable and Wireless, and electricity and coal companies. Hopkins, quoting Keynes's *General Theory* with regard to the importance of market expectations in monetary policy, thought that the issue of such

[132] What follows, except where otherwise stated, is based on her *British Monetary Policy*.
[133] Fforde, *Bank of England*, 320, 327.   [134] Eady to Bridges, 9 July 1947, T273/304.

stock at 3 per cent would be 'a confession of failure' as regards cheaper money.[135] Cripps was no less opposed than Dalton to the issue of a 3 per cent Transport Stock in January 1948, but in December 1947 the Bank had to advise that the market would not accept a long-dated 2¾ per cent stock, and the new Chancellor had to accept that compensation to the owners of railway shares would have to be at 3 per cent. The policy of reducing interest rates was at an end.

Even so the policy of cheap, as opposed to cheaper, money, pursued since 1932, continued. In May 1949 the Investment Programmes Committee warned that direct controls over investment would become progressively less effective in future, and that therefore financial controls must be made more effective. However, E. G. Compton, the Third Secretary in charge of Home Finance, responded: 'All our experience is against relying on finance as the primary instrument of investment control.' Both interest rates and capital issues control depended for their effectiveness on a firm's need to borrow, but the war had left many firms flush with cash.[136]

The clearing banks also had plenty of money, their deposits having increased from around £2,200 million to £4,800 million during the war, and to £5,600 million in 1946, the last figure being equivalent to 63 per cent of gross national product (GNP).[137] In 1948 Jay, as Economic Secretary, suggested a complicated manœuvre whereby, he believed, the budget surplus of £600 million in prospect for 1947/8 could be used to bring about a fall in the banks' reserves to the extent necessary to lead them to reduce their deposits by £600 million. Neither Treasury officials nor the Bank thought that Jay's proposals were workable, if only because the banks could easily replenish their reserves by selling or not renewing their large holdings of Treasury bills. As in the inter-war period, the Bank preferred to work towards bringing the market under control by reducing the floating debt. As a result of Jay's initiative, however, reports were prepared by the Bank and Treasury officials on the use of budget surpluses for debt reduction, and on trends in the clearing banks' assets and liabilities. The September figures showed a large rise in bank advances, and a joint working party of Bank and Treasury officials, and the Director of the Economic Section, Hall, was set up to look into the matter.

As during the war, the Treasury thought that the banks could be asked to restrict credit, and from December 1947 increased publicity was given to requests to give priority to loans for reconstruction, especially exports, and to avoid advances that might be used for speculation. However, Cobbold, the Deputy Governor of the Bank, warned the Chancellor in September 1948 that it would be 'most unwise' to set a fixed limit to bank advances; instead the Bank

---

[135] Hopkins to Bridges, 'The Gilt-edged Market', n.d., but Sept. 1947, T233/143. Hopkins referred to page 203 of the *General Theory* (*JMK*, vii).

[136] 'Comments by the Treasury (Home Finance) on IPC Report of 12 May', 23 May 1949, T229/455.

[137] Howson, op. cit., 224, compared with estimate of GNP in C. H. Feinstein, *National Income, Expenditure and Output of the United Kingdom, 1855–1965* (Cambridge, 1972), table 1.

proposed to invite them to 'shorten their advances'. When in December the Governor, Catto, heard that the Economic Section had raised the question of placing a ceiling on deposits and advances, he wrote to the Chancellor to protest that such matters should be dealt with at the highest level, and expressing his 'utmost alarm' at the proposal, which he regarded as impractical and liable to lead to 'violent deflation'. The Bank viewed a budget surplus, plus the reduction in floating debt which that would make possible, as the natural cure for inflation, and therefore looked to the Treasury to cut public expenditure, whereas the Treasury, which knew how difficult it was to secure such cuts, hankered after restrictions on bank advances as an alternative.[138]

Treasury officials included the possibility of allowing interest rates to rise as part of a deflationary package to avoid devaluation in 1949. Cobbold, now governor, was by no means opposed to higher interest rates in principle, but he advised that a tighter monetary policy would have little effect on confidence in sterling unless accompanied by large reductions in government expenditure. Once devaluation had been decided upon, Cobbold wanted to let Treasury bill rate rise so as to make Bank rate, still 2 per cent, effective[139] from the day after devaluation, but Eady prevaricated, rightly anticipating that ministers would dislike any measure that would increase the banks' profits. The outcome was another request to the banks to restrain their lending.

Gaitskell took an active interest in monetary policy, both as Minister of State and as Chancellor. He was more willing than Dalton or Cripps had been to see long-term interest rates rise, and told the Cabinet's Economic Policy Committee in June 1951 that, although the recent rise in the long-term rate from 3½ to 4 per cent had not been engineered by the monetary authorities, it had his acquiescence. He did not believe that the rate of interest was a very powerful influence on investment, but he thought that the decline in gilt-edged prices was in itself a deflationary factor (presumably because of the psychological effect on the holders of securities).[140] On the other hand, he hoped to keep short-term rates down, and overruled his senior officials when, from December 1950, they supported the Bank's case for reactivating Bank rate by making it effective and raising it to 2½ per cent. The Bank admitted that the psychological effects of such a move were uncertain, whereas higher interest rates would certainly increase the cost of government borrowing at a time when it faced large bills for rearmament and steel nationalization. Cobbold, for his part, refused in June

---

[138] Alec Cairncross, 'Prelude to Radcliffe: Monetary Policy in the United Kingdom, 1948–57', *Riv. Storia Econ.*, 2nd ser., 4 (1987), 5–7. Catto's letter of 17 Dec. and the Chancellor's reply are printed in Fforde, *Bank of England*, 367–8.

[139] Bank rate could be effective only if the clearing banks were forced to borrow from the Bank of England, but the banks could always replenish their reserves by reducing their holdings of Treasury bills, which the Bank was committed to buying in order to maintain the Treasury bill rate of ½ of 1 per cent. This 'open back door' was not closed until the ½ of 1 per cent Treasury bill rate was abandoned, after the change of government, in 1951.

[140] 'Memorandum by the Chancellor of the Exchequer', EPC(51)65, 22 June 1951, CAB134/230.

1951 to countenance Gaitskell's suggestion that the banks should be told to take up an increased quantity of Treasury bills or Treasury deposit receipts at current interest rates, as to do so would 'be a fundamental blow to British Government credit'.[141] It was at this time that Treasury officials asked the Treasury Solicitor what powers the Chancellor had to give directions to the banks under the Bank of England Act of 1946, and were told that he had none. The Governor, who did have the power, would go no further than 'requests' for restraint by the banks in making advances.

Labour's nationalization programme placed considerable strain on monetary policy. Between 31 March 1946, when only the Bank of England had been nationalized, and 31 March 1951, when Labour's nationalization programme was complete, total gilt-edged debt (including government-guaranteed issues) increased from £13,168 million to £15,280 million, the increase being broadly the same as the total for nationalization compensation issues, £2,107 million. The scale of the National Debt and post-war nationalization issues helps to explain why Treasury officials favoured cheap money, and the existence of exchange controls and controls over investment encouraged them to put Keynes's ideas for cheaper money into practice. However, even professional economists who were broadly 'Keynesian' had doubts about Labour's monetary policy: Hall agreed with a leading Bank of England official in 1948 that Keynes had left behind a set of doctrines that were quite unsuited for a period of inflation, and in the same year Meade, Hall's predecessor as Director of the Economic Section, publicly expressed his preference for the use of interest rates rather than physical controls to influence investment.[142] Cheap money, then, was adopted only partly because of Keynes's liquidity preference theory. The policy also reflected traditional Treasury concern with the National Debt, and was made possible by the existence of controls over investment and by the fact that interest rates were low throughout the world until central bank discount rates began to rise in the summer of 1950.

As Howson notes, the evidence relating to the effects of cheaper money policy on private expenditure in 1946 and 1947 is ambiguous. The ratio of money balances (M3) to national income, which had increased from 55 per cent to 70 per cent during the war, reached 79 per cent in 1946/7 before declining steadily to its pre-war level by 1952.[143] Rationing, price controls, and food subsidies prevented this increase in the money supply from having its full effect on prices, but both investment and consumer expenditure rose, to the detriment of exports

---

[141] Howson, *British Monetary Policy*, 297.

[142] Hall, *Diaries, 1947–1953*, 43; James Meade, *Planning and the Price Mechanism: The Liberal–Socialist Solution* (1948).

[143] Howson, op. cit., 331–2. M3 comprises notes and coins in circulation with the public, plus all deposits of all residents (both public and private sectors) with the UK banking sector (including sight and time deposits in sterling and foreign currencies, and time deposits with accepting houses, overseas banks, and other banks).

and the balance of payments. When the scale of the balance-of-payments problem became apparent in 1947, the Treasury had to rely on disinflationary budgetary policy as an alternative to deflationary monetary policy. (The term 'disinflationary' was coined by Cripps to distinguish his policy from deflation.)

FISCAL POLICY

Although the emphasis in what follows is on budgetary policy as a policy instrument to deal with inflation, it should be noted that the budgets of 1945–51 also had other objectives.[144] In particular, Labour Chancellors were committed to using taxation to achieve greater equality of incomes and property. For example, Dalton made significant increases in death duties in his 1946 budget, against the advice of his officials. He also wished to remove the disincentive effects of high taxation. Accordingly, in his first budget in October 1945, he reduced the standard rate of income tax from 10s. (50p) to 9s. (45p) in the pound, while revising the surtax scale to ensure that, for people on higher incomes, the income tax reliefs were offset by surtax increases, with the combined rate of income tax and surtax on the highest incomes remaining at 19s. 6d. (97½p) in the pound. In 1946 he increased earned income allowances, hoping to stimulate production, although Keynes advised that instead of 'releasing money without goods to buy', it would be better to relax import restrictions to allow in an extra £50 million of semi-luxuries, especially food, as a means of providing stimulus.[145]

In the case of profits, the need to encourage businessmen to maximize production had to be balanced against the need to assure workers, who were being asked to accept wage restraint, that there was no profiteering. Accordingly, although the wartime tax on excess profits, EPT, was cut from 100 per cent to 60 per cent in October 1945 and repealed in 1946, national defence contribution, which had been levied at 5 per cent of company profits since 1937, was renamed profits tax and levied in the April 1947 budget at 12.5 per cent on distributed profits and 5 per cent on profits put to reserve. Both rates were doubled in the November 1947 budget. The novel differentiation between distributed and undistributed profits reflected the thinking of James Meade, who believed that investment levels could be influenced by levying a lower rate on undistributed profits in times of inflation and a lower rate on distributed profits in times of deflation.

Tax changes could also be aimed at influencing firms' investment by varying

---

[144] What follows draws heavily upon Richard C. Whiting, 'Taxation Policy', in H. Mercer, N. Rollings, and J. D. Tomlinson (eds.), *Labour Governments and Private Industry: The Experience of 1945–51* (Edinburgh, 1992), 117–34.

[145] Dalton's note on Bridges to Chancellor, 23 Mar. 1946, and Keynes to Chancellor, 1 Apr. 1946, T171/388.

depreciation allowances. A scheme of 'initial allowances' was introduced in 1945 to increase the proportion of the cost of an asset that was allowed free of tax in the year of purchase. Correspondingly less was allowed in later years, so that over the whole life of the asset, the total tax relief granted for depreciation was unchanged. The idea was to compensate firms for the fact that current depreciation allowances, assessed on the original cost of the capital in use, was insufficient for its replacement at post-war prices, and to encourage firms to invest. Subsequently, with a view to raising investment, Cripps doubled the initial allowances in 1949, but in 1951 Gaitskell, confronted with the need to divert industrial materials from investment to rearmament, gave notice that initial allowances would be suspended from April 1952.

Labour ministers, as might be expected, were strongly in favour of a capital levy. Dalton thought that a graduated levy on individual net wealth could make a worthwhile reduction in the National Debt, although he accepted that any saving on interest would be largely offset by a reduction in the yield from income tax, surtax, and death duties. He believed that such a levy would be strongly anti-inflationary and would discourage rich people from living on capital. It would, moreover, 'be a brisk step towards economic and social equality'. Prior to his resignation, he was considering making a capital levy the principal feature of the 1948 budget, and he passed on his ideas to Cripps.[146]

Treasury officials, with the assistance of the Economic Section and the Board of Inland Revenue, prepared a note in which it was stated that a capital levy had not been found to be worth while when the question had been examined in 1945, and lower interest rates since then had reduced the possible savings on the National Debt, and higher tax rates had increased the amount of revenue that would be lost. The Economic Section argued that a levy would force people to sell securities, and consequently the price of securities would fall, which would be equivalent to, and would cause, a rise in the rate of interest. People would fear that the levy would be repeated and would try to get capital out of the country, particularly to South Africa, and the sterling area in its present form would be in jeopardy. The Board of Inland Revenue referred to the experience of Lloyd George's land values duties, and quoted the Colwyn Report on the need to obtain the willing assent of taxpayers to any large, complicated measure. At a meeting with Bridges, Plowden, Gilbert, Eady, Sir Eric Bamford (then a Third Secretary in the Treasury), and Hall, Cripps observed that he 'was not convinced that as much weight had been given to the "pros" for such a levy as to the "cons" in the note'. The Chancellor admitted that the administrative problems would be formidable, but also noted that the political pressures for a capital levy would be extremely strong.[147]

[146] Dalton, *High Tide and After*, 288–9.
[147] 'Budget', note of meeting of 20 Jan. 1948, T171/394; 'Note on Capital Levy', BC(48)13, 14 Jan. 1948, T171/395.

Cripps came down in favour of a scheme for levy on investment income, which was offered by officials as an alternative to a capital levy. As modified after discussion with the Chancellor, what was called a 'special contribution' took the form of a once-for-all, graduated tax, which would be largely paid out of capital, being assessed on all dividends, interest, and rents received by individuals in 1947/8. Cripps thereby avoided the major administrative problem of a capital levy: the need for a valuation of all capital assets in the country. The special contribution applied only to people whose total income exceeded £2,000, thereby excluding people of moderate means. However, the expected yield, £105 million, was a small sum in relation to the National Debt of £15,000 million.[148]

Budgets also continued to be concerned with calculations of what levels of government expenditure could be afforded at given levels of taxation. For example, a paper by Gilbert on 'The Budget of an Early Post-war Year' on 25 July 1945—the day before Labour took office—was concerned entirely with the margin that would be available, given certain assumptions about prices and national income, for defence and remission of taxation out of a balanced budget, once social insurance, health, and educational reform had taken effect, and assuming a continuation of some food subsidies to stabilize the cost of living.[149]

With the economy still converting from war to civil production, and with the need to reserve much of the latter for exports, there was a danger, as Dalton said when introducing his budget in October 1945, that 'too much money should run after too few goods'.[150] Dalton said he did not expect to achieve a genuine surplus immediately, any more than a genuine surplus had been achieved in 1919/20. However, he believed that, once the transition from war finance had been completed, the aim should be to balance the budget over a period of years, planning surpluses when trade was good, and deficits when a trade depression threatened.[151] In the event, a fall in defence expenditure of £3,556 million between 1945/6 and 1947/8 outweighed an increase in other expenditure (£1,210 million over the same period), so that Dalton was able to achieve a surplus on the conventional budget in 1947/8, with a net addition to ordinary revenue of £560 million.[152] However, taking items such as loans to local authorities and nationalized industries into account, central government remained a net borrower until 1948/9 (see Table 8.2).

Cripps introduced the concept of the overall budget surplus in 1948. The traditional budget accounts had always excluded or very partially reflected the operation of the National Insurance Fund, the Exchange Equalisation Account, or loans to local authorities and public corporations, and the last

---

[148] 449 HC Deb., 5s, 1947–8, cols. 71–2.   [149] T171/371.
[150] 414 HC Deb., 5s, 1945–6, col. 1876.
[151] Ibid., col. 1886. See also 436 HC Deb., 5s, 1946–7, cols. 54–5.
[152] Cairncross, *Years of Recovery*, 420.

TABLE 8.2. *Budget Balance for Financial Years 1945/6–1951/2 (£m.)*

	Surplus (+) or deficit (−) above the line[a]		Deficit below the line[b]	Overall surplus or deficit
	Forecast	Out-turn	Out-turn	Out-turn
1945/6	−2,300 (April and October)	−2,207	−32	−2,239
1946/7	−726	−586	−518	−1,104
1947/8	+270 (April) +318 (October)	+636	−651	−15
1948/9	+778	+831	−451	+380
1949/50	+470	+549	−487	+62
1950/1	+443	+720	−473	+247
1951/2	+39	+380	−529	−149

[a] The conventional budget balance accounting for revenue into and expenditure out of the Consolidated Fund.

[b] Payments for which Parliament had authorized the Treasury to borrow, such as loans to local authorities or capital expenditure by public utilities.

Sources: Column 1: budget speeches; columns 2–5: 'Exchequer Financing and the National Debt, 1945–51', *Economic Trends* (Dec. 1961), table 1, and Committee on the Working of the Monetary System, *Principal Memoranda of Evidence*, i. 78.

two items had grown to substantial sums in the range of £500 million to £700 million a year with Labour's housing and nationalization programmes. From 1949 such 'below-the-line' items, as they were known, were included in the Chancellor's annual Financial Statement.[153]

The extent to which the early post-war budgets were informed by Keynesian analysis, even as much as wartime ones had been after 1941, has been a matter of debate. For Cairncross, Dalton's emergency budget of November 1947 was a turning point in post-war fiscal policy, both because it was only then that the Chancellor related the additional taxation that he was imposing to excess demand as measured within a national income accounting framework, and because inflationary pressure, which had been increasing steadily through 1947, fell sharply in 1948. As already noted, the Economic Section was at its least effective while Meade was Director in 1946–7, and Booth has suggested that it was only with Dalton's emergency budget of November 1947 and Cripps's first disinflationary budget in 1948 that 'the tap of Keynesian advice was turned on again'. This focus on November 1947 has been challenged on two grounds. First, Rollings has denied that the November 1947 budget reflected an intellectual conversion by Treasury officials to Keynesian economic theory, and has instead stressed their practical reasons for aiming at a budget surplus, in particular their wish to cut government expenditure, especially food subsidies.

[153] For budget accounts see J. R. Hicks, *The Problem of Budgetary Reform* (Oxford, 1948); *Report of the (Crick) Committee on the Form of Government Accounts* (Cmd. 7969), PP 1950, vi. 1; *Reform of the Exchequer Accounts* (Cmnd. 2014), PP 1962–3, xxxi. 215.

Second, Howson has pointed out that Dalton's budget of April 1947 aimed at an anti-inflationary surplus.[154]

It is true that little was said in public about the 'inflationary gap' in the first two years after the war, but part of the reason was that the figures were so uncertain. Meade put forward estimates of the inflationary gap between national income and expenditure in an unpublished 'Economic Survey for 1946', but Keynes attacked his figures on logical and statistical grounds. In his view, some items were forecasts, but others were gaps between demand and supply that were bound to disappear as government departments cut their programmes or as inflation curbed private demand. Keynes did not trust the estimates produced by the Central Statistical Office, and certainly each year the CSO kept changing its estimates of national income. Moreover, forecasts frequently proved to be wrong, with the level of stock-building being particularly hard to predict, and even forecasts of government expenditure were remarkably inaccurate.[155] In such circumstances estimates of the inflationary gap could only provide a very rough guide as to what action should be taken in the budget, and Keynes was not alone in preferring to rely upon intuitive hunch. Meade's advice for the April 1947 budget was that fiscal policy should be used to bring total post-tax incomes closer to the total supply of goods. Dalton did not refer to the inflationary gap in his budget speech, but he justified budgeting for a surplus of £270 million by drawing attention to low unemployment and rising prices, and claimed that a surplus now would earn the right to a deficit in a future year when deflation threatened.[156] To that extent, the April 1947 budget was 'Keynesian'.

The 1947 budgets were concerned with the balance of payments as well as with the related problem of excess demand in the British economy. Dalton doubled the customs duties on tobacco in April, not so much to raise revenue as to curb dollar expenditure on imports from the United States. (He had been advised that, if consumption continued at its present rate, one-fifth of the American Loan would, quite literally, go up in smoke.[157]) The emergency budget in November was itself a response to the dollar shortage, being first conceived by Dalton in August, during the convertibility crisis, and in his speech he explained that fiscal measures were necessary to reduce purchasing power at a time when the government had decided to increase exports and reduce imports.

Dalton's speech in November still used the expression of 'too much money running after too few goods', and, claiming that not even the most skilful statistician could measure the inflationary pressure, he refused to put any precise

[154] Cairncross, *Years of Recovery*, 410, 419–20; Booth, *British Economic Policy*, 167; Rollings, 'British Budgetary Policy', 286–90; Howson, *British Monetary Policy*, 163–4, 333.

[155] Keynes to Meade, 16 Jan. 1946, T230/55. Cairncross and Watts, *Economic Section*, 192–8, 203; Cairncross, *Years of Recovery*, 413, 426.

[156] 436 HC Deb., 5s, 1946–7, cols. 54–5; J. Meade, *Collected Papers*, vol. i, ed. Susan Howson, *Employment and Inflation* (1988), esp. 279, 292, and vol. iv, 281.

[157] Burke Trend to Chancellor, 18 Jan. 1947, T171/389.

figure on the inflationary gap.[158] Nevertheless, up to a point, the concept of the inflationary gap between prospective national money expenditure and real output had informed Treasury discussions on the size of surplus to be aimed at. Bridges observed in September that the purpose of the budget was 'not the old fashioned one of extra taxation to balance the budget, but a reduction of the inflationary pressure' that threatened the external balance. Hall, who had replaced Meade as head of the Economic Section, had estimated the inflationary gap at £600 million to £650 million, and Bridges advised Dalton that a gap of that order could not be closed simply by increasing taxation. He suggested a £240 million cut in cost-of-living subsidies as well as up to £172 million in tax increases, leaving a gap of about £200 million. However, Dalton still thought that the inflationary gap was hard to quantify. He refused to agree to a reduction in expenditure on food subsidies, because raising the price of food would hit the poorest members of the community and stimulate demands for higher wages and increased social insurance benefits, although he did agree to remove subsidies on clothing and footwear.[159] In the end increased taxation and other measures in the budget left an inflationary gap of more than £400 million— equivalent to 4 per cent of gross domestic product—apparently untouched. The budget was thus, like wartime budgets, shaped by 'hunch' and by a sense of what was politically possible or desirable, as well as by very rudimentary Keynesian analysis.

Cripps, unlike Dalton, was the minister responsible for economic planning as well for financial policy, and he drew upon the advice of Plowden as well as Hall to place his budgets in the context of economic planning. The annual *Economic Survey* issued in March 1948 provided detailed background for the budget debate, starting with the balance of payments and the need to expand exports, whether or not Marshall Aid became available, and analysing the problem of inflation in terms of forecasts of national income and expenditure for the year ahead. The Economic Section estimated the inflationary gap for 1948 at £480 million, and in January the Treasury officials on the Budget Committee agreed with the Section's suggested target of an increase in the budget surplus of £200 million to £300 million, in addition to the £270 million surplus anticipated on the existing basis of taxation. In the event, the Inland Revenue revised its estimate for 1948/9, so that the prospective surplus rose to £778 million, making tax concessions possible.[160]

In September 1948 budgetary policy was reviewed by the Economic Section and the Treasury in connection with the four-year programme to be submitted

---

[158] 444 HC Deb., 5s, 1947–8, col. 393.

[159] Bridges to Chancellor of the Exchequer, 23 Sept. 1947, with Dalton's marginal comments, and 'Cuts in Expenditure', n.d., and unsigned, but by Dalton, late Oct. 1947, T171/392.

[160] *Economic Survey for 1948* (Cmd. 7344), PP 1947–8, xxii. 733. BC(48)3, 'Note on Inflation'; 'Treasury Comment on BC(48)3', and 'Budget', by Trend, 20 Jan 1948, T171/394. 449 HC Deb., 5s, 1947–8, col. 56.

to the OEEC, which was drawn up to show how Britain could become independent of Marshall Aid by 1952. Hall stressed the need for tax concessions to encourage enterprise on the part of business, describing profits tax (as opposed to graduated income tax) as 'economically wrong' in principle, and the top rate for income tax and surtax combined of 19s. 6d. (97½p) as 'penal'. Treasury officials could see no prospect of any significant reduction in government expenditure, unless there were changes in policy, and both Hall and Bridges agreed that fiscal policy should continue to be disinflationary, thereby supplementing the private savings required for industrial investment.[161]

Doubts about the wisdom of budget surpluses which were expressed in Cabinet shortly after the general election in February 1950 reduced Labour's majority to six, on the grounds that large surpluses reduced private saving rather than consumption. In a short Cabinet paper Hall had to defend what he called a 'revolution in British practice' since 1947 and 1948, warning that any serious departure from it would be regarded at home and abroad 'as an abandonment of the principle of planning'.[162]

By the time Gaitskell came to present his budget in April 1951 the problem of rising expenditure was much worse on account of rearmament. Dalton described Gaitskell's speech as the best official statement of the doctrine that closing the inflationary gap is the most important economic function of the budget.[163] However, the preparation of the budget illustrated the problems of Keynesian analysis at a time of uncertainties in various elements in the national income accounting framework, including possible changes in productivity, increases in company reserves, the balance of payments, and, not least, the level of the government's own expenditure. Treasury officials on the Budget Committee did not accept the Economic Section's estimate in February 1951 that the extra taxation required to prevent inflation was in the range £50 million to £100 million, and by the time the Chancellor came to discuss his budget with the Prime Minister in March a figure of £150 million in extra revenue or reduced expenditure was being used, with the proviso that the figure could be nearer £200 million if the underlying forecast of productivity growth proved to be too optimistic.[164] The standard rate of income tax was raised by 6d. (2½p) to 9s. 6d. (47½p), close to its wartime level of 10s. (50p). It was clear that there was very little scope for increased expenditure other than on defence, and the scene was set for a major clash in Cabinet over National Health Service expenditure (see below).

---

[161] 'Budgetary Prospects and Policy, 1948–1952', by Hall, 17 July 1948; minutes of a meeting in Bridges's room, 22 July 1948, and 'Outline of the Problems of a 4-Year Budgetary Policy', by Bridges, 10 Sept. 1948, T171/397.

[162] CP(50)35, reproduced in Kit Jones, *An Economist among Mandarins*, 205–6.

[163] Dalton, *Principles of Public Finance* (1954), 222.

[164] Howson, *British Monetary Policy*, 277–81 has a useful account of these discussions.

Budgetary policy was necessarily limited in its effectiveness in dealing with inflationary pressure in 1945–51, partly because private individuals and firms had ample liquid funds, and the propensity to save was markedly lower than either before 1939 or after 1951.[165] Excess demand was too great to be removed by increasing taxation, for direct taxation was probably close to what was electorally possible, and may well have had a disincentive effect on enterprise,[166] while increased indirect taxes, or reduced subsidies, might provoke demands for higher wages. The alternative to increasing taxation was to reduce government expenditure, but, as will be noted below, the Treasury's power to enforce cuts was very limited. In Christopher Dow's judgement, budgetary policy in 1945–51 can be credited with preventing any increase in inflationary pressure, but was not actively disinflationary.[167]

PRICES, WAGES, AND FOOD SUBSIDIES

Treasury officials were not wholly committed to holding down prices, as opposed to reducing government expenditure. In his post-budget reflections in 1946, shortly before his death in April, Keynes predicted that, given that normal budget expenditure was unlikely to fall below £2,750 million, it would not be possible to achieve a balanced budget unless prices and wages increased, thereby raising money national income and tax revenue. At a time when the official cost-of-living index was 131 (pre-war = 100), Keynes thought that it should be allowed to rise gradually to 200, and that wages might then be expected to rise from 160 to 200. To this end he advised that in 1947 subsidies holding down the cost of living should be reduced, adding that it was better to reduce both subsidies and taxation than it was to increase both.[168]

Dalton's budget speech had promised that the cost of living would be held steady for another year, but had also warned that the increasing cost of food subsidies would have to be reconsidered the following year. Three months later Meade was describing food subsidies as 'one of the great inflationary forces', in that by holding down prices to consumers they released purchasing power to be spent on other commodities. Treasury officials responded to this advice by looking for economies in subsidies on items that did not enter the cost-of-living index, while advising the Chancellor that major economies must await the outcome of an enquiry by the Ministry of Labour into the composition of the index.[169]

---

[165] R. C. O. Matthews, C. H. Feinstein, and J. C. Odling-Smee, *British Economic Growth, 1856–1973* (Oxford, 1982), 143.

[166] The *Second Report of the Royal Commission on the Taxation of Profits and Income* (Cmd. 9105), PP 1953–4, xix. 187, recognized that very high marginal tax rates on incomes probably discouraged the taking of risks, but thought that the effect was unascertainable (para. 149).

[167] Dow, *Management of the British Economy*, 210.   [168] *JMK*, xxvii. 414–17.

[169] 'The Economic Survey for 1947 and the Budget for 1947/48', n.d., and note by Trend, 22 July 1946, T171/389.

By early in 1947 it was known that the Ministry of Labour would shortly introduce a new cost-of-living index in which food would be weighted at 35 per cent of household expenditure, as against 60 per cent in the current one. Food subsidies would thus have less impact on the index. Meade suggested that cost-of-living subsidies should be reduced by £150 million, but Gilbert advised that so large a reduction would have a disruptive effect on prices and would set off another round of wage increases, and was therefore 'quite impracticable'.[170] On the other hand, Treasury officials definitely wanted to bring subsidy expenditure under control, and Dalton warned in his budget speech in April that it might be necessary to impose a ceiling on food subsidies as 'otherwise this element alone in all the total of our public expenditure might seem to be passing out of our own control'.[171] (He reluctantly did so later in the year, after the convertibility crisis, when it was stated that the April estimate of £392 million was not to be exceeded.)

Although Dalton was physically and mentally exhausted by the time he was preparing his November budget, he showed considerable resolve when resisting pressure put on him by Treasury officials to reduce subsidies.[172] In order to maintain the ceiling of £392 million in 1948/9, the Cabinet was persuaded to approve price increases to be spread between January and March 1948, but Cripps postponed most of these increases in February when Attlee appealed to all workers not to press for higher wages. Consequently, expenditure on food subsidies in 1948/9 was allowed to rise to £484.5 million. In April 1949 Cripps imposed a new ceiling of £465 million, and this ceiling was reduced to £410 million as part of the public expenditure cuts following devaluation in the autumn.

Further cuts could not be contemplated after November 1949, when the General Council of the TUC recommended a one-year stabilization of wage rates, provided that the retail price index did not increase by more than 5 per cent. Bridges urged in April 1950 that a long-term wages policy must be found, as he believed that the policy of full employment made it impossible to control the wage–price spiral through deflation. He advised that the Chancellor should tell the TUC that the government had not got a solution to the problem, but was anxious to find one, and suggested that senior officials should be authorized to enter talks with representatives of the TUC and the British Employers' Confederation.[173] However, on 28 June the General Council issued a new statement, suggesting that the vigorous restraint adopted after sterling's devaluation was no longer necessary, while calling for great moderation in view of the country's economic position, and in September the TUC conference rejected proposals for continued restraint. Treasury officials once more felt free to press for a

[170]   Gilbert to Bridges, 14 Mar. 1947, T171/389.
[171]   436 HC Deb., 5s, 1946–7, col. 44.   [172]   Rollings, 'British Budgetary Policy', 289.
[173]   'Wages Policy', by Bridges, 28 Apr. 1950, T172/2033.

reduction in food subsidies, but Gaitskell's budget in April 1951 simply re-affirmed the £410 million ceiling.

PROBLEMS OF CONTROLLING EXPENDITURE

Food subsidies were a special case of a general problem facing Treasury officials: to what extent could new forms of expenditure adopted during the war be reversed? Keynes observed in January 1946 that government current expend-iture was 'shamefully high', and would probably prevent private capital forma-tion from reaching the level forecast in the Economic Survey for the year.[174]

As after 1918, the Treasury had to reimpose discipline on spending depart-ments and try to avoid open-ended commitments. Dalton agreed with his offi-cials in 1945 that, as a step towards restoring Treasury control over expenditure, votes of credit—that is, the general funds voted by Parliament for war expend-iture—should not be continued after the end of the financial year 1945/6, and that departments should be required to submit Estimates of expenditure, year by year, in the normal way thereafter.[175] In theory the Estimates submitted by the end of one financial year put a ceiling on a department's expenditure in the coming financial year, although in practice it was often difficult for the Treasury to deny a Supplementary Estimate later. Once, when trying to bring a depart-ment's expenditure under control, Gilbert remarked to Douglas Jay that: 'I've always found that with the female members of my own family, the only way to stop people spending money is to see they don't have it.' Although Jay was com-mitted as Economic Secretary to applying advanced economic thought to pub-lic finance, the experience of Treasury work led him occasionally to allow himself what he called the 'unworthy thought' that there might be as much truth in Gilbert's 'outmoded wisdom' as in Keynesian analysis.[176]

On the whole, the forms of Treasury control seem to have been re-established with remarkably little controversy. Evidence by permanent heads of depart-ments to the Treasury Organisation Committee in 1950 suggested that spend-ing departments found the degree of delegation of control of expenditure exercised by the Treasury's Supply Services divisions was satisfactory, with the notable exception of the Ministry of Food, where there were special difficulties about the availability of foreign exchange for long-term contracts for overseas purchases.[177] Treasury control of expenditure seems to have been powerfully reinforced by the machinery of economic planning, particularly with regard to import programmes, which justified rigorous control of all expenditure involv-ing foreign exchange, and with regard to investment programmes. As early as

[174] Keynes to Proctor, 2 Jan. 1946, T230/55.
[175] Dalton to Bridges, 15 Aug. 1945, T273/325.   [176] Jay, *Change and Fortune*, 172.
[177] 'Treasury Organisation Committee: Minutes of Meetings', T273/203.

1947 it was apparent that shortage of materials and general excess demand in the economy would impose limits on public investment, and the Investment Programmes Committee was used to restrict building work connected with housing, hospitals, health centres, and schools. The 'Long-Term Programme' of 1948, which was designed to show the OEEC how Britain would achieve dollar viability, gave highest priority to investment in industry, transport, and fuel, and the lowest priority to housing and basic social services. Contrary to Correlli Barnett's thesis, industrial investment was not sacrificed to the 'New Jerusalem' of the welfare state.[178]

The dollar shortage led to an unusual case of a Treasury official advocating higher expenditure. In July 1947 Otto Clarke drew attention to the fact that increased food production by British farmers was one of the principal ways in which dollar imports could be cut. He urged that the Chancellor should be told that the Ministry of Agriculture's existing programme for increasing agricultural production was inadequate, and Dalton was subsequently advised to accept the Ministry of Agriculture's argument that an injection of £40 million a year into the aggregate net income of farmers was a necessary 'psychological stimulus' to make reasonably sure of the farmers' co-operation.[179]

As always, Treasury control was subject to policy decisions by ministers. For example, one of Dalton's first instructions to his officials when he became Chancellor was that, with regard to the building of new factories in areas that had experienced high unemployment in the inter-war period (the 'Development Areas' under the Distribution of Industry Act of 1945), the Treasury was to be 'no longer a curb, but a spur'; and it was in this context that he told Parliament that he would find all the money necessary 'with a song in my heart'.[180] (This speech drew from Lord Cherwell the comment that the words came from *The Beggar's Opera*.) Treasury officials foresaw that once financial inducements became available to firms moving to Development Areas, none would be prepared to go to one without inducement. Even so, they had to accept Cripps's ruling that further legislation on the distribution of industry in 1950 would continue to provide for Exchequer grants or loans to specific industrial undertakings, albeit in 'the most exceptional cases'. In the event, although Board of Trade expenditure in connection with regional policy peaked in 1947/8, Treasury expenditure continued to rise down to 1951/2.[181]

The major policy contradiction in relation to the level of public expenditure lay in the government's determination both that Britain should not be caught out with inadequate defence forces, as had happened in the 1930s, and that

---

[178] See Tomlinson, *Democratic Socialism*, ch. 11. The thesis, originally put forward in Barnett's *Audit of War* (1986), ch. 12, has been restated in his *The Lost Victory* (1995), chs. 7–8.

[179] 'Agriculture', by Clarke, 24 July 1947, and '£100 million Increase in Agricultural Production', by Arnold France, 4 Aug. 1947, T223/216.

[180] 421 HC Deb., 5s, 1945–6, col. 1807.

[181] Ibid., col. 1811; T228/202 *passim*; Gavin McCrone, *Regional Policy in Britain* (1969), 114.

social services should be greatly improved. At first it seemed that what became known as the 'welfare state' could be financed out of a post-war 'peace dividend', as defence expenditure fell after the war, but this trend ended in 1950 with the outbreak of the Korean War and the decision of the Labour government to embark upon a rearmament programme (see Table 8.3). Comprehensive statistics for central government expenditure on social services are only available from 1949/50, but the figures in Table 8.3 show that total central government expenditure on social services fell as a proportion of gross domestic product after that year.

TABLE 8.3. *Total Net Expenditure by Central Government on Defence, 1945/6–1951/2 and Social Services, 1949/50–1951/2*

	Defence		Social services	
	£m.	Percentage gross domestic product at market prices	£m.	Percentage gross domestic product at market prices
1945/6	4,410.0	44.7	—	—
1946/7	1,653.4	16.3	—	—
1947/8	853.9	7.8	—	—
1948/9	753.2	6.3	—	—
1949/50	740.7	5.9	1,065.7	8.5
1950/1	777.4	5.8	1,119.5	8.4
1951/2	1,110.2	7.5	1,141.0	7.8

Sources: Expenditure figures from *Annual Abstract of Statistics*, 90 (1953), tables 43 and 252; GDP from C. H. Feinstein, *National Income Expenditure and Output of the United Kingdom, 1855–1965* (Cambridge, 1972), table 3, adjusted from calendar years to financial years.

DEFENCE EXPENDITURE

As already noted, defence expenditure was a major drain on Britain's balance of payments. In February 1946 Dalton circulated to the Cabinet a memorandum, drafted by Keynes, in which it was estimated that on current trends military expenditure overseas might cost anything from £600 million to £750 million in the three years 1946–8, and, when combined with projected political expenditure, such as relief for war-devastated countries, was likely to leave nothing out of the American loan (£937 million) for food imports or capital equipment for British industry.[182] Dalton thought that Keynes's paper had made an impact on his colleagues, and hoped that, if they accepted that Britain lacked the resources to keep open the Mediterranean route in time of war, they would also agree that troops need not be maintained in the Suez Canal Zone or the rest of the Middle East.

[182] *JMK*, xxvii. 466, 478.

Attlee certainly talked of withdrawing to a line from Lagos to Kenya, but Ernest Bevin, the Foreign Secretary, strongly supported the Chiefs of Staff when they argued that Britain must remain a Mediterranean power. During 1946 and early 1947, when economic planning focused on the shortage of industrial and agricultural workers, Bevin obstinately resisted any reduction in Britain's armed forces or overseas commitments that might weaken his diplomacy, and such was Bevin's position in the Cabinet and Labour party that Attlee could not overrule him. It was not until after the convertibility crisis of July 1947 that Dalton was able to persuade Bevin that a reorganization of the defence forces ought to release 200,000 men. In September the Cabinet's Defence Committee agreed to a reduction in the strength of the armed forces from 1,217,000 to 713,000 by March 1949, a step that was said to involve 'serious risks and consequences', although the strength of the armed forced in mid-1939 had been only 480,000.[183]

Bridges had hoped in 1946 that the creation of a Ministry of Defence, with inter-service integration with regard to research and development, production, and preparation of balanced annual Estimates, would lead to a more rational allocation of resources than the pre-war procedure whereby each service had fought its own battle with the Treasury. Treasury criticism of the service Estimates continued, but the bulk of the economies, and the balance between the services, were to decided by the Ministry of Defence: for example, the Ministry of Defence was responsible for cutting the original draft Estimates for 1947/8 from £1,164 million to £963 million, and subsequent inspection by the Treasury could only secure a further £22.8 million in economies. However, in August 1947 Bridges was told by the Permanent Under-Secretary of State at the War Office, Sir Eric Speed (a former Treasury colleague), that the Ministry of Defence was not working as intended, in that the Chiefs of Staff could not agree on where the cuts necessary to bring defence expenditure within the Chancellor's target of £600 million should fall, and that it was not reasonable to expect the Minister of Defence to arrive at a balanced judgment without independent advice.[184] In the event, despite instructions from the minister, A. V. Alexander, to the three services to produce a balanced, long-term defence policy costing £600 million a year, they failed to do so, and Alexander had to impose crude ceilings on the different Estimates for 1948/9, much as a pre-war Chancellor might have done. Bridges continued to regard greater integration of the

[183] Dalton Diary, vol. 34, 18 Feb. and 23 Mar. 1946; 'Note on a Difference of Opinion', by Dalton, 20 Jan. 1947, Attlee papers dep. 49, Bodleian Library, Oxford; G. C. Peden, 'Economic Aspects of British Perceptions of Power on the Eve of the Cold War', in Josef Becker and Franz Knipping (eds.), *Power in Europe? Great Britain, France, Italy, and Germany in a Postwar World* (Berlin, 1986), 246–50.

[184] Bridges to permanent secretaries of the Air Ministry, Admiralty, War Office, and Ministry of Supply, 2 Sept. 1946, and 'Note on the Examination of Service and Supply Estimates', by Gilbert, 20 Jan. 1947, T273/280; Speed to Secretary of State for War, 27 Aug., and note by Bridges, 29 Aug. 1947, T273/281.

Ministry of Defence and the service departments as preferable to a return to pre-war procedure. However, once financial constraints were eased on account of the Cold War, and were then removed from rearmament in 1950, the defence departments returned to their pre-war habit of adding up their requirements rather than establishing policy priorities that could be achieved within the country's economic resources.[185]

The crisis atmosphere engendered by the outbreak of the Korean War on 25 June 1950 would in any case have made it difficult for Treasury officials to curb defence expenditure. However, their task was made more difficult by the fact that Hall and Plowden, who were responsible for advising on the economic impact of rearmament, were both firm believers in the view that, had Britain and her allies reacted more quickly to the Nazi menace, the Second World War might have been avoided. Consequently both gave their support to an increase in defence expenditure and strategic stocks.[186] Moreover, Gaitskell, mindful of the need for Britain to be seen as a firm ally of the United States, was also in favour of rearmament. Even he rejected the £6,000 million figure of NATO's three-year plan that Emanuel Shinwell, the new Minister of Defence, had virtually accepted in Washington in October 1950, but the Chancellor took the lead in persuading the Cabinet to accept in January 1951 a £4,700 million programme for 1951/2 to 1953/4, although only six months earlier the Cabinet had been told that £3,400 million was the maximum physically possible without special measures. There were good grounds for doubting whether, even with a strengthening of controls over investment and the allocation of industrial materials, all the money could be spent without forcing up prices. Equally there was no doubt that there would be a major diversion of resources: for example, the building work to be done would require a labour force more than half as large as that employed on the housing programme.[187]

Treasury officials were unhappy at Gaitskell's role, one remarking that 'a Chancellor has no business to be in favour of *any* expenditure programme'.[188] However, they had to accept his views, and, when reviewing the possibilities for economies in government expenditure in October 1951, Gilbert remarked that defence expenditure must be attacked not so much from the point of view of reducing it, but of getting the best value for the effort.[189] The Treasury thus found itself being drawn in to discussions about the merits of the defence departments' proposals, as before the war.

[185] 'The Organisation and Future of the Ministry of Defence', by Bridges, 25 Apr. 1949, and agreed report on 'The Financial Responsibility of the Ministry of Defence', 24 June 1950, T273/183; Anthony Gorst, 'Facing the Facts? The Labour Government and Defence Policy, 1945–1950', in Nick Tiratsoo (ed.), *The Attlee Years* (1991), 190–209.

[186] Plowden, *Industrialist in the Treasury*, 97–8.

[187] Gaitskell, *Diary*, 229; Cairncross, *Years of Recovery*, 215, 219–23.

[188] Roll, *Crowded Hours*, 76.

[189] 'Economy', 18 Oct. 1951, T273/323.

SOCIAL SERVICES

Treasury officials also had to respect Labour's major electoral commitments when examining proposals for the social services, but sometimes they found grounds for criticism. For example, Eady noted in 1947 that, if the productivity of labour in building had been at the pre-war level, 400,000 houses could have been produced a year instead of the 250,000 planned, and, even allowing for problems in securing materials, 'somewhere there is clearly a waste of resources'.[190] Part of the explanation for the discrepancy seems to have been the decision of Aneurin Bevan, the Minister of Health, who was responsible for housing, to build local authority houses of a higher standard than pre-war. Housing completions did not reach 250,000, and fell after 1948 when timber imports were cut to save foreign exchange. However, housing was an issue on which Labour ministers felt acute political sensibilities—so much so that early in 1950 Gaitskell, then Minister of State, and Jay devised what the latter called 'an amiable conspiracy' whereby they suggested to Bevan that, if he asked for an increase from 175,000 to 200,000 in the new house-building programme, they would both tell Cripps that they strongly supported it.[191] The increase was announced in the budget speech, but could not be implemented because of the diversion of building labour to defence contracts later in the year, and in 1951 the government reluctantly reduced space specifications for council houses.

Again, Treasury officials did not like the way in which the level of expenditure on education was 'bounding up' after the Education Act of 1944, but the Minister of Education, Ellen Wilkinson, successfully resisted pressure for postponement of raising the school leaving age from 14 to 15 in 1947. Dalton accepted Gilbert's advice that he should suggest to her successor, George Tomlinson, that his ministry should show 'a little more lethargy' in carrying out government policy,[192] but Tomlinson evidently did not take the hint, and education expenditure continued to rise.

National Health Service (NHS) expenditure caused concern in the Treasury from the first year of the service's operation.[193] The financial memoranda appended to the NHS Bills for England and Wales, and for Scotland, estimated the annual net cost—that is after appropriations in aid from the National Health Insurance Fund—as £134 million, but it quickly became apparent that this figure was much too low. The original Estimates for 1948/9 and 1949/50 were exceeded, and it seemed that the Exchequer had incurred an unlimited liability (see Table 8.4). When considering the sketch Estimates for 1949/50 Cripps urged Bevan to explore the whole range of possibilities for reducing the Exchequer's liability, but Bevan, wedded to the principal of a free health service, precluded the introduction of charges.

[190]   Eady to Bridges, 9 July 1947, T273/304.   [191]   Jay, *Change and Fortune*, 197.
[192]   Gilbert to Trend, 12 Mar. 1947, T171/389.
[193]   What follows draws upon Charles Webster, *The Health Services since the War*, vol. i (1988), ch. 5.

TABLE 8.4. *Parliamentary Estimates for the National Health Service,*
1948/9–1951/2 (Net Totals after Appropriations in Aid) (£m.)

	England and Wales		Scotland	
	Original	Final	Original	Final
1948/9 (9 months)	132.4	185.4	17.2	22.9
1949/50	228.4	317.9	31.3	40.6
1950/1	351.5	351.6	41.4	41.4
1951/2	355.0	355.4	43.0	44.1

Source: Charles Webster, *The Health Services Since the War*, vol. i (1988), 136.

The dollar crisis of 1949 led the Treasury to undertake a study of possible economies in the social services. Education and health services at that date accounted for £473.4 million of the £1,050 million of Supply Services expenditure for which the Treasury's 'S.S.' division was responsible. The only way of securing large, immediate economies seemed to be to reduce the pay of people employed in these services, but this was not practical politics as the principle of equality of sacrifice would demand that pay cuts be applied to all public employees. Neither was a reduction in the number of teachers or health service workers a 'very hopeful line', given that the government was already subject to criticism on account of over-large classes in schools and long waiting lists for hospital beds. The only possible approach seemed to be to cut demand. With regard to education, increased fees for grammar schools or charges for school meals were open to the objection that they might prevent promising boys and girls from receiving the education which they should, in the national interest, receive. Exchequer grants to the universities were held to be sacrosanct, as they were fixed quinquennially and could not be reduced immediately. On the other hand, it was believed that 'quite modest' charges for spectacles and dentures would probably have a marked effect on demand.[194]

Bevan was prepared reluctantly in the autumn of 1949 to accept the Treasury's suggestion of a 1s. (5p) prescription charge for pharmaceutical services, but only as a temporary expedient to discourage unnecessary medication, and even then he persuaded Attlee that action should be deferred until after the general election, which was held in February 1950. The NHS for England and Wales required a Supplementary Estimate of £89.4 million for 1949/50, a figure that Gilbert believed laid the government open to the charge that public expenditure was out of control. However, when Labour's majority was reduced to five, he recognized that radical reform of NHS finance was not practical politics. This consideration did not deter him from suggesting rigorous control over the rate of improvements to hospitals, together with charges for hospital, ophthalmic, and dental treatment. At the same time, he thought that it would be

[194] 'Possibilities of Major Economy in Social Services', 9 Aug. 1949, T273/322.

impossible to save money by having some hospital beds unused. Cripps, for his part, aware of the danger that Bevan might resign over the principle of a free health service, insisted that charges, including the prescription charges already agreed, should only be imposed if it could be shown that they were the only way to control expenditure. As it happened, Treasury officials were encouraged to hope for other economies when the President of the Royal College of Physicians, Lord Moran, visited the department, at his own request. Moran, whom Bridges knew from the war as Winston Churchill's doctor, gave examples of waste and inefficiency, such as unnecessary use of proprietary medicines, or of the ambulance service for transporting non-emergency patients.[195] There seemed, therefore, to be reason to believe that, if a ceiling could be placed on expenditure, what would now be called efficiency savings would be found.

In the run-up to the budget for 1950/1 the Cabinet accepted Cripps's proposal for a ceiling of £392 million on net NHS expenditure in Great Britain, but refused to empower him to impose charges should that limit be exceeded. From May NHS expenditure was subject to review by a Cabinet committee, in which Gaitskell and Bevan adopted intransigent positions, but nothing had been decided by October when the Treasury's Budget Committee looked at the prospects for reductions in expenditure in 1951/2. NHS expenditure was, in Gilbert's words, one of the 'four main candidates' (the others being cutting food subsidies; putting the school leaving age back to 14; and lowering housing standards).[196]

The main cause of inflationary pressure, and therefore of the need for a budget surplus in 1951/2, was defence expenditure. In January 1951 Bevan had been moved to the Ministry of Labour, where he became more familiar with the problems of implementing the rearmament programme, but without abandoning his passionate attachment to the principle of a free NHS. Gaitskell for his part aimed to keep total expenditure on social services in 1951/2 at the previous year's level, and this led him to look for economies to accommodate an increase in the old-age pension. Bevan's successor as Minister of Health, Hilary Marquand, and Hector McNeil, the Secretary of State for Scotland, agreed reluctantly to charges for prescriptions, dentures, and spectacles, but Bevan's threats of resignation led to the issue being debated in full Cabinet in March and April. In the discussion on the budget statement Bevan stressed how small the £13 million savings in charges were compared to the defence Estimates of £1,250 million, which he did not believe would all be spent, while Gaitskell stressed the need for a budget surplus to check inflation.[197] Attlee, faced with

---

[195] Memoranda by Gilbert, 1, 11, and 21 Mar. 1950, with Cripps's comment on the last, and 'National Health Service', by Bridges, 29 Mar. 1950, T273/329. Bridges concluded his memorandum: 'Lord M. also made certain comments about the handling of Health Service matters in the Ministry of Health, but this had better not be put on paper.'

[196] Budget Committee minutes, 17 Oct. 1950, T171/403.

[197] Cabinet conclusions, 9 Apr. 1951, CAB128/21.

Gaitskell's offer of resignation, decided to keep his Chancellor rather than his Minister of Labour, and Bevan subsequently resigned.

On the morning of the budget in which the NHS charges were announced Bridges told Gaitskell that: 'it is the best day we have had in the Treasury for ten years.' Gaitskell, for his part, paid tribute in his diary to the advice he had received from Bridges, Plowden, Leslie (the head of the Treasury's Information Unit), and William Armstrong, the Chancellor's principal private secretary.[198] Gaitskell's budget, with its Keynesian concept of a disinflationary budget surplus, had proved to be a powerful device to impose control on public expenditure. However, Treasury officials had wished to bring NHS expenditure under control for reasons quite independent of the size of the budget surplus.

SUMMARY

The period 1945–51 saw the Treasury become the central department of government again, with enhanced responsibility for co-ordinating economic policy. However, the enlargement of the Treasury's functions was balanced by a more equal relationship with the rest of Whitehall through a system of interdepartmental committees. Moreover, the Bank of England retained considerable autonomy with regard to supervision of the monetary system. Finally, as always, Treasury officials' influence depended upon ability to persuade ministers to accept their advice, which they were not always able to do.

The dollar shortage dominated Treasury thinking on the external balance, and therefore also on the future of the international economy and relations with the Commonwealth, the sterling area, and continental Europe. The Treasury would have preferred overseas expenditure to have been reduced more than it was after the war, but was unable to persuade the Cabinet to take drastic steps to reduce commitments, in the face of contrary advice from the Foreign Office and the Chiefs of Staff. Similar difficulties occurred when the ministries of Food and Health resisted proposals for import cuts.

The Treasury used Labour's preference for economic planning and direct controls over market mechanisms to enable ministers to judge proposals for expenditure in relation to other claims on scarce resources. The Investment Programmes Committee took decisions from 1947 which had the effect of curbing public capital expenditure, and which therefore reinforced the annual cycle of Estimates and budgets. Full employment was accepted in principle, but the immediate aims of economic policy were to finance reconstruction, hold down excess demand, and restore the external balance—hence Treasury support for priority for investment in industry and agriculture rather than social services.

[198] Gaitskell, *Diary*, 248.

Keynes's ideas influenced monetary policy and budgetary policy, but so too did other considerations, such as the size of the National Debt and the need to control public expenditure. The lack of accurate economic forecasts, or estimates of public expenditure, made it difficult to estimate the 'inflationary gap', and budgetary policy continued to be based in part on intuitive hunch. There was no doubt, however, that there was excess demand in an economy that was experiencing full employment, and therefore Keynesian analysis pointed to restriction of government expenditure, reinforcing Treasury arguments about the need to establish priorities in government policy.

CHAPTER NINE

The Treasury and the Managed Economy, 1951–1959

INTRODUCTION

The Treasury's management of the economy in the 1950s has had a bad press. Unemployment, measured as a national, annual average, exceeded 2 per cent only briefly in 1952 and 1958–9; the retail price index, which had been rising at an annual rate of about 9 per cent in 1951, owing to the effects of the Korean War, rose by less than 1 per cent in 1959; despite balance of payments problems, there was no devaluation; and the standard of living rose so that Macmillan, as Prime Minister, could claim, with some justice, in 1957 that 'most of our people have never had it so good'.[1] However, from the late 1950s, international comparisons of economic growth rates, hitherto little discussed in public, became the yardstick used by critics for the success of economic policy. In this context, the annual average growth of Britain's real national income per person employed between 1950 and 1962, 2.3 per cent, was less than half that of France (4.9 per cent) or West Germany (7.3 per cent).[2]

It was widely assumed that the reason for low economic growth compared with other European countries was relatively low industrial investment, although it was possible to argue that the level of investment reflected less rapidly expanding markets. Economists and financial journalists, followed subsequently by economic historians, castigated the Treasury for its willingness to curb industrial investment as a means of overcoming sterling crises in 1951–2, 1955, 1956, and 1957. Deflation to secure stable prices and to protect sterling, followed by reflation on the eve of elections, or when unemployment rose, as in 1955 and 1959, came to be known as 'stop–go'. It was claimed that uncertainty arising from changes of direction in policy itself discouraged investment. Economic policy was intended to provide stability by controlling the tendency of a market economy to oscillate between booms and slumps, but the Treasury was criticized for reflating when the economy was already recovering from a slump,

---

[1] The context of this claim, however, was that the British people might be living beyond their means—see Alistair Horne, *Macmillan*, vol. ii, *1957–1986* (1989), 64–5.

[2] Edward Denison, 'Economic Growth', in Richard Caves, *et al.*, *Britain's Economic Prospects* (Washington, DC, 1968), 235–6; J. Tomlinson, 'Inventing "Decline": The Falling Behind of the British Economy in the Postwar Years', *Econ. Hist. Rev.*, 2nd ser., 49 (1996), 731–57.

and vice versa.[3] An authoritative analysis by an ex-Treasury economist, Christopher Dow, did indeed suggest that economic forecasting had been defective, and that different management of fiscal and monetary policy might have avoided much of the fluctuation in the rate of growth of internal demand, and some of the fluctuations in the balance of payments. On the other hand, fluctuations in the British economy were no worse than those in other countries over the decade. It is not clear, therefore, that in this respect the management of the British economy was markedly worse than in other countries.[4]

From a rather different perspective, economic management in the 1950s was criticized by Professor Frank Paish for maintaining demand at too high a level, except in 1958 and the first half of 1959, to be consistent with long-term price equilibrium. He suggested that a margin of unused productive capacity consistent with an increase in unemployment from an average of 1.8 per cent in 1956–60 to an average of between 2 and 2.5 per cent might be sufficient to achieve equilibrium.[5] However, in the 1950s (and indeed down to the 1970s) the electoral risks associated with rising unemployment seemed to be too great for experiments to discover what economists would now call the NAIRU (the non-accelerating inflation rate of unemployment). Conservative governments in the 1950s preferred to appeal to trade unions for voluntary restraint in demanding higher wages. As will be shown below, the Treasury was well aware of the consequences for prices, the balance of payments, and ultimately employment, if these appeals for restraint were ignored.

Treasury management of the economy and control of expenditure were necessarily subject to the political goals and preferences of the government of the day. The Conservatives' majority was slender in 1951, and their success in being re-elected in 1955 and 1959 was far from inevitable. Consequently, the Conservative and Labour parties competed for the middle ground of politics, producing an apparent consensus on the welfare state, the mixed economy, and the use of demand management to maintain full employment. For example, the Conservatives outbid Labour in the 1951 election by promising to build 300,000 houses a year, compared with the 200,000 a year built by Labour, and the promise was fulfilled, despite Treasury protests about balance-of-payments difficulties. With regard to economic management, Norman Macrae, of the *Economist*, coined the term 'Butskellism' in 1954, by conflating the names of the Conservative Chancellor, R. A. Butler, and his Labour predecessor, Gaitskell, implying a degree of continuity in economic policy. It is true that the Conservative governments, like their predecessors, managed the economy with a view to controlling the rise in prices and defending the pound, while maintaining full

[3] See B. W. E. Alford, *British Economic Performance, 1945–1975* (1988) for survey of a vast literature.
    [4] J. C. R. Dow, *Management of the British Economy, 1945–1960* (Cambridge, 1964), 135–43, 392. T. Wilson, 'Instability and the Rate of Growth', *Lloyds Bank Rev.*, NS, 81 (1966), 16–32.
    [5] F. W. Paish, *Studies in an Inflationary Economy* (1962), ch. 17. Paish was son of Sir George Paish, who had advised Lloyd George when he was Chancellor of the Exchequer.

employment. On the other hand, the Conservatives were opposed to Labour's style of economic planning, and wished to decontrol the economy and reduce taxation as quickly as possible, so as to encourage private enterprise to increase prosperity (and the party's electoral popularity). It was not until 1961 that the Conservatives resorted to planning, in consultation with industry, to try to influence directly the structure and efficiency of the national economy.[6]

In these circumstances the Treasury had a key role to play, using both financial instruments and its influence over the co-ordination of government policy, to manage the overall level of demand in the economy. Although in retrospect the 1950s appear to be a time of stability, the Treasury was concerned about the effects of what was called 'creeping inflation', with prices and wages rising year by year, and therefore it took an active interest in wages policy. The Treasury was particularly concerned with what it believed to be the burden on the economy of public expenditure and taxation, and regarded the control of public expenditure as just as important a function as management of the economy.

PERSONALITIES AND ORGANIZATION

It was by no means inevitable that the Treasury would continue to enjoy the authority it had regained in the late 1940s. The Conservatives were suspicious of the machinery of government that they had inherited from Labour and, on taking office, they embarked on what Bridges later described as 'somewhat strange antics' with regard to the allocation of ministerial responsibility.[7] Churchill believed that he had received bad advice from Treasury officials and the Bank of England when he had taken the decision to return to the gold standard in 1925. He asked Sir Arthur Salter, who had been Director of the Economic and Finance Section of the League of Nations in the 1920s, and a member of the Economic Advisory Committee's Committee on Economic Information in the 1930s, to join the government, and offered him the choice of creating a new Economic Department, with himself as minister, or of joining the Treasury as its second minister. Convinced that a new ministry would have no chance of making a policy of its own effective, if that policy were opposed by the Treasury or Board of Trade, Salter chose to become Minister of Economic Affairs within the Treasury.[8] Churchill also restored the wartime arrangement whereby he received economic and other advice from Lord Cherwell, who held

[6] For 'consensus' politics and 'Butskellism' see Michael Pinto-Duschinsky, 'Bread and Circuses? The Conservatives in Office, 1951–1964', in Vernon Bogdanor and Robert Skidelsky (eds.), *The Age of Affluence, 1951–1964* (1970), 55–77; Neil Rollings, 'Poor Mr Butskell: A Short Life, Wrecked by Schizophrenia?', *20th Cent. Brit. Hist.*, 5 (1994), 183–205.

[7] Bridges to Brook, 23 Sept. 1953, T199/257.

[8] Sir Arthur Salter, *Memoirs of a Public Servant* (1961), 339; id., *Slave of the Lamp: A Public Servant's Notebook* (1967), 216.

ministerial rank as Paymaster-General, and who, as in the war, was in turn advised by Donald MacDougall and other economists in the Prime Minister's Statistical Section.

In 1951 Churchill believed that the Treasury, the Board of Trade, and the Ministry of Supply could be grouped together as economic ministries, with their ministers subordinated to an 'overlord', Sir John Anderson, who had held an analogous position during the war as Lord President of the Council. Anderson, however, thought that the proposed arrangement would be in conflict with departmental ministers' responsibility to Parliament, and declined the post. Three years later Churchill thought that he could hand over the 'home front', including economic affairs, to a Deputy Prime Minister—but he was dissuaded by Macmillan, then Minister for Housing, who believed that no Chancellor of the Exchequer could agree to surrender his responsibilities to another minister.[9]

Churchill was generally expected to appoint as Chancellor Oliver Lyttleton, a prominent City man who had been chairman of the Conservatives' Finance Committee while the party was in opposition. However, Churchill apparently dared not appoint Lyttleton because of the latter's reputation in the City as a gambler and market operator.[10] Instead he chose Butler, largely, it appears, because of his ability to handle the House of Commons. Butler had been a Cambridge history don before becoming an MP, and Churchill told him that it 'was no great matter' that he was not an economist, as he would have as his assistant 'the best economist since Jesus Christ' (Salter).[11] However, at 70 years of age, Salter was past his best, and, during the thirteen months that he was at the Treasury, his advice, tendered handwritten in green ink, seems to have been ignored by Butler and his officials. Churchill also attempted to guide Butler by appointing a 'Treasury Advisory Committee' of senior ministers, such as Lord Woolton (Lord President of the Council) and Lord Swinton (Chancellor of the Duchy of Lancaster), but again the Chancellor and his officials went their own way, and eventually the Advisory Committee was absorbed into the Cabinet's Economic Policy Committee.[12] The Chancellor of the Exchequer's pre-eminence in economic policy making was also increased when Cherwell retired, and the Prime Minister's Statistical Section was disbanded, in November 1953.

Butler lacked Gaitskell's professional understanding of economic issues and depended almost wholly on his officials' advice. Hall, from the vantage point of head of the Economic Section, thought that he was a weak Chancellor who had the utmost difficulty in making up his mind.[13] Moreover, Butler seems not to

[9] J. Wheeler-Bennett, *John Anderson, Viscount Waverly* (1962), 352; H. Macmillan, *Tides of Fortune, 1945–1955* (1969), 485, 497, 541–2.

[10] Anthony Seldon, *Churchill's Indian Summer: The Conservative Government, 1951–55* (1981), 154–5.

[11] Lord Butler, *The Art of the Possible* (1971), 156.

[12] Lord Woolton, *Memoirs* (1959), 371–4.

[13] R. Hall, *The Robert Hall Diaries, 1954–1961*, ed. A. Cairncross (1991), 56; Lord Roberthall, interviewed by Anthony Seldon, 23 Apr. 1980, British Oral Archive of Political and Administrative History, British Library of Political and Economic Science, London.

have been greatly liked by some members of the Cabinet, on the grounds that, as a junior minister at the Foreign Office from 1938 to 1940, he had been associated with appeasement. For whatever reason, he found it difficult to win battles over public expenditure, and felt that he should have resigned over the Cabinet's refusal to accept his autumn package of cuts in 1955.[14] He suffered a severe blow in December 1954 with the death of his first wife, upon whom he had relied for support. Moreover, a serious viral infection left him looking very tired before Eden, who had taken over as Prime Minister in April 1955, replaced him with Macmillan in December that year.

Macmillan, who had succeeded Eden as Foreign Secretary, would have preferred to remain at the Foreign Office, and insisted that, as Chancellor, he should have full responsibility for co-ordinating all aspects of economic policy, external as well as internal. He had established a reputation as someone who thought about economic issues in the 1930s, when the impact of unemployment on his constituency, Stockton-on-Tees, had been a traumatic experience, and when he had adopted the economics of Keynes's *General Theory*. Macmillan was predisposed towards expansionary policies to cure unemployment, and officials were said to keep a mental tally of how often he mentioned Stockton in a week. On the other hand, he was prepared to assert his authority as Chancellor by threatening resignation in February 1956 over the Cabinet's unwillingness to cut public expenditure.[15]

Macmillan hoped to be 'something of a reformer' at the Treasury[16] and, although he presented only one budget as Chancellor, he took a keen interest in budgets and economic policy after he became Prime Minister in January 1957. His first Chancellor, Peter Thorneycroft, had a lawyer's ability to master his brief, and over six years' experience of economic problems as President of the Board of Trade. Although he never claimed to be an intellectual high flier, Thorneycroft was interested in economic ideas and, along with his junior ministers, the Financial Secretary, Enoch Powell, and the Economic Secretary, Nigel Birch, he was to adopt a position on the relationship between public expenditure, the money supply, and inflation that owed nothing to Treasury advisers. It was unusual for junior ministers to be so influential in formulating policy, but all three Treasury ministers resigned in January 1958 when the Cabinet would not support fully the Chancellor's attempt to limit public expenditure (see pages 486–93).

Thorneycroft's successor, Derick Heathcoat Amory, was more pliable in his relationship with the Prime Minister, particularly when Macmillan demanded reflation before the 1959 election. Amory worked hard at economic matters, to

[14] Anthony Howard, *RAB: The Life of R. A. Butler* (1987), 216.
[15] Harold Macmillan, *Winds of Change, 1914–1939* (1966), 490–6; id., *Tides of Fortune*, 692–4; id., *Riding the Storm, 1956–1959* (1971), 13–14; Roberthall interviewed by Anthony Seldon, 13 May 1980; S. Brittan, *The Treasury under the Tories, 1951–1964* (1964), 180; Macmillan to Harrod, 31 Dec. 1955, T172/2066.
[16] Macmillan, *Tides of Fortune*, 692.

the point that, according to Hall, he was able to see things as a government economist (that is, as Hall himself) would see them. Amory's principal interest, however, lay in the field of taxation, where he relied heavily upon advice from the heads of the boards of Inland Revenue and Customs and Excise. His weakness as a Chancellor was that he was far from being a born leader and he found it very difficult to persuade his Cabinet colleagues to do things that they did not like.[17] He was initially assisted at the ministerial level by the Paymaster-General, Reginald Maudling, who was a member of the Cabinet, and whose duties for nine months after Birch's resignation included those of the Economic Secretary, a post that Maudling had held previously from 1952 to 1955. Maudling, who had studied *literae humaniores* at Oxford, took an intellectual interest in economic problems, and Hall regarded him as 'a reasonably good economist'.[18] As Paymaster-General, Maudling was principally responsible for supervising the development of policy on a European free trade area from 1957, in which role he worked amicably with both Thorneycroft and Amory.

According to Hall, senior Treasury officials thought in 1951 that a Conservative government would be more to their way of thinking than Labour had been, presumably because of Conservative rhetoric on high taxation and waste in public expenditure. Hall had described himself as a socialist in Oxford before the war, but during the 1950s he came to regard the Labour party as 'just as woolly-minded as the Tories are bloody-minded' and hoped that the Conservatives would win the 1955 election.[19] Nevertheless, ministers and officials did not always see eye to eye any more than they had done when Labour was in office. Officials found that the Conservatives in office were more reluctant to cut public expenditure than they had professed to be while in opposition. Butler, on the other hand, was critical of what he called 'a certain tendency' on the part of officials to be 'recession-minded', and told Bridges that this attitude was 'not consistent with my incumbency as Chancellor of the Exchequer'.[20] Macmillan found that officials tried to persuade him to introduce into his budget 'all sorts of methods of annoying the taxpayer, especially the well to do', and rejected some of their advice.[21]

Bridges had been due to retire as Permanent Secretary on his sixtieth birthday in 1952, and had arranged that he would be succeeded by Sir Norman Brook, the Cabinet Secretary, who would in turn be succeeded by a Treasury official, Thomas Padmore. However, Churchill, who liked to work with people he had known in wartime, insisted on keeping Brook as Cabinet Secretary, and also asked Bridges to stay on at the Treasury. Fortunately Bridges recovered

[17] Hall, *Diaries, 1954–1961*, 242; Lord Amory interviewed by Anthony Seldon, 2 Feb. 1980, British Oral Archive of Political and Administrative History.

[18] Hall, *Diaries, 1954–1961*, 11.

[19] Roberthall interviewed by Anthony Seldon, 23 Apr. 1980; Hall, *Diaries, 1954–1961*, 37, 120.

[20] Butler to Bridges, 28 Apr. 1953, T273/248.

[21] Macmillan to Amory, 2 Apr. 1958, T171/487.

from the muscular nervous complaint mentioned in Chapter 8, and regained for a time his old verve and energy. However, there is little doubt that he tried to do too much. Although the process of reviewing the machinery of government was practically moribund by the early 1950s, he had to give a good deal of time to matters arising in connection with the Royal Commission on the Civil Service, which met from 1953 to 1955. He seemed a tired man before he retired in October 1956. When asked that year how he coped with his responsibilities as official head of both the Treasury and the Civil Service, he replied that he did not—that he reckoned that 'he caught one ball in four'.[22]

Although Brook had been a protégé of Bridges, a coolness seems to have developed between the two men during Bridges' last two or three years at the Treasury. Churchill increasingly, and then Eden, relied upon Brook for advice on policy, and Bridges ceased to have much influence at 10 Downing Street. Indeed, when, shortly before his retirement, Bridges sent his private secretary to ask Brook for Cabinet committee papers relating to plans for the invasion of Egypt during the Suez crisis, the private secretary was told by an embarrassed Brook that he had strict instructions as to who was to see the papers, and that Bridges was not one of them.[23]

It had already been decided in April 1956 that, when Bridges retired, his job should be divided between two Joint Permanent Secretaries: Sir Roger Makins, who would be in charge of the home and overseas finance and Supply Services sides of the Treasury, and Brook, who would be in charge of the establishments work, as Official Head of the Civil Service, while continuing to be Cabinet Secretary (see Figure 9.1). Under this arrangement, Makins was responsible to the Chancellor of the Exchequer, and Brook handled that part of the Treasury's work that fell within the prerogative of the Prime Minister as First Lord of the Treasury, particularly senior appointments in Whitehall, but had nothing to do with the Chancellor.

Makins had entered the Foreign Office in 1928 and had experience of international economic diplomacy, having been Minister in charge of Economic Affairs at the Washington Embassy from March 1945 to February 1947, and the Assistant Under-Secretary supervising the Foreign Office's economic intelligence and economic relations departments during the negotiations on Marshall Aid. He had worked very closely in 1943 and 1944 with Macmillan, while the latter was Resident Minister at Allied Forces Headquarters in the Mediterranean theatre, and Macmillan wanted Makins to join him at the Treasury, which he did in October 1956. However, three months later Macmillan became Prime Minister, thereby defeating the original purpose of Makins' appointment.[24]

Makins sensed that it was painful for the Treasury to have someone with a Foreign Office background imposed upon them, but he found that he could

[22] P. Hennessy, *Whitehall* (1989), 144.   [23] Ibid., 143–5.
[24] Conversation with Sherfield, 9 June 1988.

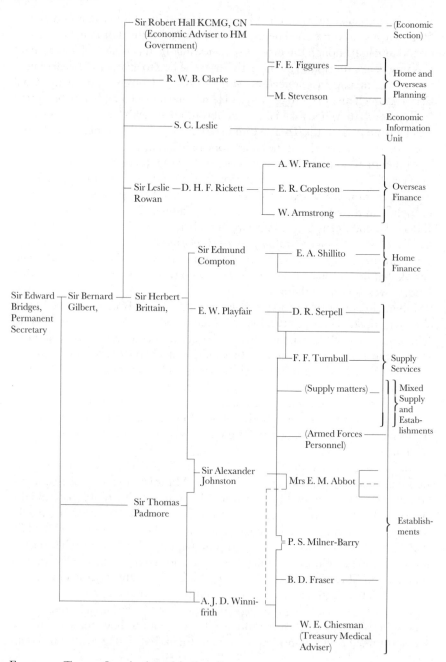

FIG. 9.1.   *Treasury Organization at March 1956*
Source: T199/702.

work amicably with all of his officials except Rowan, the Second Secretary responsible for overseas finance, who tended to give the Chancellor different advice from that given by himself. Makins found that, during Bridges' time, the Second Secretaries had got into the habit of going direct to the Chancellor, while letting the Permanent Secretary have carbon copies of their memoranda: 'I was caught in a cross-fire of flimsies,' he later recalled.[25] The Second Secretaries would seem to have exercised the same degree of independence as Controllers had done in the 1920s, and Makins and Brook reacted to the situation very much as Fisher had done then, by gradually reducing the number of officials who could tender advice directly to the Chancellor. When Brittain, the Second Secretary responsible for the home finance and Supply Services divisions, retired in 1957, and Rowan left for a job in industry in November 1958, they were not replaced. Instead, their work was handled by Third Secretaries who, unlike Second Secretaries, did not have the status equivalent to a permanent secretary in another Whitehall department, and whose advice was tendered to the Chancellor through Makins or the sole remaining Second Secretary, Sir Thomas Padmore.

Padmore was now expected to take much of the burden of supervising the home finance and Supply Services divisions, leaving Makins to concentrate on overseas finance, where his experience of economic diplomacy would be most valuable. The new arrangement did not last long. Hall thought that Makins had not really got a grasp of his job as Permanent Secretary, and indeed Makins had not wanted much to come to the Treasury; he loathed the work there, and hoped to return to the Foreign Office after three years as Permanent Under-Secretary. Instead in July 1959 he accepted the offer of the chairmanship of the UK Atomic Energy Authority, the appointment taking effect from the end of the year.[26]

It would seem, therefore, that for most of the 1950s neither Bridges nor Makins provided as effective leadership as might have been expected of men of their undoubted intellectual capacity (both were fellows of All Souls College, Oxford). Much depended upon their senior subordinates. The most senior Second Secretary under Bridges was Sir Bernard Gilbert, who had been due to retire at the age of 60 in 1951. Bridges rated Gilbert's ability so highly that he told him that he could not continue himself as Permanent Secretary unless Gilbert also stayed on, which he did, until Bridges retired. Gilbert had been responsible for the Supply Services divisions since 1944, and had also taken over responsibility for home finance in April 1952, when Eady retired. In November 1953, when Plowden left the Treasury, and after Butler had complained that there were too many officials giving advice to the Chancellor—'too many hares and

[25] Conversation with Sherfield, 9 June 1988.
[26] Hall, *Diaries, 1954–1961*, 138, 165, 170, 205–6; Macmillan diary, 24 Apr. 1956, Bodleian Library, Oxford; Sir Edward Playfair interviewed by Anthony Seldon, 20 May 1980, British Oral Archive of Political and Administrative History.

too many hounds', as he put it[27]—there was a general restructuring of the department's senior management. Gilbert's responsibilities for home finance and Supply Services were taken over by Brittain, and Gilbert was appointed Deputy to the Permanent Secretary, with responsibility for co-ordinating economic policy, and channelling advice to the Chancellor from the home finance and overseas finance divisions, while also taking over responsibility for the CEPS, although he took little interest in its work. As noted in Chapter 8, Dalton had regarded Gilbert as the wisest of his advisers, but Hall complained bitterly that Gilbert consistently threw all his weight in the direction of doing nothing, and even an official who admired Gilbert thought that by the 1950s he had become incapable of anything but critical thought. Matters were not improved by the fact that Gilbert fell ill late in 1951 and never fully recovered his health.[28] On the other hand, as noted in Chapters 7 and 8, Gilbert was sceptical of Keynesian economics, and it is not surprising that he and Hall should not have seen eye to eye.

Rowan was the other leading Second Secretary. He was one of Churchill's intimates, having been his private secretary during the war, and being a fellow member of the Other Club, where they dined together. Jock Colville, another of Churchill's intimates, thought that the reason why Rowan was not promoted to be head of the Treasury was one of Whitehall's unsolved mysteries. Rowan was an able and forceful civil servant who worked tremendously hard. However, his preference for quick decisions bordered on impulsiveness, and this characteristic, combined with a tendency to moodiness, may have limited his promotion prospects. Macmillan, when Chancellor, tried to have Rowan transferred to the War Office, and cannot have warmed to him when he not only refused to go, but also told him to his face that the appointment of Makins as Permanent Secretary had been the biggest blow the Civil Service had ever received. However, even Hall, whose relations with Rowan were poor, recognized that the latter's work in overseas finance had made him an international figure, and that the Treasury was weakened when he left in November 1958 to join Vickers.[29]

The retirements of Bridges and Gilbert in 1956, followed by that of Brittain in 1957, and then the resignation of Rowan, marked the end of a generation of pre-war officials. Makins, whose academic background was in history and law, was more inclined than they had been to rely on the Economic Section's advice. He recalled that he had to 'mug up' the financial aspects of the department's work

[27] Butler to Bridges, May 1953, Butler papers G26, Wren Library, Trinity College, Cambridge.

[28] Hall, *Diaries, 1954–1961*, 80; Playfair, interviewed by Anthony Seldon; Seldon, *Churchill's Indian Summer*, 161. Butler considered appointing Sir Oliver Franks, the British ambassador in Washington, as deputy to Bridges, but Hall advised Franks against taking the job, warning him of the jealousy of permanent civil servants against outsiders—Butler to Franks, 19 Aug. 1952, Butler papers G24, and Hall, *Diaries, 1954–1961*, 263–4.

[29] J. Colville, *The Fringes of Power: Downing Street Diaries, 1939–1955*, 764. M. Gilbert, *'Never Despair': Winston S. Churchill, 1945–1965* (1988), 749, 1289; Hall, *Diaries, 1954–1961*, 71, 165–6, 180; Amory and Playfair interviewed by Anthony Seldon. Conversation with Lord Thorneycroft, 11 May 1988.

in order to appear as principal Treasury witness before the Radcliffe Committee on the Working of the Monetary System in 1957. However, like any other Permanent Secretary, he had little time for the study of economic theory—as he remarked, he 'couldn't suddenly start reading John Stuart Mill'[30]—and, lacking any theoretical standpoint of his own, he seems to have accepted Hall's Keynesianism. The same seems to have been true of Padmore, who, down to November 1958, had been primarily concerned with the work of the establishment divisions, and who claimed to know nothing of economics or finance. Padmore was an able administrator, as might be expected of someone whom Bridges had considered to be fit to be Cabinet Secretary, but Hall thought that Padmore was not quite up to the job of running the Treasury.[31]

There was rather more economic literacy at the Third Secretary level, where Clarke (planning) and Rickett (overseas finance), who both reached that rank in 1955, had a background in economics, and William Armstrong (home finance from 1958) had been given a good grounding in economics when, as the Chancellor's principal private secretary, he had worked with the Economic Section on the budget speeches from 1950 to 1953. Armstrong was certainly more familiar with Keynesian analysis than his predecessors in home finance, Brittain, or Sir Edmund Compton, had been.[32] Economic ideas entered the Treasury through officials' private study as well as through the Economic Section. For example, Bridges cited what he called Alec Cairncross's 'admirable textbook on economics' when advising the Chancellor on monetary policy and investment in 1955.[33] Cairncross's book is highly accessible to the layman, being nonmathematical in its approach, and, written in the 1930s, and revised in 1951, it incorporated Keynesian concepts.[34]

ECONOMIC ADVICE

Nevertheless, the impetus for utilizing Keynesian analysis came from the Economic Section. Hall regarded himself as a Keynesian, but, as head of the Economic Section, he read very little theoretical economics, which he felt had little to do with the real world, and turned instead to the *Economist*, the *Financial Times*, and *The Times*. In his work he relied upon hunch much more than on figures. By 1957 he was getting tired of his job, in the sense that it no longer fascinated him

[30] Conversation with Sherfield, 9 June 1988.

[31] Hall, *Diaries, 1954–1961*, 20; Hall interviewed by Seldon, 13 May 1980.

[32] Hall, *Diaries, 1954–1961*, 165, 167. Compton, who had been a Third Secretary since 1949, was appointed Comptroller and Auditor General in 1958.

[33] Bridges to Chancellor of the Exchequer, 14 July 1955, T273/401.

[34] Alec Cairncross, *Introduction to Economics* (1st edn., 1944, 2nd and 3rd edns., 1951). Another textbook which was mentioned by an official of the period as having been useful was John R. Hicks, *The Social Framework: An Introduction to Economics* (1st edn., Oxford, 1942; 2nd edn., Oxford, 1952). The official was H. L. Jenkyns (entered Treasury 1945) in a conversation with the author on 10 Oct. 1988.

as it once had, but he had built up a staff of able young economists (many of them on secondment from universities), who did not hesitate to claim to have a better understanding of economic policy than had administrators or bankers.[35] Reflecting their Keynesian background, these economists were primarily interested in macroeconomic issues and had very little to do with the Treasury's divisions that controlled expenditure. As a result, when one member of the Economic Section did take an interest in that side of the Treasury's work in 1957 he found himself in a world of what he called 'do-it-yourself economics', where economic judgements were made on the basis of the intuitive ideas of lay people.[36]

The emphasis on short-term financial instruments, rather than on planning or direct controls, in the conduct of economic policy after 1951 placed increasing importance on the work of the Economic Section, which alone in Whitehall, after the disbanding of the Prime Minister's Statistical Section in November 1953, was able to give professional advice based on macroeconomic analysis. The Economic Section was transferred from the Cabinet Office to the Treasury in November 1953, a move that had been mooted in 1945 and again in 1950, but which had been delayed until there could be no doubt that there would be only one minister responsible for co-ordinating economic policy, and that that minister would be the Chancellor of the Exchequer. As noted in Chapter 8, Hall had already come to be treated by Treasury officials as if he were a member of the department, but he had retained the right to advise ministers other than the Chancellor, and did so in 1952 when he opposed a plan (known as 'Robot'), discussed below, for sterling convertibility. As a result, his relations with the officials responsible for the plan, Rowan and Clarke, were very bad for over a year, and their hostility, added to Hall's belief that he could improve his financial position by finding work outside Whitehall, led him to consider resignation. Butler, however, was determined to retain his services, and Bridges arranged for Hall to be given the title of Economic Adviser to Her Majesty's Government, with a salary roughly halfway between that of a Third and a Second Secretary, and a knighthood in the 1954 New Year Honours. Thereafter, until his retirement in 1961, Hall advised the Chancellor of the Exchequer only. He had a good deal of influence on Butler and Amory, and some on Macmillan, although little on Thorneycroft.[37]

---

[35] Roberthall interviewed by Seldon, 13 May 1980; Hall, *Diaries, 1954–1961*, 118. [P.] D. Henderson, 'The Use of Economists in British Administration', *Oxford Econ. Papers*, NS, 13 (1961), 5–26; I. M. D. Little, 'The Economist in Whitehall', *Lloyds Bank Review*, NS, 44 (1957), 29–40. Other economists who were in the Economic Section in the 1950s included Fred Atkinson, Christopher Dow, Jack Downie, Wynne Godley, Brian Hopkin, Kit McMahon, Robert Nield, Alec Nove, Roger Opie, Maurice Scott, and Nita Watts.

[36] P. D. Henderson, *Innocence and Design: The Influence of Economic Ideas on Policy* (Oxford, 1986), 2–10.

[37] 'Economic Section', by Brook, and Bridges to Brook, 23 Sept. 1953, T199/257; K. Jones, *Economist Among Mandarins: A Biography of Robert Hall, 1901–1988* (Cambridge, 1994), 124–5; Roberthall interviewed by Seldon, 23 Apr. and 13 May 1980; Amory interviewed by Seldon; conversation with Thorneycroft.

The Economic Section did not, however, have a monopoly of professional economic advice. Ministers could, and did, consult other economists informally, and thereby obtain a variety of views. Notwithstanding the 'Keynesian revolution' in economic thought, the economics profession did not speak with one voice. Indeed, as macroeconomic theory developed, there were growing differences between what rival economists claiming to be Keynesians taught, so that by the 1960s it could be argued that economics was further from achieving a theoretical synthesis than in the 1930s.[38] Macmillan noted that economists conducted their debates with a bitterness that matched those between theologians in earlier centuries. He himself, both as Chancellor and Prime Minister, sought the advice of an old friend, Roy Harrod, an Oxford economist, whom he described as 'a stalwart expansionist', but whom Hall described as 'completely incompetent and irresponsible'.[39] However, Macmillan was also aware of less expansionist views, including those of Frank Paish.[40] Another economist whose views commanded attention in Whitehall was Lionel Robbins, who had returned to the London School of Economics after his wartime service as Director of the Economic Section. Robbins, with some reason, denied being an *éminence grise* behind the scenes, but his belief that balance-of-payments equilibrium should be the sole test of financial policy was well known to ministers, including Macmillan and Thorneycroft. In contrast, Harrod, by the later 1950s, believed that economic policy should aim at full employment and a steady growth of output in accordance with the potential of the economy, and that policy-makers should not allow fears about the balance of payments to constrain growth.[41] Given these differences of opinion, it is hardly surprising that ministers do not seem to have been overawed by economic science. Macmillan told his Cabinet colleagues in relation to the economic situation in 1957: 'we must read the economists and take some advice from the Civil Servants; but we must decide for ourselves'.[42]

There was also a good deal of debate among economists in the 1950s about the working of the monetary system. It was not until the summer of 1959 that the Radcliffe Committee reported that changes in Bank rate were less effective in influencing investment or the level of demand than much of the economic literature of the previous thirty years had suggested, and that, insofar as monetary policy was effective, it acted upon total demand by altering the liquidity position of financial institutions and of firms and people wishing to spend, rather than through interest rates. The authors of the Report concluded that the supply

[38] Axel Leijonhufvud, *On Keynesian Economics and the Economics of Keynes* (New York, 1968), 34. For differences between what Keynes had written and the views of Keynesians see also T. W. Hutchison, *Economics and Economic Policy in Britain, 1946–1966* (1968).

[39] Macmillan, *Riding the Storm*, 705, 709; Hall, *Diaries, 1954–1961*, 193.

[40] See F. W. Paish, 'Inflation in the United Kingdom, 1948–57', *Economica*, NS, 98 (1958), 94–105.

[41] Lionel Robbins, *Autobiography of an Economist* (1971), 229; id., *The Balance of Payments* (1951); Roy F. Harrod, *Policy Against Inflation* (1958), esp. 230; id., *The Pound Sterling, 1951–1958* (Princeton, NJ, 1958), 46–9.   [42] C(57)194, 1 Sept. 1957, CAB129/88.

of money was not in itself a critical factor, but both Robbins and Harrod attached more importance than they did to the need to regulate the supply of money.[43]

The Bank of England, rather than the Economic Section, continued to be the major source of advice on monetary policy, and the Bank was not affected by Keynesian economics before the Radcliffe Report. The Bank's expertise tended to be narrow and technical, and its statistical services were limited. The Governor paid regular visits to the Chancellor and the Permanent Secretary of the Treasury, and representatives of the Treasury visited the Bank once a week, but the overseas finance divisions had more contact with the Bank than had the home finance divisions. Indeed, Macmillan was struck by the lack of contact between Bank and Treasury officials when he became Chancellor, and he instituted regular weekly meetings with three or four representatives of each institution.[44] The failure of monetary policy to check the boom of 1955 led to a joint Bank/Treasury review of monetary control in 1956, in the course of which the Chief Cashier of the Bank, Leslie O'Brien, described one paper by Hall as 'full of woolly half truths'; Hall, for his part, remarked that it was 'really almost unbelievable how little co-operation' the Treasury had had from the Bank in economic policy in recent years.[45]

In April 1957 the Chancellor announced the appointment of the Radcliffe Committee to enquire into the working of the monetary system. Thereafter, Treasury and Bank officials collaborated to ensure that their evidence to the Committee was consistent, and the general effect of their evidence was to suggest that relations between the two institutions were a good deal closer than they had in fact been. As he had done since his appointment as Governor in 1949, Cobbold had defended the Bank's prerogatives against what he saw as Treasury encroachment. For example, when Bridges had suggested in 1955 that there should be closer direct contacts between the Treasury and the clearing banks, Cobbold had told him very firmly that relations between the government and the banks were the Bank's responsibility, not the Treasury's. In September 1957, when the Chancellor, Thorneycroft, wished to impose a limit on bank credit—contrary to Bank of England advice—the advice of the Treasury Solicitor was sought on whether the Chancellor had the power to direct the Governor to give directions to bankers, or to dismiss the Bank's Court of Directors. However, as in 1951, the advice was that the Act of 1946 conferred no such powers. The Bank

[43] Lionel Robbins, *Politics and Economics: Papers in Political Economy* (1963), 179–85, 197–226; Roy F. Harrod, *Topical Comment: Essays in Dynamic Applied Economics* (1961), 240–9; Committee on the Working of the Monetary System, *Report* (Cmnd. 827), esp. paras. 385–97, 418, 428, 440–65, 471–2, PP 1958–9, xvii. 389.

[44] J. Fforde, *The Bank of England and Public Policy, 1941–1958* (Cambridge, 1992), 611–13; Macmillan diary, 13 Mar. 1956.

[45] A. Cairncross and N. Watts, *The Economic Section, 1939–1961: A Study in Economic Advising* (1989), 225–6; Hall, *Diaries, 1954–1961*, 65.

was thus confirmed in its independence in control of the banking system.[46] The Bank had not made a change in Bank rate without the Chancellor's approval since 1931 but, as the Radcliffe Committee reported in August 1959, the relationship between the Bank and the Treasury was not easy to describe in formal language with any great precision. The continuous and confidential exchanges between the two institutions were conducted in a way that left the Bank a separate organization, capable of forming views, advice, and proposals of its own.[47]

ECONOMIC PLANNING

The changes in government priorities after 1951 led to changes in the number of Treasury officials and the distribution of their duties. The Conservative government wished to reduce the size of the Civil Service, and the Treasury led by example, the number of officials of assistant secretary or higher rank falling from seventy-seven in 1951 to sixty in 1955, and remaining at about that level for the rest of the decade. The biggest reduction was made in officials, mainly those in the CEPS, engaged in one form or other of 'planning': from seventeen of assistant secretary rank or above in 1951 to six in 1956.[48] Butler persuaded Plowden to stay on as Chief Planning Officer and head of the CEPS, and appreciated his ability to interpret advice coming from the inarticulate Hall. On the other hand, the Chancellor's confidence in Plowden seems to have been reduced when, in February 1952, the latter advised Eden, then Foreign Secretary, against the Robot plan for a flexible exchange rate, which Butler favoured.[49] When Plowden left the Treasury in November 1953 to become the first chairman of the UK Atomic Energy Authority, he was not replaced.

Even before Plowden left the Treasury, 'planning' had come to mean no more than interdepartmental discussion and co-ordination with a view to ensuring that government economic policy was rational and consistent. In 1952 Butler had directed that the annual *Economic Survey* presented by the Chancellor to Parliament was to be limited to a factual report of the economic situation, and that 'prophecies, forecasts and targets' were to be avoided.[50] In 1953 the Investment Programmes Committee was wound up—to the regret of Treasury officials and Hall, as it had been an effective means of deciding priorities under Labour.[51] By 1954, Dow, then in the Economic Section, thought that 'no-one (understandably) quite knows what planning is nowadays', and drew attention

---

[46] Extract from Governor's Diary, 4 Aug. 1955, Bank of England papers, G1/73/1181/2; R. J. B. Anderson (Treasury Solicitor's Office) to William Armstrong, 5 Sept. 1957, PREM11/1824.
[47] Cmnd. 827, paras. 760–71.
[48] 'Changes in Treasury Staff Numbers', by Clarke, 10 Dec. 1958, T199/703.
[49] Butler, *Art of the Possible*, 157; R. Hall, *The Robert Hall Diaries, 1947–1953* (1989), 275–6.
[50] Economic Policy Committee minutes, 2 Apr. 1952, CAB134/842.
[51] M. Chick, *Industrial Policy in Britain, 1945–1951* (Cambridge, 1998), 205–8.

to the lack of systematic attention paid to long-term issues. The Economic Section itself was by that date concerning itself increasingly with short-term forecasting: fiscal policy was based on annual forecasts of the national income and the balance of payments, and the Treasury's interdepartmental review of public investment was likewise on an annual basis.[52]

As the work of the CEPS contracted, it was first managed by the same Third Secretary (William Strath) as officials servicing interdepartmental committees, and then merged with them in mid-1955 in a new Home and Overseas Planning Staff. At the end of 1955 Strath left the Treasury to join Plowden at the Atomic Energy Authority, and was replaced by the dynamic 'Otto' Clarke, who had left the overseas finance side of the Treasury in 1953 to take charge of the division dealing with the expenditure of the social services. Clarke's promotion to Third Secretary proved to be a turning point as regards planning in the Treasury. While studying economics at Cambridge he had met Colin Clark, who brought him into the New Fabian Research Bureau in 1932, where he had come into contact with economists such as Meade, Gaitskell, and Durbin who were interested in planning. Clarke had also written a book in which he had set out the arguments for nationalizing steel.[53] With this background, and his mastery of statistics, Clarke was well qualified to be a planner. Even Hall, who disliked Clarke personally, admitted that planning of public investment was better under him than it had been under Plowden.[54] With the Conservative government becoming more interested in policy reviews from 1956, there was more work for the Home and Overseas Planning Staff to do and in November 1958 it was replaced by two divisions, one for overseas co-ordination, and one for national resources.

THE UNITED KINGDOM'S ROLE IN WORLD AFFAIRS

It is impossible to understand Treasury management of the economy in the 1950s without understanding contemporary perceptions of Britain's world role. External constraints would have had less influence on domestic economic policy if sterling had not been an international currency, if British overseas investment had been lower, and if defence expenditure had not been as high as it was as a result of the Cold War with the Soviet Union and the problems of maintaining Britain's authority and interests in her colonies and in the Middle East. More generally, British external policy in the 1950s is only comprehensible if account is taken of policy-makers' conviction that Britain should play a leading role in world affairs. An interdepartmental policy review by officials concluded

---

[52] Memoranda by Dow on 'Long-term Planning', 6 May 1954, and 'Long-term Planning and the C.E.P.S.', 30 June 1954, T230/267.

[53] 'Ingot' (Richard Clarke), *The Socialisation of Iron and Steel* (1936).

[54] Hall, *Diaries, 1954–1961*, 46, 167.

in June 1958 that Britain could still hope to exercise substantial influence, partly in partnership with the United States, partly as the leader of the independent Commonwealth, and partly through her position as a link between Europe and the Commonwealth and the United States. In other words, Britain's external policy was related to what Churchill, in a well-known phrase, had called the 'three circles' of 'free nations': the United States, the Commonwealth, and western Europe.[55]

Treasury views on external policy were based upon the belief that the interests of the United Kingdom and the sterling area, as well as the United States, would be served by expanding world trade, and that this objective could best be achieved by reducing barriers to multilateral trade through the General Agreement on Trade and Tariffs (GATT), by international agreements to remove quantitative import controls, and by making sterling convertible, as and when it was safe to do so. The Treasury's traditional bias in favour of free trade can be seen in its support of the Board of Trade's policy of trade liberalization, although the Economic Section urged caution, on the grounds that the balance of trade would suffer if import controls were removed too quickly—as indeed appears to have happened from the mid-1950s.[56]

An economic conference of Commonwealth prime ministers in December 1952 agreed that countries in the sterling area should move progressively and collectively towards convertibility, by maintaining sound internal economic policies, and by developing resources that would strengthen the sterling area's balance of payments, in terms of dollars, and these policies were confirmed at Commonwealth finance ministers' conferences in January and October 1954. Treasury officials feared that, if Britain were to go back on what was called the Collective Approach to convertibility, Canada, which was not a member of the sterling area, and probably Australia and South Africa, which were, would develop closer economic relations with the United States than with the United Kingdom, thereby weakening the cohesion of the Commonwealth. In the event, the Collective Approach did not gain the support that Britain hoped for from the United States or European countries, and full convertibility was not achieved until December 1958. Convertibility involved the removal of the currency restrictions that had defined the sterling area since 1939. Moreover, the overseas sterling area had a growing deficit on current account with the non-sterling world from 1954 to 1958, so that Britain could no longer look to the rest of the sterling area to balance its own deficit on current account with the non-sterling world. Nevertheless, the Radcliffe Committee concluded in July 1959

[55] Norman Brook to Prime Minister, 5 June 1958, and 'The Position of the United Kingdom in World Affairs', report by officials, PREM11/2321. The review's papers are in CAB130/139. For Churchill's 'three circles' see *The Times*, 11 Oct. 1948.

[56] See Alan S. Milward and George Brennan, *Britain's Place in the World: A Historical Enquiry into Import Controls, 1945–60* (1996).

that the sterling area continued to be beneficial both from the point of view of encouraging international trade and as an important link between Britain and the Commonwealth.[57]

The Commonwealth and sterling area also influenced overseas investment policy, as it was recognized in the Treasury that freedom of capital movement was one of the main attractions of the sterling area to its members. Treasury officials also accepted that government-sponsored investment in colonial development had political benefits, and was likely to rise over time, and Treasury control was exercised from the point of view of ensuring that such investment was economically sound. Private investment through the raising of market loans was controlled by the Capital Issues Committee, which would approve projects that satisfied criteria laid down at Commonwealth economic conferences, principally concerning the need to increase the sterling area's balance of payments in terms of dollars. This was a criterion amply met by the biggest single form of overseas investment, which was by British oil companies, principally in the Middle East. However, as the dollar shortage eased, but sterling remained under pressure from 1955 to 1958, the Treasury became less willing to sanction loans to colonial borrowers, a change in attitude that has been seen in retrospect as leading logically to decolonization, but which can also be seen simply as a case of the Treasury reverting to type, given its attitude to colonial development in the inter-war period. By no means all British overseas investment was directed at the sterling area; indeed, down to 1956 at least, the Treasury was anxious to encourage British investment in Canada, to reduce that country's dependence on the United States.[58]

In retrospect, given the decline of Commonwealth links and the sterling area in the 1960s and 1970s, the Treasury's world view in the 1950s might seem to have been based upon a misperception of Britain's interests. Indeed in 1958 Andrew Shonfield argued that responsibility for the sterling area, with the concomitant freedom for British capital to be exported, led to lower levels of investment in Britain than would otherwise have taken place. However, Catherine Schenk's analysis of the sterling area between 1949 and 1958 suggests that the ratio of overseas investment to domestic capital formation was too small for there to have been a significant negative impact on British economic growth. Moreover, the sterling area did allow a degree of multilateralism which was far

---

[57] 'Future Economic Policy', memorandum by the Chancellor of the Exchequer, 15 May 1953, CAB134/848; 'External Economic Policy', n.d., but spring 1955, T273/317; A. R. Conan, *The Rationale of the Sterling Area* (1961), 1–8; Cmnd. 827, para. 657.

[58] 'Overseas Investment Policy', PR(56)40, 30 July 1956, CAB134/1315. For Treasury control of colonial development see D. J. Morgan, *The Official History of Colonial Development*, vol. iii, *A Reassessment of British Aid Policy* (1980), 187–97. For decolonization see P. J. Cain and A. G. Hopkins, *British Imperialism: Crisis and Deconstruction, 1914–1990* (1993), 281–91. For decline in Anglo-Canadian trading links see B. W. Muirhead, 'Britain, Canada, and the Collective Approach to Freer Trade and Payments, 1952–57', *J. Imperial and Commonwealth Hist.*, 20 (1992), 108–26.

from insignificant at a time when close on half the world's trade was still conducted in sterling.[59]

A more telling criticism by Shonfield concerned the heavy burden of defence expenditure, especially overseas, on the British balance of payments, and Susan Strange subsequently argued that much of this overseas defence expenditure was incurred to defend overseas investments and members of the sterling area.[60] However, the Treasury was at one with the critics regarding the need to reverse the growth of defence expenditure, which had originally been associated with the Korean War of 1950–3. Indeed, the Treasury succeeded in registering in the Defence white paper of 1957 its main point that Britain's influence in the world depended 'first and foremost' on the health of her internal economy and on the success of her exports. Otherwise, it argued, as it had done in 1937 and 1938, military power could not be sustained in the long run.[61]

In its submission to a Cabinet policy review in 1956 of the future of the United Kingdom in world affairs, the Treasury argued that successive governments since the war had tried to do too much in all aspects of policy, both at home and abroad, with the result that the country had only rarely been free from the danger of economic crisis. What had been achieved had been made possible only by loans and grants from the United States, which would now have to be repaid, adding to the burden on the balance of payments. With reserves of £800 million and short-term liabilities of £3,742 million, Britain was in no position to check a major run on sterling. The reserves in 1955 were equivalent to only 11 per cent of Britain's visible trade—lower than in 1951 when the proportion had been 12½ per cent—and thus offered inadequate protection against an adverse change in the terms of trade, such as had occurred at the time of the Korean War. The Treasury thus hoped to achieve two objectives: first, to attain a balance-of-payments surplus of £300 million a year, so as to build up the reserves to £1,700 million; and second, to raise the proportion of GNP devoted to fixed investment from 15 per cent in 1955 to 17 per cent in 1960, with an emphasis on directly productive investment, such as coal and steel, or transport, rather than on housing. The Treasury argued that these objectives could be attained only if the growth of both consumer expenditure and public authorities' current expenditure on goods and services could be held down below the growth of GNP, but also held out the prospect that higher investment would lead to higher economic growth. It was expected in 1956 that the main saving in public expenditure must come from defence, and the Treasury called for a comprehensive review of government external commitments. Thus, as regards the need to increase domestic investment and to

[59] Andrew Shonfield, *British Economic Policy since the War* (1958), ch. 6; Catherine Schenk, *Britain and the Sterling Area: From Devaluation to Convertibility in the 1950s* (1994).

[60] Shonfield, op. cit., ch. 5; Susan Strange, *Sterling and British Policy* (1971), ch. 6.

[61] *Defence: Outline of Future Policy* (Cmnd. 124), PP 1956–7, xxiii. 489, para. 6.

restrain government expenditure overseas, the Treasury anticipated Shonfield and Strange.[62]

The Suez crisis underlined both the vulnerability of sterling and the importance that was placed on the preservation of its international role, as well as Britain's dependence upon the United States. The crisis began when Colonel Nasser, the Egyptian dictator, nationalized the Suez Canal Company in July 1956, and came to a head when Britain and France, acting in collusion with Israel, responded with air attacks on Egypt on 31 October. The first part of an Anglo-French expeditionary force, which was intended to occupy the Suez Canal zone, landed at Port Said on 5 November, but the following day the United States used Britain's need for American support for sterling to insist on a cease-fire, and Britain and France were compelled to withdraw their forces in December. The role of economic diplomacy in the resolution of the crisis is well known,[63] and what follows centres on the light cast by the crisis on the work of the Treasury.

The Suez crisis is a striking example of the crucial, and in this case disastrous, role that a Chancellor of the Exchequer can play in policy. As early as April 1956 both the Chancellor, Macmillan, and the Prime Minister, Eden, had been warned by Treasury officials that foreign confidence in sterling was so weak that pressure for devaluation might become irresistible at some point between August and November that year. Inflationary pressures, manifested in the form of demands for wage increases, created doubt about Britain's capacity to compete in international markets, and the Suez crisis merely added to the uncertainty. In August and September, while ministers were considering what action should be taken to force Nasser to give up control of the canal, Bridges repeated the warning to Macmillan about the weakness of sterling, and told him that it was vital that Britain should not act without the 'maximum United States support'.[64] As already noted, Bridges was excluded from the inner councils handling policy towards Egypt; the same was also true of his successor, Makins, who took up his post on 15 October. It fell, therefore, to the Chancellor to convey the force of the Treasury's warnings to Eden and his colleagues. However, Macmillan, who was one of the ministers keenest on invading Egypt, apparently failed to do so. Indeed, he used a visit to the International Monetary Fund (IMF) in late September to have informal talks with President Eisenhower, Secretary of State John Foster Dulles, and Secretary of the Treasury George Humphrey, and, despite Dulles's warning against the use of force before the American

---

[62] 'The Future of the United Kingdom in World Affairs', PR(56)3, circulated by Norman Brook, 1 Jan. 1956, and PR(56)30, 20 July 1956, CAB134/1315.

[63] See Lewis Johnman, 'Defending the Pound: The Economics of the Suez Crisis', in T. Gorst, L. Johnman, and W. S. Lucas (eds.), *Postwar Britain, 1945–64: Themes and Perspectives* (1989), 166–81, and Diane B. Kunz, *The Economic Diplomacy of the Suez Crisis* (Chapel Hill, NC, 1991).

[64] Macmillan to Eden, 5 Apr. 1956, PREM11/1326; Bridges to Macmillan, 8 Aug. and 7 Sept. 1956, and Rowan to Macmillan, 25 Sept. 1956, T236/4188.

presidential election on 6 November, managed to convince first himself, and then Eden, that American support would be forthcoming. The decision to attack Egypt seems to have been taken on the basis of this misunderstanding.[65]

British vulnerability to American pressure was greater than it might otherwise have been owing to a failure to strengthen Britain's dollar reserves prior to the attack on Egypt. Whereas France secured an IMF standby credit of $239 million beforehand, the Treasury decided not to go to the IMF, although Rowan expected that the reserves would fall to $2,248 million by 1 November, not far above the $2,000 million regarded as a minimum working balance for the sterling area. Rowan reported to Makins, and through him the Chancellor, on 26 October that the feeling within overseas finance was that it would be better to go to the IMF while sterling was fairly strong, for then such action might be interpreted as indicative of determination to carry through with Suez and other policies. However, the Governor of the Bank, Cobbold, had warned that to follow the French example might be taken as a sign of weakness, and that it would be better to wait until the seasonal improvement in the reserves in the new year. Rowan felt that, as the object of the exercise was to improve confidence in sterling, the Treasury should not ignore the Bank's advice on likely market reactions. Neither Rowan nor Cobbold appears to have had any inkling that the Anglo-French invasion fleet was about to set sail; had they done so, their advice might have been different. Britain's dependence on American goodwill in relation to sterling was all the greater because payments, amounting to $180 million, were due in December under the Anglo-American and Canadian loan agreements, and the Bank of England advised that the waiver clause in the Anglo-American agreement could not be used without some stigma of default.[66]

On 6 November, the day after the Anglo-French landings, Macmillan was told that the Americans would neither support an application to the IMF nor give any other assistance. With heavy selling of sterling producing a drain on the dollar reserves, Macmillan felt that he had no option but to advise the Cabinet to accept American demands for a cease-fire that day, and subsequent demands for a withdrawal from Egypt. The alternative of foregoing American support would have been to allow sterling to float, but in the circumstances such action would have been the equivalent of devaluation. Both Cobbold, who had held informal talks with the governors of eight of the central banks in the Commonwealth, and Hall had already warned in October that another devaluation, coming so soon after that of 1949, would probably bring about the break-up of the sterling area.[67]

[65] For a summary of the evidence on Macmillan's role see John Turner, *Macmillan* (1994), 113–23.

[66] D. A. V. Allen to A. France, 19 Oct., and Rowan to Makins, 26 Oct. 1956, T236/4188; Bank of England papers on 'The Waiver', 25 Oct., and 'The Foreign Exchange Market', 7 Nov. 1956, T236/4189.

[67] Hall to Bridges, 2 Oct., and Cobbold to Chancellor, 17 Oct. 1956, T236/4188; Hall, *Diaries, 1954–1961*, 85.

It might have been thought that Suez would have led to a dramatic re-appraisal of Britain's overseas commitments. However, as already noted, it was in June 1958 that an interdepartmental working party of officials, chaired by Sir Norman Brook, reported to the Prime Minister that Britain could still hope to exercise substantial influence in world affairs. The officials warned that, in order to be able to exercise this influence, the foreign exchange reserves would have to be strengthened by running an annual current surplus of £350–£400 million on the balance of payments over the next few years (a more ambitious target than the £300 million set by the Treasury earlier). On the other hand, they advised that there should be no reduction in government expenditure overseas in support of foreign policy, and that there should be no further reductions in defence expenditure other than those already decided on. The message was that the desired surplus on the balance of payments, and therefore Britain's position in world affairs, depended upon reducing the share of GNP devoted to civil expenditure at home.[68]

The Treasury was well aware that Britain's position in the world depended upon the competitiveness of her exports, and that competitiveness could be undermined by the demands of public expenditure and private consumption upon productive capacity. Bridges had told Butler in 1953 that it was the duty of the Treasury—as the department responsible for general economic co-ordination—to ensure that economic conditions were favourable for exports.[69] Table 9.1 shows how Britain's share of world trade in manufactures fell from 25.4 per cent in 1950 to 20.9 per cent in 1953. However, the 1950 figure was abnormally high, owing to the temporary, war-induced dislocation of the German and Japanese economies. Moreover, the downward trend slowed after 1953, and was even reversed in 1958, so that there were still grounds then for hoping that Britain could maintain its position as a trading nation (something she signally failed to do in the 1960s). Britain's position in the world thus seemed stronger in the 1950s than hindsight would suggest.

ATTITUDES TOWARDS EUROPE

Contemporary perceptions in Whitehall of Britain's position in the world help to explain policy-makers' attitudes towards European integration in the 1950s. In 1951 the Commonwealth took 50 per cent of British exports, compared with 25 per cent going to the six European countries (France, West Germany, Italy, and the Benelux countries) that were to form the common market of the European Economic Community (EEC), and although the proportion going to the Commonwealth fell during the decade, it still stood at 43 per cent in 1957, the

---

[68] Brook to Prime Minister, 5 June 1958, enclosing report on 'The Position of the United Kingdom in World Affairs', PREM11/2321; 'Long-Term Problems', by Clarke, 21 Jan. 1959, T234/330.

[69] Bridges to Butler, 25 Feb. 1953, T273/172.

TABLE 9.1. *UK Share of Exports of Manufactures by Eleven Industrial Countries, 1937, 1950–9, and 1969*

Date	Percentage share
1937	21.3
1950	25.4
1951	21.9
1952	21.5
1953	20.9
1954	20.5
1955	19.8
1956	19.2
1957	17.9
1958	18.2
1959	17.7
1969	11.2

Source: London and Cambridge Economic Service, *The British Economy: Key Statistics 1900–1970* (1971), 17.

year the Six signed the Treaty of Rome. Although in 1956 Macmillan began to question how far it was to Britain's advantage to give preferences to Commonwealth products, when these were not the cheapest available, even he thought the problem was how to reconcile Britain's position as head of the Commonwealth and the sterling area with her place in Europe.

Questions relating to European integration were handled by interdepartmental committees with Treasury officials acting as 'non-departmental' chairmen. Membership always included representatives of the Treasury, the Foreign Office, and the Board of Trade, but might extend to the Commonwealth Relations Office, the Colonial Office, the Ministry of Agriculture, Fisheries and Food, the Ministry of Power, and the Board of Customs and Excise. Treasury and Foreign Office officials agreed that relations between their departments were much improved by this interdepartmental machinery, which ensured that officials in both departments had a full say before matters reached ministerial level, even when their advice reached the appropriate Cabinet committee via the Chancellor of the Exchequer, as the minister in charge of economic policy.[70] It is not always easy, therefore, to discern a distinctive Treasury influence on policy relating to European integration, and what follows is more concerned with showing continuities in the Treasury's world view, down to 1959, than with establishing the Treasury's responsibility for Britain's 'failure' to become a founding member of the EEC.[71]

[70] 'European Economic Co-operation: Whitehall Organisation', sent by Clarke to Max Beloff, 21 Apr. 1959, and memoranda by D. F. Hubback (Treasury), 6 Oct., and P. H. Gore-Booth (Foreign Office), 12 Oct. 1959, T199/690.

[71] See James R. V. Ellison, 'Perfidious Albion? Britain, Plan G and European Integration, 1955–56',

From the Marshall Plan onwards, British policy had been to participate in intergovernmental co-operation in Europe, for example in the OEEC, while rejecting membership of supranational bodies, such as the European Coal and Steel Community. Following the decision of the Six at their conference in Messina in June 1955 to set up the Spaak Committee in Brussels to prepare plans for a common market, Butler circulated a Cabinet paper objecting to British participation, on the grounds that a discriminatory bloc was bound to affect the obligations that Britain (and the Messina Six) had to the OEEC and GATT.[72] In the event, a senior Board of Trade official, Russell Bretherton, took part in the work of the Spaak Committee, but British policy continued to emphasize the benefits of working through the OEEC. The Treasury had no doubt in 1955 that Britain's economic interests would be adversely affected by the establishment of a common market from which she was excluded. Burke Trend, the Treasury Under-Secretary who chaired a working group between July and October on the potential effects of a common market, thought that there was an interdepartmental consensus that, on balance, it would be to Britain's 'real and ultimate interest' that the common market project should collapse. However, he was much more sceptical than the Foreign Office that the discussions in Brussels would fail, or that Britain could divert the project into the OEEC. Consequently, the interdepartmental committee of senior officials dealing with the common market project, the Economic Steering Committee, which was chaired by Gilbert, recommended in November that a study be undertaken of what Britain could put forward by way of a fresh initiative in Europe.[73]

Butler, who was still Chancellor, was uniformly negative about the common market: most notoriously, he had described the Messina conference as 'archaeological excavations', that is an attempt to dig up discredited ideas on European federalism.[74] However, his successors, Macmillan and Thorneycroft, were much keener to explore possible forms of a new policy in Europe, and in February 1956 Macmillan asked his officials to prepare a plan that would reconcile Britain's position as head of the Commonwealth and sterling area with some degree of European co-operation. Rowan, as the Second Secretary in charge of the overseas finance side of the Treasury, believed that closer co-operation with Europe was incompatible with the Collective Approach to global convertibility of currencies and multilateral trade. On the other hand, Clarke, as head of the

Contemp. Brit. Hist., 10 (1996), 1–34, and Martin Schaad, 'Plan G: A "Counterblast"? British Policy Towards the Messina Countries, 1956', *Contemp. Eur. Hist.*, 7 (1998), 39–60.

[72] 'European Integration', note by the Chancellor of the Exchequer, 29 June 1955, CAB129/76.

[73] Trend to Clarke, 'Brussels and All That', 26 Oct. 1955, and Economic Steering Committee minutes, 1 Nov. 1955, T234/181. The latter show that Sir Frank Lee, the Permanent Secretary of the Board of Trade, was of the personal opinion that on economic grounds it would be to Britain's advantage to enter the common market, but he did not press this view against the balance of opinion on the committee, the other members being Rowan and the permanent secretaries of the Foreign Office and the Ministry of Fuel and Power.

[74] Michael Charlton, *The Price of Victory* (1983), 194–5.

Treasury's Home and Overseas Planning Staff, argued that the Collective Approach was out of date, being based on Britain's position at the centre of Churchill's 'three circles': the United States, the Commonwealth, and Europe, whereas, since the Collective Approach had been adopted in 1952, the relative importance to Britain of Europe, compared with the other two circles, had increased. Clarke advocated a 'genuine plan, representing a significant and real tilting of our policy towards Europe'.[75] Clarke's view was supported by the Economic Section's analysis, which showed the potential loss of exports if Britain were to be discriminated against in the markets of the Messina Six.

By 20 April an interdepartmental committee of officials under Clarke had produced six options, A–F, of which option E, a partial free trade area with Europe, was favoured by both Macmillan and the President of the Board of Trade, Thorneycroft. Revised as Plan G, the partial free trade plan was an attempt to avert the danger of exclusion from continental markets by proposing that the Six would be linked as a single unit to a wider European free trade area for industrial (but, the British hoped, not agricultural) goods. Whereas a customs union would have involved common tariffs against imports from non-members, the free trade area envisaged in Plan G would only remove tariffs between members, thereby allowing Britain to maintain existing preferential trading arrangements with the Commonwealth.

Gilbert warned that Plan G would involve a drastic change of policy, in that it would expose British industry to much greater competition than it experienced under existing tariffs and quota arrangements. A free trade area would offer British exporters new opportunities in a market of 250 million people, but advantage could only be taken if British industry were sufficiently competitive. That in turn would depend, not only upon the success of government policies to maintain a competitive economy and a sound balance of payments, but also on the attitudes of management and labour.[76] The adoption of Plan G by ministers in the autumn of 1956 therefore enhanced the importance that the Treasury already attached to price and wage stability, and the need not to overload the economy.

The Treasury played a leading role in preparing for the negotiations with the Six, although the actual negotiations were handled by Maudling, as Paymaster General, supported by an ad hoc Free Trade Area Office. Clarke chaired the Economic Steering Committee's Sub-Committee on Closer Economic Association with Europe, and the Treasury's Home and Overseas Planning Staff was responsible for interdepartmental co-ordination. The negotiations, which began in October 1957, failed in November 1958, mainly because British insistence on preservation of Commonwealth links could not be reconciled with the EEC's

---

[75] 'European Integration', by Clarke, 11 Feb. 1956, T234/701.
[76] 'United Kingdom in Europe', 26 July 1956, T234/195, and 'Future Commercial Policy', 3 Sept. 1956, T234/197, both by Gilbert.

intention to develop a common agricultural policy that would discriminate against Commonwealth food producers, and also because Britain was reluctant to accept an implicit commitment to work towards political unity with the Six.

Between December 1958 and February 1959, a new Cabinet Committee on European Economic Questions, supported by a committee of officials under Makins, decided that Britain should try to create a free trade area without the Six. Makins welcomed the idea of a free trade area with the Scandinavian countries and Austria, Switzerland, and Portugal, which was eventually agreed in November 1959, as a base from which further progress might be made in negotiations for freer trade in Europe.[77] By 1959 a less confident view was forming in the Treasury of Britain's future role in the world than had been assumed earlier in the decade. One Under-Secretary, noting how Britain was likely to decline in terms of population in relation to the United States, the EEC, and Russia, over the next ten or twenty years, drew the conclusion that a close political as well as economic relationship with Europe would become a necessity. Referring to Churchill's concept of the three interlocking circles of the United States, the Commonwealth, and Europe, the official remarked: 'I don't know whether we shall be sufficiently skilful as a juggler to keep the three circles in the air much longer.'[78]

AIMS AND PROBLEMS OF ECONOMIC MANAGEMENT

The Treasury's world view suggests that the aims of the managers of the economy extended beyond the four conventionally listed in textbooks: full employment, stable prices, balance-of-payments equilibrium, and economic growth. Maintenance of Britain's role in world affairs was another aim. The key to achieving this aim was the balance of payments, for only if there were a substantial surplus on current account would it be possible to cover net investment abroad and to build up the reserves that would enable sterling to continue to be an international currency. As already noted, the Treasury's target for annual balance-of-payments surpluses on current account ranged from £300 million in 1953, to £350 million to £400 million in 1958. However, despite an improvement in the terms of trade, particularly when import prices fell between 1951 and 1953, and despite substantial defence aid from the United States from 1952 to 1955, the surplus came within the target range only in 1958 (see Table 9.2). Hall had no doubt that year that the failure since the war to build up the reserves in proportion either to the sterling balances or the amounts of sterling used in world trade was a fundamental weakness, for sterling was left exposed to crises in confidence.[79]

[77] Note by Makins, 16 Dec. 1958, T234/357.
[78] A. W. France to Rickett, 10 July 1959, T234/277.
[79] 'The Economic Situation', 29 Jan. 1958, T171/487.

TABLE 9.2. *Estimates of UK Balance of Payments on Current Account, 1951–1960 (£m.) surplus (+) or deficit (−)*

	Contemporary	1961	1995	Defence aid (net)
1951	−521	−419	−369	+4
1952	+291	+164	+163	+121
1953	+225	+148	+145	+102
1954	+160	+125	+117	+50
1955	−103	−156	−155	+44
1956	+245	+207	+208	+26
1957	+237	+209	+233	+21
1958	+455	+328	+350	+3
1959	+139	+111	+164	0
1960	−339	−301	−237	0

Note: A number of changes in sources and methods in compiling balance-of-payments statistics were made in 1961.

Source: Annual Abstract of Statistics.

Even full employment could be seen as a means of maintaining Britain as a world power. As Plowden explained in a paper prepared for Butler in 1952, the economic case for full employment (in addition to its social and political advantages) was that the nation's output and economic strength was maximized thereby. The problem was that, at full employment, wages tended to increase faster than output, leading to cost inflation, a loss of competitive power, and balance-of-payments difficulties. Plowden therefore advised that a wages policy to check this tendency was a necessary concomitant of full employment, while admitting that a satisfactory answer to the problem of wages had yet to be found. Full employment, he added, also required imports of raw materials, and therefore maintenance of Britain's competitive power in world markets. Economic policy, therefore, must ensure that there was a satisfactory flow of capital investment to keep British industry, public utilities, and agriculture 'in the van of technological progress'. The problem was that there was a large unsatisfied demand for social investment, such as housing and schools, and therefore there was a danger that total investment would generate inflationary pressures that would divert resources from exports. Hence, Plowden argued, the state must accept responsibility both for enforcing savings through the budget, when the volume of private savings available for investment was inadequate, and for supervising the total volume of private and public investment, to keep it in balance with the total volume of savings.[80]

However, the responsibilities which this Keynesian analysis thrust upon the state exceeded the powers of economists to forecast trends in time for appropriate fiscal or monetary action to be taken. Bridges broadly agreed with Plowden's paper, but stated that he did not believe that anyone knew enough, either by way

[80] 'Economic Policy', by Plowden, 10 Apr. 1952, T229/323.

of techniques 'or prophetic insight', to exercise complete control over an economy, which, in any case, was very dependent on external trade. The best that could be done was for the state to modify or restrain economic forces when these tended to produce conditions that were socially undesirable.[81] Some idea of the problem can be obtained by looking at balance-of-payments forecasts, which were crucial in determining the direction of demand management at a time when sterling was subject to frequent crises of confidence. As Table 9.2 shows, estimates of the balance of payments were subject to substantial revisions long after the event. In particular, a comprehensive revision in 1961 of earlier estimates, particularly of net earnings from invisibles, led Hall to reflect ruefully that his advice in recent years had been based on false views of the situation. As he remarked, it was always a problem for an economic adviser 'to know where one is at a given time', and, in retrospect, he felt that he ought to have put more weight on the need to run the economy under less pressure of demand.[82]

Hall and the Economic Section were also handicapped by the fact that, down to 1956, it was still not possible for the Central Statistical Office to compile national income and expenditure data quarterly, as was then being done in the United States. Hall advised Bridges before the 1955 budget that the British figures for fixed investment were a year out of date; information on stocks and work in progress was inadequate; full figures for industrial production were often four months late; there were serious gaps in the statistics on consumption; and very little was known about future plans for construction. At Hall's suggestion, Bridges advised Sir Harry Campion, the Director of the Central Statistical Office, that his efforts to improve the data had the Treasury's full support, but a year later Bridges was 'concerned' and Rowan was 'shocked' at the inadequacy of the statistics about economic trends on which the Chancellor had to base his economic policies.[83] Thus Macmillan's well-known remark in 1956 that lags in information meant that 'we are always, as it were, looking up a train in last year's Bradshaw' (a guide to railway timetables) expressed his officials' views as well as his own.[84] Matters improved thereafter: in particular, quarterly national income estimates became available from January 1957. However, some items, notably stocks, were so volatile that they continued to be hard to forecast.[85]

Even with better statistics it would have been difficult to manage the economy without inflationary pressures and balance-of-payments problems. Unemployment, expressed as a national annual average, exceeded 2 per cent only in 1952, 1958, and 1959, with 2.3 per cent in the last year being the highest of the

[81] Bridges to Armstrong, 22 Apr. 1952, T273/315.   [82] Hall, *Diaries, 1954–1961*, 260.
[83] 'Economic Statistics', by Hall, 3 Feb., and Bridges to Hall, 9 Feb. 1955, T273/317; Budget Committee minutes, 2 Mar. 1956, T171/469.
[84] 541 H C Deb., 5s, 1955–6, col. 867.
[85] See Sir Harry Campion, 'Recent Developments in Economic Statistics', *J. Royal Stat. Soc.*, ser. A (general), 1/1 (1958), 1–15; Sir Robert Hall, 'Reflections on the Practical Application of Economics', *Econ. J.*, 69 (1959), 639–52.

decade. As a Treasury memorandum, endorsed by Macmillan in 1956, noted, keeping unemployment as low as 2 per cent without inflation 'requires, so to speak, steering to a finer course than the ship may be capable of'.[86] Moreover, experience showed that not enough was known about the multiplier to allow it to be used in any simple way in forecasting the effects of a budget, as employers hoarded or shed labour in a variable relationship to aggregate demand in the economy.

As regards economic growth, Hall thought in 1953 that it would be unwise to aim at much more than 3 per cent a year, given 'fairly full' employment, commenting within the Economic Section that: 'I don't believe we can trust the Government with a system under more pressure than that—i.e. we will in fact be rather too inflationary if we aim too high.'[87] With compound growth of 3 per cent a year national income would double in twenty-four years, and doubtless Hall was consulted by Butler before the latter made a notable speech at the Conservative party conference in 1954 in which he set a target of doubling the standard of living over the next twenty-five years. Moreover, when setting that target, the Chancellor appealed both for restraint in short-term political commitments, and for higher levels of investment rather than of consumption in the immediate future.[88]

It is also worth noting that the Treasury and its economic advisers had to work in a world that seemed to be a good deal less stable at the time than it does in historical perspective. The Korean War and associated rearmament and stockbuilding brought about a rapid rise in import prices in 1950 and 1951, a balance-of-payments deficit on current account, and a sterling crisis. An equally precipitate fall in import prices in 1952 and 1953 eased the task of correcting the balance of payments, and took the pressure off sterling. However, in 1954 the terms of trade (the price of exports relative to the price of imports) again turned against Britain, and in 1955 there was another balance-of-payments deficit on current account and a sterling crisis. From 1955 to 1959 the terms of trade once more moved in Britain's favour, but this trend did not prevent sterling crises occurring in 1956, on account of Suez, or in 1957, when devaluation of the French franc led to expectations of a general realignment of exchange rates.

Deflationary effects on the world economy of a slump in the United States were widely feared by financial commentators as well as Treasury officials in 1953: the end of the Korean War pointed to a fall, or at least a levelling off, of American defence expenditure, at a time when consumer expenditure was thought to have peaked. In the event, the American recession had much less impact on the British economy than had been feared. Even so, in 1954 Hall wondered whether the period of economic expansion since the war was coming to an end. He pointed out that almost all of the increase in production in the

---

[86] PR(56)30, 20 July 1956, CAB134/1315.
[87] 'Long-term Economic Policy', by Hall, 17 Sept. 1953, T230/267.   [88] *The Times*, 9 Oct. 1954.

United Kingdom between 1950 and 1953 had come from expenditure on the defence and housing programmes, both of which were reaching a ceiling. The British investment boom of the mid-1950s was not foreseen by the Economic Section, although it was getting under way even as Hall was writing.[89]

Uncertainty also extended to the effectiveness of policy instruments. There was no recent experience of the effects of varying Bank rate, and fiscal policy had not previously been used to manage aggregate demand in the absence of direct controls—either physical controls over investment (through building licensing and steel allocation), consumption (through rationing), and imports, or by the Capital Issues Committee.[90] In the circumstances, it is not surprising that Treasury officials were less enthusiastic than Conservative ministers about rapid dismantling of direct controls. Butler came to office determined to do something different from his Labour predecessor: for example, when Bridges suggested a reintroduction of petrol rationing, to save dollars, in 1951, the Chancellor expressed a preference for rationing by price rather than by 'hordes of officials'.[91] He was encouraged in this attitude by his colleagues in the Cabinet's Economic Policy Committee, particularly Lyttelton, the Colonial Secretary, and Duncan Sandys, the Minister of Supply. However, the conditions of excess demand were such in 1951 and 1952 that Butler had to tell the committee that, while he would have preferred to rely mainly upon fiscal and monetary measures to influence demand, direct controls would have to continue for the time being. Indeed, the balance-of-payments crisis which the government had to deal with on taking office forced Butler to impose what Dow called 'the most spectacular of the post-war import cuts'.[92]

Plowden advised Butler that, in the circumstances of 1952, reliance solely upon monetary measures and the price mechanism would require deflation to produce bankruptcies and unemployment, in order to achieve the degree of flexibility necessary for a market economy. He argued for the use of both monetary measures and direct controls, the role of each to be determined empirically from time to time. To do away with direct controls entirely for political reasons would, he thought, be to try to solve 'most formidable problems' with one hand tied behind one's back.[93] However, as the balance of payments on current account moved into surplus, and as conditions of excess demand eased, there was a sharp decline in the coverage of direct controls between 1952 and 1954, and correspondingly greater reliance upon fiscal and financial instruments. Even so, as late as 1956 the Treasury was not convinced that the

[89] 'Some Impressions of the United States Economic and Budgetary Position', by Plowden, 8 Mar. 1953, T273/316; 'The Budgetary Problem in the Next Five Years', by Hall, 5 July 1954, T171/450.

[90] The Radcliffe Committee concluded that capital issue controls were of negligible importance except in the case of overseas issues (Cmnd. 827, paras. 965–77).

[91] Butler to Bridges, 4 Dec. 1951, T273/315.

[92] Dow, *Management of the British Economy*, 156. For pressure on Butler from his Cabinet colleagues see Economic Policy Committee minutes, 2 Jan. 1952, CAB134/842.

[93] Plowden to Butler, 10 Apr. 1952, T229/323.

economy could be managed successfully without some direct controls over imports, investment, and the allocation of materials. Both Macmillan in 1956 and Thorneycroft in 1957 considered reimposing building controls, which had been abolished in 1954, to supplement monetary and fiscal measures to curb investment.[94] In the event, the trend towards decontrol was not reversed, but some quota restrictions on dollar imports persisted until the end of 1959, a year after sterling convertibility, and controls on overseas capital issues and foreign exchange remained in place thereafter.

Not the least of the Treasury's difficulties in managing the economy lay in the exercise of its traditional responsibilities over public expenditure and revenue. Forecasts of both were, on average, less accurate in the 1950s than in the 1930s. In the case of forecasts by the Board of Inland Revenue, this state of affairs could almost entirely be accounted for by the change since the 1940s to more complex and less predictable taxes, notably purchase tax and pay-as-you-earn income tax. The reasons for less effective Treasury control of expenditure will be considered below. On average, forecasts of expenditure for the purposes of fiscal policy improved in the second half of the 1950s, but, overall, fiscal marksmanship remained defective for the purposes of managing the economy—no small matter given that the enlarged public sector had a greater influence on aggregate demand than ever before in peace.[95]

The aims and problems of economic management may now be summarized. In response to political pressures, maintenance of full employment was given high priority. Economic expansion was also desired, as Butler's target of doubling the standard of living over twenty-five years indicated. The Treasury wished to encourage investment that would make the British economy more competitive in an international economy in which currency and other restrictions on trade were being steadily removed. However, management of the economy was subject to the weakness of sterling. Price stability proved to be elusive, and deflationary measures were taken from 1955 to control the boom that had been developing since 1954. As will be discussed below, Thorneycroft was prepared in 1957 to make price stability the primary aim of policy, allowing unemployment to rise from its existing level of 1.3 per cent to about 3 per cent if necessary. In the event, 1958 turned out to be a year of minor recession and, although unemployment did not rise above 3 per cent, policy switched to reflation in 1958 and 1959.

---

[94] 'Import Controls', 2 July 1956, T273/339; Cabinet conclusions, 3 Aug. 1956, CAB128/30; 'The Economic Situation', memorandum by the Chancellor of the Exchequer, CP(56)17, 21 Jan. 1956, CAB129/79; 'Building Control', draft memorandum by the Chancellor of the Exchequer, 25 Feb. 1957, PREM11/1824.

[95] G. C. Peden, 'Old Dogs and New Tricks: The British Treasury and Keynesian Economics in the 1940s and 1950s', in M. O. Furner and B. Supple (eds.), *The State and Economic Knowledge: The American and British Experiences* (Cambridge, 1990), 233–4; P. Mosley, 'When is a Policy Instrument Not an Instrument? Fiscal Marksmanship in Britain, 1951–84', *J. Public Policy*, 5 (1985), 69–85; R. Middleton, 'The Size and Scope of the Public Sector', in S. J. D. Green and R. C. Whiting (eds.), *The Boundaries of the State in Modern Britain* (Cambridge, 1996), 89–145.

EXTERNAL FINANCIAL POLICY: ROBOT, 1951–1952

The Conservatives were left in no doubt that they had taken office in October 1951 in the midst of a balance-of-payments crisis. A note by Bridges for the new Chancellor forecast that, on current trends, the deficit on current account would be £472 million in 1951 and £540 million in 1952, as against gold and dollar reserves (to serve the whole sterling area) which had peaked at £1,381 million in June 1951. Britain was also in deficit with the other members of the EPU and was likely to have to meet the whole of any further deficit from March 1952 in gold and dollars. Bridges advised Butler that the position was worse than in 1949, and recommended that restoration of confidence in sterling and the British economy should be 'the first and most important object of Government policy'. Butler presented the note to the Cabinet, and Churchill was so impressed that he sent a copy to Attlee, in order that he might know the government's starting point.[96] It was in this context that Butler first raised Bank rate and imposed a cut of £360 million in imports, and the Cabinet agreed that all departments must reduce their expenditure, even though this would mean recasting the rearmament programme.

Despite these measures, the outlook had worsened by February 1952. By then it had transpired that earlier expectations of economic and defence aid from the Americans by the end of June 1952 would be disappointed to a total of $225 million, and accordingly the latest forecast of the date by which the reserves would fall to $1,400 million (£500 million) had to be adjusted from end of June to the end of April. It was believed in the Bank and the Treasury that with reserves at that level—the same as at the time of devaluation in September 1949—the $2.80 exchange rate could not be defended against a crisis of confidence, and that depreciation in unfavourable circumstances would mean the dissolution of the sterling area and the end of sterling as an international currency. Commonwealth finance ministers had agreed in January to co-operate in stopping the dollar drain, but Treasury officials doubted whether other sterling countries would be able or, in the case of non-Commonwealth members, willing to do all that was required of them. It seemed that the only factor that could make a substantial change to the situation would be an inflow of capital resulting from a restoration of confidence in sterling—and that would require a tightening of monetary policy; economies in public expenditure, such as housing or rearmament, where there was a high import content; and a tough budget.[97]

This was the context in which, on 13 February, the Governor of the Bank of England submitted a radical plan which incorporated ideas developed in the

---

[96] 'The Economic Position', 25 Oct. 1951, T273/315; Cabinet conclusions, 30 Oct. 1951, CAB128/23.
[97] 'Emergency Action', unsigned paper, 8 Feb. 1952, T236/3245. A. Cairncross, *Years of Recovery: British Economic Policy, 1945–51* (1985), 241 n., suggests that the author of the paper was Rowan, but Fforde, *Bank of England*, 429, states that it was drafted by Clarke, in consultation with George Bolton, of the Bank of England.

Bank and by Clarke in overseas finance for sterling convertibility. The Bank was particularly concerned by the use of inconvertible (or 'cheap') sterling, which could be bought and sold outside Britain at rates below $2.80, and which was being used on a large scale by Britain's competitors to pay for raw materials and services abroad, thereby undercutting British firms which had to buy and sell sterling at the official rate. The main features of the Bank's plan, in the form in which it reached the Cabinet, were: (i) a single, floating rate of exchange (thereby eliminating cheap sterling); (ii) compulsory funding of not less than 80 per cent of the sterling balances held by members of the sterling area, and 90 per cent of those held by non-members, except for American and Canadian accounts which were already convertible into dollars; (iii) full convertibility into gold, dollars, or other currencies of the remaining balances and any new sterling earned by non-residents. It was argued that the exchange rate, rather than the reserves, would take the strain of the balance-of-payments deficit. The intention was to use the Exchange Equalisation Account to maintain sterling within 15 per cent of $2.80—that is, within a range of $2.40–$3.20, but this intention would be revealed only to Commonwealth governments and their central banks. It was clearly expected that sterling would tend to depreciate, for it was argued that the plan would bring the economy into balance, by making imports dearer and exports cheaper. It was also argued that the funding of the sterling balances would restore confidence in sterling and make it easier to strengthen the reserves by borrowing.[98]

The plan was code-named 'Robot', presumably to suggest an automatic regulator, but the name came to be associated with the names of its principal advocates: ROwan, the Second Secretary in charge of overseas finance, George Bolton, an executive director of the Bank of England, and OTto Clarke.[99] Within the Treasury, Robot was accepted by Butler, but opposed by Salter, the Minister of State for Economic Affairs, who was advised by Plowden and Hall (the latter still attached to the Cabinet Office). Within the Cabinet, Lyttelton was a consistent supporter of the plan, and most ministers were at first inclined to go along with it, not least for the political reason that it relied upon the price mechanism to restore equilibrium to the economy, rather than on direct controls. However, Cherwell, the Paymaster-General, who was advised by Donald MacDougall and Hall, was a formidable opponent. The controversy was conducted with much bitterness, reflecting, perhaps, the temperamental personalities of Rowan and Clarke, but also the challenge that was being made by

[98] Cabinet conclusions of 28 and 29 Feb. 1952, T236/3242 (not recorded in main CAB23 series). For the Governor's paper see Fforde, *Bank of England*, 431–4.

[99] What follows draws upon the accounts by Lord Birkenhead, *The Prof in Two Worlds* (1961), 283–90; Butler, *Art of the Possible*, 158–60; Cairncross, *Years of Recovery*, ch. 9; Edmund Dell, *The Chancellors* (1996), 166–81; Fforde, *Bank of England*, 417–51; D. MacDougall, *Don and Mandarin: Memoirs of an Economist* (1987), 85–105; E. Plowden, *An Industrialist in the Treasury: The Post-War Years* (1989), 143–58, and Salter, *Slave of the Lamp*, ch. 15, as well as Hall's *Diaries, 1947–1953*, and overseas finance files (T236).

economists to the primacy of Treasury and Bank officials in giving advice on monetary policy.

Both Bolton and Clarke had argued previously against a floating rate, Bolton as recently as January 1952. Clarke had claimed in March 1951 that it would be bad for traders and planners, involve 'a complete destruction of the IMF', and would be incompatible with exchange control. In 1952, however, he took the view that the fall in the reserves had created a situation in which sterling could no longer be maintained as an internationally acceptable currency on an inconvertible basis, and that Robot was the only way in which convertibility could be achieved and sterling preserved. Surprisingly, given his earlier views, he hoped that, despite breaching IMF rules, Britain would be able to draw on the Fund once 'the international exchange situation had settled down', and envisaged no significant change in exchange control regulations. There would have to be a 'substantial' rise in short-term interest rates, both for domestic 'disinflation' and to discourage people overseas from borrowing short-term in London, but Clarke thought that these measures would be necessary anyway.[100]

Within the Treasury the balance of advice to the Chancellor on 19 February seems to have been that the Governor's version of the plan, which envisaged action after the budget, required further study. However, Butler dined that evening with Churchill, Cobbold, and the Leader of the House, Harry Crookshank, and the Prime Minister insisted that it would be wrong to introduce a budget that gave no hint of the plan: if radical measures were to be adopted, they should be announced on budget day. As it had already been announced that the budget would be brought forward from early April to early March (to introduce measures to deal with the crisis), and as Commonwealth countries would have to be informed in advance, a decision on Robot was required in about ten days—an impossibly short time for proper study of the plan's far-reaching and complex implications. As these implications included an end to British participation in the EPU, with possibly damaging effects on relations with western European countries and the United States, ministers decided that Eden, the Foreign Secretary, who was then at a conference in Lisbon, must be consulted.

It was decided to delay the budget for a week, and two senior officials, one from the Treasury (Sir Herbert Brittain) and one from the Foreign Office, were sent to Lisbon to explain the plan to Eden. Bridges, who saw Robot as a 'chance of remaining in control of the position', wrote to Plowden, who was also at the conference, to express the hope that he would feel the same and would help the officials 'to expound the matter to the Foreign Secretary'.[101] However, Bridges also allowed Hall, whom he knew to be unhappy at the haste with which the matter was being decided, to consult Professor Robbins, who agreed with Hall that Robot should not be adopted until other measures, especially raising Bank

---

[100] Fforde, op. cit., 425–6; Cairncross, op. cit., 237; 'Plan for "Overseas Sterling"', by Clarke, 19 Feb. 1952, T236/3245.   [101] Bridges to Plowden, 22 Feb. 1952, T236/3240.

rate, had been tried first. Hall wrote to Plowden, outlining the objections to Robot, and Plowden, finding himself, as usual, in agreement with Hall, persuaded Eden that Robot should be very much a last resort, and that more time should be spent in examining alternatives. According to Hall, Bridges was very cross with Plowden for 'intriguing' with the Foreign Secretary against the Chancellor.[102]

The economic arguments against Robot were, briefly, that a floating exchange rate would tend to fall sharply initially, and the reserves might be used up as rapidly in defending a rate of $2.40 as $2.80. A fall in the exchange rate would raise the price of imports, possibly precipitating a wage–price spiral. At all events, given that there was no slack in the economy with which to expand exports, the net effect of a rise in import prices would be to widen the trade gap. Indeed, depending upon the exchange rate, Robot might give other countries an incentive to convert sterling into dollars rather than to buy imports from Britain. There was a danger of unemployment if Britain could not export enough to pay for raw materials for its industry, or if the economy were to be deflated to create the slack in the economy necessary to expand exports.

Doubts certainly existed within the Treasury about the wisdom of Robot. Burke Trend, an Under-Secretary on the home finance side, observed that higher Bank rate would have indiscriminate effects and, if unemployed labour were not quickly absorbed by export industries, 'abstract economics' would be 'at odds with politics'.[103] Dennis Rickett, who was in Washington at the time as Economic Minister in charge of the Treasury and Supply Delegation, thought that convertibility along the lines of Robot would lead countries outside the sterling area to discriminate against sterling. E. G. Coppleston, who, like Clarke, was an Under-Secretary on the overseas finance side, thought the probable result of Robot would be the utter disruption of Britain's trade, the disintegration of the sterling area and Commonwealth, and the economic collapse of Europe.[104]

In presenting Robot to the Cabinet, Butler admitted that the plan involved serious risks, including 'some measure' of unemployment and an end to stability of prices and wages, as well as disruption of the EPU and the possible defection of one or two members of the sterling area. Ministers were understandably reluctant to take such risks before it was clear that other measures had failed, and decided the time had not yet come to make sterling convertible. Meanwhile the Chancellor would have to act through domestic monetary policy and fiscal policy, and by persuading his colleagues to make further cuts in defence production and in imports.[105]

[102] Hall to Plowden, 22 Feb., and Plowden to Chancellor, 25 Feb. 1952, T236/3240; 'Note for the Record', by Hall, 4 Mar. 1952, T236/3245; Hall, *Diaries, 1947–1953*, 207.
[103] Trend to Eady, 15 Feb. 1952, T171/409.
[104] Conversation with Rickett; Dell, *Chancellors*, 168.
[105] Cabinet conclusions, 28 and 29 Feb. 1952, T236/3242.

The Cabinet's decision on 29 February was not an end of the matter. Within the Treasury Clarke continued to urge the case for Robot. A group of ministers considered the plan again on 30 June, after the Governor of the Bank had predicted a renewed sterling crisis in August unless Robot were adopted. However, Butler himself was becoming doubtful about Robot's merits, and the matter was not put to Cabinet. The threatened crisis did not develop; the terms of trade improved, and the reserves rose to £1,850 million by the end of 1952, £469 million above their 1951 peak. In fairness to Rowan and Clarke, such a favourable outcome must have seemed unlikely in February, or even later. A more telling criticism of Treasury officials' advice is that the alarmist manner in which it was given reversed the usual relationship between civil servant and ministers, whereby Cherwell in particular had to temper the enthusiasm of Rowan and Clarke for a radical change in policy. Even the normally cautious Bridges seems to have lost his sense of what was politically possible and to have allowed his inexperienced Chancellor to be exposed to a damaging defeat in Cabinet over an inadequately prepared scheme.

EXTERNAL FINANCIAL POLICY: APPROACHES TO CONVERTIBILITY, 1952–1958

External policy in the 1950s was marked by persistent efforts by the Bank to move towards convertibility, but the Treasury was able to exercise restraint until it was convinced that conditions were right. The Bank was primarily concerned with technical aspects of money markets, while stressing the need for the necessary restraint in internal economic policy to maintain balance-of-payments equilibrium. The Treasury agreed with the need for sound internal economic policy, but preferred to wait for the results of that policy, and meanwhile placed more faith than the Bank in the efficacy of exchange controls.[106] However, considerations of the prestige of sterling as an international currency, itself an element in maintaining Britain's role in world affairs, weighed with the Treasury as well as with the Bank, and neither a deliberate devaluation nor a large-scale downward float in the exchange rate was considered as an alternative to sound domestic monetary and fiscal policies.

In his memoirs, Butler expressed the belief that the absence of a floating exchange rate robbed chancellors of an external regulator of the balance of payments, and thereby threw a greater strain on the internal regulators, principally Bank rate, leading to 'stop–go'.[107] However, the shelving of Robot did not in

---

[106] For example, the Treasury overruled the Bank in July 1957 by insisting on the closure of the free dollar market which had hitherto been tolerated in Hong Kong—see Catherine Schenk, 'Closing the Hong Kong Gap: The Hong Kong Free Dollar Market in the 1950s', *Econ. Hist. Rev.*, 2nd ser., 47 (1994), 335–53.   [107] Butler, *Art of the Possible*, 158–9.

itself remove the possibility of convertibility with a floating exchange rate at a later date. Robot was replaced by the Collective Approach, which was drafted by an interdepartmental working party, including Hall and MacDougall (although neither of them liked the Collective Approach very much). Hall and Plowden doubted whether ministers would agree to the severe internal measures stated to be necessary to achieve convertibility. Bridges, on the other hand, 'speaking as a layman', thought that a more stringent internal economic policy was necessary anyway to escape from the vicious circle of excessive public expenditure, leading to (a) 'crushing taxation', which in turn had an adverse effect on savings, and (b) shortages, which in turn made the maintenance of direct controls necessary, to the detriment of individual initiative.[108]

The plan was put, without any firm British commitment, to a meeting of Commonwealth officials in September 1952, and revised subsequently in the light of their comments. Then a meeting of Commonwealth prime ministers in December agreed to conversations between Britain and the United States on the basis of the Collective Approach, the conversations being conducted by Butler in Washington in March 1953. As with Robot, convertibility would be limited to non-residents, and the pound would be allowed to float. The Collective Approach differed from Robot in not being intended as a emergency action in response to balance-of-payments difficulties; the goal now was freer international trade and payments. Sterling balances were no longer to be blocked, but the United States was to be asked to lend about 2,000 million dollars to the IMF to enable the latter to provide a stabilization fund to supplement the sterling area's reserves and drawing rights. The United States was also to be asked to pursue 'good creditor' policies, including lending abroad and removing restrictions on imports, while tolerating continued quantitative controls on British imports of American goods for about a year after convertibility, with only the promise of negotiations on new trade rules thereafter. Butler was warned in Washington that there was no immediate prospect of Congress voting funds to support sterling. Moreover, when members of EPU were consulted by Rowan in the spring of 1953, it became plain that they had no wish to participate; not all of them were ready for convertibility, and they did not wish the EPU to be divided between countries with convertible exchange rates and those without. Moreover there was a risk that a European country that tied its exchange rate to a floating pound could find its internal financial stability threatened if sterling depreciated.[109]

The Collective Approach remained the agreed policy of the Commonwealth, but was overtaken by initiatives by the Bank of England. The Bank

[108] 'The Collective Approach and All That', by Bridges, 24 Oct. 1952, T273/377.
[109] For detailed accounts of the moves leading to convertibility between 1953 and 1958 see Fforde, *Bank of England*, 475–605; J. J. Kaplan and G. Schleiminger, *The European Payments Union: Financial Diplomacy in the 1950s* (Oxford, 1989), chs. 10–12 and 17; and Stephen Proctor, 'Towards Convertibility: The Sterling Policy of the Conservative Governments, 1951–1958', Ph.D. (Bristol, 1990).

progressively brought all non-dollar, non-resident sterling into a single transfer-able account area. Balances on transferable accounts could be used for any purpose, capital or current, within the non-dollar area, but control on payments to the dollar area remained. By March 1954 there was a regular market abroad with a single rate for transferable sterling. Within the Treasury, this simplification of exchange control was supported by Rowan and Bridges, although opposed by Hall and Strath, who were concerned about easing control when the outlook for the balance of payments was uncertain. Then, in January 1955, when sterling began to weaken and the gap between the transferable rate and the official rate of $2.80 tended to widen, the Bank intervened to keep the transferable rate about $2.72. The Governor sought the Chancellor's authority: (a) to bring the two rates close together, to reduce the scope for dealings in cheap sterling, and (b) to apply to the IMF for permission to widen the dealing spread for the official rate to $2.70–$2.90, instead of the $2.78–$2.82 normally allowed. Rowan thought that the Governor's proposals amounted in practice to the convertibility of sterling on external account, and, with Hall's support, advised that, unless firm internal action were taken to curb inflation and restore confidence in sterling, they would merely lead to a fall in the exchange rate. A balance-of-payments deficit on current account was forecast, and the prospect of a general election in 1955 was a source of uncertainty. By mid-February there was a sterling crisis. Although acknowledging that 'the Bank are the experts' in money markets, Bridges advised Butler against the wider margins, and the Treasury agreed to intervention in the transferable market, without changing the official fixed rate, only as a means of curbing speculation and protecting the reserves.[110]

At this stage, both the Bank and the Treasury still believed that convertibility would have to be introduced with a flexible rate of exchange. Nevertheless, from 24 February sterling was *de facto* convertible for non-residents at only a small discount on the official fixed rate. A weakening of the balance of payments in 1955 fed rumours that sterling would be floated (downwards), or that the spread in the rate would be widened, and pressure on the reserves in July and again in September, forced the Chancellor on both occasions to deny any intention to do either. Hall warned in July that convertibility with a fixed exchange rate would be like going back to the gold standard in 1925, in that in present circumstances deflation would be required to maintain the exchange rate. Rowan, however, thought that, given the choice between full employment and maintaining the exchange rate, public opinion would insist on full employment. Nevertheless, he added, the discipline of maintaining a spread of $2.70–$2.90 'could be a good thing to get governments to take unpopular measures'.[111]

---

[110] 'Exchange Policy', memoranda by Rowan and Hall, 10 Feb., and Bridges to Butler, 19 Feb. 1955, T273/379.
[111] 'Exchange Rate Policy', memoranda by Hall, 26 July, and Rowan, 27 July 1955, T273/379.

In August 1955, and again in April 1956, Treasury officials rejected pressure from the Bank to unite the official and transferable rates, mainly on the grounds that it would be impossible to pass off unification as anything other than convertibility, which would lead to pressure on Britain to abandon discrimination against the dollar at a time when only about half of imports from North America were free of quantitative restrictions.[112] The possibility of convertibility with a floating rate or a wider spread remained on the agenda, notably at the time of Suez, when a temporary adoption of a flexible rate was seen as less damaging to sterling's reputation as an international currency than a devaluation would be, and again in August 1957, when a devaluation of the franc led speculators to expect sterling to be allowed to depreciate against the dollar and the mark.

On the latter occasion, however, in response to a request from the Prime Minister, Macmillan, for contingency plans, the Treasury and the Bank advised that the $2.80 rate should be defended if at all possible, partly because devaluing the currency in which the sterling area held its reserves would risk breaking up the sterling area, which would be an 'appalling' prospect, both economically and politically. Moreover, flexible rates with weak reserves would encourage speculation. In contrast to 1952, it was no longer believed by the Bank or the Treasury that a flexible rate would automatically correct an imbalance between imports and exports. In the light of lack of success with wages policy (see below), it was now argued that, when a flexible rate fell and import prices rose, domestic prices and wages would also rise, whereas when a flexible rate rose again and import prices fell, wages and domestic prices would remain at the higher level. A flexible exchange rate would therefore remove the need for deflationary measures only if it were a permanently sinking rate.[113]

In 1958 there was a substantial surplus on the balance of payments on current account and, in contrast to 1952, there was no need to consider convertibility in the context of 'emergency action'. Once more Macmillan raised the possibility of a floating rate, but Rowan and the Bank restated the case against. The Commonwealth Trade and Economic Conference in Montreal in September reaffirmed the objective of making sterling fully convertible as soon as the necessary conditions had been achieved. Rowan, Hall, and the Bank were all of the view that, with inflation in Britain apparently under control, the world dollar shortage at an end, and the gold and dollar reserves rising, the time was ripe. Despite the suspension of negotiations over the British proposal for a European free trade area in November, the French government proved to be co-operative about a general move to convertibility, which was made on 29 December. Britain was thereby committed to maintain a rate of $2.80 with a 1 per cent margin either side.[114]

[112] 'Exchange Policy', by Rickett, 19 Apr. 1956, T236/3940.
[113] 'Economic Situation: Sterling', note by the Treasury, 16 Sept. 1957, PREM11/1824.
[114] Hall, *Diaries, 1954–1961*, 170; Fforde, *Bank of England*, 585–602.

DOMESTIC MONETARY POLICY, 1951–1957

There were disagreements between the Bank, the Economic Section, and the Treasury about how monetary policy worked in the 1950s. Down to 1955 the Bank seems to have thought about monetary measures mainly in non-quantitative terms of effects on money markets and expectations, whereas the Economic Section thought mainly in terms of effects on investment and aggregate demand. Treasury officials, while accepting that interest rates and expectations were important, considered control of bank advances to be the most effective way of restricting investment. When monetary measures did not have their hoped-for impact in 1955, the Treasury called for a reappraisal, which led, via an unpublished joint Bank/Treasury report on 'Monetary Organisation', completed in June 1956, to the Radcliffe Report of July 1959.[115]

Notwithstanding their differences, Bank and Treasury officials were able to agree on the connection between monetary policy and the finance of government expenditure. Treasury bills were the clearing banks' most important liquid asset, as they had been since the First World War. When government expenditure had to be financed through the issue of Treasury bills, the Bank would, if necessary, provide the banks with enough cash to enable them to take up Treasury bills without contracting their other loans or changing the proportion that they normally maintained between cash and total deposits. When the government's contractors were paid, they would deposit the money with the banks. Government expenditure financed through the issue of Treasury bills thus increased the supply of money in circulation almost as much as if the expenditure had been financed directly by the Bank through Ways and Means advances, except that in the latter case the expenditure would have led to an increase in the banks' holdings of cash—in the form of deposits at the Bank of England—rather than of Treasury bills. Consequently, the Bank would urge restraint in public expenditure at times when tax receipts and long-term borrowing were insufficient to meet the government's needs.[116] On the other hand, the Treasury was inclined to believe that exhortation could dissuade the banks from increasing advances to the public, even when the banks had plenty of money to lend.

In October 1951 both the Bank and the Treasury had proposals prepared for the new Chancellor for monetary and other measures to deal with the balance-of-payments crisis. The Conservatives were rightly expected to be more

---

[115] 'Monetary Organisation', by Sir Edmund Compton and Hall (Treasury) and Leslie O'Brien and Maurice Allen (Bank), 25 June 1956, T230/472. What follows is based mainly on papers on the development of monetary policy in T230/384 and 385, and the Bank of England's Chief Cashier policy files C40/688/1696/4, C40/689/1697/1, and C40/692/1698/1; 'Monetary Policy and the Control of Economic Conditions', Treasury Memorandum No. 6, Aug. 1957, (Radcliffe) Committee on the Working of the Monetary System, *Memoranda of Evidence*, vol. i (1960).

[116] 'Monetary Organisation', 25 June 1956, T230/472.

sympathetic than Labour had been to the use of Bank rate. Butler announced an increase in Bank rate from 2 per cent to 2½ per cent, on 7 November, along with import cuts, a reduction in the investment programme, and a search for economies in government expenditure. The clearing bankers agreed with the Governor to increase lending rates and to make credit harder to obtain; the Capital Issues Committee was instructed to give priority to projects that were essential to rearmament or helpful to the current balance of payments; and a letter from the Chancellor asked the banks to limit finance for hire purchase, and not to make advances for capital expenditure, as well as repeating earlier injunctions against making advances for speculative purposes.

Bank rate was raised again, to 4 per cent, on 11 March 1952, along with Butler's first budget, and gave an appearance of toughness which the budget itself lacked. Although drastic use was made of direct controls to reduce imports and investment, it was the use of Bank rate that attracted most comment, and the swing in the balance of payments back into surplus on current account, and the slowing down in the rise of the retail price index that followed, encouraged both the Bank and the Treasury to believe that monetary policy was an effective deflationary instrument. Members of the Economic Section were more sceptical, arguing that fixed investment had risen in 1952 by the same amount as in the previous year, and that there was no close, direct relationship between bank advances and the fall in stocks that had occurred, while the slowing down in the rise of the retail index had been caused by a fall in import prices. Treasury officials agreed with the Economic Section that the circumstances of 1952 were so abnormal that events then were of little value as a guide to future policy, but continued to believe that a tight monetary policy could be effective. Hall was inclined to agree with them, but commented that 'we don't really know a great deal about how Bank rate changes work'.[117]

The years 1953 and 1954 provided little practical experience of how monetary policy could be made to work. Reductions in Bank rate occurred in 1953 and 1954, at the Bank's initiative, in response to changes in money market conditions, but the banks were told that the Chancellor's requests about restricting advances still applied. In 1955 the Third Secretary in home finance, Sir Edmund Compton, could still describe the operation of monetary policy in the post-war economy as 'experimental'.[118] Nevertheless, monetary measures were the main policy instrument used to restrain the boom in 1955, given the reduction in direct controls since 1952, and given the decision to use the budget in 1955 to reduce direct taxation rather than to curb demand (see next section).

The monetary authorities responded to increased pressure on sterling in February 1955 by raising Bank rate from 3½ per cent to 4½ per cent, only a month after it had been increased from 3 per cent to 3½ per cent, and restrictions on

[117] Cairncross and Watts, *Economic Section*, 220.
[118] 'Monetary Policy', 24 Oct. 1955, T230/384.

hire-purchase sales were reintroduced. These measures were intended to tighten credit conditions and improve the balance of payments, and, for a time, the loss of reserves was checked. The Bank of England had warned the Treasury in January that control of credit through the banks would not be as severe as formal control by the Capital Issues Committee on the issue of shares. Nevertheless, Butler felt able in his budget speech on 19 April to claim that monetary policy was curbing domestic demand sufficiently to leave a margin of production available for exports, and thereby to correct the balance of payments on current account.[119]

It was realized in the Treasury that it would take time for credit control to show results but, from informal contacts which each of them had with clearing bank chairmen, Hall and Rowan had reason to doubt claims by the Governor, Cobbold, that he was being tough with the banks. By July the inflationary boom seemed as strong as ever and the balance of payments was still weakening. Treasury officials were so concerned about the rapid rise in bank advances in the first half of 1955 that, most unusually, the Bank of England agreed to Gilbert, Brittain, and Hall meeting representatives of the clearing banks, in the presence of senior Bank officials, on 13 July. It transpired that the Bank had relied upon the increase in Bank rate to act as a 'storm signal', and had given the banks no specific instructions other than asking them to restrict advances for hire-purchase transactions.[120]

The clearing banks were prepared to reduce their lending, provided that the government made a public request for them to do so. Accordingly, the Chancellor made a statement on 25 July asking for a reduction in advances, using the words 'positive and significant' suggested by Cobbold, rather than the figure of 10 per cent by the end of the year proposed by Treasury officials. Credit restriction was reinforced by tightening of hire-purchase restrictions, and was to be balanced by efforts by government to reduce its own expenditure, especially overseas, and by appeals to local authorities and nationalized industries to postpone capital expenditure.[121] Meanwhile Butler had accepted Cobbold's advice that an increase in Bank rate (which the Economic Secretary of the Treasury, Edward Boyle, had suggested) would give the impression of a crisis measure, especially to overseas opinion, at a time when the exchange rate was under pressure.[122]

The Treasury also had difficulty in Cabinet, where it was argued on 12 July that measures to correct the balance of payments should concentrate on restricting consumption, on the grounds that restrictions on investment, either by the private sector or by nationalized industries, were bound to harm export

[119] Governor's memorandum of conversation with Edmund Compton (Treasury), 25 Jan. 1955, Bank of England papers, C40/688/1696/4; 540 HC Deb., 5s, 1954–5, col. 55.

[120] Note of meeting held in the Bank, 13 July 1955, Bank of England papers, G1/73/1181/2.

[121] A. Cairncross, 'Prelude to Radcliffe: Monetary Policy in the United Kingdom, 1948–57', *Riv. Storia Econ.*, 2nd ser., 4 (1987), 16.

[122] 'Bank Rate Changes', by Margaret Gowing, 15 Aug. 1957, T230/385.

industries and to delay efforts to make the economy more competitive. With Hall and Strath's backing, Bridges protested to Butler that the whole point of the credit policy which had been adopted was to moderate the tempo of industrial expansion. Not all investment projects were equally valuable at a given point of time, and the rapid increase in investment since 1954 made it necessary to induce a more cautious attitude towards accumulation of stocks and marginal projects for fixed investment.[123]

The banks did reduce their advances to the private sector after 25 July, but demand from local authorities and nationalized industries for bank advances continued to rise until the autumn. Continued public sector borrowing raised the capacity of the banks to lend. In the second half of 1955 over £500 million of Treasury bills were issued, partly to cover the seasonal Exchequer deficit (before the normal inflow of tax receipts in the last quarter of the financial year), but also to finance borrowing by the nationalized industries. The alternative of selling long-term stock was not pursued, owing to weakness in the gilt-edged market, and the Bank's advice that people would not buy if they thought that the prices of gilt-edged securities were going to fall further. There was continued evidence of inflationary conditions, with an adverse trade balance and with wages rising in a tight labour market.

Butler had to resort to an autumn budget and, belatedly, cuts were made in public investment programmes. At a meeting of the Budget Committee on 15 December Bridges said that monetary measures were 'on trial', and the only alternatives (other than tighter fiscal policy) would be 'unpalatable measures' such as direct controls on building and imports.[124] Also in December the Economic Section began to think in terms of raising the long-term rate of interest to influence fixed investment. However, Compton pointed out that, for a year at least, local authorities and nationalized industries must raise capital to meet maturing commitments, whatever the rate of interest, and, to avoid raising the cost to the Exchequer of borrowing for public investment, action on long-term interest rates was delayed until 1957.[125] In February 1956 Bank rate was raised to 5½ per cent and in the course of that year the economy responded to a series of deflationary measures, including cuts in subsidies and public expenditure programmes. Early in 1957 heavy demand by the banking system for Treasury bills, at a time when the supply was decreasing, led to a fall of about half a per cent in short-term rates in the money market, and Bank rate was reduced to 5 per cent in February, despite Rowan and Hall's fears that this move would suggest that the monetary authorities thought that the situation was fully under control, when it was not.

---

[123] Cabinet conclusions, 12 July 1955, CAB128/29; note of meeting in Chancellor's room, 12 July, T172/2097, and 'Monetary Policy and Investment', 14 July 1955, T273/401.
[124] T171/469.
[125] 'Long-term Rate of Interest', memoranda by F. J. Atkinson, 16 Dec., and Compton, 19 Dec. 1955, with comments by Hall, T230/384.

Policy from July 1955 depended upon the goodwill of the banks, because refusing advances for credit-worthy purposes damaged their relations with their customers. The banks agreed as a short-term measure not to compete among themselves by offering overdrafts to would-be borrowers who had been refused by other banks, but the banks disliked this self-denying ordinance, and it was with reluctance that it was renewed for three-month periods at a time in April and July 1957. In the light of experience, the key to controlling bank lending was seen by both the Treasury and the Bank to be a reduction in the volume of Treasury bills in the banking system. This reduction could be achieved by reducing the government's borrowing requirement, by cutting public expenditure, including investment by nationalized industries, or by raising taxation, and the Bank tended to urge greater restraint in public expenditure than the Treasury thought possible. The alternative was to fund debt by selling gilt-edged securities, but inflationary pressures weakened demand for securities at a given interest rate, on account of fears about the fall in the value of money. The Treasury and the Bank agreed that the key to creating a strong gilt-edged market was to create expectations that inflation would be controlled. Thus monetary policy relied upon sound fiscal policy and restraint in public expenditure, and also on restraint in demands for wage increases.

TABLE 9.3. *Budget Balance for Financial Years, 1951/2–1959/60 (£m.)*

	Surplus (+) or deficit (−) above the line[a]		Deficit below the line[b]	Overall surplus or deficit
	Forecast	Out-turn	Out-turn	Out-turn
1951/2	+39	+380	−529	−149
1952/3	+510	+88	−524	−436
1953/4	+109	+94	−391	−297
1954/5	+10	+433	−501	−68
1955/6	+148	+397	−538	−141
1956/7	+460	+290	−621	−331
1957/8	+462	+423	−635	−212
1958/9	+364	+377	−559	−182
1959/60	+102	+386	−700	−314

[a] The conventional budget balance accounting for revenue into and expenditure out of the Consolidated Fund.
[b] Payments for which Parliament had authorized the Treasury to borrow, such as loans to local authorities or capital expenditure by nationalized industries.

Sources: Budget speeches and (Radcliffe) Committee on the Working of the Monetary System, *Principal Memoranda of Evidence*, i. 78.

FISCAL POLICY, 1951–1957

As a comparison of Table 9.3 with Table 8.2 shows, fiscal policy placed a greater burden on monetary policy in the 1950s than had been the case between 1947 and 1950. As Chancellor, Cripps had aimed at an overall surplus, whereby the surplus above the line more than balanced the deficit below the line. The overall deficits of the 1950s had to be financed by selling gilt-edged securities or by increasing the Treasury bill issue, and, as noted above, an increase in the floating debt could frustrate a restrictive monetary policy, a factor that was to have some influence on fiscal policy in the light of experience in 1955. Economists writing about fiscal policy have been primarily concerned with its contribution to demand management, and the responsiveness of ministers and officials to advice from the Economic Section.[126] However, fiscal policy was not decided solely according to the Economic Section's estimates of what was required to control the level of aggregate demand. Other aims included: effective control of public expenditure; maintenance of confidence in sterling; and reductions in direct taxation to provide incentives for industry to increase output.

The budget continued to have its traditional, constitutional function of an account rendered to Parliament of annual expenditure related to annual votes of taxation, on a strict cash basis of payments into and out of the Exchequer. Gaitskell had set up a working party under Hall to consider the case for preparing the budget accounts according to the macroeconomic significance of all government transactions, and not simply cash flows into and out of the Exchequer. However, when Hall's working party reported in 1952 in favour of a new, economic classification in line with national income statistics, Treasury officials on the Budget Committee agreed to its use only for internal purposes, and opposed publication both then and in subsequent years until the Exchequer accounts were reformed in the 1960s. As Gilbert remarked in 1952, the existing form of the budget 'was honest in that it dealt entirely with cash and all the items were ultimately audited', whereas the economic classification included items, such as estimates of the nation's savings and investment, that could never be finally ascertained. The Treasury's opposition to publication was confirmed when the economic classification forecast a deficit on current receipts less current expenditure for 1954/5, although the conventional budget showed a surplus above the line.[127]

The Treasury was reluctant to see the link between central government expenditure and taxation broken, for experience suggested that ministers would spend borrowed money with a lighter heart than they would if taxes had to be raised immediately for a given purpose. For example, in an echo of the Asquith doctrine of 1906, the Treasury resisted a suggestion in 1954 that the cost of major public offices or prisons should be met by borrowing, instead of from revenue. A memorandum drafted for a Cabinet Committee on Civil Expenditure argued that control of expenditure would be weakened thereby, since the annual loan

---

[126] The best examples of this approach are Cairncross and Watts, *Economic Section*, ch. 16, and Dow, *Management of the British Economy*, chs. 7, 15, and 16.

[127] Budget Committee minutes, 28 May 1952, T171/431; 'The Form of Budget Accounts', BC(54)26, T171/437; N. Rollings, 'The Control of Inflation in the Managed Economy: Britain, 1945–53', Ph.D. (Bristol, 1990), 189–92.

charges would be so much smaller than the capital sum, and consequently the Treasury would be faced with the argument in any particular case that it was 'only a little one'. Moreover, the Treasury claimed, if capital expenditure were to be taken below the line, revenue from capital, such as death duties, ought also to be taken below the line. Yet financial opinion, including foreign holders of sterling, had got used to 'the sleeping dogs' of capital items being charged or credited above the line, and, in the interests of confidence in public finance, radical disturbances in the traditional basis of the budget should be avoided.[128]

On the other hand, the 1954 Finance Act abolished the permanent annual charge to redeem the National Debt. By that date even so conservative an official as Sir Herbert Brittain could recognize that any kind of fixed sinking fund was incompatible with the idea that the size of the budget surplus or deficit should be determined by broad economic considerations. Moreover, the change also reflected the expectation that in future the National Debt would no longer represent only unproductive expenditure related to war, and that Exchequer commitments to finance capital development programmes of the nationalized industries and other public bodies would produce a money return which would enable the new debts to be paid off—a principle that Sir Richard Hopkins would have recognized.[129]

The unreformed nature of the budget accounts meant that the overall deficit had no direct relevance to demand management as it was conceived by Keynesian economists. Moreover, the items included in outgoings below the line varied over the decade. Up to October 1955 most local authority loan expenditure (mainly for housing) was financed by obtaining funds from the Public Works Loan Board, which in turn was financed from loans from the Exchequer, but thereafter only local authorities that could show that they were unable to borrow in the market had access to the Board, as a last resort. On the other hand, the 1956 Finance Act legislated for the capital requirements of all the nationalized industries to be financed out of the Exchequer (as had always been the case with the National Coal Board), in place of issues of guaranteed stock outside the budget. The only economic significance of the overall deficit, apart from its effects on financial confidence, was the effect on the size of the floating debt, and hence on monetary policy. On becoming Chancellor, Macmillan found that Treasury officials rejected any fixed formula regarding the overall budget balance; on the other hand, they believed that total investment, including both private and public, should be financed by 'savings', whether in the form of profits that were reinvested, 'genuine' private savings, or revenue surplus. Genuine private savings were broadly identified with the sale of gilt-edged securities.[130]

[128] 'Borrowing for Capital Expenditure', 1 July 1954, CAB134/785.
[129] H. Brittain, *The British Budgetary System* (1959), 203.
[130] Macmillan, *Riding the Storm*, 27.

Insofar as the budget was used as an instrument for demand management, attention for most of the period focused on the balance between income and expenditure above the line, the expenditure being on items for which Parliament had not specifically authorized borrowing. Down to 1952, national income forecasts had been able to assume that the growth in output was restricted by supply factors, such as labour, and in these circumstances the function of the budget was the same as it had been since 1941, to reduce or close the inflationary gap of excess demand, implying a surplus above the line. In 1952 a margin of spare capacity appeared, and with it the possibility that the growth in output, and employment, could be influenced by reducing government revenue relative to expenditure, or increasing expenditure relative to revenue.[131] Indeed, in 1953 and 1954 the Budget Committee debated whether there should be a deficit above the line, and Hall complained in 1954 that Butler, Bridges, Gilbert, Rowan, and Brittain had reverted to pre-war principles, and that he had difficulty in explaining to them that demand management might require a deficit. However, Hall agreed with them that a deficit would have an adverse effect on confidence in sterling, at a time when the balance of payments was far from robust.[132]

The need to maintain confidence in sterling also restricted what was possible with regard to taxation. When Butler was being pressed by Cabinet colleagues to cut taxes in 1953, the Governor of the Bank of England wrote to him to point out that external opinion would be more concerned about whether the budget was balanced than with what would now be called 'supply-side' arguments in favour of tax cuts.[133] On the other hand, Churchill and what Butler called 'inner ministers' would review the political implications of budget proposals. For example, the Chancellor told the Budget Committee in February 1952 that the Prime Minister and the Foreign Secretary (Eden, Churchill's heir apparent) were very much against an increase in the standard rate of income tax from 9s. 6d. (47.5p) to 10s. (50p), which Bridges had suggested as an element in the deflationary package designed to ease the strain on the balance of payments.[134]

From the 1952 budget onwards the Federation of British Industries pressed for a reduction in government expenditure in order to allow taxation to be reduced without creating inflationary conditions. The Federation argued that the burden of high marginal rates of direct taxation on medium and larger incomes both discouraged British industrialists from matching the enthusiasm and drive of their rivals in the United States and Germany, and reduced the incentive to save, and thereby the funds available for investment. These

[131] 'National Income in 1953', summary report of the National Income Forecasts Working Party, circulated by Hall as appendix to BC(53)15, 9 Feb. 1953, T171/413.

[132] Hall, *Diaries, 1954–1961*, 8. See also N. Rollings, 'British Budgetary Policy, 1945–1954: A "Keynesian Revolution"?', *Econ. Hist. Rev.*, 2nd ser., 41 (1988), 295–7.

[133] Rollings, op. cit., 296.

[134] Record of meeting in Chancellor's room, 16 Feb. 1952, T171/408; Butler to Bridges, 10 Mar. 1954, T171/437.

arguments were supported in the Cabinet's Economic Policy Committee and elsewhere by Peter Thorneycroft, then President of the Board of Trade; indeed Thorneycroft was of the opinion that fiscal policy was a more potent means of improving productivity than anything his ministry could achieve by seeking to act directly on industry—for example, by encouraging the adoption of work study methods.[135]

Treasury officials broadly shared the Federation's position on taxation. In a note setting out for Butler the Treasury's underlying philosophy on profits and taxation, Bridges, Gilbert, and Hall took as given the government's belief that energetic and efficient management of industry was best provided by private enterprise. It was also agreed that Britain's future depended upon increasing investment that would keep industry up to date and competitive. As Hall had noted in discussions leading to the 1953 budget, the dynamic had to come from industry itself—hence the need for a reasonable return on risk capital. While much of the capital for investment was provided by ploughing back profits, Treasury officials also accepted that there must be a free supply of capital for new enterprises, and that taxation of profits and dividends should not normally interfere with decisions by private enterprise about how to allocate funds. This belief was balanced by two propositions: first, that when industry had provided funds for expansion at the rate required by the national interest, and an adequate return for risk capital, further potential increases in profits should be passed on to the consumer in the form of lower prices; and second, in an oblique reference to industrial relations, that the community would suffer if workers felt that their share of the product of industry was too low in relation to profits being distributed to shareholders. However, Treasury officials believed that it was impractical to have statutory limitation of dividends and that taxes on excess profits were in general unsatisfactory, as they worked unfairly as between different types of capital.[136]

An excess profits levy was imposed in the 1952 budget, in accordance with the Conservative election manifesto, to limit profits made as a result of rearmament, as in 1937, and to make other measures, such as a cut in food subsidies, politically acceptable. However, at the same time the existing rates of profits tax were reduced, so that the average rate for industry as a whole for income tax, profits tax, and excess profits levy combined was about 60 per cent, compared with 57 per cent for income tax and profits tax combined at the pre-budget rates.[137] Moreover, although the levy was originally intended to be applied over

---

[135] Thorneycroft's comments on draft report of the Productivity and Conditional Aid Committee, Feb. 1954, Board of Trade papers, series 64, file 4742. For FBI arguments see 'Representations of the Federation of British Industries to the Chancellor of the Exchequer', Dec. 1952, T171/413.

[136] Bridges to Butler, 20 Oct. 1954, enclosing 'Underlying Philosophy', T273/311. See also Hall, 'The Economic and Budgetary Problem in 1953', 9 Feb. 1953, T171/413.

[137] Inland Revenue note for the Chancellor on FBI memorandum on the excess profits levy, 9 Apr. 1952, T171/408.

three years, it was ended on 31 December 1953, as soon as what Butler called 'moral reasons' allowed.[138]

Throughout the 1950s much of the Budget Committee's deliberations focused on the need to remove the disincentive effects of taxation on enterprise, and on the need for tax reliefs designed to encourage investment. In particular, the standard rate of income tax was reduced from 9s. 6d. (47.5p) to 9s. (45p) in 1953; 8s. 6d. (42.5p) in 1955; and 7s. 9d. (38.75p) in 1959. However, even in 1959/60 the top marginal rate of income tax and surtax stood at 17s. 9d. (88.75p), compared with 15s. (75p) in 1938/9. In 1953 Butler restored the initial allowances for the depreciation of new capital assets, which Gaitskell had suspended in 1951, albeit at a rate of 20 per cent rather than the 40 per cent that Cripps had set in 1949. In 1954 Butler substituted a new allowance called the 'investment allowance', which gave tax relief at a fixed rate throughout the life of the asset, whereas initial allowances had given extra relief in the first year in which investment was undertaken, at a cost of smaller allowances in later years. The rates on investment allowances were selective, being 20 per cent of expenditure on new plant and machinery, but only 10 per cent on new buildings, a difference that the Board of Inland Revenue regarded as being in breach of an important principle of taxation whereby all taxpayers should be treated alike. However, Hall, Bridges, and Gilbert combined to persuade the Chancellor to disregard the Board's advice, on the grounds that investment in plant and machinery was a higher priority than investment in buildings.[139] The balance-of-payments crisis of 1955 led to the withdrawal of the investment allowances in 1956, but the old initial allowances were reinstated in their place. When the balance-of-payments constraint eased in 1958, the rate on initial allowances was increased to 30 per cent in July and the investment allowances were restored in the 1959 budget, this time in addition to initial allowances.

On the other hand, Treasury officials saw the direct taxation of working-class incomes in a rather different light. In 1950, when the Royal Commission on the Taxation of Profits and Income was set up, Hall had had no doubt that high marginal rates of income tax influenced workers' willingness to work overtime. However, by February 1953 a social survey by the Treasury's Information Unit and the Royal Commission suggested that only a minority of workers understood the relationship between tax rates and net pay well enough to influence their attitude to working overtime, and that consequently changes in the tax structure were unlikely to have any direct effect on productivity.[140] Moreover, even before the results of the survey, both Bridges and Gilbert thought that, from a 'civic point of view', the liability of large numbers of workers to income

[138] Butler's comment on Plowden to Chancellor, 18 Feb. 1953, T171/414.

[139] Minutes of meeting in Chancellor's room, 5 Mar. 1954, T171/449.

[140] Hall to Plowden, 18 May 1950, T171/427; 'Comment on Social Survey on P.A.Y.E. etc', by C. Leslie, n.d., but Feb. 1953, T171/414. See also *The Second Report of the Royal Commission on the Taxation of Profits and Income* (Cmd. 9105), PP 1953–4, xix. 187, paras. 38–41.

tax (in contrast to the position before the Second World War) should not lightly be given up, even though there were administrative advantages in reducing the number of people who paid tax.[141] Presumably the officials believed that the political temptation to spend public money could be tempered by ensuring that a high proportion of the electorate would bear some part of the cost.

Treasury officials also saw the advent of a Conservative government as an opportunity to pursue their long-standing campaign against food subsidies. The Conservative's election manifesto had stated that food subsidies could not be radically changed 'in present circumstances', but held out the prospect 'later on' of targeting the needy through family allowances and tax changes rather than by subsidies for all consumers. However, the balance-of-payments crisis of 1952 provided a strong case for an immediate reduction in food subsidies in the budget, in order to deflate the economy.[142] Such a policy ran the risk of stimulating inflationary wage claims. Nevertheless, in conjunction with officials in the Ministry of Food and the Ministry of National Insurance, Bridges and Gilbert drafted proposals for what, as classical scholars, they called 'Operation Diogenes', to reduce food subsidies, and Diogenes's converse, 'Operation Senegoid', to provide compensatory benefits.[143] Operation Diogenes originally envisaged a £200 million cut in food subsidies, but Bridges remarked that it was necessary not to upset the TUC seriously, and he proposed that if food subsidies were reduced by £150 million, between £70 and £80 million should be given back in the form of increases in family allowances and national insurance benefits.[144] The Treasury sought to reduce food subsidies year by year, but prime ministers were sensitive to the wider political implications: for example, Churchill said in 1954 that he was dead against cutting bread subsidies, mentioning as he did so not only likely TUC opposition but also his own Liberal past.[145]

It is against this background of fiscal policy having a range of functions that its use as an instrument of demand management must be considered.[146] The 1952 budget was intended to restore confidence in sterling, and, although the Treasury was unable to secure all the cuts in public expenditure it hoped for, unemployment rose, from an annual average of 281,000 (1.2 per cent of the labour force) in 1951 to 463,000 (2.1 per cent) in 1952. The 1953 and 1954 budgets were likewise constrained by the need to maintain confidence in sterling and, as already noted, Hall accepted in the Budget Committee that tax cuts should be

---

[141] Bridges to Chancellor, 14 Feb. 1952, and record of meeting held in the Chancellor's room, 16 Feb. 1952, T171/408.   [142] The *Economist*, 1 Dec. 1951, filed in T171/409.

[143] Diogenes was an ancient Greek philosopher who taught that happiness is attained by satisfying one's natural needs in the cheapest and easiest way.

[144] Record of meeting in Chancellor's room, 16 Feb. 1952, T171/408. The original proposal is in BC(52)14, 6 Feb. 1952, T171/409.   [145] Butler to Bridges, 10 Mar. 1954, T171/437.

[146] What follows draws heavily upon Alan Holmans's 'Policy to Control the Level of Demand', Treasury Historical Memorandum No. 8, July 1965, T267/12.

restricted to what would leave a small surplus above the line, although the national income forecasts pointed to a deficit. As it happened, the forces making for expansion of demand were greater than what had been allowed for in the forecasts, and, somewhat fortuitously, the Treasury's reluctance to incur budget deficits was justified in the event by the inflationary pressure that had built up in the economy by 1955.

On the other hand, Butler's decision to give £134 million in tax reliefs in 1955, principally by cutting the standard rate of income tax by 6d. (2.5p) to 8s. 6d. (42.5p), has generally been seen as an economic blunder, given that the economy was booming, with unemployment (seasonally adjusted) as low as 1.1 per cent, and that the balance of payments on current account was moving into deficit. It was not difficult to believe that these tax concessions were at least partly related to the fact that a general election was to be held shortly after the budget.[147] According to Butler, Churchill had wanted the whole of the prospective budget surplus to be given away to increase incentives, and he himself had begun discussions on the budget in July 1954 by telling his advisers that he was minded to do something to help middle-class taxpayers.[148] However, Butler was more cautious than Churchill and other ministers who wanted tax cuts; by October 1954 unemployment, at about 254,000, was already below the 1951 level, and in November the Chancellor warned the Cabinet's Economic Policy Committee that there were symptoms of shortages of materials and skilled labour that would make it difficult to contemplate budgetary concessions which would increase purchasing power. At that date Hall thought that there was no real evidence of a deterioration in the balance of payments, but he advised against giving way to Cabinet pressure before reductions in public expenditure had been secured to accommodate both tax cuts and increased industrial investment.[149]

In December the surplus above the line in 1955/6, on the existing basis of taxation, was forecast at £171 million, and senior officials in the Budget Committee agreed with Bridges when he said that 'the rare opportunity provided by a large surplus should be used to reduce the standard rate of income tax by sixpence' (2½p).[150] By February a deficit of £70 million in the balance of payments on current account was forecast, in contrast to the November forecast of a surplus of £155 million. Hall warned on 22 February that the evidence pointed to the need for a stiffer budget than had at first been hoped, and it was decided on 28 February to delay the budget to see what effects the recent increase in Bank rate, hire-purchase restrictions, and intervention in the transferable rate for sterling would

[147] See, for example, Brittan, *Treasury under the Tories*, 177, and Pinto-Duschinsky, 'Bread and Circuses?', 64–9.

[148] Butler, *Art of the Possible*, 176; note of meeting in the Chancellor's room, 28 July 1954, T171/450.

[149] Economic Policy Committee minutes, 18 Nov. 1954, CAB134/850; Hall, 'The State of the Economy', 22 Nov. 1954, T273/316.

[150] 'Policy to Control the Level of Demand', 19, T267/12.

have. At a meeting at which the Chancellor was not present, it was minuted that 'it should not be forgotten that the gold and dollar reserves existed to be used', but by April Rowan, representing the views of the overseas finance side of the Treasury, said he was becoming much more doubtful about the proposal to reduce the standard rate of income tax because of the inflationary effect. On 6 April, by which time there was still no clear evidence of the effects of credit restrictions, officials agreed with Hall that the economic situation indicated a standstill budget. However, for reasons that the Budget Committee minutes do not make clear, it was agreed that, if there were to be an early election, the proposed reduction in the standard rate should go ahead. Only Butler could have said definitely how important electoral strategy was in this decision, for the minutes also indicate that officials believed that the Bank of England could be firmer than it had been in imposing credit restrictions. In his diary, however, Hall admitted that he thought that the government had a right to take some chances to win the election, and also that he believed that there would have been a violent run on sterling if Labour had won. There seems little doubt that Treasury officials, anxious for supply-side reasons to reduce income tax, and placing hope in an as yet untried monetary policy, chose not to advise against an electioneering budget.[151]

The budget speech on 19 April tried to suggest that the Chancellor was being prudent by giving away less than half of his prospective surplus on the existing basis of taxation. How much would be added to domestic demand was uncertain; Butler said he trusted that those benefiting from tax cuts would save rather than spend the money. In any event, he claimed, there were the 'resources of a flexible monetary policy' in reserve ('flexible' in the sense that, unlike taxation, which required a budget, normally once a year, monetary policy could be changed at any time).[152] Press comment, apart from the Labour party's *Daily Herald*, was generally favourable: the *Economist*, while recognizing that by strict economic reasoning 1955 was a poor year for tax cuts, commented that 'no one can say with any dogmatism . . . that Mr Butler's guesses will not come out right', and Harrod, in the *Financial Times*, thought that tax reliefs totalling £134 million, or little more than 1 per cent of consumers' expenditure, would not have an appreciable effect on inflationary pressure. Harrod held to this view even after pressure on sterling forced Butler to introduce a second, deflationary, budget in October, arguing that confidence in sterling had been undermined by talk in London about a flexible exchange rate, and by upward pressure of wage rates.[153]

As already noted, the Budget Committee had been too optimistic about the ability of monetary policy to curb demand when government itself was borrowing to fund its capital expenditure. The government's victory in the general election in May did not prevent a run on sterling in the summer, whatever Hall

---

[151] Notes of meetings of 22 and 28 Feb., 9 Mar., and 1 and 6 Apr. 1955, T171/450; Hall, *Diaries, 1954–1961*, 71.   [152] 540 HC Deb., 5s, 1954–5, cols. 55, 58–61.
[153] The *Economist*, 23 Apr. 1955, and *Financial Times*, 23 Apr. and 28 Oct. 1955.

may have thought about financial markets preferring the Conservatives to Labour. By July rumours regarding the future parity of sterling, buoyant investment and consumer expenditure, and increased industrial unrest, had all contributed to a sterling crisis, and it was clear that monetary policy was not being applied as strictly as the Treasury had hoped. On the 26th, the day after the Chancellor made his statement asking for a reduction in bank advances, Bridges warned Butler that an autumn budget might be necessary, and suggested that contingency plans be made 'in deepest secrecy' with the boards of Inland Revenue and Customs and Excise.[154]

An autumn budget was not something to be undertaken lightly, the only previous twentieth-century examples being associated with war (1914, 1939, and 1945) or an exchange crisis (1931 and 1947). Nevertheless, Bridges warned Butler that the need to maintain confidence in sterling did not allow delay, and on 26 October the Chancellor introduced a budget that increased purchase tax by £75 million, and profits tax by £40 million (both calculated for a full year), while leaving the standard rate of income tax untouched. As a further deflationary measure, the Exchequer subsidy to local authorities for housing was withdrawn, except for schemes connected with slum clearance and overcrowding. The new Prime Minister, Eden, had favoured a temporary capital gains tax, in reaction to the Stock Exchange boom, but the Board of Inland Revenue advised that the necessary legislation required would have been too complex to be introduced at short notice.[155]

Continued pressure on sterling in 1956 and 1957 inhibited any further major reductions in direct taxation until 1959. Macmillan was tempted to make the theme of his budget in 1956 one of 'slosh the speculator', but accepted the Inland Revenue's advice that a capital gains tax could not be introduced in 1956/7.[156] He contemplated reversing Butler's 6d. (2.5p) cut in the standard rate of income tax, provoking the latter to phone Bridges and other officials 'in a state of considerable excitement'. Butler considered that such an action would be so damaging to his reputation that he would have to resign from his Cabinet post as Lord Privy Seal. Treasury officials gave Macmillan conflicting advice at a meeting on 29 March: Rowan, with his passionate concern for defending sterling, was in favour of increasing income tax; Gilbert, Brittain, and Hall were against; and Bridges was undecided. Macmillan himself accepted the political argument that reversing Butler's tax cut would be to admit that it had been a mistake.[157] Instead he made 'savings' his theme, and his budget is best remembered for introducing Premium Bonds as a means of mopping up surplus purchasing power in the hands of people who had not been attracted to more conventional forms of National Savings.

[154] Bridges to Chancellor, 26 July 1955, T273/317.
[155] Eden's interventions in the preparation of the budget can be found in PREM11/887.
[156] Macmillan to Bridges, 31 Jan. 1956, T171/473.
[157] Macmillan diary, 26, 28, and 29 Mar., and 8 Apr. 1956.

However, the principal alternative to a tax increase as a means of defending sterling was a reduction in public expenditure. Macmillan wished to save £61 million by abolishing the bread subsidy and by raising the price of milk by a half penny a pint. Eden was absolutely opposed to these measures but, faced with Macmillan's threat to resign, agreed in February to a compromise whereby the bread subsidy was to be reduced in stages, and the increase in the price of milk was to go ahead as Macmillan wished. This compromise has been presented by David Carlton as a significant political victory for the Chancellor, but Macmillan hesitated before agreeing to it, and apparently did so only after accepting the advice of Bridges and the Governor of the Bank of England that resignation would cause a panic in the City. Moreover, with savings on bread and milk reduced to £38 million, Macmillan believed that he had to look elsewhere for ways of reducing inflationary pressure, and opted for a suspension of the tax allowances on investment that Butler had introduced in 1954. It is true that the majority of the Treasury's Budget Committee, with the notable exceptions of Hall and Rowan, had thought as early as January that suspension of the allowances was a logical corollary of other measures to control inflation, but in his memoirs Macmillan said he thought that it had been wrong to withdraw encouragement of investment even during a boom.[158]

The 1957 budget was prepared in the wake of Suez, with its concomitant sterling crisis. Officials recommended an increase of 6d. in the standard rate of income tax as well as an increase in petrol duty,[159] but once more an increase in direct taxation was unacceptable to a Conservative government. With a large overall deficit forecast for 1957–8, the need to cut public expenditure was accepted by the Cabinet in principle, although, as usual, it was not easy to identify politically acceptable cuts.

Deflationary fiscal policy from the autumn of 1955 had a marked effect on industrial production, which was no higher in the spring of 1957 than it had been eighteen months earlier. However, unemployment, although higher in 1957 than in 1955, was still below 2 per cent, and upward pressure of wages led Thorneycroft to address the problem of what was called 'cost-push' inflation in his budget speech. He rejected 'savage deflationary policies' that would depress demand to the point where employers could not grant pay increases, but did so in the hope that people would exercise voluntary restraint.[160] At this point it is convenient to break off from the story of demand management to look at the Treasury's attitude towards full employment, prices, and wages.

[158] 'The Economic Situation', 21 Jan. 1956, CAB129/79; Macmillan to Eden, 11 Feb., and confidential annex to Cabinet conclusions, 15 Feb. 1956, PREM11/1324; David Carlton, *Anthony Eden* (1981), 396; Budget Committee, 19 Jan. 1956, T171/469; Macmillan, *Riding the Storm*, 14–15; Macmillan to Eden, 5 Apr. 1956, PREM11/1326.

[159] Budget Committee minutes, 27 Nov. 1956, T171/478.

[160] 568 HC Deb., 5s, 1956–7, cols. 969–70.

FULL EMPLOYMENT, PRICES, AND WAGES, 1951–1958

The Conservatives took office in October 1951 in a highly inflationary situation: in the fourth quarter of 1951 retail prices were rising at an annual rate of 21.1 per cent and wages at an annual rate of 11 per cent. The rise in prices partly reflected rising import prices, and partly excess domestic demand, to which government itself, with its rearmament programme, was a major contributor. Deflationary measures were taken, but Treasury officials were well aware of the political dangers of unemployment, and indeed it was partly because of the risks to full employment that ministers rejected Robot. Nor did the economic advice available suggest that unemployment was an acceptable answer to 'cost-push' inflation: Hall advised Bridges in November 1951 that 'experience suggests that very high levels of unemployment indeed are necessary to put a really effective stop on wage increases', and four months later gave a figure of 600,000 (or 2.7 per cent of the labour force) as the level at which the economic advantages of releasing labour for transfer into export industries were offset by loss of output and by social unrest.[161] Down to the summer of 1957, when Thorneycroft made price stability a primary aim of policy, deflationary measures were a reaction to balance-of-payments difficulties, not rising prices or wages.

Unemployment, expressed as an annual national average, rose from 281,000 (1.2 per cent) in 1951 to 463,000 (2.1 per cent) in 1952, well within the 3 per cent employment standard adopted by the Labour government. However, fears of a recession spreading from the United States led the Conservative government to review plans for remedial measures. In the course of 1953 the Treasury effectively opposed plans for either non-remunerative public works or reductions in national insurance contributions, although both measures had been included in the 1944 White Paper on *Employment Policy*. The main forum for official discussion was the Economic Steering Committee's Working Group on Employment Policy, which included representatives of the Board of Trade, the Ministry of Labour, and the Scottish Office, with Gilbert representing the Treasury, Strath the Central Economic Planning Staff, and Hall the Economic Section, and with Plowden as chairman. The working group considered that fiscal policy, which could take the form of an autumn budget, would be a speedier and more effective response to unemployment that public works. Even so, the group's report advised against reductions in national insurance contributions, on the grounds that it would be politically difficult to raise them again.[162]

Ministers did invite the Ministry of Works to prepare a paper on what could be done with a reserve of public works, but Gilbert argued that 'it is

[161] Cairncross and Watts, *Economic Section*, 338; Hall to Bridges, 13 Mar. 1952, T273/315.

[162] J. Tomlinson, *Employment Policy: The Crucial Years, 1939–1955* (Oxford, 1987), 151–5. The working group's papers are in CAB134/890.

fundamental that the measures adopted and held in reserve against a recession should be directed to inspiring confidence. The best insurance of this is to
concentrate on building up industrial efficiency.'[163] Such words echoed the
Treasury's arguments against Keynes before the war—unsurprisingly since
Gilbert had helped to draft these arguments. The sum made available by the
Treasury for the Ministry of Works' study was limited to £50,000, an effective
administrative device to ensure that not very much was done. The Treasury's
preferred solution to unemployment arising from a recession spreading from
the United States would have been international collaboration to maintain
international credit and to avoid a chain reaction of import restrictions, with
a flexible rate for sterling, if necessary, to absorb changes in Britain's external
position.[164]

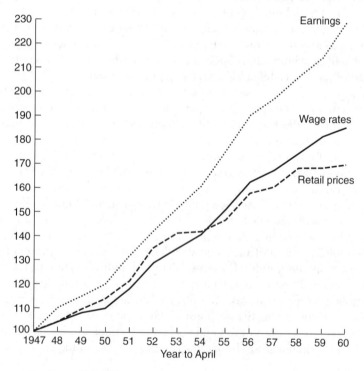

FIG. 9.2. *Earnings and Wage Rates, 1947–1960*
Source: T267/7.

[163] Marginal comment on 'Reserve of Works', 5 Dec. 1953, T229/818.
[164] 'Measures to Combat a Recession in the United States and to Strengthen the Economy', by Chancellor of the Exchequer, 1 Oct. 1953, CAB134/848.

Far more pressing than plans to solve future unemployment, in the Treasury's view, was the need to prevent rising costs from pricing British goods out of markets. As Figure 9.2 shows, the Ministry of Labour's indices of money earnings and wage rates showed a steep rise from 1950 to 1955, and although the rise slackened thereafter, money earnings continued to rise more quickly than retail prices. Unemployment was below 2 per cent of the labour force between 1953 and 1957, and in the privacy of his diary Hall wished that it was higher. However, he was not impressed by the evidence, put forward by the economist A. W. Phillips in 1958, for a close historical relationship between the level of unemployment and the rate of inflation. The Phillips curve, as this relationship became known, suggested that, if unemployment were about 2½ per cent, prices would be stable, but Hall thought that Phillips had taken insufficient account of the increased bargaining power of trade unions. Rather than advocate higher unemployment, Hall became the chief proponent within Whitehall of the view that the problem of rising wages and prices should be tackled, not by deflation, but by government guidance on the general levels of wage increases that could be afforded, if cost-push inflation were to be avoided and the competitiveness of British goods maintained. His belief that wage restraint was a necessary concomitant of full employment was subsequently endorsed by major Keynesian economists.[165]

It was one thing to identify the problem, and quite another to find a practical solution. Policy on wages and prices was co-ordinated by the Cabinet's Economic Policy Committee, but departmental responsibility for matters relating to wages lay with the Ministry of Labour. Bridges confessed to being 'irritated beyond measure', at times, by the Ministry of Labour's dogma that wages must be settled between the two sides of industry, or by an arbitrator, and that any action by government was bound to make the situation worse. On the other hand, he himself did not advocate any radical change in wage bargaining, preferring instead moderate disinflation to stiffen employers' resistance to wage claims, and unobtrusive attempts to educate public opinion as to the consequences of wage demands. At the end of his period as Permanent Secretary, in October 1956, he had to admit that 'the difficulty of finding any effective means of handling wage claims has in effect become the Achilles' Heel of our economy'.[166]

Conservative ministers pressed on with derationing and reductions in food subsidies (albeit hesitantly with regard to the latter) even after these measures

[165] Hall, *Diaries, 1954–1961*, 23 (27 Oct. 1954); Jones, *Economist Among Mandarins*, 149. For Phillips curve see A. W. Phillips, 'The Relation Between Unemployment and the Rate of Change of Money Wage Rates in the United Kingdom, 1861–1957', *Economica*, NS, 25 (1958), 283–99. For Keynesian belief that a successful wages policy is necessary for full employment see James Meade, *Stagflation*, vol. i, *Wage-fixing* (1982) and David Worswick, *Unemployment: A Problem of Policy* (Cambridge, 1991).

[166] 'Prices, Wages and Costs', and 'Wages and Prices: Organisation', by Bridges, 12 Oct. 1956, T234/675.

were cited by the TUC as reasons for not co-operating with government to help with wage restraint. As Chancellor of the Exchequer, Butler made three attempts to win over the TUC, two directly and one through the National Joint Advisory Council, but to no avail, even when the analysis of costs was extended to profits and dividends as well as wages. When sterling came under pressure in 1955 the wages problem came to the fore but, following talks with the Prime Minister, the Chancellor, and the Minister of Labour before the autumn budget, the TUC blamed the lack of wage restraint on Butler's decision in the spring to reduce income tax rather than to stabilize prices by reducing purchase tax on essential goods.[167]

Meanwhile, within Whitehall, there had been a series of attempts from December 1951 to draft a white paper that would alert public opinion to the need for wage restraint, with the Economic Section taking the lead in arguing that wage increases were normally justified only by increased productivity. However, the Ministry of Labour objected to anything that might upset the unions, while Butler and senior Treasury officials feared that unduly vigorous warnings about inflation causing excessive imports, and consequently balance-of-payments problems, might undermine confidence in sterling. A white paper, much of it drafted in the Economic Section, but edited by Burke Trend, was finally approved by the Cabinet on 22 November 1955, with a view to publication in mid-December. However, six days later Butler characteristically decided that he needed more time in which to study the possible political repercussions of the white paper. He may well have been influenced by critical comments on its contents by the Conservative Research Department, which later sent to the Economic Secretary, Sir Edward Boyle, an eight-page note setting out amendments that it believed to be necessary to remove any suggestion of left-wing bias, or that the government had no policy. The Treasury accepted a number of drafting points, but refused to extend the white paper by enclosing passages that would have suggested that a stricter financial policy would put an end to cost inflation.[168]

It was not until March 1956, after Macmillan became Chancellor, that the white paper, *The Economic Implications of Full Employment*, was eventually published.[169] In it the government repeated the undertaking of 1944 to maintain full employment, but, at a late stage of the drafting, Gilbert inserted a passage pointing out that a combination of low unemployment and continually rising prices was not a viable alternative to wage restraint and price stability, for, if British goods were priced out of world markets, it would not be possible to import the raw materials necessary for full employment.[170] This amendment underlined the arguments developed in earlier sections of the white paper, where attention

---

[167] For Butler's relations with TUC see T273/396 and T172/2061.
[168] T234/94 *passim*.   [169] Cmd. 9725, PP 1955–6, xxxvi. 565.
[170] Gilbert to Petch, 9 Mar. 1956, T273/320.

was drawn to Britain's declining share of world trade in manufactures, and to the need not only to keep costs in line with competitors, but also to sustain investment. Investment, at full employment, in turn depended upon a willingness to forgo consumption and upon a stable relationship between borrower and lender, both of which, the Treasury believed, could be undermined by inflation. The white paper served as a guide to the thinking that underlay the management of the economy, but it also reflected acceptance by the Treasury of the Ministry of Labour's attitude towards industrial relations. The white paper stated that there would be no government interference with wage bargaining (or the levels of dividends) and simply called for realism in relation to prices and incomes, without offering guidance as to what levels of increased incomes represented realism.

Bridges and Hall recognized that the TUC leaders were moderate men who accepted the economic arguments in the white paper, but who would have difficulty in persuading their members to exercise restraint so long as prices were rising. As it happened, the deflationary measures adopted since the autumn of 1955 had included increasing prices under government control, and in the spring of 1956 there were still increases in Post Office charges and in the prices of tobacco, bread, milk, transport fares, coal, gas, electricity, and steel to come. Macmillan believed that there was no hope of avoiding a further round of wage claims in the autumn, but he hoped to slow down the spiral of wages and prices.[171] Hall advised that the impending price increases were essential as part of the deflationary policy, but that, once they had taken place, the government should announce that there would be no need for further price increases so long as wages did not rise. This policy of a wage and price 'plateau' led to ministers securing undertakings from the chairmen of nationalized industries for price freezes for coal, electricity, and gas, and the Federation of British Industries recommended its members to exercise great restraint in pricing. Nevertheless, the TUC conference in the autumn rejected wage restraint, and the wage–price spiral continued.

From the spring of 1957 Hall argued that the government should indicate what it thought would be a fair increase in average wages each year, based on the expected average increase in productivity—a policy that came to be known as the 'guiding light'. However, although both Thorneycroft and Heathcoat Amory were willing to adopt this idea, the Cabinet was not. Most ministers were reluctant to interfere with collective bargaining, and doubted whether all wage increases could be related to a single criterion. On the other hand, the Cabinet did accept that an independent advisory body might prove to be valuable in educating public opinion, and in August 1957 the Council on Prices, Productivity and Incomes was established with a law lord, Lord Cohen, as chairman, and

---

[171] Bridges to Chancellor, enclosing note by Hall on talks with TUC, 1 Mar. 1956, T273/396; Macmillan to Eden, 27 Mar. 1956, PREM11/1324.

a City accountant, Sir Harold Howitt, and the economist and wartime Treasury adviser Sir Dennis Robertson, as members. The Council's first report, in February 1958, rejected any single percentage figure by which money wages could increase without damage to the economy, on the grounds that such a figure would become a minimum rather than an average. Moreover, although the Council's terms of reference stated that full employment was a desirable objective, the report endorsed deflationary measures taken by Thorneycroft, in the previous autumn, and remarked that no one should be surprised if unemployment rose 'somewhat further' than its current level of 1.8 per cent.[172]

THE THORNEYCROFT EPISODE, 1957–1958

Thorneycroft's brief Chancellorship was notable on three accounts. First, there was his publicly propounded belief that the supply of money must be controlled—a doctrine that was anathema to many Keynesian economists, who saw inflation in terms of excess demand rather than in terms of the quantity theory of money. Secondly, there was his deflationary response, known as the 'September measures', to inflationary pressure and a run on the pound: on 19 September 1957 Bank rate was raised from 5 to 7 per cent, and it was announced that public sector investment programmes would be held at the 1957/8 level for the next two financial years and that the clearing banks had been asked to hold advances to the private sector for the next twelve months at the average level for the previous twelve months. Thirdly, there was the Chancellor's resignation, along with the Financial Secretary, Enoch Powell, and the Economic Secretary, Nigel Birch, in January 1958, when the Cabinet would not agree in full to the Chancellor's demands for economy in public expenditure.

Thorneycroft's policies in 1957–8 have been described by the official historian of the Bank of England as 'early-day monetarism'.[173] However, the thinking behind the September measures was not monetarist, in the sense of being based on a belief that money could be defined and measured, or having anything to do with the revival in the 1950s of the quantity theory by Milton Friedman at Chicago. Insofar as Thorneycroft and the junior Treasury ministers were influenced by economic theory, the relevant economists were Dennis Robertson and Lionel Robbins, neither of whom could be described as a monetarist, as that term has since come to be understood. Indeed, both Robertson and Robbins believed that, even if the quantity of money were to be held steady, the monetary authorities could only influence indirectly the velocity with which money changed hands, and thereby the effective demand for goods and labour. What Thorneycroft and those who thought like him were concerned with was

---

[172] *First Report of the Council on Prices, Productivity and Incomes* (1958).
[173] Fforde, *Bank of England*, 586.

the level of bank advances and the level of bank liquidity arising from the financing of government expenditure through the sale to the banks of Treasury bills; no attempt was made to measure the money supply as a whole. Thorneycroft later recalled that he, Powell, and Birch were guided by 'sheer common sense', and there had not been a lot of theory behind their ideas. Birch had a City background and had dealt in gilt-edged securities. Powell had made a private study of economics, including Robertson's book on *Money*, which referred to the experience of 1915–20 in showing how government borrowing could lead to an increase in the supply of money. It is anachronistic to think of Thorneycroft's policies in 1957 as an early version of the monetarism adopted by the Thatcher government in 1979; at most they represented what Powell later called 'a gleam in the eye' of monetarism.[174]

It would also be misleading to identify Thorneycroft's ideas with Treasury official thinking. The three ministers came independently to the view that something had to be done about inflation, and began talking to each other, but their ideas were not congenial to Hall or senior officials in home finance. Indeed Hall twice considered resignation rather than be associated with what he considered to be the oversimplified economic ideas expressed by the Chancellor, and had to be dissuaded by Makins, who told Hall that it would not be long before there was a new Chancellor. Makins thought that Thorneycroft was 'a bit of a bull in a china shop'. Treasury officials, including Hall, were responsible for helping the Chancellor to draft papers and speeches, but most officials sought to moderate his enthusiasm for drastic measures. One exception was Rowan, who, according to Hall, was 'temperamentally' on the side of Thorneycroft and Robertson, and, as one might expect, there was strong support in the Supply Services divisions for measures to curb the growth of public expenditure.[175]

Thorneycroft's deflationary measures were a response to a perceived need to reverse inflationary expectations. The hope that he had expressed in his budget speech in April 1957 that inflation would be halted by voluntary wage restraint failed to evoke much in the way of a response: although retail prices rose by just over 3 per cent in the year to June 1957, the summer saw railway workers secure a 5 per cent increase, after rejecting a tribunal's award of 3 per cent, while strikes by shipbuilding and engineering workers were settled at 6½ per cent. The *Financial Times* expressed a view that was widely shared in financial circles when

[174] Conversations with Thorneycroft, 11 May 1988, and Enoch Powell, 27 Oct. 1988. Friedman was developing the modern quantity theory of money in the 1950s, but there is no evidence that anyone in the Treasury took any notice of his work at that time; the first formal commitment by a British government to monetary targets did not occur until 1967, and then at the behest of the International Monetary Fund—see David Smith, *The Rise and Fall of Monetarism* (1987). For Robertson's views on the money supply see his *Money* (Cambridge, 1948 edn., repr. 1956). For Robbins's views see his *Politics and Economics*, 166–96. Thorneycroft subsequently developed his ideas in an Institute of Economic Affairs volume, edited by Arthur Seldon, *Not Unanimous: A Rival Verdict to Radcliffe's on Money* (1960), 1–14.
[175] Hall, *Diaries, 1954–1961*, 122, 165; Lord Roberthall interviewed by Anthony Seldon, 13 May 1980; conversations with Powell, Sherfield, and Thorneycroft.

it commented on 20 July that the government had 'given up the fight against inflation', and the spread of inflationary expectations led to a fall in demand for gilt-edged securities.

The Chancellor was very far from having given up the fight. On 20 June he had told his senior officials that he 'had an uncomfortable feeling that the government's control over the economy was weakening'—citing the increase in bank advances, although he was told by the officials that there was evidence that bankers were responding to the request he had made in his budget for a credit squeeze. On 17 July he presented a paper on inflation to the Cabinet, expressing the view that, while rising wages dwarfed all other aspects of the problem, economy in public expenditure was the biggest contribution that the government could make towards solving inflation.[176] Thorneycroft's concern about public expenditure can only have been increased when, later in July, he was told (correctly as it turned out) by the Governor of the Bank of England that the whole of the Exchequer deficit for the year would have to be financed by selling Treasury bills, which would increase the liquidity of the banks and make it harder to control credit.[177]

Towards the end of July the exchange rate fell ominously to $2.78½, only half a cent above the lower level normally allowed under IMF rules, and speculative pressure on sterling increased after a devaluation of the franc in August fed expectations of a realignment of European currencies downwards against the deutschmark. On the other hand, the outlook for Britain's balance of payments on current account was considered to be satisfactory, and the rate of loss of the dollar reserves was declining in the latter part of August. Neither Treasury nor Bank officials who reviewed the sterling situation early in September thought that severe deflation was called for, but Thorneycroft, in sending their draft report to Macmillan on 13 September, claimed that the stress it laid on maintaining sterling's parity pointed to the need for internal measures—and Macmillan agreed with him.[178]

Down to September 1957 Thorneycroft had every reason to believe that he had the Prime Minister's support. He and Macmillan were agreed on the need for curbs on public expenditure to make room for non-inflationary tax cuts that would stimulate enterprise, and give some relief to taxpayers who supported the Conservative party. Prime Minister and Chancellor also shared a concern about the political effects of inflation, believing that the fall in the value of money was bitterly resented by the people who formed the hard core of the Tory party, and that disaffection in the constituencies could lead to defeat in the next election. On 19 July Thorneycroft raised in Cabinet the possibility of new measures to control the monetary system, but he observed that direct controls over

---

[176] Note of meeting 20 June 1957, T230/385; C(57)168, CAB129/88.

[177] Fforde, *Bank of England*, 675.

[178] Draft report on 'Sterling', 9 Sept., with Chancellor's covering note to Prime Minister, 13 Sept. 1957, T236/3944.

the money supply had hitherto been considered to be inconsistent with the Conservatives' political principles, and that there would certainly be pressure to apply any new measures to the public as well as the private sector.[179] Subsequently Macmillan agreed to circulate a minute on 10 August to ministers asking each of them to limit his department's current civil expenditure in 1958/9 to the 1957/8 level.

Thorneycroft had been encouraged to believe that more deflation was needed by Robertson, in the course of a conversation when the Chancellor was asking him to join the Council on Prices, Productivity and Incomes. Subsequently Hall, who was on leave, was extremely upset in September to discover that Thorneycroft had also been consulting Robbins, who had confirmed the Chancellor in his belief that the money supply was the key to controlling inflation. According to Robbins, the monetization of the government's debt had made the Treasury rather than the Bank the arbiter of the total volume of cash plus deposits, a view that pointed to the need to avoid increasing the floating debt by issuing more Treasury bills. Hall placed much less emphasis on control of the money supply, and much more emphasis on the need for a successful wages policy. Yet it is possible to overstate the differences of opinion between Hall and Robbins; despite different theoretical approaches, there was some common ground as to what measures the situation required. Hall believed that there was over-full employment, and that it would be better to aim at running the economy less flat out than hitherto. He also believed that the government had lost control of the supply of money and should regain it. On the other hand, he believed that the effects of the policy on employment would not be felt in time to affect the current wage round, and that ministers were wrong to believe that deflation would cure the wage–price spiral without forcing the government to face up to the unions over wages policy.[180]

Macmillan was at first if anything even more attracted to basing policy on controlling the money supply than Thorneycroft. On 1 September the Prime Minister presented to the Cabinet 'some thoughts' which had 'occurred' to him during a short holiday. He compared the rival theories of inflation, 'cost-push' brought about by the power of the trade unions (which he called 'the Harrod

[179] Cabinet conclusions, CAB128/31.

[180] Hall, *Diaries, 1954–1961*, 123–6, 135, 137. Robbins, *Politics and Economics*, 182. The Economic Section's advice in October was that the yield on gilt-edged securities had been lower during the previous six years than it would have been if people buying gilts had been rational and had foreseen the rates of inflation and economic growth that had occurred in 1951–7. As a consequence, fewer people were prepared to hold gilts as a long-term investment, and it was thus harder to control the banks' liquidity through the traditional means of funding debt. The Section also advised that the supply of money had to be limited directly because it cost the banks nothing to create money by extending credit, and they would always meet whatever demand there was for credit at any rate that would yield them a moderate profit (J. Downie to Compton, 11 Oct. 1957, T230/385). Hall's analysis was that savings and investment were fairly well matched, and that the government's policy, if successful, would restrict investment and reduce savings by reducing profits. However, he accepted that the objective of policy was to curtail demand in order to discourage employers from granting wage increases ('Bank Rate', by Hall, 22 Nov. 1957, ibid.).

school'), and 'demand inflation' caused by too much money created in the attempt to do too many things at once ('the Robbins school') to the argument as to which came first, the chicken or the egg. Drawing upon the Robbins school's view that the amount of money in circulation should be restricted in order to reduce pressure on the labour market, Macmillan suggested both direct control of bank advances to the private sector and curbs on public expenditure. He thought there was little scope for further economies in current public expend-iture, other than defence, but that government borrowing could be restricted by rephasing capital investment programmes such as school building or housing. His enthusiasm for direct controls over credit even led him to believe that it would be possible to dispense both with a budget surplus above the line (thereby allowing reductions in taxation) and with high Bank rate. Indeed, the tenuous hold that conventional Keynesian ideas on demand management had on Macmillan at this time is illustrated by his remark that he had 'always disliked the theory that the budget should be "an instrument of economic policy" ', a theory he attributed to 'Cripps and the economists'.[181]

A follow-up paper by Thorneycroft on 7 September was a somewhat more sober production, reflecting, no doubt, the moderating influence of Hall and Padmore (whom Hall described as the paper's 'editor'). The Chancellor's paper suggested that the country might well be suffering from both cost-push and demand inflation. Nevertheless, it reflected his belief that appeals to employers and unions for restraint would be ineffectual so long as it was felt that the gov-ernment would 'always make enough money available to support full, and indeed over-full, employment', regardless of price and wage increases. Like Macmillan, Thorneycroft believed that direct controls on bank advances to the private sector would also be necessary to cut the total of such advances by the amount that he wanted—5 per cent—but, unlike the Prime Minister, he did not dismiss the possibility of raising Bank rate. As for the problem of Exchequer financing, he proposed to introduce what would later be called 'cash limits': he asked the Cabinet to agree that total investment by public authorities—central government, local authorities, and nationalized industries—should be held in each of the years 1958/9 and 1959/60 to the same level as it was expected to rise to in 1957/8, that is £1,500 million, which would involve a 10 per cent reduction in existing programmes. The government, he said, must be prepared to see unemployment rise from just over 1 per cent to around 3 per cent, and at this stage Macmillan was prepared to give Thorneycroft his support, despite reser-vations by a number of ministers that the policy proposed would be seen as a departure, for the first time, from the 1944 commitment to full employment.[182]

[181] C(57)194, 'The Economic Situation: Memorandum by the Prime Minister', 1 Sept. 1957, CAB129/88.

[182] C(57)195, 'The Economic Situation: Memorandum by the Chancellor of the Exchequer', 7 Sept. 1957, CAB129/88; Cabinet conclusions, 10, 12, 17, and 19 Sept. 1957, CAB128/31; Hall, *Diaries, 1954–1961*, 125.

The Bank of England was not the source of Thorneycroft's ideas on monetary policy. The Governor had urged him from January to curb government
expenditure, so as to reduce the dependence of Exchequer financing on Treasury bills, and thereby strengthen the gilt-edged market. However, the Bank's
favoured monetary device was not direct control of bank advances, but a drastic increase in Bank rate, which Cobbold had first advocated on 22 August.
Against Macmillan's inclination, Thorneycroft agreed to a rise from 5 per cent
to 7 per cent (the highest level since 1921), the rise being announced on
19 September along with cuts in public sector investment programmes and the
extension of the credit squeeze. Confidence in sterling was thereby restored,
largely, it would seem, because the authorities had shown their determination
to defend the $2.80 rate. The Bank thought that the kind of control of the total
of advances that ministers were looking for would be extremely difficult to
apply, and that a public collision between the monetary authorities and the
banks would have damaging consequences for overseas confidence in the banking system and the exchange rate. Relations between the Chancellor and
the Bank were extremely strained in September, when, as already noted, the
Treasury Solicitor was asked whether the Chancellor had the power to tell the
Governor to give directions to the banks, and was told that he did not.[183]
Makins was said by Hall to be horrified at the prospect of the Chancellor having such power, on the grounds that the effect on financial confidence would
lead to a debacle over sterling.[184]

Thorneycroft then set up a working group of Bank and Treasury officials,
including Hall, together with Robbins, under the chairmanship of the Economic Secretary, Birch, to consider how to get effective control of the credit
base. The working party had the disadvantage of not knowing the conclusions
of the Radcliffe Committee on the working of the monetary system. Moreover,
the Governor, as might be expected, sought to preserve as much of the Bank's
autonomy as possible. Rather than allow the control of credit to pass to the
Treasury, he accepted a scheme, put forward by Robbins, for requiring the
banks to deposit funds with the Bank, which would then lend them to the Treasury, as a means of reducing the government's dependence on Treasury bills for
Exchequer financing. However, although the principle of what became known
as Special Deposits was agreed in October, the necessary legislation was not
introduced until the following year.[185]

Before that happened, Thorneycroft had resigned, along with Birch and
Powell, over the issue of public expenditure. Macmillan's support for his Chancellor began to ebb in the autumn. He was being advised by Harrod against
deflation as a long-term policy, even before the September measures had been
announced, and resolved after the increase in Bank rate not to give way to

---

[183] Fforde, *Bank of England*, 672–88.   [184] Hall, *Diaries, 1954–1961*, 127.
[185] The papers of the Working Group on Credit are in T230/337.

pressure for deflationary measures indefinitely. He described as 'rot' Thorneycroft's claim that Treasury control of public expenditure was essential if the Cabinet was to have an overall picture of how individual ministers' desires were related to resources, and take rational choices as to priorities.[186] The Chancellor, on the other hand, regarded holding public expenditure in 1958/9 at the 1957/8 level as a matter of principle. When the annual Estimates were put forward to the Treasury by spending departments in December, it was found that, in spite of the Prime Minister's minute of 10 August, the total for civil Estimates was £275 million above the original 1957/8 Estimates, the largest increase ever recorded in peacetime, or £175 million above the total Estimates (including Supplementary Estimates). The Chancellor was advised by his officials that the usual Treasury scrutiny of the 1958/9 Estimates would perhaps produce savings of £40 million. Further savings, however, would involve changes in policy.[187]

Thorneycroft asked for, and was granted, a Cabinet Committee on Civil Expenditure to examine both administrative economies and policy changes. However, both in the committee and later in Cabinet, the Chancellor could make only limited progress towards his goal. In particular, the Cabinet refused to accept a proposal to withdraw family allowances from the second child in each family—a measure that was designed to save £68 million, but which also seemed likely to provoke demands for compensatory wage increases. By 6 January there was still a gap of £50 million between what the Chancellor demanded and what his colleagues would agree to. Makins did not regard such a sum as sufficient to justify resignation, but, encouraged by Birch and Powell, Thorneycroft decided to go.[188]

Hall's own assessment of the economic outlook at the end of 1957 was that a policy of full employment would point to tax reliefs in the 1958 budget, or some relaxation of monetary policy. On the other hand, if the government were to continue its present policy of combating inflation, he thought that the budget surplus in 1958 should be the same as in 1957. Hall was therefore sympathetic to the Chancellor's stand on the Estimates, but felt that it was a mistake to be too rigid when £50 million would have no significant macroeconomic effect. However, as Hall was aware, Thorneycroft was concerned with the psychological effect on financial markets, at home and abroad, of failing to hold public expenditure at its 1957/8 level. Moreover, Thorneycroft had been concerned since the previous summer about future budgetary prospects, as he rightly saw that there was a danger that public expenditure would rise sharply over the next few years unless the Cabinet was prepared to impose economy on the spending

---

[186] Macmillan, *Riding the Storm*, 355–7; Turner, *Macmillan*, 240. For Harrod's views, see his *Policy Against Inflation*.   [187] C(57)295, 27 Dec. 1957, CAB129/90.
[188] Cabinet Committee on Civil Expenditure, CAB130/139; Cabinet conclusions, 3 and 5 Jan. 1958, CAB128/32; Macmillan diary, 6 Jan. 1958; conversation with Sherfield, 9 June 1988.

departments.[189] Thorneycroft's resignation was related to a much broader question of political economy—could government control its own expenditure?—than the precise figure of £50 million seemed to imply.

The Thorneycroft episode highlights the importance to a Chancellor of having the support of his Cabinet colleagues and especially that of the Prime Minister. Without that support, Treasury control could not be exercised to the point of effecting changes in policy. Likewise, the episode shows that a Chancellor could require his officials to help him to carry out a policy that he had decided upon, but he could not convert them to his views on the importance of the supply of money. The differences of views between Thorneycroft, Birch, and Powell on the one hand, and Makins on the other, about the need for ministers to resign over public expenditure, also points to the danger of assuming that the Treasury, as a department, believed in the 1950s in the need for rigid targets for public expenditure. In retrospect, however, Sir Leo Pliatzky, an official with considerable experience of the control of public expenditure from the 1940s to the 1970s, thought that the Chancellor's defeat in 1958 had seriously undermined the authority of the Treasury.[190]

CONTROL OF PUBLIC EXPENDITURE: GENERAL PROBLEMS

Although not all Treasury officials thought in 1958 that experience of control of public expenditure in the 1950s had been unsatisfactory, a number, of whom 'Otto' Clarke was the most senior, felt strongly that the Treasury was being defeated in Cabinet far too often, with consequent damage to the department's prestige. Clarke had been the head of the division dealing with expenditure on the social services from 1953 to 1955, before taking charge, as a Third Secretary, of the Treasury's planning staff, and he became convinced that the whole system of Treasury control had to be revised to ensure that ministers could take a more strategic view of policy priorities and expenditure commitments than was possible with the existing system of annual Estimates. In particular, he advised Makins in 1956 that more attention had to be paid in making expenditure decisions to the effects on the long-term strength of the economy, compared with the attention paid to its short-term balance.[191]

In terms of the modern convention of measuring public expenditure as a ratio of GDP, Treasury control seems to have been working well enough in the

[189] Budget Committee minutes, 13 Dec., and 19 Dec. 1957, T171/487; Hall, *Diaries, 1954–1961*, 136, 144; C(57)168, 17 July 1957, CAB129/88.
[190] Leo Pliatzky, *Getting and Spending: Public Expenditure, Employment and Inflation* (Oxford, 1982), 35.
[191] Clarke to Makins, 28 Dec. 1956, T234/330. What follows draws upon other papers by Clarke in that file; Sir Richard Clarke, *Public Expenditure, Management and Control*, ed. Alec Cairncross (1978), 1–40, and H. Heclo and A. Wildavsky, *The Private Government of Public Money: Community and Policy inside British Politics* (1974), 203–9.

TABLE 9.4. *Expenditure on Defence and Social Services in Financial Years 1951/2–1959/60*

	Defence		Social Services[a]	
	£m.	Percentage gross domestic product	£m.	Percentage gross domestic product
1951/2	1,110.2	(7.5)	2,134.7	(14.5)
1952/3	1,403.7	(8.8)	2,416.1	(15.2)
1953/4	1,364.5	(8.0)	2,532.5	(14.8)
1954/5	1,435.9	(7.9)	2,614.8	(14.5)
1955/6	1,404.9	(7.2)	2,801.8	(14.4)
1956/7	1,525.1	(7.3)	3,010.9	(14.4)
1957/8	1,429.7	(6.5)	3,172.1	(14.4)
1958/9	1,467.7	(6.4)	3,477.9	(14.7)
1959/60	1,475.7	(6.1)	3,718.3	(15.3)

[a] Net expenditure by central government and local authorities.

Sources: Expenditure figures from *Annual Abstract of Statistics 1960*, tables 299 and *1964*, table 37; GDP from C. H. Feinstein, *National Income Expenditure and Output of the United Kingdom, 1855–1965* (Cambridge, 1972), table 3, adjusted from calendar years to financial years.

1950s, in that the ratio fell from 46.6 per cent in 1952 to 41.0 per cent in 1957. However, these years were marked by exceptional reductions in defence expenditure, following the easing of the international tension that had been caused by the Korean War. Social service expenditure, on the other hand, was higher as a percentage of GDP in 1958/9 than it had been in 1951/2 (Table 9.4). There was evidence that the traditional system of controlling expenditure on Supply Services was under strain. Whereas Supplementary Estimates had been exceptional before the war, they had come to be accepted as the inevitable consequence of drawing up Estimates at February prices in a period when prices were rising; but the readiness of the Treasury to grant Supplementary Estimates weakened the discipline imposed by annual Estimates. A spending department which underestimated the cost of a new proposal could reasonably hope to obtain further funding later on. Moreover, since the war, there had been an expansion of public expenditure which could be financed by loans: in particular, there were the development programmes of the nationalized industries, and there was the growth of local authority expenditure, particularly on housing and education. There was good reason, therefore, for Clarke and like-minded officials to fear in the 1950s that the long-term, upward trend in public expenditure would soon be resumed.

The concepts of public expenditure used in the 1950s did not make it easy for the Treasury to express trends in terms of a simple ratio in relation to GDP. Clarke recalled that the distinction between Supply expenditure (above the line in the Chancellor's budget) and loans to nationalized industries and local authorities (below the line) led to misunderstandings within Whitehall, as did the distinction between the Exchequer contribution to national insurance funds and gross expenditure from the funds (which included employers' and employees' contributions). Treasury divisions dealing with Supply Services dealt separately with each spending department. Clarke commented:

In retrospect, the main characteristic of the system was its diffuseness and decentralisation. The management and control of government expenditure was seen as the examination of a mass of spending proposals from departments, each to be considered 'on its merits', with a Judgement Day in January when the Estimates (over 2000 sub-heads) were added up and a view taken whether the budget prospect called for special 'economy' action and if so (as in 1958), how much, and emergency action initiated accordingly.[192]

'Emergency action' created tension between the Treasury and the spending departments, and led to battles in Cabinet, where the Chancellor would find himself forced to make concessions, even when macroeconomic indicators pointed to a need for greater economy in public expenditure. Clarke had never been enthusiastic about attempts to manage the economy by decreasing or increasing public expenditure, particularly public sector investment, in the short term. Instead, he wanted a new system of Treasury control, in which public expenditure would be treated as a whole, with less emphasis on a single financial year, and more emphasis on the need to look ahead over a period of years to ensure that spending departments kept their planning within the resources that were likely to be available to them, thereby reducing the need for emergency action. There were long-term programmes for public investment, including roads, and regular 'forward looks' for defence expenditure, but only one forward survey (in 1955–6) of the cost of the social services.

In July 1958 the House of Commons Select Committee on Estimates, briefed by Treasury officials who thought like Clarke, concluded that the existing system of Estimates submitted annually to Parliament led to insufficient consideration of future commitments and consequences arising from decisions on new proposals.[193] The Select Committee recommended that there should be an independent committee to report on the theory and practice of Treasury control but, in the event, the committee that was appointed in September 1959 under Lord Plowden was very much an insider enquiry, with Treasury officials acting as assessors.[194] Clarke did so much of the drafting that it would be fair to say that the report reflected his views. How far did the report reflect the Treasury's experience in the 1950s, and how different was that experience from earlier decades in the twentieth century?

Like Warren Fisher in 1919, the Plowden Committee concluded that the level of government expenditure was ultimately the consequence of government

---

[192] Clarke, *Public Expenditure*, 3.

[193] *Treasury Control of Expenditure: Sixth Report from the Select Committee on Estimates* (HC 254), PP 1957–8, v. 663.

[194] See Rodney Lowe, 'Milestone or Millstone? The 1959–61 Plowden Committee and its Impact on British Welfare Policy', *Hist. J.*, 40 (1997), 463–91.

policies. It also agreed with Clarke that, under the traditional system of Treasury control, it was only when the annual Estimates were being considered that the Cabinet was in a position to relate public expenditure decisions to what the country could afford, and to the relative importance of one form of expenditure against another; at other times, decisions were made ad hoc, with the Cabinet being involved only when a minister appealed against a decision by the Chancellor of the Exchequer. The Plowden Committee believed that public opinion was no longer as effective a constraint on the growth of public expenditure as it had been in the past, and noted that decisions on many public sector activities involved contractual or moral commitments for several years ahead. Moreover, the scale and complexity of the public sector was greater than ever before, and Keynesian management of the economy meant that the annual budget was no longer seen as a simple balancing of receipts against expenditure; instead taxation and expenditure were used as instruments to influence the economy. For all these reasons, the Committee agreed with Clarke that there was a need for more regular surveys of public expenditure as a whole, and for forecasts of prospective resources, over a period of years ahead, and for means to be found for providing the Chancellor of the Exchequer with more support in Cabinet.[195]

At first sight, it might seem surprising that government policies should be regarded as problematic, from the point of view of Treasury control, given the Conservatives' rhetoric in 1951 on the need to bring public expenditure under control. The government was certainly quick to demand cuts in the size of the Civil Service, and the Treasury was prepared to conduct a fierce inquisition into such 'unsolved riddles' as why the Admiralty needed a staff of 32,000 in 1951 for a fleet that was much smaller than that with which a staff of 8,000 had dealt competently in 1935; or why the Foreign Office had more than quadrupled its establishment over the same period.[196] However, as regards policies, matters went somewhat differently. Churchill certainly gave his support to Treasury demands for short-term economies in public expenditure to deal with the sterling crisis of 1951–2, but an attempt by Bridges in August 1952 to persuade the Prime Minister that decisions also had to be taken about the long-term burden on the economy got nowhere; indeed, Bridges was left 'pretty badly puzzled' as to whether Churchill did not understand the position, 'or was just not going to'. In 1955 Butler was subject to a 'whispering campaign' by some backbenchers who alleged that he was soft on public expenditure, but, as he pointed out to one MP, 'whatever item you suggest for economy, there is always a vocal body of Conservatives whose thrifty principles stop short of that particular item, whether it be agriculture, roads, or subscriptions to the United Nations'.[197]

[195] *Control of Public Expenditure* (Cmnd. 1432), PP 1960–1, xx. 713, paras. 8–12, 31–2.
[196] Alec Johnston (Third Secretary, Treasury) to Bridges, 13 Nov. 1951, and Bridges to Butler, 19 Nov. 1951, T273/323.
[197] Bridges to Butler, 12 Aug. 1952, Butler papers G24; Butler to Mrs Evelyn Emmet, Emmet papers, MS. Eng. hist. C1055, Bodleian Library, Oxford.

The government had also inherited commitments from its Labour predecessor, commitments that could not be easily reduced even when Conservative principles suggested that they should be. The Conservatives did denationalize the steel industry[198] and some road transport services, but had to accept continuing responsibility for the efficiency, and therefore for the investment programmes, of the coal, electricity, and gas industries, the railways, and the airlines. The electricity and gas industries were asked by the Treasury in July 1955 to slow down their investment programmes, and cuts were made in all the nationalized industries' programmes in 1956 and 1957—although an element of these cuts was on paper only since, for practical reasons, the industries were not always able to spend the full amount planned. The Asquithian principle that public capital expenditure should produce a money return sufficient to pay off the capital and interest could not always be applied to the nationalized industries. When Leo Pliatzky, then a junior Treasury official, looked at the railways' modernization plan, he could not see how there could be so much capital expenditure when current revenue was so small.[199] In the event the principle of writing off nationalized industries' debts with Exchequer funds was introduced with the Transport (Railway Finances) Act of 1957.

As already noted, the Treasury made repeated attempts to reduce subsidies on bread and milk, but encountered opposition from the Ministry of Labour, on the grounds that cuts would antagonize the TUC and provoke demands for wage increases, and Macmillan only gained most of the cuts that he wanted in 1956 by threatening resignation. It proved to be even harder to deal with agricultural subsidies. The annual Farm Price Review attempted, in consultation with the farmers' unions, to determine the subsidy that the Exchequer would have to pay to guarantee prices at a level that would enable farmers to maintain their standard of living. One reason why the Treasury did not like this system was that the level of subsidy depended upon fluctuating prices of imports, and was therefore unpredictable. Another reason, however, concerned efficiency in the allocation of resources; as one Treasury official remarked: 'in order to make it possible for a man to scratch out a living from a Welsh hillside' the government guaranteed 'quite unnecessarily high prices for the produce of farmers of the rich soil of East Anglia'.[200]

At Hall's suggestion, Gilbert set up a Treasury working party on agricultural policy, with input from the Economic Section, in April 1955. The Treasury had favoured subsidizing home food production in the late 1940s as an alternative to spending dollars on imports, but, with the easing of the dollar shortage, balance-of-payments arguments were no longer considered to be as important as they had been. Likewise strategic arguments were given short shrift, on the

[198] For the Treasury's role in the denationalization of steel see Kathleen Burk, *The First Privatisation: The Politicians, the City and the Denationalisation of Steel* (1988).
[199] Conversation with Pliatzky.   [200] P. Nicol to Trend, 10 Aug. 1955, T223/290.

grounds that the advent of nuclear weapons made the need to prepare for a long blockade unnecessary. The working party concluded that the level of subsidy was unnecessarily high for the savings to the balance of payments, and recommended that the Ministry of Agriculture carry out a study of the optimum level and distribution of subsidy.[201] However, the Ministry (in the Treasury's view) stalled on the matter, and the total cost to the government of subsidies to agriculture rose from £208.4 million (1 per cent of GDP) in 1955/6 to £288 million (1.27 per cent) in 1957/8. Clarke thought in January 1958 that agriculture was the 'biggest government expenditure scandal', but thereafter the Ministry did change the balance of subsidies from supporting prices to encouraging production and improvements, and the total cost fell to £245.5 million (1.03 per cent of GDP) in 1958/9.[202] The subsidies were political in nature, and could only have been reduced earlier and further if the Conservative party's opposition to subsidies had extended to agriculture.

TABLE 9.5. *Public Expenditure on Selected Social Services*[a] *in Financial Years 1951/2–1959/60*

	Housing		Education		National Health Service	
	£m.	Percentage gross domestic product	£m.	Percentage gross domestic product	£m.	Percentage gross domestic product
1951/2	417.3	(2.8)	416.1	(2.8)	493.9	(3.3)
1952/3	504.8	(3.2)	449.0	(2.8)	497.7	(3.1)
1953/4	544.0	(3.2)	472.3	(2.8)	508.9	(3.0)
1954/5	525.9	(2.9)	517.7	(2.9)	537.0	(3.0)
1955/6	501.6	(2.6)	567.4	(2.9)	583.1	(3.0)
1956/7	490.0	(2.3)	671.3	(3.2)	639.2	(3.1)
1957/8	446.6	(2.0)	756.8	(3.4)	684.7	(3.1)
1958/9	412.7	(1.7)	810.4	(3.4)	731.6	(3.1)
1959/60	445.2	(1.8)	882.3	(3.6)	787.7	(3.2)

[a] All public authorities, eliminating transfers from one public authority to another, to avoid double counting.

Source: Expenditure figures from *Annual Abstract of Statistics 1964*, table 37; GDP from C. H. Feinstein, *National Income, Expenditure and Output of the United Kingdom, 1855–1965* (Cambridge, 1972), table 3, adjusted from calendar years to financial years.

The Treasury's major battles over public expenditure, however, concerned defence and social services, which accounted for approximately 70 per cent of the Supply votes. While the management of the economy, and in particular the balance of payments, would have benefited from lower levels of public expenditure, the figures in Tables 9.4 and 9.5 do not suggest that the Treasury had altogether lost its grip in the 1950s. Increased expenditure on the social services

---

[201] The papers of the working party are in T223/290.
[202] Clarke to Makins, 9 Jan. 1958, T234/330; Gavin McCrone, *The Economics of Subsidising Agriculture* (1962), 46. See also J. K. Bowers, 'British Agricultural Policy since the Second World War', *Agricultural Hist. Rev.*, 33 (1985), 66–76.

was offset by reduced defence expenditure, and, within social services, increased expenditure on education after 1954/5 was offset by lower expenditure on housing. The proportion going to the National Health Service was lower in 1959/60 than it had been in 1951/2. It would seem that the Plowden Report, however perceptive it may have been about the need to reform Treasury control of expenditure, gave a somewhat lugubrious impression of the ability of the Treasury to resist political pressures in the 1950s for higher public expenditure. Such pressures were hardly new, having been experienced throughout the period covered by this book, and, notwithstanding the drama of Thorneycroft's resignation, the traditional system of control through annual Estimates could still concentrate the mind of a Cabinet that had set its heart on tax cuts.

On the other hand, Treasury control was not concerned simply with controlling aggregate expenditure on the different categories of public expenditure. As Sir James Crombie, the Third Secretary in charge of the control of Supply Services expenditure noted in 1953, the Treasury had always advised against arbitrary cuts, as these would be a confession of failure to deal with the problem of government expenditure on merits, and would be inequitable, 'in that the just suffer with the unjust'.[203] To an economist like Ely Devons, the procedure whereby spending departments were cross-examined by the lay critics of the Treasury added little or nothing to the control that should be exercised by the departments' own finance officers.[204] However, it is not clear how otherwise Treasury officials could learn what was going on, and be in a position to advise the Chancellor before policies were debated in Cabinet. Assessment of Treasury control, therefore, also has to deal with the Treasury's influence on Cabinet decisions.

CONTROL OF PUBLIC EXPENDITURE: DEFENCE

As noted in Chapter 8, the Ministry of Defence was responsible for co-ordinating defence policy, and therefore for the balance of expenditure between the Admiralty, the Air Ministry, and the War Office. However, until 1957, central direction of policy, either by the Minister of Defence or the Cabinet's Defence Committee, was weak, and defence strategy at any given time tended to be a compromise embodying the ambitions of the separate defence departments. The Treasury examined the services' Estimates from the point of view of getting the best value for money within the strategic policy laid down by the Defence Committee, and could and did point out what seemed to be extravagances. For example, Humphreys-Davies, the head of the Treasury's Defence Materiel (DM) division, noted in 1953 that the Air Ministry planned to have 240 long-range

---

[203]   Crombie, 'Expenditure 1953/54', 5 Jan. 1953, T273/316.
[204]   Ely Devons, 'Treasury Control' in id., *Essays in Economics* (1961), 87–102.

bombers by 1958 and commented that there was no prospect of enough atomic bombs being produced for such a force by that date 'even on the assumption that no atom bomber ever returns'.[205] Such criticisms probably had little direct influence on the defence departments, who seem to have taken much the same disdainful view of Treasury laymen as the Admiralty had done before the First World War. However, briefed by his officials, the Chancellor could and did use his membership of the Cabinet's Defence Committee to challenge the defence departments' demands. For example, in 1957, Thorneycroft was able to persuade the Minister of Defence, Duncan Sandys, to accept a reduction in the RAF's bomber programme.[206]

The DM division devoted its main effort to attempting to persuade the individual defence departments to keep their expenditure within an annual total agreed between the Treasury and the Ministry of Defence. This task was by no means easy: the growing sophistication of weapons systems, requiring long-drawn-out research and development programmes in a period of rising prices, led to many examples of costs being underestimated, and consequent criticism by the Parliamentary Committee of Public Accounts and the Select Committee on Estimates.

It was responsibility for management of the economy that gave the Treasury its strongest arguments for controlling defence expenditure. The balance-of-payments deficit in 1951 gave the Treasury the opportunity to call for a review of the rearmament programme that the Conservatives had inherited from Labour, particularly with a view to reducing demand on metal-using industries in order to release capacity for exports. The review revealed that the programme could not be completed by March 1954, as planned, and that defence expenditure was likely to continue to rise until at least 1955/6, when, unless something were done, it would reach £1,867 million, compared with the original programme's peak of £1,694 million in 1953/4. It was clear that the scale of the rearmament programme was incompatible with an economic policy that aimed to strengthen Britain's balance of payments. Eventually, after the Chancellor had failed to persuade the Minister of Defence to accept a ceiling of £1,600 million for 1953/4, the Cabinet set up a 'radical review' by a committee under Sir Norman Brook, the Cabinet Secretary, which concluded that defence expenditure could only be kept at its current level if there were major changes in policy, such as reducing commitments outside Europe and cutting down on research and development. Such changes did not come immediately, but by 1954 it was accepted in Whitehall that the defence programme should be worked out on at least a three-year basis.[207] Churchill raised the possibility of a

[205] Humphreys-Davies to Crombie and Gilbert, 30 Apr. 1953, T234/276.

[206] Martin S. Navias, *Nuclear Weapons and British Strategic Planning, 1955–1958* (Oxford, 1991), 166–72.

[207] G. R. M. Hartcup, 'History of the Defence Budget 1946–71', Treasury Historical Memorandum (1971), 4–8, T267/23. For the impact of the Treasury's economic arguments on the navy see E. J. Grove, *Vanguard to Trident: British Naval Policy since World War II* (Annapolis, Md., 1987), ch. 3.

Defence Loan, on the precedent of 1937, but Treasury officials advised Butler that there could be no certainty that such borrowing would be temporary, since the development of new weapons was always likely to lead to a need to replace defence equipment; that borrowing was suitable only for revenue items; and that to start borrowing for defence might impair financial confidence.[208] In the event Churchill did not pursue the idea.

As Minister of Defence in 1954 and 1955, Macmillan became convinced that there was no effective defence against the hydrogen bomb. As Chancellor from 1955 to 1957 he accepted Treasury officials' arguments on the defence programme's detrimental effects on the balance of payments: 'it is defence expenditure which has broken our backs', he told the Prime Minister. Macmillan believed that the air defence of the United Kingdom, insofar as it was practicable at all, would depend less and less upon manned fighters, which the Air Ministry had ordered in large numbers, and more and more on the use of guided weapons. He warned Eden that 'when the story of the aeroplanes finally comes out, it will be the greatest tragedy, if not scandal, in our history'.[209] The Defence Committee agreed that the defence departments should assess the consequences of reducing defence expenditure to £1,450 million in 1958/9 and later years, but the defence staffs' attention was diverted by the Suez crisis. It was not until Macmillan became Prime Minister, and appointed Duncan Sandys as Minister of Defence, that the defence departments were forced to accept radical changes in strategic policy. With Thorneycroft pressing hard for cuts in defence expenditure, the outcome was the 1957 white paper, *Defence: Outline of Future Policy*, which sought to reconcile strategy with economics by emphasizing nuclear deterrence, and by reducing the conventional forces and abolishing conscription.[210]

The Treasury's task was to ensure that the impact of the new policies was felt in the defence Estimates. The Ministry of Defence hoped to bring the Estimates for 1958/9 down to £1,450 million but came up with a figure of £1,511 million at the end of 1957, partly because of rising costs, and partly because the Admiralty, at a late date, wished to retain more ships than originally planned. In the event, the Treasury succeeded in bringing the Estimates down to £1,483 million. More significantly, in April 1958 it agreed with the Ministry of Defence that in future defence expenditure would be considered on the basis of three-year programmes, with long-term costings to take account of likely increases in pay and prices.

In general, the case of defence expenditure presents a picture of growing effectiveness of Treasury control of expenditure over the decade. The Treasury had had little control over the defence departments down to about 1955–6, since

[208] Crombie, 'Defence Review', 22 Oct. 1954, T225/440.
[209] Macmillan to Eden, 23 Mar. 1956, PREM11/1326.
[210] Cmnd. 124, PP 1956–7, xxiii. 489. See also S. J. Ball, 'Harold Macmillan and the Politics of Defence', *20th Cent. Brit. Hist.*, 6 (1995), 78–100.

there had been no firm ceilings on expenditure in future years, and a proposal excluded from the annual Estimates in one year could be held over for another. However, acceptance by the Cabinet that there must be ceilings for defence expenditure, and the introduction of long-term costings, together enabled the Treasury both to participate in the formulation of policy and to advise ministers on ceilings on expenditure for a number of years ahead.

CONTROL OF PUBLIC EXPENDITURE: SOCIAL SERVICES

The Conservatives entered office pledged to maintain the standards of the social services, which implied a rising level of expenditure, given the effects of the post-war bulge in the birth rate on the cost of education, and of the increasing proportion of the population above retirement age on the cost of pensions and other cash benefits. In addition, there was the Conservative election pledge to increase house building. It was therefore extraordinarily difficult for the Treasury to achieve any cuts in social service expenditure that involved changes in policy, even when, as from 1955 to 1958, the government had agreed in principle that economies in public expenditure were necessary, both to find room in the budget for tax cuts and to protect sterling.

As an alternative to what had proved to be ineffectual annual economy exercises, Clarke suggested in May 1955 that the Treasury should initiate a review of social services expenditure for the next five years, with a view to keeping its growth in line with the growth of GNP, and thereby strengthening Treasury control, by making the social services ministers compete for a share of a given percentage of GNP. In the event, although the review showed that social services expenditure under existing policies would increase more quickly than the Treasury's estimate of the likely increase in GNP, and although the Cabinet appointed a Social Services Committee, chaired by Butler, to examine the issues raised by the review, six months of ministerial wrangling from January to July 1956 produced economies totalling only £16.6 million against the Treasury's target of £137 million. Indeed, the principal effect of the exercise was to provide an opportunity for the social services ministers to argue political cases against economies in the welfare state.[211] Clarke continued to believe that it would be possible to contain the growth of social services expenditure if decisions could be taken far enough ahead,[212] but the exercise of reviewing social services expenditure over the next five years was not repeated in the 1950s.

Proposals for expenditure on the individual social services tended therefore to be considered on their merits, and ministers were as much concerned with

---

[211] See R. Lowe, 'Resignation at the Treasury: The Social Services Committee and the Failure to Reform the Welfare State, 1955–57', *J. Social Policy*, 18 (1989), 505–26. The committee's papers are in CAB134/1327.   [212] Clarke to Makins, 28 Dec. 1956, T234/330.

political as with economic arguments. Housing was a striking case in point, since there was a direct conflict between the Conservatives' electoral commitment to have 300,000 houses built each year (compared with 200,000 under the Labour government) and the government's declaration in the King's speech in 1951 that the balance-of-payments crisis was its first priority. More building implied more imports of timber, and diversion of labour from exports. However, as Minister for Housing and Local Government, Macmillan enjoyed Churchill's full support against the Treasury's efforts to secure economies in his programme for housing completions, which projected targets of 230,000 for 1952, 260,000 for 1953, and 300,000 for 1954, these figures to include both local authority and private building. Butler argued in Cabinet in December 1951 that the goal of 300,000 completions was unrealistic, but Macmillan's programme was approved, subject only to accepting limitations, which could not readily be enforced, on labour and raw materials. Battle was joined again in June 1952, when Butler called for the housing programme for 1953 to be slowed down in order to direct resources towards productive investment and exports, but the Cabinet refused to hold back on its most popular policy. By May 1953 Macmillan was so confident in his dealings with the Treasury that he issued what the Financial Secretary, John Boyd-Carpenter, called 'a direct challenge' to Butler's authority as Chancellor, by making it clear that he intended to exceed his Estimates, which had been agreed only four or five months earlier, and saying that he would 'get in touch' once he required a Supplementary Estimate.[213] There were 326,000 completions in 1953, against the target of 260,000. Macmillan agreed with Butler to limit the 1954 programme to 300,000, but, then quietly authorized his officials to exceed this ceiling to avoid having to place severe restrictions on local authority building to accommodate expanding output by private developers. As a result, there were 354,000 completions in 1954. In his memoirs, Macmillan admitted that in his battles with the Treasury he had got 'rather more than my fair share of resources'.[214]

Treasury officials did not feel able to challenge the 300,000 target until after the 1955 election, by which date private developers were responsible for over a third of all completions, compared with an eighth in 1951. It was government policy to promote housing for owner-occupation, and to encourage local authorities to restrict their activities to slum clearance, overcrowding, and provision for the elderly. Exchequer subsidies ceased to be available for construction for general needs from the end of 1956, and local authority completions fell from 171,000 in that year to 125,000 in 1959. Thus the Treasury was eventually able to apply the brake to public expenditure on housing, but only once government priorities had changed.

[213] 'Ministry of Housing and Local Government—Treasury Control of Expenditure', by Boyd-Carpenter, 3 June 1953, T273/323. For Butler's battles with Macmillan see Harriet Jones, 'The Conservative Party and the Welfare State, 1942–1955', Ph.D. (London, 1992), 236–42, 251–8.
[214] Macmillan, *Tides of Fortune*, 375.

A further example of the limits of the Treasury's ability to influence policy relates to the development of New Towns by Development Corporations, which had access through the Ministry of Housing and Local Government to Exchequer finance at the same interest rate as loans from the Public Works Loan Board to local authorities. In 1953 Butler and Macmillan agreed that there should be as much investment as possible by private developers in New Towns, to reduce demands on the Exchequer. However, by 1955 it had become apparent that the value of property in the centres of New Towns was likely to rise considerably as the latter were developed, and the Treasury urged on the Ministry a policy of encouraging the New Town Development Corporations themselves to build commercial premises for rent, with a view to the state reaping the increase in the value of property. However, although the Treasury could exempt the New Towns from restrictions on public investment in the autumn of 1955, it could not dictate policy to the Ministry, which supported the New Town Development Corporations in seeking to involve private capital in the development of New Town centres. Treasury control was better adapted to restraining public enterprise than it was to promoting it.[215]

In the early 1950s priority for the housing programme held back investment in schools, except in new housing areas. The Treasury also sought economies in current expenditure on education, and various economy measures, such as raising the school entry age, reducing the leaving age, or the introduction of fees, were considered and rejected by a ministerial Committee on Supply Expenditure chaired by the Chancellor in 1953. In the light of this experience, Crombie concluded that these measures were not worth while pursuing thereafter for political reasons.[216] As it happened, the replacement of Florence Horsbrugh as Minister of Education by Sir David Eccles in October 1954 made the Treasury's quest for economies even harder. Horsbrugh had not enjoyed the Prime Minister's support; Eccles did. He presented education as a means both of creating greater equality of opportunity and of meeting business's demands for a more technically aware workforce. Moreover, he adopted tactics used by Macmillan in his housing drive: targets were set and widely publicized, making it impossible for the Treasury to cut back on educational building even in 1955, when there was pressure on sterling.[217] As a result, expenditure on all forms of education rose from 2.9 per cent of GDP in 1954/5 to 3.4 per cent in 1957/8.

In contrast, public expenditure on the National Health Service, measured as a percentage of GDP, remained remarkably stable in the 1950s. Unlike the ministers of housing and education, ministers of health lacked Cabinet rank, and the political priority given first to housing and then to schools, and the

---

[215] Carol E. Heim, 'The Treasury as Developer-Capitalist? British New Town Building in the 1950s', *J. Econ. Hist.*, 50 (1990), 903–24.

[216] Crombie, 'Economy 1954/55', 11 Nov. 1953, T273/323.

[217] See Dennis Dean, 'Preservation or Renovation? The Dilemmas of Conservative Educational Policy, 1955–1960', *20th Cent. Brit. Hist.*, 3 (1992), 3–31.

Treasury's constant pressure for economy, ensured that capital expenditure on hospitals in the 1950s was 'manifestly inadequate', even according to a Treasury witness to the Select Committee on Estimates.[218] However, current expenditure on hospitals continued to rise; ministers were reluctant to take unpopular measures, and there were very strong pressures within the NHS for higher pay. While preparing the 1952/3 Estimates, officials in the Treasury and the health departments agreed on a range of possible economy measures, but ministers shied away from the imposition of hospital charges on patients or the partial abolition of the dental or ophthalmic services, and the Cabinet reduced the target for savings on the NHS from £38 million to £25 million, to be achieved mainly through prescription charges. In the event, these savings were more than offset by an award, through arbitration, of improved remuneration to general practitioners, which required a Supplementary Estimate of £40 million in 1952/3.

Confronted in November 1952 with increased Estimates for the cost of the hospital service, Treasury officials cast about for ways in which to bring expenditure under control. Edward Playfair, a Third Secretary, who came from a medical family and read medical journals, commented on how a free health service had made physicians' professional standards the sole consideration in determining the standard of treatment, 'although we all know perfectly well that there is a wide variety, both of amenity of treatment and actual choice of methods of treatment, within which one can choose without endangering life and limb'. Since it was impossible for laymen, be they civil servants or politicians, to challenge professional experts, Playfair took up the idea, apparently originally the Chancellor's, of an independent enquiry into the financing of the NHS. Playfair's first thought was that the chairman should be an eminent scientist who knew the medical world, but who was not a clinical doctor. However, no such person could be found with time in which to do the work as quickly as the Treasury wanted, and Butler chose Claude Guillebaud, a Cambridge economist.[219]

The Guillebaud enquiry proved to be a major disappointment to the Treasury. Its report was not published until January 1956, and meanwhile consideration of major economy measures had to be delayed. Moreover the Guillebaud Committee was influenced by the weight of evidence, which it took from representatives from all parts of the NHS, in favour of a period of stability in order to allow existing arrangements to settle down. Even worse, from the Treasury's point of view, Guillebaud asked the National Institute of Economic and Social Research to undertake an economic analysis of the costs of the NHS, and this analysis showed that the current net cost of the NHS in England and Wales to

---

[218] Charles Webster, *The Health Services since the War*, vol. i. (1988), 342. What follows draws upon ch. 6. of that work.
[219] Playfair to Gilbert, 21 Nov. 1952, T273/329, and Playfair to Gilbert, 11 Mar. 1953, T227/333.

public funds, expressed as a percentage of GNP, was lower in 1953/4 than it had been in 1949/50. The Guillebaud Committee concluded that there was no opportunity for making recommendations that would produce major savings in expenditure or new sources of income; indeed, in the interests of future efficiency, it recommended replacing older buildings by increasing hospital capital expenditure in England and Wales from £9.4 million in 1953/4 to £30 million a year over the seven years starting in 1958/9.[220] The Treasury was already committed to a programme which would rise to £21 million for Great Britain, but thought that the programme could be held there. Coming as the Guillebaud Report did at a time when the Treasury was struggling to hold down public investment for macroeconomic reasons, it is hardly surprising that Sir Herbert Brittain described it as 'pretty awful', or that Macmillan, as Chancellor, insisted that the publication of the report should be accompanied by a statement that 'in view of the economic situation the government cannot undertake any additional financial commitments in respect of the Health Services at the present time'.[221]

In the event, the Treasury's pressure was maintained down to 1957, when Thorneycroft was able to hold the hospital capital development budget for England and Wales to £19 million for 1958/9, and £21 million for 1959/60, compared with the Ministry of Health's bids for £20 million and £25 million respectively. However, the longer-term consequence of restraint in capital expenditure on hospitals in the 1950s was the need, accepted even by the Treasury in 1962, for a ten-year, £500-million programme—which was presented to Parliament, ironically enough, by Enoch Powell, as Minister of Health. NHS Expenditure as a whole increased by 13.3 per cent in volume terms between 1950 and 1958, but it is difficult to disagree with the official historian that this rate of increase was inadequate for a service faced with growing demand from demographic change and the need for modernization.[222] The Treasury in the 1950s successfully prevented the health service from becoming an open-ended commitment, but at the cost of delaying capital expenditure to a period when there would be no more slack in the economy than there had been in the 1950s.

Old-age pensions represented another possibly open-ended commitment, owing to the growing numbers of dependent elderly people and the increasing tendency for people to retire from paid employment when they reached the age when they qualified for pensions (65 for men; 60 for women). The low level of unemployment since the war had allowed the National Insurance Fund to remain in surplus, but a joint study by the Treasury, the Ministry of National Insurance, the Government Actuary, and the Economic Section in

---

[220] *Report of the Committee of Enquiry into the Cost of the National Health Service* (Cmd. 9663), PP 1955–6, xx. 833; The National Institute's analysis was published as Brian Abel-Smith and Richard Titmuss, *The Cost of the National Health Service in England and Wales* (Cambridge, 1956).

[221] Webster, op. cit. 210–11. The Treasury's reactions are in T227/424.

[222] Webster, *The Health Services since the War*, vol. ii (1996), 6, 92–106.

1952 showed that from 1954/5 there would be a growing excess of outgoings over income from contributions from employers, workers, and the Exchequer at current rates. The calculations assumed an average rate of unemployment of 4 per cent from 1955/6 (compared with current levels of about 2 per cent) but, even so, old-age pensions, which represented over 60 per cent of the out-goings from the Fund in the early 1950s, were expected to account for over 70 per cent by 1977/8. Gilbert observed that an increase of national income of very nearly 1½ per cent a year would be necessary simply to maintain the stand-ard of living of pensioners relative to average earnings—a situation he com-pared to Alice and the Red Queen in *Through the Looking Glass* having to run very fast in order to keep in the same place.[223]

The National Insurance Act of 1946 provided for quinquennial reports by the Government Actuary on the financial condition of the fund, with the first review due by 1954, but Treasury officials hoped that legislation would follow the election expected in 1955 or 1956, when ministers could be expected to be more willing to make controversial changes in policy. Treasury policy was to make what Playfair called 'a slow but steady push' towards raising the effective retirement age, thereby bringing into employment nearly 300,000 fit but unoccu-pied men between the ages of 65 and 70. The Ministry of National Insurance favoured an enquiry by the National Insurance Advisory Committee under Sir Will Spens, to give the topic the publicity the Ministry thought it deserved, but the Treasury feared that such a course would lead to 'an old people's charter' and preferred an enquiry by a committee which would include an economist, and which would focus on economic problems of supporting ever-increasing numbers of old people. In May 1953 Butler secured the Cabinet's agreement to an independent committee of enquiry, chaired by Sir Thomas Phillips, a former Permanent Secretary of the Ministry of National Insurance, and including Professor Alec Cairncross, an economist with experience of working in Whitehall, as well as representatives of the TUC and other interested parties.[224]

From an actuarial point of view, the problem with the National Insurance Fund was that full rates of pension had been conceded to older entrants whose period of making contributions was shorter than those who entered at age 16. However, in his evidence to the Phillips Committee, Gilbert adopted what might be called a Keynesian position, when it was suggested to him that a sink-ing fund might be set up to deal with the prospective deficit. He argued that the modern budget sought to equate national savings with capital investment, and any funding scheme would have to lead to a large increase in capital investment

[223] 'Finance of the National Insurance Fund', joint memorandum by the Treasury, Ministry of National Insurance, Government Actuary and Economic Section, with comment by Gilbert, 1 Dec. 1952, T227/166.
[224] K. E. Couzens to J. G. Owen, 3 June 1952; Owen to Gilbert, 19 June 1952; Butler to Osbert Peake (Minister of National Insurance), 29 July 1952; and Playfair to Gilbert, 28 Oct. 1952, T227/165.

over and above what would otherwise have taken place. He believed that the present need was for lower taxation, and preferred to treat the prospective deficit on the fund as a future budgetary problem. He consulted Clarke and Hall, who advised that the extra taxation required for a sinking fund would be deflationary, and that the only way in which the present generation could relieve the burden on the next was by increasing the nation's productive power, so that the next generation would have better capital resources and higher productivity.[225]

The Phillips Committee's report was thus generally in line with the Treasury's views in recommending that increases to national insurance contributions should be calculated with reference to the benefits to be enjoyed by new entrants, and not to the cost of paying increased benefits to existing pensioners, and also in recommending that the minimum pension ages for men and women should be gradually raised to 68 and 63 respectively. However, the reservations by the TUC representatives on raising the retirement ages made it clear to the Treasury that it would be extremely difficult to implement this recommendation. The Cabinet agreed that there should be no public statement that would prejudice the line that the government would take, and invited Osbert Peake, the Minister of Pensions and National Insurance, to consider with the Chancellor what should be said in Parliament. However, instead of doing so, Peake introduced his National Insurance Bill in December 1954 with the remark that he was sceptical whether there would be any gain, either to the Insurance Fund or to the economy, from raising the retirement age. Thus, Butler had to avoid any clear statement of the Treasury's views when he came to take part in the debate on the Phillips Report, and the most that Treasury officials could hope for was that an increase in the retirement age would not be ruled out in future.[226]

In the event, this hope was not to be fulfilled, and subsequent discussion on national insurance legislation turned on the levels of contributions necessary for improved benefits, and on the assumptions embodied in the actuarial calculations. In 1957 the Government Actuary raised the question of whether the assumption of 4 per cent unemployment should be continued, pointing out that if the assumed rate were reduced to 3 per cent the actuarial contribution for employers and employed persons would be reduced. However, although the Treasury at that time was privately assuming unemployment of $1\frac{1}{2}$ per cent, officials advised against any change in the published assumption that would make it difficult for ministers to raise contributions.[227] By the end of the year it was anticipated that expenditure from the National Insurance Fund would, for

[225] Gilbert's evidence of 8 Oct. 1953, and Clarke and Hall's advice to Gilbert, 24 and 27 Nov. 1953, T227/265.

[226] *Report of the Committee on the Economic and Financial Problems of the Provision for Old Age* (Cmd. 9333), PP 1954–5, vi. 589; Cabinet minutes, 6 Dec. 1954, CAB128/27; 535 HC Deb., 5s, 1954–5, cols. 964–5, and memoranda by K. Whalley, 3 Dec., Gilbert, 9 Dec. 1954 and Clarke, 18 Jan. 1955, T227/416.

[227] Sir George Maddox to B. D. Fraser, 24 July, and Fraser to Whalley, 6 Aug. 1957, T227/446.

the first time, exceed income from contributions (including normal Exchequer supplements) in 1958/9. Treasury officials were perfectly aware that the insurance basis of the scheme was largely a fiction, but they were opposed to the use of the Fund's balances to meet the prospective deficit of £14 million, since then there would be pressure for the balances to be used for improved benefits. Instead they took their stand on the economic argument that the deficit represented the extent to which the purchasing power of one section of the community (the pensioners) would not be offset by a reduction in the purchasing power of other sections (the contributors), and would therefore be inflationary unless matched by increased contributions or taxation.[228] In effect, the principle of an actuarially sound scheme was explicitly replaced with one in which current contributions directly financed current outgoings.

The Treasury's experience in relation to housing, education, the National Health Service, and old-age pensions suggests that its direct influence on policy was limited, and that its ability to control expenditure depended upon Cabinet priorities. On the other hand, the influence of Keynesian thought on the welfare state was not perhaps what one might expect: given the level of aggregate demand, and the need to strengthen the balance of payments, management of the economy pointed to restriction on public expenditure where there was no high political priority. A further effect of Keynesian analysis was the demise of the actuarial principles that had underlain Lloyd George's and Beveridge's approaches to national insurance.

REFLATION 1958–1959: A 'KEYNESIAN' TREASURY?

From the summer of 1955 to the beginning of 1958 the Treasury had pursued a policy of moderate disinflation. There followed a period of stable prices, with the retail price index rising by less than a percentage point between April 1958 and April 1960. On the other hand, there were fears in 1958 about the effects on the British economy of a recession in the United States. By the summer of 1958 industrial production in Britain was lower than a year earlier. Investment was declining, and, with considerable capacity under-employed, there seemed to the Economic Section to be a risk of a further, serious decline.[229] Unemployment had risen from 1.7 per cent in March 1957 to 2 per cent by the time of the budget speech in 1958, and reached 2.8 per cent in January 1959, close to Gaitskell's figure of 3 per cent for full employment. By-election defeats in the spring of 1958 convinced Macmillan that his party would be vulnerable in a general election, and, encouraged by Harrod, he began to press his new

[228] K. Whalley to F. F. Turnbull, 19 Dec. 1957; W. Armstrong to Turnbull, 23 Dec. 1957, and Turnbull to B. D. Fraser, 8 Jan. 1958, T227/915.
[229] Dow, *Management of the British Economy*, 104–5.

Chancellor, Heathcoat Amory, to consider reflationary measures. As Chancellor, Macmillan had told the Cabinet in 1956 that: 'the methods of reversing a deflation which has gone too far are well known and because they involve spending or tax concessions are likely to be only too easy from a political point of view.'[230] As Prime Minister, he was more willing to risk inflation, especially when the Opposition chose in October 1958 to make unemployment the major issue at the opening of what seemed likely to be the last session of Parliament before the general election. He had more understanding of economics than most politicians, but as he noted in his diary: 'the trouble is that Economics is not a science—hardly even an Art. It's a gamble.'[231]

Hall deplored Harrod's influence, and the tendency of ministers to panic over unemployment, but he himself had warned as early as June 1958 that unemployment would reach a politically sensitive level if nothing were done soon. Moreover, the Economic Section underestimated both the boom that developed in 1959 and the associated problems with the balance of payments.[232] Hall did tell the Chancellor in February 1958 that it would be unwise to reverse the government's anti-inflationary policy too soon, and persuaded him, and through him the Prime Minister, that a change in policy from 'restraint to gradual expansion' should be conditional on a solution to the wages problem. In the event, ministers seem to have been content with the fact that, on average, wages were rising no more rapidly in 1958 than in 1957 (see Figure 9.2). Preparations for reflation were put in hand before the 1958 budget, but the budget speech itself on 15 April stated that it was too soon to contemplate a general relaxation of economic policy, and warned that expanding economic activity at home would be an inappropriate, and possibly ruinous, response to a loss of exports due to a world recession.[233]

Treasury officials believed in February and March 1958 that the first step should be help for exports, through export credits (which were already available), followed by an easing of restrictions on private investment. In the event Bank rate was reduced from 7 per cent to 6 per cent on 20 March, and then by $\frac{1}{2}$ per cent steps from May to 4 per cent in November; restrictions on bank advances were removed in July; hire-purchase controls were first relaxed in August and September, and then removed in October; and finally capital issues control was suspended, except for overseas issues, in February 1959. Clarke also suggested in February 1958 that there could be government credits or government-guaranteed loans for private-sector projects that would strengthen the industrial equipment of the community, such as dry docks or a steel mill, where

[230] CP(56)17, 21 Jan. 1956, CAB129/79.   [231] Macmillan diary, 4 Oct. 1958.
[232] Hall, *Diaries, 1954–1961*, 178–9, 193, 207, 210.
[233] Note of meeting in the Chancellor's room, 12 Feb., Prime Minister's minute to Chancellor of the Exchequer, 5 Mar. and Budget Committee minutes, 2 Apr. 1958, T171/487, and Macmillan on 'Gradual Expansion', n.d., but 20 Feb., and Hall on 'Economic Situation', 25 Feb. 1958, T234/372. 586 HC Deb., 5s, 1957–8, col. 50.

these were being held up for lack of finance, and he thought that the budget speech could express willingness to provide increased funds for projects under the Distribution of Industry Act. Indeed, measures to deal with regional unemployment were seen in the Treasury as pre-empting political pressure for general reflation. On the other hand, Clarke thought there was little point in dealing with regional unemployment by housing and non-remunerative public works, since the effect was to raise costs and to make it harder to initiate 'real industrial projects'.[234]

Clarke advised very strongly against any general expansion in public investment. He noted in February 1958: 'we have striven for years to get control over public investment, and to get it properly phased on a long-term basis'. Treasury control, he thought, would be 'irrevocably prejudiced' if the government were suddenly to tell departments, local authorities, and nationalized industries to forget about economy and go in for expansion, for then considerations of profitability and economic justification would easily slip out of sight. However, by July he accepted that there would have to be some departure from Thorneycroft's principle of stability in public sector investment in 1958/9 and 1959/60. Underspending, mainly because of lower-than-expected costs, had resulted in the 1957/8 figure being £1,431 million, instead of the estimated £1,500 million, and the out-turn for 1958/9 was expected to be £1,425 million. Clarke therefore suggested that the ceilings for 1959/60 and 1960/1 be raised by £75 million steps to £1,500 million and £1,575 million, compared with departmental bids of about £1,520 million and £1,670 million respectively (all at constant prices). Although the proposed rates of increases in public sector investment, 5.26 per cent in 1959/60 and 5 per cent in 1960/1, were about double the expected rates of growth in GDP in these years, Hall thought that Clarke's figures were perhaps on the low side. Nevertheless, both he and ministers were more concerned with measures to prevent unemployment rising sharply in the coming winter rather than with the level of investment in 1959/60 or 1960/1, and Clarke's figures for the long-term public sector investment programme were accepted by the Cabinet on 24 July 1958 as a reasonable basis for discussion between the Treasury and the departments which would be responsible for the programmes.[235]

As early as April officials had been identifying investment and maintenance expenditure that could be carried out between October 1958 and September 1959, if approval were given by June 1958, and on 31 July the Cabinet approved the Chancellor's proposals for additional expenditure of £30 million on projects expected to provide work quickly, half of that figure representing authorization of 7,500 additional local authority houses. By October ministers were becoming

[234] Clarke, 'Gradual Expansion', 21 Feb. 1958, T234/372, '1958 Budget Speech', 14 Mar. 1958, T171/487, and 'Unemployment in Scotland', 19 Dec. 1958, T234/343.
[235] Clarke and Hall to Makins, both 8 July 1958, T234/372; Cabinet conclusions, 24 July 1958, CAB128/32.

impatient for results, and the informal ministerial committee that Macmillan set up under his own chairmanship to review reflationary measures seems to have taken little account of the fact that many of the measures that had been approved had not had time to have an effect on employment, although Padmore had pointed this out to the Financial Secretary. The July reflation exercise was followed in November by a second one, costed at £42 million, made up of investment and maintenance that met four criteria set by the Chancellor: the work could be carried out quickly; it would be drawn as far as possible from schemes scheduled for 1960/1; it would have a high labour content; and it could be directed towards areas or sectors of industry where unemployment was high. In December the public sector investment programme for 1959/60 was revised upwards from Clarke's figure of £1,500 million in July to £1,585 million. By January 1959 there still seemed to be no sign of a substantial improvement in employment, with private investment showing little sign of revival, apart from house-building. Macmillan disagreed with Treasury officials' advice that the danger was a boom rather than a slump, and the lack of accurate economic forecasts made it impossible for the latter to resist further authorizations of public sector investment, totalling £30 million, to be carried out by March 1960.[236]

Meanwhile, with Hall taking the lead, the Budget Committee was considering substantial reductions in taxation. The unemployment figures for February 1959 had been lower than for January, but Hall felt that the figures for one month did not mean much. The Budget Committee wished neither to take risks with the balance of payments, which at last seemed quite sound, nor to get the economy moving so quickly that it would be hard to rein back when unemployment had fallen again. On the other hand, officials welcomed the opportunity to make tax reliefs that would encourage private sector investment—hence the reduction of the standard rate of income tax by 9d. (3.75p) to 7s. 9d. (38.75p) and the reintroduction of investment allowances (see above p. 475). The prospect of greater reliance on Treasury bills for Exchequer financing, and therefore of providing greater liquidity with which to expand advances, was regarded, somewhat optimistically, as a process that was readily reversible through the new Special Deposits scheme, whereby the banks could be required to deposit funds with the Bank of England.[237] On the other hand, Hall had to accept that the Chancellor could not bear the idea of a deficit above the line, even though he (Hall) regarded such an attitude as 'quite inconsistent with the principle on which all post-war budgets had been constructed'.[238] Indeed, Heathcoat Amory was anxious to avoid making tax reliefs in 1959 that would be so substantial that

---

[236] Macmillan, *Riding the Storm*, 726–8; 'Reflation Diary', 17 Nov. 1958, T234/372.

[237] Hall, 'Economic Outlook for 1959', 17 Dec. 1958, T171/501; Budget Committee minutes, 25 Feb. 1959, T171/496; Hall, *Diaries, 1954–1961*, 191, 194–5; Board of Inland Revenue and Treasury briefs for budget debates, T171/671.

[238] 'Economic Outlook for 1959', by Hall, T171/501.

they would have to be followed by tax increases in 1960, on the grounds that such a course would be 'unfortunate politically'[239]—a reference, no doubt, to Butler's experience in 1955.

The outcome of the reflationary measures suggests that Treasury reluctance to give way fully to ministerial pressure to expand public investment was justified. It is not possible to disaggregate the effects of the different measures taken in 1958 and 1959, but the overall effect, together with a largely unforeseen demand for exports, placed a great strain on the labour market. After the middle of 1959 a rising proportion of consumer demand was met by increasing imports, and the balance of payments deteriorated markedly, notwithstanding the rise in exports. Bank rate had to be raised from 4 per cent to 5 per cent in January 1960, and to 6 per cent in June. A 'no-change' budget in April was followed at the end of the month by the reimposition of hire-purchase restrictions, and the first call for Special Deposits from the clearing banks. However, the banks responded to the latter by selling investments, and advances continued to expand until there was a further call for Special Deposits in June. Much of the increased public sector investment approved in 1958 and 1959 had its full reflationary effect in 1960, when the policy had been reversed. This experience reinforced the Treasury's view that normally the extent to which the level of public investment could be varied within a year was limited to about £30 million (representing employment for an additional 15,000 people), and that, while larger variations might be possible in certain circumstances, an increase of more than £50 million would involve serious risk of damage to efficiency and control. The conclusion drawn in the Treasury was that monetary and fiscal measures should be the main policy instruments, complemented by only marginal adjustments in public investment.[240]

In what sense, then, could the Treasury be described as 'Keynesian' in 1959? One economic historian has claimed that there never was a Keynesian revolution in economic policy, on the grounds that such a revolution required the legitimization of budget deficits to stimulate aggregate demand when necessary to maintain employment.[241] The reluctance of Butler in 1953 and 1954, and Heathcoat Amory in 1959, to contemplate budget deficits above the line may be taken as evidence in support of this view. On the other hand, even Hall, who was committed in theory to budget deficits when necessary, feared the psychological effects of such deficits on financial markets and on confidence in sterling. Moreover, at no time in the 1950s was there an overall budget surplus such as Cripps had achieved from 1948/9 to 1950/1, and the budget accounts were such that there could be considerable reflation through loan-financed expenditure below

[239] Minutes of meeting of Treasury ministers and officials, 9 Mar. 1959, T171/496.

[240] 'Reflation', paper prepared by Economic Section and Home Finance, n.d., but June 1962, T230/588. See also *Public Investment in Great Britain* (Cmnd. 1203), PP 1960–1, xxvii. 1049.

[241] J. Tomlinson, 'Why Was There Never a "Keynesian Revolution" in Economic Policy?', *Econ. Society*, 10 (1981), 72–87.

the line, such as occurred with the expansion of public investment in 1959/60 (see Table 9.3). However, it cannot be said that Treasury officials were enthusiastic converts to the use of public investment to increase employment, fearing as they did the effects on efficiency and Treasury control. As Rollings has pointed out, the arguments used by officials in 1958 and 1959 were very similar to those used by their predecessors in the inter-war period and at the time of discussions on the 1944 white paper on employment policy.[242]

The Treasury, guided by the Economic Section, had been using Keynesian macroeconomic analysis continuously since 1947 to inform the budget judgement, but other factors entered into fiscal policy: in particular, tax reliefs in 1959 represented a resumption of a long-term policy intended to stimulate enterprise, and were therefore not simply aimed at increasing aggregate demand. When the time came to check the growth of aggregate demand, and protect sterling, in 1960, monetary measures were deployed rather than tax increases. Indeed, the use made of Bank rate from 1951 onwards was more in accord with the views of Hawtrey than those of Keynes, although in other respects, notably the absence of a sustained effort to fund floating debt, one can see Keynes's influence. No one can know what advice Keynes would have given in 1959: what one can say is that, through the Economic Section, his ideas were an important influence on policy, but they were not the only influence. Treasury officials continued to be concerned with maintaining rules of public finance which would protect ministers or their departments from the temptation to spend money freely. When Macmillan suggested in October 1958 that roads should be put below the line in the budget (where they could be financed by borrowing) in order to permit increased expenditure without disturbing the balance above the line, Treasury officials objected that such a step would weaken parliamentary (and, by implication, Treasury) control.[243] The tradition whereby central government expenditure, which did not produce a direct revenue, should be paid for out of taxation remained as a curb on Keynesian deficit finance.

SUMMARY

The goals of the managed economy were maintenance of British power and influence, full employment, stable prices, a sound balance of payments, and increased prosperity. The problems with which the Treasury was confronted in managing the economy were not simply intellectual, although ministers and senior officials had varying degrees of comprehension of economic theory, or

[242] Neil Rollings, 'Butskellism, the Postwar Consensus and the Managed Economy', in Harriet Jones and Michael Kandiah (eds.), *The Myth of Consensus: New Views on British History, 1945–64* (1996), 104.
[243] 'Above- and Below-the-Line Accounting', by E. H. Boothroyd, 29 Oct. 1958, T171/501. Boothroyd was a junior official (a principal) but the memorandum incorporated current Treasury doctrine.

technical, although economic forecasts, and the data upon which they were based, were imperfect, and experience of the effects of policy instruments was limited. Professional economists, both inside and outside the Treasury, enjoyed considerable influence on policy, although they did not speak with one voice. However, economic theory had to be applied to given political objectives, both in relation to Britain's and sterling's role abroad, and to social policy at home. There was conflict between economic and political objectives, as when the government in 1951 made the balance of payments its first priority, but also approved a major expansion in housing, with its high import content. Moreover, responsibility for policy was in the hands of ministers, and concern with the Conservatives' chances of re-election influenced Butler's policy on taxation in 1955, Thorneycroft's policy on inflation in 1957, and Heathcoat Amory's (or, more accurately, Macmillan's) policy on unemployment in 1958 and 1959.

Effective management of the economy depended upon effective control of public expenditure. Public expenditure was one of the elements in aggregate demand, and had to be kept within the limits set by the available resources (insofar as these could be calculated) to meet that demand. Moreover inaccurate forecasts of public expenditure compounded the problems facing those responsible for making the economic forecasts upon which budgets were based. The level of public expenditure limited the scope for tax reliefs, although Treasury officials were keen to reduce high rates of direct taxation, so as to encourage enterprise and investment in the private sector. When public expenditure was financed by borrowing, the extent of reliance upon Treasury bills determined the liquidity of the clearing banks, and therefore the ability of the Bank and the Treasury to impose a credit squeeze. There were other inflationary influences in the economy, including the boom in private investment from 1954 to 1957, or trade unionists' demands for higher wages, but public expenditure was what the Treasury should, in theory, have found easiest to control.

As before, however, the Treasury found it difficult to control expenditure programmes that enjoyed political support, notably housing and education, or where the expert could not easily be contradicted, as with defence. The maintenance of balanced budgets above the line, however archaic they might seem to Keynesian economists, had the merit of making ministers think about priorities in current expenditure, while the introduction of long-term programmes for defence expenditure and public investment programmes provided the possibility that ministers would think about policy priorities beyond the annual budget cycle. The traditional system of public finance was under strain, and it is not surprising that at the end of the 1950s the Treasury should have been seeking ways in which to improve its control over expenditure.

CHAPTER TEN

Conclusion

INTRODUCTION

By the 1950s the Treasury was using Keynesian macroeconomic concepts to manage the British economy. On the other hand, Chancellors and officials continued to regard control of public expenditure as an equally important function of the department. Indeed, the two functions were not separate and distinct, because public expenditure was one of the hardest variables to forecast and control. Keynesian economics did not displace the traditional goals of public finance; rather macroeconomic analysis was deployed to persuade ministers to decide priorities in policy in much the same way as had occurred in the days of balanced budgets. Responsibility for managing the economy made the Treasury more dependent upon professional economic advice, but traditional currents of Treasury thought persisted: for example, in the belief that public expenditure and taxation should be held at levels that would not damage private enterprise; in the priority given to maintaining a stable exchange rate; and in the bias in favour of removing restrictions on international trade. The persistence of these attitudes is hardly surprising, given that officials were trained 'on the job', working beside experienced colleagues who had entered the department long before the Keynesian revolution in economic thought. Moreover, high levels of demand in the long post-war boom made inflation rather than unemployment the more pressing problem to be faced, and Keynesian economic management generally required that public expenditure be held down, a task in line with the Treasury's traditional role. What follows reviews the ways in which the Treasury responded to changes in the responsibilities of government between 1906 and 1959, and offers some answers to the questions raised in Chapter 1.

PUBLIC FINANCE

Gladstonian public finance had been based on balanced budgets, the gold standard, and free trade. Treasury officials had been aware even before 1914 that politicians might misuse budgets for electoral reasons. Balanced budgets could not be sustained in wartime, but during the First World War the McKenna rule ensured that revenue would be sufficient to service the enlarged National Debt, and subsequently forecasts of taxation necessary to balance the budget in a 'normal year' were used to curb ambitious reconstruction programmes. Despite dubious accounting practices employed by Churchill and other Chancellors, balanced budgets were a real constraint on spending departments' ambitions in the inter-war period, until borrowing began for rearmament in 1937.

During the Second World War, and under the Labour governments of 1945–51, planning, particularly manpower planning, allied to controls over imports, production, and consumption, displaced the annual cycle of Estimates and the budget as the focus of decision-making. However, budgets, informed by Keynesian macroeconomic analysis, were used to restrict expenditure in the community as a whole. Dalton was prepared to contemplate deliberately having a budget deficit to offset a depression, but in practice the problem he faced was one of excess demand. His successor, Cripps, achieved overall budget surpluses—that is, not only above the line, as Chancellors traditionally had done, but also even after deducting the deficit below the line, which was incurred for purposes for which Parliament had authorized borrowing, such as loans to local authorities and nationalized industries. In modern parlance, he had a negative Public Sector Borrowing Requirement—something his successors in the 1950s failed to achieve.

Despite the use of new economic concepts, Treasury officials defended the traditional form of the budget accounts as a means of controlling public expenditure, and stressed the need to maintain a surplus above the line to sustain confidence in sterling. Politicians accepted the need for budgetary discipline, and, should they be tempted to do otherwise, there was the further discipline of financial markets, where the prices of gilt-edged stock and the sterling exchange rate were determined. Politicians were aware of the electoral benefits of tax cuts and other measures to create what is now called the 'feel-good factor' before an election, and risks were taken in the budgets of 1955 and 1959 that would not have been taken at other times. On the other hand, the risks taken were not great, and the discipline of a fixed exchange rate may help to explain why the statistical evidence for a political business cycle is weak.[1]

The overall budget was in deficit in the 1950s on account of below-the-line financing of local authorities and nationalized industries. However, there were safeguards against a loss of control over public expenditure. The doctrine, propounded by Asquith in 1906, that central government expenditure which would not produce a money return should be paid for out of taxation rather than by borrowing was preserved by keeping such expenditure above the line. The Treasury had powers to withhold sanction for local authority borrowing. Nationalized industries were required by statute to generate sufficient revenue, on an average of good and bad years, to meet interest and redemption of

---

[1] For evidence, or lack of it, for political business cycles see Paul Whiteley, *Political Control of the Macroeconomy* (1986), 66–83.

capital, although some failed to do so. An attempt was made to clarify the obligations of nationalized industries in this respect in 1961, when the period over which their surpluses should be at least sufficient to cover deficits was fixed at five years.[2]

On the other hand, the management of the National Debt changed markedly over the period. The Debt had traditionally been regarded as the price of past wars, and its repayment as a means of releasing capital for private enterprise. The inclusion of a fixed debt charge in the annual budget was also seen by Bradbury as an incentive to economy in public expenditure. However, systematic debt redemption, such as had been carried out under the Sinking Fund Act of 1875 until the First World War, or under the Sinking Fund Act of 1923, was reduced to a minimum in the 1930s, on account of the difficulty of achieving a balanced budget in the wake of the depression. Once it came to be accepted in the 1940s that the size of a budget surplus, or deficit, depended on the balance of demand and supply in the whole economy, the concept of a fixed debt charge became outmoded. Moreover, the National Debt was no longer associated with unproductive expenditure, the bulk of the increase in the Debt after the Second World War being associated with the creation of real assets, such as houses and schools by local authorities, or capital development by nationalized industries. Consequently, the permanent annual charge was abolished in the Finance Act of 1954.

Likewise, relations between the Treasury and the Bank of England underwent considerable changes over the period. Under the pre-1914 gold standard the Bank enjoyed complete independence, with interest rates being determined by the need to maintain a fixed exchange rate. During the First World War the Treasury became the dominant partner in both external and domestic monetary policy. The restoration of the gold standard in 1925 once more allowed the Chancellor to disclaim responsibility for interest rates, but matters changed with its suspension in 1931. Although the Bank was responsible for the execution of monetary policy, it was the Treasury that determined policy in relation to sterling's floating exchange rate and cheap money in the 1930s. The Bank retained its independence, however, to the point that Governor Norman thought that no man could serve both the Bank and the Treasury without suffering from a divided allegiance. Despite nationalization of the Bank in 1946, Governor Cobbold likewise pursued his own agenda from 1949, with the Bank urging restraint in public expenditure as a precondition both for successful domestic monetary policy (including funding short-term debt inherited from the Second World War) and for maintaining confidence in sterling, which was once more exposed to full convertibility, with a fixed exchange rate, at the end of 1958. The Treasury had its own reasons for doing what the City wanted it to do. Ministers could be persuaded to take unpopular measures for the sake of

---

[2] *The Financial and Economic Obligations of the Nationalised Industries* (Cmnd. 1337), PP 1960–1, xxvii. 975.

sterling, and convertibility (which occurred only when the Treasury had decided that the time was ripe) also fitted in with the Treasury's bias in favour of removing obstacles to an expansion of international trade.

Free trade, the third feature of Gladstonian public finance, was, like the gold standard, a casualty of the 1931 crisis. However, Treasury officials continued to fear that protection would make British industry less competitive, even after they had been persuaded of the advantages of tariffs and other restrictions on trade from the point of view of restoring a sound balance of payments, and the Treasury's sympathies remained predominantly towards freer trade. With the reduction in wartime import controls in 1949–50, and again after 1952, Britain once more became an open economy, apart from the need to protect British agriculture. In 1959 only about 4 per cent of total Customs and Excise revenue was accounted for by Customs duties designed primarily to protect British manufacturers from foreign competition.[3]

ECONOMIC MANAGEMENT

A consistent theme in Treasury management of the economy was that Britain lacked natural resources, apart from coal, and that the country had to earn essential imports, both by its industry being competitive in export markets and from 'invisible' exports in the form of international financial services and shipping. It is true that the return to the gold standard in 1925 seemed to indicate a higher priority for finance than for industry, but on that occasion the degree of adjustment in industrial prices and wages had been miscalculated. In the 1930s the exchange rate was deliberately held down to help British exporters. Further doubt about a Treasury prejudice in favour of the City rather than industry arises from restrictions, formal or informal, on overseas investment for most of the inter-war and post-war periods.

Although the Treasury was concerned in the first instance with finance, officials also thought in terms of real resources, as arguments deployed both in the First World War and during the period of rearmament in the 1930s show. Officials assumed that normally the government should compete as little as possible with private enterprise in bidding for loanable funds, because they believed that government expenditure tended to be on unproductive things, and resources had to be left available for private enterprise to use for productive purposes. In the inter-war period this 'Treasury view' had led them to oppose Keynes's ideas on employment policy, and had spurred him to write the *General Theory*, but, as Keynes himself had observed in that book, the differences between him and pre-Keynesian economists disappeared when the economy was at full employment, as it was during and after the Second World War.[4]

---

[3] H. Brittain, *The British Budgetary System* (1959), 80.   [4] *JMK*, vii. 378.

The same view of government expenditure likewise informed Treasury attitudes towards taxation. It is true that before 1914 officials like Blain and Bradbury had supported increased reliance on income tax, but they did so on grounds of equity and in defence of free trade. By 1918, when it was clear that post-war budgets could balance only with much higher tax rates than had prevailed before the war, Blackett stressed the importance of not 'strangling enterprise' with taxation, a concern shared by his successors. However, at all times Treasury officials insisted that reductions in public expenditure should precede tax cuts. Their first priority was sound finance.

The development of the Treasury's role in economic management may be seen as a series of responses to challenges to classic doctrines of laissez-faire. In 1919 the challenge was inflation, and the Treasury and Bank of England responded by using interest rates to curb demand in the private sector, while taking steps to balance the budget, so as to enable the Bank to begin to regain control of money markets by funding debt. In the 1920s unemployment led to demands for loan-financed public works, but the Treasury insisted, successfully, that expenditure should be confined to projects that would help to make Britain more competitive in the world economy—for example, by reducing transport costs. The Treasury's preferred route to economic recovery was by lowering interest rates, although by 1937 Phillips was prepared to admit that counter-cyclical public works had a limited role to play in stabilizing employment. Monetary policy also had a role to play in managing prices and expectations, at least in the special circumstances of the fall in world prices after 1929, in that the depreciation of sterling in 1931 and 1932 was intended to help to restore prices to their pre-depression level, thereby altering the balance of advantage between holding paper assets, on the one hand, and investing in productive assets, on the other, to the disadvantage of the rentier. It is hard to reconcile monetary policy between 1932 and 1939 with claims that the Treasury was biased in favour of the City.

It was the challenge of financing rearmament, not employment policy, that led the Treasury to adopt a measure of fiscal management in the April 1939 budget, when tax increases were withheld in the hope that economic recovery would be stimulated thereby, and revenue increased as the economy moved towards full employment. However, deficit finance was still seen as a temporary expedient, and the intention was to restore budget to balance in 1942/3, and to use mon-etary policy to prevent unemployment thereafter.

It was inflationary pressure in the Second World War that led the Treasury to adopt Keynes's macroeconomic analysis in fiscal policy. However, both during the war and the period of Labour government that followed it, the budget was only one policy instrument, and it was less important than direct controls over consumption, investment, and imports down to 1949, and arguably down to 1952. The reduction in direct controls over investment was compensated for by a revival of use of Bank rate from 1951, and the way in which monetary policy was conducted by the Bank was not entirely to the liking of Hall or Keynesian economists who gave evidence to the Radcliffe Committee. As for variations in levels of public expenditure, which had been advocated by Keynes as a means of evening out booms and slumps, the Treasury's traditional scepticism was endorsed by the Plowden Committee on the control of public expenditure in 1961, when it reported that the possibilities of useful short-term action had been overestimated, and recommended that the goal should be stability in expenditure policy.[5]

The enlargement of the public sector as a result of nationalization, and the need to stabilize prices and wages at full employment, brought the Treasury closer to industrial problems than hitherto. Treasury officials had long preferred government to have a hands-off relationship with industry, except in wartime—for example, in 1918 they had opposed the use of public funds to finance private electricity-generating plants that were not required for war production, and in the inter-war period, when rationalization was being discussed, they had urged that government should not become directly responsible for closures of firms. From the late 1940s, however, the Treasury had to ensure that the nationalized industries had the finance necessary for capital developments. The Treasury also found that it had become involved in wages policy to a degree hitherto confined to wartime. The 1956 white paper, *The Economic Implications of Full Employment*, spelt out the need for moderation in price and wage increases as a condition of full employment in a world in which British goods had to compete in export markets, if the imports necessary to sustain an expanding economy were to be paid for. However, it remained unclear at the end of the decade what, if any, effective action could be taken by government to secure the required degree of moderation.

ECONOMIC ADVICE

Any history of the Treasury and the development of economic management must give a good deal of attention to the increasing importance of advice from professional economists in the course of the twentieth century. However, one must not overlook the continuing influence of the Bank of England, and through the Bank, the City of London. There was less intimate contact between the Treasury and industry, but the views of industrialists, or even of trade unionists, in their own fields were not considered in the Treasury to be less important than the views of economists or financiers.

Keynes did succeed in making the Treasury pay close attention to developments in economic theory and their implications for public policy. Even so, Treasury officials tended to use their considerable critical powers to think up

---

[5] *Control of Public Expenditure* (Cmnd. 1432), PP 1960–1, xx. 713, paras. 22–3.

objections to his ideas on public works, and fiscal and monetary policy. It was the use of macroeconomic analysis in budgetary policy from 1941 that made the Treasury dependent on advice from professional economists, for only they knew how to calculate the economic variables. Although there were different schools of thought among economists, none of those consulted by Treasury ministers or officials could be accurately described as 'monetarist'. The so-called 'monetarism' of Thorneycroft in 1957 and 1958 was not an alternative that found favour with officials, other than Rowan, who was probably influenced chiefly by his responsibilities for overseas finance rather than by economic theory.

Even so, while recognizing the primacy of Keynesian economics from the 1940s to the 1970s, one has also to remember that Treasury willingness in 1945 to consider Keynes's approach to the National Debt depended not only upon his theory of liquidity preference, but also on an assumption that investment would be subject to effective direct controls. There is no evidence that Treasury officials were in a hurry to remove these controls in order to rely solely upon financial instruments. On the contrary, officials regretted the winding up of the interdepartmental Investment Programmes Committee in 1952 because it had been seen as a means of identifying excess pressure on particular industries, and of persuading ministers to make decisions about priorities.

Nor was Keynesian economic analysis used with any degree of precision for some considerable time after the war. Early estimates of national income were rough and ready. The Treasury did not acquire its own statistical division until 1947, and then only because of dissatisfaction with data relating to sterling in the convertibility crisis of that year. By the mid-1950s senior Treasury officials, stung by criticism of the 1955 budget, did become concerned about lack of adequate data for managing the economy, but the problem persisted. In 1961 Hall was to lament that new balance-of-payments figures showed that the economy had been under excess pressure, and that more emphasis ought to have been put on deflation in the 1950s. In this context, the budgets of 1955 and 1959 can be seen as the products of inadequate data, and a long-felt need to reduce direct taxation so as to provide incentives, as well as of short-run electoral calculation.

Economic science, then, did not develop to the point where fine tuning of the economy, with only about 2 per cent of the labour force unemployed, was practical. Nevertheless, the increased reputation of economists, both in the Economic Section and outside Whitehall, meant that ministers had a new source of advice. Whereas Churchill had little choice but to accept views of his officials and the Bank of England on the question of the return to the gold standard in 1925, ministers confronted with the Robot plan in 1952 could look elsewhere for professional advice, and reject the views of the Treasury and Bank of England. Likewise, later in the 1950s, Macmillan could draw upon the advice of Harrod in favour of a greater degree of reflation than Treasury officials or Hall thought wise.

CONTROL OF EXPENDITURE

Recurrent balance-of-payments problems suggest that the Treasury was right to believe that the economy was overburdened in the 1940s and 1950s, and that there was a need for parsimony in public expenditure. It is debatable whether the same can be said for the whole of the inter-war period, but there was ample evidence of weakness in the balance of payments in the 1930s. In any case, the Treasury's reasons for parsimony were not related to macroeconomic considerations alone. Traditionally Treasury control was a means of securing value for money, by putting spending departments under pressure both to choose which of their proposals mattered most, and to execute them as economically as possible. The increased scale of public expenditure meant that in the 1920s, and again after 1945, more responsibility for the control of expenditure had to be delegated to spending departments themselves. However, traditional Treasury criticism of proposals for expenditure helped both to ensure that new policies were carefully thought out, and that ministers could be made aware of the disadvantages as well as the advantages of a particular course of action.

At all times the Treasury could only exercise control when the Cabinet allowed it to do so. Normally Treasury officials were expected to be good at counting candle ends, but matters of high policy had to be referred to ministers. Even Cabinets committed to economy in principle were apt to deviate from that principle in particular cases. In practice, effective Treasury control was only possible when ministers accepted the need to keep within the constraint of a balanced budget, or within the constraints of managing the economy to ensure stable prices and a sound balance of payments. Given the uncertainties of data related to economic management, there was inevitably more scope for disagreement as to what size of budget surplus above the line might be required in the 1950s than had been the case when a precise cash balance between revenue and expenditure was the goal.

Moreover, although expenditure was subject to the discipline of annual Estimates and budgets, many new proposals, even before 1914, involved commitments in future years. Warships, once laid down, could not easily be left half-completed (although some were in the 1940s and 1950s); national insurance against interruption of earnings resulting from ill health or unemployment involved contractual obligations, which governments might subsequently adjust, but which, as experience in the inter-war period showed, could not be disowned altogether. The increasing complexity of weapons systems (and the concomitant difficulty in forecasting their costs) and the increased scope of welfare services inevitably led to a reappraisal of the effectiveness of Treasury control. However, the principal difficulty in the 1950s was that Conservative Chancellors had the greatest difficulty in persuading their Cabinet colleagues to agree to curbs on the growth of public expenditure, even when there was inflationary pressure in the economy.

The Plowden Report of 1961 concluded that decisions on public expenditure should never be taken without consideration of (a) what the country could afford over a period of four or five years, having regard to prospective resources, and (b) the relative importance of one kind of expenditure compared with another.[6] Even in the inter-war period the Treasury had, from time to time, looked forward a number of years in connection with revenue and expenditure, but neither estimates of revenue nor expenditure were related to forecasts of national income (as opposed to government revenue) prior to discussions during the Second World War about the financial consequences of the Beveridge Report. The real genesis of long-term planning of public expenditure in relation to prospective resources lay in the proposal in 1955 by 'Otto' Clarke for a five-year review of social service expenditure, which led, via the Plowden Report, to the Public Expenditure Survey Committee (PESC) system of the 1960s and 1970s, with its five-year programmes for social services, defence, and public sector investment.

It should be added that the PESC system was not, in the long run, any more successful than traditional Treasury control had been in curbing political pressures to spend money. The attempt was made to relate expenditure to growth in national income over a period of time. Unfortunately, neither estimating national income nor measuring public expenditure was an exact science. Ministers had been able to dispute Treasury figures for national income when these had been calculated on a pessimistic basis in 1955. On the other hand, from 1963 growth of national income was assumed to be what rather optimistic forecasts by the National Economic Development Council, which Macmillan had created in 1961, or the Labour government's National Plan of 1965, said it would be. As a result, when national income grew more slowly in relation to forecasts than public expenditure did, public expenditure rose as a proportion of national income, contrary to Treasury hopes.[7]

SOCIAL SERVICES

Much of the literature on social policy assumes that the Treasury has always been hostile to the development of the social services. Yet, as Chapter 2 shows, the Treasury under Asquith and Lloyd George played an active role in setting up old-age pensions and national insurance against ill health and poverty. Even in the inter-war period, when the problem of balancing the budget led to

---

[6] Cmnd. 1432, para. 7.

[7] For the PESC system and its history see R. Clarke, *Public Expenditure, Management and Control*, ed. A. Cairncross (1978); Samuel Goldman, *The Developing System of Public Expenditure Management and Control* (1973); L. Pliatzky, *Getting and Spending: Public Expenditure, Employment and Inflation* (Oxford, 1982); Colin Thain and Maurice Wright, *The Treasury and Whitehall: The Planning and Control of Public Expenditure, 1976–1993* (Oxford, 1995), ch. 3.

major cuts in social services under the Geddes 'axe' and after the May Report, Treasury officials had to accept that the cost of social services would tend to rise subsequently. What they disliked were open-ended commitments where the cost of a social service depended solely upon the demand for it. Major examples of the Treasury acting to curb such commitments can be found in regard to cash benefits for the unemployed in 1931, the suppression of Beveridge's 'subsistence' principle in policy towards social insurance in 1944, and the ceiling placed on National Health Service expenditure in 1951.

The Treasury's attempts to curb the growth of expenditure on the social services in the 1950s had the support of Hall's Keynesian analysis, on the grounds that there was excess demand in the economy. Even so, the Treasury sought to organize an economy drive based upon general principles rather than attempt to impose arbitrary cuts. Moreover, while Treasury officials may have exaggerated when they claimed in the mid-1950s that expenditure on the social services was rising more rapidly than national income, subsequent experience suggests that their fears were not entirely misplaced. For example, the cost of the NHS was to rise from 3.16 per cent of GDP in 1964 to 4.59 per cent in 1975; the corresponding figures for education were 2.82 per cent and 4.79 per cent.[8] These increases could be attributed partly to demographic trends—rising numbers of old and young people in the population. There was another factor, however: with the creation of the welfare state, the normal tendency of spending departments to expand their programmes was strengthened by the increasing number of experts in health or education whose natural ambition to achieve excellence in their fields was less restrained than hitherto by a sense that the public purse was limited.

DEFENCE POLICY

It was always difficult for Treasury laymen to challenge experts in the defence departments. New weapons systems, once invented, could not be ignored, even in peacetime. Moreover, the Treasury's financial arguments were likely to be disregarded by the Cabinet at times of international tension, and it was impossible to sustain Treasury control in wartime. While Treasury parsimony sometimes had adverse effects on Britain's preparedness for war—for example, as regards munitions capacity in 1914—it was also the case that the absence of effective Treasury control could result in wasteful expenditure, such as resulted from a lack of co-ordination between the Admiralty, the Ministry of Munitions, and the War Office during the First World War. Financial restraint put pressure on the experts in the defence departments to establish priorities and to look for

[8] J. F. Wright, *Britain in the Age of Economic Management: An Economic History since 1939* (Oxford, 1979), 166.

value for money, but inter-service rivalry, even after the creation of a Ministry of Defence, meant that defence expenditure was not always as well co-ordinated as it might have been. Chancellors, notably Lloyd George, Churchill, Neville Chamberlain, and Macmillan, found themselves drawn into debates on defence strategy in their quest for economy, and they relied on their officials to provide them with arguments that would persuade defence departments to review their policies.

The key Treasury argument, both in the 1930s and the 1950s, was that scarce resources, especially in the engineering industry, were being diverted from strengthening the national economy, and in particular the balance of payments, to create larger armed forces than the economy could sustain. In retrospect, this argument seemed less than wise in relation to the situation that the country faced at the time of Munich and then subsequently after Dunkirk. Consequently, it was harder for the Treasury to argue for restraint at the time of the Korean War. However, the Cold War produced a situation where there was a classic trade-off between strong defence forces and a strong economy over an indefinite period, and many of the problems of the defence departments and their suppliers, especially the aircraft industry, in the later 1950s arose from the need to slim down programmes that had been conceived on too large a scale at the beginning of the decade.[9]

INTERNATIONAL RELATIONS

The 1930s also cast a shadow over the Treasury's reputation in the conduct of international relations. Despite Fisher's break with Neville Chamberlain over the terms of the Munich agreement, the association in the public mind of the Treasury with the policy of appeasement was not altogether unjustified. However, even in the 1930s the Treasury could not dictate to the Foreign Office, and its real influence on foreign policy was the indirect one of drawing ministers' attention to the weakness of Britain's economic position. While there will probably always be debate about the policy of appeasement in the 1930s, Britain's position would not necessarily have been improved by ministers ignoring the Treasury's economic advice. In 1956 Bridges' warnings about Britain's need for financial support from the United States, if there were to be a conflict over the Suez Canal, failed to prevent Macmillan supporting Eden's decision to attack Egypt, and the consequence was humiliation at the hands of the United States and the United Nations.

The Treasury's true *métier* in international relations was financial diplomacy. In the First World War, and again in the Second, it had to negotiate the best possible terms for financing munitions and other supplies from the United States

---

[9] See, for example, David Edgerton, *England and the Aeroplane* (1991), 88–105.

and other allies. Between the wars there was the long-drawn-out haggling over war debts and reparations. Few members of the Foreign Office would have argued that such technical matters should have been left exclusively to traditional diplomats. On the other hand, as at the Hague conference in 1930, there could be conflict between the Treasury's determination to secure the best possible financial terms (in that case a share of German reparations), and the Foreign Office's hopes of conciliating a foreign power (France). In the Second World War financial diplomacy broadened out into planning the post-war international monetary system, with Keynes playing a leading role. In the 1940s and 1950s relations between the Treasury and the Foreign Office appear to have improved markedly, probably partly because of the common experience of the frustrations of being treated as a junior partner by the United States, and partly because of Bridges' success in co-ordinating economic with other aspects of international relations through interdepartmental committees. In the post-war period the Treasury and Foreign Office shared the same views on the need to maintain British independence and to limit Britain's liabilities in relation to Marshall Aid, the OEEC, the European Coal and Steel Community, and the European Common Market.

OFFICIALS AND MINISTERS

The relationship between civil servants and ministers depended a good deal on personalities, and on the agenda of the government of the day. In 1959, as in 1852, Treasury officials had the influence arising from giving the Chancellor the figures he needed for his budget. On the other hand, ministers could set the agenda, as happened when Lloyd George set out to wage war on poverty before the First World War, or Churchill insisted on a measure of derating for industry in the 1920s, or Macmillan insisted on reflation in 1959. Ministers were not pawns in their officials' hands. Indeed, a Permanent Secretary's lot was not a happy one when confronted by a Lloyd George or a Churchill, although normally relations between minister and officials were amicable.

Although one can trace continuity in Treasury views—for example, on taxation or employment policy—official advice had to take account of what the government of the day could be expected to accept. Since Treasury officials regarded themselves as guardians of the taxpayer's interests, one would expect there to have been less scope for differences of values and attitudes between officials and Conservative ministers. However, officials certainly preferred to work with Snowden rather than Churchill, and Cripps was another austere Labour figure with whom officials seem to have had much in common, even if he regarded them as unsympathetic to his more socialist beliefs. There were, of course, issues on which officials and Labour ministers did not readily agree— for example, on the advisability of a capital levy. However, it is worth noting that, while Dalton and Cripps were reluctant to accept officials' advice on food subsidies in the 1940s, so too were Churchill and Eden in the 1950s.

Thus, although the Treasury did have its own attitudes and aims in relation to public finance regardless of which party was in office, ultimately officials could only advise ministers. The importance of winning interdepartmental battles in Cabinet meant that officials had a consistent preference for strong Chancellors who could articulate Treasury arguments, but Thorneycroft's experience suggests that officials did not expect a Chancellor to be totally uncompromising. On the contrary, notwithstanding the critical tone that they adopted towards other departments' arguments, Treasury officials' training inclined them to compromise and to make the best of collective decisions.

CONTROL OF THE CIVIL SERVICE

Claims that the Treasury made improper use of control of staffs in spending departments to influence policy have not been substantiated. On the other hand, criticisms that the Treasury was insufficiently interested in responding to the increasingly managerial role of the Civil Service in the 1940s are not without foundation. Bridges seems to have aimed at completing Fisher's work in promoting teamwork in a service of generalists, rather than at making far-reaching changes in training or organization and methods. The question arises whether the Treasury was the appropriate body to control the Civil Service, given the department's historic mission to control public expenditure. If one assumes that the Treasury's attitude to public expenditure was essentially negative, then the answer would seem to be no. On the other hand, if one accepts that the Treasury aimed at value for money, then it is not clear why it should have been backward in adapting the Civil Service to a managerial role, since good management aims at maximizing the use of scarce resources. Perhaps one reason for the absence of change before the 1960s was that management training had not yet become very advanced either in British business or in British universities. Another reason was that the Treasury itself in the 1950s was still manned largely by generalist officials, with only about a dozen economists in the Economic Section. The Treasury was only likely to see a need to change the nature of the Civil Service as a whole if it accepted a need to change itself, something which it had not done to any marked degree by 1959.

HOW GOOD WAS THE TREASURY'S ADVICE ON POLICY?

The range, and changing nature, of the Treasury's responsibilities, and the variety of political and economic circumstances with which officials had to deal, between 1906 and 1959, makes it almost impossible to make general statements about the quality of the department's advice. However, some observations can be made. The Treasury failed to undertake or promote any systematic compilation of statistics before the Central Statistical Office began work on regular series during the Second World War, and although considerable improvements were made in national income data in the later 1950s, substantial gaps in financial information were identified by the Radcliffe Committee at the end of the decade. Down to 1940, despite the existence of Hawtrey's Financial Enquiries branch, the data used by the Treasury tended to be compiled on an ad hoc basis, and what official series existed, like the Board of Trade's index of wholesale prices or the Ministry of Labour's working-class cost-of-living index, were not always suitable for the purposes for which they were used in measuring trends.

Another criticism that may be applied to the period as a whole was that, although, or perhaps because, the Treasury stressed the importance of officials who were all-rounders, the department was always short of officials who were competent to advise on financial policy or to conduct financial negotiations. In practice, once officials had reached senior rank on the finance side of the department, they tended to stay there, and officials who moved into that side late in their careers, like Eady or Wilson Smith, do not seem to have been able to achieve the competence of a Chalmers, Bradbury, Hopkins, or Phillips.

On the other hand, a case can be made for generalists in the Treasury's work related to the control of expenditure. Here officials had to be able to see problems of government as a whole, in contrast to the views of officials or experts seeing a problem from a particular point of view. In this respect Treasury officials normally had experience of a range of different government policies, either from having served in different divisions within the Treasury, or (after 1919) from having served in other departments, and were to that extent trained for a managerial role. Arguments prepared for the Chancellor by his officials may often have been wrong, but if they were, other departments had the opportunity to contradict them, either in discussion with the Treasury, or in the Cabinet or one of the Cabinet's committees.

The breadth of the Treasury's responsibilities placed a huge burden on the Permanent Secretary. Even in 1907 Hamilton could draw Asquith's attention to the different qualities required of an administrator, like his fellow Joint Permanent Secretary, Murray, and a 'financial man' like himself. In 1919 Fisher had thought there was a danger that the Treasury would break up into three separate departments, dealing respectively with finance, control of Supply expenditure, and the Civil Service. Fisher, who was an outstanding civil servant, could only exercise very general supervision of most of the Treasury's work, relying heavily upon senior subordinates, especially Hopkins. The same was true of the even more impressive Bridges, who, however, lacked a Hopkins to lean on. Both Bridges and his deputy, Gilbert, showed signs of stress as the amount of work done in the department increased. No official after 1919 found time to match Sir Thomas Heath's achievement of writing a major work on Greek mathematics.

Nevertheless, by acting as the central department of government, the Treasury brought together many streams of official, and some unofficial, advice. Fisher and his successors genuinely sought to promote interdepartmental collaboration, even if Fisher's personality sometimes gave offence. Bridges accepted that the enlargement of the Cabinet Office, over which he had presided during the war, meant that the centre of government must be shared between the Treasury and the Cabinet Office. While there were always disputes between the Treasury and each spending department on particular policies, government was carried on in a more coherent fashion than if each department had gone its own way. Treasury officials did not exercise control over the political wishes of elected politicians; rather they drew the Chancellor's attention to cases where other ministers were acting in ways which were at variance with what had been agreed in Cabinet. Treasury control may not have been the ideal brake on the tendencies in democratic government and bureaucracies identified by public choice theory, but it was certainly better than the alternative of leaving all financial responsibility to the spending departments themselves.

Within the sphere of economic policy there is ample scope for criticism of the Treasury's advice, although even now economic historians do not agree on the extent to which sterling was overvalued in the 1920s, or the extent to which unemployment could have been reduced by more adventurous policies than those adopted in the inter-war period. As part of his technique of persuasion, particularly in the press or pamphlets, Keynes was inclined to imply that economic problems had simple solutions, and too many economists and economic historians have adopted his rhetorical style. The Treasury's counter-arguments were likewise designed to justify policies, and should not be accepted uncritically. Even so, accusations that the Treasury had a 'contempt for production'[10] are hard to square with the Treasury's advice, both in the inter-war and post-war periods, that government expenditure should impinge as little as possible on resources required for productive purposes by industry. That advice was not always taken—for example, the Conservative government preferred to withdraw investment allowances in 1956 rather than abolish the bread subsidy.

The reasons for Britain's poor economic performance relative to most other industrial countries for most of the twentieth century do not by any means lie wholly within the sphere of public policy. However, insofar as public policy could have contributed to a higher growth rate, the Treasury's advice in the 1950s on the need to divert scarce resources from defence to civil production, especially for export, would not seem to be misplaced. Moreover, whereas critics of the Treasury have focused on its responsibility for Britain's economic decline relative to other industrial countries, much less thought has been given to the effects of economic decline on policy. One problem facing the Treasury after 1945 was the unwillingness of successive governments to adapt Britain's

---

[10] S. Pollard, *The Wasting of the British Economy: British Economic Policy 1945 to the Present* (1982), ch. 4.

international role to its straitened economic circumstances. The main failure of economic management in the 1950s lay in the continued weakness of the external balance, and the paucity of Britain's gold and dollar reserves, but this failure by no means reflected the balance of the Treasury's advice. The weakness of the reserves itself reflected the difficulty of controlling public expenditure, at a time when government was committed both to improving the condition of the British people through the welfare state, and to maintaining the armed forces and international commitments of a world power.

SUMMARY

At all times the Treasury sought to maintain rules of public finance that would restrict the propensity of ministers to spend money, and focus their minds on the need to make choices. Keynesian economics was absorbed into official thinking in the 1940s and 1950s, but in ways that reflected the Treasury's traditional concerns about sound finance and control of public expenditure. In addition to the traditional argument that a given proposal for expenditure represented so much on the income tax, officials could use macroeconomic analysis to show that public expenditure commitments were too high in relation to prospective resources. Much had changed in the Treasury during the transition from Gladstonian to Keynesian public finance, but there were continuities—for example, a preference for private enterprise rather than public expenditure, and for an open rather than a closed economy. Nor were the changes necessarily in the direction of less restraint. Whereas traditionally Chancellors had aimed at a balanced budget, with a small surplus to pay off some of the National Debt, post-war Chancellors aimed at a surplus above the line that would offset at least part of the borrowing below the line. The gold standard had gone, but its place had been taken by the discipline of a fixed exchange rate that could be adjusted only in exceptional circumstances. Officials like Bridges and Gilbert retired in 1956 from a very different institution from the one which they had first entered in 1917 and 1914 respectively, but it had by no means lost touch with its traditional aims and attitudes.

Bibliography

All publishers have London offices, unless otherwise stated.

ARCHIVAL SOURCES

Public Record Office, London

Records of the following:

Board of Trade
Cabinet Office
Foreign Office
Prime Minister's Office
Treasury; the Treasury's records include papers of the following officials:

    Bradbury, Sir John (T170)
    Bridges, Sir Edward (T273)
    Hamilton, Sir Edward (T168)
    Hawtrey, Sir Ralph (T208)
    Hopkins, Sir Richard (T175)
    Leith-Ross, Sir Frederick (T188)
    Niemeyer, Sir Otto (T176)
    Phillips, Sir Frederick (T177)

Bank of England

Norman diaries (ADM20)
Chief Cashier's policy files (C40)
London Exchange Committee (C91)
Secretary's files (G15)
Secretary's letter books (G23)

National Archives, Washington, DC

Department of the Treasury: Records of the Bureau of Accounts (RG39)
General Records of the Department of the Treasury (RG56)
Department of State: Decimal Files (RG59)
Department of State: Inter- and Intradepartmental Committees (RG353)

Other Archives

Asquith, H. H., Bodleian Library, Oxford
Attlee, Clement, Bodleian Library, Oxford

Baldwin, Stanley, Cambridge University Library
Brand, R. H., Bodleian Library, Oxford
Butler, R. A., Wren Library, Trinity College, Cambridge
Cairncross, Sir Alec, Glasgow University Archives
Chamberlain, Sir Austen, Birmingham University Library
Chamberlain, Neville, Birmingham University Library
Churchill, Sir Winston, Churchill College, Cambridge
Clay, Sir Henry, Nuffield College, Oxford
Dalton, Hugh, British Library of Political and Economic Science, London
Emmet, Evelyn, Bodleian Library, Oxford
Fisher, Sir Warren, British Library of Political and Economic Science, London
Hamilton, Sir Edward, British Library, London
Hankey, Sir Maurice, Churchill College, Cambridge
Harcourt, Lewis, Bodleian Library, Oxford
Hawtrey, Sir Ralph, Churchill College, Cambridge
Henderson, Sir Hubert D., Nuffield College, Oxford
Kennet, Lord, Cambridge University Library
Keynes, J. M., King's College, Cambridge
Law, Andrew Bonar, House of Lords Record Office, London
Lloyd George, David, House of Lords Record Office, London
Lothian, Lord, National Archives of Scotland, Edinburgh
McKenna, Reginald, Churchill College, Cambridge
Macmillan, Harold, Bodleian Libray, Oxford
Montagu, E. S., Wren Library, Trinity College, Cambridge
Morgenthau, Henry, Franklin D. Roosevelt Library, Hyde Park, New York
Simon, Sir John, Bodleian Library, Oxford
Steel-Maitland, Sir Arthur, National Archives of Scotland, Edinburgh
Weir, Viscount, Churchill College, Cambridge, and Glasgow University Archives
Worthington-Evans, Sir Laming, Bodleian Library, Oxford

PUBLISHED DIARIES, LETTERS, AND PAPERS

Asquith, H. H., *Letters to Venetia Stanley*, ed. M. Brock and E. Brock (Oxford, 1982).
Bridgeman, W., *The Modernisation of Conservative Politics: The Diaries and Letters of William Bridgeman*, ed. P. Williamson (1988).
Cairncross, A., *The Wilson Years: A Treasury Diary, 1964–1969* (1997).
Chamberlain, A., *The Austen Chamberlain Diary Letters: The Correspondence of Sir Austen Chamberlain with his Sisters Hilda and Ida, 1916–1937*, Camden 5th ser., vol. v, ed. R. C. Self (Cambridge, 1995).
Churchill, W. S., *Winston S. Churchill*, ed. M. Gilbert, vol. iv companion, part 2 (1977).
—— *Winston S. Churchill*, ed. M. Gilbert, vol. v companion, part 1 (1979).
Colville, J., *The Fringes of Power: Downing Street Diaries, 1939–1955* (1985).
Crossman, R., *The Diaries of a Cabinet Minister*, vol. i, *Minister of Housing, 1964–66* (1976).
Dalton, H., *The Political Diary of Hugh Dalton, 1918–40, 1945–60*, ed. B. Pimlott (1986).
—— *The Second World War Diary of Hugh Dalton, 1940–45*, ed. B. Pimlott (1986).

Documents on British Foreign Policy, 1919–1939, 1st ser., series 1A, 2nd ser., and 3rd ser.
Documents on British Policy Overseas, 1st and 2nd ser.
Gaitskell, H., *The Diary of Hugh Gaitskell, 1945–1956*, ed. P. Williams (1983).
Hall, R., *The Robert Hall Diaries, 1947–1953*, ed. A. Cairncross (1989), and *1954–1961* (1991).
Henderson, H. D., *The Inter-war Years and Other Papers*, ed. H. Clay (Oxford, 1955).
Hobhouse, C., *Inside Asquith's Cabinet: From the Diaries of Charles Hobhouse*, ed. E. David (1977).
Jones, T., *Whitehall Diary*, 3 vols., ed. K. Middlemas (1969, and 1971).
Keynes, J. M., *Collected Writings of John Maynard Keynes*, 30 vols., ed. E. Johnson and D. Moggridge (1971–89).
Meade, J., *The Collected Papers of James Meade*, vol. i, ed. S. Howson, *Employment and Inflation* (1988); vol. iv, ed. S. Howson and D. Moggridge, *The Cabinet Office Diary, 1944–46* (1990).
Robbins, L., and J. Meade, *The Wartime Diaries of Lionel Robbins and James Meade, 1943–45*, ed. S. Howson and D. Moggridge (1990).
Stevenson, F., *Lloyd George: A Diary by Frances Stevenson*, ed. A. J. P. Taylor (1971).

OFFICIAL PUBLICATIONS

Council on Prices, Productivity and Incomes, *First Report* (1958).
House of Commons Debates
House of Lords Debates
(Macmillan) Committee on Finance and Industry, *Minutes of Evidence*, 2 vols. (1931).
Parliamentary Papers
Public Accounts Committee, *Epitome of the Reports from the Committee of Public Accounts 1857 to 1937 and of Treasury Minutes Thereon* (1938).
(Radcliffe) *Committee on the Working of the Monetary System: Principal Memoranda of Evidence*, 3 vols. (1960).
Royal Commission on Unemployment Insurance, *Evidence*, vol. i (1932).

UNPUBLISHED TREASURY HISTORIES

Hawtrey, R. G., 'Financial History of the War', n.d., Public Record Office, London (T208/204). There is another copy at Churchill College, Cambridge.

Treasury Historical Memoranda, Public Record Office, London (series T267):

Bretherton, R., 'The Control of Demand, 1958 to 1964' (1971).
Ellis-Rees, H., 'The Convertibility Crisis of 1947' (1962).
Hartcup, G. R. M., 'History of the Defence Budget, 1946–1971' (1974).
Holmans, A. E., 'Policy to Control the level of Demand 1953–58' (1965).
Ogilvy-Webb, A. K., 'The Government and Wages, 1945–1960, 4 vols. (1962).
—— 'Long-term Economic Planning, vol. i, 1945–51' (1964).

INTERVIEWS

Author's conversations with the following:

Lord Jay, 11 Nov. 1988
Henry Jenkyns, 10 Oct. 1988
Sir Thomas and Lady Rosalind Padmore, 15 Mar. 1975 and 13 Feb. 1978
Sir Edward Playfair, 21 Apr. 1975 and 17 Sept. 1979
Sir Leo Pliatzky, 9 June 1988
Enoch Powell, 27 Oct. 1988
Sir Denis Rickett, 15 Feb. 1989
Lord Sherfield, 9 June 1988 and 26 July 1990
Lord Thorneycroft, 11 May 1988
Lord Trend, 26 June 1975
Sir John Winnifrith, 31 Jan. 1975

Typescripts of Anthony Seldon's interviews of the following (all in British Oral Archive of Political and Administrative History, British Library of Political and Economic Science, London):

Lord Amory, 2 Feb. 1980
Sir Edward Playfair, 20 May 1980
Lord Roberthall, 23 Apr. and 13 May 1980

NEWSPAPERS

Economist
Financial Times
Listener
Statist
The Times

MEMOIRS

Asquith, H. H. [Earl of Oxford and Asquith], *Memories and Reflections*, 2 vols. (1928).
Braithwaite, W., *Lloyd George's Ambulance Wagon*, ed. H. Bunbury (1957).
Butler, R. A., *The Art of the Possible* (1971).
Chamberlain, A., *Down the Years* (1935).
Chatfield, E., *It Might Happen Again* (1947).
Churchill, W. S., *The World Crisis, 1911–1914*, 4 vols. (1923).
Dalton, H., *High Tide and After: Memoirs, 1945–1960* (1962).
Davidson, J. C. C., *Memoirs of a Conservative: J. C. C. Davidson's Memoirs and Papers, 1910–37*, ed. R. R. James (1969).
Grigg, P. J., *Prejudice and Judgement* (1948).
Jay, D., *Change and Fortune* (1980).
Leith-Ross, F., *Money Talks* (1968).
Lloyd George, D., *War Memoirs*, 6 vols. (1933–6).

Lloyd George, D., *The Truth About the Peace Treaties*, 2 vols. (1938).

MacDougall, D., *Don and Mandarin: Memoirs of an Economist* (1987).

McFadyean, A., *Recollected in Tranquillity* (1964).

Macmillan, H., *Memoirs*, vol. i, *Winds of Change, 1914–1939* (1966); vol. iii, *Tides of Fortune, 1945–1955* (1969); vol. iv, *Riding the Storm, 1956–1959* (1971).

Martindale, H., *From One Generation to Another, 1839–1944* (1944).

Maudling, R., *Memoirs* (1978).

Meynell, A., *Public Servant, Private Woman* (1988).

Plowden, E., *An Industrialist in the Treasury: The Post-War Years* (1989).

Robbins, L., *Autobiography of an Economist* (1971).

Roll, E., *Crowded Hours* (1985).

Salter, A., *Memoirs of a Public Servant* (1961).

—— *Slave of the Lamp: A Public Servant's Notebook* (1967).

Simon, J., *Retrospect* (1952).

Snowden, P., *Autobiography*, 2 vols. (1934).

Walker, C., *Thirty-six Years at the Admiralty* (1934).

Woolton, Lord, *Memoirs* (1959).

OTHER BOOKS AND ARTICLES

Abel-Smith, B., and R. Titmuss, *The Cost of the National Health Service in England and Wales* (Cambridge, 1956).

Addison, P., *The Road to 1945: British Politics and the Second World War* (1975).

—— *Churchill on the Home Front, 1900–1955* (1992).

Aldcroft, D., 'British Monetary Policy and Economic Activity in the 1920s', *Rev. Int. d'Hist. de la Banque*, 5 (1972), 277–304.

Alford, B. W. E., *British Economic Performance, 1945–1975* (1988).

—— R. Lowe, and N. Rollings, *Economic Planning, 1943–1951: A Guide to Documents in the Public Record Office* (1992).

Allen, W. Gore, *The Reluctant Politician: Derick Heathcoat Amory* (1958).

Alt, J. E., and K. A. Chrystal, *Political Economics* (Brighton, 1983).

Anderson, J., *The Organisation of Economic Studies in Relation to the Problems of Government* (1947).

Andrews, L., *The Education Act, 1918* (1976).

Anon., 'Sir Richard Hopkins', *Public Admin.*, 34 (1956), 115–23.

Ashworth, W., *Contracts and Finance* (1953).

Atkin, J., 'Official Regulation of British Overseas Investment, 1914–1931', *Econ. Hist. Rev.*, 2nd ser., 23 (1970), 324–35.

Balderston, T., 'War Finance and Inflation in Britain and Germany, 1914–1918', *Econ. Hist. Rev.*, 2nd ser., 42 (1989), 222–44.

Balfour, C., 'The Anglo-American Loan Negotiations: The US Viewpoint', in J. Fforde, *The Bank of England and Public Policy, 1941–1958* (Cambridge, 1992), 807–22.

Ball, S. J., 'Harold Macmillan and the Politics of Defence: The Market for Strategic Ideas during the Sandys Era Revisited', *20th Cent. Brit. Hist.*, 6 (1995), 78–100.

Balogh, T., 'The Apotheosis of the Dilettante', in H. Thomas (ed.), *The Establishment* (1959), 83–126.

Barkai, H., 'Productivity Patterns, Exchange Rates and the Gold Restoration Debate of the 1920s', *Hist. Pol. Econ.*, 25 (1993), 1–37.

Barker, R. S., 'Civil Service Attitudes and the Economic Planning of the Attlee Government', *J. Contemp. Hist.*, 21 (1986), 473–86.

Barnett, C., *Audit of War: The Illusion and Reality of Britain as a Great Nation* (1986).

—— *The Lost Victory: British Dreams, British Realities, 1945–1950* (1995).

Barro, R. J., 'Government Spending, Interest Rates, Prices and Budget Deficits in the United Kingdom, 1701–1918', *J. Monetary Econ.*, 20 (1987), 221–47.

Bastable, C. F., *Public Finance* (1892).

Beenstock, M., F. Capie, and B. Griffiths, 'Economic Recovery in the United Kingdom in the 1930s', in Bank of England Panel of Academic Consultants, *The UK Economic Recovery in the 1930s*, panel paper 23 (1984).

Beer, S. H., *Treasury Control: The Co-ordination of Financial and Economic Policy in Great Britain* (Oxford, 1956).

Beloff, M., 'The Whitehall Factor: The Role of the Higher Civil Service', in G. Peele and C. Cook (eds.), *The Politics of Reappraisal, 1918–1939* (1975), 209–31.

Bennett, G., 'British Policy in the Far East, 1933–1936: Treasury and Foreign Office', *Mod. Asian Stud.*, 26 (1992), 545–68.

Birkenhead, Lord, *The Prof in Two Worlds: The Official Life of Professor F. A. Lindemann, Viscount Cherwell* (1961).

Black, R. D. Collinson, 'Ralph George Hawtrey', *Proc. Brit. Acad.*, 63 (1977), 363–97.

Blake, R., *The Unknown Prime Minister: The Life and Times of Andrew Bonar Law, 1858–1923* (1955).

Blaug, M., 'Second Thoughts on the Keynesian Revolution', *Hist. Pol. Econ.*, 23 (1991), 171–92.

Blum, J. M., *From the Morgenthau Diaries*, 3 vols. (Boston, Mass., 1959, 1965, and 1967).

Boadle, D. G., 'The Formation of the Foreign Office Economic Relations Section, 1930–1937', *Hist. J.*, 20 (1977), 919–36.

Bond, B., *British Military Policy between the Two World Wars* (Oxford, 1980).

Booth, A., 'An Administrative Experiment in Unemployment Policy in the Thirties', *Public Admin.*, 56 (1978), 139–57.

—— 'The "Keynesian Revolution" in Economic Policy-making', *Econ. Hist. Rev.*, 2nd ser., 36 (1983), 103–23.

—— 'Economic Advice at the Centre of British Government, 1939–41', *Hist. J.*, 29 (1986), 655–75.

—— 'Britain in the 1930s: A Managed Economy?', *Econ. Hist. Rev.*, 2nd ser., 40 (1987), 499–522.

—— *British Economic Policy, 1931–1949: Was There a Keynesian Revolution?* (1989).

—— 'The British Reaction to the Economic Crisis', in W. R. Garside (ed.), *Capitalism in Crisis: International Responses to the Great Depression* (1993), 30–55.

—— and A. W. Coats, 'Some Wartime Observations on the Role of the Economist in Government', *Oxford Econ. Papers*, NS, 32 (1980), 177–209.

—— and M. Pack, *Employment, Capital and Economic Policy: Great Britain, 1918–1939* (Oxford, 1985).

Boothby, R., *Recollections of a Rebel* (1978).

Bowers, J. K., 'British Agricultural Policy since the Second World War', *Agricultural Hist. Rev.*, 33 (1985), 66–76.

Bowley, A. L., *Studies in the National Income, 1924–1938* (Cambridge, 1942).

Bowley, M., *Housing and the State, 1919–1944* (1945).

Boyce, R. W. D., *British Capitalism at the Crossroads, 1919–1932: A Study in Politics, Economics and International Relations* (Cambridge, 1987).

—— 'Creating the Myth of Consensus: Public Opinion and Britain's Return to the Gold Standard in 1925', in P. L. Cottrell and D. E. Moggridge (eds.), *Money and Power: Essays in Honour of L. S. Pressnell* (1988), 173–97.

Boyle, E., 'Who Are the Policy Makers? Minister or Civil Servant?', *Public Admin.*, 43 (1965), 251–9'.

Brand, R. H., *War and National Finance* (1921).

Bridge, A., *Permission to Resign* (1971).

Bridges, E., *Portrait of a Profession: The Civil Service Tradition* (Cambridge, 1950).

—— *Treasury Control* (1950).

—— *The Treasury* (2nd edn., 1966).

Brittain, H., *The British Budgetary System* (1959).

Brittan, S., *The Treasury under the Tories, 1951–1964* (1964).

Broadberry, S. N., 'Fiscal Policy in Britain during the 1930s', *Econ. Hist. Rev.*, 2nd ser., 37 (1984), 95–102.

—— *The British Economy Between the Wars: A Macroeconomic Survey* (Oxford, 1986).

—— 'Cheap Money and the Housing Boom in Interwar Britain: An Economic Appraisal', *Manchester School*, 55 (1987), 378–91.

—— 'Purchasing Power Parity and the Pound-Dollar Rate in the 1930s', *Economica*, NS, 54 (1987), 69–78.

—— 'The Emergence of Mass Unemployment: Explaining Macroeconomic Trends in Britain during the Trans-World War I Period', *Econ. Hist. Rev.*, 2nd ser., 43 (1990), 271–82.

—— and N. F. R. Crafts, 'The Implications of British Macroeconomic Policy in the 1930s for Long Run Growth Performance', *Riv. Storia Econ.*, NS, 7 (1990), 1–19.

Brown, A. J., *The Great Inflation, 1939–1951* (Oxford, 1955).

Buchanan, J. M., and R. E. Wagner, *Democracy in Deficit: The Political Legacy of Lord Keynes* (New York, 1977).

—— J. Burton, and R. E. Wagner, *The Consequences of Mr Keynes* (1978).

Budd, A., *The Politics of Economic Planning* (1978).

—— 'Unemployment Policy Since the War—The Theory and the Practice', in B. Corry (ed.), *Unemployment and the Economists* (Cheltenham, 1996), 89–135.

Burk, K., 'Great Britain in the United States, 1917–1918: The Turning Point', *Int. Hist. Rev.*, 1 (1979), 228–45.

—— 'J. M. Keynes and the Exchange Rate Crisis of July 1917', *Econ. Hist. Rev.*, 2nd ser., 32 (1979), 405–16.

—— 'The Treasury: From Impotence to Power', in id. (ed.), *War and the State: The Transformation of British Government, 1914–1919* (1982), 84–107.

—— *Britain, America and the Sinews of War, 1914–1918* (1985).

—— 'Britain and the Marshall Plan', in C. Wrigley (ed.), *Warfare, Diplomacy and Politics: Essays in Honour of A. J. P. Taylor* (1986), 210–30.

—— 'Finance, Foreign Policy and the Anglo-American Bank: The House of Morgan, 1900–31', *Hist. Research*, 61 (1988), 199–211.

—— *The First Privatisation: The Politicians, the City and the Denationalisation of Steel* (1988).

—— *Morgan Grenfell, 1838–1988: The Biography of a Merchant Bank* (Oxford, 1989).

—— 'The House of Morgan in Financial Diplomacy', in B. J. C. McKercher (ed.), *Anglo-American Relations in the 1920s: The Struggle for Supremacy* (1991), 125–57.

—— 'American Foreign Economic Policy and Lend Lease', in A. Lane and H. Temperley (eds.), *The Rise and Fall of the Grand Alliance, 1941–5* (1995), 43–68.

Buxton, S., *Mr Gladstone as Chancellor of the Exchequer: A Study* (1901).

Cain, N., 'Hawtrey and the Multiplier Theory', *Australian Econ. Hist. Rev.*, 22 (1982), 68–78.

Cain, P. J., 'Political Economy in Edwardian England: The Tariff Reform Controversy', in A. O'Day (ed.), *The Edwardian Age: Conflict and Stability, 1900–1914* (1979), 35–59.

—— and A. G. Hopkins, *British Imperialism: Crisis and Deconstruction, 1914–1990* (1993).

Cairncross, A., *Introduction to Economics* (1st edn., 1944; 2nd edn., 1951).

—— 'Economic Forecasting', *Econ. J.*, 79 (1969), 797–812.

—— *Years of Recovery: British Economic Policy, 1945–51* (1985).

—— *Economics and Economic Policy* (Oxford, 1986).

—— *The Price of War: British Policy on German Reparations, 1941–1949* (Oxford, 1986).

—— *A Country to Play With: Level of Industry Negotiations in Berlin, 1945–46* (Gerrards Cross, 1987).

—— 'Prelude to Radcliffe: Monetary Policy in the United Kingdom, 1948–57', *Riv. Storia Econ.*, 2nd ser., 4 (1987), 1–20.

—— 'Reflections on Economic Ideas and Government Policy: 1939 and After', *20th Cent. Brit. Hist.*, 1 (1990), 318–40.

—— *The British Economy since 1945* (Oxford, 1992).

—— *Austin Robinson: The Life of an Economic Adviser* (1993).

—— 'Economists in Wartime', *Contemp. Eur. Hist.*, 4 (1995), 19–36.

—— and B. Eichengreen, *Sterling in Decline: The Devaluations of 1931, 1949 and 1967* (Oxford, 1983).

—— and N. Watts, *The Economic Section, 1939–1961: A Study in Economic Advising* (1989).

Campion, H., 'Recent Developments in Economic Statistics', *J. Royal Stat. Soc.*, ser. A (general), 1/1 (1958), 1–15.

Capie, F. H., 'The British Tariff and Industrial Protection in the 1930s', *Econ. Hist. Rev.*, 2nd ser., 31 (1978), 399–409.

—— 'Tariffs, Elasticities and Prices in Britain in the 1930s', *Econ. Hist. Rev.*, 2nd ser., 34 (1981), 140–2.

—— *Depression and Protectionism: Britain between the Wars* (1983).

—— 'Effective Protection and Economic Recovery in Britain, 1932–1937', *Econ. Hist. Rev.*, 2nd ser., 44 (1991), 339–42.

—— and M. Collins, 'The Extent of British Economic Recovery in the 1930s', *Econ. and Hist.*, 23 (1980), 40–60.

—— and A. Webber (eds.), *A Monetary History of the United Kingdom, 1870–1982*, vol. i (1985).

Capie, F. H., T. C. Mills, and G. Wood, 'Debt Management and Interest Rates: The British Stock Conversion of 1932', *Applied Econ.*, 18 (1986), 1111–26.

—— T. Mills, and G. Wood, 'What Happened in 1931?', in F. Capie and G. Wood (eds.), *Financial Crises and the World Banking System* (New York, 1986), 120–48.

Carlton, D., *MacDonald versus Henderson: The Foreign Policy of the Second Labour Government* (1970).

—— *Anthony Eden: A Biography* (1981).

Casson, M., *Economics of Unemployment: An Historical Perspective* (Oxford, 1983).

Catterall, R., 'Attitudes to and the Impact of British Monetary Policy in the 1920s', *Rev. Int. d'Hist. de la Banque*, 12 (1976), 29–53.

Caulcott, T. H., 'The Control of Public Expenditure', *Public Admin.*, 40 (1962), 267–88.

Central Statistical Office, *Statistical Digest of the War* (1951).

Chapman, R. A., *Leadership in the British Civil Service: A Study of Sir Percival Waterfield and the Creation of the Civil Service Selection Board* (1984).

—— *Ethics in the British Civil Service* (1988).

—— *The Treasury in Public Policy-making* (1997).

—— and J. R. Greenaway, *The Dynamics of Administrative Reform* (1980).

Charlton, M., *The Price of Victory* (1983).

Chester, D. N. (ed.), *Lessons of the British War Economy* (Cambridge, 1951).

—— [Sir Norman Chester], *The Nationalisation of British Industry, 1945–51* (1975).

—— [Sir Norman Chester], *The English Administrative System, 1780–1870* (Oxford, 1981).

Chick, M., *Industrial Policy in Britain, 1945–1951: Economic Planning, Nationalisation and the Labour Governments* (Cambridge, 1998).

Churchill, R., *Winston S. Churchill*, vol. ii (1967).

Churchill, W. S., *Great Contemporaries* (1937).

Clapham, J., *The Bank of England: A History*, vol. ii (Cambridge, 1944).

Clarke, P., 'The Politics of Keynesian Economics, 1924–1931', in M. Bentley and J. Stevenson (eds.), *High and Low Politics in Modern Britain* (Oxford, 1983), 154–81.

—— *The Keynesian Revolution in the Making, 1924–1936* (Oxford, 1988).

—— 'The Treasury's Analytical Model of the British Economy between the Wars', in M. O. Furner and B. Supple (eds.), *The State and Economic Knowledge: The American and British Experiences* (Cambridge, 1990), 171–207.

—— 'The Twentieth-Century Revolution in Government: The Case of the British Treasury', in F. B. Smith (ed.), *Ireland, England and Australia: Essays in Honour of Oliver MacDonagh* (Canberra and Cork, 1990), 159–79.

—— 'Churchill's Economic Ideas, 1900–1930', in R. Blake and W. R. Louis (eds.), *Churchill* (Oxford, 1993), 79–95.

—— 'Keynes in History', *Hist. Pol. Econ.*, 26 (1994), 117–35.

—— 'The Historical Keynes and the History of Keynesianism', in T. C. W. Blanning and D. Cannadine, *History and Biography: Essays in Honour of Derek Beale* (Cambridge, 1996), 203–26.

—— 'The Keynesian Consensus and its Enemies: The Argument over Macroeconomic Policy in Britain since the Second World War', in D. Marquand and A. Seldon (eds.), *The Ideas That Shaped Post-War Britain* (1996), 67–87.

—— 'Keynes, Buchanan and the Balanced-Budget Doctrine', in J. Maloney (ed.), *Debt and Deficits* (Cheltenham, 1997), 60–83.

Clarke, R., *Public Expenditure, Management and Control*, ed. A. Cairncross (1978).

—— *Anglo-American Economic Collaboration in War and Peace, 1942–1949*, ed. A. Cairncross (Oxford, 1982).

Clarke, S. V. O., *The Reconstruction of the International Monetary System: The Attempts of 1922 and 1933* (Princeton, NJ, 1973).

—— *Exchange-Rate Stabilization in the Mid-1930s: Negotiating the Tripartite Agreement* (Princeton, NJ, 1977).

Clavin, P., 'The World Economic Conference 1933: The Failure of British Internationalism', *J. Eur. Econ. Hist.*, 20 (1991), 489–527.

Clay, H., *Lord Norman* (1957).

Coats, A. W. (ed.), *Economists in Government: An International Comparative Study* (Durham, NC, 1981).

Collins, M., 'Did Keynes Have the Answer to Unemployment in the 1930s?', in J. Hillard (ed.), *J. M. Keynes in Retrospect: The Legacy of the Keynesian Revolution* (Aldershot, 1988), 64–87.

Colvin, I., *Vansittart in Office* (1965).

—— *The Chamberlain Cabinet* (1971).

Conan, A. R., *The Rationale of the Sterling Area* (1961).

Constantine, S., *The Making of British Colonial Development Policy, 1914–1940* (1984).

Cooke, C., *The Life of Richard Stafford Cripps* (1957).

Corry, B. A., 'The Theory of the Economic Effects of Government Expenditure in English Classical Political Economy', *Economica*, NS, 25 (1958), 34–48.

—— (ed.), *Unemployment and the Economists* (Cheltenham, 1996).

Costigliola, F. C., 'Anglo-American Financial Rivalry in the 1920s', *J. Econ. Hist.*, 37 (1977), 911–34.

Crafts, N. F. R., 'Long-term Unemployment and the Wage Equation in Britain, 1925–1939', *Economica*, NS, 56 (1989), 247–54.

Crammond, E., 'The Economic Relations of the British and German Empires', *J. Royal Stat. Soc.*, 77 (1914), 777–807.

Cripps, S., 'Can Socialism Come by Constitutional Methods?', in C. Addison *et al.*, *Problems of a Socialist Government* (1933), 35–66.

Croham, Lord, 'The IEA as Seen from the Civil Service', in A. Seldon (ed.) *The Emerging Consensus: Essays on the Interplay between Ideas, Interests and Circumstances in the First 25 Years of the IEA* (1981), 207–15.

Crombie, J., *Her Majesty's Customs and Excise* (1962).

Cromwell, V., and Z. Steiner, 'Reform and Retrenchment: The Foreign Office between the Wars', in R. Bullen (ed.), *The Foreign Office, 1782–1982* (1984), 85–106.

Cronin, J. E., *The Politics of State Expansion: War, State and Society in Twentieth-Century Britain* (1991).

—— 'Power, Secrecy, and the British Constitution: Vetting Samuel Beer's *Treasury Control*', *20th Cent. Brit. Hist.*, 3 (1992), 59–75.

Cross, C., *Philip Snowden* (1966).

Crowther, A., *British Social Policy, 1914–1939* (1988).

Dalton, H., *Principles of Public Finance* (1923 and 1954).

Daunton, M. J., 'How to Pay for the War: State, Society and Taxation in Britain, 1917–24', *Eng. Hist. Rev.*, 111 (1996), 882–919.

Daunton, M. J., 'Payment and Participation: Welfare and State-Formulation in Britain, 1900–1951', *Past and Present*, 150 (1996), 169–216.

Davidson, R., *Whitehall and the Labour Problem in Late Victorian and Edwardian Britain: A Study in Official Statistics and Social Control* (1985).

—— 'The Measurement of Urban Poverty: A Missing Dimension', *Econ. Hist. Rev.*, 2nd ser., 41 (1988), 299–301.

Dayer, R. A., *Finance and Empire: Sir Charles Addis, 1861–1945* (1988).

Dean, D., 'Preservation or Renovation? The Dilemmas of Conservative Educational Policy, 1955–1960', *20th Cent. Brit. Hist.*, 3 (1992), 3–31.

Deane, P., and Cole, W. A., *British Economic Growth, 1688–1959* (Cambridge, 1962).

Dell, E., *The Chancellors: A History of the Chancellors of the Exchequer, 1945–90* (1996).

Denison, E., 'Economic Growth', in R. Caves, *et al.*, *Britain's Economic Prospects* (Washington, DC, 1968), 231–78.

Deutscher, P., *R. G. Hawtrey and the Development of Macroeconomics* (1990).

Devons, E., 'An Economist's View of the Bank Rate Tribunal Evidence', *Manchester School*, 27 (1959), 1–16.

—— 'Treasury Control', in id., *Essays in Economics* (1961), 87–102.

—— *Papers on Planning and Economic Development*, ed. A. Cairncross (Manchester, 1970).

Dilks, D., *Neville Chamberlain*, vol. i, *1869–1929* (Cambridge, 1984).

—— ' "We Must Hope for the Best and Prepare for the Worst": The Prime Minister, the Cabinet and Hitler's Germany, 1937–1939', *Proc. Brit. Acad.*, 73 (1987), 309–52.

Dimand, R. W., *The Origins of the Keynesian Revolution: The Development of Keynes's Theory of Employment and Output* (Aldershot, 1988).

Dimsdale, N. H., 'Keynes and the Finance of the First World War', in M. Keynes (ed.), *Essays on John Maynard Keynes* (Cambridge, 1975), 142–61.

—— 'British Monetary Policy and the Exchange Rate, 1920–38', *Oxford Econ. Papers*, NS, 33, supplement (1981), 306–42.

—— 'Employment and Real Wages in the Inter-war Period', *Nat. Institute Econ. Rev.*, 110 (1984), 85–93.

—— S. J. Nickell, and N. Horsewood, 'Real Wages and Unemployment in Britain during the 1930s', *Econ. J.*, 99 (1989), 271–92.

Dobson, A. P., *US Wartime Aid to Britain, 1940–46* (1986).

Dow, J. C. R., *The Management of the British Economy, 1945–1960* (Cambridge, 1964).

Dowie, J. A., '1919–20 is in Need of Attention', *Econ. Hist. Rev.*, 2nd ser., 28 (1975), 429–50.

Drummond, I. M., *Imperial Economic Policy, 1917–1939: Studies in Expansion and Protection* (1974).

—— *London, Washington, and the Management of the Franc, 1936–39* (Princeton, NJ, 1979).

—— *The Floating Pound and the Sterling Area, 1931–1939* (Cambridge, 1981).

Durbin, E., *New Jerusalems: The Labour Party and the Economics of Democratic Socialism* (1985).

Dutton, D., *Austen Chamberlain: Gentleman in Politics* (Bolton, 1985).

—— *Simon: A Political Biography of Sir John Simon* (1992).

Edgerton, D., *England and the Aeroplane: An Essay on a Militant and Technological Nation* (1991).

Eichengreen, B., *Sterling and the Tariff, 1929–32* (Princeton, NJ, 1981).

—— *Golden Fetters: The Gold Standard and the Great Depression, 1919–1939* (Oxford, 1992).

—— 'The Origins and Nature of the Great Slump Revisited', *Econ. Hist. Rev.*, 2nd ser., 45 (1992), 213–39.

—— and J. Sachs, 'Exchange Rates and Economic Recovery in the 1930s', *J. Econ. Hist.*, 45 (1985), 925–46.

Ellison, J. R. V., 'Perfidious Albion? Britain, Plan G and European Integration, 1955–56', *Contemp. Brit. Hist.*, 10 (1996), 1–34.

Fanning, R., *The Irish Department of Finance, 1922–58* (Dublin, 1978).

Feiling, K., *The Life of Neville Chamberlain* (1946).

Feinstein, C. H., *National Income, Expenditure and Output of the United Kingdom, 1855–1965* (Cambridge, 1972).

—— 'Britain's Overseas Investments in 1913', *Econ. Hist. Rev.*, 2nd ser., 43 (1990), 288–95.

Ferguson, N., 'Public Finance and National Security: The Domestic Origins of the First World War Revisited', *Past and Present*, 142 (1994), 141–68.

Ferris, J., 'The Theory of a "French Air Menace", Anglo-French Relations and the British Home Defence Air Force Programmes of 1921–25', *J. Strategic Stud.*, 10 (1987), 62–83.

—— 'Treasury Control, the Ten Year Rule and British Service Policies, 1919–1924', *Hist. J.*, 30 (1987), 859–83.

—— *The Evolution of British Strategic Policy, 1919–26* (1989).

Fforde, J., *The Bank of England and Public Policy, 1941–1958* (Cambridge, 1992).

Floud, R., and D. McCloskey (eds.), *The Economic History of Britain since 1700*, vol. ii (Cambridge, 1981).

—— (eds.), *The Economic History of Britain since 1700*, 2nd edn., vols. ii and iii (Cambridge, 1994).

Flux, A. W., 'Gleanings from the Census of Production Report', *J. Royal Stat. Soc.*, 76 (1913), 557–85.

Forbes, N., 'London Banks, the German Standstill Agreements, and "Economic Appeasement" in the 1930s', *Econ. Hist. Rev.*, 2nd ser., 40 (1987), 571–87.

Foreign and Commonwealth Office Historians [Gill Bennett], *Nazi Gold: Information from the British Archives*, FCO History Notes No. 11 (Sept. 1996) and 12 (May 1997).

—— *British Policy Towards Enemy Property During and After the Second World War*, FCO History Notes No. 13 (Apr. 1998).

Foreman-Peck, J., 'The British Tariff and Industrial Protection in the 1930s: An Alternative Model', *Econ. Hist. Rev.*, 2nd ser., 34 (1981), 132–9.

Freeden, M., *The New Liberalism: An Ideology of Social Reform* (Oxford, 1978).

French, D., *British Economic and Strategic Planning, 1905–1915* (1982).

—— *British Strategy and War Aims, 1914–1916* (1986).

—— *The Strategy of the Lloyd George Coalition, 1916–1918* (Oxford, 1995).

Fry, G. K., *Statesmen in Disguise : The Changing Role of the Administrative Class of the British Home Civil Service, 1853–1966* (1969).

—— *Reforming the Civil Service: The Fulton Committee on the British Home Civil Service of 1966–1968* (Edinburgh, 1993).

Furner, M. O., and B. Supple (eds.), *The State and Economic Knowledge: The American and British Experiences* (Cambridge, 1990).

Gardner, R. N., *Sterling–Dollar Diplomacy: The Origins and Prospects of Our International Economic Order* (New York, 1969).

Garside, W. R., *British Unemployment, 1919–1939: A Study in Public Policy* (Cambridge, 1990).

Garside, W. R., and J. J. Greaves, 'Rationalisation and Britain's Industrial Malaise: The Interwar Years Revisited', *J. Eur. Econ. Hist.*, 26 (1997), 37–68.

Gibbs, N. H., *Grand Strategy*, vol. i (1976).

Gilbert, B. B., *David Lloyd George: A Political Life. The Architect of Change, 1863–1912* (1987); *Organizer of Victory* (1992).

Gilbert, M., *Winston S. Churchill*, vol. v, *1922–39* (1976).

—— *'Never Despair': Winston S. Churchill, 1945–65* (1988).

Glynn, S., and A. Booth (eds.), *The Road to Full Employment* (1987).

Goldman, S., *The Developing System of Public Expenditure Management and Control* (1973).

Gordon, G. A. H., *British Seapower and Procurement between the Wars* (1988).

Gorst, A., 'Facing the Facts? The Labour Government and Defence Policy, 1945–1950', in N. Tiratsoo, *The Attlee Years* (1991), 190–209.

Green, E. H. H., 'The Influence of the City over British Economic Policy, *c.*1880–1960', in Y. Cassis (ed.), *Finance and Financiers in European History, 1880–1960* (Cambridge, 1992), 193–218.

Green, S. J. D., and R. C. Whiting (eds.), *The Boundaries of the State in Modern Britain* (Cambridge, 1996).

Greenaway, J. R., 'Warren Fisher and the Transformation of the British Treasury, 1919–39', *J. Brit. Stud.*, 23 (1983), 125–42.

Grigg, J., *Lloyd George: The People's Champion, 1902–1911* (1978).

Grove, E. J., *Vanguard to Trident: British Naval Policy since World War II* (Annapolis, Md., 1987).

Hall, H. Duncan, *North American Supply* (1955).

Hall, P. A. (ed.), *The Political Power of Economic Ideas: Keynesianism Across Nations* (Princeton, NJ, 1989).

Hall, R., *The Economic System in a Socialist State* (1937).

—— 'The Place of Economists in Government', *Oxford Econ. Papers*, 7 (1955), 119–35.

—— 'Reflections on the Practical Application of Economics', *Econ. J.*, 69 (1959), 639–52.

—— 'The End of Full Employment', in C. P. Kindleberger and G. di Tella (eds.), *Economics in the Long View*, vol. iii (1982), 155–74.

Ham, A., *Treasury Rules: Recurrent Themes in British Economic Policy* (1981).

Hamilton, E., *Conversion and Redemption* (1889).

Hamilton, H. P., 'Sir Warren Fisher and the Public Service', *Public Admin.*, 29 (1951), 3–38.

Hammond, R. J., *Food*, vol. i (1951).

Hancock, W. K., and M. M. Gowing, *British War Economy* (1949).

Harris, J., *Unemployment and Politics: A Study in English Social Policy, 1886–1914* (Oxford, 1972).

—— *William Beveridge: A Biography* (Oxford, 1977).

—— 'Bureaucrats and Businessmen in British Food Control, 1916–19', in K. Burk (ed.), *War and the State* (1982), 135–56.

—— 'The Transition to High Politics in English Social Policy, 1880–1914', in M. Bentley and J. Stevenson (eds.), *High and Low Politics in Modern Britain* (Oxford, 1983), 58–79.

—— 'Society and the State in Twentieth-century Britain', in F. M. L. Thompson (ed.), *Cambridge Social History of Britain, 1750–1950*, vol. iii (Cambridge, 1990), 63–117.

—— 'War and Social History: Britain and the Home Front during the Second World War', *Contemp. Eur. Hist.*, 1 (1992), 17–35.

Harrod, R. F., *The Life of John Maynard Keynes* (1951).

—— *Policy Against Inflation* (1958).

—— *The Pound Sterling, 1951–8* (Princeton, NJ, 1958).

—— *Topical Comment: Essays in Dynamic Applied Economics* (1961).

Hatton, T. J., 'The Outlines of a Keynesian Solution', in S. Glynn and A. Booth (eds.), *The Road to Full Employment* (1987), 82–94.

Hawtrey, R. G., *Good and Bad Trade* (1913).

—— 'The Gold Standard', *Econ. J.*, 29 (1919), 428–42.

—— *The Exchequer and the Control of Expenditure* (Oxford, 1921).

—— *Monetary Reconstruction* (1923).

—— 'Public Expenditure and the Demand for Labour', *Economica*, 5 (1925), 38–48.

—— *Currency and Credit* (1928).

—— *Trade Depression and the Way Out* (1931).

—— *A Century of Bank Rate* (1938).

Headlam, M. F., 'Sir Thomas Little Heath', *Proc. Brit. Acad.*, 26 (1940), 425–38.

Heath, T., *The Treasury* (1927).

—— and P. E. Matheson, 'Lord Chalmers, 1858–1938', *Proc. Brit. Acad.*, 25 (1939), 321–32.

Heclo, H., and A. Wildavsky, *The Private Government of Public Money: Community and Policy inside British Politics* (1974).

Heim, C. E., 'The Treasury as Developer-Capitalist? British New Town Building in the 1950s', *J. Econ. Hist.*, 50 (1990), 903–24.

Helsby, L. N., 'Recruitment to the Civil Service', *Pol. Quart.*, 25 (1954), 324–35.

Henderson, H. D., 'The Anglo-American Financial Agreement', *Bull. Oxford Univ. Institute Stat.*, 8 (1946), 1–13.

Henderson, [P.] D., 'The Use of Economists in British Administration', *Oxford Econ. Papers*, NS, 13 (1961), 5–26.

—— *Innocence and Design: The Influence of Economic Ideas on Policy* (Oxford, 1986).

Hennessy, P., *Cabinet* (Oxford, 1986).

—— *Whitehall* (1989).

Hennock, E. P., *British Social Reform and German Precedents: The Case of Social Insurance, 1880–1914* (Oxford, 1987).

Hicks, J. R., *The Problem of Budgetary Reform* (Oxford, 1948).

—— *The Social Framework: An Introduction to Economics* (Oxford, 1942; Oxford, 1952).

Hicks, U., *British Public Finances: Their Structure and Development, 1880–1952* (1958).

—— *The Finance of British Government, 1920–1936* (Oxford, 1970).

Higgs, H., 'Treasury Control', *Public Admin.*, 2 (1924), 122–30.

Hogan, M. J., *The Marshall Plan: America, Britain and the Reconstruction of Western Europe* (Cambridge, 1987).

Honigsbaum, F., *Health, Happiness and Security: The Creation of the National Health Service* (1989).

Horne, A., *Macmillan*, vol. i, *1894–1956* (1988); vol. ii, *1957–1986* (1989).

Howard, A., *RAB: The Life of R. A. Butler* (1987).

Howson, S., ' "A Dear Money Man"?: Keynes on Monetary Policy, 1920', *Econ. J.*, 83 (1973), 456–64.

—— *Domestic Monetary Management in Britain, 1919–38* (Cambridge, 1975).

Howson, S., *Sterling's Managed Float: The Operations of the Exchange Equalisation Account* (Princeton, NJ, 1980).

—— 'Slump and Unemployment', in R. Floud and D. McCloskey (eds.), *The Economic History of Britain since 1700*, vol. ii (Cambridge, 1981), 265–85.

—— 'Hawtrey and the Real World', in G. C. Harcourt (ed.), *Keynes and His Contemporaries* (1985), 142–88.

—— 'The Origins of Cheaper Money, 1945–7', *Econ. Hist. Rev.*, 2nd ser., 40 (1987), 433–52.

—— 'Cheap Money and Debt Management in Britain, 1932–51', in P. L. Cottrell and D. E. Moggridge (eds.), *Money and Power* (1988), 227–89.

—— 'The Problem of Monetary Control in Britain, 1948–51', *J. Eur. Econ. Hist.*, 20 (1991), 59–92.

—— *British Monetary Policy, 1945–51* (Oxford, 1993).

—— and D. Winch, *The Economic Advisory Council, 1930–1939: A Study in Economic Advice during Depression and Recovery* (Cambridge, 1977).

Hubback, D., 'The Treasury's Role in Civil Service Training', *Public Admin.*, 35 (1957), 99–109.

—— 'Sir Richard Clarke—1910–1975: A Most Unusual Civil Servant', *Public Policy and Admin.*, 3 (1988), 19–34.

Hurst, A. W., 'The Place of Finance Departments, Committees and Officers in Administrative Control', *Public Admin.*, 5 (1927), 418–30.

Hutchison, T. W., *Economics and Economic Policy in Britain, 1946–1966* (1968).

Ingham, G., *Capitalism Divided? The City and Industry in British Social Development* (1984).

James, H., *The German Slump: Politics and Economics, 1924–1936* (Oxford, 1986).

—— 'Financial Flows Across Frontiers During the Interwar Depression', *Econ. Hist. Rev.*, 2nd ser., 45 (1992), 594–613.

—— *International Monetary Cooperation Since Bretton Woods* (Oxford, 1996).

Jeffreys, K., *The Churchill Coalition and Wartime Politics, 1940–1945* (Manchester, 1991).

Jenkins, R., *Asquith* (1986).

—— *Baldwin* (1987).

—— *The Chancellors* (1998).

Jennings, I., *Cabinet Government* (Cambridge, 1961).

Johnman, L., 'Defending the Pound: The Economics of the Suez Crisis', in T. Gorst, L. Johnman, and W. S. Lucas (eds.), *Postwar Britain, 1945–64: Themes and Perspectives* (1989), 166–81.

Johnson, P. B., *Land Fit for Heroes: The Planning of British Reconstruction, 1916–1919* (Chicago, 1968).

Johnston, A., *The Inland Revenue* (1965).

Jones, J. H., *Josiah Stamp, Public Servant: The Life of the First Baron Stamp of Shortlands* (1964).

Jones, K., *An Economist Among Mandarins: A Biography of Robert Hall, 1901–1988* (Cambridge, 1994).

Jones, M. E. F., 'The Regional Impact of an Overvalued Pound in the 1920s', *Econ. Hist. Rev.*, 2nd ser., 38 (1985), 393–401.

Jones, R., *Wages and Employment Policy, 1936–1985* (1987).

Kahn, R. F., 'The Relation of Home Investment to Unemployment', *Econ. J.*, 41 (1931), 173–98.

Kaldor, N., 'The White Paper on National Income and Expenditure', *Econ. J.*, 51 (1941), 181–91.

Kalecki, M., 'The Budget and Inflation', in Oxford University Institute of Statistics, *Studies in War Economics* (Oxford, 1947), 86–7.

Kaplan, J. J., and G. Schleiminger, *The European Payments Union: Financial Diplomacy in the 1950s* (Oxford, 1989).

Kelsall, R. K., *Higher Civil Servants in Britain from 1870 to the Present Day* (1955).

Kent, B., *The Spoils of War: The Politics, Economics, and Diplomacy of Reparations, 1918–1932* (Oxford, 1989).

Keynes, J. M., 'War and the Financial System, August 1914', *Econ. J.*, 24 (1914), 460–86.

—— 'The Balance of Payments of the United States', *Econ. J.*, 56 (1946), 171–87.

Keynes, M. (ed.), *Essays on John Maynard Keynes* (Cambridge, 1975).

Kirkaldy, A. W. (ed.), *British Finance During and After the War* (1921).

Kitson, M., and S. Solomou, *Protectionism and Economic Revival: The British Interwar Economy* (Cambridge, 1990).

—— —— and M. Weale, 'Effective Protection and Economic Recovery in the United Kingdom during the 1930s', *Econ. Hist. Rev.*, 44 (1991), 328–38.

Kunz, D. B., *The Battle for Britain's Gold Standard in 1931* (1987).

—— *The Economic Diplomacy of the Suez Crisis* (Chapel Hill, NC, 1991).

Kynaston, D., 'The Bank of England and the Government', in R. Roberts and D. Kynaston (eds.), *The Bank of England: Money, Power and Influence* (Oxford, 1995), 19–55.

Laybourn, K., *Philip Snowden: A Biography* (Aldershot, 1988).

Lee, J. M., 'Reviewing the Machinery of Government, 1942–1952' (Civil Service Department, 1977).

Leijonhufvud, A., *On Keynesian Economics and the Economics of Keynes* (New York, 1968).

Leffler, M. P., *The Elusive Quest: America's Pursuit of European Stability and French Security, 1919–1933* (Chapel Hill, NC, 1979).

Lewis, R., *Enoch Powell: Principle in Politics* (1979).

Little, I. M. D., 'The Economist in Whitehall', *Lloyds Bank Review*, ns, 44 (1957), 29–40.

Loebl, H., *Government Factories and the Origins of British Regional Policy* (Aldershot, 1988).

Lowe, R., 'The Erosion of State Intervention in Britain, 1917–24', *Econ. Hist. Rev.*, 2nd ser., 31 (1978), 270–86.

—— 'The Failure of Consensus in Britain: The National Industrial Conference, 1919–1921', *Hist. J.*, 21 (1978), 649–75.

—— *Adjusting to Democracy: The Role of the Ministry of Labour in British Politics, 1916–1939* (Oxford, 1986).

—— 'Resignation at the Treasury: The Social Services Committee and the Failure to Reform the Welfare State, 1955–57', *J. Soc. Policy*, 18 (1989), 505–26.

—— 'The Second World War, Consensus and the Foundation of the Welfare State', *20th Cent. Brit. Hist.*, 1 (1990), 152–82.

—— 'Milestone or Millstone? The 1959–61 Plowden Committee and its Impact on British Welfare Policy', *Hist. J.*, 40 (1997), 463–91.

—— 'Plumbing New Depths: Contemporary Historians and the Public Record Office', *20th Cent. Brit. Hist.*, 8 (1997), 239–65.

McCrone, G., *The Economics of Subsidising Agriculture* (1962).

—— *Regional Policy in Britain* (1969).

McDonald, A., 'The Geddes Committee and the Formulation of Public Expenditure Policy, 1921–22', *Hist. J.*, 32 (1989), 643–74.

MacDonald, C. A., 'Economic Appeasement and the German "Moderates", 1937–1939: An Introductory Essay', *Past and Present*, 56 (1972), 105–35.

McFadyean, A., *Reparation Reviewed* (1930).

McKenna, S., *Reginald McKenna, 1863–1943: A Memoir* (1948).

McKibbin, R., 'The Economic Policy of the Second Labour Government 1929–31', *Past and Present*, 68 (1975), 95–123.

Macleod, I., *Neville Chamberlain* (1961).

MacLeod, R. M., *Treasury Control and Social Administration: A Study of Establishment Growth at the Local Government Board, 1871–1905* (1968).

Macnicol, J., *The Movement for Family Allowances, 1918–45* (1980).

—— *The Politics of Retirement in Britain, 1878–1948* (Cambridge, 1998).

Maddison, A., *Dynamic Forces in Capitalist Development* (Oxford, 1991).

Maier, C. S., *Recasting Bourgeois Europe: Stabilization in France, Germany and Italy in the Decade after World War I* (Princeton, NJ, 1975).

Maisel, E., *The Foreign Office and Foreign Policy, 1919–1926* (Brighton, 1994).

Mallet, B., *British Budgets, 1887/88 to 1912/13* (1913).

—— and C. O. George, *British Budgets, 1913/14 to 1920/21* (1929).

—— —— *British Budgets, 1921/22 to 1932/33* (1933).

Maloney, J., 'Gladstone and Sound Victorian Finance', in id. (ed.), *Debt and Deficits: An Historical Perspective* (Cheltenham, 1997), 27–46.

Marder, A. J., *From Dreadnought to Scapa Flow: The Royal Navy in the Fisher Era, 1904–1919*, vol. i (1961).

Marks, S., 'The Myths of Reparations', *Central Eur. Hist.*, 11 (1978), 231–55.

—— 'Reparations in 1922', in C. Fink, A. Frohn, and J. Heideking (eds.), *Genoa, Rapallo and European Reconstruction in 1922* (Cambridge, 1991), 65–76.

Marquand, D., *Ramsay MacDonald* (1977).

Masterman, L., *C. F. G. Masterman: A Biography* (1939).

Matthews, K. G. P., 'Was Sterling Overvalued in 1925?' *Econ. Hist. Rev.*, 2nd ser., 39 (1986), 572–87.

—— 'Could Lloyd George Have Done It?', *Oxford Econ. Papers*, NS, 41 (1989), 374–407.

Matthews, R. C. O., C. H. Feinstein, and J. C. Odling-Smee, *British Economic Growth, 1856–1973* (Oxford, 1982).

Meade, J., *Planning and the Price Mechanism: The Liberal–Socialist Solution* (1948).

—— *Stagflation*, vol. i, *Wage-fixing* (1982).

Mercer, H., N. Rollings, and J. D. Tomlinson (eds.), *Labour Governments and Private Industry: The Experience of 1945–51* (Edinburgh, 1992).

Middlemas, K., *Power, Competition and the State*, vol. i, *Britain in Search of Balance, 1940–61* (1986).

—— and J. Barnes, *Baldwin: A Biography* (1969).

Middleton, P., 'Economic Policy Formulation in the Treasury in the Post-war Period', *Nat. Institute Econ. Rev.*, 127 (1989), 46–51.

Middleton, R., 'The Constant Employment Budget Balance and British Budgetary Policy, 1929–39', *Econ. Hist. Rev.*, 2nd ser., 34 (1981), 266–86.

—— 'The Treasury in the 1930s: Political and Administrative Constraints to Acceptance of the "New" Economics', *Oxford Econ. Papers*, NS, 34 (1982), 48–77.

—— 'The Treasury and Public Investment: A Perspective on Inter-war Economic Management', *Public Admin.*, 61 (1983), 351–70.

—— 'The Measurement of Fiscal Influence in Britain in the 1930s', *Econ. Hist. Rev.*, 2nd ser., 37 (1984), 103–6.

—— *Towards the Managed Economy: Keynes, the Treasury and the Fiscal Policy Debate of the 1930s* (1985).

—— 'Britain in the 1930s: A Managed Economy? A Comment', *Econ. Hist. Rev.*, 2nd ser., 42 (1989), 544–7.

—— 'Keynes's Legacy for Post-war Economic Management', in A. Gorst, L. Johnman, and W. S. Lucas (eds.), *Poswar Britain, 1945–64: Themes and Perspectives* (1989), 22–42.

—— *Government versus the Market: The Growth of the Public Sector, Economic Management and British Economic Performance, c.1890–1979* (Cheltenham, 1996).

—— 'The Size and Scope of the Public Sector', in S. J. D. Green and R. C. Whiting (eds.), *The Boundaries of the State in Modern Britain* (Cambridge, 1996), 89–145.

—— *Charlatans or Saviours: Economists and the British Economy from Marshall to Meade* (Cheltenham, 1998).

Milward, A. S., *The Reconstruction of Western Europe, 1945–51* (1984).

—— and G. Brennan, *Britain's Place in the World: A Historical Enquiry into Import Controls 1945–60* (1996).

Moggridge, D. E., *British Monetary Policy, 1924–1931: The Norman Conquest of $4.86* (Cambridge, 1972).

—— 'The Keynesian Revolution in Historical Perspective', in O. F. Hamouda and J. N. Smithin (eds.), *Keynes and Public Policy After Fifty Years*, vol. i, *Economics and Policy* (Aldershot, 1988), 50–60.

—— *Maynard Keynes: An Economist's Biography* (1992).

—— and S. Howson, 'Keynes on Monetary Policy, 1910–1946', *Oxford Econ. Papers*, NS, 26 (1974), 226–47.

Morgan, D. J., *The Official History of Colonial Development*, vol. iii, *A Reassessment of British Aid Policy* (1980).

Morgan, E. V., *Studies in British Financial Policy, 1914–1925* (1952).

Morgan, K., *Labour in Power, 1945–1951* (Oxford, 1984).

—— and J. Morgan, *Portrait of a Progressive: The Political Career of Christopher, Viscount Addison* (Oxford, 1980).

Mosley, P., 'When is a Policy Instrument Not an Instrument? Fiscal Marksmanship in Britain, 1951–84', *J. Public Policy*, 5 (1985), 69–85.

Muirhead, B. W., 'Britain, Canada, and the Collective Approach to Freer Trade and Payments, 1952–57', *J. Imperial and Commonwealth Hist.*, 20 (1992), 108–26.

Murray, B. K., *The Peoples's Budget, 1909/10: Lloyd George and Liberal Politics* (Oxford, 1980).

—— '"Battered and Shattered": Lloyd George and the 1914 Budget Fiasco', *Albion*, 23 (1991), 483–507.

Navias, M. S., *Nuclear Weapons and British Strategic Planning, 1955–1958* (Oxford, 1991).

Nevin, E., *The Mechanism of Cheap Money: A Study of British Monetary Policy, 1931–1939* (Cardiff, 1955).

Newton, S., 'Britain, the Sterling Area and European Integration, 1945–50', *J. Imperial and Commonwealth Hist.*, 13 (1985), 163–82.

Newton, S., *Profits of Peace: The Political Economy of Anglo-German Appeasement* (Oxford, 1996).

—— and D. Porter, *Modernization Frustrated: The Politics of Industrial Decline since 1900* (1988).

Niskanen, W. A., *Bureaucracy and Representative Government* (New York, 1971).

—— *Bureaucracy: Servant or Master?* (1973).

O'Brien, D. P., *Lionel Robbins* (1988).

O'Brien, P. K., 'Britain's Economy between the Wars: A Survey of a Counter-revolution in Economic History', *Past and Present*, 115 (1987), 107–30.

Offer, A., *Property and Politics, 1870–1914: Landownership, Law, Ideology and Urban Development in England* (Cambridge, 1981).

—— 'Empire and Social Reform: British Overseas Investment and Domestic Politics, 1908–1914', *Hist. J.*, 26 (1983), 119–38.

O'Halpin, E., 'Sir Warren Fisher and the Coalition, 1919–22', *Hist. J.*, 24 (1981), 907–27.

—— *Head of the Civil Service: A Study of Sir Warren Fisher* (1989).

Orde, A., *British Policy and European Reconstruction after the First World War* (Cambridge, 1990).

Packer, I., 'The Liberal Cave and the 1914 Budget', *Eng. Hist. Rev.*, 111 (1996), 620–35.

Paish, F. W., 'Inflation in the United Kingdom, 1948–57', *Economica*, ns, 98 (1958), 94–105.

—— *Studies in an Inflationary Economy* (1962).

Parker, R. A. C., 'British Rearmament 1936–9: Treasury, Trade Unions and Skilled Labour', *Eng. Hist. Rev.*, 96 (1981), 306–43.

—— 'The Pound Sterling, the American Treasury and British Preparations for War, 1938–1939', *Eng. Hist. Rev.*, 98 (1983), 261–79.

—— *Chamberlain and Appeasement: British Policy and the Coming of the Second World War* (1993).

Peacock, A., *The Economic Analysis of Government and Related Themes* (Oxford, 1979).

—— and J. Wiseman, *The Growth of Public Expenditure in the United Kingdom* (1961).

Pechman, J. (ed.), *The Role of the Economist in Government: An International Perspective* (1989).

Peden, G. C., *British Rearmament and the Treasury, 1932–1939* (Edinburgh, 1979).

—— 'Sir Warren Fisher and British Rearmament Against Germany', *Eng. Hist. Rev.*, 94 (1979), 29–47.

—— 'Keynes, the Treasury and Unemployment in the Later Nineteen-thirties', *Oxford Econ. Papers*, ns, 32 (1980), 1–18.

—— 'Keynes, the Economics of Rearmament and Appeasement', in W. J. Mommsen and L. Kettenacker (eds.), *The Fascist Challenge and the Policy of Appeasement* (1983), 142–56.

—— 'Sir Richard Hopkins and the "Keynesian Revolution" in Employment Policy, 1929–45', *Econ. Hist. Rev.*, 2nd ser., 36 (1983), 281–96.

—— 'The Treasury as the Central Department of Government, 1919–1939', *Public Admin.*, 61 (1983), 371–85.

—— 'A Matter of Timing: The Economic Background to British Foreign Policy, 1937–1939', *History*, 69 (1984), 15–28.

—— 'The "Treasury View" on Public Works and Employment in the Interwar Period', *Econ. Hist. Rev.*, 2nd ser., 37 (1984), 167–81.

—— *British Economic and Social Policy: Lloyd George to Margaret Thatcher* (Deddington, 1985; Hemel Hempstead, 1991).

—— 'Economic Aspects of British Perceptions of Power on the Eve of the Cold War', in J. Becker and F. Knipping (eds.), *Power in Europe? Great Britain, France, Italy and Germany in a Postwar World* (Berlin, 1986), 237–61.

—— *Keynes, the Treasury and British Economic Policy* (1988).

—— 'Britain in the 1930s: A Managed Economy? A Comment', *Econ. Hist. Rev.*, 2nd ser., 42 (1989), 538–43.

—— 'Old Dogs and New Tricks: The British Treasury and Keynesian Economics in the 1940s and 1950s', in M. O. Furner and B. Supple (eds.), *The State and Economic Knowledge: The American and British Experiences* (Cambridge, 1990), 208–38.

—— 'The Road to and from Gairloch: Lloyd George, Unemployment, Inflation and the "Treasury View" in 1921', *20th Cent. Brit. Hist.*, 4 (1993), 224–49.

—— 'Economic Knowledge and the State in Modern Britain', in S. J. D. Green and R. C. Whiting (eds.), *The Boundaries of the State in Modern Britain* (Cambridge, 1996), 170–87.

—— 'The Treasury View in the Interwar Period: An Example of *Political* Economy?', in B. Corry (ed.), *Unemployment and the Economists* (Cheltenham, 1996), 69–88.

Pelling, H., *Britain and the Marshall Plan* (1988).

Peters, J., 'The British Government and the City–Industry Divide: The Case of the 1914 Financial Crisis', *20th Cent. Brit. Hist.*, 4 (1993), 126–48.

Phillips, A. W., 'The Relation Between Unemployment and the Rate of Change of Money Wage Rates in the United Kingdom, 1861–1957', *Economica*, NS, 25 (1958), 283–99.

Pigou, A. C., *Wealth and Welfare* (1912).

—— *Aspects of British Economic History, 1918–1925* (1947).

Pimlott, B., *Hugh Dalton* (1985).

Pinto-Duschinsky, M., 'Bread and Circuses? The Conservatives in Office, 1951–1964', in V. Bogdanor and R. Skidelsky (eds.), *The Age of Affluence, 1951–1964* (1970), 55–77.

Pitfield, D. E., 'The Quest for an Effective Regional Policy, 1934–37', *Regional Studies*, 12 (1978), 429–43.

Playfair, E., 'Who Are the Policy Makers? Minister or Civil Servant?', *Public Admin.*, 43 (1965), 260–8.

Pliatzky, L., *Getting and Spending: Public Expenditure, Employment and Inflation* (Oxford, 1982).

Pollard, S. (ed.), *The Gold Standard and Employment Policies between the Wars* (1970).

—— *The Wasting of the British Economy: British Economic Policy 1945 to the Present* (1982).

Post, G., jnr., *Dilemmas of Appeasement: British Deterrence and Defence, 1934–1937* (Ithaca, NY, 1993).

Postan, M. M., *British War Production* (1952).

Powell, J. Enoch, 'Treasury Control in the Age of Inflation', *Banker*, 108 (1958), 215–19.

—— 'Plan to Spend First; Find the Money Later', *Lloyds Bank Rev.*, 52 (1959), 19–34.

Pressnell, L. S., '1925: The Burden of Sterling', *Econ. Hist. Rev.*, 2nd ser., 31 (1978), 67–88.

—— *External Economic Policy since the War*, vol. i, *The Post-War Financial Settlement* (1986).

Ranki, G., *The Economics of the Second World War* (Vienna, Cologne, and Weimar, 1993).

Reading, Marquess of, *Rufus Isaacs, First Marquess of Reading*, 2 vols., *1860–1914* (1942) and *1914–1935* (1945).

Redmond, J., 'An Indicator of the Effective Exchange Rate of the Pound in the Nineteen-thirties', *Econ. Hist. Rev.*, 2nd ser., 33 (1980), 83–91.

—— 'The Sterling Overvaluation in 1925: A Multilateral Approach', *Econ. Hist. Rev.*, 2nd ser., 37 (1984), 520–32.

Reynolds, D., *The Creation of the Anglo-American Alliance 1937–41: A Study in Competitive Co-operation* (1981).

Ritschel, D., *The Politics of Planning: The Debate on Economic Planning in Britain in the 1930s* (Oxford, 1997).

Robertson, D., *Money* (Cambridge, 1948 edn.; repr. 1956).

Robbins, L., *The Balance of Payments*, Stamp Memorial Lecture (1951).

—— *Politics and Economics: Papers in Political Economy* (1963).

Robinson, E. A. G., *Economic Planning in the United Kingdom: Some Lessons* (Cambridge, 1967).

—— 'The Economic Problems of the Transition from War to Peace', *Cambridge J. Econ.*, 10 (1986), 165–85.

—— 'The Beginning of the Economic Section of the Cabinet Office', *Cambridge J. Econ.*, 15 (1991), 95–100.

Roll, E., *The World After Keynes: An Examination of the Economic Order* (1968).

—— *The Uses and Abuses of Economics and Other Essays* (1978).

—— 'The Influence of Ideas on Economic Policy', *Contemp. Brit. Hist.*, 10 (1996), 186–98.

Rollings, N., 'The "Keynesian Revolution" and Economic Policy-making: A Comment', *Econ. Hist. Rev.*, 2nd ser., 38 (1985), 95–100.

—— 'British Budgetary Policy, 1945–1954: A "Keynesian Revolution"?', *Econ. Hist. Rev.*, 2nd ser., 41 (1988), 283–98.

—— ' "The Reichstag Method of Governing"? The Attlee Governments and Permanent Economic Controls', in H. Mercer, N. Rollings, and J. D. Tomlinson (eds.), *Labour Governments and Private Industry: The Experience of 1945–1951* (Edinburgh, 1992), 15–36.

—— 'Poor Mr Butskell: A Short Life, Wrecked by Schizophrenia?', *20th Cent. Brit. Hist.*, 5 (1994), 183–205.

—— 'Butskellism, the Postwar Consensus and the Managed Economy', in H. Jones and M. Kandiah (eds.), *The Myth of Consensus: New Views on British History, 1945–64* (1996), 97–119.

Rowland, P., *Lloyd George* (1975).

Roseveare, H., *The Treasury: The Evolution of a British Institution* (1969).

Roskill, S., *Naval Policy between the Wars*, vol. i, *The Period of Anglo-American Antagonism, 1919–1929* (1968); vol. ii, *The Period of Reluctant Rearmament, 1930–1939* (1976).

—— *Hankey, Man of Secrets*, 3 vols. (1970, 1972, 1974).

Routh, T., *British Protectionism and the International Economy: Overseas Commercial Policy in the 1930s* (Cambridge, 1993).

—— 'The Political Economy of Protectionism in Britain, 1919–1932', *J. Eur. Econ. Hist.*, 21 (1992), 47–97.

Rowan, L., *Arms and Economics: The Changing Challenge* (Cambridge, 1960).

Sabine, B. E. V., *A History of the Income Tax* (1966).

—— *British Budgets in Peace and War, 1932–1945* (1970).

Sanderson, M., 'Education and Economic Decline, 1890–1980s', *Oxford Rev. Econ. Policy*, 4/1 (1988), 38–50.

Sayers, R. S., *Financial Policy, 1939–1945* (1956).

—— 'The Return to Gold, 1925', in S. Pollard (ed.), *The Gold Standard and Employment Policies between the Wars* (1970), 85–98.

—— *The Bank of England, 1891–1944*, 3 vols. (Cambridge, 1976).

Schaad, M., 'Plan G: A "Counterblast"? British Policy Towards the Messina Countries, 1956', *Contemp. Eur. Hist.*, 7 (1998), 39–60.

Schenk, C., *Britain and the Sterling Area: From Devaluation to Convertibility in the 1950s* (1994).

—— 'Closing the Hong Kong Gap: The Hong Kong Free Dollar Market in the 1950s', *Econ. Hist. Rev.*, 2nd ser., 47 (1994), 335–53.

Schremmer, D. E., 'Taxation and Public Finance: Britain, France and Germany', in P. Mathias and S. Pollard (eds.), *The Cambridge Economic History of Europe*, vol. viii (Cambridge, 1989), 315–494.

Schuker, S. A., *The End of French Predominance in Europe: The Financial Crisis of 1924 and the Adoption of the Dawes Plan* (Chapel Hill, NC, 1976).

—— *American 'Reparations' to Germany, 1919–33: Implications for the Third-World Debt Crisis* (Princeton, NJ, 1988).

Seabourne, T., 'The Summer of 1914', in F. Capie and G. E. Wood (eds.), *Financial Crises and the World Banking System* (New York, 1986), 77–116.

Searle, G. R., *The Quest for National Efficiency: A Study in British Politics and Political Thought, 1899–1914* (Oxford, 1971).

Seldon, Anthony, *Churchill's Indian Summer: The Conservative Government, 1951–55* (1981).

Seldon, Arthur (ed.), *Not Unanimous: A Rival Verdict to Radcliffe's on Money* (1960).

Self, R., 'Treasury Control and the Empire Marketing Board: The Rise and Fall of Non-Tariff Preference in Britain, 1924–1933', *20th Cent. Brit. Hist.*, 5 (1994), 153–82.

Sharp, A., 'The Foreign Office in Eclipse, 1919–22', *History*, 61 (1976), 198–218.

Shay, R., *British Rearmament in the Thirties: Politics and Profits* (Princeton, NJ, 1977).

Shonfield, A., *British Economic Policy since the War* (1958).

Skidelsky, R., *Oswald Mosley* (1975).

—— 'Keynes and the Treasury View: The Case For and Against an Active Unemployment Policy, 1920–1939', in W. Mommsen (ed.), *The Emergence of the Welfare State in Britain and Germany* (1981), 167–87.

—— *John Maynard Keynes: Hopes Betrayed, 1883–1920* (1983).

—— *John Maynard Keynes: The Economist as Saviour, 1920–1937* (1992).

—— *Keynes and Employment Policy in the Second World War*, Mathur Memorial Lecture (Aberystwyth, 1998).

Smith, D., *The Rise and Fall of Monetarism* (1987).

Snowden, P., *Labour and National Finance* (1920).

—— *Labour and the New World* (1921).

—— *If Labour Rules* (1923).

—— *The Truth about Protection: The Worker Pays* (1930).

Spender, J. A., and C. Asquith, *Life of Herbert Henry Asquith, Lord Oxford and Asquith*, 2 vols. (1932).

Spiers, E., *Haldane: An Army Reformer* (Edinburgh, 1980).

Stamp, J., *British Incomes and Property: The Application of Official Statistics to Economic Problems* (1916).

Stamp, J., 'The Special Taxation of Business Profits in Relation to the Present Position of National Finance', *Econ. J.*, 29 (1919), 407–27.

—— *Wealth and Taxable Capacity* (1922).

—— *The Financial Aftermath of War* (1932).

—— *Taxation During the War* (Oxford, 1932).

Stone, R. (ed.), *Inland Revenue Report on National Income 1929* (Cambridge, 1977).

Strange, S., *Sterling and British Policy* (1971).

Sumida, J. T., *In Defence of Naval Supremacy: Finance, Technology and British Naval Policy, 1889–1914* (1989).

Tawney, R. H., 'The Abolition of Economic Controls, 1918–21', *Econ. Hist. Rev.*, 13 (1943), 1–30.

Taylor, M. P., 'The Dollar–Sterling Exchange Rate in the 1920s: Purchasing Power Parity and the Norman Conquest of $4.86', *Applied Economics*, 24 (1992), 803–11.

Thain, C., 'The Treasury and Britain's Decline', *Political Studies*, 32 (1984), 581–95.

—— and M. Wright, *The Treasury and Whitehall: The Planning and Control of Public Expenditure, 1976–1993* (Oxford, 1995).

Thane, P., 'Non-contributory versus Insurance Pensions, 1878–1908', in id. (ed.), *The Origins of British Social Policy* (1978), 84–106.

Theakston, K., *The Labour Party and Whitehall* (1992).

Thomas, M., 'Rearmament and Economic Recovery in the Late 1930s', *Econ. Hist. Rev.*, 2nd ser., 36 (1983), 552–79.

Thomas, T., 'Aggregate Demand in the United Kingdom, 1918–45', in R. Floud and D. McCloskey (eds.), *The Economic History of Britain since 1700*, vol. ii (Cambridge, 1981), 332–46.

Thorneycroft, P., 'Policy in Practice', in A. Seldon (ed.), *Not Unanimous: A Rival Verdict to Radcliffe's on Money* (1960), 1–14.

Tiratsoo, N., and J. Tomlinson, *Industrial Efficiency and State Intervention: Labour, 1939–51* (1993).

Tolliday, S., *Business, Banking and Politics: The Case of British Steel, 1918–1939* (Cambridge, Mass., 1987).

Tomlinson, B. R., 'Indo-British Relations in the Post-Colonial Era: The Sterling Balances Negotiations, 1947–49', *J. Imperial and Commonwealth Hist.*, 13 (1985), 142–62.

Tomlinson, J., 'Why Was There Never a "Keynesian Revolution" in Economic Policy?', *Econ. Soc.*, 10 (1981), 72–87.

—— *Employment Policy: The Crucial Years, 1939–1955* (Oxford, 1987).

—— 'The Attlee Government and the Balance of Payments, 1945–51', *20th Cent. Brit. Hist.*, 2 (1991), 47–66.

—— 'Planning: Debate and Policy in the 1940s', *20th Cent. Brit. Hist.*, 3 (1992), 154–74.

—— 'Inventing "Decline": The Falling Behind of the British Economy in the Postwar Years', *Econ. Hist. Rev.*, 49 (1996), 731–57.

—— *Democratic Socialism and Economic Policy: The Attlee Years, 1945–1951* (Cambridge, 1997).

Trachtenberg, M., *Reparation in World Politics: France and European Economic Diplomacy, 1916–1923* (New York, 1980).

Trebilcock, C., 'War and the Failure of Industrial Mobilisation', in J. M. Winter (ed.), *War and Economic Development: Essays in Memory of David Joslin* (Cambridge, 1975), 139–64.

Trend, B., 'Policy and the Public Purse', *Times Literary Supplement*, 16 July 1982, 755.

Trevithick, J. A., 'The Monetary Prerequisites for the Multiplier: An Adumbration of the Crowding Out Hypothesis', *Cambridge J. Econ.*, 18 (1994), 77–90.

Tsokhas, K., 'The Australian Role in Britain's Return to the Gold Standard', *Econ. Hist. Rev.*, 2nd ser., 47 (1994), 129–46.

Tullock, G. A., *The Vote Motive: An Essay in the Economics of Politics* (1976).

Turner, A., 'Anglo-French Financial Relations in the 1920s', *Eur. Hist. Quart.*, 26 (1996), 31–55.

—— 'British Holdings of French War Bonds: An Aspect of Anglo-French Relations during the 1920s', *Financial Hist. Rev.*, 3 (1996), 153–74.

—— *The Cost of War: British Policy on French War Debts, 1919–1931* (Brighton, 1998).

Turner, J., *Lloyd George's Secretariat* (Cambridge, 1980).

—— *Macmillan* (1994).

Turner, P., 'Wealth Effects and Fiscal Policy in the 1930s', *Econ. Hist. Rev.*, 2nd ser., 44 (1991), 515–22.

Van Dormael, A., *Bretton Woods: Birth of a Monetary System* (1978).

Waley, D., 'The Treasury during World War II', *Oxford Econ. Papers*, NS (1953), supplement on Sir Hubert Henderson, 47–54.

Watt, D. C., *Personalities and Policies: Studies in the Formulation of British Foreign Policy in the 20th Century* (1965).

—— *How War Came: The Immediate Origins of the Second World War, 1938–1939* (1989).

Webster, C., *The Health Services since the War*, vol. i, *Problems of Health Care. The National Health Service before 1957* (1988); vol. ii, *Government and Health Care. The National Health Service, 1958–1979* (1996).

Weir, M., 'Ideas and Politics: The Acceptance of Keynesianism in Britain and the United States', in P. A. Hall (ed.), *The Political Power of Economic Ideas: Keynesianism Across Nations* (Princeton, NJ, 1989), 53–86.

—— and Skocpol, T., 'State Structures and the Possibilities for "Keynesian" Responses to the Great Depression in Sweden, Britain, and the United States', in P. B. Evans, D. Rueschemeyer, and T. Skocpol (eds.), *Bringing the State Back In* (Cambridge, 1985), 107–63.

Wendt, B.-J., ' "Economic Appeasement"—A Crisis Strategy', in W. J. Mommsen and L. A. Kettenacker (eds.), *The Fascist Challenge and the Policy of Appeasement* (1983), 157–72.

Wheeler-Bennett, J., *John Anderson, Viscount Waverly* (1962).

Whiteley, P., *Political Control of the Macroeconomy: The Political Economy of Public Policy Making* (1986).

Whiteside, N., 'Welfare Legislation and the Unions during the First World War', *Hist. J.*, 23 (1980), 857–74.

—— 'Private Agencies for Public Purposes: Some New Perspectives on Policy Making in Health Insurance between the Wars', *J. Soc. Policy*, 12 (1983), 165–94.

Whiting, A., 'An International Comparison of the Instability of Economic Growth: Is Britain's Poor Economic Performance Due to Government Stop–go Induced Fluctuations?', *Three Banks Review*, 109 (1976), 26–46.

Whiting, R. C., 'The Labour Party, Capitalism and the National Debt, 1918–24', in P. J. Waller (ed.), *Politics and Social Change in Modern Britain: Essays Presented to A. F. Thompson* (Brighton, 1987), 140–60.

Whiting, R. C., 'Taxation and the Working Class, 1915–24', *Hist. J.*, 33 (1990), 895–916.

—— 'Taxation Policy', in H. Mercer, N. Rollings, and J. D. Tomlinson (eds.), *Labour Governments and Private Industry: The Experience of 1945–51* (Edinburgh, 1992), 117–34.

—— 'The Boundaries of Taxation', in S. J. D. Green and R. C. Whiting (eds.), *The Boundaries of the State in Modern Britain* (Cambridge, 1996), 146–69.

—— 'Income Tax, the Working Class, and Party Politics, 1948–52', *20th Cent. Brit. Hist.*, 8 (1997), 194–221.

Williamson, J., 'Keynes and the International Economic Order', in D. Worswick and J. Trevithick (eds.), *Keynes and the Modern World: Proceedings of the Keynes Centenary Conference* (Cambridge, 1983), 87–113.

Williamson, P., 'A "Bankers' Ramp"? Financiers and the British Political Crisis of August 1931', *Eng. Hist. Rev.*, 99 (1984), 770–806.

—— *National Crisis and National Government: British Politics, the Economy and Empire, 1926–1932* (Cambridge, 1992).

Wilson, K. M., *The Policy of the Entente: Essays on the Determinants of British Foreign Policy, 1904–1914* (Cambridge, 1985).

Wilson, T., 'Instability and the Rate of Growth', *Lloyds Bank Rev.*, NS, 81 (1966), 16–32.

—— *Churchill and the Prof.* (1995).

Winch, D., *Economics and Policy: A Historical Study* (1969).

—— 'Britain in the 'Thirties: A Managed Economy?', in C. H. Feinstein (ed.), *The Managed Economy: Essays in British Economic Policy and Performance since 1929* (Oxford, 1983), 47–67.

—— 'Keynes, Keynesianism and State Intervention', in P. A. Hall (ed.), *The Political Power of Economic Ideas: Keynesianism Across Nations* (Princeton, NJ, 1989), 107–27.

Winnifrith, A. J. D., 'Treasury Control of Establishments Work', *Public Admin.*, 36 (1958), 9–17.

—— 'Edward Ettingdean Bridges—Baron Bridges', *Biographical Memoirs of Fellows of the Royal Society*, 16 (1970), 37–56.

Withers, H., *Our Money and the State* (1917).

Wolcott, S., 'Keynes Versus Churchill: Revaluation and British Unemployment in the 1920s', *J. Econ. Hist.*, 53 (1993), 601–28.

Woods, J., 'Treasury Control', *Pol. Quart.*, 25 (1954), 370–81.

Woods, R. B., *A Changing of the Guard: Anglo-American Relations, 1941–1946* (Chapel Hill, NC, 1990).

Worswick, G. D. N., 'The Sources of Recovery in the UK in the 1930s', *Nat. Institute Econ. Rev.*, Nov. 1984, 85–93.

—— *Unemployment: A Problem of Policy* (Cambridge, 1991).

Wright, J. F., *Britain in the Age of Economic Management: An Economic History since 1939* (Oxford, 1979).

—— 'Britain's Inter-war Experience', *Oxford Econ. Papers*, NS, 33, supplement (1981), 282–305.

Wright, M., 'Treasury Control, 1854–1914', in G. Sutherland (ed.), *Studies in the Growth of Nineteenth-Century Government* (1972), 195–226.

Young, E. Hilton, *The System of National Finance* (2nd edn., 1924).

Young, J. W., *Britain, France and the Unity of Europe, 1945–51* (Leicester, 1984).

Zimmeck, M., 'Strategies and Strategems for the Employment of Women in the British Civil Service, 1919–1939', *Hist. J.*, 27 (1984), 901–24.

THESES

Bradbury, J., 'The 1929 Local Government Act: The Formulation and Implementation of the Poor Law (Health Care) and Exchequer Grant Reforms for England and Wales', Ph.D. (Bristol, 1992).

Chester, A., 'Planning, the Labour Governments and British Economic Policy, 1943–51', Ph.D. (Bristol, 1983).

Gibbon, H. R. G., 'Butler and His Budgets. The Chancellorship of R. A. Butler, 1951–55: A Study in Economic Policy-making in Britain', M.Litt. (Oxford, 1989).

Hay, J. R., 'British Government Finance, 1906–1914', B.Litt. (Oxford, 1970).

Hemery, J. A., 'The Emergence of Treasury Influence in British Foreign Policy, 1914–1921', Ph.D. (Cambridge, 1988).

Janeway, W. H., 'The Economic Policy of the Second Labour Government, 1929–31', Ph.D. (Cambridge, 1971).

Jones, H., 'The Conservative Party and the Welfare State, 1942–1955', Ph.D. (London, 1992).

Jones, R., 'The Wages Problem in Employment Policy, 1936–48', M.Sc. (Bristol, 1983).

McDonald, A., 'The Formulation of British Public Expenditure Policy, 1919–1925', Ph.D. (Bristol, 1988).

O'Brien, P. P., 'The Cabinet, Admiralty and Perceptions Governing the Formation of British Naval Policy, 1909, 1921–22, 1927–36', Ph.D. (Cambridge, 1992).

Price, N. G., 'The Relationship of the Home Office and the Ministry of Labour with the Treasury Establishment Division, 1919–1946. An Evaluation of Contrasting Needs', Ph.D. (London, 1991).

Proctor, S., 'Towards Convertibility: The Sterling Policy of the Conservative Governments, 1951–1958', Ph.D. (Bristol, 1990).

Roberts, R., 'The Board of Trade, 1925–1939', D.Phil. (Oxford, 1987).

Rollings, N., 'The Control of Inflation in the Managed Economy: Britain, 1945–53', Ph.D. (Bristol, 1990).

Schaad, M., 'Anglo-German Relations during the Formative Years of the European Community, 1955–61', D.Phil. (Oxford, 1995).

Short, M., 'The Politics of Personal Taxation: Budget-making in Britain, 1917–31', Ph.D. (Cambridge, 1985).

Stacey, S., 'The Ministry of Health, 1919–1929: Ideas and Practice in a Government Department', D.Phil. (Oxford, 1984).

Index